Gaelic in Scotland

Gaelic in Scotland
Policies, Movements, Ideologies

Wilson McLeod

EDINBURGH
University Press

To Alex

Edinburgh University Press is one of the leading university presses in the UK. We publish academic books and journals in our selected subject areas across the humanities and social sciences, combining cutting-edge scholarship with high editorial and production values to produce academic works of lasting importance. For more information visit our website: edinburghuniversitypress.com

© Wilson McLeod, 2020

Edinburgh University Press Ltd
The Tun – Holyrood Road
12 (2f) Jackson's Entry
Edinburgh EH8 8PJ

Typeset in 10.5/13pt Sabon by
Servis Filmsetting Ltd, Stockport, Cheshire

A CIP record for this book is available from the British Library

ISBN 978 1 4744 6239 6 (hardback)
ISBN 978 1 4744 6241 9 (webready PDF)
ISBN 978 1 4744 6242 6 (epub)

The right of Wilson McLeod to be identified as author of this work has been asserted in accordance with the Copyright, Designs and Patents Act 1988 and the Copyright and Related Rights Regulations 2003 (SI No. 2498).

Contents

Abbreviations	vi
Acknowledgements	viii
Introduction	1
1 Historical and Sociolinguistic Background	6
2 Policy, Ideology and Discourse	27
3 Foundations, 1872–1918	56
4 Transition, 1919–44	112
5 Stirrings, 1945–74	137
6 Revitalisation, 1975–96	174
7 Restructuring, 1997–2005	242
8 Institutionalisation, 2006–20	274
Conclusion	330
Notes	337
Appendix: Timeline of Gaelic Policy from 1871	351
Bibliography	353
Index	437

Abbreviations

ACG	An Comunn Gàidhealach
AG	*An Gàidheal*
BnG	Bòrd na Gàidhlig
CCES	Committee of Council on Education in Scotland
CCG	Comataidh Craolaidh Gàidhlig
CnaG	Comunn na Gàidhlig
CNCA	Comunn na Cànain Albannaich
CnE	Comhairle nan Eilean
CnES	Comhairle nan Eilean Siar
CnES–SnG	An unpublished document held by Sgioba na Gàidhlig, Comhairle nan Eilean Siar
CNSA	Comhairle nan Sgoiltean Àraich
CoE	Council of Europe
CTG	Comataidh Telebhisein Gàidhlig
CUP	Cambridge University Press
DCMS	Department of Culture, Media and Sport
DG	*An Deo-Gréine*
EUP	Edinburgh University Press
GB	*Guth na Bliadhna*
GH	*Glasgow Herald*
GLS	Gaelic League of Scotland
GME	Gaelic-medium education
GMS	Gaelic Media Service
GRG	Gaelic Report Group
GSI	Gaelic Society of Inverness
GSL	Gaelic Society of London
HC	Highland Council
HIDB	Highlands and Islands Development Board

Abbreviations

HMSO	Her/His Majesty's Stationery Office
HO	Home Office
HoC	House of Commons
IC	*Inverness Courier*
MP	Member of Parliament (Westminster)
MSP	Member of the Scottish Parliament
NLS	National Library of Scotland
NRS	National Records of Scotland
OUP	Oxford University Press
P&J	*Press & Journal* (Aberdeen)
PS	Parliamentary Secretary
SE	Scottish Executive
SED	Scottish Education Department
SG	Scottish Government
SG	*Stornoway Gazette*
SGS	*Scottish Gaelic Studies*
SDD	Scottish Development Department
SHHD	Scottish Home and Health Department
SMO	Sabhal Mòr Ostaig
SNP	Scottish National Party
SO	Scottish Office
SoS	Secretary of State
SQA	Scottish Qualifications Authority
SSPCK	Society in Scotland for Propagating Christian Knowledge
TESS	*Times Education Supplement Scotland*
TGSI	*Transactions of the Gaelic Society of Inverness*
UWP	University of Wales Press
WCM	An unpublished document in the possession of the author and not held in any public repository
WHFP	*West Highland Free Press*

Acknowledgements

This book has been long in the gestation and I have received a great deal of support and assistance along the way. I am very grateful to the Arts and Humanities Research Council for awarding me a research fellowship which allowed me to carry out foundational archival research and interviews with numerous activists and policy-makers, and to the Gaelic Books Council for awarding a publication grant. For giving me access to different kinds of archival materials, I am indebted to Alasdair MacLeod, Dolina MacLeod and David Powell (CnES), Joyce Seymour Chalk and Tommy MacAskill (GSL), Douglas Ansdell and Stuart Pescodd (Scottish Government), Gordon Cameron (Royal Celtic Society/Stuart & Stuart, Edinburgh) and Professor Donald Meek (formerly of the universities of Aberdeen and Edinburgh). Kirsty Blackhall, Alasdair MacCaluim and Fiona MacDougall helped with the transcription of interviews. My thanks to Ronald Black, William Gillies, Sheila Kidd, Ian MacDonald, Jennifer McHarrie, Matthew MacIver, Hugh Dan MacLennan, Peadar Morgan, Gillian Munro, Fiona O'Hanlon, Tadhg Ó hIfearnáin, Peadar Ó Muircheartaigh and Colin Williams, who assisted me with enquiries or practical requests of different kinds. I am especially grateful to all those who gave of their time to be interviewed in connection with this book: Allan Campbell, Kenna Campbell, Duncan Ferguson, Michael Forsyth, Neil Fraser, Norman Gillies, John Angus Mackay, Kenneth MacKinnon, Malcolm Maclean, Aonghas MacNeacail, Annie MacSween, Donald Martin, Donald Meek, Lindsay Paterson, Peter Peacock, Roy Pedersen, Boyd Robertson, Mina Smith, Iain Taylor, Mike Watson, Brian Wilson and the late Duncan MacQuarrie. Particular thanks are due to Ewen Cameron, Rob Dunbar, Alasdair MacCaluim and John Walsh, who provided valuable comments on an earlier draft of the manuscript. Finally, a special note of gratitude to Konstanze and Mànus for their patience and forbearance throughout. Mo thaing chridheil dhuibh uile.

Introduction

WRITING IN 1958, THE distinguished linguist Kenneth Jackson, Professor of Celtic at the University of Edinburgh, expressed his 'belie[f] that Scottish Gaelic will be quite extinct by the middle of the next century, unless some new factor is introduced which radically alters the present situation' (Jackson 1958: 230). Jackson predicted that the Isle of 'Lewis seems likely to be the last refuge of the language, and those who wish to study it in the middle of next century may still find there a few people who can remember it' (Jackson 1958: 232). Viewed sixty years later, Jackson's prognosis appears strikingly pessimistic and the position of Gaelic in Scotland looks much more favourable, greatly if perhaps not fundamentally altered. Especially since the 1980s, a wide range of policies and programmes to support and sustain the language have been introduced, and Gaelic plays a more important role in Scottish life than it has in many centuries. At the same time, however, the number of Gaelic speakers continues to decline and indifference or hostility to the language remains entrenched.

How and why did this shift occur? This study endeavours to explain the trajectory of Gaelic in modern Scotland, considering the policies of government and other powerful institutional actors, the work of the movements, activists and campaigners that sought to maintain and promote the language, and the competing ideologies that have worked to drive the decline, marginalisation and revitalisation of Gaelic. The account begins in 1872, when state education was introduced in Scotland, but it is necessary to begin with a longer perspective, reaching back into medieval history. To a perhaps surprising extent, arguments about the appropriate place of Gaelic in modern Scotland often draw upon understandings (or misunderstandings) of its place in centuries past. Chapter 1 gives a historical overview of Gaelic in Scotland, including an analysis of its spread in the Middle Ages and the course of demographic decline and language shift in recent centuries. Chapter 2 then presents several key issues and themes that have affected the position of Gaelic throughout the modern period, including the aims of state language policy in Scotland and the wider United Kingdom, the relationship between Gaelic and national and group identities, competing ideological interpretations of the value of Gaelic and the characteristics of Gaelic organisations. Different historical stages are then covered in separate chapters, with the emphasis on the period from 1975 onwards, which has seen much more focused development activity in relation to the language and much greater attention from policy-makers of different kinds. Each of these chapters begins with a consideration of the social, political and cultural contexts that shaped the policy environments of different periods and then proceeds to consider the principal developments of these decades in relation to official policy, development and planning, education, media provision and other key fields of activity.

Chapter 3 describes the first wave of Gaelic revival activity from the late eighteenth century onwards, with a focus on the period from 1872 to 1918. This era saw significant controversy concerning the role of Gaelic in the state education system, newly established by the *Education (Scotland) Act 1872*,[1] widespread agitation for land rights in the Gaelic-speaking areas, and the establishment of the first modern Gaelic organisation, An Comunn Gàidhealach.[2] Chapter 4 considers the position of Gaelic in the challenging decades following the First World War, including issues involving the implementation of the *Education (Scotland) Act 1918*, which brought about a somewhat increased role for Gaelic in the education system. Chapter 5 covers the period from 1945 to 1974, a period of significant social and cultural modernisation in Scotland and, from the mid-1960s onwards, renewed campaigning energy on behalf of Gaelic. Chapter 6 considers the period from 1975 to 1997, which was the crucial turning point in institutional provision for the language, when significant government support for Gaelic development and the basis of a modern language planning regime began to emerge. Chapter 7 begins in 1997 with the election of the 'New Labour' government and the referendum on the establishment of the Scottish Parliament, which opened in 1999. The main development of this period was the enactment by the Scottish Parliament of the *Gaelic Language (Scotland) Act 2005*, following a lengthy campaign. Finally, Chapter 8 addresses the period from 2006 to the present, with an emphasis on the implementation of the *Gaelic Language Act* and the role of the Gaelic television service BBC ALBA, which was established in 2008.

The case of Gaelic poses a number of analytical problems, which are introduced below and then teased out through the individual chapters. The position of the language in modern Scotland is complex, indeed contradictory in some respects, and resists straightforward categorisations or explanations. Gaelic has often been presented as a national language of Scotland, or indeed the national language, but today only 1.1 per cent of Scots can speak it (NRS 2014, Table QS211SC) and it has not been spoken by a majority of the population for well over five hundred years. National(ist) movements in Scotland have generally placed little emphasis on Gaelic, and many Scots have little awareness of the language. At the same time, Gaelic clearly has a significant national resonance in Scotland and cannot plausibly be regarded merely as a regional language or the language of a discrete cultural minority. In relation to the recent period of revitalisation, overarching interpretive narratives about the growth of regionalism in Europe or the modern 'ethnic revival' (Smith 1981) fit the Gaelic situation only loosely and are significantly under-explanatory, as are linkages to conventional analyses of the economic and social factors that have diminished Scots' attachment to Britain and Britishness in the post-1945 period (Keating 2010a).

This book is first and foremost a diachronic study of language policy, with its principal focus on the demands of language advocates and the response of public institutions, and it reflects its author's legal background. Although it addresses many historical, political and social questions, it may occasionally prove frustrating to historians, political scientists and sociologists, who might approach such topics in different ways, and although it is informed by recent work in sociolinguistics, it rarely engages directly with conceptual frameworks or theoretical debates in that field. Little direct attention is given to consideration of the social and linguistic dynamics of Gaelic communities or to developments and debates involving different aspects of Gaelic culture, except to shed light on the ways in which these factors have affected the shaping and implementation of language policy. The book is intended for an international readership and thus provides rather more foundational explanation of various Scottish matters than a Scottish reader might expect.

THE RESEARCH CONTEXT

There has been surprisingly little research on the evolution of Gaelic language policy and movements in Scotland. To date there have been two general books, both written for a popular audience (MacKinnon 1974,

1991; Hutchinson 2005; Hutchinson with Dick 2005),[3] and a single book on the history of An Comunn Gàidhealach, the principal Gaelic organisation during the period between 1891 and 1984 (Thompson 1992), as against more than two dozen studies of the counterpart Irish organisation, Conradh na Gaeilge (the Gaelic League) (e.g. McMahon 2008; Ó Fiannaí 1995). There are very few detailed studies of specific historical issues or events relating to Gaelic policy or movements, and most of these relate to the nineteenth and early twentieth centuries rather than the more recent period (e.g. Cruickshank 2002; Fairney 2006; M. K. Macleod 1981; Scott 2014). There has, however, been a significant growth in research on Gaelic sociolinguistics, applied linguistics and language policy in the last two decades (e.g. McLeod 2006; Munro and Mac an Tàilleir 2010; Cox and Armstrong 2011; M. MacLeod and Smith-Christmas 2018), work that sits within a wider international context of much-increased academic engagement with questions of language shift and language revitalisation (e.g. Hogan-Brun and O'Rourke 2019) and language policy more generally (e.g. Spolsky 2012).[4]

General works on modern Scottish history (e.g. Cameron 2010; Findlay 2004; Harvie 1998; C. Macdonald 2009), politics and government (e.g. Keating 2010b; McGarvey and Cairney 2008), society (McCrone 2017) and culture (Craig 2018) tend to treat issues relating to Gaelic in a cursory fashion, if at all. One interpretation of this omission is that it amounts to an objective assessment of the importance of Gaelic in the social, political and cultural affairs of Scotland as a whole, reflecting the consensus view of a range of scholars working independently in different disciplines. On the other hand, there can be a simplistic tendency to assume that the importance of Gaelic for Scotland corresponds directly to its demographic density (e.g. Harvie and Jones 2000: 3; Hussain and Miller 2006: 128). It must also be borne in mind that negative or dismissive attitudes towards Gaelic are so deeply ingrained in Scotland that some writers may simply take for granted that the language is insignificant and unworthy of attention. There may also be something of a vicious circle in operation, by which the dearth of detailed studies on Gaelic policy and history means that scholars producing works of synthesis find little useful secondary literature to draw upon, and skirt around the topic as a result (Paterson 2011). In contrast, this book draws on a diverse, indeed eclectic, range of different kinds of primary sources, including public reports and other documents produced by public bodies and Gaelic organisations, internal government papers, articles in diverse newspapers and periodicals, and interviews with a number of key policy-makers and activists. The great majority of relevant published sources are in English, although relevant Gaelic sources are also drawn upon. This pattern reflects the diglossic position of Gaelic, by which the language was long excluded from most formal domains and the scope of writing and publishing was limited. Today many relevant texts are published bilingually, but as this book is written in English the English versions are quoted and cited here. Similarly, although Gaelic speakers often use Gaelic forms of their names when using Gaelic and English forms when using English, the English forms are given here except for the few individuals who always prefer(red) the Gaelic form.

ESTABLISHING THE CONTEXT

Between 1872 and 2020 the number of Gaelic speakers in Scotland dropped by more than four-fifths and the language steadily weakened as a living community vernacular. Yet in recent decades the position of Gaelic has become increasingly contradictory, with this ongoing decline in the total number of Gaelic speakers and the intensity of Gaelic use coexisting with a dynamic of revitalisation, heightened recognition and increased public status. To understand the evolution of Gaelic policy in its proper context, a foundation in the history and sociolinguistics of Gaelic and an explication of overarching discourses and ideological positions concerning the role of Gaelic in Scotland is required. The following two chapters lay this foundation.

1

Historical and Sociolinguistic Background

THIS CHAPTER PRESENTS AN overview of the history of Gaelic in Scotland from the Middle Ages to the present and analyses the changing sociolinguistic situation of the language over time. Gaelic slowly emerged as the dominant language of Scotland in the central Middle Ages but following language shift it became confined to the northwest of the country. In the subsequent centuries Gaelic became stigmatised as a language of poverty, backwardness and even barbarism. Since the middle of the eighteenth century, against the background of severe economic and social disruption, language shift from Gaelic to English in the traditional Gaelic area gathered pace, so that the position of Gaelic as a community vernacular is now weaker than ever before.

THE SHIFTING POSITION OF GAELIC IN SCOTLAND

For a small country, Scotland has an unusually complex linguistic history, and some important issues in the historical trajectory of Gaelic in Scotland remain less than entirely clear. Scotland in the first millennium was a multi-ethnic, multilingual land, in which identities and affinities were often fluid. The modern borders were not fixed until the fifteenth century and a considerable portion of what is now 'Scotland' was not part of the Scottish kingdom at the time that Gaelic reached its maximal geographical spread.

Gaelic belongs to the Celtic family of the Indo-European languages and is closely related to Irish and Manx, although it has been recognised for centuries as a distinct variety (Gillies 2008). Most scholars hold that the language was originally brought to Scotland by settlers from Ireland in the early centuries of the common era (Clancy 2011), but it may actually be most appropriate 'to imagine Ireland and Western Scotland as a

Historical and Sociolinguistic Background

single linguistic zone in which Gaelic evolved' (Márkus 2017: 79). The principal early Gaelic settlement in Scotland was associated with Dál Riata, a small kingdom in the northeast of Ireland that came to establish a beachhead in Argyll, in the west of Scotland. The Pictish people dominated northern Scotland until the early ninth century, however, and Dál Riata seems generally to have functioned as a vassal kingdom, or constellation of kingships, under Pictish control (Fraser 2009; Woolf 2007).

The Britons, who were dominant in the south of the country, and the Picts spoke 'P-Celtic' language varieties that appear to have been fairly closely related to each other (and to modern Welsh), if rather more distant from Gaelic (a so-called 'Q-Celtic' language) (James 2013).[1] Both Brittonic and Pictish had probably gone out of use by 1100 (Gondek 2007: 71; Clancy 2015: 7). From the seventh century, northern Old English (a Germanic variety) became established in the southeast of the country, following the Anglo-Saxon migration across the North Sea, and then became the dominant language in Scotland from the late Middle Ages onwards. In the later Middle Ages this language variety became more distinctively Scottish and became known as Scots, but the linguistic relationship between Scots and English is close and complex, as discussed below (p. 48). From the end of the eighth century Scotland also experienced Scandinavian settlement, concentrated in the far northeast and along the western seaboard (Fraser 2009; Woolf 2007), with Norse speech surviving in Shetland until the eighteenth century (Knooihuizen 2005). Gaelic was thus only one of several languages spoken in Scotland, and has never existed in isolation or near-isolation. Any claims about the status of Gaelic as a national language of Scotland, or as *the* national language – and the choice of indefinite or definite article is significant – should therefore be framed with great care.

By the eleventh century, Gaelic had spread from Argyll throughout almost all of what is now mainland Scotland, although this process of diffusion was complex and its dynamics varied considerably from region to region (Clancy 2011). Crucially, Gaelic became the language of the first unified Scottish monarchy, the kingdom of Alba that emerged in the ninth century with its heartland in the east of the country, in the former Pictland, which had slowly become Gaelicised (Woolf 2007). The kingdom of Alba then expanded southwards, taking over the Lothian region, and establishing the modern border with England after 1018. 'Alba' is now the ordinary Gaelic word for 'Scotland', although its original meaning was the island of Britain (Dumville 1996) and the kingdom of Alba was not co-extensive with modern Scotland. Gaelic language and culture then reached their zenith in Scotland during the eleventh and early twelfth centuries, when Gaelic was the language of the court and government, of the aristocracy, clergy and intelligentsia. This period of Gaelic dominance is important for Gaelic language advocates, driving a narrative that Gaelic was the original language of Scotland. The evidence of Gaelic place names in almost every part of Scotland testifies to the former spread of the language, a factor often cited by supporters of Gaelic (e.g. Kavanagh 2011).

Yet this period of Gaelic dominance was short-lived. From the middle of the twelfth century onwards, Gaelic language and culture began a long decline in Scotland. Norman French and Latin came to take the place of Gaelic as the languages of authority, before yielding in turn to Scots in the fourteenth and fifteenth centuries. Feudal institutions of Continental origin, including legal and administrative structures, largely came to replace Gaelic ones. The Gaelic language was displaced as a language of institutional and socio-economic power and slowly replaced by Scots throughout the east and south of the country (with the exception of Galloway and Carrick in the southwest). It is important that this process of language shift away from Gaelic took place within the independent Scottish kingdom and not, as was the case with Welsh in Wales and Irish in Ireland, as a consequence of foreign invasion or conquest.

It is not possible to give an accurate estimate of the proportion of the Scottish population that would have spoken Gaelic at the maximal point (which was probably in the twelfth century), but it seems clear that it would have been a substantial arithmetic majority. While the language became deeply rooted in many areas of Scotland, in parts of the southeast Gaelic may have been used only for a relatively short period by the landowning class (Nicolaisen 2001: 173–4) and it is not known how widely knowledge of Gaelic would have diffused throughout the population. In the pre-modern period rulers were generally unconcerned about the language use of the labouring classes (Wright 2016: 28) and little evidence on this point can be gleaned from the surviving sources that shed light on the sociolinguistic dynamics of the time.

This process of de-Gaelicisation in southern and eastern Scotland remains incompletely understood, and some familiar interpretations are rather misleading. St Margaret, the Anglo-Saxon wife of king Máel Coluim III (1054–93), who instituted a range of church reforms along Continental lines while placing little value on older Gaelic institutions, was long identified as a key player in this transformation (Stephens 1976: 55–6; see Keene 2013). Importance has also been assigned to the Northumbrian and Anglo-Norman lords who were placed in prominent positions throughout the country by Máel Coluim III and his successors, especially David I (1124–53); but many of these nobles, particularly those outside the core of the kingdom, actually adapted to the Gaelic milieu and became assimilated into Gaeldom (Clancy and Crawford 2001: 81–90; Stringer 2005). In fact, institutional and structural changes were probably more determinative than the actions of a few key individuals. The slow penetration of new feudal structures and institutions certainly played a role, but the most important factor, it seems, was the growth of the new royally chartered trading burghs from the early twelfth century onwards. These trading centres were populated largely by speakers of Germanic varieties (Scots/English, Flemings and Germans), so that Scots, rather than Gaelic, became the principal language of commerce. The burghs, concentrated on the east coast, appear to have served as beachheads of language and culture shift, and Gaelic was slowly pushed back into the hinterland. By 1200, Gaelic had probably disappeared from the core of the Scottish kingdom in Lothian and the Forth valley; by 1400, the language shift probably extended to the entire east coast. Overall, the processes of language and culture shift from the twelfth century onwards remain incompletely understood, but recent research suggests that the process of de-Gaelicisation was more gradual and diffuse than once supposed (Neville 2010; Taylor and Márkus 2012).

From the late fourteenth century onwards, a cultural and linguistic division between 'Highland' and 'Lowland' Scotland, marked by a so-called 'Highland Line', seems to have been perceived, at least by those in the newly defined 'Lowlands', the now de-Gaelicised region of southern and eastern Scotland. Although this distinction may appear to be a natural consequence of geography and geology, given that a boundary fault clearly delineates the mountainous northwest of Scotland, no such division between 'Highlands' and 'Lowlands' had previously been known; the concept 'had simply not entered the minds of men' (Barrow 2003: 332). Earlier polities had straddled east and west; the southern border, not the western, had been most problematic.

By the end of the fourteenth century, the language shift of the late medieval period seems to have been substantially complete. Scots/English was spoken in the more agriculturally productive and economically dynamic regions of the country and Gaelic effectively confined to the less favoured Highlands.[2] The linguistic border between the Gaelic- and Scots/English-speaking zones was then fairly stable until the middle of the eighteenth century, when language shift began in earnest within the Highlands, as discussed in the next section. It is not clear why the process of language shift did not simply continue steadily through this period. Some tentative explanations involve the limited reach of burgh-based trading zones in interior river basins and the impact of the Black Death in the mid-fourteenth century, which eased population pressure and led to an abandonment of upland zones, thereby widening the gap between Highland and Lowland populations (Grant 1991: 200–2).

Even as the language was declining in some areas of Scotland during the late Middle Ages, it was strengthening in others. In particular, the Hebridean islands, which today are perceived as the heartland of Gaelic language and culture in Scotland, were under Norse control at the time the Gaelic kingdom of Alba was expanding and were not incorporated into the kingdom of Scots until 1266. The Hebrides then became more strongly Gaelic in linguistic and cultural terms during the late Middle Ages, and the powerful 'Lordship of the Isles' posed a serious threat to the Scottish kings at the height of its power in the fifteenth century (Oram 2014). As late as 1500, Gaelic was probably still spoken by about half the population of Scotland, but this proportion has dropped steadily, especially since c. 1750, as discussed below (Withers 1984).

Beginning in the late 1300s, if not earlier (Broun 2009), commentators from the Lowlands began to assert strongly negative attitudes towards the people of the Highlands, whom they had come to consider backward, violent, even barbarous (MacGregor 2009). The most famous expression of this view is that of the historian John of Fordun, usually dated to around 1380:

> The customs and habits of the Scots differ according to the difference of language; for two languages are in use, the Scottish [Gaelic] and the Teutonic [Scots/English]. The latter is the language of those living by the sea coast and in the plains, while the race of Scottish speech inhabits the highlands and outlying islands. The people of the coast are home-loving, civilised, trustworthy, tolerant and polite, decently attired, affable and pacific, devout in their worship of God, yet always ready to resist an injury at the hands of their enemies. The highlanders and people of the islands, on the other hand, are a wild and untamed race, primitive and proud, given to plunder and the easy life, clever and quick to learn, handsome in appearance, though slovenly in dress, consistently hostile to the people and language of the English, and, when the speech is different, even to their own nation. They are, however, loyal and obedient to their king and country, and provided they be well governed they are obedient and ready enough to respect the law.[3]

Fordun's rhetoric is typical of medieval western European discourse on the struggle between 'civilisation' and 'barbarity', a discourse that echoes conventional classical descriptions of barbarian peoples. His depiction of Lowlanders and Highlanders may therefore be understood, to some extent at least, as a redeployment of stereotyped tropes rather than an original ethnographic observation on the cultural politics of late medieval Scotland (Boardman 2005; MacGregor 2009).

Fordun continued to use the term 'Scottish' (*lingua Scotica*)[4] to refer to Gaelic, but from the fifteenth century onwards the term 'Irish' became dominant in Lowland usage and 'Scots' came to be used (alongside 'Inglis') as a label for the Germanic vernacular of the Lowlands (MacGregor 2009). Only in the later eighteenth century did the term 'Gaelic' fully replace 'Irish' (or 'Erse', in its Scots form) as the ordinary word for the language in Scotland.

The Gaelic terms corresponding to 'Highlands' and 'Lowlands' are *Gàidhealtachd* and *Galldachd* – the Gaelic culture-region and the non-Gaelic culture-region – but these expressions did not come into general use until well after the Highland/Lowland divide had emerged (McLeod 1999). The semantics of the term Gàidhealtachd have also become somewhat less clear over time. Sometimes it is now used to refer to the mainland Highlands only, so that the Hebrides, although now perceived as the Gaelic 'heartland', are sometimes excluded from the Gàidhealtachd,[5] but in the Scottish context it is rare for it to have the meaning of the corresponding term *Gaeltacht* (formerly spelled *Gaedhealtacht*) in modern Ireland, that of a geographical area in which the Gaelic language is spoken (Ó hIfearnáin 2008: 557–64).

Anti-Gaelic prejudices intensified in the later sixteenth century, when the Reformation transformed Lowland Scotland into a bastion of reformed Protestantism, and new ideologies of kingship and government gave new impetus to the imposition of 'civility' on the Gàidhealtachd, particularly under the reign of King James VI and I (1567–1625) (Cowan 2000).[6] James saw the Gaels as consisting of 'two sorts of people: the one that dwelleth in our maine land, that are barbarous for the most parte, and yet mixed with some shewe of civilitie: the other, that dwelleth in the Iles and are alluterlie barbares, without any sorte or shewe of civilitie' (Craigie 1944: I, 71). Increasingly repressive measures were adopted, notably the Statutes of Iona (1609), which placed strict restrictions upon the Highland chiefs and required them to have their heirs educated in the Lowlands, with the requirement that they 'may be found able sufficiently to speik, reid and wryte Englische' (Withers 1984: 22–30; MacGregor 2012). While some Highland clans such as the MacDonalds resisted these centralising processes, others such as the Campbells, conventionally labelled 'progressive', worked closely with the Lowland authorities and came to serve as regional power brokers (Macinnes 1996).

After 1603 the crowns of Scotland and England were united and a full union of parliaments followed in 1707. From the 1640s onwards the Gàidhealtachd became increasingly connected to wider British politics, especially the various conflicts concerning royal succession and the powers of the monarchy. Many, though by no means all, Highlanders became royalists, supporters of the Stuart dynasty, known as Jacobites following the overthrow of King James (*Jacobus* in Latin) VII and II in 1688. When the final Jacobite rising was crushed at the battle of Culloden in 1746, severe repressive measures were imposed upon the Gàidhealtachd to ensure that the region would never again pose a threat to the British state. Military occupation and scorched-earth tactics were followed by the so-called Acts of Proscription of 1747,[7] which outlawed the wearing of the traditional Highland dress and the carrying of arms. Contrary to widespread misconception, however, there was no prohibition on the bagpipes or the use of the Gaelic language (MacDonald 2017).

In the view of the distinguished Gaelic scholar William Gillies, 'the defeat of the Jacobite army at Culloden became burned into the collective memory of Gaelic speakers everywhere, irrespective of religion or political persuasion. [. . .] Important as the battle was at the time in terms of human loss, it became even more important as a symbol – the symbol of something like the end of independent Gaelic action' (Gillies 1991: 40). Traditional Gaelic institutions were shattered, and there was a pervasive sense of demoralisation.

The period following Culloden also saw an intensification of processes of economic and cultural assimilation. From the late eighteenth century onwards the Industrial Revolution dramatically transformed Scotland, but industrial development was overwhelmingly concentrated in the central Lowlands, prompting many Gaels to migrate to the rapidly growing Lowland cities, especially under the pressure of agricultural restructuring in the Gàidhealtachd, as discussed below (Withers 1998). At the same time, the expansion of the British Empire from the middle of the eighteenth century brought attractive new opportunities overseas, not least through participation in the British military (MacKillop 2001; Dziennik 2015). The Highland regiments became a key element in the imperial and 'British' loyalties that became deeply entrenched in Scottish Gaelic identity (McLeod 2013c; Maciver 2018).

Although some parts of the Gàidhealtachd, particularly in Argyll and the far north, adopted Protestantism in the sixteenth century, it was only in the later eighteenth century, as evangelical movements spread, that many areas embraced the new religion with enthusiasm (Meek 1996:

23). Some areas remained Catholic, following Counter-Reformation initiatives in the seventeenth and eighteenth centuries (Meek 1996: 16–18). In 1843 the established Church of Scotland (Calvinist in its theology and Presbyterian in its structure) underwent a schism, known as the Disruption, with the breakaway of the Free Church of Scotland. Particularly in the northern parts of the Gàidhealtachd, the Free Church became the dominant denomination, not least because one of the principal issues that gave rise to the Disruption was the right of congregations, rather than the local landowner, to choose the local minister (Ansdell 1998). In some minds, Gaelic became associated with a gloomy, oppressive kind of Calvinism and this perception forms part of the (typically negative) stereotyping applied to Gaelic speakers down to the present (e.g. Galloway 2008).

From the 1760s onwards, different strands of Romanticism began to influence perceptions of Gaelic in Scotland, with the now-pacified Gaels perceived as noble savages of a sort (Stroh 2017: 113–40). Central to this process were the heroic prose-poems published by James Macpherson from 1760 onwards, which he attributed to a third-century Gaelic poet called Ossian. These works were substantially the creation of Macpherson himself, though reworked from authentic Gaelic material, and were challenged as forgeries by Dr Samuel Johnson and others. Nevertheless, Ossian had an immense impact in Britain and across Europe and was instrumental in establishing the idea of the Gael as a noble ancestor of Scotland (Moore 2017). The once-banned Highland garb became newly fashionable, especially following the visit of King George IV (1820–30) to Scotland in 1822, which was choreographed by the novelist Sir Walter Scott (Cheape 2010: 21–2). As a result of these competing understandings and discourses, by the middle of the nineteenth century Lowland attitudes towards the Highlands had become a complex mix of 'contempt, sympathy and romance' (Fenyö 2000). But if the Gaelic language could sometimes be perceived as the 'quintessence of Scottish culture' and the 'spiritual substance of the nation' (Chapman 1978: 12–13), the Gaelic-speaking areas were 'never seen in any widespread way as being a treasure-house of [national] cultural revival or a repository of aphoristic wisdom', in the manner of the Irish Gaeltacht (Titley 2011: 405).

Educational initiatives by church and state had a very significant long-term impact on Gaelic and the Gàidhealtachd. Unlike many European minority languages, Gaelic has a very long history as a written language. The earliest surviving Gaelic texts date from the eighth century and the first Gaelic book was published in 1567 (Ó Baoill 2010). There was a flourishing Gaelic learned culture in the Middle Ages, concentrated in professional schools organised by hereditary learned families and sustained by aristocratic patronage and strong links to Ireland, but this broke down during the seventeenth century following the final English conquest of Ireland (McLeod 2004a).

Although various plans and initiatives had been announced throughout the seventeenth century, notably the 1616 *Act for the Settlement of Parochial Schools*, only in the eighteenth century, following the enactment of the *Act for settling of schools* in 1696, did the authorities succeed in establishing schools in the Gàidhealtachd in a meaningful fashion. Instrumental in these efforts was the Society in Scotland for Propagating Christian Knowledge (SSPCK), founded in 1709, which had set up over three hundred schools in the region by 1795, aiming to educate children in the 'Reformed Protestant Religion' by instructing them in reading, 'especially the Holy Scriptures', writing and arithmetic (Kelly 2016: 2). The extent of the SSPCK's hostility to Gaelic has sometimes been overstated, but it initially focused on English literacy exclusively, and the ideology underpinning the initial phase of the SSPCK's activity was summarised in a memorial (formal submission) in 1716 as 'reducing these Countries to order [. . .] making them usefull to the Commonwealth [. . .] teaching them their duty to God, their King and Countrey, and rooting out their Irish Language' (quoted in Durkacz 1983: 50–1).

A Gaelic translation of the Bible was not made available until 1767 (New Testament) and 1801 (Old Testament), following an initiative by the SSPCK and other educational institutions (Meek 1990).[8] The availability of the Bible, and the spread of new kinds of schools affiliated with different religious organisations (see pp. 75–6 below), effected a significant increase in Gaelic literacy rates in the first part of the nineteenth century. This growth in the Gaelic reading public led to a wave of publication initiatives, including the first Gaelic periodicals from 1803 onwards. Only seventy Gaelic books were published in the 1700s (forty-five of them in the 1780s and 1790s), but the number exceeded a thousand in the following century (Thomson 1983b: 245–6). The position of Gaelic was much less favourable than that of Welsh: in Wales, the first translation of the Bible was published as early as 1588, helping to establish a standard form of the language (as Martin Luther's Bible did for German) and to build a much stronger culture of publishing and literacy (Davies 2014: 39–41, 48–9).

The transformation of the Gàidhealtachd from the middle of the eighteenth century onwards also involved massive changes to the regional economy, particularly in terms of land use, which had the consequence of triggering out-migration on a huge scale, some of it voluntary, some otherwise. Traditional smallholdings were eliminated to create large-scale commercial sheep farms, a process that required the wholesale eviction of the existing population, sometimes forcibly. This process, known as the Highland Clearances, meant that tens of thousands of people left the region, through emigration to Canada or elsewhere in the Empire or by migration to the expanding industrial cities. Others remained on inferior new holdings, often in 'desperately exposed' and 'grimly inhospitable' places on the coast (Hunter 2000: 4). Following the Clearances, which lasted from approximately 1780 to 1860, the population of the Gàidhealtachd fell steadily for more than a century. A large proportion of the Gàidhealtachd population was subsisting in extreme poverty, sometimes outright destitution, especially during the famine of the 1840s (Devine 1988). In some activist accounts the Clearances are even characterised as 'bordering on genocide' (Thompson 1985: 4), although this view has not received scholarly approbation (Small 2018).

Clearance and emigration led to the establishment of numerous Gaelic-speaking communities in different parts of the world in the eighteenth and nineteenth centuries, especially in Canada, the United States, Australia and New Zealand. These opportunities for emigration and overseas settlement were integrally linked to British imperialism and colonialism. By far the largest and best-sustained of these emigrant communities was in eastern Nova Scotia, especially Cape Breton Island (Kennedy 2002). Traditional native speakers have now nearly disappeared from Cape Breton, but there has been increasingly vigorous revival activity in recent years (Province of Nova Scotia 2019: 18–20). The social and institutional trajectory of Gaelic in the distinct context of Nova Scotia exceeds the scope of this book, however.

New urban Gaelic communities also developed in the cities and towns of the Lowlands, especially Glasgow, which became known in Gaelic as 'Baile Mòr nan Gàidheal' (City of the Gaels) (Withers 1998; Kidd 2007). This process of out-migration has continued in the twentieth and twenty-first centuries, and these urban Gaelic communities have played an important role in Gaelic movements and cultural initiatives. However, as is typical of languages in migration contexts (Fishman 1978), intergenerational transmission of Gaelic in urban communities was weak: the language tended to 'evaporate[] in the next generation', like 'a river flowing into a desert or sinking into the sand' (Grant 1984: 4).

The Clearances had come to an end by the late 1850s but the land question continued to be controversial in the later nineteenth century. There had been different forms of resistance to the Clearances earlier in the 1800s, but this intensified considerably from 1874 as a so-called 'Crofters' War' broke out. This involved significant unrest in many parts of the Gàidhealtachd, notably the islands of Skye, Lewis and Tiree, as tenants mobilised to improve their conditions by organising rent strikes and resisting evictions. The government responded to these pressures by setting up the Royal Commission on the Crofters and Cottars in the Highlands and Islands of Scotland (the Napier Commission), to take evidence concerning the tenants' situation and make policy recommendations (Royal Commission 1884; Cameron 1986). The subsequent *Crofters Holdings (Scotland) Act 1886* granted important new rights to the crofters (traditional subsistence tenants in designated areas of the Highlands and Islands). The most important of these rights involved security of tenure and the right to have the rent level determined by an independent body (the Crofters' Commission). But the Act did not address the crofters' fundamental demand, that landlords release land for the creation of new holdings. The land question remained controversial in the following decades, particularly through the practice of land raids, by which cottars and crofters occupied farms and established smallholdings of their own, triggering evictions and high-profile legal cases. The effect of the new crofting system in stabilising communities, and the solidaristic experience of the 'making of the crofting community' (Hunter 2000), played a very important role in Gaelic language maintenance. Indeed, crofting came to be 'revalorized as the essential embodiment of the "Gaelic way of life"' (Burnett 2011: 271).

The introduction of the Crofters Act was one of several measures that reflected the government's new sense that the Highlands and Islands (a new term which came into use during this period) should be treated as a 'special policy area' requiring distinct policies (Cameron 1997). These included the establishment in 1897 of the Congested Districts Board to support the development of the regional economy and infrastructure. As discussed in subsequent chapters, the issue of Highland underdevelopment was a major policy preoccupation for most of the twentieth century. The problem has diminished since the 1960s, largely due to the success of policies adopted by the Highlands and Islands Development Board and its successor, Highlands and Islands Enterprise. The connection between the vitality of the Gaelic language and the socio-economic development of the Gàidhealtachd has also been an important theme since the nineteenth century, although arguably this linkage has become less prominent in the twenty-first century, as Gaelic development has begun to focus more on promoting the language in distinct sectors and contexts across Scotland.

THE PROCESS OF LANGUAGE SHIFT

Following several centuries in which the Gaelic/English linguistic border along the 'Highland Line' was fairly stable, language shift within the Gàidhealtachd began in earnest in the eighteenth century and has progressed steadily since. This was driven by the destructive combination of circumstances summarised above: military repression, drastic economic change, heavy, sometimes forced emigration, persistent material deprivation, and continuous Anglicising cultural pressures (Withers 1984). Against this background, the influential *Cor na Gàidhlig* report of 1982, discussed below (pp. 192–4), observed that 'the cause for wonder may be, not that decline has been so rapid, but that the language survived at all' (GRG 1982: 14).[9]

By the middle of the eighteenth century, language shift was evidently under way in southern and eastern parts of the Highlands, especially those areas nearest the Highland Line. In such districts transitional bilingualism developed as younger generations acquired English, through formal schooling or experience of seasonal work in the Lowlands, and with the breakdown of intergenerational transmission the language tended to pass out of community use relatively soon thereafter. Language shift processes slowly worked their way north and west in the nineteenth century, driven by improved transport links and increased social and economic interaction with the English-speaking world. However, 'the decline of Gaelic . . . should not be seen as the simple "retreat" north-westwards of a Gàidhealtachd in which Gaelic was uniformly spoken and common in all domains'; rather, the Gàidhealtachd as a whole became 'less and less strongly Gaelic', as English became more widely known everywhere and penetrated into an increasing range of domains (Withers 1998: 326–8). Gaelic was very slow in disappearing altogether, however: when fieldwork was conducted for the Gaelic Section of the Linguistic Survey of Scotland in the 1950s and 1960s, field investigators were still able to locate Gaelic speakers native to almost every parish in the traditional Gàidhealtachd (Gillies 1997: vii).

Although the academic literature concerning language shift is very extensive, there is no consensus as to how these sociolinguistic processes may best be understood (Dorian 2011: 469; Mufwene 2017). Kenneth MacKinnon has offered four models to explain the language shift in the

Gàidhealtachd, all of which played a role in the process and all of which can be connected to the Clearances to one degree or another:

1. The 'Clearance' model, in which substantial numbers of the native population have been through force or other inducement removed from an area.
2. The 'Economic Development' model, in which new forms of economic organisation bring about cultural changes requiring language shift (e.g. introduction of English as a commercial or technical language).
3. The 'Changeover' model operating at the demographic level. New people come in to an area to undertake new activities. Opportunity for the local population to retain the stability of its traditional socio-economic infrastructure diminishes and the local people die out or leave.
4. The 'Social Morale' model. Changes occur in the power relationship between social groups. The local community loses confidence in its system of values, e.g. through religious or educational proselytisation. The local language as symbolic of superseded local values is shifted in favour of the language in which the new values have been mediated (1977: 35).

The last of these models is probably the most important and long-standing in its impact, although it is the least susceptible to objective detection and measurement. The pervasive sense of demoralisation within the Gaelic community in the nineteenth century was famously expressed by the campaigning journalist and land rights activist John Murdoch in his testimony to the Napier Commission in 1883:

> The language and lore of the Highlanders being treated with despite [sic], has tended to crush their self-respect, and repress that self-reliance without which no people can advance. When a man was convinced that his language was a barbarism, his lore as filthy rags, and that the only good thing about him – his land – was, because of his general worthlessness, to go to the man of another race and another tongue, what remained [...] that he should struggle for? (Royal Commission 1884: 3083)

In the twentieth century, Gaelic commentators wrote repeatedly of an 'inferiority complex' afflicting the community (e.g. Mac na Ceàrdaich 1928; Murchison 1955: 16; Macrae 1957: 103), 'a deep and subtle feeling that English must be superior to Gaelic' (Smith 1986: 37).

MacKinnon's models relate primarily to the nineteenth century and arguably do not provide an entirely satisfactory explanation for the ongoing language shift of recent decades, whose dynamics have only been explored to a limited extent. Sharon MacDonald has pointed to the impact of English-language mass media (especially television), the increased uptake of (English-medium) secondary and tertiary education, the increase in linguistically mixed marriages (in which only one partner speaks Gaelic), increased levels of in-migration to Gaelic communities, and changing community norms concerning English language use, by which English slowly became accepted and normalised in previously solidly Gaelic domains (MacDonald 1997: 222–3). It is also important in this context to bear in mind how deeply rooted negative perceptions and attitudes can become within minority language communities and how slow they can be to change, even when more favourable policies are adopted by the authorities and a more supportive environment develops (Ó hIfearnáin 2013: 118).

Before 1881, when questions concerning Gaelic were first placed on the national census, evidentiary sources for the demography of the language are relatively thin, although Charles Withers's landmark study (1984) analysed them comprehensively. The *Old Statistical Account* (1791–9) and *New Statistical Account* (1831–45) provide invaluable information about the linguistic dynamics of the different Highland parishes, revealing a complex and variegated situation across the region, and often recording significant sociolinguistic changes in the decades between the two surveys (Withers 1984: 73–6, 87–90, 297–323). The best estimate suggests that there were just under 300,000 Gaelic speakers at the start of the nineteenth century, approximately one-fifth of the population of Scotland (Withers and MacKinnon 1984: 111).

The subsequent collapse in the Highland population due to out-migration had very significant demolinguistic consequences. The most obvious and direct effect 'was simply the loss of great numbers of Gaelic speakers and the resultant decline in intensity of the language within the Gàidhealtachd' (Withers 1984: 110). In the Isle of Tiree and the mainland district of Morvern, the population has declined by more than 85 per cent since 1831, and even in Lewis and Harris, where the population continued to rise until 1911, the level has since fallen by almost 40 per cent.

The 1881 census showed a total of 231,594 Gaelic speakers, a mere 6.2 per cent of the national population, which had grown significantly during the era of industrial expansion in the Lowlands. The 1881 census is not considered reliable, however, as it asked whether respondents were 'in the habit of making colloquial use of the Gaelic language'. The census of 1891 (and subsequent iterations until 1961) asked whether

Table 1 Historical demography of Gaelic[10]

Date	Total Gaelic speakers in Scotland	Proportion of total Scottish population (%)	Intercensal change (%)
1500	150,000?	50?	
1755	290,000	22.9	
1806	297,823	18.5	
1881	231,594	6.2	
1891	254,415	6.3	
1901	230,806	5.2	−9.3
1911	202,398	4.3	−12.3
1921	158,779	3.5	−21.6
1931	136,135	3.0	−14.3
1951	95,447	1.9	−29.9[11]
1961	80,978	1.6	−15.3
1971	88,892	1.7	+9.8
1981	82,620	1.6	−7.1
1991	65,978	1.3	−16.8
2001	58,652	1.2	−11.1
2011	57,602	1.1	−2.2

respondents spoke Gaelic and returned a figure of 254,415 speakers aged three and over, 6.3 per cent of the Scottish total (Thomas 1998: [1]; Withers and MacKinnon 1983: 10–11). This figure may well represent an undercount, however, particularly in the Western Isles (Withers 1984: 210–11).[12] Just under a fifth of Gaelic speakers recorded in 1891 (43,738 persons) were not able to speak English; more than two-thirds of these were concentrated in the Western Isles, Skye and Tiree (Census Office 1893: Table I).

Out-migration meant that Gaelic spread out beyond the traditional Gàidhealtachd; in 1891 more than a quarter of Scotland's Gaelic speakers were living in the Lowlands (Census Office 1893: Table I). In addition, as a result of overseas emigration, a significant proportion of the overall Gaelic-speaking population lived outside Scotland at the end of the nineteenth century. In 1901 there were some 50,000 Gaelic speakers in Nova Scotia alone (more than a fifth of the total recorded in Scotland in that year) (Kennedy 2002: 63).

By 1931 the number of Gaelic speakers had fallen to 136,135 (3.3 per cent of the national population), with only 6,716 monoglots remaining, and in most Highland parishes only a minority of the population could speak Gaelic. In much of the southern and eastern Gàidhealtachd the Gaelic-speaking population had dropped below a quarter, sometimes even below a tenth. Conversely, most of the northern and western

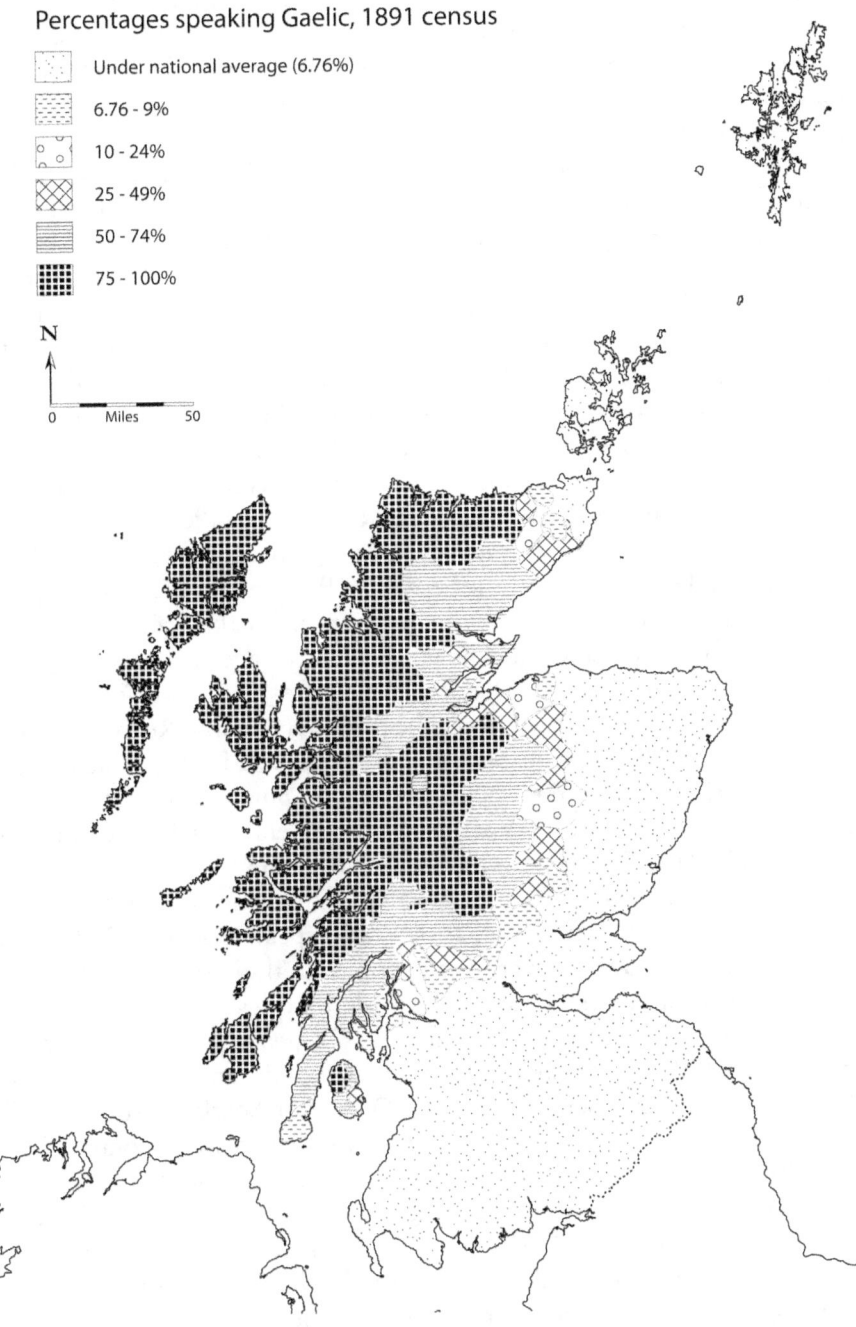

Density of Gaelic speakers in Scottish parishes in the 1891 Census. © Kenneth MacKinnon; used with permission.

mainland, as well as most of the Hebridean islands, remained over 70 per cent Gaelic speaking, and eleven parishes, in the Western Isles, Skye and Tiree, stood at over 90 per cent (Thomas 1998: Table 2). But in the following decades, language shift continued almost without interruption, as shown in Table 1.

The number of Gaelic speakers fell by almost three-quarters over the course of the twentieth century, and most areas in the Gàidhealtachd have become entirely English-speaking. The 2011 census showed 57,602 Gaelic speakers aged three and over in Scotland, a mere 1.1 per cent of the national population.[13] Of these, 32,191 people could speak, read and write Gaelic; 18,966 could speak Gaelic but not read or write it; 6,218 could speak and read Gaelic but not write it; 1,678 had other combinations of skills in Gaelic; and a further 23,357 could understand Gaelic but not speak, read or write it (NRS 2014, Table QS211SC; see NRS 2015). The rate of decline has now slowed considerably, however. Between 2001 and 2011 the number of Gaelic speakers decreased by only 2.2 per cent, following an 11.1 per cent drop between 1991 and 2001 and a 16.8 per cent drop between 1981 and 1991. The proportion of Gaelic speakers in the younger sections of the Scottish population (those between three and nineteen years of age) increased slightly between 2001 and 2011, probably as a result of Gaelic-medium school education, which has developed since 1985 (General Register Office for Scotland 2005, Table 4; NRS 2014, Table DC2120SC; MacKinnon 2004: 24, 27). Even so, the Gaelic-speaking population remains skewed to older age groups, with 52 per cent of speakers in 2011 aged fifty or over (NRS 2014, Table DC2120SC; see NRS 2015).

Today, the densest concentration of speakers is in the Western Isles, where 52 per cent of the population could speak Gaelic in 2011, but with proportions over 80 per cent in some rural districts. The proportion of Gaelic speakers in the Western Isles had dropped rapidly in the preceding decades, however, down from 78 per cent in 1971 and 62 per cent in 2001, as a result of both language shift and in-migration by English monoglots (General Register Office for Scotland 2005: Table 1; MacKinnon 1978: 29). Some Inner Hebridean islands, notably Skye and Tiree, also still contain dense concentrations of Gaelic speakers (29 per cent and 38 per cent respectively), while the highest level of any mainland parish in 2011 was only 19.3 per cent, in Ardnamurchan. The share of Gaelic speakers living in the Lowlands now stands at approximately 48 per cent, with significant concentrations in the larger urban areas, particularly greater Glasgow (home to some 10,000 speakers) (NRS 2014: Table QS211SC; see NRS 2015). In these Lowland

Historical and Sociolinguistic Background

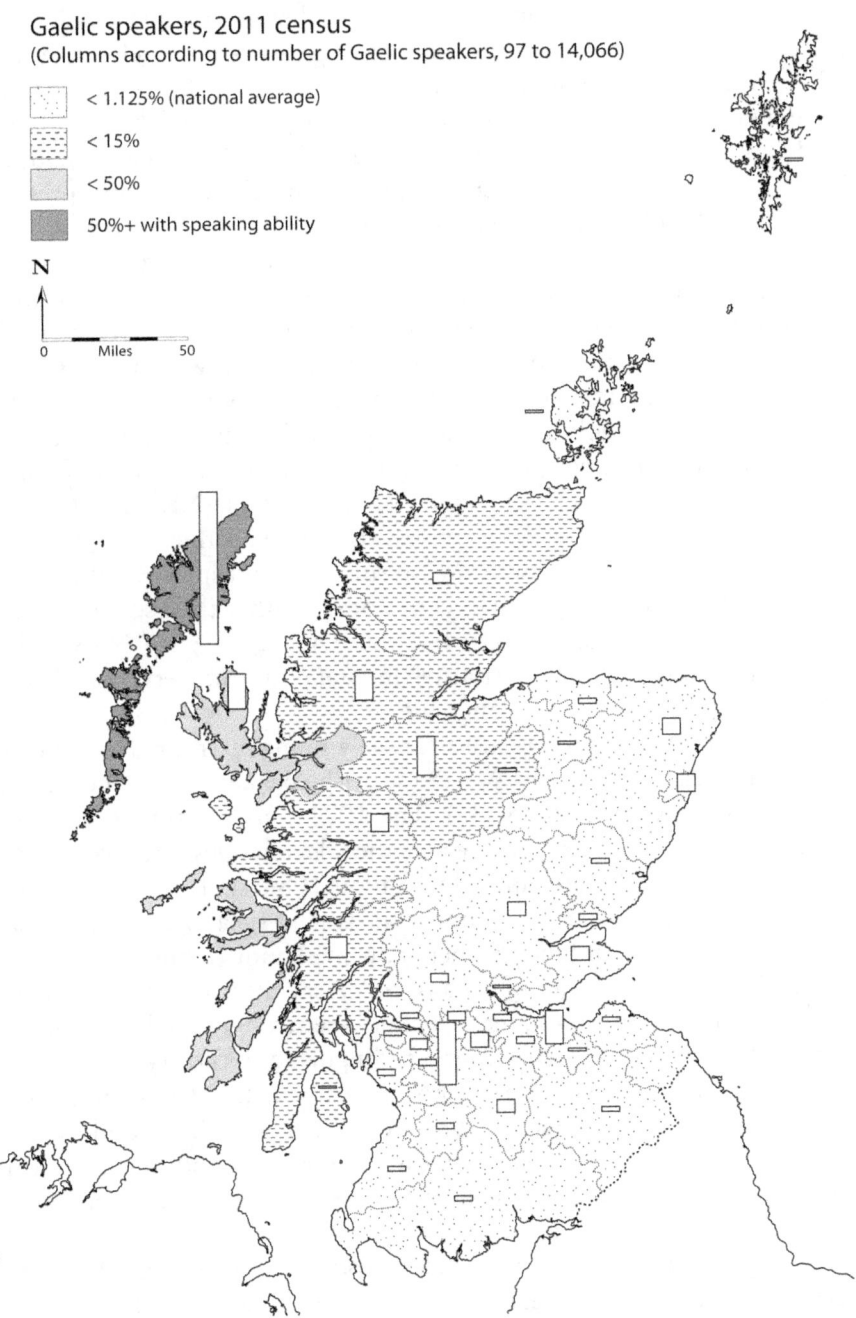

Density and numbers of Gaelic speakers in Scottish local authorities in the 2011 Census. © Bòrd na Gàidhlig; used with permission.

areas, however, the proportion of Gaelic speakers in the population is extremely low, generally 1 per cent or below. In 2011 only 24.3 per cent of Gaelic speakers were living in parishes in which more than 50 per cent of the population could speak Gaelic, while 43.3 per cent were living in parishes in which less than 1.1 per cent of the population could speak Gaelic (NRS 2015: 7, 72–82; NRS 2014: Table KS206SC). The dispersed nature of the contemporary speech community presents significant challenges for Gaelic development efforts.

Intergenerational transmission of the language is weak. According to the 2011 census, only 72.2 per cent of children aged between three and fifteen who were living with two Gaelic-speaking parents could speak Gaelic, as against 39.4 per cent of those living with a lone Gaelic-speaking parent and a mere 26.8 per cent of those living with two parents, of whom only one could speak Gaelic (this last arrangement being the most common, comprising some 64 per cent of the families in which at least one parent could speak Gaelic) (NRS 2014: Table CT_0217_2011).[14] The 2011 census also showed that only 29.5 per cent of the 3–4 age group in the Western Isles could speak Gaelic, which gives a rough indicator of the level of home- (rather than school-) based language acquisition (NRS 2014: Table DC2120SC; see NRS 2015). Gaelic thus appears to be seriously threatened in the very last districts where it remains a majority language.

All Gaelic speakers today are effectively bilingual in English, as is the case with Welsh speakers in Wales and Irish speakers in Ireland (Davies 2014: 103: Ó Riagáin 2018: 35). The 1971 census returned only 477 monoglot Gaelic speakers, after which the relevant question was removed from the census (Withers and MacKinnon 1983: 111; NRS 2015: 19). During the last few decades almost all Gaelic-speaking children have acquired English in infancy rather than in school (Lamb 2008: 44–6; Gillies 2008: 299). Although many older speakers can be considered Gaelic-dominant, most younger speakers are strongly English-dominant (Lamb 2008: 44–6). In this context, 'linguistic authority' tends to be 'conferred on fluent speakers' who grew up in the 1940s and 1950s when community language use was much stronger. These model speakers are perceived as retaining traditional grammar and idiom, in contrast to the 'reduced' 'English-influenced usages of the younger generation' (Bell et al. 2014: C199–200).

Perhaps as much as 25 per cent of today's speaker population are second-language (L2) speakers, i.e. people who have acquired the language through formal education or some other mechanism besides family transmission. It is impossible to give a reliable figure, however, as the census does not seek this information and no other relevant national surveys have been conducted. This relatively low proportion reflects the traditional exclusion of Gaelic from the Scottish education system, but it is clear that the numbers of L2 (or 'new') speakers have increased significantly in recent years due to the expansion of Gaelic-medium education and the growing number of adults who have learned the language to fluency (McLeod and O'Rourke 2015).

These sociolinguistic trends mean that the significance of the figures reported in the census has changed over time. Those who were recorded as Gaelic speakers in the late nineteenth century would overwhelmingly have been first-language speakers who used Gaelic as their main means of communication, whereas today those indicating an ability to speak Gaelic might include people with a wide range of competences, probably including some with limited ability in Gaelic who are motivated by a desire to express support for the language for attitudinal or political reasons. This has long been a difficulty with the census in Ireland, where the number of speakers recorded in the census hugely exceeds the number of fluent, active speakers (Ó hIfearnáin 2010: 36–7). At the same time, some 'diffident' native speakers may choose not to record themselves as Gaelic speakers in the census, considering themselves 'lapsed' or insufficiently fluent (MacKinnon 1985: 10).

Literacy levels in Gaelic are also low: according to the 2011 census, only 67 per cent of Gaelic speakers could read Gaelic and only 56 per cent could write it (NRS 2014: Table QS211SC). Moreover, many of those who can read and/or write Gaelic do not necessarily do so frequently or comfortably (Lamb 2008: 49–50). Given that English literacy is nearly universal in Scotland, these low levels of Gaelic literacy are a strong indicator of the limited role Gaelic has had in the education system.

The 2011 census included a question concerning language use for the first time. Respondents were asked whether they used a language other than English at home, and 24,974 people indicated that they used Gaelic in this context, some 43 per cent of the total number of speakers (NRS 2014, Table KS206SC). This census question was open to different interpretations (how, for example, should someone living on their own answer the question?) and this figure may be less than entirely reliable. The low figure for Gaelic is nevertheless understandable in view of the fact that less than one Gaelic speaker in five lives in a household in which everyone speaks Gaelic (MacKinnon 2009: 166). The census data on usage showed significant variation in different parts of Scotland; as might be expected, in areas with dense concentrations of Gaelic speakers the proportion who reported using the language at home was much higher than in areas of low density. 77.3 per cent of Gaelic speakers in the Western Isles reported using the language at home, while the proportions in Lowland Scotland varied between 10 per cent and 40 per cent (NRS 2014: Table KS206SC). The census is a blunt instrument for measuring the dynamics of language use, but there has never been any kind of national Gaelic language use survey of the kinds conducted in Wales and the Basque Country, for example (Welsh Government and Welsh Language Commissioner 2015; Basque Autonomous Community 2013).

Additional evidence from recent sociolinguistic studies makes it abundantly clear that Gaelic is in severe decline as a community language. These studies show a significant and ongoing decrease in the level of community Gaelic use in the Western Isles since the 1970s (MacKinnon 2006; NicAoidh 2006; Mac an Tàilleir, Rothach and Armstrong 2010; Rothach, Mac an Tàilleir and Dòmhnallach 2016; BBC Naidheachdan 2019). Disturbingly, survey evidence indicates that many Western Isles residents tend to use English even in circumstances or settings where they are aware it is possible for them to use Gaelic (NicAoidh 2006, 79, 85; Western Isles Language Plan Project 2005: 23–4). Language shift in the islands is now at an advanced stage, and even in the strongest rural districts, where Gaelic was the normal language of social interaction until the 1960s and beyond, community use of the language has declined very considerably and intergenerational transmission appears to have nearly ceased.

In summary, every sociolinguistic indicator suggests that Gaelic is now in a severely weakened state and that this decline is ongoing, in spite of the revitalisation initiatives of recent years. Policies and programmes to strengthen the position of Gaelic therefore function within a very challenging sociolinguistic context.

2

Policy, Ideology and Discourse

Through the centuries, official policy in Scotland in relation to Gaelic has been driven by overarching aims and underpinned by important assumptions, but these have more often been tacit rather than explicit. This chapter introduces some of the key elements of Gaelic policy provision and the main factors that have shaped or constrained its development, along with an overview of the nature of the principal ideological debates and activists' demands in relation to the language. In different ways at different times, these structural and ideological factors have had important impacts on what was offered and what was sought, as discussed in detail in the following chapters.

The term 'language ideology' is widely used in academic work on language policy and sociolinguistics, although it may not be familiar outside this context. A useful explanation of the concept was given by Annette Boudreau and Lise Dubois (2008: 104):

> Language ideologies are usually defined as a set of beliefs on language or a particular language shared by members of a community. . . . These beliefs come to be so well established that their origin is often forgotten by speakers, and are therefore socially reproduced and end up being 'naturalized', or perceived as natural or as common sense, thereby masking the social construction processes at work. Ideologies become political when they are embedded in the social principles on which a community organises itself institutionally.

In the Gaelic context, perceptions of the language rest on a range of assumptions about its role, its significance and its value. Some of these perceptions are typical of minority languages in general while others are specific to the Scottish context, some of them rooted in centuries-old discourses and others having emerged more recently.

GAELIC LANGUAGE POLICY IN SCOTLAND: AN OVERVIEW

The fundamental goal of state language policy in Scotland, as in other parts of the United Kingdom and elsewhere in Europe, was to establish and spread the state language, English, and to ensure that all the population had a knowledge of that language. In the case of Gaelic, this goal can be said to have been fulfilled by the 1980s, with the passing of the last monolingual speakers, but it had effectively been achieved much earlier than this. This aim has rarely been expressly articulated, however, and the methods used to accomplish this end have varied a good deal over time, largely as a result of the increasing capacity of government institutions. There are few direct statements setting out any kind of general government policy in relation to Gaelic until the end of the twentieth century, by which time a much more favourable regime of public support for the language was gradually being put in place. Of course, language policies are often covert rather than overt (Shohamy 2006), implicit rather than explicit, and the failure of the authorities to engage carefully with the issue of Gaelic can be seen as reflecting an understanding that the matter was insufficiently important to merit such attention.

Crucially, the fundamental aim of securing universal knowledge of the state language does not necessarily determine the nature of the government's policy towards the ongoing survival and use of other languages among the citizenry. Once the pre-eminence of the state language as the medium of public and economic life in the national territory has been ensured, the authorities may sometimes be willing to allow a limited space for minority languages and to adopt measures to facilitate their retention or indeed development. In other cases, there can be an insistence on monolingualism in the state language, with the continuing use of a minority language characterised as inherently inimical to the government's authority or founding principles (Wright 2016: 49). A classic statement of this latter view was given by Bertrand Barère in 1794, in the context of revolutionary France:

> Le fédéralisme et la superstition parlent bas-breton; l'émigration et la haine de la République parlent allemand; la contre-révolution parle l'italien, et le fanatisme parle le basque. Cassons ces instruments de dommage et d'erreur. [. . .] Citoyens, la langue d'un peuple libre doit être une et la même pour tous.
>
> Federalism and superstition speak Breton, emigration and hatred of the Republic speak German, counter-revolution speaks Italian and fanaticism speaks Basque. Let us break these instruments of injury and error. Citizens, the language of a free people must be one and the same for all. (Barère 1794)

A softer version of the French republican ideology emphasised universalism and the need to eradicate barriers and differences, including linguistic barriers and differences, to give practical effect to the concept of equality (Grégoire 1794). The British inflection of this universalising ideology was classically expressed by Matthew Arnold, celebrated poet, essayist and educationalist, who asserted, in a report to the education authorities in Wales in 1852, that 'it must always be the desire of a Government to render its dominions, as far as possible, homogeneous, and to break down barriers to the freest intercourse between the different parts of them' (Arnold 1889: 13). Expounding on this theme in his famous 1867 volume *On the Study of Celtic Literature*, Arnold wrote:

> The fusion of all the inhabitants of these islands into one homogeneous, English-speaking whole, the breaking down of barriers between us, the swallowing up of separate provincial nationalities, is a consummation to which the natural course of things irresistibly tends; it is a necessity of what is called modern civilisation, and modern civilisation is a real, legitimate force; the change must come, and its accomplishment is a mere affair of time. The sooner the Welsh language disappears as an instrument of the practical, political, social life of Wales, the better; the better for England, the better for Wales itself. (Arnold 1867: 12)

The dominant version of assimilationist language ideology in Britain, however, tended to place more emphasis on the advantages of economic mobility and access to opportunities than on matters of identity and belonging (e.g. MacArthur 1885: 253–4). The command of English allowed access to the labour market not only in the economically dynamic areas of Britain but also throughout the British imperial dominions. Sometimes these two ideas were intertwined, and the economic rationale could appear as an instrumental justification for a deeper form of assimilationism, as the Registrar-General for Scotland proclaimed in 1874:

> The Gaelic language may be what it likes, both as to antiquity and beauty, but it decidedly stands in the way of the civilisation of the natives making use of it, and shuts them out from the paths open to their fellow-countrymen who speak the English tongue. It ought, therefore, to cease to be taught in all our national schools; and as we are one people, we should have but ONE language. (Census Office 1874: II, xx)

The pre-eminent nineteenth-century political philosopher John Stuart Mill made clear his view that this process of linguistic and cultural assimilation was not a matter of the merger of equals to create a greater whole, as Arnold had suggested, but the absorption and improvement of backward, 'half-savage' relic populations:

> Experience proves it is possible for one nationality to merge and be absorbed in another; and when it was originally an inferior and more backward part of the human race the absorption is greatly to its advantage. Nobody can suppose that it is not more beneficial to a Breton, or a Basque of French Navarre, to be brought into the current of the ideas and feelings of a highly civilised and cultivated people – to be a member of the French nationality, admitted on equal terms to all the privileges of French citizenship, sharing the advantages of French protection, and the dignity and prestige of French power – than to sulk on his own rocks, the half-savage relic of past times, revolving in his own little mental orbit, without participation or interest in the general movement of the world. The same remark applies to the Welshman or the Scottish Highlander as members of the British nation. (Mill 1991 [1861]: 294–5)

Yet the policies and rhetoric of the Victorian era had already softened considerably from the approach of earlier periods. In the late sixteenth and seventeenth centuries the government in Scotland had expressed an aggressive policy of linguistic assimilation – if not extirpation – in relation to the Gaelic language. The most direct statement in this respect is the Scottish Privy Council's 1616 *Act for the Settlement of Parochial Schools*:

> Forsamekle as, the Kingis Majestie haveing a speciall care and regaird that the trew religioun be advanceit and establisheit in all the pairtis of this kingdome, and that all his Majesties subjectis, especiallie the youth, be exercised and trayned up in civilitie, godlines, knawledge and learning, that the vulgar Inglishe toung be universallie plantit, and the Irishe language, whilk is one of the cheif and principall causis of the continewance of barbaritie and incivilitie amongis the inhabitantis of the Iles and Heylandis, may be abolisheit and removit; and quhairas thair is no meane more powerfull to further this his Majesties princelie regaird and porpois than the establisheing of scooles in the particular parrocheis of this kingdome whair the youthe may be taught at the least to write and reid, and be catechiesed and instructed in the groundis of religioun; thairfore the Kingis Majestie, has thocht it necessar and expedient that in everie parroche of this kingdome whair convenient meanes may be had for interteyning a scoole, that a scoole salbe establisheit, and a fitt persone appointit to teache the same ... (Masson 1891: 671–2)

This assertion of a causal connection between the Gaelic language and 'the continuance of barbarity and incivility' signalled a new intensification of anti-Gaelic sentiment and policy on the part of the Lowland authorities. Even so, there was never any formal legal enactment in Scotland establishing the English language in public life or barring Gaelic speakers from holding public office, as had been the case in Wales under legislation from 1536 (Roberts 1997).[1] Certainly there was no official 'ban' on Gaelic at any point, although this has become a well-established misconception in Scotland (e.g. McKenna 2011).

Through the seventeenth century and beyond, government and church institutions continued to express the aim of 'rooting out' the Gaelic language, a goal the Scottish Parliament characterised as a 'pious use' in its 1695 *Act and remitt in favour of the synod of Argyll*. Attitudes began to soften after the Highlands ceased to pose any kind of military threat to the state after the defeat of the last Jacobite rising in 1746. Already by the early nineteenth century, there was no longer any perception of Gaelic as seditious or symbolically oppositional to the state, in the way, for example, that Irish was seen by the Stormont regime in Northern Ireland after 1921 (Andrews 1997).

From the 1870s until as late as the 1960s, official policy towards Gaelic was characterised by two basic principles, pragmatism and liberalism. The principal objective of achieving universal competence in English was steadfastly pursued, but there was less and less evidence of the kind of forceful assimiliationism expressed by the Registrar-General in 1874, partly because of the manifest success of the state schools in securing the acquisition of English by the Highland population. From at least the start of the twentieth century, official expressions of outright hostility to Gaelic become rare, although patronising or faintly contemptuous attitudes remained endemic. The authorities would authorise the use of Gaelic in public contexts when this was felt to be genuinely necessary, and made no point of principle of monolingualism for its own sake, while the use of Gaelic in private contexts would be accepted and even encouraged in appropriate circumstances, especially for purposes of cultural expression. But the broader matter of language maintenance was not perceived as a government responsibility; this was essentially a matter for Gaelic speakers themselves (e.g. SO 1975).

In the crucial sphere of education – the principal policy mechanism for the spreading of English from the 1616 Act onwards – various concessions were made from the 1870s to allow a limited role for Gaelic in the school curriculum. The *Education (Scotland) Act 1872* brought universal state education – the principal aim of education reform in nineteenth-century Western societies – to Scotland but did not address the issue of Gaelic at all. The most important concession was an amendment to the *Education (Scotland) Act 1918* which required education authorities to make 'adequate provision' for teaching Gaelic in 'Gaelic speaking areas', a mandate which was carried over into subsequent Education Acts, including the Act of 1980, which remains in effect as the basic legal framework for the delivery of education in Scotland. As discussed in detail in chapter 4, the determination of which areas were 'Gaelic speaking' and what level of provision was deemed 'reasonable' was left up to individual education authorities. In practice, teaching of the language was very limited in terms of class hours and confined to areas where a significant proportion, typically a large majority, of the school pupils came from Gaelic-speaking homes. From the 1950s onwards, as discussed in chapter 5, formal national education policy became progressively more open towards Gaelic, but there was little institutional steering of these changes and no systematic and programmatic implementation. By the early 1970s Gaelic remained marginal to the curriculum even in the most strongly Gaelic-speaking areas. Until 1947 the language was not taught outside the Highland area, and teaching was almost entirely focused on native speakers until the 1960s, when dedicated examinations for Gaelic learners were introduced. There has never been any move to add Gaelic to the general school curriculum in Scotland, so that even today less than one-tenth of secondary schools offer instruction in Gaelic and the overwhelming majority of Scottish pupils have no contact with the language at any point in their education. The contrast with Welsh in this regard is striking; following the implementation of the *Education Reform Act 1988*, all pupils in Wales must study Welsh until age sixteen.

By far the most important development in relation to educational provision for Gaelic has been the growth of Gaelic-medium education since 1985. Following a pioneering 'bilingual project' in the Western Isles from 1975 to 1982 (Murray and Morrison 1984), Gaelic 'units' were launched in two primary schools in Glasgow and Inverness in 1985. Today almost five thousand pupils in many different parts of Scotland receive Gaelic-medium education (GME) (BnG 2019b). A crucial development that facilitated the growth of GME was the government's decision in 1986 to establish a system of 'specific grants' to help education authorities fund the development of Gaelic education. The trajectory of this major policy shift is discussed in detail in chapters 6, 7 and 8.

Outside the realm of education, and a limited radio service, there was effectively no provision for Gaelic by public agencies until the 1960s; the unstated policy was one of thoroughgoing monolingualism. Until the 1980s, for example, almost no government publications were issued in Gaelic; Gaelic was used only in a small number of notices or leaflets relating to public health or law and order, which the authorities were concerned to ensure were understood by all. In the 1960s the government expressed a willingness to make adjustments 'where the shoe pinches' (SO

1966a: [2]), that is, where Gaelic speakers could be shown to have suffered 'genuine difficulties' when dealing with the monolingual English state (SO 1970b; Scottish Home and Health Department 1980). But requests for Gaelic versions of official documents were typically dismissed on the grounds that any pinching was insufficiently painful: that costs would be excessive given the small number of monolingual Gaelic speakers (e.g. SO 1969, 1980b). There was, however, no insistence that only the state language could be used for public functions as a matter of principle. Similarly, there was no formal prohibition on Gaelic in the courts, but litigants or witnesses were only permitted to use Gaelic when they were unable to speak English (a stricture that remains in place in criminal cases and all but a very few civil cases) (see pp. 201 and 261 below).

The government did make a small but important shift in policy in the 1960s by awarding direct support for Gaelic organisations for the first time, implicitly recognising that Gaelic language maintenance was, to some extent at least, a responsibility of government. Over time, government funding for different kinds of Gaelic initiatives has grown immensely in scale and scope, typically by the incremental growth of particular programmes, but occasionally by leaps and bounds, most notably with the annual injection of £9.5m for Gaelic television production from 1992 onwards. In 2018–19 total Scottish Government funding for Gaelic was £28.5m, of which £12.8m was dedicated to broadcasting (SG 2018c). In a similar way, the number and range of publications and documents produced in Gaelic by public authorities has increased steadily since the 1980s.

The government's approach to Gaelic issues was typically responsive rather than programmatic, so that decisions were rarely based on general or formally articulated principles and the rationales offered by the authorities tended to shift over time. In 1984 the Montgomery Committee, which considered the governance of Scotland's islands, 'sought to establish what national policy on Gaelic had been pursued in recent years' but concluded:

> We found no concrete evidence of an explicit national policy. Government action on Gaelic matters seems to have been largely reactive, in response to initiatives from Gaelic organisations. There appears to be no set of objectives or allocation of responsibility at a national level for what, if anything, needs to be done to protect or develop the Gaelic language. (Committee of Inquiry 1984: 65)

From the 1960s Gaelic campaigners became increasingly aware of the situation of other minority language communities in Europe, especially the Welsh. As the increasingly militant Welsh language movement began to win significant concessions from the authorities in relation to legal status, public signage and broadcasting (Phillips 2000), Gaelic activists often backed their claims for improved provision for Gaelic by making comparisons with the counterpart provision for Welsh. Although the government attempted to rebuff such claims by pointing to the much larger size of the Welsh-speaking community,[2] the point of principle was difficult to ignore entirely. As the disparity between provision for Welsh and Gaelic grew ever greater, the government found itself 'embarrassed' into taking some measures in Scotland (e.g. SED 1981b, 1982b).

With the reorganisation of local government in Scotland in 1974, a new authority was created for the Western Isles, the Gaelic 'heartland'. The new council, Comhairle nan Eilean, adopted a bilingual policy in 1975 (CnE 1975). This was a move of historic significance in terms of the public status of Gaelic, even if the language did not become institutionalised over time in the Western Isles as Welsh did in north Wales, where newly created local authorities, especially Gwynedd, also began to bilingualise their operations (Carlin 2013). Another key initiative by the council was the establishment of the pioneering bilingual education project referred to above.

From the late nineteenth century onwards, the distinct social and economic needs of the Highlands and Islands were recognised by the government and the economic development of the region became a defined official priority (see Cameron 1996, 1997), but language issues tended to have little explicit role in these policy processes and the debates that accompanied them. The goals and assumptions of policy were set within a narrowly modernisationist paradigm (Walsh 2011), and Gaelic was implicitly understood as the cultural reflex of the outdated economic structure that needed to be replaced. The most important decision in relation to regional development policy was the establishment in 1965 of the Highlands and Islands Development Board, a dedicated public agency with responsibility for the economic and social development of the region. In its early years the HIDB placed little emphasis on Gaelic, but from the late 1970s it began to play a crucial role in the fundamental policy shift in relation to Gaelic that took place in the mid-1980s. The success of Gaelic-related community initiatives in the Western Isles and elsewhere convinced key individuals in the HIDB that Gaelic could actually function as a motor of confidence-building and economic dynamism for the region. With the 1982 report *Cor na Gàidhlig* (Gaelic Review Group 1982), HIDB had a blueprint for Gaelic development, including, crucially, the establishment of a dedicated language planning agency, Comunn na Gàidhlig (CnaG) (see pp. 192–4).

As explored in detail in chapter 6, a thickening of Gaelic development initiatives followed. Alongside the expansion of GME, there was significant progress with the Gaelic arts and, most strikingly, Gaelic television provision. The lack of coordination between these initiatives prompted efforts to 'secure the status' of the language from the mid-1990s onwards. These took the form of a demand for a Gaelic Language Act (CnaG 1997a, 1999), inspired in part by the *Welsh Language Act 1993*, which required that Welsh and English be 'treated on a basis of equality' in public life in Wales. Eventually this demand was fulfilled by the *Gaelic Language (Scotland) Act 2005*, which expressed the ambitious aim of 'securing the status of Gaelic as an official language of Scotland commanding equal respect with the English language' (preamble). The principal motor of the Act is a statutory language planning agency, Bòrd na Gàidhlig, which is required to produce a National Gaelic Language Plan every five years and empowered to compel Scottish public authorities to produce Gaelic language plans to promote the language. Since the passage of the Act the Bòrd has become the principal actor in Gaelic policy and the successive National Plans and individual organisations' Gaelic plans the main mechanism of policy. The implementation of the Act and the work of the Bòrd are considered in chapter 8.

The other major development of recent years has been the establishment of a dedicated Gaelic television channel, BBC ALBA, in 2008. Here too, improved provision came only after a long campaign that was driven by the perception that the existing structure was inadequate. The Gaelic Television Fund, created in 1992, led to the production of approximately two hundred hours of Gaelic television programming per year, but with no coherent mechanism for its transmission (Dunbar 2010: 406–7). The campaign for a dedicated Gaelic channel coincided with the technological revolution of digital television, so that it was only in 2011 that the new service became universally available.

Just as the current policy regime for Gaelic bears almost no relation to that of the 1960s, the range of actors involved in shaping Gaelic policy has increased considerably over the years. For a large part of the period under study in this book, there is very little to say about the activity of most arms of government and other important public and private bodies as they made no provision of any kind for Gaelic and probably never contemplated doing so. For many decades Gaelic language policy in Scotland could be assessed almost entirely in terms of the actions of the Scottish Office, especially its Education Department, and to a lesser extent the Highland education authorities and the BBC. In twenty-first-century Scotland, however, Gaelic language policy is situated in the actions of the Scottish Government and Parliament (which were established following legislative devolution in 1999), in the thirty-two Scottish local authorities, in the dozens of public authorities that have prepared statutory Gaelic language plans, and a wide range of public and private organisations ranging from charitable groups to supermarkets and snow sports centres that have produced Gaelic publications, erected bilingual signs or made other kinds of formal provision for the language. Describing and analysing the nature of policy and provision for Gaelic has thus become a great deal more complex.

GAELIC AND THE SCOTTISH NATION

The ideological principles of Gaelic language policy, today as in the past, are inextricably linked to ideas and discourses concerning the role of the language in Scottish history and society. These matters have always been contested in different ways, even if the prevailing language ideologies and the principal tropes of discourse have changed over time. It is indisputable that despite its demographic decline Gaelic has become much more prominent in Scottish public life in recent decades and has come to enjoy much greater public and institutional attention and support. It is equally indisputable that this shift is related to the increasing sense of Scottish cultural distinctiveness and the stronger demands for Scottish self-government that have developed over the last half century. Yet the connection between these phenomena is anything but straightforward, and the relationship between Gaelic and Scottish nationhood and nationalism is complex and in some ways contradictory.

A central issue is the relationship between the Scottish nation and the Gaelic language and the Gaelic-speaking community. Many diverse perspectives have been presented on the extent to which Gaelic should be considered the national language of Scotland (or 'a' national language, with indefinite article) or as having merely regional or even minority ethnic significance. A traditional Gaelic point of view, expressed by Gaelic poets from the sixteenth century onwards, characterised Gaelic as the original language of Scotland, latterly abandoned and betrayed by the Lowlanders (McLeod 2003: 98–100). The first collection of Gaelic poetry, published in 1751 by Alasdair mac Mhaighstir Alasdair (Alexander MacDonald), bore the provocative title *Ais-eiridh na Sean Chanóin Albannaich* (Resurrection of the Old Scottish Language) and opened with a long poem praising Gaelic as the former language of

Scotland's kings, nobles and even the Lowland peasantry, but now beset by 'gò / is mì-rùn mòr nan Gall' (the deceit and great ill-will of the Lowlanders) (Thomson 1996: 75–82, ll. 587–8). The phrase 'mì-rùn mòr nan Gall' is still commonly used today to refer to hostility towards Gaelic and its speakers.

According to Gaelic historian and folklorist John MacInnes, the Gaels came to perceive themselves as 'the disinherited, the dispossessed' of Scotland (2006: 46). Yet this interpretation did not have the aim of, or propose any strategy for, taking repossession, other than a vague messianic hope of restoration (MacInnes 2006: 44). Although contempt for ignoble 'Lowland churls' (*bodaich Ghallda*) was frequently expressed, the Gaels never developed any antipathy to the Scottish nation or its monarchy, and retained an unquestioning commitment to the integrity of Scotland (MacInnes 2006: 39). This traditional view found modern expression in a pamphlet published by An Comunn Gàidhealach in 1966, which argued that the Gaels 'were [. . .] the first Scots [. . .] and [. . .] could well claim, as they did in the past, to be the most Scottish of all Scots' (MacKay 1976). This understanding differs significantly from that of many linguistic and ethnic minorities in Europe which see themselves as fundamentally distinct from the dominant people and polity that absorbed them.

Alongside this traditional understanding, from the late nineteenth century onwards certain writers and intellectuals have pressed claims for the recognition and promotion of Gaelic as the true national language of Scotland. Underpinning these claims has been the idea attributed to German romantic philosophers, including Johann Gottfried Herder and Johann Gottlieb Fichte, that nationality and nationhood are most fundamentally expressed in the distinctiveness of a national language (Edwards 2009: 205–11). A corollary of this view is that any nation and national movement must necessarily have a distinct language, a role for which Gaelic was selected by Scottish nationalists of this stripe. The manifesto issued c. 1912 by the short-lived nationalist organisation Clann na h-Alba (The League of Scottish Nationalists) gave succinct expression to this idea:

> It is therefore the duty of all Scotsmen and Scotswomen to support in all possible ways the revival of that Scottish Gaelic tongue which, alone among languages, can mark us out as a nation apart. (Clann na h-Alba 1912(?))

For these nationalists, Gaelic has been adopted or appropriated as a uniquely powerful symbolic marker of Scottish distinctiveness.

In the early decades of the twentieth century, the most militant writers pressed for the full re-Gaelicisation of Scotland as the logical extension of this nationalist view. The central figure here was Ruaraidh Erskine of Marr, a perfervid nationalist activist and founder of and prolific contributor to a number of important periodicals in Gaelic and English (see p. 70). Similarly, most of the writers associated with the interwar literary movement known as the 'Scottish Renaissance', most notably Hugh MacDiarmid (Christopher Murray Grieve), were strong supporters of Gaelic, even if few ever attained full competence in the language (McCulloch 2004: 270–316). In the 1960s and 1970s, renewed claims for Gaelic as Scotland's true national language were pressed, notably by Seumas Mac a' Ghobhainn, who wrote in 1977 that 'A' Ghàidhlig – the Scottish language – is the very essence of Scottish nationality and the living symbol of its unity' (Mac a' Ghobhainn 2000: [17]). The sharpest critique of this position was articulated by the activist Norman Easton in 1982:

> Oor modern Pretend-Gaels inherit thon racial/linguistic notion of nationalism. Oor nation maun [must] hae ane 'True Scots' language that oor 'True Scots' saul be rediscoverit. National *Cultural* Puritie maun be restored. [. . .]
>
> The Pretend-Gaels [. . .] fix on the Gaelic language like Popeye fixit on spinach. It's the grit restorer. Dinna be a puny Scots weakling! Get the Gaelic and ye kin be a muckle [huge] grit Fingalian[3] hero!
>
> Gaelic is selectit for the 'true' language simply because it is sae obviouslie distinct fae English, the evil tongue o English pouer. (Easton 1982: 18)

Significantly, since the modern revitalisation movement gathered force in the 1980s and began to advance concrete programmes of action in fields such as education and broadcasting, sweeping nationalistic claims about Gaelic have become less functional and now form a much less prominent element in the rhetoric of language activists than was the case in the 1960s and 1970s. A small linguistic move demonstrates the rhetorical shift. In 2011 Arthur Cormack, chair of Bòrd na Gàidhlig, told the Scottish Parliament's Education Committee that the Bòrd recognises the role of Scots and other languages in Scotland and 'promotes Gaelic as *an* official language of Scotland. We have not, and will not, promote Gaelic as *the* language of Scotland' (Cormack 2011). Yet the phrase 'language of Scotland', used in the Gaelic Language Act itself, clearly implies a 'national' status for Gaelic, and Gaelic development since the 1980s has become increasingly national, i.e. Scotland-wide, in its approach.

Those arguing for Gaelic's status as language of the Scottish nation have had to confront the obvious difficulty that few Scots know it.

Gaelic activists have tended to tackle this problem in two slightly different ways. The first is to argue that regardless of its current position, Gaelic is the original language of Scotland and its displacement reflects a historical wrong turn that ought to be reversed. In the older view of the Gaelic poets, summarised above, Gaelic was betrayed far back in the Middle Ages, but particularly in the early twentieth century, many intellectuals, including Erskine of Marr and writers such as Fionn MacColla and Compton Mackenzie, tended to identify the Reformation as the great wrong turn in Scotland's history, a disastrous move away from Scotland's Catholic, Gaelic past that cut Scotland off from the mainstream of European culture (*GB* 1904, 1905; Macdonald 2009: 267–8). The second strategy can be described as a kind of 'cultural amnesia' (or 'false consciousness') argument: that more Scots, especially Lowlanders, would be awakened from their indifference to Gaelic and would come to realise the importance of the language if only they had a better understanding of Scottish history and the central role of Gaelic within it (e.g. Mac a'Ghobhainn 2000: [17]). The ongoing failure of such claims to gain general acceptance within the Scottish population means that there is a numbing repetitiveness to Gaelic activists' arguments in this vein; very similar contentions are made decade after decade. Even in 2011, one of a series of articles on 'Scotland's Language Myths' included a lengthy rebuttal of the view that 'Gaelic has nothing to do with the Lowlands' (Kavanagh 2011), replete with arguments that would have been familiar from the activist press a century and more earlier (e.g. MacNeacail 1920).

Several overlapping reasons explain the limited impact of claims for Gaelic as national language of Scotland. It is true that a significant portion of the Scottish population has simply been unaware of the history of Gaelic in Scotland and the extent to which it was once spoken in 'Lowland' areas. Notwithstanding proposals by advisory bodies and policy experts over the decades (Advisory Council on Education 1946: 80; Lo Bianco 2001: 78–84), the linguistic history of Scotland has never been systematically taught in Scottish schools, so that misconceptions and misinformation are widespread and frequently aired in public discussions. The typical rhetorical expression of this rejectionist view, a commonplace of letters to newspaper editors and now of social media and online comments sections (McEwan-Fujita 2018), is the claim that Gaelic was 'never spoken here' (although the historical presence of Gaelic in the area in question may actually be well attested) and thus to argue that public provision for Gaelic 'here' is inappropriate. To an extent that is perhaps surprising, public discussions of current initiatives and proposals concerning Gaelic often involve semi-informed arguments over medieval linguistic history and the evidence of place names. In this regard it is significant that even a maximal interpretation of Gaelic's former presence in Scotland cannot be said to provide a particularly strong basis to justify current action on behalf of the language in Lowland areas; in Lowland Scotland, Gaelic was probably spoken for a total period of between 150 and 500 years and has not been widely spoken for seven hundred years or more. The situation is quite different from that of Wales or Ireland, where the 'national' language was spoken, at least residually, across a very large proportion of the national territory within the last two centuries, and a very high proportion of the population have an awareness of a relatively recent family connection to the language.

An alternative response is to accept the status of Gaelic in earlier times but to interpret its significance differently, characterising the marginalisation of Gaelic from mainstream Scottish society and culture in recent centuries as the consequence of historical injustice, citing in particular the repression that followed Culloden and the brutality of the Clearances (McLeod 2019). Particularly when combined with a post-Ossianic view of Gaelic Scotland as distant and somehow romantic, versions of this interpretation have probably played a considerable role in shaping public perceptions of Gaelic over time.

Prevailing understandings of the role of Gaelic have operated in the context of the deep-rooted Highland–Lowland divide, with many of the claims for Gaelic's national status seeking to undermine the view that Gaelic is of importance only for the Highlands rather than Scotland as a whole. Although this divide has become a great deal less significant than it once was, the continuing resistance to arguments about Gaelic's relevance to the Lowlands testifies to its residual vitality. Importantly, the perception of Gaelic as a Highland phenomenon does not necessarily indicate hostility to the language; one strand of support for the language may depend on sympathy for what is perceived as a mistreated periphery or a distinct and romantic space.

An extreme but once widely accepted interpretation of Scotland's history and the role of Gaelic within it was to conceptualise Scotland as divided on the basis of 'race', with the Lowlanders belonging to the dominant Teutonic (or 'Gothic') race and the Highlanders to a separate, inferior Celtic race (Stroh 2017: 185–211). Most notably in the work of John Pinkerton (1758–1826), this supposed racial distinction was used to explain, and justify, the poverty and underdevelopment of the Highlands. In contemporary Scotland, however, this interpretation is very largely forgotten, and Scotland as a whole is conventionally depicted as a 'Celtic' country.

An alternative view of Gaelic and nationhood might consider the Gaels to constitute a separate nation, distinct from Scotland. John MacInnes argued that '[t]he Gaels in Scotland for most of our history have been a nation' but 'the processes of decline have produced what can only be regarded now as the detritus of a nation' (MacInnes 1975: 1). MacInnes's analysis is redolent of Friedrich Engels's dismissive assertion in 1849 that the Gaels in Scotland were but one of many 'relics of a nation' and 'ruined fragments of peoples' to be found throughout Europe (Engels 2010: 234; see Davidson 2001). The concept of a Gaelic 'nation' is occasionally noted in modern revivalist discourse (e.g. Buchanan 2002: 271), but without any close analysis of its conceptual suitability (McLeod 2014). At no point, however, has there ever been any kind of 'Gaelic separatist' movement, the idea that the Gaels' linguistic and cultural distinctiveness required self-determination and the establishment of a separate Gaelic polity, in accordance with the principles of linguistic nationalism articulated by Herder and Fichte. The connection between the Gàidhealtachd and the rest of Scotland was too tight and the Gàidhealtachd manifestly too small to have functioned as an independent state (Wright 2015: 40–1; Davidson 2001: 299).

Although the term 'the Gaelic people' was once widely used, only occasionally have Gaelic activists conceptualised the Gaels as an ethnic minority within Scotland (e.g. D. J. MacLeod 1969: 8). Nevertheless, this framework clearly has some theoretical potential in light of the social history of the Gaelic community (McLeod 1998); a recent report on hate crime in Scotland concluded that 'there is a fairly strong argument that Gaelic speaking Gaels belong to an "ethnic group"' distinct from the general Scottish population in terms of language, culture, sense of tradition and way of life (SG 2018a: 52). This conceptualisation probably conflicts somewhat with the traditional idea that the Gaels are the essence of the Scottish nation.

There is a tension between attempts to conceptualise the Gaelic language in national or ethnic terms and the prevailing understandings in modern Gaelic communities, which tend to be narrower in their scope. Ethnographic studies of Hebridean communities in the later twentieth century 'all reveal remarkably consistent conceptions of Gaelic-speaking as a local practice in the nexus of home, family and crofting community' (McEwan-Fujita 2010a: 175). Such restricted understandings appear to reflect the cumulative effect of policies that worked to marginalise Gaelic:

As English became the exclusive language of the state, the schools, and literacy in Gaelic-speaking areas, it seems likely that many Gaelic speakers in local community contexts gradually stopped seeing Gaelic as the language of knowledge, learning, and a wider Gàidhealtachd or Gaelic-speaking region, and instead began to see Gaelic as only a local, spoken language most suitable for interaction with kin and neighbours. (McEwan-Fujita 2010b: 93)

Against this background, some traditional Gaelic speakers may resist or reject revitalisation initiatives that challenge these understandings of the appropriate role of the language. Such initiatives may be perceived as artificial, unnatural or simply uncomfortable, and speakers may come to feel that the language no longer belongs to them (Macdonald 1997: 217–18; McEwan-Fujita 2008).

GAELIC, NATIONALISM AND UNIONISM

In recent decades the question of the constitutional status of Scotland has come to occupy centre stage in Scottish politics, especially since the Scottish National Party took control of the Scottish Parliament in 2007 and organised an unsuccessful referendum on Scottish independence in 2014. Yet issues of language and culture have never been prominent in Scottish national movements, in marked contrast to most other European countries. In conventional understandings, Scottish national distinctiveness and autonomy inhered primarily in the national institutions that were retained following the Union of 1707, principally the separate Church of Scotland and the distinct Scottish legal and educational systems (Craig 2018: 73–4). Recent debates concerning Scottish self-government have focused on economic and social issues and questions of democratic representation and participation rather than cultural matters (Williams 1999: 272). Gaelic (and indeed Scots, discussed below) has played a distinctly limited role in these discussions. Many nationalist organisations in the early twentieth century placed considerable emphasis on Gaelic, but from the mid-1930s onwards the newly created SNP began to de-emphasise linguistic and cultural issues and focus more on socio-economic matters (Finlay 1994; Craig 2018: 20–1). The situation in Wales was very different; the absorption of Wales into England effectively removed any distinctive national institutions, leaving the language as the principal badge of nationhood, and the SNP's sister party, Plaid Cymru, has always made the promotion of the Welsh language a major priority (McAllister 2001). In any event, until the late 1960s, when the SNP began to achieve significant electoral success, 'nationalism occupied the margins of the margins of Scottish politics' (Kidd 2008: 24–5). The SNP began to give Gaelic somewhat more attention than it had in the immediate post-war decades, but it remained at the periphery of the party's programme. By the late 1970s historians could conclude that Gaelic was 'hardly an issue' in Scottish nationalism and that 'for the vast majority of Scottish nationalists, the language issue hardly existed' (Webb 1977: 91; Brand 1978: 15).

Since coming to power in 2007, the SNP government has not effected any significant changes in relation to Gaelic policy (as discussed in chapter 8). There has actually been substantial policy continuity in relation to Gaelic from the 1980s onwards, as successive Labour and SNP governments have effectively built on the foundations laid by the Conservative government in the 1980s. It has been an article of faith among Gaelic activists that Gaelic should receive support from all political parties and not be associated with any single strand of political opinion (Campbell 2002: Ross 2018: 48–9). There is evidence that supporters of Gaelic are somewhat more likely to support Scottish independence, but even so, a large proportion of those who support independence do not have favourable views of Gaelic (Paterson et al. 2014).

Just as Scottish nationalism did not become strongly associated with Gaelic, the Gaelic cause has not been perceived as inherently oppositional to the British state and incompatible with support for the union between Scotland and England. Unionism has come in different incarnations over time but has typically been flexible rather than monolithic, readily accommodating different kinds of diversity, including – within certain parameters – linguistic diversity (Kidd 2008). Thus, the fact that the crucial steps towards a more favourable government policy towards Gaelic were taken in the 1980s under a Conservative, firmly unionist government is not inherently peculiar or intellectually problematic.

A telling indicator here is the support of the British monarchy for Gaelic initiatives, including the annual Mòd of An Comunn Gàidhealach, the pre-eminent Gaelic cultural festival, which has been designated as the 'Royal National Mòd' since 1992 (see pp. 60–2). The reigning monarch, Queen Elizabeth II,[4] is the official Patron of the Mòd and members of the Royal Family have formally visited the Mòd on many occasions, most recently Prince Charles, current heir to the throne, in 2010.[5] This royal support for Gaelic goes back to King George IV (1820–30), who became patron to the Society for the Support of the Gaelic Schools in the Highlands and Islands (Mudie 1822: 309), but was particularly strong in the case of Queen Victoria (1837–1901), who had great affection for the Highlands, especially her home at Balmoral in Aberdeenshire, and who had two volumes of her Highland diaries translated into Gaelic

(Victoria 1878, 1886). In 1849 she wrote to the Lord President of the Privy Council expressing her hope that Gaelic be taught in Highland schools alongside English, explaining that 'being very partial to her loyal good Highlanders, [she] takes much interest in what she thinks will tend more than anything to keep up their simplicity of character, which she considers a great merit in these days' (Benson and Esher 1908: 255). Within Gaeldom there has been little opposition or hostility to these royal connections and trappings, and a British identity was accepted and highly valued by most.

There is some evidence of a shift in unionist opinion concerning Gaelic, at least among those characterised as 'ultras', in the polarised political environment that followed the 2014 independence referendum (*Herald* 2018a). Where unionism traditionally has allowed substantial latitude for Scottish distinctiveness within the union, including cultural distinctiveness, some now assert that the promotion of Gaelic in Scotland, most notably in the form of bilingual signage, is intended to manufacture artificial difference between Scotland and England as part of a separatist agenda (*Scotsman* 2018; *Herald* 2019b). Other unionists have criticised this interpretation (*Herald* 2018a; Massie 2019), however, and it remains to be seen how much traction it will gain over time.

THE VALUE OF GAELIC

Much of the ideological debate concerning Gaelic in modern Scotland has involved competing visions of the utility and value of the language. Like other European minority languages, Gaelic has been a 'despised language' (Grillo 1989: 174), associated with a deep-rooted 'ideology of contempt' (Cooper 1990) that can be traced back to the anti-Highlander discourse that emerged in the late Middle Ages. The nature of this ideology has mutated considerably over time but at its core, at least since the eighteenth century, is a perception of Gaelic as an outdated, underdeveloped language unsuited to the modern world and destined to die out, whose speakers are socio-economically disadvantaged and restricted in their life opportunities. Maintenance and revitalisation efforts on behalf of the language are thus 'competitively depicted and regarded as social mobility contraindicated, parochial and anti-modern', in the words of the leading sociolinguist Joshua Fishman (2001: 21).

From the eighteenth century onwards, a discourse of modernisation, improvement and progress became dominant in relation to Gaelic. Gaelic monolingualism was said to hold Gaelic speakers back, preventing them from accessing opportunities and from participating fully in civic and cultural life. In 1760 a report submitted to the General Assembly of the Church of Scotland argued as follows:

> In the western Highlands and islands [...] the common people can carry on no transactions with the more southern part of Great Britain, without the intervention of their superiors, who know the English language, and are thereby kept in that undue dependence, and unacquaintance with the arts of life, which have long been the misery of these countries. Till the partition arising from different languages be removed, and the common language of Great Britain be diffused over the Highlands, the inhabitants will never enjoy, in their full extent, the benefits of religion and civil government.[6]

Arguments to similar effect were legion throughout the nineteenth century, with an additional emphasis on the connection between English, economic opportunity and mobility. A leader column published in the Edinburgh newspaper *The Scotsman* in 1824 was particularly forceful in this regard:

> The use of the Gaelic prolongs the existence of a thousand associations that fetter the native genius of the Highlander, who never figures to advantage till he quits his native mountains. Teach him English if you wish him to adopt the industrious and enterprising habits of the people of England, and to throw off his hereditary indolence and apathy. The new language will give him new ideas, and new wants – above all it will place him in a state of communication and sympathy with those portions of his fellow subjects from whom he has much to learn, and to whom he is at present nearly as much a stranger as he is to the Danes or Dutch. The Highlands are in fact a moral and intellectual waste; but extirpate the Gaelic, and you do more to carry civilization and the spirit of improvement into these districts, than if you levelled the Grampians. (*Scotsman* 1824)

Significantly, this vision of Gaelic as lacking in practical value has been widely accepted among Gaelic speakers and unquestionably represents the single most important factor that has driven language shift from the late eighteenth century onwards. Despite the revitalisation initiatives of recent decades, 'unstated but deeply felt emotions and anxieties' (Dauenhauer and Dauenhauer 1998: 62) about the value of the language appear to retain considerable force in Gaelic communities, with important consequences for decisions concerning language transmission, educational choices and policy priorities.

Thus many Gaelic language advocates have accepted, indeed even sometimes celebrated, the idea of the language having limited usefulness. Activists of the late nineteenth and early twentieth centuries routinely conceded that Gaelic had little or no 'commercial value' (e.g. *Northern Chronicle* 1882; Ross 1925: 191; GSI 1929: 61). A classic statement of this view that Gaelic was best suited to private and cultural contexts and had no role in commercial or other functional domains was given by James Shaw Grant, publisher of the *Stornoway Gazette* (the principal local newspaper in the Western Isles), at the Mòd in 1972:

> The value of Gaelic lies precisely in the fact that it is *not* the language of commerce and technology, it is *not* the language in which we pay our income tax, it is *not* the language of the mass media.
>
> It is the language into which one can retire from the hurly-burly of an over busy world. It offers an escape from canned, pre-packaged entertainment, from the superficiality of instant news and instant comment.
>
> Gaelic adds an extra dimension to life. It is a folk language, in which people still make their own songs and write their own poetry [. . .] Gaelic has no material value whatsoever and thank God for it. It is *not* the language of the rat race. That is its supreme value.
>
> An Comunn has its priorities right when it puts the emphasis on culture, music, religion and education rather than debasing Gaelic by trying to make it an ordinary work horse for business and administrative purposes. (Grant 1972)

This 'reactionary view of the language as a docile relic of a prelapsarian rural Scotland' (Hutchinson 2005: 100) began to be significantly challenged in the 1970s, however, and a counter-narrative that Gaelic could actually be a vehicle for economic and community development began to take hold. As discussed in chapter 6, this alternative view was an important driver for the changes to institutional policy that began in the 1980s.

As Gaelic both continued its demographic decline and began to receive greater institutional support, critics began to assert the purported 'uselessness' of Gaelic in somewhat different ways. In effect, the decline of Gaelic became a self-fuelling argument: action to promote the language was deemed a waste of money either because it was destined to die out anyway or illegitimate because with so few speakers the costs of provision would outweigh any benefits (MacKinnon 2012). In a common metaphor, governmental support for Gaelic constitutes a 'life-support system', and some commentators contend that it is time 'to pull the plug' (Linklater 2002; Fry 2007). Opponents of provision for Gaelic in the education system often argue that other, more 'useful' languages (either languages of international stature such as Spanish or languages associated with immigration to Scotland such as Polish) should be taught instead of Gaelic (McLeod 2019). A related, somewhat less aggressive challenge to the value of Gaelic asserts that the language merits a place as an object of academic study but should not be supported for practical purposes as a living language. This argument is by no means novel but has been pressed in different contexts since the nineteenth century (Gillies 1989a: 10; Aitken 2004).

Particularly before the Second World War, Gaelic advocates tended to make the case for Gaelic by emphasising group heritage, identity, cultural pride, self-respect and duty rather than pragmatic concerns. Arguments were often expressed in romantic terms, as when the Rev. G. W. Mackay told the Pan-Celtic Congress in 1917:

> We base the claims of Gaelic on its inherent worth. [...] It is a noble and highly developed tongue. It is the key to the heart of the Gael; it enshrines within itself ideals of feeling and ways of looking at men and affairs that are peculiar to him. (Mackay 1917: 21)

As John Edwards observes, however, appeals that rest 'upon abstract pillars of cultural continuity and tradition [...] can often seem empty or [...] of a rather low priority' to many members of the language group (Edwards 2010: 69). Thus Gaelic advocates frequently lamented – or denounced – the assimilationist impulses of other Gaels and their indifference to the language (e.g. 'Ian' 1904; MacPhaidein 1917). With the significant improvements in the status of Gaelic in recent decades, attitudes of Gaelic speakers towards the language now appear much more favourable, although residual doubts evidently remain (MacKinnon 2001).

THE ISSUE OF SCOTS

Efforts to elevate the status of Gaelic in Scotland have also been complicated by the presence of another linguistic variety, Scots, that also holds national significance in Scotland. The linguistic dynamic in Scotland is more complex than in Wales, for example, where the Welsh language serves as a talisman of national identity and no other language variety holds comparable symbolic significance. On the other hand, while the issue of Scots often confounds public discussion and discourse concerning Gaelic, the Scots factor has actually had very little practical impact on the development of Gaelic policy, as there has been very little formal provision for Scots (except in relation to matters like the preparation of dictionaries) and very little organised demand for such provision. Arguments that it would be more appropriate to promote Scots than Gaelic are routinely advanced (e.g. McIlvanney 2000; P&J 2014b), but sometimes, it appears, as a rhetorical device to block provision for Gaelic rather than a serious effort to advance the position of Scots.

This disparity in the levels of provision, and demand for provision, is difficult to understand at one level, given that Scots appears to be much more widely spoken than Gaelic today. A question concerning Scots was included in the census for the first time in 2011 and 1,541,693 respondents claimed that they could speak Scots, as opposed to 57,602 for Gaelic (NRS 2014: Table KS206SC).

An important obstacle that has hindered the promotion of Scots is the view that it does not constitute a distinct language but a mere 'dialect' of English. The issue is complex. Scots and English developed independently from the speech of the Anglo-Saxon settlers who arrived in Britain from the sixth century onwards, and following the decline of Gaelic in the late Middle Ages Scots became the language of the Scottish court and the main language of administration and commerce in Scotland. Following the Reformation, however, which spread the influence of written English, and the unions of 1603 and 1707, Scots steadily lost status and the influence of standard English continued to spread, especially through the education system (see Craigie 1924; Millar 2018). Today the distinctiveness of Scots is seen to be fading, most obviously with the loss of vocabulary, and many believe that over time it 'will essentially disappear, replaced by a form of colloquial English which contains token features derived from the former dialects' (Millar 2018: 216). There is a linguistic spectrum from so-called 'Broad' Scots at one end to Scottish Standard English at the other, and the boundary between the two is often unclear, not least in the minds of ordinary speakers. While many in Scotland accept the designation of Scots as a language rather than a variety of English, sometimes on grounds that are more political than linguistic, many scholars disagree with this interpretation (Kirk 2011: 193–5) and a large proportion of the Scottish public appears to concur. A survey commissioned by the Scottish Government in 2010 found that 64 per cent of respondents agreed with the proposition 'I don't really think of Scots as a language, it's more just a way of speaking', while only 30 per cent disagreed (TNS-BMRB 2010: 15).

Another major problem is that of internal diversity within Scots: many speakers reject the overarching label 'Scots' in favour of regional alternatives such as 'Doric' (in northeast Scotland) and 'Orcadian' (in Orkney), and there is strong resistance to the development of an agreed standard written form (Costa 2017). This is a significant barrier to any potential institutional development for Scots.

For many of its proponents, however, Scots should properly be understood as the national language of Scotland, a claim that effectively requires the 'erasure' of Gaelic and its relegation to regional status, as something belonging to the Gàidhealtachd only (Costa 2009). The argument is largely theoretical, however, as Scots activists have never developed an effective campaign to embed Scots in public institutions so that the authorities might be presented with competing claims on resources. In contrast to Gaelic, there is no legislation to protect and promote Scots, there are very few Scots organisations, there are no Scots media services, there is no Scots-medium education and there are no significant initiatives to use Scots in official documents or public signage. As a result, government expenditure on Scots is minimal in comparison to Gaelic: £270,000 per year as against £28.5m in 2018–19 (SG 2018c). There is actually more institutional provision for Ulster Scots in Northern Ireland than for Scots in Scotland, but this reflects the very different linguistic politics of Northern Ireland, by which promotion of Irish is often perceived as being linked to Republicanism and Ulster Scots is therefore promoted as a countervailing expression of support for Unionism or Loyalism (Mac Póilin 2018). In 2019–20 there appeared to be a thickening of grass-roots activity in relation to Scots, but it remains to be seen whether this will yield lasting results.

CHARACTERISTICS OF GAELIC LANGUAGE MOVEMENTS

The term 'movement' is not especially well suited to the Gaelic context, and is not often used by Gaelic organisations or activists, either today or in past decades. Indeed, the Irish scholar Colm Ó Baoill, based in Scotland since the 1960s, once referred to Scottish Gaelic as 'Gaeilge gan ghluaiseacht' (Gaelic without a movement), making an implicitly negative comparison to the situation in Ireland (Ó Baoill 1974). The most widely used term is *saoghal na Gàidhlig*, literally 'the Gaelic world', referring loosely to those individuals and organisations who are professionally involved or otherwise actively engaged with Gaelic language and culture.

Most of the Gaelic organisations established in the nineteenth century, most importantly An Comunn Gàidhealach, stated goals that focused on furthering relatively narrow cultural objectives and did not link the language issue to a wider programme of social or political change. From its establishment in 1891, An Comunn stated that its work would be non-political, but there were different interpretations of what 'non-political' meant in practice; it certainly did not mean a total withdrawal from engagement with public policy. For example, in 1918 An Comunn organised a petition demanding provision for Gaelic in the schools in

Gaelic-speaking areas and successfully lobbied Parliament to adopt a legislative amendment to this effect (see pp. 84–6).

Setting aside the claims of those militants who advocated the wholesale re-Gaelicisation of Scotland – a view that has effectively disappeared from public discourse in recent decades – there has been little debate in Gaelic circles about the ultimate goal of Gaelic revitalisation activity. As is common in many language revitalisation contexts (Sallabank 2014: vii–viii), the aims of Gaelic organisations and activists have typically been stated in very general, often defensive terms: 'keeping Gaelic alive' and the like. Bòrd na Gàidhlig's *National Gaelic Language Plan 2007–2012* set out its 'vision for Gaelic':

> Our vision is to create a sustainable future for Gaelic in Scotland in which the language will be the preferred language of an increasing number of people in Scotland[,] the mother tongue of an increasing number of speakers[,] supported by a dynamic culture in a diverse language community. (BnG 2007: 12)

These goals can hardly be considered transformational, and are phrased so broadly that no supporter of the language could really disagree with them. The most recent National Plan (2018–23) is more general still, giving no greater statement of purpose than 'our aim is that Gaelic is used more often, by more people and in a wider range of situations' (BnG 2018a: 6, 15).

A distinctive feature of Gaelic language movements from the late nineteenth century has been the absence of fundamental ideological disagreement; the phenomenon of the 'ideological split' is almost unknown in the Gaelic context. A key issue here may be lack of critical mass; the number of Gaelic activists has always been too small and scattered to sustain a multiplicity of organisations. An Comunn came under attack almost from its inception from critics who challenged its non-political stance and general lack of vehemence, but although various campaigning organisations emerged at different stages, all of them proved short-lived. Nor have there been divisions in the Gaelic movement connected to other political or cultural fault lines (left versus right, nationalist versus unionist, secular versus religious). Individual disagreements and rivalries are hardly unknown among Gaelic activists and intellectuals, but these have not been structural in nature.

Mainstream Gaelic groups have tended to eschew militant rhetoric and tactics. Discussions concerning Gaelic in the political and cultural journals of the late 1960s and 1970s often used a vocabulary of oppression, cultural imperialism and the like (e.g. Mulholland 1972; Thompson

1973). Such vehement rhetoric is rarer today, although claims for Gaelic in the wider public domain are often presented in terms of righting historical injustices, sometimes with reference to the Statutes of Iona, Culloden or the Clearances (e.g. *Herald* 2003; McKenna 2011).

In contrast to Welsh, there has been very little in the way of direct action on behalf of Gaelic. There was a brief spate of painting out monolingual English road signs in the late 1970s and early 1980s, but no violence to persons or property has been involved at any stage. There have been very few public demonstrations pressing claims for Gaelic. The first street protests, seeking improved provision for Gaelic broadcasting, were held in 1974–5 and there have probably been no more than twenty such demonstrations altogether, the great majority of them held in either Edinburgh or Glasgow rather than the Gàidhealtachd. The largest of these, a march in Edinburgh in 1981, mobilised only five hundred people. Nor have Gaelic movements made much use of the legal system as a mechanism to advance particular claims. In this respect the situation of Gaelic is very different from that of French in Canada, and to a lesser extent Māori in New Zealand and Irish in Ireland, where tactical use of litigation has played an important role in shaping language policy (Martel 1999).

Gaelic organisations and activists have often struck a somewhat defensive stance, concerned about weak support within the Gaelic community. In 1968, for example, the educationalist John A. Smith wrote that the majority of Gaelic-speaking parents, 'while kindly disposed, are apathetic and some are either secretly or actively hostile' to the teaching of the language (Smith 1968: 65). More recently, Allan Campbell, former chief executive of Comunn na Gàidhlig and Bòrd na Gàidhlig, observed that Gaelic activists and leaders have tended to underestimate the extent of deep-seated unease or negativity in Gaelic communities in relation to the language (Campbell 2011). Similarly, Gaelic advocates have also been constrained by concern that provision for Gaelic might bring a 'backlash' from the English-monoglot majority.

Since the 1980s, when significant government support for Gaelic development began, the number of Gaelic organisations active in different fields has grown very considerably. All of these bodies, however, are substantially or entirely dependent on public funding; there is little private finance for Gaelic initiatives and no national organisations rely principally on membership dues. This structure tends to constrain the work of different organisations, as there are constant concerns about satisfying funding bodies and 'the scope for tactical manoeuvring is extremely limited' (Dunbar 2000: 81). There is also an issue of co-optation, by which many of the most articulate and engaged Gaelic speakers take up employment in the Gaelic sector and are concerned about speaking out publicly.

In addition, the absence of independent campaigning groups – a radical wing, so to speak – has tended to weaken the hand of Gaelic organisations seeking to win concessions from the authorities (N. Gillies 2011; Mackay 2011). In the absence of such pressure, attempts to improve provision have been advanced by 'working within the system' and accepting the constraints this brings. This approach differs dramatically from the highly oppositional approach of Irish-language activists in Northern Ireland from the 1970s onwards (Muller 2010).

Within the Gaelic community, this organisational structure has tended to induce a degree of passivity and over-reliance on official bodies in relation to Gaelic initiatives. Rob Dunbar described this approach as 'let [the funded groups] do it, after all, they are the ones who are getting paid to promote the language' (Dunbar 2000: 84). A broader issue is the weakness of participation, democracy, ownership and accountability in relation to Gaelic development, which can lead to disconnection or even alienation in the wider Gaelic community in relation to Gaelic organisations and professionals. Decisions are sometimes seen as being made by well-salaried people working in comfortable offices far away from the Gaelic heartlands (e.g. Morrison 1997). Bòrd na Gàidhlig in particular has been repeatedly criticised for its perceived lack of engagement with the Gaelic community (Jones et al. 2016).

Since the late nineteenth century, Gaelic language movements have been driven mainly by bourgeois elements from the Gàidhealtachd, though these have tended to be upwardly mobile individuals who have benefited from educational opportunity rather than members of a more established elite. In the late nineteenth and early twentieth centuries, members of the Highland aristocracy also played an active role in Gaelic organisations,[7] a presence that may have limited the effectiveness of these bodies in the core Gaelic communities of the Hebrides and northwest Highlands, where hostility to the landowner class was often strong. Particularly since the 1970s, Gaelic initiatives have been driven principally by first-generation university graduates with close ties to Hebridean crofting communities. Native rather than second-language speakers of Gaelic have been dominant at all stages, although some of the key players in An Comunn in the pre-war period were learners of Gaelic and second-language speakers have become more prominent in Gaelic organisations since the 1980s, though very rarely in senior leadership roles. Even in recent years, most leadership positions have been filled by men, although there are important exceptions, especially in the field of broadcasting.

The relationship between urban and rural Gaelic speakers has often proved somewhat fraught. Although the great majority of speakers lived in the Gàidhealtachd, in some respects urban Gaelic speakers held a dominant position. Until the 1960s An Comunn maintained its headquarters in Glasgow, and Donald John MacLeod observed in 1970 that 'it is indisputable [...] that virtually every development of significance in Gaelic literature during this century has emanated from the Lowland-based Gaelic intelligentsia' (D. J. MacLeod 1970: 25). A rather circular debate has rolled through the decades about the relative priority to be accorded to Gaelic initiatives in different parts of Scotland. One established and frequently articulated view is that maintaining Gaelic in the heartland areas is essential for the survival of the language and that Gaelic activity in the Lowlands is of secondary importance (e.g. MacLeòid 1944: 26–7; AG 1962: 79; MacCaluim 2007b). Unlike in Ireland (Nig Uidhir 2006; Mac Póilin 2007), there have been no serious efforts to establish any kind of intentional Gaelic-speaking community, either in rural areas or as a new 'urban Gàidhealtachd'.

Over time, Gaelic has slowly become somewhat more associated with the political left, and some sections of the extreme left became passionate supporters of Gaelic (e.g. Fingal 1967–8). On the other hand, the mainstream left in Scotland has paid little attention to Gaelic, and some leftist activists and commentators have even expressed hostility to the language. Conversely, some conservative politicians and commentators have given strong support (e.g. Gove 2009; Rifkind 2016). This pattern demonstrates the extent to which Gaelic is effectively de-politicised, not connected to distinct views on divisive socio-economic or cultural issues. Since the 1980s, all the political parties in Scotland have tended to express support for Gaelic but none of them have given it much prominence (Chhim and Bélanger 2017: 934–6; Bélanger et al. 2018: 79–82). Certain individual politicians in different parties tend to be perceived by Gaelic organisations as friends of the language, reflecting a clientelist model by which progress for the language is achieved by working with key individuals rather than securing deeper structural change. There is much resistance to the idea that Gaelic might become a 'political football', to use the prevailing metaphor (Cameron 2018; see Robertson 2016: 21). This may well reflect a recognition that in such a competition no party is likely to give much prominence to the language.

In contrast to many other minority language movements in Europe, and indeed to Scots, corpus planning (work concerning the development or regulation of the language itself) has not been a prominent issue for Gaelic organisations and activists. There has been relatively little contention concerning dialect variation and issues of orthography, and certainly none of the intense conflict seen in relation to Breton or Cornish (Wmffre 2007). To some extent, this reflects the relatively limited internal variation within Gaelic in linguistic terms and the successes of orthographic standardisation processes in the late eighteenth and early nineteenth centuries (Black 2010; McLeod 2017). In further contrast to Occitan and some other minority languages with powerful dynamics of regionalism or localism (Eckert 1983), there has also been a strong sense of cultural and linguistic unity across the Gaelic community and a common 'ethnolinguistic consciousness' (McLeod 2003). These unifying factors have been broadly beneficial to the Gaelic cause.

For much of the twentieth century, Gaelic organisations, especially An Comunn, tended to conduct their affairs in English, and most Gaelic periodicals were actually bilingual rather than all-Gaelic. Since the 1970s, however, a stronger ideology of language use has taken root within Gaelic organisations, particularly as a result of the work of the Gaelic college Sabhal Mòr Ostaig in Skye, and the proactive use of Gaelic for formal purposes has become institutionalised and indeed somewhat politicised (McEwan-Fujita 2008; see pp. 235–6).

Compared to other European minority languages, the Gaelic periodical press has been distinctly underdeveloped. This has had significant consequences for Gaelic language movements in terms of limiting the opportunities for ideological, policy and cultural debates. Romansch and Sorbian both have fewer speakers than Gaelic, yet both have a daily newspaper, while even weekly or monthly newspapers have proved unsustainable in Gaelic.[8] The longest-running and most influential periodicals were An Comunn's monthly *An Deò-Ghréine/An Gaidheal* (1905–67) and the quarterlies *Guth na Bliadhna* (1904–25) and *Gairm* (1952–2002). Following the closure of *Gairm*, two literary/cultural journals, *Gath* and *STEALL*, have appeared, but only about a dozen issues have been published between them. On the other hand, Gaelic television is now well developed; no other minority language in Europe with a comparable number of speakers has such an extensive service. Given that the budget for Gaelic broadcasting is now over £20 million per year, the weak state of Gaelic periodical publishing is a striking indicator of priorities.

A related phenomenon is the lack of institutional and community memory in relation to the work of previous generations of Gaelic activists and organisations. Here the dynamic contrasts sharply with Ireland

and the Basque Country, where past achievements are celebrated, even mythologised (Urla 2012: 23). There are no obvious examples of canonical texts that inspired Gaelic activists, in the way Douglas Hyde's 1892 lecture 'The Necessity for De-Anglicising Ireland' (Hyde 1894: 115–61) motivated the Gaelic Revival in Ireland or Saunders Lewis's 1962 radio address 'Tynged yr Iaith' (The Fate of the Language) (Lewis 1986, 1971) precipitated a wave of direct action on behalf of the Welsh language.

Over time, Gaelic movements have been only moderately interested in and connected to efforts on behalf of other minority languages and 'small nations'. Throughout the twentieth century, for example, Gaelic periodicals published many reports on developments concerning minority communities elsewhere in Europe, but this coverage was rarely sustained and detailed. Without doubt, the main foci of interest and linkage have been the fellow 'Celtic' countries of Ireland and Wales. In relation to Ireland, these connections have mostly been cultural in nature, while Wales has been looked at enviously as the main source of policy innovation and energy. The emulation of Wales has been particularly strong since the 1960s, and most of the policies and initiatives that have been put in place for Gaelic, most notably the *Gaelic Language Act* of 2005, can be understood as smaller or weaker versions of existing provision for Welsh.

CONCLUSION

Historical geographer Charles Withers argued that attempts to restore Gaelic 'to a respected position as one of Scotland's languages must contend with centuries of alienation in education and public life, linguistic retreat, economic decline and lack of social status' (Withers 1984: 251). Campaigns for improved provision have brought about very considerable changes in the public role of Gaelic in Scotland, particularly since the 1980s, yet these deep-rooted structural and ideological factors continue to play a significant constraining role. Many Gaelic speakers still retain doubts about the value of the language and discourses of rejection remain vigorous among some elements of the wider Scottish population. As the following chapters demonstrate, policy and provision for Gaelic, and the social position of the language more generally, have undergone considerable evolution over the last century and a half, but important fundamentals remain in place.

3

Foundations, 1872–1918

THE YEAR 1872 IS chosen as a starting point for this study because the passage of the Education Act in that year ushered in an important new phase in educational provision for the Gàidhealtachd and triggered a wave of controversy concerning the status of the Gaelic language over the following decades. The issue of Gaelic in the schools gained public prominence through the emergence of key organisations and publications in the early 1870s that championed the language in different ways, including the Gaelic Society of Inverness, the magazine *An Gaidheal* (1871–7) and the newspaper *The Highlander* (1873–81). At the same time, the land question became highly politicised from the mid-1870s onwards, and for many there was a strong connection between the campaign for land rights and demands for improved provision for Gaelic. The first dedicated Gaelic language organisation, An Comunn Gàidhealach, was established in 1891, with its Mòd or cultural festival staged for the first time in 1892. An Comunn's campaigning work in its early decades concentrated on improving provision for Gaelic in the schools, efforts which culminated in the adoption of a clause in the *Education (Scotland) Act 1918* which required education authorities to make reasonable provision for Gaelic in Gaelic-speaking areas. With the passage of the Act, and the conclusion of the First World War, an important foundational phase in Gaelic development came to an end.

GAELIC ORGANISATIONS

The first Gaelic organisations were established in the eighteenth century, and although they functioned principally as mutual aid societies for Gaels, they also played an important cultural role in various fields (Black 1986; Fairnie 2006). Almost all of these bodies were based in Lowland towns and cities, serving the new Highland communities that had developed from the eighteenth century onwards (Withers 1998). The first society of this kind was the Glasgow Highland Society, founded in 1727, with the Gaelic Society of London (later the Highland Society of London) following in 1778 and the Highland Society of Edinburgh in 1784 (Black 1986; Fairney 2006). The last part of the nineteenth century saw the emergence of a range of new organisations, including new Gaelic societies in Inverness (established in 1871), Perth (1880), Glasgow (1887), the Celtic Union in Edinburgh (1894) and Ceilidh nan Gaidheal in Glasgow (1896); a range of associations connected to particular islands and Highland districts in Glasgow, Edinburgh and elsewhere; and most importantly An Comunn in 1891. These organisations briefly came together after 1878 under the banner of the Federation of Celtic Societies, which held several annual conventions, but this overarching structure did not prove long-lasting and the Federation's activities were limited to 'vague statements of intent and rather inconclusive meetings' (Cameron 2000: 71).

These Gaelic organisations had varying aims, but their membership tended to be heavily bourgeois in their social composition, with some support from members of the aristocracy. These bodies generally served as mutual support societies, facilitating upward mobility and, implicitly, assimilation for their members (Withers 1998), although some of them became involved in famine relief in the middle of the nineteenth century or the land agitation of later decades. By no means were they committed to a transformation in the societal status of the Gaelic language; many, even most of them, held their events and meetings and conducted their written affairs in English. Some activists denounced the societies' tendency to use English and to curry favour with the landowning classes (L. L. 1898; *GB* 1908a). At the same time, these urban societies and their cultural gatherings played an important role in promoting a sense of common Gaelic identity and cultural unity among diaspora urban Gaels, even if this identity often had elements of sentimentality or nostalgia (Bateman 2015: 173, 186).

Of these organisations, the Gaelic Society of Inverness played an especially important public role. Its objectives included cultural aims such as 'the cultivation of the language, poetry, and music of the Scottish Highlands' and 'the rescuing from oblivion of Celtic poetry, traditions, legends, books, and manuscripts', but also encompassed 'the vindication of the rights and character of the Gaelic people; and, generally, the furtherance of their interests, whether at home or abroad' (*TGSI* 1872: v). These last two objectives, with their references to 'rights' and 'interests', could be interpreted as incorporating social and economic issues, including the land question, but the principal emphasis of the Society was on less contentious cultural matters. Although its core was clearly bourgeois (Gillies 1989b: 9–10), the Society noted that its membership included 'many of the most influential landed proprietors and other gentlemen in the North of Scotland' (*TGSI* 1884: 51), and the clan chief Cluny MacPherson of Cluny was appointed as its first Chief. From the outset English was its main working language, and English was used for the great majority of the papers read at its meetings and subsequently published in its *Transactions* (beginning in 1872 and continuing to the present). The same preference for English was apparent in the case of the Gaelic Society of Glasgow (Comunn Gailig Ghlascho 1891). Over time, the Inverness society became less activist in its ethos; studying its *Transactions*, Anne Lorne Gillies detected 'gradually decreasing political bite, and proportionately increasing bias towards scholasticism in its articles, imperialism in its rituals and polemic' (Fraser 1989: 52). For much of the twentieth century, the Gaelic Society of London was often the most politically engaged of the Gaelic societies.

The term 'activist' as a label for those involved in Gaelic promotional and cultural activity during this period can be somewhat obscurantist. Many of those involved did not aim at any fundamental change in the social role of Gaelic in the Gàidhealtachd, or in Scotland more generally, and often their goal was no more than to celebrate the language in certain narrowly defined cultural contexts and prevent it from dying out. This dynamic can be observed in other minority language situations, such as those of Catalan and Occitan: literary and cultural figures who are conventionally characterised as champions of the language actually tended to be bilinguals who acquiesced in the prevailing linguistic hierarchies and the sociolinguistic restriction of the dominated language (Marfany 2004). As explained above (pp. 45–6), Gaelic writers and cultural activists during the late nineteenth and early twentieth centuries almost all conceded that Gaelic had no 'commercial value'. A classic statement in this regard came from Dr John MacGregor, a Stornoway-born military surgeon and poet who was active in Gaelic circles in London, Edinburgh and Glasgow at the turn of the twentieth century (McLeod 2008b). In 1897 MacGregor wrote:

> It is true enough that English has cut a short march, as it were, on Gaelic, as the business language of bread and butter, which unfortunately we cannot do without. And however devoted to the Gaelic we may be, we should never under-value the advantage and even the necessity for Highlanders to know English, without which they cannot nowadays make much headway in the world. But if we Highlanders have such small heads as to be capable of

containing only one language, we are not the kind of people that we claim to be. [. . .]

It is the duty of every Highlander to do his best to uphold the language, not only as a true and faithful servant, but also in order that, if the heroic language of a heroic people be doomed to die, its last days may be its best; and that it may perish like a gallant man-o'-war sinking in the ocean, with her flags flying, and fighting to the last. (MacGregor 1897: 9)

MacGregor's characterisation of Gaelic as 'the heroic language of a heroic people' had obvious Ossianic overtones, as did the prospect of its glorious death. This was by no means a prospectus for language revival.

AN COMUNN GÀIDHEALACH

An Comunn Gàidhealach,[1] which went on to become by far the most important Gaelic organisation until the onset of the new language planning regime of the mid-1980s, was established in Oban in 1891. Its focus from the beginning, indeed its initial *raison d'être*, was on the organisation of a Gaelic musical and cultural festival, which became known as the Mòd. An Comunn's Mòd was inspired by the national Eisteddfod, the great Welsh cultural festival, which had been established as a national event in 1861 (Edwards 1990: 20). The idea of a Gaelic counterpart to the Eisteddfod had been floated as early as 1874 (AG 1874a), but this proposal did not bear fruit; the immediate impetus for An Comunn's Mòd was a visit to Wales by Professor David Masson of the University of Edinburgh, which prompted Masson to urge the development of a counterpart Scottish festival. The Eisteddfod authorities then provided advice to An Comunn in the preliminary stages of organising the first Mòd (Thompson 1992: 11).

The first public meeting to establish the new organisation was held in Oban on 30 April 1891. All but one of the nine officers and twenty-six Executive Council members were male and the overwhelming majority came from Oban or other parts of northern Argyll, greater Glasgow, Edinburgh or London (Thompson 1992: 14). Their class composition was firmly bourgeois (including five ministers, five educationalists, four local office-holders from Oban, three solicitors and two doctors). The first president was Lord Archibald Campbell, son of the eighth Duke of Argyll, and the ten patrons also included four aristocrats, including the Duke and Duchess of Sutherland (Thompson 1992: 14). Particularly at a time when the land question was a matter of intense controversy, this class composition meant that from the outset there was a gulf between An Comunn and the bulk of ordinary Gaels, especially in the poorer and more isolated areas of the Gàidhealtachd. An Comunn's emphasis on gaining the support of the upper classes was made explicit in 1904, when its Oban branch adopted a resolution 'that the forward movement in favour of Gaelic would be greatly assisted by the support and example of the chiefs, landed proprietors and the professional classes' (*EEN* 1904). Although the clan chiefs had been progressively Anglicised from the seventeenth century onwards, many members of the Highland aristocracy developed an interest in Gaelic language and culture during the later nineteenth century, with many of them learning the language in childhood from Gaelic-speaking nannies and servants (McLeod 2018: 81). The Royal Family's support for Gaelic played a role here: Prince Albert began learning Gaelic in 1849 and the future Edward VII was also required to take Gaelic lessons as a boy (Queen Victoria's Journals 1849; *EEN* 1901). Some Highland aristocrats made a significant contribution to Gaelic culture during this period, most notably in relation to folklore collecting (McLeod 2018), but this interest by no means signified a commitment to transformative change in the socio-economic conditions of the ordinary Gaelic-speaking people. As the activist Ruaraidh Erskine of Marr (himself the son of a baronet) summarised the situation, 'the presence in our ranks of so many of the aristocracy and landed gentry serves to impart a somewhat conservative air to our movement' (Erskine 1901: 83).

An Comunn's leadership was also overwhelmingly male, and the role of women in the Gaelic movement during this period was tightly circumscribed (Scott 2014). One significant exception was Margaret Burnley Campbell, an important activist who served as president of the organisation between 1907 and 1909, among various other leadership roles over several decades (Scott 2014: 43–8). Although two of the seven presidents who preceded her were women (both of them aristocrats), the twenty who followed until 1995 would all be male.

Following its initial meeting, the Executive Council of An Comunn published a Manifesto setting out five Objects for the organisation. The first three were, in order:

1 To promote the cultivation of Gaelic Literature and Music and Home Industries in the Highlands.
2 To encourage the Teaching of Gaelic in Highland Schools.
3 To hold an Annual Gathering, at which competitions shall take place, and prizes be awarded. (ACG 1891)

The third of these aims, the organisation of an annual gathering, took precedence. Following extensive debate, the name 'mòd' was chosen for this event, a word of Norse origin (cognate with the English noun *moot*) signifying a gathering (Murchison 1955: 24). The first Mòd was held in September 1892 in Oban. It has continued annually ever since (except during the World Wars), since 1895 in a different town each year, and is still recognised as the pre-eminent Gaelic cultural event in Scotland. In addition to the national Mòd, there are also regional or local mòds, as many as seventeen of them in the late 1960s (ACG 1968: 27). The emphasis of the Mòd has been on musical competitions of different kinds, especially singing, although drama was introduced in 1909 (Ross 2016: [2]).

Over the years, the Mòd has attracted frequent and often fierce criticism, typically on the grounds that too much English is used at the event, with 'many parrots mouthing Gaelic yet understanding nothing of what they sing' (*Times* 1955), and that the Gaelic music presented at the Mòd was adulterated to suit Edwardian 'parlour sensibilities' and diverged from authentic Gaelic tradition (Caimbeul 2011). Criticisms became commoner after the First World War (e.g. MacFarlane 1929; *P&J* 1932) and have continued to the present (e.g. Ross 1991; *Scotsman* 2007). Other criticisms included the lack of emphasis on literary competitions, which, unlike music, held the potential for language development (*Alba* 1920b). More generally, critics were concerned that too much emphasis was given to the Mòd to the detriment of other kinds of promotional activity. The Rev. Kenneth MacLeod famously asked in 1912, 'Tha an Comunn an déidh bliadhna air fhichead de cheol a thoirt duinn – nach toir e dhuinn a nis bliadhna air fhichead de Ghàidhlig?' (An Comunn has given us twenty-one years of music – will it not now give us twenty-one years of Gaelic?) (MacLeòid 1912: 188).

An Comunn did organise other kinds of events besides the Mòd, notably a great Féill in Glasgow in 1907, a major fundraising bazaar with the patronage of various Highland aristocrats (ACG 1907a; Thompson 1986: 29). This was followed by the organisation of an idealised Highland *clachan* (village) at the Scottish Exhibition of National History, Art and Industry in 1911 (Thompson 1986: 32). Although these events involved the promotion of Highland home industries such as tweed weaving and basket-making, and generated not inconsiderable funds, they served to reinforce the sense of disconnection between the bourgeois leadership of An Comunn and the ordinary population of the Gàidhealtachd.

Membership of the organisation was slow to grow and from 1902 onwards An Comunn began to place greater emphasis on establishing a network of branches in different parts of the Gàidhealtachd, particularly in Argyll. Gaelic scholar and activist Ella Carmichael characterised this as a 'new and more aggressive policy' and a 'new and welcome stimulus' (Carmichael 1912: 95). From a mere 191 in 1904, by 1912 membership approached four thousand, in some seventy branches (Murchison 1955: 62; Thompson 1986: 24, 36–8). By way of comparison, at its peak in 1906 the Irish counterpart to An Comunn, Conradh na Gaeilge, had 964 branches and a membership estimated at between 48,000 and 67,000 – a powerful marker of the greater reach of the Irish language movement (McMahon 2008: 88–9).

One important area where An Comunn did not have any significant impact was the Western Isles, where for many years the only branch was in Lewis. This indicated a lack of connection between An Comunn and the core of the Gaelic-speaking community in the crofting townships of the Hebrides. For Professor Derick Thomson, the leading Gaelic intellectual of the later twentieth century, this omission was understandable; 'in Harris', for example, 'it might have seemed just as sensible to found an Association for the Encouragement of Breathing as to found a Branch of An Comunn. They spoke Gaelic anyway, just as they breathed' (*AG* 1962: 79). Instead, the headquarters of An Comunn was located in Glasgow rather than a Gaelic heartland area, which served to intensify this disconnect (MacDonald 1958: 18–19; Hutchinson 2005: 86).

In 1912 Margaret Burnley Campbell identified three kinds of members of An Comunn: non-Gaelic speakers 'who love the Highlands of Scotland' but with perhaps only an 'abstract' association with the Gaelic language; those of Highland stock who were concerned with 'Highland matters politically and socially', but not resident in the Gàidhealtachd and perhaps not native Gaelic speakers; and 'by far the most important', 'our own Gaelic-speaking Highland people, who after many decades of suppression of all that concerns their Gaelic nationality, are at last finding an opportunity of voicing the feelings which have so long lain dumb and dormant in their breasts' (Burnley Campbell 1915). Developing an effective strategy to appeal to such a diverse membership was obviously difficult.

Although An Comunn campaigned vigorously to improve provision for Gaelic in the educational sphere, as discussed in detail below, these efforts were focused almost entirely on native-speaking schoolchildren, and the organisation did not assign significant priority to the teaching of Gaelic to adults (or to non-native-speaking children). This approach stands in sharp contrast to the approach of Conradh na Gaeilge, which organised Irish classes in all parts of Ireland and attracted many thousands of students. Even if these students rarely reached fluency in the language, this initiative was immensely significant in building a broad base of personal and political support for the language in the Irish population as a whole (McMahon 2008: 126). Between 1910 and 1939, An Comunn did organise summer schools for adult learners in different parts of the Gàidhealtachd (*Celtic Review* 1912: 96; *AG* 1939). These schools did not develop deep roots, unlike in Ireland, where 'Gaelic colleges' in different parts of the Gaeltacht were established in the early years of the twentieth century, some of which have continued in existence for over a century (Ó Ceallaigh 2006).

Compared to Conradh na Gaeilge, the vision and ambition of An Comunn were much more circumscribed; certainly there was no general goal of national language restoration, as in the Irish case. Three principal factors underpinned the difference. First, at this time, the leadership of An Comunn tended to view Gaelic as a regional language, or the language of a distinct ethno-cultural minority, within Scotland, rather than a national language for all of Scotland (e.g. *P&J* 1922). Second, and relatedly, the work of Conradh na Gaeilge was connected – more and more directly so over time – to a nationalist movement that was much more powerful than its Scottish counterpart. Finally, the demographic decline of Irish in the nineteenth century had been much more rapid and dramatic than that of Gaelic, so that there was a much greater sense of urgency in relation to the language, even if the situation of Gaelic in Scotland was obviously very challenging (McLeod 2008a: 92–3).

From its inception it was agreed that An Comunn should be non-political, but it was never agreed exactly what this stricture meant and what kinds of activities were to be avoided. A maximal interpretation seemed to mean that the organisation should 'leave politics severely alone',[2] not engaging with any issues of public policy and focusing exclusively on cultural matters. A narrower view was that this stricture related only to 'opinions on sectarian religion and present-day party politics' (ACG 1904). Yet almost from its foundation, and continuously thereafter, An Comunn was regularly involved in lobbying the education authorities and local and national politicians, principally concerning education matters, and participated in electoral politics by urging voters to select candidates for different kinds of offices who were supportive of Gaelic (e.g. *DG* 1909b; [Reid] 1910; ACG 1918a, 1928). During wartime the organisation's journal published strongly pro-war editorial columns (e.g. [MacPhie] 1914; [M. Macleod] 1942), but this was not a divisive issue.

The question of the language used by An Comunn in its meetings and general operations was a matter of ongoing controversy. From the beginning An Comunn included a number of non-Gaelic speakers in key roles, including its first president, Lord Archibald Campbell, who was criticised by one commentator as 'ha[ving] so little interest in "the language of the heroic age" that the innumerable Gaelic tutors who tried to teach him the language completely failed to give him a mastery of it' (*Oban Times* 1891). English rather than Gaelic was used not only at public events such as the Mòd but also for internal purposes such as meetings of the organisation's Executive Council. More generally, the emphasis on music, especially choir performances, encouraged an ongoing influx of people who did not speak Gaelic and were not necessarily concerned to acquire it beyond a basic level.

Attempts to establish Gaelic as the organisation's working language became such a regular occurrence that in 1934 Alexander McKechnie could describe them as a 'hardy annual crop[]' (McKechnie 1934: 40). For example, motions at the annual meetings of 1911 and 1912 that all members of the Executive Council should be Gaelic speakers were narrowly rejected (*Scotsman* 1911, 1912). The thinking of those who opposed such moves was expressed by the outgoing president, William Mackay, in 1912, who declared that 'it would be committing suicide to adopt the motion' and reiterated that the cultivation of Gaelic was only one of the objects of An Comunn (*Scotsman* 1912). Meetings of An Comunn's Executive Committee in 1933, 1938 and 1939 were conducted entirely in Gaelic, but the fact that this procedure was deemed reportable in the press (*Scotsman* 1933, 1938, 1939b) indicates the extent to which English had been institutionalised as the language of the organisation's operations. In 1938 a series of compromises was agreed: Gaelic would be the ordinary language at meetings, but English was permitted; at least one Executive Council meeting per year would be held in Gaelic; minutes of Executive Council meetings would be written in Gaelic; at least half of each publication would be in Gaelic; and Mòd proceedings would be conducted in Gaelic 'as far as reasonably possible' (ACG 1938a: 7, 9, 35).

English was also the language used for most of An Comunn's printed material. In 1911 the Executive Council rejected a motion that would have required at least half of An Comunn's publications to be in Gaelic (*Oban Times* 1911). The most important of these was a monthly magazine launched in 1905, initially entitled *An Deò-Ghréine*. This publication was bilingual but preponderantly in English. The vision for the magazine, as set out in an appeal letter circulated in 1904 (ACG 1904), was strikingly ambitious:

The Gaelic people must therefore be organised and welded into one strong brotherhood. The mainspring and motive power already exists in the Comunn. By help of the periodical now proposed, and particularly by the forming of branches, it ought, in a few years, to have a widespread and powerful organisation, able to impose its will, in the interests of the Gaelic language, upon School Boards, the Education Department, and, if need be, on Parliament itself.

In a word, the main object of the Magazine is to preserve the race individuality in a sane condition and, by so doing, to increase the chances of the Units of the Race being able to reach and maintain a like condition. (ACG 1904)

An Comunn continued to publish the magazine until 1967, with two changes of title: *Gailig* for several issues in 1923 and *An Gaidheal*[3] from 1923 onwards. This publication is the single most important source concerning Gaelic movements and policy in the first two-thirds of the twentieth century, but it has never been analysed in a single study of the kind done for counterpart Irish publications (Nic Pháidín 1998; Uí Chollatáin 2004). Irrespective of its content, however, the magazine never achieved significant popularity in the Gaelic community and consistently ran at a loss (Thompson 1986: 105).

The language issue was also controversial in other Gaelic organisations at this time, notably Ceilidh nan Gaidheal, a social group established in Glasgow in 1896 after an existing group, Ceilidh na h-Ard-Sgoile, amended its rules so as to allow for a greater use of English in its work. A minority of members, described as 'luchd na fìor Ghàidhlig' (the true Gaelic people), then split away and formed the new organisation, with a clear stricture that only Gaelic would be used (Ceilidh nan Gaidheal 1947: 13–14). Over the following decades Ceilidh nan Gaidheal, which later included branches in Oban, Edinburgh and Inverness, organised a programme of lectures and other events, always in Gaelic, and even the minutes of meetings were kept in Gaelic. This strong Gaelic policy was very much an outlier among Gaelic organisations, however.

OTHER CULTURAL MOVEMENTS

The Gaelic movement spearheaded by An Comunn functioned within a wider cultural context in *fin-de-siècle* Scotland that was attracted to, and drew upon, Gaelic and Gaelic culture in various different ways. A 'Celtic Revival' movement found expression in a variety of forms, including art and design as well as literature, but most of those involved knew no Gaelic and had little direct connection to the Gaelic movement and no meaningful interest in the development of Gaelic as a living language (Shaw 2020). Moreover, much of the 'Celtic' material that inspired the movement was medieval rather than contemporary, or Irish or Welsh rather than Scottish. An important exception was Alexander Carmichael's celebrated *Carmina Gadelica*, a compilation of prayers, charms, blessings and other folkloric material collected mostly in the Western Isles and published in six beautifully produced volumes beginning in 1900. While the material in *Carmina Gadelica* was largely authentic (Black 2008), its wider public appeal was principally due to its presentation of a way of life and set of spiritual values that were very different from those of the modern city. Carmichael's work can also be understood as a contribution to the 'vindication of the Gael', a concern of Gaelic intellectuals that dated back to the Ossianic controversy and Dr Samuel Johnson's attacks on the value of Gaelic culture. Carmichael expressed his motivation as follows:

> Everything Highland is becoming of interest. Let us try to meet this interest and to show the world that our dearly beloved people were not the rude, barbarous, creedless, godless, ignorant men and women that prejudiced writers have represented them. It is to me heart breaking to see the spiteful manner in which Highlanders have been spoken of. (Campbell 1978: 1)

One of the most prominent figures in Scotland's Celtic Revival movement was William Sharp, who adopted the pen name 'Fiona MacLeod' and wrote under the guise of a Gaelic woman.[4] Scotland's Celtic Revival was linked to the better-known Irish movement of this period, in which William Butler Yeats and Lady Augusta Gregory were the most prominent notable figures. Yeats popularised the term 'Celtic Twilight' with his 1893 folklore collection of that name, and 'Fiona MacLeod' adopted this crepuscular rhetoric with enthusiasm:

> When I speak of the Gaelic people of Ireland and Scotland, I speak, alas! only of the small Gaelic remnant in the Scottish Highlands and in the Isles, and of the remnant in Ireland. This people is unable or unwilling to accept the bitter solace of absorption in the language, the written thought, the active, omnipresent, and variegated energy of the dominant race. It has to keep silence more and more, and soon it too will be silent.
>
> It is a strange thing: that a nation can hold within itself an ancient race, standing for the lost, beautiful, mysterious ancient world, can see it fading through its dim twilight, without heed to preserve that which might yet be preserved, without interest even in that which once gone cannot come again. The old Gaelic race is in its twilight indeed; but now, alas it is the hastening twilight after the feast of Samhain, when winter is come at last, out of the hills, down the glens, on the four winds of the world.

> There are some, however, who do care. There are some whose hearts ache to see the last pathetic stand of a retreating people, and who would gladly do what yet may be done to preserve awhile the beautiful old-world language and the still more beautiful and significant thought and legend and subtle genius enshrined in that language ... (Sharp 1910 [1900]: 224–6)

The term 'revival' seems inapposite in relation to Sharp, who was evidently more taken with the decline and disappearance of Gaelic rather than the prospects for its revitalisation.

The Mòd and the musical styles it fostered reflected the prevailing fashions and cultural dynamics of the era. This approach was most famously seen in the work of Marjory Kennedy-Fraser, whose *Songs of the Hebrides* (published in three volumes beginning in 1909, with the Rev. Kenneth MacLeod as her Gaelic cultural advisor) reworked traditional Gaelic material to suit the drawing-room taste of the day. Her work enjoyed great popularity, even in 'official' Gaelic circles (*DG* 1914b), but it bore little connection to authentic Gaelic tradition (Ahlander 2009) and became widely derided in the post-war period, when new emphasis was placed on 'authentic' Gaelic performance styles (Blankenhorn 2018).

All these movements touched in different ways on Romantic interpretations of Gaelic culture, ultimately connected to Macpherson's Ossian and later interpretations of 'Celtic' culture. If *Carmina Gadelica* and *Songs of the Hebrides* achieved some valorisation for Gaelic culture, this was tightly circumscribed and backward-looking and could not provide meaningful support for a programme of language revitalisation or cultural modernisation.

A different kind of cultural revival with relevance to Gaelic involved the development and codification of the traditional game of shinty (*camanachd*), especially following the foundation of Comunn na Camanachd (the Camanachd Association) in 1893. Comunn na Camanachd had little connection to An Comunn, however, or to other strands of the Gaelic movement, including the Gaelic nationalists of the early twentieth century (MacLennan 1998: 398, 423, 461 fn. 20; Reid 2013). By the same token, there was very little connection between the Gaelic movement and the revival of traditional Highland gatherings and games during this period (Jarvie 1991). The situation was very different in Ireland, where Cumann Lúthchleas Gael (the Gaelic Athletic Association), founded in 1884, maintained strong links to the Irish language movement and had a much more profound impact on Irish society (Billings 2017).

ERSKINE OF MARR AND GAELIC NATIONALISM

From the turn of the twentieth century a very different strain of Gaelic activism emerged in connection with the Scottish nationalist activity that began to gather force after 1886. This group of 'Gaelic nationalists' was strongly influenced by the language-centred understanding of nationhood which dominated nationalist thinking in Europe in the nineteenth century, placing great emphasis on language as a marker of national distinctiveness (May 2012: 60–2). The most important of these Gaelic nationalists was Ruaraidh Erskine of Marr. Born Stuart Richard Erskine, son of the fifth Baron Erskine of Restormel Castle, he learned Gaelic as a child from a family nurse from Harris and later adopted the name Ruaraidh Erskine of Marr, although his family was only distantly related to the earls of Mar (Thomson 2004).[5]

Most of those agitating for greater political autonomy for Scotland in the late nineteenth and early twentieth centuries were working towards 'home rule' within the United Kingdom, with a parliament in Scotland, and did not seek to establish a separate Scottish state. The Gaelic nationalists were therefore at the margins of those who were seeking autonomy, and the movement for home rule had limited political impact in any event (Cameron 2010: 63, 100). Their role within the Gaelic movement was more important, however, and their language ideology is worthy of study in its own right.

One early expression of the new 'Gaelic nationalist' viewpoint was the 'Brosnachadh' ('incitement' or 'encouragement') issued published by the London-based 'Clann na h-Alba' (The League of Scottish Nationalists), a leaflet issued in connection with the school board elections in 1912. The leaflet characterised Gaelic as 'the national language of Scotland' and the only language that 'can mark us out as a nation apart'. It began with a prologue in Gaelic, which included the claims that '[m]a gheibh a Ghàidhlig bàs, gheibh Albainn mar dhùthaich air leth, bàs cuideachd' and '[m]a thig aiseirigh na seann chànain Albannaich,[6] thig leasachadh mòr air ar duthaich fèin' ('if Gaelic dies, Scotland as a separate country will also die' and 'if a resurrection of the ancient Scottish tongue comes, a great improvement will come to the country'). To further these ends, the 'Brosnachadh' argued for the much greater use of Gaelic in education, including its introduction in schools in Lowland Scotland.

An earlier 'Brosnachadh' was promulgated in 1907 under the name of 'John, Earl of Mar', but, like the Clann na h-Alba leaflet, it appears to have been the work of Ruaraidh Erskine (Hanham 1969: 125).[7] This document called for the establishment of a new Scottish Party

('Buidheann tur Albannach'), which included among its objectives '[t]o give first place to the Gaelic language', to make the teaching of Gaelic mandatory in all Highland schools, to require all holders of public office in Scotland to 'have a knowledge of the Gaelic' and '[t]o return to the old system of Highland ruling' (Napier 1907; see *GB* 1907a). These proposals, especially the recommended stricture in relation to public office holders, were strongly criticised by another nationalist activist of the time, Theodore Napier, who argued such an 'aggressive policy' in favour of Gaelic would 'prove a fatal one', and could even provoke '*civil war* in Scotland' (Napier 1907: 6 (emphasis in original)). An editorial in the *North Star and Farmers' Chronicle* (1907) gave a more measured criticism of the proposal to make Gaelic mandatory, noting the extent of language shift in many parts of the Highlands and parents' overwhelming concern that their children acquire a firm command of English.

The Gaelic nationalists' emphasis on Gaelic as a national language for all of Scotland included efforts to demonstrate how widely spoken Gaelic had been in Lowland Scotland during medieval times. Although many in Scotland still remain unaware of this history, in the early twentieth century the notion of a rigid distinction between Highlands and Lowlands was much more entrenched and assertions of this kind all the more challenging to prevailing understandings. In 1920 Erskine's associate H. C. MacNeacail wrote:

> Gaelic was the language of the builders of the Scottish nation [...] who strove to mould the various states and principalities of our country into one Gaelic-speaking nation. In the eleventh and twelfth centuries, Gaelic was spoken from north to south, and from east to west of the country.

Based on this interpretation, MacNeacail asserted that Gaelic was the 'only [...] living language entitled to be styled the Scottish language' and dismissed Scots, which 'owed its spread to English or pro-English influences' (MacNeacail 1920: 59–60).

In keeping with his national view of Gaelic, Erskine urged that Gaelic should be promoted on a Scotland-wide basis and not limited to the Gàidhealtachd: 'To confine the Gaelic movement to the "Highlands" would be, even if it were practicable – which it is not – a truly suicidal policy' (Erskine 1912: 496). Sometimes his arguments to this end were clearly exaggerated; for example, he claimed in 1900 that '[t]here are probably more Gaelic-speaking people in Glasgow than there are in the whole of Argyll-shire and Inverness-shire combined; whilst the Gaelic-speaking populations of other important towns and cities in Scotland are increasing by leaps and bounds' (Erskine 1900).[8]

These claims about the national status of Gaelic and its critical importance to Scottish nationality appear to have rarely drawn any kind of refutation.[9] This is in marked contrast to the pattern in recent decades, whereby this fundamental issue is a matter for endless debate, generally formulaic and repetitive in nature, most commonly in the letters sections of newspapers. The vision of Gaelic restoration in Scotland was sometimes challenged, however. In a leader column in 1908 opposing Gaelic amendments to the education bill that was then going through Parliament (discussed below, pp. 83–4), *The Scotsman* dismissed:

> The notion of [. . .] 'ousting English from the dominating position it holds in Celtic Scotland and relegating that tongue to a secondary and subordinate status' is a dream, and a mischievous dream. If it be capable of part realisation in Ireland and in Wales, so much the worse in the end for those sections of the 'Celtic fringe'. In Scotland, even in the Highlands of Scotland, the plan of using Gaelic to dam back English is recognised to be as hopeless as that of trying to keep out the Atlantic with a broom. (*Scotsman* 1908)

Erskine was also concerned to 'bring[] written Gaelic into the modern world' and develop it as 'an effective political language' (Thomson 1997–8: 287; Thompson 1971–2: 86). His most important publication was *Guth na Bliadhna* ('The Voice of the Year'), which ran from 1904 to 1925 and was described by Donald John MacLeod as 'a political and literary review of an uncompromisingly avant-garde and cosmopolitan nature, edited from a Gaelic-nationalist or otherwise radical point of view' (D. J. MacLeod 1970: 41). Other publications established by Erskine included the short-lived weekly newspaper *Alba* (1908–9 and 1920–1), and the literary periodicals *Am Bàrd* (1901–2), *An Sgeulaiche* (1909–11) and *An Ròsarnach* (1917–30). In 1914 Erskine also became editor of the *Scottish Review*, an established English-language periodical which had been in abeyance since 1900 (Thompson 1971–2: 86).

As well as adopting a distinct position on the national significance of Gaelic, the Gaelic nationalists were generally more militant in their approach to the promotion of the language and regularly attacked An Comunn for its perceived timidity. In 1904 *Guth na Bliadhna* criticised those who

> regard the language movement as something that may be played with – as a hobby suitable for dull winter evenings, or as an excuse for 'social gatherings' at which tea and gossip (for the most part in English) may be indulged in to the weak heart's unbounded content. [. . .] It is now full time that we ceased junketing – that we put an end for ever to all our sentimental

do-nothing twaddle about clans and 'Bonnie Prince Charlie' and seriously addressed ourselves to business. (*GB* 1904b: 202, 206)

Erskine and others in his circle also asserted a strong link between Gaelic and Catholicism, presenting Catholicism as the true Gaelic faith and the Reformation as a disastrous wrong turn in Scottish history (Powell 2011; *GB* 1905: 303–4). The first article in the first issue of *Guth na Bliadhna* in 1904 declared:

> Presbyterianism is not a plant indigenous to Celtic Scotland, but was an importation which had to be forced on the people [. . . .] No Gael [. . .] can escape the reflection, however disagreeable it may be, that the position of his race was infinitely better under Catholic than it is under Protestant auspices. [. . .] Pray, what has he done that is worthy to be mentioned since he accepted Protestantism or, rather, since the Teutonic persuasion was forced on him? He has emigrated, and he has helped to rivet his own political fetters by fighting the battles of his political masters; but he has done little (if anything) else. (*GB* 1904: 2–5)

A related issue was the connection between Scottish Gaeldom and Ireland. Gaelic organisations and activists of different kinds built links to the Irish language movement that gathered pace from the 1890s onwards (O'Leary 1986), and they also took an active role in the pan-Celtic movement which emerged at the turn of the twentieth century (De Barra 2018). Pan-Celticism aimed to build cultural and political links between the various territories that had become identified as 'Celtic' (Scotland, Ireland, Wales, the Isle of Man, Cornwall and Brittany). Pan-Celtic activity before the First World War did not cause controversy among Gaelic activists in Scotland, in contrast to Ireland, where many Irish language activists saw Pan-Celticism as a distraction from the specific problems of Ireland and the Irish language (De Barra 2018: 121–54).

Scottish Gaels continued to be involved in the second wave of pan-Celtic activity from 1917 onwards. By this stage, however, there was a split in the Scottish committee connected to members' views on the Irish question, which had become much more divisive in the wake of the Easter Rising of 1916. Eventually Erskine and the other nationalists withdrew from the organisation (De Barra 2018: 204–14). The Celtic Congress continued over the course of the following decades (e.g. [Ross] 1930) and indeed down to the present, although the event now has a low profile.[10]

Erskine and other Gaelic nationalists, notably Liam MacGille Ìosa, were particularly keen to promote links with their Irish counterparts

(Witt 2013; Hunter 1975: 192–4). Writing in the Irish revivalist paper *An Claidheamh Soluis* in 1905, Erskine proposed 'reciprocity' between Scotland and Ireland, and its editor, the leading Irish activist Patrick Pearse (who was later executed for his role in the Easter Rising of 1916), proposed 'an entente cordiale between the Gael of Scotia Major [Ireland] and the Gael of Scotia Minor' (Erskine 1905; Pearse 1905),[11] and in 1906 spoke of a 'Gaelic confederation' (*GB* 1906). Some elements in the pan-Celtic movement recommended an even closer alignment, including a somewhat fanciful 1903 contribution which proposed 'the annexation of the Highlands' to an Irish-dominated 'Gaelic empire' (Pan-Celtic Congress 1903). Erskine and MacGille Ìosa gave strong support to the cause of Irish independence (e.g. MacGille Iosa 1920) and even contemplated a counterpart Scottish rising in 1920 (Witt 2013).

Among Scottish Gaels more generally, attitudes to Ireland and the Irish were coloured by anti-Catholic prejudice and distaste for Irish nationalism. Scotland experienced heavy immigration from Ireland during the nineteenth century, principally in the industrial areas, and Irish immigrants and their descendants suffered significant hostility and discrimination. Economic competition and religious differences meant that interaction between Scottish Gaelic and Irish incomers in cities such as Glasgow were not always harmonious (Sloan 1991, 1994). The majority of Scottish Gaels were steadfast Protestants, and even the Catholics among them were sometimes resentful of Irish-dominated church institutions (Burnett 1998; Coogan 2002: 236–40). Mainstream British opinion, including Highland opinion, was profoundly hostile to Irish nationalism, especially its 'physical force' strain. Many Scottish Gaels had become firmly and enthusiastically attached to the British state and empire and had little sympathy for Irish nationalism and indeed the Irish more generally (Meek 2004).

GAELIC AND SOCIAL MOVEMENTS

The Gaelic language issue played very little role in the labour and socialist movements that developed in Scotland during the late nineteenth and early twentieth centuries (Young 1983: 143). There was almost no sense that demands for improved provision for Gaelic and attempts to strengthen its role in public life were linked to demands for improving the socio-economic position of either rural or industrial workers. The areas of Scotland that became industrialised in the nineteenth century had not been Gaelic-speaking for several centuries, although Gaelic speakers of Highland origin were certainly prominent in the workforce in some sectors, especially in the larger towns and cities such as Glasgow and Dundee. For Tony Dickson, the fact that Gaelic was not the 'majority language' 'for the whole of the period in which it is meaningful to talk about a Scottish working class (roughly, from 1750 onwards)' is 'precisely why the "language question" has never been a major issue in working-class political action in Scotland' (Dickson 1985: 332). The situation was different from that in Wales, where most of the areas in which industry (especially mining) developed were strongly Welsh-speaking and Welsh continued as the language of community institutions (including some trade unions) following industrialisation (Jenkins 1998).

One minor exception to this pattern was the slate-quarrying industry at Ballachulish in Argyll, where bitter industrial disputes broke out in 1902 and 1905, pitting the Gaelic-speaking workforce against an aggressive management (Kirk 2007). During the First World War, Gaelic was the language of the labour force in some Glasgow munitions factories (Scott and Cunnison 1924: 3), but this was not a long-lasting or large-scale phenomenon.

There were also some limited individual exceptions. In the last stage of his life, John Murdoch, an important voice in the crofters' cause and a champion of Gaelic, became involved in the labour movement in Ayrshire and chaired the first meeting of the Scottish Labour Party in 1888. Murdoch was not an important figure in the party, however, and the Gaelic issue per se was not a concern. Robert Smillie, vice-president of the Miners' Federation of Great Britain between 1912 and 1921 and first chairman of the Scottish Trades Union Congress, became aligned with Erskine and his fellow Gaelic nationalists and wrote to MacGille Ìosa in 1918, 'I am with you heart and soul for the revival of the Gaelic language' (Diack 1918: 172). John Carstairs Matheson, a Gaelic-speaking teacher who helped found the Socialist Labour Party and who edited the journal *The Socialist*, made some symbolic use of Gaelic in his writings. Yet Matheson tended to view Gaelic society as highly peripheral in Scotland (Davidson 2001: 296–7), speaking dismissively of 'Comun[n] nan Albannach, Gaelic Scotch nationalists' and the 'backward agrarian struggle [. . .] for the repatriation of the [. . .] rocks of the Hebrides and the West Highlands', which he viewed as irrelevant to the socialist cause (Burnett 2016: 61).

James D. Young speculated that if the leading socialist campaigner John Maclean had acquired Gaelic from his parents, Highland Gaelic speakers who had migrated to Glasgow, the role of Gaelic within labour and socialist movements at this time might have been different (Young

1983: 143). As a first-generation English monoglot, Maclean himself was representative of the urban Gaelic experience: as is typical of (im)migrants to urban areas, intergenerational transmission of the language in Scotland's towns and cities was weak. Maclean did speak hopefully of the possibility that agitation on the land issue in the Highlands could lead to 'a real Gaelic revival' and 'a Gaelic movement to clear all landlords out of the Highlands', but such notions were on the margins of his political thinking, which focused on the urban working class (Maclean 1978: 220; Howell 1986: 170).

Both Maclean and Erskine endeavoured to find in the traditional structure of Gaelic or Celtic society, especially the model of the clan, something that could be understood as 'Celtic communism' (Howell 1986: 213). Maclean expressed the view that 'the old communal traditions of the clans must be revived and adapted to modern conceptions and conditions' to help shape a model of Scottish 'national communism' (Maclean 1978: 219). Erskine wrote several articles for Maclean's paper *The Vanguard* in 1920 explaining his own concept of 'Celtic Communism', although he had previously rejected the secularism of communism and what he perceived as its disregard for the traditional family (*GB* 1907b).

This intersection between elements of the Gaelic movement and socialist movements in industrial communities was short-lived and by the 1930s it had effectively dissipated. This pattern was to continue in the period after 1945; Gaelic has been connected at different stages to efforts to promote the economic and social development of the Highlands and Islands, but has not played any meaningful role in left-wing politics in Scotland more generally, although some far-left sects have symbolically appropriated Gaelic from time to time, as discussed in subsequent chapters.

GAELIC AND THE SCHOOLS

The *Education (Scotland) Act 1872*, which built the framework for a new system of state schools in Scotland, was without question a landmark in the history of Scottish education, yet in the Gaelic context the Act is usually characterised as a disaster for the language. This criticism is arguably misplaced, however, partly because it is based on a misunderstanding of the nature of the 1872 Act. Nevertheless, it is clear that the state education system as a whole marginalised Gaelic and functioned as a very important motor in the process of language shift in the Gàidhealtachd. As the prominent writer George Mackay Brown summarised the educational experience of his mother and those like her, 'the subtly insinuated suggestions, repeated over and over, that English was the language of authority and business and the ascendancy, tore Gaelic to tatters in a few generations' (Brown 2008: 16).

It is difficult to go behind the official policies and practices and get a meaningful sense of the nature of the education system as it was experienced and perceived by ordinary Gaels, and then to assess its cumulative impact on Gaelic communities. The consensus of Gaelic intellectuals has certainly been highly critical. For example, in 1972 Donald MacAulay, later Professor of Celtic at Glasgow University, wrote that 'the 1872 Act destroyed the movement towards Gaelic literacy spearheaded by the Gaelic schools societies and produced generations of people, virtually illiterate in their own language and taught by the practice of the most pervasive institutions in their community that their culture was of no value' (MacAulay 1972; see MacKinnon 1974: 54).

The state education system of the late nineteenth century had forerunners going back to the early eighteenth century. By 1811 the SSPCK had 290 schools in the Gàidhealtachd, with 16,000 pupils (MacKinnon 1991: 63). Beginning in 1811, a further group of schools was established in the Highlands, run by a diverse range of charitable organisations, affiliated to the Church of Scotland or the Free Church, including the Church of Scotland Ladies' Gaelic School Association, the Free Church Ladies' Association and several local societies which became amalgamated as the Gaelic Schools Society (M. K. MacLeod 1981: 28–30, 83). These new establishments, which came to be known as *sgoilean Chrìosd* (literally 'schools of Christ'), had the purpose of spreading evangelical religion and were not schools in the conventional sense; they placed a heavy emphasis on teaching Gaelic literacy in order to facilitate reading the Bible in Gaelic (MacKinnon 1991: 64). It has been estimated that at least 90,000 Gaels learned to read at these schools in the period up to 1872 (MacThòmais 1958: 270). Literacy in Gaelic was higher than in English at that point (Nicolson 1866: 14), but declined significantly among the generations who received their schooling after 1872.

The educational focus of the Gaelic societies' schools was narrow in its range, with a heavy emphasis on religious topics, and did not prepare pupils well for working life and the possibility of out-migration to English-speaking areas. When state education was introduced after 1872, it was accepted that schools should prepare pupils in a more practical fashion, and debates about the position of Gaelic in the curriculum need to be understood against this backdrop (Thomson 1981: 12).

Following the 1872 Act the new state schools slowly replaced the existing networks of private schools. This process was not immediate: in 1874 there were still sixteen schools, with 861 pupils, run by the Church of Scotland Ladies' Gaelic School Association in operation, but these numbers were declining rapidly given 'the apparently spreading conviction that the Act had entirely superseded the necessity of private charitable effort in the cause of education' (*AG* 1874). By 1895 the association had essentially ceased its activity in relation to elementary education, while the Gaelic Schools Society was formally wound up in 1892 (M. K. MacLeod 1981: 84–5).

The 1872 Act followed a similar measure for England and Wales, the *Elementary Education Act 1870*, and resulted from a series of three reports issued between 1865 and 1868 by the Education Commission, more commonly known as the Argyll Commission (Education Commission 1865, 1867, 1868). Although the Argyll Commission was chaired by, and took its name from, a leading Highland landowner, the eighth Duke of Argyll, the Commission's main report took no cognisance of the Gaelic question. The issue of Gaelic was instead considered in a chapter in the report on elementary schools that dealt with the specific problems of the Hebrides and Western Highlands (Education Commission 1867: lxiii–lxxvi), and built on a separate report on the state of education in the Hebrides, prepared by the Skye-born, Gaelic-speaking lawyer Alexander Nicolson (Nicolson 1866). Along with addressing many pressing practical problems affecting the region, including physical isolation, inadequate school accommodation and difficulties of teacher recruitment, the Argyll Commission's report warned against appointing English-monoglot teachers in Gaelic-speaking areas. In the view of the Commission, 'it seems obvious that, in districts where Gaelic alone is understood, the teacher should be able to communicate in a language the meaning of which they can comprehend. [. . .] It is a mistake to overlook the difficulties of the scholar who is sent to learn what to him is a foreign language without having first acquired the art of reading his own' (Education Commission 1867: lxx–lxxi). Unfortunately, in the succeeding decades this advice was often not followed, as discussed below.

As many critics have pointed out over the years, sometimes in a polemical fashion, the 1872 Act made no mention of Gaelic. However, the Act actually did not address the content of the school curriculum, other than elementary instruction in reading, writing and arithmetic. The Act dealt instead with the structure of school governance, with curricular matters being regulated by the Code of Regulations (often known as the Schools Code), adopted in 1873 and amended thereafter, which set out the conditions upon which government grants would be paid to school boards. Campaigns seeking an increased role for Gaelic in school education were therefore focused in the first instance on securing amendments to the Schools Code rather than amending the underlying Education Act. The Act also created a supervisory Board of Education for Scotland, but the main government agency was the Scotch (later Scottish) Education Department (SED).[12]

Neither the 1872 Act nor the Schools Code imposed any kind of ban on the teaching or use of Gaelic in the state schools, or any requirement that only English could be used. The policy was therefore different from that followed in France, for example, where an 1851 memorandum on the implementation of the Fallou educational law of 1850 required that only French could be used as a language of instruction (Judge 2007: 22–3). The question of provision for Gaelic was instead left to the 984 local school boards that were created by the Act in each parish and burgh. Although the franchise for these boards was considerably wider than for parliamentary elections (Cameron 2000: 70), the boards were, according to one Gaelic advocate, mainly 'composed of lairds, factors, clergymen, doctors, and sheep-farmers – classes which generally have very few Celtic sympathisers, indeed a strong desire to have the whole race Saxonized right off' (Cameron 1877: 186). Crucially, as one of the main elements in the system for financing schools was local property taxation, the school boards in impoverished Highland areas often had very limited resources and costs were borne by a small number of local ratepayers, who often had to pay much higher rates than was typical in the Lowlands. Highland school boards were thus in a very weak financial position, with many of them actually becoming bankrupt by the late 1880s (Anderson 1995: 182–4; Day 1918: 159). In this context, in the absence of additional government funding, any costs that might result from improved provision for Gaelic would fall directly on this small group of ratepayers, who tended to have little interest in promoting the language.

In 1876 the Gaelic Schools Society presented a memorial (formal petition) to the Lord President of the Council[13] urging the payment of special government grants to encourage the teaching of Gaelic in Gaelic-speaking areas. In response, the SED sent a circular to 103 school boards in Argyll, Caithness, Inverness, Perthshire, Ross & Cromarty and Sutherland to seek their views on the teaching of Gaelic as a subject within schools, on the relative difficulty of recruiting Gaelic teachers, and the names of schools and numbers of pupils who would benefit from such provision (SED 1877; AG 1877: 155–6). Ninety replies were received, with sixty-five school boards in favour of providing Gaelic-language teaching and twenty-five opposing it. Fifty-three of the boards who supported the proposal indicated that suitable teachers were available, as did fourteen of those opposing it. The potential reach of provision by the supportive school boards was 16,331 pupils across 208 schools (*AG* 1877: 158). All of the eight boards in the Western Isles supported the proposal, as did 16 of the 20 Inner Hebridean boards that responded. On the mainland, the boards in Inverness-shire and Perthshire were more supportive (15 of 18 and 7 of 8 in favour) than those in Argyll, Caithness, Ross & Cromarty and Sutherland (32 of 49) (*AG* 1877: 156–8). In 1876 the Board of Education also supported the teaching of Gaelic literacy in predominantly Gaelic-speaking areas, recommending that schools with qualified staff offer one or more Gaelic-language lessons each week to Gaelic-speaking pupils on a voluntary basis (Board of Education 1876: xxv).

This strong showing of potential demand for Gaelic education probably surprised the SED (Cameron 2000: 69–70) and it did not take any real action as a result of its findings (Macleod 1963: 322). Actual provision in the decades following was therefore very limited. From 1875 a series of minor 'concessions' concerning the role of Gaelic was secured on an incremental basis, as discussed below. The first of these concessions involved a provision in the Code of Regulations to allow for the testing of the intelligence of Gaelic-speaking children by having them explain in Gaelic a passage read to them in English (SED 1875: 8 (s. 19 C 3)). But children were still assessed 'by the same standards as if English were their mother tongue' (MacKinnon 1875), and this concession had very little practical impact as few of the school inspectors in the Gàidhealtachd at the time could speak Gaelic (M. MacLeod 1963: 321).

In 1878 the new version of the Code of Regulations included two new concessions relating to Gaelic, both of them set out in footnotes (Royal Commission 1884: 79–80). The first of these authorised the payment of part of the salary of a Gaelic teacher from a school's grant funding and the second allowed Gaelic to 'be taught during the ordinary school hours, either by the certificated teacher or by any person specially appointed for the purpose'.[14] In principle at least, there was no limit to the amount of teaching time that could be dedicated to Gaelic; this decision was left to the determination of individual school boards (*TGSI* 1878a: xiv). No additional funding was provided to support Gaelic teaching; this had to be met out of existing budgets. But because Gaelic was not a specific subject assessed by examination or included in the scope of school inspections, there was little incentive for school boards to expand provision.[15]

Although its main focus was the land question, the report of the Napier Commission, published in 1884, included a strongly worded section on the issue of education in the crofting areas, including the place of Gaelic. One of the commissioners was Alexander Nicolson, author of the 1886 report on education in the Hebrides, and it was probably he who wrote this section of the report (Anderson 1995: 183). The Commission condemned what it described as 'the discouragement and neglect of the native language in the education of Gaelic-speaking children' and issued a series of recommendations concerning the role of Gaelic in the schools, including the reinstatement of special bursaries for students training as teachers and the provision of additional grants to support the salaries of Gaelic teachers. In terms of the curriculum, the Commission argued that all children with Gaelic as their mother tongue should be taught to read and write Gaelic and that Gaelic was 'entitled to something more than permissive recognition, and a place in a footnote along with drill and cookery' (this being a reference to the concession in the 1878 Code of Regulations (CCES 1878: 8)). The Commissioners also argued that a knowledge of Gaelic 'ought to be considered one of the primary qualifications of every person engaged in the carrying out of the national system of education in Gaelic-speaking districts, whether as school-inspectors, teachers, or compulsory officers' (Royal Commission 1884: 80–1).

Most of the recommendations in relation to education by the Commission, which probably exceeded its remit, were ignored by the authorities, but a new report on Highland education was commissioned, written by Sir Henry Craik, who would soon become the first secretary of the SED (Craik 1884a). Craik's report led to the promulgation of the so-called 'Highland Minute' of 1885 (SED 1885), which authorised Gaelic as a specific subject for examination and created a dedicated grant for teaching Gaelic (in the amount of ten shillings per pupil per year). Even with this new concession, as late as 1898 Gaelic was still only being taught in twenty-five schools (CCES 1885; Hansard 1898). Although Irish had been added to the secondary Leaving Certificate in 1878, Gaelic was not included until 1905 (at the Lower level). An additional grant of £10 per year to schools that employed Gaelic teachers was introduced in 1906 (SED 1905: 19–20), and by 1907–8, 158 schools were in receipt of the new Gaelic grant (*DG* 1908c). The Higher examination in Gaelic was not introduced until 1915, following another campaign by An Comunn and other bodies (*DG* 1916a). Twenty-six candidates sat the Higher exam in the first year, and the average uptake in the following decades remained modest, approximately thirty-five pupils per year (*AG*

1952). Following its addition to the Leaving Certificate, between 1908 and 1911 Gaelic also became a subject for preliminary examination and bursary competitions in the universities of Aberdeen, Edinburgh and Glasgow (M. K. MacLeod 1981: 209–10).

In addition, from 1893 onwards Gaelic was included as a subject in the schedule of subjects in the code of regulations for evening continuation classes. These served as a substitute for post-primary education for adults, a precursor of modern further education (e.g. SED 1893: 11). This did not lead to a large-scale expansion of provision in this sector, however; by 1914 there were only twelve such classes running, with 275 students. Some of these were in unlikely locations, notably the east coast port of Arbroath (*Dundee Evening Telegraph* 1916). By 1930, however, many more continuation classes were running; twelve of these were in the Glasgow area, with an enrolment of almost four hundred (MacMaster Campbell 1930: 52–3).

Despite making these various concessions over the decades, the SED did little to coordinate or supervise the teaching of Gaelic. For example, between 1907 and 1911 the department issued nine memoranda on the teaching of particular school subjects (Bone 1968: 169); one of these dealt with languages, but there was no mention of Gaelic in the document (SED 1907b). The first memorandum dealt with the teaching of English, which did make passing reference to the needs of Gaelic-speaking children (as well as those whose mother tongue was Scots), recommending that teachers allow the use of Gaelic (or Scots), and even use it themselves, to facilitate the initial phase of elementary education (SED 1907a: 9). The omission of Gaelic in these documents could of course be justified on the grounds that few schools taught the language, although such an argument is ultimately circular.

Similarly, senior management of the SED provided little support for Gaelic. Craik, the department's first secretary, was firmly opposed to the expansion of Gaelic education. In his 1901 survey of Scottish history he argued that the 'one essential condition' for progress in the social conditions of the Highlands was 'the spread of the English language – an opinion which the sentimentalists of our own generation have vainly tried to controvert' (Craik 1901: 23), while his lengthy chapter on education in Scotland in his 1884 book *The State in its Relation to Education* (Craik 1884b) did not mention Gaelic at all. In 1918, as a Member of Parliament, Craik opposed the ultimately successful amendment to include the 'Gaelic clause' in the Education (Scotland) Bill (*Aberdeen Daily Journal* 1918). Craik's successor, Sir John Struthers, was probably even less supportive than Craik (M. K. MacLeod 1981:

301). Even so, Gaelic activists of the period did not necessarily perceive the SED as inimical; Ella Carmichael wrote in 1912 that 'whatever it may have been in the past, there is no reason to suppose that at the present time the [SED] is hostile to Gaelic' (Carmichael 1912: 95–6).

The overall official position was made clear in 1911 at a conference on bilingualism in education in the British Empire attended by representatives from Canada, India, Jersey, Malta and South Africa as well as Britain. The SED representative, W. H. Warre Cornish, asserted in relation to Scotland's approach to Gaelic in education that 'the problem has been successfully left to settle itself on the spot', dealt with by local school boards, with the SED 'refrain[ing] from laying down the law'. Warre Cornish noted that '[o]f course, there are enthusiasts for the Gaelic language and extremists who may make their voice heard sometimes, but there has been very little complaint from the parents that that language is not receiving sufficient attention' (*Report of the Imperial Education Conference 1911*: 257, 258). In her 1926 study of bilingual education and nationalism, South African scholar Anna Jacoba Aucamp quoted Warre's phrase 'settle itself on the spot' in relation to Gaelic education policy in Scotland and characterised the nineteenth-century policy as one of '"laissez-faire" that led to indifference, and often total neglect of the language' (Aucamp 1926: 40–1).

Although a broadly similar pattern could be seen in Wales and Ireland in the decades following the introduction of state education, the concessions there were more significant and wide-ranging, so that by 1914 the level of provision for Welsh and Irish was a good deal more extensive than that for Gaelic (M. K. MacLeod 1981: 304–9). In addition, the concessions obtained in Scotland were all permissive rather than mandatory in nature, so that the take-up was generally low and the impact limited.

From the perspective of the Scottish education authorities, there seems to have been a 'tacit assumption that Gaelic-speaking Scots form such a small minority than no special administration is needed' (Smith 1948: 9). In Wales, the language issue was much more prominent by virtue of the much higher proportion of Welsh speakers in the national population (54.5 per cent in 1891, the first census to incorporate a question on language, compared to 6.8 per cent for Gaelic in Scotland (Parry and Williams 1999: 11)).

In significant part the difference in outcomes from campaigns for improved provision for Gaelic and Welsh was the result of relative political weight rather than any fundamental difference of strategy or tactics. Substantially similar campaigns and demands for Welsh and

Gaelic proved successful in Wales but were defeated or ignored in Scotland. In Ireland, the strength of the nationalist movement meant that lobbying on behalf of Irish in the education system was backed by broad support in civil society across the country (M. K. MacLeod 1981: 308–9, 346). In Frank Thompson's view, An Comunn lacked 'key figures who were willing to stand up and be counted' and 'people, embedded in the national establishment, who were willing to challenge authority and make waves' against 'the deeply entrenched Anglicisation of the Scottish establishment' (Thompson 1986: 43). Instead, the typical pattern was that An Comunn, the GSL or other organisations would send periodic deputations[16] to meet with senior officials in London or Edinburgh, where they would receive 'tea and sympathy' (Thompson 1986: 75) but rarely anything more. Typically officials would deflect the organisations' proposals by suggesting they direct their demands for improved provision to the school boards in the first instance (M. MacLeod 1914: 367–8; Fairney 2006: 100). At the same time, as late as 1909 some school boards contended that they had no authority to allow the teaching of Gaelic ([Reid] 1909).

In terms of Gaelic language maintenance, the reality of educational provision on the ground in the Gàidhealtachd was probably more important than the formal regulatory framework. Despite the concerns expressed by the Argyll Commission, in many cases teachers with no knowledge of Gaelic were appointed to work in schools in areas where the children came to school with no knowledge of English (e.g. Rea 1997 [1964]: 17). Typically this was simply a consequence of the shortage of certificated Gaelic-speaking teachers rather than any kind of deliberate practice. Few Gaelic speakers had the requisite qualifications to gain admission to the teacher training colleges, largely because there was almost no access to secondary education in the stronger Gaelic areas (M. K. MacLeod 1981: 219). Even so, this situation was not considered sufficiently intolerable that urgent action was required to increase the numbers of Gaelic speakers entering the teaching profession. Indeed, in 1884 Alexander Walker, schools inspector for Perthshire, argued that the practice of appointing English-monoglot teachers in Gaelic areas was actually educationally advantageous. According to Walker, the Gaelic-speaking pupils with the best facility in English were those who had learned from a teacher with no knowledge of Gaelic, as this required the children to use English at all times and required the teacher to be flexible and creative in the use of English in order to be understood (CCES 1884: 165).

The low value of land in the Highlands meant that it generated very low rate income, with the result that school facilities were very poor and it was difficult to attract highly qualified and motivated teachers, irrespective of whether they could speak Gaelic. There was no national salary scale at this time and local boards simply paid what they could – a system which disadvantaged the Highland boards (M. K. MacLeod 1981: 53–4). In some cases teachers accepted posts in the Gàidhealtachd because they could not find work in more central locations and came to develop 'a bitter anti-Gaelic complex' (Murchison 1955: 17). The problem of recruitment was exacerbated by the impact of the wider social conditions of the region. The poverty of the crofting communities meant that scholars attended only irregularly, which reduced the money available for teachers' salaries since they were partly dependent on fees from the pupils and an assessment of average attendance (M. K. MacLeod 1981: 61–3, 71).

Beginning in 1904, as plans for a new Education Bill were being circulated, An Comunn and the GSL began to press for a legislative amendment to improve provision for Gaelic. This included organising a conference at the House of Commons to formulate suggestions for Gaelic amendments, followed by a deputation, along with representatives of other Gaelic and Highland societies, to the Secretary for Scotland (*DG* 1906). In addition, from 1905 onwards An Comunn organised annual conferences on Gaelic education, which allowed for focused discussion concerning the way forward (e.g. ACG 1907b).

In 1908 An Comunn launched a 'vigorous campaign' for the inclusion of clauses requiring improved provision for Gaelic in the bill that became the *Education (Scotland) Act 1908* (*DG* 1908b). The proposed amendments would have required school boards in 'Gaelic-speaking districts' to make 'adequate provision' for 'the instruction of Gaelic-speaking children in reading and writing the Gaelic language'. Further, the amendments would have conditioned school boards' ability to access any surplus funding on having made such provision (*DG* 1908b).

This proposal was controversial and drew opposition even from some Gaelic organisations, whom An Comunn characterised as 'pseudo-friends': 'the fact that they have now become hostile shows that the movement is making itself felt' (*DG* 1908b: 184). While the GSL backed the proposals (*IC* 1908a), William Mackay, Chief of the Gaelic Society of Inverness, described the amendment as 'ill-considered' and 'a grave tactical error', for requiring school boards to make provision for Gaelic without allocating additional financial resource would have had a seriously adverse impact on their overall provision (*TGSI* 1915b: 43). A number of school boards in the Gàidhealtachd opposed the amendment on this basis, as did some branches of the Educational Institute of Scotland (EIS, the teachers' union), who were also concerned about the possibility of non-Gaelic-speaking teachers losing their jobs (*IC* 1908a, 1908b, 1908c). An Comunn's perceived mismanagement of the campaign was characterised by *Guth na Bliadhna* (1908b) as a 'crisis in the Gaelic movement'.

After the rejection of these amendments at the committee stage (*Scotsman* 1908; *IC* 1908d), later in the legislative process An Comunn arranged for the introduction of an alternative, less stringent amendment which would have provided additional funding to school boards in Gaelic-speaking areas for teaching Gaelic reading and writing and created additional bursaries for Gaelic-speaking pupils intending to become teachers (*DG* 1908f). This amendment received more support from Highland school boards but was nevertheless defeated by 192 votes to 109. Although only one of the seventy-two Scottish MPs intentionally voted against the amendment, only nineteen voted in favour; a sobering indicator of the weak support for Gaelic across Scotland as a whole (*DG* 1909a; see M. K. MacLeod 1981: 235–40, 314–26). Despite the rejection of these amendments, the 1908 Act did include one provision relating to Gaelic. This authorised (rather than required) school boards in 'Gaelic-speaking districts' to provide continuation classes in 'Gaelic language and literature', within the framework of the wider duty that the Act imposed on school boards 'to make suitable provision of continuation classes for the further instruction of young persons above the age of fourteen years' (s. 10(1)).

A decade later, the prospect of another new Education Act gave Gaelic activists another opportunity to seek improved provision for Gaelic after the failure of the 1908 campaign. An Comunn took the lead in these efforts, organising a petition requesting Gaelic teaching in schools that was signed by more than 20,000 people (Watson 1923: 51). The petition had four demands: that in schools attended mainly by Gaelic-speaking children, Gaelic should be a mandatory subject of instruction and should be available to all children; that provision should be made for training Gaelic teachers; that teacher salaries should be increased to give teachers incentives to remain in or return to the Gàidhealtachd; and that a dedicated Education Board for the Highlands should be established. The SED rejected these proposals, however, requiring An Comunn to seek the introduction of an amendment to further the first objective (ACG 1918b). Comunn nan Gàidheal (the Scots National League) published a ferociously worded attack on the education bill as introduced, charging that it had 'aon cheann-rùin a tha soilleir eadhoin do leth-amadan, agus se sin a' Ghàidhlig a chlaoidh, a gheur leanmhuinn, agus a thachdadh mar chù salach gun mheas gun fheum' ('a single purpose that is clear even to a half-wit, and that is to torment, persecute and strangle Gaelic like a filthy, disrespected useless dog') (Comunn nan Gàidheal 1918: 80).

The legislation replaced the school boards with a new set of education authorities. An Comunn's proposals would have required these authorities to 'make the teaching of Gaelic an essential part of the curriculum in every school which is mainly attended by Gaelic-speaking children' and to 'provide that in other schools within their area attended by Gaelic-speaking children instruction in Gaelic shall be available as desired'. Reflecting its difficulties in having to deal with individual school boards over the decades, An Comunn demanded a broad, rights-based approach: 'the decision as to whether the language is or is not taught should not be left to the Local Authorities. The position of Gaelic as the native speech should be recognised by Parliament, and the principle laid down that Gaelic-speaking children should by right have instruction provided for them in their own language' (ACG 1918b).

An Comunn proposed to limit the teaching of Gaelic to 'Gaelic-speaking areas' (a phrase already included in the 1908 Act, as noted above), arguing:

> it will not be necessary to define these [Gaelic-speaking] areas; the school, and its composition as to scholars, and not the area will be the determining factor. It will be easy to determine whether a school is attended mainly by Gaelic-speaking scholars or not, only in these schools need instruction in Gaelic be essential; in other schools provision need only be made if it is desired by the parents. There is no desire to force Gaelic teaching on children who speak English only. (ACG 1918b)

As with the 1908 campaign, An Comunn's proposals provoked considerable opposition within the Gàidhealtachd (M. K. MacLeod 1981: 328–42). Although the churches were broadly supportive, several prominent churchmen wrote to the Secretary of the SED to express their opposition. The Rev. Angus Maciver of Drumnadrochit argued that such a requirement would 'be the source of divisions injurious to Education' in the Gaelic areas, and attributed support for the proposal to the influence of 'certain enthusiasts, with perhaps a limited horizon' (Maciver 1918). School inspector D. Munro Fraser criticised the role of what he called 'the high-fliers of the Gaelic Movement' 'who live in the South and not the North of the Kingdom' and discounted the significance of the petitions collected by An Comunn: 'they are to be found in the shops in Oban' (Munro 1918). More substantively, concerns were expressed that requiring the teaching of Gaelic would interfere with the discretion of the education authorities and have an adverse impact on teacher recruitment.

The actual amendment introduced on behalf of An Comunn was less ambitious than its original proposal. In contrast to 1908, An Comunn was much more successful in securing support among Scottish MPs, including J. Iain Macpherson, Secretary of State for Ireland, who seconded the amendment. With the support of Macpherson and then Scottish Secretary Robert Munro, the amendment was accepted (M. K. MacLeod 1981: 339–41). The Act as passed required education authorities to 'prepare and submit for the approval of the [SED] [. . .] a scheme for the adequate provision [. . .] of all forms of primary, intermediate and secondary education in day schools (including adequate provision for teaching Gaelic in Gaelic-speaking areas' (s. 6(1)). The Act also replaced the existing school boards with new education authorities for each burgh and county (s. 1). The failure of the Act to define and delimit the term 'Gaelic-speaking areas' has been frequently criticised, but less attention has been given to the term 'adequate provision', which is arguably at least as important. In particular, there was no attempt to benchmark 'adequacy' in terms of educational outcomes such as imparting oral and written language skills.

The so-called 'Gaelic clause' in the 1918 Act has been retained, with minor modifications, in subsequent education acts. In the *Education (Scotland) Act 1945* the relevant provision states that education authorities must 'secure that adequate and efficient provision is made [. . .] of all forms of primary, secondary and further education (including the teaching of Gaelic in Gaelic-speaking areas)' (s. 1(1)). This wording was retained in the *Education (Scotland) Act 1962* and the *Education (Scotland) Act 1980*, although the structure of the relevant sections has changed somewhat. The 1980 Act continues to serve as the basic statutory framework for education in Scotland, but the 'Gaelic clause' has played no meaningful role in developments in Gaelic education in recent decades.

PROHIBITION AND PUNISHMENT

It is noteworthy that the issue of corporal punishment did not emerge as an issue in public debates concerning the role of Gaelic in the education system in the late nineteenth and early twentieth centuries. Modern popular accounts of the decline of Gaelic tend to place heavy emphasis on the 'beating out' of Gaelic – the enforcement of formal prohibitions on the use of Gaelic in the classroom (or elsewhere on the school grounds) by inflicting physical punishment on offending pupils (e.g. MacKinnon 1974: 55). Although there is certainly considerable evidence indicating that punishment of this kind was widespread (*pace* Durkacz 1983: 224–6; Chapman 1992: 103), the extent of these practices is nevertheless less systematic than such accounts would suggest. Those urging the increased use of Gaelic in the education system in the decades following 1872 only referred to the role of corporal punishment very occasionally, and when the issue was mentioned it was usually presented as something belonging to the past, rather than an ongoing practice that required reform. Certainly there is no evidence that education authorities at national or local level adopted a broad policy in the period following 1872 to prohibit the use of Gaelic at school and authorise the use of corporal punishment on pupils to enforce such a ban (Durkacz 1983: 224).

In contrast, in 1753 the SSPCK had enacted an 'Act anent Schoolmasters', which provided that 'Hereafter the Scholars attending the Charity Schools be Discharged, Either in the Schoolhouse, or when playing about the Doors thereof, to speak Earse, under the pain of being chastised, and that Schoolmasters appoint Censors to note down and report to them such as Transgress the Rule' (quoted in Mason 1954: 8). In 1766, however, the Society changed its practice and required its schoolmasters in Gaelic-speaking areas to teach their pupils to read both English and Gaelic (Macleod 1963: 310; Kelly 2016: 13). Similarly, the Gaelic Society schools that were established after 1811 emphasised Gaelic literacy and used Gaelic as a teaching medium, and obviously had no systemic antipathy to the use of Gaelic in the school environment.

Decisions to impose punishments for using Gaelic might have been taken at different levels: by a school board, by a head teacher at a particular school or by an individual classroom teacher. In 1876 the Lochalsh school board instructed its clerk 'to write to all the teachers under the Board's authority enjoining them to forbid scholars from using the Gaelic while under their control' (*Scotsman* 1876). The fact that this incident was reported in the national press, and criticised by a Member of Parliament, Charles Fraser Mackintosh ('Z' 1876), might suggest that this was an isolated occurrence, but it is not possible to be certain. A different kind of prohibition comes from the (second-hand and undated) report of an acting head teacher at Dull, near Aberfeldy, who observed an entry in the school logbook: 'Caught the children speaking G[aelic] in the playground this morning, they were punished and warned they are only to speak the Queen's English while at school' (Sinclair 1981). The fact that this incident was formally recorded suggests that the stricture was well established and normalised at that school at that time, but no wider conclusion can be drawn.[17] In 1885 John MacArthur suggested that prohibitions on Gaelic in schools were widespread at that time but that enforcement by means of corporal punishment was the exception rather than the rule, commenting that 'some [teachers] even go so far as to thrash any of their scholars who may be convicted of conversing in it on the playground, or anywhere in the neighbourhood of the school buildings' (MacArthur 1885: 303).

It is very difficult to get an accurate sense of the extent to which corporal punishment was used to discourage the use of Gaelic in the late nineteenth century or the twentieth century. Almost all the detailed accounts relate to the early part or middle of the nineteenth century, before the introduction of state education. The most famous of these was given by William Mackay, one of the founders of the Gaelic Society of Inverness, describing the practice of schoolteacher Daniel Kerr in Glen Urquhart about 1800:

> He made it his first duty, after the opening prayer, to hand to one of the boys a roughly carved piece of wood, which was called 'the tessera.' The boy transferred it to the first pupil who was heard speaking Gaelic. That offender got rid of it by delivering it to the next, who, in his turn, placed it in the hand of the next again. And so the tessera went round without ceasing. At the close of the day it was called for by Mr Kerr. The child who happened to possess it was severely flogged, and then told to hand it back to the one from whom he had received it. The latter was dealt with in the same manner; and so the dreaded tessera re-traced its course, with dire consequences to all who had ventured to express themselves in the only language they knew. (Mackay 1893: 403)

This use of a symbolic block of wood to facilitate the ban on the language was similar to the notorious 'Welsh Not' in Wales, although this too seems not to have been as widely used as often believed (Davies 2014: 75–6).

The poet Evan MacColl described how he and his schoolmates (in the 1810s) were regularly forced to wear a horse's skull around their neck and beaten if caught speaking Gaelic; but when he published this account in 1886 he expressed bewilderment as to '[h]ow Highland parents with the least common sense, could approve of all this is to me now inexplicable,' suggesting that circumstances by then had changed considerably (MacColl 1886: 6; see also Robertson 1979: 204, 208). Similarly, in 1923 Professor W. J. Watson noted that in the decades after 1872, 'children were punished in a variety of ways for talking Gaelic, even in the playground' but commented that 'the thing sounds incredible nowadays' (Watson 1923: 67; see Carmichael 1907). A correspondent to *The Scotsman* in 1907 expressed this sense of changing times more forcefully:

> The day has passed when parson and laird frowned upon Gaelic as a hindrance to the progress and enlightenment of the Highlanders. The writer knows a veteran parochial schoolmaster who imposed humiliating punishment upon the unfortunate child who was known to speak a Gaelic word within school hours. The culprit was compelled to wear a pair of ram's horns around his neck until he discovered some other pupil who committed a similar breach of discipline. And this was done with the approval of the educational authorities! But now, under the fostering care of the Comunn Gaidhealach a complete change has taken place in the status of Gaelic. ('Rob Roy' 1907)

Gaelic writers and activists educated in the decades following 1872 provide sharply contrasting accounts of their educational experiences. Angus MacLellan, born in South Uist in 1869, noted that pupils were allowed to speak Gaelic in his school and Neil Shaw, born in 1881, reported that all the subjects in his school in Jura were taught through Gaelic (Mac 'Ill Fhialain 1972: 5; Shaw 1955: 103). In contrast, Duncan Livingstone, born in Mull in 1877, stated that students were beaten if they spoke Gaelic in the classroom or the playground and Angus Henderson, born in Ardnamurchan in 1866, described being beaten on the hand with the tawse (a kind of thong) for speaking Gaelic on the playground (MacDhunlèibhe 1961; Henderson 1937). Although Angus Campbell, born in Lewis in 1903, did not report in his autobiography that corporal punishment was used to discourage Gaelic, he described a brutal school environment in which the treatment of Gaelic was profoundly negative:

> Cha d' fhuair mise leasan Gàidhlig san sgoil riamh agus 's e faireachadh a bha agad gun dh'àlaich do chànan, d' fhine is do dhualchas ann an treubhan ainreiteach, borb, aineolach agus ma bha dùil agad slighe shoirbheachail a dhèanamh san t-saoghal, gum b' e do bhuannachd an dì-chuimhneachadh gu tur.
>
> I never got a single Gaelic lesson in school and the feeling you got was that your language, your people and your heritage had descended from ignorant, barbarous, violent tribes and that if you wanted to make a successful path in life, it would be to your benefit to forget them entirely. (Caimbeul 1973: 22)

If the evidence of pupils being beaten for speaking Gaelic in school is not as extensive as sometimes believed, and the causal link between corporal punishment and language shift is not clear, there can be no doubt that such practices had a significant impact over time. As Michael Newton argues, 'we should see memories of beatings in school as a symbol articulating the sense of oppression and injustice of alien institutions' (Newton 2000: 233).

GAELIC AND EDUCATION: ARGUMENTS AND IDEOLOGIES

A heated debate about the appropriate role of Gaelic in the education system developed following the passage of the 1872 Act and has continued ever since, even if the specific issues and lines of argument have changed over time. In the late nineteenth century, the question at hand was the fundamental one of whether Gaelic should be taught at all in the state schools. A range of positions was set out, with proponents typically arguing that children should be educated in their mother tongue and opponents insisting that teaching Gaelic would impede the effective teaching of English, which all parties accepted was a much higher priority. Some opponents buttressed their arguments by challenging the inherent worth of Gaelic, and a smaller group presented the teaching of Gaelic as a threat to national unity. Participants in these debates included Gaelic activists and journalists of different stripes but some of the most important contributions came from school inspectors, who set out strikingly divergent positions in their formal annual reports. Significantly, the overwhelming majority of the contributions to this long-running debate were made in English rather than Gaelic, with only a few Gaelic columns and articles appearing (e.g. MacLauchlan 1875). Sometimes opinions were expressed in forceful terms, as when the Rev. Archibald Farquharson of Tiree 'denounce[d] those schools, where the Gaelic is the language spoken by the people, and where it is not taught, as the schools of Antichrist' (Farquharson 1875: 18).

One of the main arguments made by opponents of teaching Gaelic in the schools was simply that Highland parents did not want this provision. One 'Gaelic-speaking Highlander', writing in 1897, asserted that '[i]t would not be easy to find in the Highlands at this moment one parent in a thousand [...] desirous of having his children instructed in' Gaelic (*GH* 1897). Supporters of Gaelic generally conceded this point, repeatedly lamenting the 'apathy' of Highland parents in relation to the language (e.g. GSI 1885: xv; MacFarlane 1906: 150; *DG* 1916b). Against this background, those who opposed an increased role for Gaelic, such as schools inspector Donald Ross, were able to characterise Gaelic advocates as 'outsiders' who were attempting to 'thrust' the language on an unwilling populace ('W' 1884: 436). In particular, critics sometimes associated the promotion of Gaelic education with 'aggressive city Gaels' ('Sandy' 1908).

The overwhelming concern of Highland parents was to ensure their children acquired English. Activists were therefore keen to promote bilingualism, conceding the necessity of English acquisition but arguing that this need not be at the expense of Gaelic, yet the prevailing popular understanding of bilingualism at this time was that the development of Gaelic might be at the cost of English and might hold children back (e.g. Watson 1906; Robertson 1923: 19–20).

The most commonly articulated positions in these debates tended to cluster in the middle, so to speak. No one took a maximal position in relation to Gaelic, for example that it should be the principal medium of instruction at all stages of education (or indeed any stage) as part of a full programme of societal Gaelicisation. Conversely, arguments that Gaelic should be banned for political reasons, as a threat to national unity, were very rare; the claim of Charles Stewart, in a controversial letter to *The Times* in 1906, that teaching Gaelic might 'sow the seed' of 'separatism' and be 'unfavourable to National and Imperial unity' was an outlier (Stewart 1906). Instead, most arguments involved different perceptions of the educational benefits of including Gaelic in the school curriculum, which tended to rest upon competing assessments of the general worth and usefulness of Gaelic. Some simply saw no value whatsoever in the language; in the most notorious anti-Gaelic screed of the era, the publisher William Chambers declared that 'we are [. . .] warranted in characterising Gaelic as a NUISANCE, which every one should aid in removing with all reasonable speed' (Chambers 1877: 691).

Beyond the overarching issue of whether Gaelic should be taught, several more specific points were pressed. For example, among those who supported increased provision for Gaelic in elementary education some argued that English literacy should be taught first and some Gaelic. Similarly, advocates rarely specified the level of Gaelic literacy that was sought. W. J. Watson, the second Professor of Celtic in the University of Edinburgh, thought merely that children in Gaelic-speaking areas should be taught at least to the level where they could 'read their Gaelic Bible' and 'write an ordinary Gaelic letter' (*TGSI* 1915a: 11). This was a good deal less than the elementary schools were expected to deliver in relation to English literacy.

Even the strongest advocates of Gaelic were very clear that Highland children needed to acquire English, particularly in order to prepare them for working life in the Lowlands or overseas. The Rev. Thomas MacLauchlan, a leading Gaelic scholar of the period, wrote in 1873 that if the Gaels were without English it would as well for them to be without a tongue (MacLauchlan 1873: 17). Arguments in support of introducing Gaelic were typically presented in terms of its usefulness for facilitating the acquisition of English rather than something of value in itself. A related argument, first articulated in the Rev. Alexander Stewart's Gaelic grammar of 1801, was that teaching Gaelic should be accepted as an interstitial measure so long as Gaelic

> continues to be the common speech of multitudes, – while the knowledge of many important facts, of many necessary arts, of morals, of religion, and of the laws of the land, can be conveyed to them only by means of this language, – it must be of material service to preserve it in such a state of cultivation and purity, as that it may be fully adequate to these valuable ends; in a word, that while it is a living language, it may answer the purpose of a living language. (Stewart 1801: 1)

Other commentators presented the demise of Gaelic as a positive outcome that could be more rapidly achieved if the language were used tactically in the education system. Donald MacKinnon, later to become the first Professor of Celtic at Edinburgh, expressed the view that the 'practical advantages' of replacing Gaelic with English in the Highlands 'will more than compensate for the loss sustained through the demise of Gaelic' and stated his 'firm conviction that the quickest and most effective method of extirpating the Gaelic language is to make a freer use of it in educating Highland children' (MacKinnon 1875: 24, 27).

Only a few voices urged the teaching of Gaelic in order to build confidence and pride in Gaelic culture and identity. One of these was John Murdoch, who argued that the Gael should be 'taught to value his language, his traditions, his race, his circumstances' (*Highlander* 1879: 2; see also *GB* 1906: 98–9).

The lengthy statements of the school inspectors working in the Highland counties in the late 1870s are especially valuable in revealing the varying views and assumptions of officials in this era. Above and beyond their value as evidence of prevailing discourses and ideologies, these statements had very important practical ramifications, as the school inspectors played a critical role in determining the actual provision for Gaelic in the schools during this period.

These statements were given within the annual reports of the Committee of Council on Education in Scotland, which were the principal national reports on education until 1947. Of these inspectors, Donald Sime, the Inspector for Ross, Caithness and Sutherland, took the strongest negative position, declaring in 1879, 'I should regard the teaching of Gaelic in schools, in any shape or form, as a most serious misfortune' (CCES 1879: 222). Sime decried the 'sentimentalists and "patriots" who [...] dream of a virtuous peasantry dwelling by the northern seas, whose speech should be Gaelic, and for whom the Grampian passes should be as the pillars of Hercules'. In Sime's view, '[t]here was but one way whereby the Highlander can have the world before him where to choose [...] and that is knowledge of English. [...] Gaelic is not, and never will be of the slightest value in conducting the business of this world, and there can be no commercial reasons for teaching it.' Sime also challenged the viability of bilingual teaching, as it would require children to alternately 'suppress' and 'encourage' Gaelic, to 'blow hot and cold with the same breath': 'I cannot imagine a more suicidal form of education' (CCES 1879: 223).

Donald Ross, the Inspector for Renfrew, Bute and Argyll, articulated a slightly softer position than Sime, proposing that Gaelic be added to the list of 'special subjects' and thus given the same curricular status as Latin or Greek (CCES 1879: 193). Ross also believed that Gaelic might 'very usefully be employed by teachers in remote corners to explain their lessons to the children, just as Broad Scotch is employed in several parts of the country' (CCES 1879: 195). But he expressed concern that the issue of Gaelic in the schools had become politicised in the context of 'the Gaelic revival [that] is passing over the northern part of the island' (CCES 1879: 192), with school boards placed under pressure from 'irresponsible outsiders and confused opinion' (CCES 1879: 193). Ross also argued that language shift was sufficiently far advanced that teaching Gaelic was no longer necessary, claiming that the great majority of Gaelic speakers were actually bilingual (CCES 1879: 194).

Ross was particularly forceful in his dismissal of the value of Gaelic culture, even though he was a Gaelic speaker himself. 'There is no great poem, no great history, no work on philosophy in Gaelic', he declared; 'every existing fragment is essentially barbarous and the product of barbarous conditions'. In terms of 'quality', Ross opined, the existing Gaelic literature 'finds its parallel every Saturday in the year, in the columns of the provincial press' (CCES 1879: 194). He considered Gaelic to be 'almost infinitely inferior to English', which 'has one of the most expansive and noblest literatures in the world' (CCES 1879: 195, 194). Ross's views on the cultural supremacy of English echoed the notorious 'Minute on Education' submitted to the Governor General of India by Lord Macaulay in 1835, in which Macaulay urged the British authorities to exclude the use of native languages from education in India, denigrating their cultural value and extolling the vast superiority of the English language (Bureau of Education, India 1920: 102–31; Durkacz 1983: 205).

William Jolly, the Inspector for Inverness, the Western Isles, Nairn and Elgin, expressed the most favourable view of Gaelic. Jolly was not a Gaelic speaker, although he was actively involved in the GSI (CCES 1880: 140). Jolly argued that 'Gaelic should be used orally in the teaching of English from the first, in order to get at and train the intelligence of Gaelic children, and to make the teaching of English more thorough' (CCES 1878: 171). At the early stages, 'Gaelic would require to be used exclusively [. . .] [b]ut in all cases, care should be taken to use English more and more' as the children progressed (CCES 1878: 171). Like Ross, Jolly advocated the teaching of Gaelic as a specific subject in upper elementary school, which 'would afford the important intellectual gymnastic of inter-translation between two languages' and 'give the child a better knowledge of English at this riper age' (CCES 1880: 142).

There were clear limits to Jolly's support, however. He argued that reading should be introduced in English first, not in Gaelic, despite the 'theoretic grounds for learning to read the native language before a foreign one'. Given the greater importance of English and the difficulty associated with teaching an additional language, he thought that children should be given more time to learn it. 'But by beginning with English, Gaelic may be read with ease in a short time when a child is able to read English, for he has merely to apply the power of reading which he has acquired to the knowledge he knows and uses' (CCES 1878: 171). This understanding is close to that developed for Gaelic-medium education at the end of the twentieth century, in which pupils, the great majority of whom are learners of the language, acquire Gaelic literacy first but rapidly develop their English literacy skills once English is introduced (O'Hanlon, Paterson and McLeod 2010).

In contrast to Ross, Jolly also pressed '[t]he importance of Gaelic literature as an instrument of culture to the Gaelic people', describing it as 'abundant, varied and powerful, full of fine sentiment, pleasant humour, lyrical beauty, deep feeling, practical wisdom, and natural life' (CCES 1878: 171). Yet he expressed disappointment that 'the Highlander does not sufficiently perceive and plead for' the value of Gaelic (CCES 1878: 172), even going so far as to argue that if parents 'had so far degenerated as to despise their mother tongue while speaking it, their opinion should be disregarded, and their children treated better than their parents desire and deserve' (CCES 1880: 149).

More fundamentally, Jolly did not champion the long-term maintenance of Gaelic, suggesting that 'Gaelic dying out as a spoken tongue

[...] in many ways would be an advantage to the people' (CCES 1878: 172) and that teaching Gaelic 'intelligently' in the schools would 'undoubtedly hasten' the demise of the language, by ensuring the more effective acquisition of English (CCES 1878: 171). Jolly saw the use of Gaelic as a transitional proposition, a matter of 'simple justice, if not higher wisdom', 'while Gaelic is [...] the hourly language of nearly half a million of our people' (CCES 1878: 172).

These strikingly different positions demonstrate the clear lack of consensus among those who developed and implemented policy concerning Gaelic in the early years of state education in Scotland. These divergences continued to be apparent in later decades in relation to the use of Gaelic as a teaching medium. In 1898 one school inspector went so far as to declare that '[f]or all real educational purposes, the use of Gaelic in the general instruction of the school is strenuously encouraged' (CCES 1898: 430), while the following year his deputy took the opposite view, stating that he was 'thoroughly convinced that much less good is done to Gaelic-speaking children by teachers who make too much use of their Gaelic than by teachers who have none at all' (CCES 1899: 523). Taken as a whole, however, the school inspectors were generally negative towards Gaelic and they played an important constraining role on provision for the language (Durkacz 1983: 174).

GAELIC IN THE UNIVERSITIES

In addition to school education, another focus of the Gaelic movement of the late nineteenth century was improved provision for Gaelic in Scotland's universities (then four in number). Above and beyond its practical value in educational terms, recognition for the language by these prestigious national institutions was understood as symbolically important for the status of Gaelic. The principal achievement on this front was the successful campaign to establish a chair of Celtic at the University of Edinburgh in 1882.

Attempts to establish a university chair of Celtic began as far back as 1786, when the Highland Society of London made the first of several proposals (Fairney 2005: 63–4). Petitions seeking to create a chair in one university or another were lodged in Parliament in 1836, 1838 and 1839 (Kelta 1836; *Scotsman* 1838, 1838b, 1839). The creation of the Scottish Universities Commission in 1859 provided an opportunity for the submission of several requests for Celtic chairs (Scottish Universities Commission 1863: 122, 127, 132). Some of these proposed to establish the chair in Aberdeen, Glasgow or St Andrews instead of Edinburgh, but none of them bore fruit. In Ireland, in contrast, the first chair of Irish was established at Trinity College Dublin in 1838, with other professorships in Belfast, Cork and Galway created in the decades following. In 1877 a Celtic chair was also established at Jesus College, Oxford, which had a strong Welsh connection (Ó Cuív 1989: 397; Wallace 2006: 272).

The ultimately successful campaign for the Edinburgh chair began in the 1860s but took a number of years to bear fruit. The University's General Council approved the chair in principle in 1872, subject to the raising of a £10,000 endowment. The fundraising campaign was led by John Stuart Blackie, Professor of Greek in the University, a polymath who was not only interested in the Gaelic language but actively involved in the crofters' movement. With 'abundant energies', 'tireless eloquence' and 'flamboyant style' (Gillies 1989b: 12), Blackie launched an extensive fundraising drive throughout Ireland, England and the Highlands, drawing contributions from large numbers of ordinary crofters, with the support of John Murdoch's radical newspaper *The Highlander*. Queen Victoria and the dukes of Argyll and Sutherland, among other aristocrats, also made donations. By 1881 the chair campaign had succeeded in raising almost £14,000, and in 1882 Donald MacKinnon, a schoolmaster originally from Colonsay, was appointed the first Professor of Celtic in the University (Wallace 2006: 272–5).

Once the chair was established, however, the Celtic classes did not attract large numbers of students. Between 1892 and 1909, for example, the numbers attending the various Celtic classes ranged between five and fourteen (University of Edinburgh 1898: 9; 1902: 9). Graduates of the department did have a positive impact on the Gaelic community, however, notably in relation to ministers who benefited from 'the enlightened study of Gaelic and its literature' in the University and 'discovered the cultural value of the old language in the class-room' (Watson and Nicholson 1929: xii).

Following the creation of the Celtic chair in Edinburgh, campaigning and fundraising activity led to provision for Gaelic at other universities. The teaching of Gaelic began at the University of Glasgow in 1901, with a series of lectures, and a full-time lecturer was then appointed in 1906 (The Gaelic Story 2019). In 1916 a lectureship at the University of Aberdeen was created, with the authorities noting a recent SED circular indicating the view that 'a course of study in Gaelic at a University [i]s an essential part of the equipment of every teacher of the subject' (*Aberdeen University Review* 1916). However, it took much longer for professorial chairs to be established in those universities – 1956 in the case of Glasgow and 1991 in Aberdeen (see pp. 130–1; Meek 2013a).[18] As had been the case with the Edinburgh chair, the appointment of Gaelic lecturers in other institutions depended on fundraising on the part of Gaelic organisations, as in Glasgow in 1905–6 (The Gaelic Story 2019). Gaelic was also taught at King's College London in 1897 (Caber-Feidh 1897) and in several Canadian institutions from 1879 onwards, most notably St Francis Xavier University in Nova Scotia, which continues to maintain a Celtic Studies department (Nilsen 2010: 99). At different times in the twentieth and twenty-first centuries, Gaelic has also been taught at universities in Wales, Ireland, Germany, Norway, the United States, Australia and New Zealand.

Efforts to secure provision for Gaelic in the Scottish universities were neither as controversial nor as successful as they were in Ireland. Following a major campaign by Conradh na Gaeilge, it was agreed in 1910 that all entrants to the National University of Ireland would be required to have a knowledge of Irish (McMahon 2008: 81). This requirement remains in place to this day, and continues to ensure a strong presence for Irish in the school system as well as a much greater role in tertiary education than Gaelic enjoys in Scotland.

An important element in the push for recognition of Gaelic by the universities was the increasing academic interest in Celtic linguistics in the later nineteenth century. This new academic prestige not only served to bring these languages to greater public attention, but also to reduce some of the stigma that had previously been attached to them. Academic study was able to place the Celtic languages into their true context as important European languages and to disprove long-standing myths concerning their supposed barbarity and disconnection from European and classical civilisation (Charles-Edwards 2007). Particularly influential in this regard was Johann Kaspar Zeuss's *Grammatica Celtica* of 1853, a landmark in philology and Celtic scholarship. In the Scottish context, W. F. Skene's three-volume study *Celtic Scotland* (1876–80) drew new attention to the Celtic aspect of Scottish history, while the *Scottish Celtic Review*, published between 1881 and 1885, was the first major scholarly journal in the field. Popular interest in Celtic matters such as place names and personal names also increased as a by-product of this growing academic activity (Blackie 1876: 8). Through all of this, Gaelic was able to secure a new form of prestige that served to improve its overall status.

GAELIC IN LAW, ADMINISTRATION AND POLITICS

The role of Gaelic in the formal domains of law and public administration in the nineteenth century was extremely circumscribed. Gaelic did receive a minimal recognition in Scots law; for example, nineteenth-century court rulings established that slanderous statements made in Gaelic were legally actionable[19] and wills written in Gaelic were enforced (*Dundee Evening Telegraph* 1879). On the other hand, statutes enacted in 1847 and 1868 specifically required that property deeds in Scotland had to be 'expressed in the English language' (*Crown Charters (Scotland) Act 1847*, s. 25; *Titles to Land Consolidation (Scotland) Act 1868*, s. 90).

The judicial system in Scotland made very little room for the use of Gaelic, although unlike in Ireland or Wales there was no statute establishing English as the language of the courts.[20] Instead, the requirement to use English was imposed by judicial rulings, especially the Court of Justiciary's 1841 *Alexander McRae* decision, which held that it was improper to allow a witness to testify in Gaelic, through an interpreter, when the witness could speak English 'with perfect distinctness'. The defendant in that case asserted that his English was not as good as his Gaelic and unsuccessfully sought permission to use Gaelic to defend himself against a murder charge. In subsequent cases, sheriffs[21] and judges often allowed testimony in Gaelic and the use of interpreters, but such permission was a matter of judicial discretion and the preferences of litigants and witnesses were sometimes overruled, even to the point of imprisoning witnesses for contempt of court if they declined to use English, as occurred in a debt case in Nairn in 1870 (*GH* 1870; see *EEN* 1893). In one highly unusual, but effectively symbolic, instance in Inverness Police Court in 1881, an entire criminal case was conducted in Gaelic when the presiding officer (the Dean of Guild, Alexander MacKenzie, editor of *The Celtic Magazine*) determined that the accused, all witnesses and the prosecutor all understood Gaelic ([MacKenzie] 1881).

Gaelic campaigners of this era did not seek to establish a legal right to use Gaelic in court proceedings, but rather pressed demands that officers appointed to key posts in the legal system should have a knowledge of the language. These attempts were consistently rebuffed by the authorities and no concessions were made. Gaelic speakers were sometimes appointed through the conventional procedures, however; there were three Gaelic-speaking sheriffs serving in 1893, for example (*Scottish Highlander* 1893).

The Napier Commission argued that 'the important qualification of a knowledge of Gaelic should not be lost sight of' in making appointments as sheriff and procurator fiscal (Royal Commission 1884: 73). In 1885 Alexander Mackenzie decried 'how often we have seen Gaelic-speaking witnesses bullied and threatened with all sorts of pains and penalties [...] for declining, or exhibiting any reluctance, to give evidence in English' and argued that 'preference should be given to Gaelic speakers in appointments to sheriffships and other public offices in Highland districts' ([Mackenzie] 1885: 444). In 1892 the Lord Advocate rebuffed a parliamentary question seeking an assurance that a Gaelic speaker would be appointed to a vacant procurator fiscal[22] post in Ross & Cromarty, asserting that 'there are, in my opinion, other qualifications of more importance' (*Times* 1892). Repeated efforts were made in later decades, all of them unsuccessful. It is notable that these demands for the appointment of Gaelic speakers were concerned only with senior officials and not directed to all public-facing staff.

Rather more provision was made for Welsh in the legal system during this era. There was more latitude to give evidence in Welsh and from 1872 'it became the general policy to appoint Welsh-speaking county court judges and registrars throughout Wales', except in the urban southeast (Davies 2000: 218). Of course, it is very important in this context that the proportion of Welsh speakers in the Welsh population was more than eight times as high as for Gaelic in Scotland; Welsh speakers were the majority in eight of the thirteen counties as against three of thirty-four in Scotland.[23]

Although the authorities consistently refused to make accommodation for Gaelic in relation to the appointment of judges, sheriffs and prosecutors, from 1886 onwards a number of statutes required that appointees to certain administrative bodies should be Gaelic speakers. The *Crofters Holdings (Scotland) Act 1886* stipulated that at least one of the four members of the Crofters Commission should be a Gaelic speaker, and this requirement has been retained in legislation concerning the second Crofters Commission (now Crofting Commission), which was established in 1955 (Crofters Acts of 1955, 1993 and 2010). A similar provision was included in the *Small Landholders (Scotland) Act 1911* and its successor statute, the *Scottish Land Court Act 1993*, requiring that at least one of the seven members of the Land Court, which deals with disputes concerning crofting land in the Highlands and Islands as part of its national remit, should be a Gaelic speaker. There has been some pressure in recent decades to remove this requirement (R. J. MacLeod 2012), and it is noteworthy that the most recent legislation concerning Highland land ownership and use (the *Land Reform*

(*Scotland*) *Act 2016*) does not require a Gaelic-speaking member of the Scottish Land Commission, only that 'every reasonable step' is taken to ensure that such a member is appointed (s. 11(2)).

As Gaelic was very widely spoken in the crofting communities in 1886 (other than those in Orkney and Shetland), this provision concerning membership was intended to make the Crofters Commission appear more accessible and legitimate to those it served. The legislation did not specify that Gaelic could be used by litigants, although this was '[t]he clear implication' (Evans 1982: 286), or in the workings of the Commission itself. Originally many Commission cases were conducted in Gaelic (see Crofters Commission 1888: viii–x, xii) but because of the drastic decline in the number of Gaelic speakers over the last century, Gaelic now has almost no role even though its use is still permitted. Similarly, although Land Court cases were sometimes heard in Gaelic (*Laws of Scotland* 2017: Courts and Competency para. 244), parties and witnesses were often dissuaded from using Gaelic; 'English was emphatically the language of the Court' (R. J. MacLeod 2012: 102).

During this period, Gaelic was only used for a very limited range of official purposes, yet at the same time there was never any formal statement that only the state language, English, was acceptable for use in the public sphere as a matter of principle. Only occasionally was a specific demand to make use of Gaelic rebuffed, as with a proposal in 1908 to issue pensions regulations in Gaelic (Hansard 1908); far more often, the possibility of using Gaelic was simply not raised or considered. In his four-hundred-page study of public administration in the Highlands and Islands, published in 1918, John Percival Day referred to Gaelic only in a few specific contexts (the schools, the Crofters Commission and the Land Court) but gave no suggestion at all that a bilingual system of administration might be introduced or even contemplated (Day 1918).

Although no general statement of policy was ever given, in practice the authorities used Gaelic only when it was deemed essential that all citizens understood the information being communicated. One such context was that of policing and law enforcement. For example, a written warning from the local sheriff-substitute invoking the Riot Act was printed in Gaelic to the land-hungry crofters who raided the farm at Aignish in Lewis in 1888.[24] A more unusual example was the Gaelic notice by the Registrar-General of Births, Deaths and Marriages explaining the procedural changes required by the *Registration of Births, Deaths and Marriages (Scotland) Act 1854*.[25] In 1882 the Chamberlain's Office in Stornoway issued a bilingual notice concerning the penalties for parents who failed to ensure that their children attended school.[26]

More commonly, Gaelic was used when health and safety were at issue. Leaflets were prepared in Gaelic by the County Medical Officers for Inverness-shire and Ross-shire for certain public health purposes, such as information concerning the spread of infectious diseases (Local Government Board for Scotland 1910: lxvi). The authorities responsible for farm regulation also issued Gaelic versions of leaflets concerning animal and crop diseases (Board of Agriculture and Fisheries 1913: 50; Board of Agriculture for Scotland 1921: xcviii). A more unusual circumstance was the requirement that licences for the storage, transport, sale and use of nitroglycerine should include safety instructions in Gaelic and Welsh (HO 1873: 428). The pattern in relation to the official use of Welsh during this period was broadly similar to that of Gaelic, although there were rather more exceptions to the rule (Davies 2000: 219–20).

Some public bodies, such as the Commissioners of Inland Revenue, made a point of employing Gaelic-speaking staff in order to deal with Gaelic speakers (Commissioners of HM Inland Revenue 1909: 195; Board of Agriculture for Scotland 1919). In 1865 the Inspector of Constabulary for Scotland reported that all the constables in Inverness-shire and Ross-shire were 'required to be thoroughly acquainted with the Gaelic as well as the English language', with the consequence that 'the chief constable has a much more limited number of candidates to choose from than in the Lowland counties' (HM Inspector of Constabulary 1865: 18, 23). In 1848 the Board of Supervision for Relief of Poor adopted a rule that in any 'parish in which it was found necessary to provide religious instruction to the people in the Gaelic language [. . .] the inspector [of poor] should be capable of communicating [. . .] in that language' (Board of Supervision for Relief of Poor 1849: iv). In 1867 an inspector of poor in Knapdale was duly removed from office because his command of Gaelic was inadequate (Board of Supervision for Relief of Poor 1867: Appendix A, 2). Between 1845 and 1870, Gaelic was specified as a mandatory or desirable attribute in at least fifty-six advertisements for medical officers, twenty-five for inspectors of poor and seven for poorhouse employees (Kidd 2015). Of course, advertisements for teaching posts in the Highlands often stipulated that Gaelic speakers were preferred, and this practice was also quite common in relation to certain kinds of private employment, especially domestic service.[27]

From 1921 Gaelic was listed as one of the languages that could be taken by candidates in examinations for posts in the civil service, alongside Welsh, Irish, Latin, Greek, French and German (and later Spanish) (Civil Service Commissioners 1921). This regulation did not, and was not intended to, lead to any strategic development of the capacity of the civil service to operate through Gaelic or deliver services to the public through Gaelic, as was the case in Ireland after 1922. Indeed, in 1948 the Commissioners reported that in twenty years only two candidates sat the Gaelic examination, so that it was dropped as an option (ACG 1948: 9). Subsequent efforts to reinstate Gaelic proved unsuccessful (*GH* 1962; Grant 1965: 130–1).

Without question, the government institution with the longest-standing practice of accommodating Gaelic was the armed forces. Use of the language was generally tolerated on an informal basis, but sometimes more specific measures were adopted. In 1914 the Army Council issued instructions that soldiers could freely converse in Gaelic, Welsh or Irish while on duty, although when on parade all orders would be given in English (*Aberdeen Daily Journal* 1914). In the Second World War, soldiers were permitted to write letters home in Gaelic and the authorities made specific censorship arrangements (*GH* 1939). Highland regiments sometimes designated particular posts as 'Gaelic desirable' (*Aberdeen Daily Journal* 1903) and recruitment notices were occasionally issued in Gaelic (e.g. Inspector-General of Recruiting 1870: 2). While there were no Gaelic counterparts to the numerous Welsh-language recruitment posters published during the First World War, this was evidently a matter of linguistic demography and not principle.[28] Since the eighteenth century the armed forces had made a practice of appointing Gaelic-speaking chaplains and in the First World War there were twelve of them in service (*Scotsman* 1915). In 1915 An Comunn launched a successful fundraising campaign to establish a separate ward for Gaelic-speaking war wounded, staffed by Gaelic-speaking nurses, at the Glasgow military hospital, but despite an agreement with the War Office and the Red Cross Society, no Gaelic speakers were actually assigned to the ward. An Comunn considered demanding a refund of the contributions, but eventually decided not to press this claim (*DG* 1916c). Despite these various accommodations of Gaelic, considered as a whole the British military was an overwhelmingly English-dominant institution and functioned as a powerful force for the linguistic and cultural assimilation of the Gaelic speakers who participated in it.

Following an unsuccessful request in 1871, in 1881 the GSI presented a memorial to the Home Secretary urging the government to include a question concerning the Gaelic-speaking population of Scotland in the census that was to be conducted that year (Thompson 1992: 34). The society argued that this 'would be of great practical value in connection with several important questions affecting the Highlands, and would hereafter be considered a valuable historical record' (*TGSI* 1884: 51).

While there had been a counterpart question in relation to Irish in Ireland since 1851, for Gaelic in Scotland there were only estimates. The most recent and important of these was that made by E. G. Ravenstein in 1879, which suggested a figure of 301,000 Gaelic speakers (Ravenstein 1879: 606). The timing of the Society's request was difficult, as the papers for the census planned for that year had already been printed. Charles Fraser Mackintosh MP argued the case publicly, and the Home Office eventually acceded to the request (*TGSI* 1884: 51; Cameron 2000: 71–2). Questions concerning Gaelic have remained in every subsequent census, although their form has changed somewhat over time (Thomas 1998).

Gaelic was also used as a language of political participation to a considerable extent in the nineteenth and early twentieth centuries, as far back as 1832 but especially after 1884, when the franchise was extended to crofters (Kidd 2008, 2010). Accounts in the press indicate that Gaelic was regularly used for election speeches and meetings (e.g. Cameron 2000: 154; *Scotsman* 1909; *Perthshire Advertiser* 1914b; *P&J* 1950), although the fact that such usage was deemed notable by newspapers suggests that it was far from normalised. Newspapers began to print articles in Gaelic concerning elections and other political matters in the 1870s, although only infrequently (Kidd 2008). A variety of political leaflets and newspaper advertisements were issued in Gaelic by candidates of different parties,[29] and organisations ranging from An Comunn to the short-lived Society of the Friends of the Gaels of Scotland distributed leaflets and manifestos in Gaelic urging voters to support pro-Gaelic candidates (*EEN* 1906). Usage of Gaelic in these electoral contexts was mainly for communicative rather than symbolic purposes, in contrast to the practice of more recent decades; significant numbers of voters were more comfortable with Gaelic than with English, and using Gaelic was simply the most effective way of reaching them. The pattern of language use in relation to politics thus aligned with that of other public domains: Gaelic was permitted and tolerated, but English was normal, unmarked and overwhelmingly dominant.

Gaelic was also sometimes used in publications concerning social and political questions such as disestablishment (*Dundee Evening Telegraph* 1891), temperance (MacNéill [1892]) and Irish home rule (Ulster Loyalist Anti-Repeal Union 1886), and in political meetings outside the context of elections, particularly in relation to the land question (e.g. *EEN* 1891). Usage of the language for such purposes could be controversial; in 1884 the Earl of Dunmore denounced those men of the educated classes familiar with the language who have taken advantage of it to feed the flame of discontent among the ignorant and uneducated by applying the mischievous bellows of agitation[.] I say the Gaelic language has never been put to more unworthy and unpatriotic or wicked use than when it was employed, not as a means of tranquilising the poor people by reasoning with them in a spirit of pacification and conciliation in their own tongue, but, on the contrary, in urging them to rebellion and crime. (*TGSI* 1884: 3)

The difficulty for the earl, however, was not the use of Gaelic in a political context, but its use to express ideas and encourage action that he disfavoured.

GAELIC AND THE CHURCHES

The social role of religion in the Gàidhealtachd (and Scotland as a whole) is difficult to overstate, and the institutional responses of the churches to Gaelic can be considered an important element in the overall matrix of language policy. The religious domain was also of immense significance for the development of the Gaelic language itself, in terms of the spreading of literacy and the creation of formal registers and styles (Meek 1990). In 1869 there were regular weekly Gaelic services in 461 churches in Scotland, more than 13 per cent of the total (Murchison 1955: 4).[30]

The Church of Scotland can be considered the first institution to establish a policy to promote the use of Gaelic. From 1643 it instituted a system of preferring Gaelic speakers for bursaries, and from 1696 onwards it began taking steps to ensure that Gaelic-speaking ministers would be assigned to parishes in Gaelic-speaking areas (Durkacz 1983: 10–11). As Victor Durkacz pointed out, 'to those concerned with "civilising" the Highlands, the shortage of Gaelic clergy in the 1600s and 1700s meant that the Gaelic population remained irreligious and, in the period 1689 to 1745 in particular, politically dangerous' (Durkacz 1983: 261). Later, the Kirk established the practice of designating certain parishes as 'Gaelic essential' or 'Gaelic desirable' in relation to the appointment of ministers. Over the course of the twentieth century the number of designated parishes declined considerably: in 1912 156 parishes were designated Gaelic-essential and 137 Gaelic-desirable, but by 1966 this had declined to 82 and 82 (*DG* 1912a; MacLeòid 1968). These changes were largely the result of language shift, which diminished the demand for Gaelic services, although the shortage of Gaelic-speaking ministers also played a significant role. Sometimes, too, Gaelic speakers opted to attend an English service even when a Gaelic-speaking minister was available (M. Macleod 1944: 74).

In 1930 the Rev. Malcolm Macleod, later to become president of An Comunn, gave a despondent summary of the situation:

> Before the beginning of this century the Highland people began to show a decided tendency to worship in English. The newness of many knowing English for the first time in a district, and their own native Gaelic being associated with what was poor and depressing, made them worship in English. This tendency began fifty or sixty years ago, and has been going on with a continuous momentum till the present day. [...] Unless a complete change comes over the habits of the Gaelic people there will soon be no Gaelic Pulpit at all, except in the Outer Hebrides. The Gaelic Pulpit is fast disappearing from the mainland, and has made a sad beginning in the Inner Hebrides. (M. Macleod 1930: 13)

Difficulties in recruiting Gaelic speakers for ministerial training and appointments to individual parishes were noted as early as 1883 (*EEN* 1883) and continued to surface regularly thereafter (e.g. *Ross-shire Journal* 1912; Macdonald 1958: 19). The position in the Roman Catholic church was rather healthier, with a more coordinated approach to the recruitment and training of priests (*DG* 1917). However, the overall demand for Gaelic-speaking ministers and priests was diminishing as a result of language shift. As early as 1910 there were no parishes in Perthshire where Gaelic was regularly preached (*DG* 1910).

The linguistic situation in Highland parishes was complex, however, and went beyond the simple Gaelic/English binary. Even when Gaelic speakers were able to speak English they sometimes expressed a strong preference for worship and pastoral support in Gaelic, 'the language best understood by them and closest to their hearts' (*GH* 1888). Demand for Gaelic-speaking ministers and the use of Gaelic as a spiritual language might continue well after Gaelic had ceased to be the ordinary vernacular of the community (Durkacz 1983: 261). Similarly, the ability to speak colloquial Gaelic did not necessarily entail command of the formal register required for preaching; as early as 1888 complaints were made about the linguistic shortcomings of certain 'Gaelic-speaking' ministers, and this concern has continued since (*GH* 1888). Almost all Gaelic-speaking ministers were native speakers, although a few learned the language in order to carry out their duties.

On various occasions the churches urged the SED to improve provision for Gaelic in the schools, with a view to attracting more candidates to ministerial training (M. K. MacLeod 1981: 176–9). Even so, An Comunn expressed concern that the churches were insufficiently proactive in this regard (*DG* 1917c). An Comunn sometimes engaged in direct lobbying of the churches, sending delegations to church assemblies to promote support for the language and urge proactive measures to ensure the training of future ministers (*DG* 1912b, 1914a). In 1917 the Church of Scotland responded to these entreaties by publishing a detailed scheme of bursaries and targeted recruitment in order to generate 'a steady supply of Gaelic-speaking licentiates', and that same year a joint delegation of the Presbyterian churches and An Comunn met with the Scottish Secretary to present a list of proposals concerning Gaelic education (*DG* 1917c: 188; Mackay 1917: 22–3).

It is also notable that provision for Gaelic in higher education began in the theological colleges. The first Gaelic classes were offered at the Free Church College in Glasgow in the mid-1860s and the University of Edinburgh's divinity faculty, New College, in 1871, more than a decade before the Chair of Celtic was established at Edinburgh (Gillies 1989b: 4; *AG* 1872).

The churches also contributed to Gaelic development through publications of different kinds. These included a wide range of theological works and also periodicals, particularly Gaelic supplements to church magazines. The first of these periodicals was the Free Church's *An Fhianuis*, first published in 1845, with the Church of Scotland, the Free Presbyterian Church, the United Free Church and the Catholic Church following in later decades (*Life and Work* 2017). During the First World War, nineteen short books for Gaelic-speaking soldiers were prepared by a joint committee of the Presbyterian churches and distributed among the forces (*AG* 1946). Another series of religious publications was produced for the forces in the Second World War (*AG* 1946).

Many individual churchmen were active in a variety of fields involving Gaelic language development, even as elements within the Presbyterian churches were ambivalent or hostile towards aspects of secular Gaelic culture (Meek 1996), with some going so far as to proclaim 'cuideachd an diabhuil cuideachd a' mhòid' (the people of the mòd are the devil's people) ([Ross] 1926: 178). Although ministers had played a lead role in Gaelic scholarship in the eighteenth and most of the nineteenth centuries, this had already diminished by the early twentieth century (Meek 2001a: 317). Some Church of Scotland ministers also played an important role in An Comunn, notably the Rev. Neil Ross, president between 1930 and 1934 and editor of *An Gàidheal* between 1923 and 1936. The role of Catholic priests in these fields was rather less prominent; important examples were the lexicographer Father Ewen MacEachen (1769–1849) and the folklorist Father Allan McDonald (1859–1905) (Roberts 2006).

DEVELOPMENTS IN CORPUS PLANNING AND PUBLISHING

Corpus planning was not a significant concern for Gaelic language activists during this early revival period. This is somewhat atypical of minority language movements more generally; the requirements of language modernisation often demand considerable attention and spark considerable controversy, particularly in the initial phase of mobilisation (Fishman 1993: 2006). At the turn of the twentieth century in Ireland, for example, there were protracted debates about the appropriate spelling of Irish, the font that should be used for writing and printing Irish, and the very form of the language itself (i.e. whether it should be based on the literary language of the seventeenth century or the living dialects that were still spoken after the language shift of the eighteenth and nineteenth centuries) (Ó Conchubhair 2009: 145–235; Ó Háinle 1994). In Scotland, however, the Gaelic of the Bible served as a standard form for many purposes (Meek 1990), while the orthography of the language had largely been settled as a result of the evolving practices of the eighteenth and early nineteenth centuries, so that subsequent reform initiatives have involved marginal adjustments to the system rather than wholesale revision (Black 2010). The issue of internal variation within Gaelic did not prompt significant controversy; there appears to have been an unstated consensus concerning the essential unity of the Scottish Gaelic language, and no real difficulties appear to have emerged in practice as speakers of different dialects engaged each other (McLeod 2017). Again the contrast with Irish is very striking; in that case there were real problems of mutual intelligibility between different dialects, and the issue of managing the internal diversity of the language has been an important issue in Irish language policy ever since (McLeod 2008a, 97–8; Ó hIfearnáin 2010: 41).

Discussion of corpus planning matters in the early revival period was largely confined to attempts at elaborating new terminology and registers, especially technical terms of different kinds (e.g. Argathalian 1876; O Dughaill 1918). In the early twentieth century the Mòd even included competitions for the creation of new vocabulary in specified practical fields. It was recognised that a programme for the dissemination and adoption of such new terms would be required (such as a range of school textbooks) (M. MacLeod 1915: 28), but no such measures emerged, and thus this initial phase of terminological development had little practical impact. It was not until the 1980s, with the development of the Gaelic college Sabhal Mòr Ostaig and of Gaelic-medium education in the schools, that such efforts began to gather momentum (see pp. 272–3).

A Gaelic academy, Àrd Chomhairle na Gàidhlig, was established in 1912, aiming 'to retrieve and preserve the purity of the Gaelic language and to settle debatable points with regard to grammar and idiom' (Mac a' Ghobhainn 1972). The Gaelic scholar H. Cameron Gillies was chosen as its chair, and Erskine of Marr and Liam MacGille Ìosa also played an active role. The First World War precluded any meaningful work on the part of the Àrd Chomhairle, however, and activity did not resume after the war (Henderson 1918: 6; Thompson 1971–2: 87). To this day there has never been a language academy for Scottish Gaelic, in contrast to many other European minority languages such as Basque, Frisian and Sorbian, and recent undertakings by Bòrd na Gàidhlig have been limited in scope (BnG 2007a; p. 328 below).

Comunn Litreachas na h-Albann (the Society of Scottish Letters) was also established shortly before the First World War, with the aim of encouraging Gaelic literature, and publishing and producing editions of important Gaelic texts (Thompson 1971–2: 87). Erskine of Marr became its first chair. Although the organisation secured an impressive list of supporters, ranging from Prince Arthur of Connaught to the principals of the four Scottish universities, it failed to produce any outputs due to the war, and like Àrd Chomhairle na Gàidhlig did not resume activity thereafter (*Perthshire Advertiser* 1914a; Henderson 1918: 6). A similar organisation, the Scottish Gaelic Texts Society, was eventually established in 1934 and remains in existence, but the great majority of its publications (thirty volumes in all) have been in English, in line with the established pattern by which English was used in writings about Gaelic literature and culture, a practice which has only begun to break down in the twenty-first century (McLeod 2013b).

Responsibility for the production of textbooks and other resources for the schools largely fell to An Comunn. These included a grammar handbook (ACG 1893), a Gaelic dictionary for schools (MacFarlane 1912), and four elementary books for primary schoolchildren, which were intended to form 'a complete graded course' to 'put beginners on their feet as regards Gaelic reading and writing' (M. C. MacLeod 1912).

Resources for adult learners of Gaelic had begun to be produced from the late 1870s onwards. In addition to general instructional books (e.g. Macbean 1876; D. C. MacPherson 1879; J. MacLaren 1923), Malcolm MacFarlane published a guide to Gaelic phonetics in 1889 and J. G. MacKay published a handbook of *Easy Gaelic Syntax* in 1899 (MacFarlane 1889; MacKay 1899). Duncan Reid's *A Course of Gaelic Grammar* (1895), which became *Elementary Course of Gaelic* in later incarnations, went through nine editions and was reprinted as late as

1968. Most of these books were intended for Gaelic speakers but others were explicitly intended for learners of the language, an indication of its increasing status.

The most important achievement in relation to Gaelic corpus planning during this period was Edward Dwelly's *Illustrated Gaelic–English Dictionary*, published between 1902 and 1911, which continues to serve as the basic lexicographical resource for Gaelic and has recently been made available in electronic format (McLeod 2013a; www.dwelly.info). Remarkably, Dwelly was a learner of Gaelic, originally from Kent, who became a piper in the Seaforth Highlanders and married a Gael. Although Dwelly worked almost entirely on his own, gathering words from multiple sources over many years, his work was supported in part through the award of a civil list pension, apparently granted by King Edward VII (Ellis 2001 xvii–xix).

A major shortcoming of Gaelic development in this early period of revival was the failure to develop a lively periodical press in Gaelic, much in contrast to the situation of Welsh and indeed Māori (Hughes 2017; Paterson 2010). Gaelic periodicals were short-lived and had small circulations, and no secular periodicals at all were published between 1877 and 1892. Low levels of Gaelic literacy were an obvious impediment. The first all-Gaelic newspaper, *Mac-Talla* (Echo), was published weekly in Sydney, Nova Scotia, between 1892 and 1904, under the editorship of Jonathan G. MacKinnon. The paper carried an eclectic range of material from Scotland as well as Canada (and other diaspora communities) and circulated widely in Scotland. *Mac-Talla* addressed topical contemporary issues, including reports and analyses of the state of the language, alongside diverse items of literary and cultural interest (Dunbar 2019). In the editorial for the last issue, MacKinnon expressed frustration that the Gaels did not really want a Gaelic paper and 'gu bheil iad riaraichte le bhi comharraichte mar an aon chinneach Criosdail a th' air thalamh nach cosd ri paipeir a chumail suas na 'n cainnt féin' (were satisfied to be marked out as the only Christian people in the whole world who will not pay to maintain a paper in their own language) (*Mac-Talla* 1904). Erskine of Marr launched the all-Gaelic newspaper *Alba* in 1908 and again in 1920, but this proved even more short-lived. The editor, Angus Henderson, echoed MacKinnon's frustration, declaring that its difficulties 'proved that most of those who, in showy tartans, loved to attend Gaelic Mòds and join lustily in the empty shout of "Suas leis a' Ghàidhlig" were not prepared to lay out a penny a week on the only Gaelic paper ever published in our country' (Henderson 1918: 5).

Several English-medium periodicals dealt with Gaelic issues, however, not least the land question, and some of these had some Gaelic-language content. Important among these were *The Highlander* (1873–82), *The Celtic Magazine* (1875–88; see Stewart 2015), *The Scottish Highlander* (1885–98) and *The Celtic Monthly* (1892–1915). Highland newspapers, notably the *Oban Times* and the *Northern Chronicle*, also gave extensive coverage to Gaelic issues. In bilingual publications, however, during this period and later, Gaelic tended to be used mainly for literary or folkloric material, with English used for 'serious discussion of current affairs' (D. J. MacLeod 1974–6: 203). In all, 'there was little or no attempt [. . .] to develop Gaelic into an effective political language and a vehicle of political dissent, nor was there much effort to develop the register of Gaelic' (M. K. MacLeod 1981: 156).

The weakness of the periodical press was a symptom of the underdevelopment of Gaelic publishing more generally. In the early nineteenth century only about five books were published per year; this rose to about seventeen by 1870 following the increase in Gaelic literacy resulting from the Gaelic schools movement, but then slipped back again to about eleven per year by the end of the nineteenth century (D. J. MacLeod 1970: 27). Book publishing was also very limited in its range; a large proportion of the material published consisted of poetry collections or different kinds of religious works.

There was no significant Gaelic literary revival in the late nineteenth century, and even the deliberate promotional efforts of Erskine of Marr in the early twentieth century did not give rise to any lasting modernisation or transformation (MacLeòid 2011: 14–15). The first novels, short stories and plays were produced during this period, some of them through Erskine's proactive development programme. In this regard the situation of Gaelic was rather different from that of other minoritised languages in Europe, for which literary revival played a central role, most famously in relation to the Félibrige movement in Occitan (Thomas 2015). The real literary revival in Gaelic did not begin until the 1940s (see pp. 119–20, 143). This periodicity is not unlike that seen in relation to Irish, however, where despite the greater force of the language movement from the 1890s onwards, and the impressive achievements of the English-language writers of the Irish literary revival, the modern literary period really only began in the 1940s with the poetry of Máirtín Ó Direáin and the fiction of Máirtín Ó Cadhain (Ní Annracháin 2003).

CONCLUSION

The period from 1872 to the end of the First World War can be seen as a foundational era in Gaelic policy. The institutional structures built during this period remained in place for many decades following, and the ideological and structural constraints that impeded Gaelic development would also prove long-standing. Most obviously in relation to education, there was a mismatch between the potential and actual role of Gaelic. Although formal high-level national policies permitted a considerably greater role for the language in schools, blockage by policy managers, particularly school inspectors and school boards, meant that relatively little was done in practice. At the same time, the evident 'indifference' or 'apathy' of many Gaelic speakers was a disappointment to language activists and a constraint to the expansion of provision for the language. Certainly a stronger expression of demand on the part of Gaelic-speaking parents could have produced earlier and more meaningful concessions from the education authorities, as happened in Ireland and Wales.

These decades also set a pattern by which one particular organisation would emerge as the lead body promoting Gaelic development, and with this to become a lightning rod for criticism. An Comunn continued to play this central role until the mid-1980s, when it was superseded by Comunn na Gàidhlig and then by Bòrd na Gàidhlig.

With the outbreak of the First World War, much Gaelic activity, including the Mòd, came to a halt and was 'allow[ed] [. . .] to drift into [a] moribund state', as the activist and editor Malcolm C. MacLeod complained (M. C. MacLeod 1919: 2). The era that followed the war brought social and economic hardship to the Gàidhealtachd and continuing challenges for the Gaelic language movement, especially in connection with the implementation of the 'Gaelic clause' in the 1918 Education Act, as discussed in the next chapter.

4

Transition, 1919–44

Following the disastrous disruption of the First World War, the interwar period in Scotland was a time of social and economic crisis. Established industries went into long-term decline and more than 400,000 people – almost a tenth of the national population – left the country during the 1920s alone (Anderson 2012: 52). In the Gàidhealtachd, the problems of population decline and long-term underdevelopment posed an immense challenge to the collective confidence of the people. According to Alexander Nicolson, secretary of the Gaelic Society of Inverness, 'the depopulation which is steadily going on is slowly but surely extinguishing the Gaelic language, as well as scattering the Gaels to the uttermost parts of the earth' ([Nicolson] 1927: xii). In the Western Isles, the names of three ships – the *Iolaire*, the *Marloch* and the *Metagama* – have come to symbolise the hardship of the period. Gàidhealtachd communities suffered immensely from the losses of the First World War, but these were tragically compounded in Lewis and Harris by a further disaster, when the troopship *Iolaire*, carrying soldiers returning from the war, was wrecked on the rocks on the approach to Stornoway on New Year's Day 1919, with the loss of 205 men (J. Macleod 2015). In the following years, emigration became increasingly attractive, and in April 1923 the *Marloch* and the *Metagama* took some six hundred emigrants to Canada from Lewis, Harris and Uist. The key challenges facing the Gàidhealtachd, then, were social and economic, and the language question was not always a priority. Language shift was particularly rapid during this period, especially on the mainland; the number of Gaelic speakers declined by more than half between 1911 and 1951.

GAELIC AND HIGHLAND DEVELOPMENT

Given the hardships of the interwar period, social and economic issues came to the fore in the Gàidhealtachd. In the period immediately following the conclusion of the war, the land question returned to prominence with a wave of land raids, as returning servicemen in Lewis, Harris, Raasay and other areas occupied estates, frustrated that land was not being released for smallholdings (Leneman 1991). The *Land Settlement (Scotland) Act 1919* gave the Board of Agriculture for Scotland powers to break up farms and estates into smallholdings, but the land released was insufficient to meet demand.

The issue of Highland development policy gained new prominence from the 1930s onwards. In 1936 the Highland Development League was established, with the aim 'to inform and mobilise public opinion in support of comprehensive reconstruction of the Highlands and Islands and unified resource development' (*GH* 1936). One of its founders was Dr Lachlan Grant, who published an influential pamphlet in that year entitled *A New Deal for the Highlands*, echoing the title of President Franklin D. Roosevelt's economic and social recovery plan in the United States (Grant 1936). Although the pamphlet dealt mostly with practical matters such as infrastructure and transport, Grant expressed a strongly 'Gaelic nationalist' perspective, calling for a 'new Gaeldom' and the 'wholesale reconstruction of our Highland areas as the one and only way that can save our glorious heritage and ensure its vigorous preservation down the ages' (Grant 1936: 22–3). The Hilleary Report of 1938, produced by a committee of the Scottish Economic Council, recommended the establishment of a Highland Development Council (Scottish Economic Council 1938), but this proposal was not taken forward due to the outbreak of war in 1939. Grant's perspective was exceptional; Gaelic played a minimal role in most of the proposals and discussions concerning Highland development, and debates and policy papers were always in English only. To the extent that Gaelic was considered in these proposals and debates, language maintenance was generally not presented as an aim in itself; it was essentially taken for granted that retaining the population in Gaelic areas would mean retaining the language. As a general proposition, however, it is naïve to assume that economic development will automatically halt language shift within a community (McLeod 2002); among other things, development may bring about an influx of workers who do not speak the minority language and accelerate the spread of the majority language. This was seen in Lochaber and Kinlochleven with the development of hydroelectric installations and aluminium smelters. Some commentators expressed concern about the impact of such changes, sometimes in ethnocentric terms: the Rev. Lauchlan MacLean Watt worried that the new industrial facilities could become 'denationalizing centres', bringing 'all kinds of alien influences among our people, with forms of thought and speech and outlook entirely at variance with our own' (Watt 1937).[1] Conversely, for others the maintenance of Gaelic was no longer really in question; the novelist and activist Naomi Mitchison expressed the view that 'it is almost certainly too late to save the language as a living means of culture' (Mitchison 1942).

As in previous decades, Gaelic organisations in this period generally continued to downplay the economic significance of Gaelic. The GSL conceded in 1930 that Gaelic had little 'efficacy in the worship of Mammon' but argued that 'as the vehicle of dreams, of unsubstantial visions, of airy nothings, it will remain treasured when the halls of commerce have vanished and empires have crumbled' (*Scotsman* 1930b). The idea that Gaelic language revitalisation could assist or accelerate economic regeneration was some decades away.

GAELIC AND POLITICS

Gaelic played a very limited role in Scottish politics during the interwar period, perhaps even less so than before the First World War. Between the 1920s and the late 1940s, Gaelic became steadily less important in Scottish national movements. Although Gaelic militants such as Erskine and MacGille Ìosa played an important role in the strongly pro-independence Scottish National League from its founding in 1919–20 (Mitchell 1996: 82), they were 'gradually isolated' as 'class interest had become the dominant issue' in Scottish politics and 'the pragmatists began to form more bread and butter policies and strategies' (Finlay 2004b: 135–6). This was increasingly the case following the creation of the National Party of Scotland in 1928. The new Scottish National Party (SNP), which resulted from a merger in 1934 between the National Party of Scotland and the more right-wing Scottish Party, gave still less emphasis to Gaelic, especially after a divisive party conference in 1942 (Finlay 1994). Even so, it is noteworthy that both the SNP's first leader, Sir Alexander MacEwen, and its first national secretary, John MacCormick, were Gaelic speakers. MacEwen also held leadership positions in An Comunn, the Gaelic Society of Inverness and the Gaelic League of Scotland (discussed below), and urged the linguistic and cultural re-Gaelicisation of the Highlands (MacEwen 1932: 210).

MacEwen's successor, Andrew Dewar Gibb, wrote favourably of Gaelic and the 'precious gift of bilingualism', even if he rejected the suggestion of making Gaelic mandatory in Scottish schools (Gibb 1930: 167–8). As discussed in chapter 5, the SNP paid less attention to Gaelic in the postwar decades, before renewing its interest – albeit to a relatively modest extent – from the late 1960s onwards.

In any event, the SNP and its predecessor organisations were of minimal significance in electoral terms in the interwar decades. Its sole electoral victory came at a by-election in Motherwell in April 1945, but this seat was promptly lost to Labour at the General Election three months later. It was not until 1967 that the party won another parliamentary by-election and not until 1970 that it won a seat at a General Election (in the Western Isles, the most strongly Gaelic constituency in Scotland) (Lynch 2013).

The dominant parties in Scotland during this period – the Unionist Party and the Labour Party – did not adopt any formal policy on Gaelic. The Western Isles elected a Labour MP in 1935, Malcolm Macmillan, but he rarely took any public stand on Gaelic matters until the late 1950s, when he began to respond to new pressures from Gaelic organisations.

Although the Gaelic element in nationalist politics faded in the interwar period, and Erskine himself left the scene in the mid-1930s, some activists continued to press the view of Gaelic as an essential element in Scottish national identity. Notable among them was Seumas MacGaraidh, who wrote in 1935:

> Gaelic is the language of our country's infancy, the tongue of our forefathers when our country was a free, independent and prosperous nation [. . .] It was the native speech, it was universally in use; in fine it was the National language until the time of the Anglo-Saxon encroachments. [. . .] Retention of the National language is calculated to regenerate in the Scottish mind *a wish to be free* from English domination. (MacGaraidh 1935 (emphasis in original; see Sìol nan Gaidheal n.d. (c))

Only very occasionally did Gaelic become connected to the major political issues of the 1930s. The leading Gaelic organisations remained avowedly non-political, and no Gaelic factions and activists aligned themselves with either the far left or the far right. Some elements in the nationalist movement struck more extreme positions: the poet Hugh MacDiarmid flirted with both Communism and Fascism at different stages, while the poets Douglas Young and George Campbell Hay sometimes expressed quasi-fascist sympathies. But 'Fascist Scotland' as a whole was a small-scale phenomenon (Boyd 2013), and Gaelic played a minimal role within it. In the early 1930s, Gaelic was used as the drill language for the short-lived paramilitary Scottish Defence Force, and for the name[2] of Clann Albain, a short-lived crypto-fascist organisation associated with MacDiarmid (Boyd 2013: 133–5, 141; Lorimer 1997: 289–91), but there was no Gaelic counterpart to the openly fascist Breiz Atao organisation in Brittany (Carney 2015).

The Communist left in Scotland, meanwhile, tended to see the Gaelic movement as a reactionary phenomenon. Writing in *Communist Review* in 1932, R. MacLennan expressed the view that 'despite the artificial attempts to stimulate the language by the holding of classes, it can readily be said that it [Gaelic] is a dead language', confined to remote areas and spoken by only a very small proportion of the population. The Gaelic movement was dismissed as an example of how 'capitalism, in decline, in the throes of crisis, attempts to resurrect the dead in order to bolster up its decaying system' (MacLennan 1932: 508–9).

In a similar vein, the left-wing novelist James Barke, writing in the early 1930s, found little reason for optimism in the contemporary Gaelic scene:

> In the modern capitalist state the *Gael finds himself an anachronism* – almost an extinct species. The few of them who are articulate turn, therefore, to a hopeless backward looking, backward longing. A decayed economic system can produce only a decayed culture. The present attempts to revive this culture are therefore doomed to failure. [...] The death rattle of Gaelic culture may be amplified by all sorts of bodies and committees. They delude themselves, however, in thinking that by doing so they are performing an act of resurrection. (Grassic Gibbon 2001 [1934]: 1367)

One of the more notorious incidents of politicisation in relation to Gaelic in the interwar period arose in a most unlikely context, when in 1934 the Australian authorities used Gaelic to try to exclude the communist activist Egon Kisch from the country (Mason 2014). Kisch had been invited to Australia to address an anti-fascist rally in Melbourne. Australia's *Immigration Restriction Act 1901*, the cornerstone of the notorious 'White Australia' policy, required applicants seeking to enter the country to demonstrate that they were literate in a 'European language'. The particular language used for this test could be selected by the Australian authorities. Aware that Kisch knew several European languages, the authorities required him to transcribe the Lord's Prayer as read out in Gaelic by a police officer who had emigrated from Scotland some decades previously. Following Kisch's challenge to this procedure, the High Court of Australia ruled that Gaelic did not constitute 'an European language' within the meaning of the 1901 Act, as it was not 'a standard form of speech recognized as the received and ordinary means of communication among the inhabitants in a European community for all the purposes of the social body' (R. v. *Wilson ex parte Kisch* (1934): 241).³ Gaelic activists viewed this interpretation as a 'slur' and a 'sneer' at the language (*P&J* 1935).

Another somewhat embarrassing intersection between Gaelic and international politics arose in 1939, when the Fort William branch of An Comunn sent a telegram to the President of Czechoslovakia asking that £1,000,000 of the £10,000,000 that was paid by the UK to Czechoslovakia following the Munich Agreement of 1938 should be given instead to An Comunn. In an extraordinarily misjudged statement, Dr Isa H. McIver of An Comunn argued that the UK 'gave £10,000,000 to the Czechs as the price of betrayal, but we have never paid for the crime of the Highland clearances, beside which Hitler's anti-Jewish drive seems play' (*P&J* 1939).

Although more ambitious than An Comunn in terms of its revivalist ambitions for Gaelic, the Gaelic League of Scotland (discussed below, pp. 122–4) also did not engage meaningfully with the overriding economic and social issues of the day. Gaelic became sufficiently displaced from such political concerns that in 1947 the poet George Campbell Hay, a militant nationalist, drew attention to the 'queer belief, once common with Left wing people' but 'seldom met with now', 'that the Highlander is a reactionary, cringing ghillie and that Gaelic is the unprogressive tongue of a society once ultrafeudal [...] and now ultra-Sabbatarian, Highland Regimental and True-Blue – something that would never fit in with the dogs, the cinema and the communal crèche' (Hay 1947: 104).

GAELIC AND CULTURAL DEVELOPMENT

Against the background of economic crisis, interwar Scotland was a period of cultural dynamism and innovation, especially in the literary movement known as the Scottish Renaissance. Gaelic played a significant role in many of the cultural initiatives, debates and discussions of the period, although these tended to involve a small number of activist intellectuals and did not give rise to any large-scale popular mobilisation.

The beginning of the Scottish Renaissance is conventionally dated to 1922, with the launch of *The Scottish Chapbook*, whose 'programme', set out in its first issue, announced the intention to 'bring Scottish Literature into closer touch with current European tendencies in technique and ideation', that is, the cultural movement now known as Modernism (McCulloch 2004: xii). In terms of language, however, the main emphasis of the Scottish Renaissance was not on Gaelic but on Scots (or 'Lallans'). The leading figure in the Scottish Renaissance, Hugh MacDiarmid, perceived 'the Scots Vernacular' as the mechanism for bringing Scotland 'into the mainstream of European letters', describing it as 'a vast storehouse of just the very peculiar and subtle effects which modern European literature in general is assiduously seeking' (Grieve 2004 [1923]: 27–8). The term 'vernacular' was somewhat misleading, for MacDiarmid emphasised not the varieties in actual use but what he called 'synthetic Scots', which drew on words from the full range of Scots dialects and revived obsolete words from older literary texts (Glen 1964: 33). The Scottish Renaissance was literary in its orientation, however, and did not involve any meaningful effort to promote the revitalisation of Scots in public life. Some advocates urged the authorities to make provision for Scots in the education system (e.g. Craigie 1924: 37–8), but these calls did not lead to any kind of mobilisation, let alone substantive changes in policy.

MacDiarmid had a strong interest in Gaelic, taking the position that 'the revival of Scots is only a half-way house [. . .] an intermediate step on the way [. . .] back to Gaelic' (MacDiarmid 1977 [1929]). Even so, MacDiarmid never acquired a real knowledge of Gaelic and never wrote in the language (although he published various essays under the Gaelic version of his legal name, 'Gillechriosd Mac a' Ghreidir' (e.g. Mac a' Ghreidir 1929)). He wrote scathingly of the mainstream Gaelic movement of the time, which he characterised as 'divorced from reality' and marked by 'a pseudo-patriotism in their coteries in grotesque contrast with the actual conditions obtaining in the districts they claim to represent' (Grieve 1926: 248). But MacDiarmid was less interested in the actual language than in what he identified as the 'Gaelic Idea', a purely abstract 'intellectual conception' of national self-assertion that built upon Dostoyevsky's 'Russian Idea'. MacDiarmid wrote expressly that

> This Gaelic Idea has nothing in common with the activities of An Comunn Gaidhealach, no relationship whatever with the Celtic Twilight. It would not matter so far as positing it is concerned whether there had never been any Gaelic language or literature [. . .] From the point of view of the Gaelic idea, knowledge of, or even the existence of, Gaelic is immaterial. (Grieve 1968 [1931]: 67–9)

More generally, Gaelic was important to many lines of cultural narrative during the Scottish Renaissance period as it was considered to represent a purer form of Scottishness, more aligned with Scotland's un-Anglicised, pre-Union, pre-Calvinist past (Tange 2000: 42–3). The Scottish Renaissance period spawned a large number of literary and cultural periodicals, many of them short-lived, which provided a forum for extensive discussion and debate (McCulloch 2004). Language politics and the role of Gaelic featured fairly prominently, although substantive issues tended to be considered in English, with Gaelic mainly confined to literary and folkloric contexts.

Not all Scottish writers of the period were sympathetic to political and cultural nationalism and the role of language within it, however. Poet Edwin Muir was particularly dubious of the literary potential of Scots, characterising it as a mere 'half-way house', but considered Gaelic to be, like English, 'a complete and homogenous language' (Muir 1982: 111; see also Linklater 1938: 811). The novelist Lewis Grassic Gibbon, meanwhile, expressed cynicism towards the role of Gaelic revivalism within the nationalist movement:

> It will profit Glasgow's hundred and fifty thousand slum-dwellers so much to know that they are being starved and brutalized by Labour Exchanges staffed exclusively by Gaelic-speaking, haggis-eating Scots in saffron kilts and tongued brogues, full of such typical Scottish ideals as those which kept men chained as slaves in the Fifeshire mines a century or so ago. (Grassic Gibbon 2001: 108)

The Scottish Renaissance did not align directly with Gaelic literary and cultural initiatives of the period, although many of the key figures in the movement, not only MacDiarmid himself but also the novelists Neil Gunn and Fionn MacColla, took a keen interest in Gaelic. Erskine of Marr's initiatives in Gaelic publishing were nearing their end in the 1920s as the Scottish Renaissance began to gather pace: *Guth na Bliadhna* ceased publication in 1925 and the fourth and final volume of *An Ròsarnach* came out in 1930. MacDiarmid and Erskine nevertheless had a close relationship; Erskine contributed two Gaelic plays to MacDiarmid's *Scottish Chapbook* (Erskine 1923a, 1923b) and MacDiarmid wrote an essay praising Erskine's efforts to modernise Gaelic letters in his 1926 collection *Contemporary Scottish Studies* (Grieve 1926: 244–50). But the modern Gaelic literary renaissance did not develop until the late 1930s, after the first phase of the Scottish Renaissance, with the arrival of the poets Sorley MacLean and George Campbell Hay. The publication of MacLean's collection *Dàin do Eimhir agus Dàin Eile* (Poems to Eimhir and Other Poems) in 1943 is now viewed as an immensely important literary and cultural milestone, but

MacLean's work was little known until after the Second World War and the main impact of *Dàin do Eimhir* would not be felt until the 1970s (Black 1999: xxx).

Foundational modern academic work on Gaelic literature, linguistics and folk tradition began in earnest in the 1920s and 1930s. This included the establishment of the journal *Scottish Gaelic Studies* (1926–), scholarly editions of important literary texts (particularly by the Scottish Gaelic Texts Society, established in 1934), scientific work on Gaelic dialects, and significant initiatives involving the collection of traditional songs and tales (Thomson 1997–8).

THE WORK OF AN COMUNN

An Comunn Gàidhealach remained the main Gaelic organisation in the interwar period, continuing its work in the cultural field and especially in relation to education, where the implementation of the 'Gaelic clause' in the *Education (Scotland) Act 1918* was the principal challenge, as discussed in detail below. Throughout the interwar period, Gaelic activists of different stripes repeatedly criticised An Comunn for its perceived ineffectiveness. The main line of attack was that Gaelic was 'being sung to death' (Brown 1934): that the organisation placed too much emphasis on the Mòd and cultural activities in general and failed to give sufficient attention to the socio-economic problems facing the Gaelic community (e.g. Grant 1934; *P&J* 1937). In 1934 Angus Clark, former president of the GSL, attacked An Comunn in scathing terms:

> The attitude of what remains of our Highland population to this question [the decline of Gaelic] is a growing indifference, spiritless apathy, and dull despair [. . .] It is inconceivable that a language movement which has stubbornly refused to take cognisance of the social and economic problems of the Highlands could hope to succeed [. . . An Comunn has] sought to justify its policy by childishly chanting 'No politics' and pathetically clinging to a policy which will neither help nor protect our own land, our language, or our people. (*Courier & Advertiser* 1934)

A writer using the nom de plume 'Earra-Ghaidheal' (Argyll) was more scathing still, declaring that 'Gaelic is dying, and dying rapidly, and its assassin is An Comunn' (Earra-Ghaidheal 1933).

For the novelist Compton Mackenzie, the answer lay in linking the Gaelic cause to Scottish nationalism: '[t]he sooner that the members of An Comunn grasp that the future of Gaelic rests entirely on the achievement of national independence the better chance there is of saving the language before it is too late' (Mackenzie 1933; see also Brown 1934). Despite the frequency and diversity of these criticisms, however, An Comunn did not fundamentally change its approach; and with the exception of the Gaelic League of Scotland, discussed below, no rival language organisations were established during this period with a different ideological basis or programmatic orientation.

Given the magnitude of the socio-economic and sociolinguistic challenges that were presented, some of these criticisms of An Comunn's cautiousness were somewhat unreasonable, and the organisation also had numerous defenders, with some Gaelic activists expressly criticising broad language restoration aims. In 1927 Professor Magnus MacLean set out a conservative position:

> [S]ome well-meaning enthusiasts may be in danger of fostering extravagant notions, and propounding visionary schemes for the resuscitation of the Gaelic as the one language of the North, and the restoration of it to its ancient sway. Gaelic was the fitting medium of expression in the old order which is passing away, but while it may still be preserved to exert its influence on the life and thought of the people, and to have an important place in the education of the young, that place can be wisely determined only by accepting the fact that the old language is not adequate to the new order. (MacLean 1927: 295)

As in the pre-war period, An Comunn repeatedly noted the resistance of some Gaels to the teaching of Gaelic and the promotion of the language more generally, which served as a significant brake on progress (e.g. MacGille Sheathanaich 1936: 105; MacThòmais 1928: 30).

An Comunn was by no means indifferent to the material needs of Gaelic communities during this period, however. A Relief Fund was established in 1923 to provide assistance to alleviate hardship in the Highlands and Islands, which raised more than £40,000 (Thompson 1986: 53, 56). Another fundraising Fèill like that of 1907 was organised in 1927, again with strong aristocratic backing, which generated almost £9,000 (Thompson 1986: 56). Over the decades, An Comunn's magazine *An Gaidheal* regularly included reports and editorials on social and economic issues affecting the Gàidhealtachd, including the land question and proposals for regional development.

One important new area of activity that developed in the interwar period, supplementing An Comunn's work on Gaelic in the schools, was youth work, including the organisation of youth brigades and summer camps. The ongoing controversy concerning the use of Gaelic in An Comunn's activities led to the foundation in 1929 of an exclusively

Gaelic subgroup within the organisation, Clann an Fhraoich (literally 'Children of the Heather') (ACG 1935: 12). In 1935 a youth group, Comunn na h-Òigridh, was formed within Clann an Fhraoich. Comunn na h-Òigridh described itself as 'a Gaelic-speaking movement seeking to stimulate the use of the Gaelic language, and to promote and encourage cultural, social and recreational activities suited to the Gaelic environment' (Comunn na h-Òigridh 1955: 3). By 1939 Comunn na h-Òigridh had more than three thousand members in local *Feachdan* (brigades); the organisation went into abeyance during the war but resumed operation in 1945 and by 1947 it had 7,500 members (*Scotsman* 1939b; Hay 1947: 104). Comunn na h-Òigridh summer camps were organised from 1936 at Sonachan in Argyll, and in 1954 a house was purchased, Cnoc nan Ros, near Tain (Comunn na h-Òigridh 1937, 1955: 7). From 1950 onwards, there were camps for Gaelic learners as well as fluent speakers (*AG* 1951). The Comunn na h-Òigridh camps ran until the mid-1960s and some commentators consider them one of the most valuable things An Comunn ever did (MacLeòid 2012: 13). Even so, Comunn na h-Òigridh and later youth programmes never came close to having a broad-based societal impact in terms of language revitalisation: the number of children participating was simply too small. These initiatives cannot be compared to the Urdd (the Welsh League of Youth) in Wales or the *coláistí samhraidh* (summer colleges for secondary school pupils) in the Irish Gaeltacht, which operated at a much larger scale (Jones, Merriman and Mills 2016; MacGill-Fhinnein 1965–6: 201–5, 255–9).

These initiatives in youth work were followed by the establishment in 1950 of the Committee for Informal Education, which involved the education authorities in Argyllshire, Inverness-shire, Ross & Cromarty and the SED as well as An Comunn. The Committee aimed 'to promote and encourage in Gaelic-speaking areas, especially among young people, cultural and social and recreational activities suited to a Gaelic environment' (Committee for Informal Education 1950a). Significantly, this remit included learners as well as native speakers (Committee for Informal Education 1950b); from the 1950s onwards, learners became a significant presence in the schools (see pp. 165–8 below). Although three regional organisers were appointed, there were difficulties in the recruitment and retention of staff, and it was evident that the decline of Gaelic in many areas had reduced the number of Gaelic-speaking young people to the point where organising group work was very challenging (SED 1951b, 1953a, 1953b, 1953c).

The only important new Gaelic organisation to emerge in the interwar period was the Gaelic League of Scotland (Dionnasg Gàidhlig na h-Alba), which was established at Glasgow University in 1930 out of frustration with An Comunn's approach to Gaelic development (Glasgow University 1934: 156–7). The name chosen for this body obviously echoed the leading Irish language revival organisation and signalled the League's more political approach to Gaelic. In contrast to An Comunn, the GLS took a strongly revivalist and firmly national view of Gaelic as the language of Scotland. Its constitution stated the aims of the organisation as follows:

> the restoration of Gaelic as the national language of Scotland; the restoration of Gaelic to its former status as a European speech; the renewal of cultural relations between Scotland and the other Celtic nations; the promotion of international good fellowship between Scotland and the other Celtic nations; the promotion of international good fellowship between Celtic Scotland and the other nations of Europe; the fostering of Celtic music, art, literature, history, drama and games. (GLS 1931)

Despite these wide-reaching and broadly political aims, in terms of its bourgeois social composition the League was broadly similar to An Comunn, and it also drew support from the aristocracy (including the Duke of Argyll as its Honorary President). In addition, like An Comunn it did little to engage with the socio-economic challenges facing Scotland during this period, or with the great political questions confronting Europe more generally.

Commensurate with its strong revivalist stance, the most important activity of the GLS was the teaching of Gaelic to learners of the language. This aim was described, rather polemically, as 'an attempt to amend a lamentable situation in the country today – the lack of any facilities for the bulk of the people of Scotland to acquire a speaking knowledge of the language of their ancestors' (GLS 1935). By 1935 the League was running five weekly Gaelic classes in Glasgow. It expressed the goal of establishing branches 'throughout the country to afford the same opportunities to the rest of Scotland', but never succeeded in this objective (GLS 1935). The League also established a Gaelic rambling club, with annual summer camps in Ballachulish (Mac a' Ghobhainn 1973: 4), and produced a range of Gaelic learning materials, most notably *Gaelic Made Easy*, a series of instructional booklets, written by John M. Paterson, the organisation's long-standing president.

In 1938–9 the League produced a monthly all-Gaelic newspaper, *Crois-Tara*, edited by Paterson. This was the first Gaelic newspaper since Erskine of Marr's short-lived *Alba* in 1920–1 (Mac a' Ghobhainn 1973: 5). *Crois-Tara* combined reporting and commentary on Gaelic affairs with a range of European and international coverage, although it did not adopt any clear positions on the major political questions of the day. The outbreak of war in September 1939 brought publication to an end, although it resumed briefly after the war in a different format and with less substantial content. The League continued as a substantial organisation, however – over two thousand people attended the League's Annual Caledonian Gathering in Glasgow in 1948 (*An Ceum* 1948b) – although it slowly withered away in the decades following.

THE IMPLEMENTATION OF THE 'GAELIC CLAUSE'

Gaelic activists held high hopes in relation to the implementation of the 'Gaelic clause' in the 1918 Education Act. Alexander MacDonald of the Gaelic Society of Inverness described the clause as 'the *Magna Charta* of Gaelic education', and Murdo Morrison, Director of Education for Inverness-shire, expressed the belief in 1920 'that before long no young child of Gaelic-speaking parents who reached the age of 15 would leave school without being able to read and write his own language' (*TGSI* 1924: 94, 96). Yet when questions about Gaelic literacy were asked for the first time in the 1971 census, the results were sobering: only 51 per cent of Gaelic speakers in the Western Isles aged between 15 and 44 (and so having entered school between 1931 and 1961) indicated that they could read and write Gaelic (MacKinnon 1978: 60–1).[4] Given these poor outcomes, it could well be argued that the authorities' 'provision for Gaelic' was not 'adequate' within the meaning of the Act; had pupils' education failed to produce basic literacy in English, it is difficult to imagine it would have been considered 'adequate'.

Implementation of the clause was left to the individual education authorities[5] in the Highland counties, and their approaches differed considerably. An Comunn endeavoured to coordinate this provision and find overarching solutions to the various practical problems that arose, but met with only limited success. The SED itself did not take responsibility for implementation at a national level, in contrast to the approach in Wales, where in 1925 the SED's counterpart, the Board of Education, convened a departmental committee 'to inquire into the position of the Welsh language and to advise as to its promotion in the educational system of Wales'. The Board's subsequent report, *Welsh in Education and Life* (Board of Education 1927), made seventy-two principal recommendations, most of them involving the education system; as An Comunn complained at the time (*AG* 1927), there was no comprehensive strategic document of this kind in Scotland.

Implementation of the Gaelic clause did lead to a rapid and substantial increase in the number of pupils being taught Gaelic in the years after 1918, but there were significant divergences and anomalies in the pattern of delivery. Before 1918 the number of schools that taught Gaelic was probably under 20 (ACG 1930: 3), but at the end of 1920 the language was being taught to approximately 4,820 pupils, almost two-thirds of them (3,120) in Inverness-shire (*Scotsman* 1922). Professor W. J. Watson reported in 1923 'that already there are certain schools in purely Gaelic-speaking districts in which all instruction is given from the beginning in and through Gaelic' (Watson 1923: 83). By 1929 Gaelic was being taught to 8,977 pupils at 309 elementary schools (3,777 pupils at 136 schools in Inverness-shire, 3,400 pupils at 66 schools in Ross-shire and 1,600 pupils at 92 schools in Argyll). In Sutherland, however, only 200 pupils were being taught Gaelic, at just 15 schools, and there was no provision at all in Perthshire[6] (*Scotsman* 1930a). Gaelic was also taught at one school in Buteshire (on the Isle of Arran) in the mid-1920s (*AG* 1925: 74).

In response to a request from the GSL, the Scottish Secretary issued a statement in May 1922 concerning the delineation of the 'Gaelic-speaking areas' for purposes of the 1918 Act (*Scotsman* 1922). In October 1919 the Argyll education authority had agreed to define the whole of the county as a Gaelic-speaking area. There was no similar formal action in the other Highland counties, but the schools inspectorate set out a detailed list of what it considered to be the 'Gaelic-speaking areas'. All the island areas were included, but the designation of mainland parishes was rather more of a patchwork, especially in Inverness-shire, where some districts of the strongly Gaelic west coast parishes were excluded while other, more Anglicised areas further east such as Drumnadrochit and Kiltarlity, near Inverness, were included. Ongoing language shift meant that the Gaelic-speaking areas shrank over time; in 1961 the SED stated that the Gaelic-speaking areas 'may be broadly defined as the Outer and Inner Hebrides and some of the more remote coastal districts of the counties of Sutherland, Ross and Cromarty, Inverness and Argyll', but that 'the rest of the mainland of these counties can no longer be regarded as Gaelic-speaking' (SED 1961: 37).

An important issue was the extent to which Gaelic instruction should be limited to pupils having Gaelic as a mother tongue or extended to children who had not learned it at home. Although the legislation referred to 'Gaelic-speaking areas', it was by no means the case, given the dynamics of language shift, that all the schoolchildren in such areas were first-language Gaelic speakers. Article 16(6) of the *Code of Regulations for*

Day Schools addressed this issue by providing that the scheme of work should make reasonable provision for the instruction of Gaelic-speaking children (SO 1930b; Hansard 1932). This approach to the legislation would have meant that even in Gaelic-speaking areas there would be no requirement to teach the language to children who did not already speak it. Conversely, in a few instances Gaelic was taught in areas where the language was no longer widely spoken, to classes consisting almost entirely of children who could not speak the language.[7]

Staffing sometimes presented a challenge, and there were different aspects to the problem. Sometimes there was simply an outright shortfall of teachers with Gaelic, but in Inverness-shire in 1923 it was 'reported that the majority of the teachers are Gaelic-speaking, but an appreciable percentage have little literary knowledge of the language', a legacy of their own deficient Gaelic education which meant they were unable to teach the language effectively (*Scotsman* 1922). In other cases, Gaelic-speaking teachers employed by the local authority expressed unwillingness to move to Gaelic-speaking areas elsewhere in the county. By 1936 considerable regional variations were reported, with Inverness-shire and Ross-shire reporting little or no difficulties recruiting Gaelic teachers, while Argyll and Sutherland struggled (ACG 1936: 5).

Proponents of Gaelic education repeatedly bemoaned the lack of support from parents (e.g. Urchardainn 1927: 247). Usually this reluctance was attributed to the view that English should be prioritised given its greater practical importance, but sometimes more straightforwardly negative views were suggested, with Gaelic depicted as an outright hindrance. Lewis primary school headmaster James Thomson[8] suggested in 1923 that many Lewis parents 'attributed their failure to find the rosy paths of life more to the possession of Gaelic than to the lack of English' (Ross 1923: 11). On the other hand, a 'lost generation' phenomenon was sometimes reported; parents who had not been taught Gaelic themselves 'bitterly regretted the opportunities they had lost' and 'were strongly in favour of giving their children the advantage that was denied themselves' (Ross 1923: 12). There was no strategic programme to inform or persuade parents, however; *The Scotsman* proposed simply that if parents 'do not wish their children to speak or study Gaelic, they should be reasoned into a wiser mood' (*Scotsman* 1937c).

Gaelic campaigners often spoke favourably of bilingualism and repeatedly emphasised its benefits. In 1927, for example, Professor Magnus MacLean argued that 'it should be constantly impressed upon Highland parents that bi-lingualism gives increased intellectual power' (MacLean 1927: 296). To some extent these arguments may have been tactical, as they worked to deflect the argument that teaching Gaelic would detract from the acquisition of English. This positive view of bilingualism did not always sit well with the conventional wisdom of the time, and indeed some of the prevailing academic views, although this would change in the 1960s, as discussed below (pp. 168–9).

In addition to monitoring the extent of teaching in different areas and pressing the education authorities to improve their provision, An Comunn held several educational conferences and organised annual training courses for teachers (Watson 1923, AG 1930). The most successful training course, in 1920, involved 150 teachers (Watson 1923: 98). An Comunn also took charge of the production of Gaelic schoolbooks, including a series of elementary readers (*TGSI* 1932: 260), poetry and prose anthologies for secondary schools (Watson 1915, 1918) and numerous grammar books and editions of literary texts. Concerns were sometimes raised about the suitability and quality of An Comunn's schoolbooks, however (ACG 1936: 5; Campbell 1950: 83–4).

In 1936 An Comunn appointed a Special Committee to consider current provision for the teaching of Gaelic in schools and colleges (ACG 1936). The fact that this investigation fell to a voluntary organisation rather than the SED or the education authorities is telling in itself. The committee's convener (chair) was Lord Strathcarron, formerly Iain Macpherson MP, who had played a key role in securing the 'Gaelic clause' in the 1918 Act, as discussed above (p. 86). As part of its investigation, the Committee sent a questionnaire to the Directors of Education in the four Highland counties and to the heads of all schools there. This survey revealed that Gaelic was being taught to 7,129 elementary pupils in 284 schools, of which 5,743 (80.6 per cent) were in the islands and only 1,386 (19.4 per cent) on the mainland. Of the mainland pupils, 577 were in Argyll, even though Gaelic was significantly weaker there than in Inverness-shire, Ross-shire and Sutherland (where the corresponding figures were 337, 318 and 154), reflecting a more proactive approach on the part of the Argyll authorities. Gaelic was still not being taught in any schools in Perthshire. Among secondary pupils, 864 were being taught Gaelic at 22 schools, none of them in Sutherland, but at some of these schools the number of pupils studying Gaelic was very small (e.g. 23 out of 500 at Inverness Royal Academy and 9 out of 85 in Kingussie) (ACG 1936: 12).

The headline figure of 7,129 represented a large decline from the 8,977 that had been reported in 1930, causing a degree of consternation. In its 1936 report, An Comunn's Special Committee asserted that the 1929 figures might have been overestimated and that the apparent drop was 'almost incredible', but gave no explanation as to why this should have been the case (ACG 1936: 12). Three years later, in 1938–9, only 4,259 primary school pupils were reported as receiving instruction in Gaelic (Hansard 1943), an implausible decline of 40 per cent in three years. Evidently there was a lack of rigour in data-collection processes, which testifies to a lack of seriousness of purpose on the part of the authorities.

In a leader column responding to the 1936 report, *The Scotsman* commented that '[t]he sharpness of this decline is distinctly disquieting [. . .] the number of those able to read and write Gaelic is progressively decreasing and [. . .] unless steps are taken to arrest this decline, Gaelic will in course of time become a dead language or survive merely as a patois' (*Scotsman* 1936b). The newspaper urged better inspection arrangements for Gaelic, more use of Gaelic as a teaching medium and attention to the issue of teacher supply, but reiterated that '[a] revival of Gaelic can come only from within the Gaelic-speaking area' through 'a strenuous effort' by 'the inhabitants of the Highland counties', even if there was increasing support for the language across Scotland and more non-native speakers learning it.

The headline numbers of children being taught Gaelic disguised great differences in practice on the ground, however. Most importantly, the number of hours per week devoted to Gaelic teaching varied considerably. The average was a mere 1.25 hours per week, but many schools limited it to half an hour a week (ACG 1936: 4). The fact that Gaelic was often not considered within the scope of formal inspections made it 'the Cinderella of the curriculum' (ACG 1936: 3). An Comunn president John Bannerman amplified this metaphor in 1937: 'sometimes she must get up early in the morning to get in before the other subjects had risen, or remain cowering in a corner until other subjects had received time-honoured deference' (*Scotsman* 1937b). Moreover, although Gaelic was 'very generally used as the medium of instruction, especially in the Infant Department of schools where the pupils are native speakers', formal instruction in the language did not begin before Junior I, when children were aged nine, and in some schools did not begin until Senior I, when children were twelve (ACG 1936: 6, 4). The nature of the instruction left much to be desired; the committee found that the teaching of Gaelic was 'arid, academic and given through the medium of English' (ACG 1936: 5); the basic model was that used for the classical languages, with a strong emphasis on translation into English (F. MacLeod 1976: 1). Many teachers were not qualified to teach the language, so that 'no provision [wa]s made for writing Gaelic in a large list of schools'

(ACG 1936: 5). 'With very few exceptions', it was reported, 'Gaelic is not taught to pupils ignorant of the language', although Argyll had developed a scheme for non-native speakers. 'The reports from several schools [. . .] generate the suspicion that the presence in a class of even a few children who know English only is made the pretext for neglecting instruction in Gaelic altogether' (ACG 1936: 5, 6). Several teachers referred to 'indifference' and indeed 'actual antagonism on the part of parents' concerning the teaching of Gaelic (ACG 1936: 8).

The report made eighteen recommendations. These included devoting more time to Gaelic, ideally 2.5 hours per week; introducing Gaelic reading no later than the Junior II stage (age ten); extending the teaching of the language to non-native speakers; strengthening provision at secondary level, 'even outwith the Highlands'; and improving inspection arrangements and training provision (ACG 1936: 9–11). The relevant authorities accepted very few of these recommendations, however (Campbell 1950: 82).

Provision for Gaelic in individual schools depended to a considerable extent on the support and enthusiasm of school heads and individual teachers. In many schools, supportive teachers worked hard to encourage the language. For example, the head teacher of Cornaigmore school in Tiree from 1938 onwards was an An Comunn activist and took pains to encourage Gaelic in the school, even mandating the use of Gaelic on designated days of the week (Tiree & Coll Gaelic Partnership 2011: 19–20). In other cases there was evidence of indifference and even hostility to the teaching of Gaelic on the part of head or classroom teachers. Yet the very fact of such variegation – which would not have been evident in relation to the teaching of English reading or of mathematics – demonstrates that there was no overarching policy concerning the teaching of Gaelic, and that the subject attracted no real priority from the authorities.

Compared to the period before 1918, there was less opposition to the teaching of Gaelic, or pressure to limit it. The principal Scottish newspapers – which may be taken as reflections of 'establishment' opinion – published several leader columns in support of Gaelic teaching in the Highlands (e.g. *Scotsman* 1936b). But resistance came from various quarters, including some teachers in Gaelic areas (*Alba* 1920a) and certain public figures. In 1921 Sir John Lorne MacLeod, president of the Tìr nam Beann Society in Edinburgh, expressed the view that 'there is not the slightest warrant for any movement which would seek to compel children who do not desire to learn Gaelic to submit to instruction in that language', which 'can only mean retarding their intellectual progress'

(*Aberdeen Daily Journal* 1921). In 1937 Sir Murdoch MacDonald, MP for Inverness, expressed his opposition to a proposal to introduce Gaelic-medium education in the Gàidhealtachd (Hay 1937), declaring that '[t]he English language has conquered in the same way that a motor vehicle supersedes a horse and cart', and that attempting to strengthen the role of Gaelic was 'fantastic and undesirable' (*Oban Times* 1937).

GAELIC IN HIGHER EDUCATION

Although it was nowhere near as prominent as the issue of teaching Gaelic in the schools, the question of Gaelic provision in the universities attracted new attention in the 1930s, especially in connection with the proposal to create a Chair of Celtic in the University of Glasgow, following the precedent set in Edinburgh, and the possibility of establishing a Gaelic college in the Highlands.

In 1933 An Comunn's president, the Rev. Neil Ross, suggested that a Gaelic lectureship should be created at St Andrews, building on the limited provision at Aberdeen, Edinburgh and Glasgow (see pp. 95–7 above). In a leader the *Glasgow Herald* criticised this suggestion, arguing that 'the present facilities for the teaching of Gaelic [. . .] seem adequate to the country's need' and that 'at the present moment and perhaps for some time to come' emphasis should be on 'consolidating' and 'strengthen[ing] existing provision' (*GH* 1933). In 1936 J. Carmichael Watson, lecturer in Celtic at the University of Glasgow and later Professor of Celtic in Edinburgh, declared that 'it was absurd that in all three Universities where Celtic was taught, the whole of that subject should be entrusted to one man' (*Scotsman* 1936a). Student numbers in the universities remained very low, however: An Comunn's 1936 education survey included the universities and recorded only 36 students in Glasgow, 14 in Edinburgh and none at all in Aberdeen (ACG 1936: 13).[9]

The proposal for the Glasgow Chair was launched in 1937 by the Glasgow University Ossianic Club (The Gaelic Story 2019). In line with the approach taken by An Comunn and the Gaelic League of Scotland, support was sought from supportive 'gentlemen' and the dukes of Argyll, Montrose and Sutherland, among others, agreed to become patrons of the campaign. In a leader in 1937, *The Scotsman* lent its support to the proposal and suggested that a Chair of Celtic would also be appropriate in Aberdeen and possibly St Andrews as well (*Scotsman* 1937b).

By early 1939 £1,100 of the required £25,000 had been raised, but the outbreak of war put a halt to fundraising efforts. In 1943 Glasgow

University Principal Sir Hector Hetherington said there was not enough money to endow a Chair of Celtic at that time but 'that he was sure that sooner or later it would happen' (*GH* 1943a). The Glasgow University Ossianic Club issued a renewed public funding appeal in 1946. Following a substantial donation of £12,500 in 1955, the chair was eventually created in 1956, when Angus Matheson became the first Professor (The Gaelic Story 2019). Following Matheson's untimely death in 1962, Derick Thomson was appointed Professor and went on to become not only the central figure in Gaelic academia but in Gaelic development more generally, described by Donald Meek as 'a colossus of twentieth-century Scotland' (Meek 2012).

The most prominent issue involving further or higher education in the interwar period did not relate to the existing universities, however, but rather to the proposal to create a Gaelic college on the symbolically important island of Iona, where St Columba founded his influential monastery in 563. In 1913 An Comunn had explored the idea of establishing a university college and an agricultural and technical college in the Highlands, but this proposal was not taken forward (Thompson 1986: 39–40). A new proposal was developed from 1923 onwards. An Comunn president Angus Robertson claimed that the college on Iona could become a Gaelic 'Mecca' (*P&J* 1923). Funding of US$10 million – approximately £65 million today – was sought for the project and an American Iona Society was established in New York, which included influential members such as the president of Columbia University, the president of the New York Chamber of Commerce and the editor of *The New York Times*. Robertson visited the United States in 1924 and 1927 to discuss the proposal and on his second visit met with President Calvin Coolidge (*New York Times* 1927). The college was proposed to have twenty-two departments, combining Celtic history, language and literature with more vocational subjects, with residential facilities for five hundred students. As the scale of ambition grew, locations other than Iona were considered, including sites on the West Highland mainland or in Perthshire (Cameron 2017: 15; MacKay 2002: 34–6). The crash of 1929 put a halt to fundraising efforts. In 1931 educationalist Hugh Gunn argued the case for a Gaelic university based in Inverness (Gunn 1931). Various discussions continued for several years, but the plan never materialised.

Another failed initiative in the 1930s involved a plan to develop a folk high school (more akin to a further education college) in the Highlands to train young people 'in a Gaelic atmosphere in an endeavour to promote economic development in the Highlands' (*Dundee Courier and Advertiser* 1938). This would have involved training in modern agricultural methods and other forms of technical education, as well as classes on Gaelic history, literature and music. The concept was taken from Denmark, where such schools were well-established and successful, and was taken forward by Sir Alexander MacEwen (1931: 52). The plan was to open a prototype school on the Isle of Canna, which had been bought by the Gaelic folklorist and activist John Lorne Campbell. But An Comunn decided against providing funding for the scheme, on the grounds that Canna was too remote a location for the school to be viable (*Scotsman* 1939a), and the plan fell into abeyance with the outbreak of war.

GAELIC IN THE PUBLIC SECTOR

In addition to its work involving education and culture, in the interwar period An Comunn continued to campaign to improve the position of Gaelic in public life, particularly in relation to the appointment of Gaelic speakers to judicial and administrative posts in the Gàidhealtachd. These efforts bore little fruit. In 1930 An Comunn submitted a formal memorial to the Scottish Secretary and the Lord Advocate urging them to issue regulations to 'ensure that in the Gaelic-speaking areas of Scotland it will be a condition of the appointment of Judicial and quasi-Judicial officers that they should be persons who can speak the Gaelic language' (ACG 1930: 4). An Comunn argued that there were many parties and witnesses in legal cases who could not speak English, or could not speak it well, or who felt that they could 'express themselves with greater accuracy in Gaelic' (ACG 1930: 2). The Scottish Office rejected the memorial summarily, asserting that 'it is not practicable to give effect thereto'; although An Comunn's representations would be kept in mind when making future appointments, it was made clear that 'the Secretary of State must not be regarded as committing himself to the view that the lack of a knowledge of Gaelic on the part of the Judges and the officers of Court is prejudicial to the due administration of justice in Gaelic-speaking areas' (SO 1930b).

An internal Scottish Office minute noted the refusal of similar requests to the Lord Advocate in 1893 and 1895, and the negative views of sheriffs expressed in response to concerns about trials conducted in English in Stornoway in 1910 and in Lochmaddy in 1927 (SO 1930a). The Lochmaddy trial had attracted controversy as it involved the conviction of five Gaelic-speaking ex-servicemen who had been involved in a land raid in Scaristaveg, Harris, one of several such incidents following the end of the First World War. The forced use of English at their trial was raised in Parliament by Neil MacLean, Labour MP for Glasgow Govan, who asked the Scottish Secretary, Sir John Gilmour, 'when future appointments as sheriffs are made in the Highlands, to arrange that a knowledge of Gaelic will be one of the qualifications'. Gilmour rejected the proposal, claiming that there was 'no evidence that [such] a requirement [. . .] would be justified on the ground that there is any considerable number of people in the Highlands who know only Gaelic' (Hansard 1927).

The issue of court practice arose again in 1935 when a sheriff in Stornoway rebuked four witnesses who requested interpreters despite having what he considered 'a perfect command' of English (*Scotsman* 1935). The controversy prompted a resolution by An Comunn and a question in Parliament but once again did not lead to any action on the part of the authorities (*Courier and Advertiser* 1935). The issue of the use of Gaelic in court was to be raised again in the 1960s, as discussed below (pp. 153–4), but again to no effect.

Following the adoption of the *Education (Scotland) Act 1918*, Inverness-shire County Council stipulated that a knowledge of Gaelic would be required for its education authority's new Chief Executive Officer, but a similar proposal was narrowly defeated in Argyll. In the other Highland counties it was merely recommended that applicants have Gaelic (Thompson 1992: 46). An Comunn again drew attention to the issue of public appointments in its 1936 report on the teaching of Gaelic in schools and colleges, which included a recommendation that 'a knowledge of Gaelic should be required of officers in the public service in Gaelic-speaking areas' (ACG 1936: 11). In 1937 controversy broke out in relation to the appointment of a new Director of Education in Inverness-shire. Although a knowledge of Gaelic had been required when the post was filled in 1919 (Thompson 1992: 46), the Education Committee rejected an amendment by the Rev. Neil Ross (one of the committee members as well as president of An Comunn) to make it a 'strong recommendation' that applicants have a knowledge of Gaelic rather than a mere 'recommendation' (*Scotsman* 1937a). Ross later unsuccessfully attempted to block the appointment of a non-Gaelic speaker to the post (*Scotsman* 1937e).

An Comunn and other Gaelic activists also made limited efforts to push the government to make official publications available in Gaelic. In 1936 An Comunn wrote to the Ministry of Transport asking for the Highway Code to be made available in Gaelic, noting that there were over seven thousand people in Scotland with no English, but the request was rebuffed (*Scotsman* 1936a). During the Second World War, no Gaelic poster 'to silence dangerous gossip' was produced in connection with the government's public information campaign, ostensibly due to lack of demand (*Daily Record* 1940). Activists such as Compton MacKenzie pressed the case for the official use of Gaelic, writing in 1936 that 'there is the imperative need of taking practical measures, not merely for the preservation, but for the advancement of Gaelic. We do not intend to rest until every official communication in the Outer Isles is printed in Gaelic and in English' (MacKenzie, 1998 [1936]: 25). These demands were consistently ignored by the authorities, however, and no unrest ensued.

THE DEVELOPMENT OF GAELIC BROADCASTING

Broadcasting emerged as a new field of development and controversy for Gaelic in the interwar period, and the issue of media provision has been important for Gaelic language development ever since. Perhaps surprisingly, provision for Gaelic began very soon after the establishment of the British Broadcasting Corporation; the first Gaelic radio broadcast, a sermon by the Rev. John Bain, was made in December 1923, only thirteen months after the corporation's first English broadcast. In the early years, much of the Gaelic output consisted of songs 'dominated by Kennedy-Fraser material and by the influence of the Mòd', presented in English and aimed primarily at an urban, English-speaking audience (MacPherson 2003: 256). The Gaelic programmes were broadcast from Lowland cities, mainly Glasgow, and much of the Highlands and Islands did not receive an adequate radio service in the early decades, due to geography and limits on the network of transmitters, although these problems had been overcome by the 1940s ([Murchison] 1946).

Over time the range of Gaelic radio programming grew more diverse. The first regular programme entirely in Gaelic was *Sgeulachdan agus Orain* (Stories and Songs). In 1933 the first Gaelic play, *Dùnach*, was broadcast, and drama became an important element of the Gaelic radio programming in the years that followed. In 1934 Gaelic lessons were introduced, initially on a weekly basis and then fortnightly, an initiative that signalled that interest in Gaelic extended beyond the native-speaking community. The BBC's Programme Director in London had initially expressed opposition to this proposal, stating that it was 'better not to do anything which would stimulate the spread of "native" languages at a time when we are doing all we can for the English language' (Brown and Uribe-Jongbloed 2013: 9). In 1936 a series of programmes on Gaelic poets was broadcast, along with the series *Am Measg nam Bodach*, which involved a variety of speakers from different areas of the Gàidhealtachd discussing local folklore and tradition, which led to the publication of an accompanying book (ACG 1938b). A weekly news bulletin was introduced in 1937 and Gaelic commentary on shinty matches followed in 1938 (BBC 1939: 10).

In 1938 the BBC established a Gaelic Department and appointed Hugh MacPhee as the BBC's first Gaelic assistant. Production and transmission of the Gaelic programming shifted from Aberdeen to Glasgow, where the headquarters of the BBC in Scotland was and still is located. In 1939 the output was increased to fifty-five minutes per week (Thompson 1992: 53). In 1940 An Comunn requested an increase of output to two news programmes and a children's programme each week. This was refused, which resulted in questions being raised in the House of Commons. By 1944, output had been reduced to forty-five minutes per week, as against two hours and fifty-five minutes for Welsh (MacCurdy 1944: 42). The disparity between provision for Gaelic and Welsh would become greater, and more controversial, in the 1960s and beyond. Gaelic programmes were often broadcast late in the evening, an unpopular slot given the largely agricultural employment of much of the Gaelic-speaking audience (*Daily Record* 1944).

As early as 1946, the value of Gaelic broadcasting for Gaelic language development was noted. The Rev. T. M. Murchison, editor of *An Gaidheal*, praised the value of the BBC radio service in terms of providing access to high-register Gaelic, spreading new terminology and allowing listeners to become familiar with other dialects ([Murchison] 1946, 1950). These impacts would becoming more significant in later decades as provision expanded (see pp. 226, 272 and 315).

CONCLUSION

The interwar period appears as a kind of interregnum in terms of Gaelic policy, in which the overwhelming social and economic challenges involving underdevelopment, unemployment and depopulation in the Gàidhealtachd worked to preclude significant advances on behalf of the language. Activists' disappointment concerning the less than vigorous implementation of the 'Gaelic clause' in the *Education Act 1918* must be understood against this background.

Although An Comunn was continually criticised for not engaging with social and economic questions, it is not obvious that a different strategy on the part of the organisation would have brought better outcomes. As Murchison argued in 1949, An Comunn was 'the only body concerned with Gaelic in a big way', while there were a number of other organisations with more specific expertise that were attempting to deal with the political, economic and social affairs of the Gàidhealtachd. Had it widened its remit, An Comunn might have achieved less on the language front without making an effective impact on social and economic policy (*AG* 1949: 159). Issues of Highland development attracted ever more attention from policy-makers in the following decades, but it was not until the 1970s that a more effective linkage was made between Gaelic language promotion and the socio-economic development of the Gàidhealtachd, as discussed in chapter 7 (pp. 234–6).

5

Stirrings, 1945–74

IN THE PERIOD FOLLOWING the Second World War there were significant changes in the dynamics of Gaelic activism against a background of far-reaching social, cultural and political change in Scotland, developments which were often international in their scope. Scotland as a whole, and the Gàidhealtachd in particular, became increasingly absorbed in wider British administrative structures as the central state expanded its reach through important UK-wide institutions such as the National Health Service. At the same time, however, from the 1960s there was a renewed emphasis on Scotland's political and cultural distinctiveness, and within this Gaelic came to receive greater attention and respect. Important steps were taken to modernise the Highland economy in these decades, and development policy increasingly involved high-level regional planning structures and strategies. Compared to the pre-war period, the Gaelic movement became more connected to its grassroots in the core Gaelic areas, and activists from these social backgrounds came to assume positions of institutional and cultural leadership. Wider international developments, such as new understandings of human rights in general and minority rights in particular, also played an important role in helping Gaelic advocates analyse their situation and frame their demands.

There was significant progress in relation to Gaelic education in these decades, as the SED signalled a more favourable view of Gaelic at the national level, education authorities in the Gàidhealtachd took preliminary steps to introduce bilingual education and some urban authorities began to offer Gaelic in their schools for the first time. Gaelic organisations also secured a few concessions from the government in terms of the public role of Gaelic. Although demands for systematic bilingualisation were resisted, the government began to provide direct funding to promote Gaelic development initiatives, beginning a policy trajectory that would accelerate dramatically in the 1980s.

CHANGING CULTURAL CONTEXTS

Various wider developments in Scottish culture in the post-war decades had an impact on the Gaelic movement and worked to generate more favourable perceptions of Gaelic in the wider Scottish society. Some of the more important developments came in the early 1970s and contributed to the sense of energy and empowerment of the post-1975 period, as discussed in the next chapter.

An important folk music revival developed in Scotland from the 1950s onwards, influenced by similar movements in England and the United States. This movement brought renewed attention to the wealth of Scotland's cultural heritage and the risks of loss. Although this revival had a Gaelic dimension from the outset, Gaelic music did not play a particularly prominent role overall (M. MacLeod 1996; Munro 1991: 139–45) and there was no significant emergence of political song-making in Gaelic in the 1960s and 1970s, as was the case with Welsh (Thomas 1971: 14–15) or indeed Scots. The most important contribution to Gaelic cultural and political awakening came from the group Runrig, formed in 1974 and discussed in the next chapter (p. 177).

The post-war period also saw increased attention to Gaelic culture and folk tradition, with a new emphasis on authenticity and 'unimproved' material, in strong contrast to the reworkings of Marjory Kennedy-Fraser earlier in the century (see p. 67). The short-lived Folklore Institute of Scotland, established in 1947, set the stage for the School of Scottish Studies, founded at the University of Edinburgh in 1951, which launched a large-scale field collection programme, much of it in the Gàidhealtachd (Cheape 2014; Mackay 2013). A number of important collections of songs, stories and folklore gathered from tradition-bearers in Gaelic communities were published during this period (e.g. Campbell 1936, 1939; Craig 1944, 1949; Shaw 1955).

It is significant, however, that this wave of collection and preservation activity coincided with social changes in Gaelic communities that worked to bring about the slow disappearance of the key contexts for the creation and transmission of traditional cultural material (Challan 2012; MacAilpein 2017). The *cèilidh*-house tradition had effectively dissipated, as had the practices of waulking the tweed and transhumance (the use of shielings for the summer pasturage of animals). The collecting work of the 1950s and 1960s may thus be best understood as a form of 'salvage' rather than as part of a project of revitalisation (MacDonald 2011).

New understandings of Scottish history, and the experience of the Gaels within it, also came to the fore in this period. The most influential popular historian was John Prebble, whose books on Culloden, the Clearances and the Glencoe massacre helped build an increased sense in the wider Scottish population that the decline of Gaelic was the result of historical injustice, even if academic historians found Prebble's works 'uncritical, emotive and polemical' (Burnett 2011: 31). John Lorne Campbell's *Gaelic in Scottish Education and Life*, first published in 1945 and revised in 1950, gave a trenchant history of the marginalisation of Gaelic through the centuries.[1] This was the first work of its kind and helped inspire radical interpretations in the subsequent decades, including Kenneth MacKinnon's influential *The Lion's Tongue* of 1974. In the late 1960s and 1970s, Gaelic began to receive considerable attention in the radical political and cultural journals that flourished during this period, building an awareness of Gaelic issues among a wider readership in Scotland (Paterson 2011).

The establishment of the radical campaigning newspaper the *West Highland Free Press* in Skye in 1972 was another important development. The *Free Press* (known as the 'Pàipear Beag' ('Wee Paper') in Gaelic) gave extensive coverage and strong backing to Gaelic from its inception, even if very little of its content was actually written in Gaelic. With the exception of the short-lived *Crùisgean* (1977–80), the same was true of the various community newspapers that were set up in the Western Isles in the 1970s, which tended to have Gaelic titles but very little Gaelic content (GRG 1982: 46). This pattern was very different from that seen in Wales, where a large network of Welsh-language community newspapers have played an important role in reinforcing language maintenance (Davies 2014: 136).

INITIATIVES IN HIGHLAND DEVELOPMENT

The issue of Highland development continued its prominence in the post-war period and by the end of the 1960s the regional economy had been placed on a much stronger footing. In 1943 the government established the North of Scotland Hydro-Electric Board, which introduced a major programme of electrification in the Highlands and Islands, and then in 1947 it created the Advisory Panel on the Highlands and Islands. In 1950 the Labour government published a *Programme of Highland Development*, which emphasised the importance of developing transport infrastructure and basic services and encouraging agriculture, forestry, fisheries and tourism, exploiting natural resources and promoting manufacturing (Scottish Home Department 1950: 21–2). In 1954 the report of the Royal Commission on Scottish Affairs included an extensive discussion of Highland development (Royal Commission 1954); although the Conservatives had returned to power in 1951 they continued the same broad approach to the 'Highland problem' that had been set out in the 1950 programme (Burnett 2011: 120). Also in 1954, a Commission of Enquiry into Crofting Conditions, chaired by Sir Thomas Taylor, published its report (Department of Agriculture 1954), which led to the creation of a new Crofters Commission with powers to guide the strategic development of the crofting sector. In 1959 the government published a *Review of Highland Policy* (SO 1959). None of these important official policy documents made any direct reference to Gaelic; as had been the case before the war, language maintenance was simply not an explicit objective within economic development strategy during this period.

These discussions culminated in the government's decision to establish a Highlands and Islands Development Board, which began work in 1965. The agency was created under the *Highlands and Islands Development (Scotland) Act 1965*, which made no reference to Gaelic, in marked contrast to counterpart Irish legislation of this period, the *Gaeltacht Industries Act, 1957*, which established a development agency, Gaeltarra Éireann, whose specified duties included 'an obligation to encourage the preservation and extension of the use of Irish as a vernacular language' (s. 4(2)). Although HIDB would go on to play an extremely important role in Gaelic development in the late 1970s and 1980s, as discussed in the next chapter, in its early years of operation its principal emphasis was on the development of 'growth poles' in the more urbanised parts of the Highlands, especially the Moray Firth area and Lochaber (Pedersen 2019: 51). There was a particular focus on large industrial facilities, including an aluminium smelter in Invergordon in Easter Ross (Lotz 1969). This approach aligned with the regional development strategy that was being implemented for Scotland as a whole at this time, which sought to develop large industrial operations such as steel production and car manufacturing (Cameron 2010: 276–7). Conversely, the development of the more outlying (and strongly Gaelic) areas of the Gàidhealtachd received less attention from HIDB, so that economic underdevelopment and out-migration continued.

Gaelic itself was no priority for the HIDB in its early phase. The first chair of the Board, Sir Robert Grieve, took the view that Gaelic was a relic that retarded the development of the region, telling An Comunn officials in 1966 that 'the rot had gone too far' to make revitalisation efforts viable (HIDB 1966b: 12). Grieve warned that any 'determined effort' by An Comunn to institutionalise Gaelic in the courts and public administration in the Highlands would deter potential investors from the region (HIDB 1966b: 2). Grieve's views can be understood as a typical modernist understanding of the role of minority languages in the economy (Walsh 2011), yet HIDB's approach was different from contemporary initiatives in the Gaeltacht in Ireland, where the language issue always had some prominence given that the Gaeltacht was specifically defined in linguistic terms.

From 1966 onwards, however, HIDB did make a number of grants to An Comunn to support Gaelic development, beginning with a 'social grant' of £990 to help establish a Gaelic Information Centre near Inverness (HIDB 1966a). From the late 1970s, HIDB became much more supportive of Gaelic initiatives, and indeed the organisation was to play a critical role in the transformative developments of the early 1980s (see pp. 192–5).

CENSUSES AND SURVEY RESULTS

Most commentators on the sociolinguistic situation of Gaelic in the immediate post-war period expressed pessimism about its long-term prospects. In 1948 D. F. Mackenzie wrote that 'nothing short of a miracle will prevent the disappearance of spoken Gaelic from Scotland within the next sixty years'. Ten years later, Finlay J. MacDonald, co-founder of the journal *Gairm*, concurred, predicting that 'Gaelic will be dead as a spoken language in fifty years from now' (Mackenzie 1948: 63; MacDonald 1958: 15). But John Macdonald, Reader in Celtic at the University of Aberdeen, challenged these 'wise prognosticators' and their 'false prophesying', asserting 'that in every area to-day there is a return to Gaelic' (Macdonald 1957).

In 1948 a major study of public attitudes in Scotland included a question concerning views on Gaelic ([Drever] (1948). Respondents were asked to what extent they agreed with the proposition that 'it is a good thing that the Gaelic[2] in Scotland is dying out'. Of all the respondents, 24 per cent agreed, 55.6 per cent disagreed and 20.4 per cent had no opinion. The proportion of those disagreeing was much higher in the north of Scotland (78 per cent). Outright hostility to Gaelic would of course explain some respondents' agreement with this harsh proposition, but another interpretation is that the disappearance of Gaelic was perceived by many people as a marker of modernisation, economic progress and the end of rural isolation and backwardness. As discussed below (pp. 279–80), more recent surveys, conducted in 1981 and from 2003 onwards, show much more favourable public attitudes to the language (MacKinnon 1981; Market Research UK 2003; West and Graham 2011; Paterson and O'Hanlon 2015).

While the census of 1961 recorded a continuing decline in the number of Gaelic speakers, from 95,447 in 1951 to 80,004 in 1961, the 1971 census showed an increase of over 10 per cent, up to 88,415 (General Register Office 1975: ix). This was the only occasion an increase has been indicated since 1891. However, this rise was based entirely on increasing numbers in Lowland areas, and most commentators attributed this growth to the more favourable cultural climate for Gaelic, which might have encouraged more urban Gaelic learners and a greater propensity for migrants from Gaelic areas to 'remember' their Gaelic abilities (MacKinnon 1978: 7; Thomson 1981: 10). Speaker numbers in the main Gaelic areas continued the long-standing pattern of decline, falling by 12 per cent in Ross & Cromarty, Inverness-shire and Argyll (General Register Office 1975: ix). In retrospect, the 1971 increase can be seen as a false dawn, but at the time it served as something of a boost to morale for Gaelic activists.

As noted earlier), the 1971 census returned only 477 monoglots, and subsequent censuses removed the 'Gaelic only' option from the language question. It also asked about Gaelic reading and writing skills for the first time (see p. 124), thus providing additional data that could be taken into account in language planning strategies.

NEW PATTERNS OF CULTURAL LEADERSHIP

Scholars have attributed an important role to the native intelligentsia in the minority rights movements that emerged in numerous countries in the post-war period, pointing to 'their self-defined mission-destiny' and ability to focus and mobilise the aspirations of the community (Williams 1999: 267). This factor was clearly evident in the Gaelic context. In the 1950s the key development was the establishment of the quarterly journal *Gairm* in 1952. *Gairm* was to run for fifty years, making it by far the longest-running Gaelic publication ever. Although the focus of the journal was increasingly literary in its later years (Meek 2013b), *Gairm* provided a very important forum for the discussion – in Gaelic – of political and cultural issues affecting the Gaelic community, including issues of language development and language policy. This was increasingly the case from the mid-1960s onwards, when more 'radical and controversial' contributions began to appear (D. J. MacLeod 1970: 510 n. 67).

Underpinning this shift, the literary revival that began in the 1940s, with Sorley MacLean and Derick Thomson as key figures, helped to create the intellectual culture that provided a foundation for progress. According to Donald John MacLeod, the literary revival 'encouraged the rising post-war generation of university-educated Gaels to conclude that Gaelic was not a thing of the past but very much a language of their time with which they wanted to be involved' (MacLeòid 2011: 51). MacLeod characterised this new group as 'highly intellectual, paradoxically nativistic and cosmopolitan', and very different from the established leadership of An Comunn (D. J. MacLeod 1969: 49). The authorities were aware of the changing dynamics; in 1966, for example, a Scottish Office civil servant was alert to the possibility of 'trouble from very articulate academic and literary quarters' if the question concerning Gaelic ability were to be removed from the 1971 census (SO 1966c).

In the later 1960s there were increasing tensions between the rising generation of Gaelic intellectuals and the urban Gaelic establishment of An Comunn and the Gaelic associations. Writing in 1966, poet and academic Donald MacAulay criticised the urban leadership, noting that it was at once assimilationist and resistant to cultural innovation that did 'not coincide with or promote its "ideals"' of a static Gaelic homeland 'or, indeed, recognise its self-appointed role as guardian of Gaelic culture' (MacAulay 1966: 137). Most of the new generation of writers, including MacAulay himself and Derick Thomson, had left the Hebrides for the cities and the role of the exiled intellectual became an important theme in their work. Notably, the leading writers of the period were often profoundly hostile to the social role of the Presbyterian churches (Meek 2002).

In an important manifesto-like lecture entitled 'The Role of the Writer in a Minority Culture' (1964), Thomson described how certain activists

> are anxious to strengthen many aspects of the Gaelic society: to strengthen, for example, the language by using it [. . .] in as wide a range of situations as possible, and by adding to its range and flexibility; to strengthen the educational provision in Gaelic; to strengthen the sense of local responsibility and initiative; to strengthen the Gaelic musical tradition, and so on. . . .

This included a particular obligation for the politically engaged Gaelic writer:

> There must be a greater than ordinary degree of effort, of dedication, of fervour even on the part of the writers, than would be required within a majority culture, with its readier media of publication and its quicker and more generous rewards for the writer. In all these instances, although in varying degrees, the minority culture gathers strength, and feels in itself an increase in prestige, as new work is completed. One often senses, among writers in such a situation, a feeling of common responsibility and pride in the work they are doing. The role of the writer acquires some extra-literary characteristics. He feels that he is helping in a work of rebuilding, and that his contribution will not ultimately be judged in isolation but as part of a communal effort, as the masons and joiners who took part in the rebuilding of the Abbey at Iona, while taking pride in their individual tasks also shared the vision of a completed building, and the satisfaction of taking part in a kind of crusade. I do not think that it is over-fanciful to see the work of writers in a minority culture as a kind of crusade, although no doubt we should also be conscious of the dangers of such an attitude. (Thomson 1964–6: 267–8)

In different ways, Thomson's vision of political and cultural engagement was also applicable to the activists of the 1970s and 1980s, whose work helped build the structure of modern Gaelic development, as discussed in the next chapter.

GAELIC AND THE NATIONAL QUESTION

From the mid-1960s onwards, a different group of activists began to reassert claims about the centrality of Gaelic to Scottish culture and identity and to challenge deeply rooted beliefs about the lack of connection between Gaelic and the Lowlands. Among those pressing these claims, which echoed the arguments made by Erskine of Marr and others earlier in the century, were the London-based activist Seumas Mac a' Ghobhainn and William Neill, who became a prominent poet in Scots as well as Gaelic. As before, activists of this stripe tended to be learners of Gaelic from outside the Gàidhealtachd. A typical argument in this vein was that most Scots 'have been successfully alienated from their own language', and 'deprived [. . .] of any knowledge of their cultural identity', as the novelist Fionn MacColla argued in 1975 (MacColla 1975: 9). Mac a' Ghobhainn, the most prolific of these activists, was inclined to particularly militant rhetoric, speaking of the need for 'fanatics for the language' and 'cultural freedom fighters' (Mac a' Ghobhainn 1969).

As with earlier claims of this kind these arguments in support of Gaelic had relatively little impact, and Gaelic continued to play a very minor role in national politics, notwithstanding the wider growth of

Scottish nationalism during this period. The SNP began to emerge as a significant force in Scottish politics from the early 1960s onwards and especially from 1967, when Winnie Ewing won a parliamentary by-election in Hamilton. In 1970 the party won its first seat at a General Election, when Donald Stewart was elected for the Western Isles. The party's major electoral breakthrough came in the General Elections of February 1974, when it won seven seats, and October 1974, when it won eleven seats and received almost a third of the popular vote (Lynch 2013).

From the late 1940s to the late 1960s the SNP had paid very little attention to Gaelic, but it began to address the language issue more frequently from the late 1960s onwards. SNP MPs, especially Stewart, began to raise parliamentary questions concerning Gaelic matters with some regularity, yet even so, some Gaelic activists in the 1970s decried the party's lack of commitment to the language and criticised perceived hostility among some of its members (MacColla 1975; Thompson 1971–2: 946; Thompson 1978). In 1978 the SNP adopted a Gaelic policy for the first time; this provided for the use of Gaelic in a range of bills and regulations and official documents of various kinds, greater accommodation of Gaelic in the courts, and the expansion of Gaelic education (SNP 1978).

The issue of 'devolution' – the proposed creation of a legislative assembly in Edinburgh with powers over certain specified matters – dominated Scottish politics in the 1970s, but the Gaelic issue was quite invisible within these debates. In 1978 historian Jack Brand could write that the average Scottish Nationalist would not have known that the language question existed (Brand 1978: 15), while the leading Labour Party advocate of devolution, John P. Mackintosh, asserted categorically that language was 'not a factor' in Scottish 'national feeling' (Mackintosh 1974).

GAELIC AND POLITICAL SECTS

From the late 1960s some elements in the radical left in Scotland began to take an increased interest in Gaelic as part of a more favourable (if sometimes ideologically incoherent) attitude towards nationalist symbolism in Scotland. This shift was part of a wider ideological strategy emerging in this period through which cultural distinctiveness was deployed for its potential counter-hegemonic value in the anti-capitalist struggle (Scothorne and Gibbs 2018: 170–1). For example, the Workers' Party of Scotland (Marxist-Leninist), founded in 1967, published several pro-Gaelic articles in its paper *Scottish Vanguard* ('Fingal' 1967–8) and issued a Gaelic translation of 'Three Constantly Read Articles' by Mao Tse-tung. In 1975 the Scottish Workers Republican Party declared official status for Gaelic to be an essential plank in their manifesto (F. MacThòmais 1975: 5).

Certain fringe nationalist organisations also began to adopt Gaelic names around the same time. In the early 1970s Inverness architect William Bell formed a new party, 'Fine Gaidheil', with the stated aim of improving the status of Gaelic. As one of six defendants charged with conspiracy to rob banks, destroy power supplies and steal arms and explosives in support of the 'Scottish Army of the Provisional Government', Bell attempted to take his oath in Gaelic, but was rebuffed by the judge (*Daily Record* 1975). The campaigning group Comunn na Cànain Albannaich (discussed below, pp. 150–1) denounced Bell and the use of violence in support of the Gaelic cause (MacAoidh 1975a). Another republican extremist, Adam Busby, founder of the Scottish Republican Socialist Party, established An Comunn Albannach in 1977, which issued a manifesto 'For a Gàidhlig Scotland', which declared 'the Scottish (a' Ghàidhlig) language' to be 'the vehicle of the continuity of national existence' and sought to 'restore' it 'to its former position as the official and vernacular language in use throughout Scotland'. It 'utterly reject[ed]' the role of Scots, 'condemn[ing] the activities' of Scots language activists who were 'attemp[ting] to foist an English provincial identity on the Scottish nation' (An Comunn Albannach 1977). An Comunn Albannach did not appear to have had any genuine organisational existence, let alone any impact on Gaelic policy, but Busby went on to become involved in the Scottish National Liberation Army, which was responsible for a number of letter-bombing incidents in 1982–3 (Dinwoodie 1993).

The best-known extremist nationalist group was Sìol nan Gaidheal ('Seed of the Gael'), which had its origins 'as an Ultra-Nationalist reaction to the frustrations of the great devolution debate' of the late 1970s (Sìol nan Gaidheal n.d. (a)). Having gone through different incarnations, the organisation continues to exist and to maintain a website but now has a low public profile. Sìol nan Gaidheal expressed very strong support for Gaelic, characterising the language as 'a true expression of Scottishness [. . .] without [which] we cease to be Scots in the truest possible sense' (Sìol nan Gaidheal n.d. (b)).

All of these organisations highlighted Gaelic for essentially ideological reasons, for its perceived symbolic value within a wider nationalist vision, and did little if anything in terms of programmatic campaigning for the language. It is notable that none of them appear actually to have used Gaelic in their publications or membership activities. Mainstream Gaelic organisations and campaigners generally paid little attention to these organisations, which had minimal political impact in any event.

MINORITY RIGHTS AND SMALL NATIONS: THE INTERNATIONAL CONTEXT

The period from the late 1950s onwards into the 1970s witnessed the international phenomenon known as the 'ethnic revival' (Smith 1981; Fishman et al. 1985). Marginalised ethnic and (sub-)national groups asserted their identity more forcefully and presented rights claims of different kinds. These movements were often interpreted as a reaction to 'the homogenizing and de-personalizing tendencies of industrialization and urbanization' in the post-war period (Lotz 1969: 385). In the Gaelic context, An Comunn director Donald John MacKay expressed concern in 1968 about how 'rootless industrialised society racked on the economic treadmill called progress' was producing 'blandness and conformists' (Thompson 1968: 12). The situation of Gaelic in the post-war period does not sit particularly comfortably within the conventional paradigm of the ethnic revival, however. It is easier to use this framework to account for the changing situation of Welsh, where the language rights campaigns of the 1950s gathered momentum from the early 1960s and prompted a series of concessions from the authorities, shifts that aligned with the electoral rise of the nationalist party Plaid Cymru. In the Gaelic case, there were important stirrings from the mid-1960s onwards but it was only from the mid-1980s that there were significant developments in terms of policy. The key difference between the two cases, of course, is the respective position of the two languages in the nationalist movements of Wales and Scotland; as noted earlier, Plaid Cymru always made the Welsh language an important issue in a way that was by no means true of the SNP.

From the mid-1960s Gaelic campaigners began to make their arguments within the context of international law and Europe-wide initiatives to safeguard minority communities and languages. Minority language activists found 'surprise and pleasure in the discovery that so many language groups spread all over Europe were working with problems of common interest' (Hanoa 1969: 9–10). Minority rights in general, and minority language rights more specifically, had begun to receive specific recognition in international law during this period (de Varennes and Kuzborska 2019: 27–32). Chief among these was section

27 of the United Nations' *International Covenant on Civil and Political Rights*, which was adopted in 1966 and entered into force in 1976. This section provides that 'in those States in which ethnic, religious or linguistic minorities exist, persons belonging to such minorities shall not be denied the right in community with the other members of their group, to enjoy their own culture, to profess and practise their own religion, or to use their own language'. International gatherings of minority language communities began to be organised, drawing together activists and intellectuals who learned from each other and drew inspiration from parallel struggles (e.g. Holmestad and Lade 1969). Gaelic campaigners, notably Frank Thompson and Donald John MacKay, took an active role in these networks, particularly through the Celtic League, an inter-Celtic political organisation that was established in 1961 (e.g. Thompson 1963; *Sruth* 1967). An important contribution to these efforts was Peter Berresford Ellis's and Seumas Mac a' Ghobhainn's 1971 book *The Problem of Language Revival*, which analysed the successful revitalisation of twenty languages around the world, mainly in Europe, to help guide 'the Celts and any other people undertaking the task of cultural and linguistic revival' (Ellis and Mac a' Ghobhainn 1971: 9).

Alongside these developments, the academic field of language planning began to develop from the mid-1960s, with landmark contributions from Einar Haugen (1966) and others. Much of this work (e.g. Rubin and Jernudd 1971) focused on the linguistic challenges faced by newly independent states in Africa and Asia that were engaged in post-colonial nation-building, an effort with which the more radical elements among Gaelic activists, such as Frank Thompson, identified strongly. Work on language planning itself built on the foundational work of Charles Ferguson, Joshua Fishman and William Labov in the emerging discipline of sociolinguistics (Spolsky 2010). Taken together, these wider developments all helped to create a more favourable environment for initiatives in support of Gaelic in Scotland.

GAELIC ORGANISATIONS: ACTIVITY AND CRITIQUES

An Comunn remained the principal Gaelic organisation in the postwar period, although the GSL and Comunn na Cànain Albannaich also undertook important campaigning activity at different points. An Comunn's membership increased from 1,479 in 1948 to 3,512 in 1958, and the number of branches had reached sixty-two in 1970, but this nevertheless represented a decline from the pre-First World War peak (ACG 1948: 11; 1958: 9; 1970, 5–9; see p. 62). As in the interwar decades, the organisation continued to attract criticism and blame for every kind of difficulty and disappointment relating to Gaelic (Bannerman 1954; *AG* 1964). This dynamic changed somewhat after 1965 when An Comunn appointed its first full-time director, Donald John MacKay, and entered an important if brief period of modernisation. This appointment became possible as a result of the government's decision to award regular grant funding to the organisation, a significant development discussed below. MacKay had a business background and brought a new spirit and energy to the organisation, making it 'comparatively militant and adventurous' (MacLennan 1966: 68). He was also well-attuned to new ideas and developments in other minority language jurisdictions. Under MacKay's direction, An Comunn began to press the authorities for formal recognition for Gaelic, as discussed below, and put in place a range of new initiatives, including moving the headquarters from Glasgow to Inverness, establishing a Gaelic information centre, producing a range of new publications and merchandise, and pressing the authorities for legal status and other kinds of recognition (*AG* 1966). MacKay resigned at the end of 1969, however, as his 'business-honed management style did not mix well with the ways of a voluntary body run by a complex network of committees and branches' (MacLeòid 2011: 54). The director post was retained, however, and additional funding allowed for the appointment of a deputy director, based in the Western Isles, in 1970 (MacKinnon 1991: 104).

In 1968 An Comunn issued a policy statement clarifying that it had a 'duty' to Gaelic speakers and not simply to the language itself. This included a specific commitment to give attention to the 'social and economic development' of the Gaelic-speaking areas (ACG 1968: 25). It also began to place greater emphasis on the Western Isles as the core of the Gaelic community. An Comunn was also coming into better alignment with the social mainstream of Gaeldom by virtue of the slow disappearance of the aristocratic element which had been prominent in the organisation earlier in the century (*Sruth* 1968).

In the 1960s An Comunn produced an eclectic series of twenty-six 'Highland Information Pamphlets' that demonstrated its somewhat scattershot approach to the promotion of Gaelic language and culture. Some of them dealt with issues involving history and identity but other titles included 'Close-up on Peat', 'Highland Cookery' and 'Highland Weapons' (ACG 1972). More importantly, between 1967 and 1970 An Comunn published a bilingual weekly newspaper, *Sruth*, edited by the activist Frank Thompson, whose content was often critical of the organisation and politically radical in its overall outlook. But like all its predecessors, the paper was not financially viable and proved short-lived.

In 1969 a new campaigning group, Comunn na Cànain Albannaich (the Scottish Language Society) was established. It characterised itself as 'a radical organisation free from the fetters of royal patronage and [. . .] an aura of respectability' (MacLabhruinn 1970: 10). It took its name from the highly successful Welsh Language Society (Cymdeithas yr Iaith Gymraeg), which had been founded in 1962 (Phillips 2004). With the exception of London-based Seumas Mac a' Ghobhainn, the founding members of CNCA were connected to Glasgow University, and the great majority of them were learners of Gaelic (Meek 2011). The objectives of CNCA included the following:

a) – To work for the restoration of Gaelic as the national language of Scotland;
b) – To promote by all means available Gaelic as a medium of instruction in education and to further its use in all aspects of modern life in Scotland;
c) – To co-operate with all Gaelic-based and Celtic-based bodies for the furtherance of the interests of the language. (CNCA [1971a])

Although it proposed direct action and 'radical' measures in some of its public statements, in practice CNCA confined itself to letter-writing and similar low-key tactics. This included a 'campaign of irritation' 'aimed at bringing to official notice the fact that Gaelic, as a language, Gaelic-based culture, and Gaelic speakers are being deprived of their identity and characteristics'. CNCA criticised An Comunn for a supposed 'catalogue of inaction' and for being 'so inward-looking that a splinter group had to be formed to bring the Gaelic cause forward into the light of the present day' (CNCA 1971b). In 1973 CNCA produced a detailed five-year plan for Gaelic, setting out a step-by-step programme of what it described as 'easily attainable goals', ranging from the establishment of Gaelic playgroups and nursery schools in Gaelic-speaking areas to the setting up of local Gaelic radio stations (*Welsh Nation* 1973).

Relations between CNCA and An Comunn, and its new director Norman Burns in particular, grew increasingly fractious. In 1974 Thompson charged An Comunn with 'crimes against Gaelic', and declared that its 'record in the past four years is dismal, compared with the record of work and achievement in the same period when the previous Director was in office' (CNCA 1974). 'Support for CNCA was sporadic and not widespread', however (Ellis 1985: 52); Kenneth MacKinnon (2011) estimated that there were only 20–30 genuinely active members. In particular, the combination of a small membership and geographical dispersal across Scotland (MacIllechiar 2012) meant that any strategy of direct action was unworkable. By 1976 the organisation had been dissolved. It was followed a few years later by new campaigning organisations which proved equally short-lived, a pattern which has continued down to the present, with the most recent arrival being Misneachd in 2016.

Partly in response to pressure from CNCA, An Comunn did produce a policy on Gaelic in 1975. This policy enumerated six 'fundamental rights' in relation to Gaelic, including the rights of Gaelic speakers to 'a full education through the medium of' Gaelic, 'adequate coverage in Gaelic in the mass media', 'planned economic development in the Gaelic speaking areas', 'to deal with all organs of Government, both local and national, in Gaelic' and 'access to the Law in Gaelic'. In addition, 'all Scots' would have 'the right of access to Gaelic culture' (ACG 1975: [2]). An Comunn proposed a regional approach, with the strongest provision in a core 'Gaidhealtachd' area, less extensive provision in a 'Breac [Part] Gaidhealtachd' area and limited provision in Glasgow and Inverness (ACG 1975: [3–5]). In the event, An Comunn's document did not play a significant role in the development of policy on the ground, although it contributed to the newly focused and programmatic thinking concerning Gaelic development that was gathering momentum from the mid-1970s onwards, as discussed in the next chapter.

PUBLIC APPOINTMENTS AND OFFICIAL STATUS

After some decades of dormancy, the issue of the role of Gaelic in public administration gained renewed attention from activists in the 1960s and 1970s. The improved provision made for Welsh during this period – triggered by sustained campaigning activity – was an important inspiration for Gaelic activists, demonstrating the kinds of concessions that linguistic minorities could secure from the public authorities in Britain. The counterpart campaigns and outcomes in Scotland were significantly less dramatic, but the strategic shift that began in this period would eventually bear fruit in the 1980s. Following the Welsh lead, a key demand was formal legal status for the language. Through the 1960s and 1970s, however, the government rejected demands for legal status and other forms of official recognition for Gaelic, and endeavoured to find ways to differentiate the Welsh case.

From 1936 and especially after 1962, the Welsh language movement undertook a range of campaigns and protests and secured a succession of concessions from the authorities. In 1936 three activists, including the writer Saunders Lewis, set fire to a Royal Air Force bombing school at Penyberth in northwest Wales. Protests following their conviction at the High Court in London led to the enactment of the *Welsh Courts Act 1942*, which provided 'that the Welsh language may be used in any court in Wales by any party or witness who considers that he would otherwise be at any disadvantage by reason of his natural language of communication being Welsh' (s. 1). High-profile campaigns of the 1950s drew attention to the language issue. Campaigners fought unsuccessfully to prevent the flooding of the Welsh-speaking village of Capel Celyn in the Tryweryn valley that was to supply water to Liverpool Corporation, and the activists Eileen and Trefor Beasley resisted multiple prosecutions for refusing to pay tax bills that were written in English only (Davies 2014: 113, 120). In 1962 Lewis delivered a radio address, 'Tynged yr Iaith' (The Fate of the Language) (Lewis 1971, 1986), in which he called for 'revolutionary methods' to defend the language, which he warned was at risk of extinction. Lewis's address inspired the creation of Cymdeithas yr Iaith Gymraeg in 1962, which undertook a programme of direct action. This prompted the government to establish a commission in 1963 to assess the legal status of the Welsh language. The commission's report, known as the Hughes Parry Report (Welsh Office 1965), led to the enactment of the *Welsh Language Act 1967*, which expanded the right to use Welsh in the courts beyond what had been allowed under the 1942 Act and authorised the publication of official forms in Welsh.

In the 1950s and early 1960s, the demands and successes of the Gaelic movement were very modest in comparison. In 1955 the GSL, in the context of plans to establish a new Crofters Commission, urged that the new commission include at least one Gaelic-speaking member, and the subsequent *Crofters (Scotland) Act 1955* contained a requirement to this effect, mirroring the provision in the 1886 Act (s. 1(4)).[3] On the other hand, there was no such requirement for the new Highlands and Islands Development Board. During the House of Commons debate on the Highland Development (Scotland) Bill (later enacted as the *Highlands and Islands Development (Scotland) Act 1965*), Scottish Secretary William Ross famously declared that 'for two hundred years the Highlander has been the man on Scotland's conscience' and that '[n]o part of Scotland has been given a shabbier deal by history from the '45 onwards' (Hansard 1965a). It was striking that this 'conscience' was not seen to demand efforts to redress the decline of the Highlander's language as part of the less shabby deal that the government was offering.

In 1953 the Ministry of Defence decided to open a rocket range in South Uist, a plan which involved bringing in a large cohort of English-monoglot military personnel. The proposal provoked considerable controversy, with An Comunn and many activist intellectuals expressing concern about the negative impact the development might have on the culture of the island, which was perceived as perhaps the single most important repository of Gaelic tradition (e.g. *AG* 1955: 114–15; [MacThòmais and MacDhòmhnaill] 1955b; MacDonald 2011). Although the editors of *Gairm* went so far as to describe the rocket range as the greatest threat to Gaelic since Culloden ([MacThòmais and MacDhòmhnaill] 1955a), the issue never became a *cause célèbre* comparable to that of Tryweryn. There were important differences between the two cases in any event: the Uist rocket range did not involve the displacement of local people and actually created positive economic impacts and infrastructural improvements for the island.

Following the publication of the Hughes Parry report, Gaelic organisations began to press for parallel recognition for Gaelic, including different kinds of practical measures in public administration. The first significant push came in late 1965, when Scottish Secretary William Ross responded to a parliamentary question from Malcolm Macmillan MP asking him to appoint a committee to clarify the legal status of Gaelic by indicating that he would be willing to receive representations on the issue (Hansard 1965b). Macmillan's question had been put at the urging of An Comunn, and in February 1966 An Comunn submitted a detailed memorandum to Ross setting out eight proposals for changes in government policy on Gaelic. These included recommendations to make publications and regulations 'for the Gaelic speaking areas' available in Gaelic as well as English; that '[w]herever possible public and official business discussions and correspondence, should be conducted in Gaelic'; that district councils in Gaelic areas should conduct their business bilingually; and that civil servants in Gaelic areas should be bilingual or given 'financial inducements' 'to acquire a working knowledge of' Gaelic (ACG 1966).

Taking the view that questions of cost were more important than any issues of principle, SED officials reacted to these proposals by proposing to 'yield, if at all, in relation to the demands for larger financial subventions for the encouragement of Gaelic', on the grounds that 'concessions in the direction of improving the formal status of Gaelic would be likely to be far costlier than any ad hoc sum that could reasonably be expected for the subsidy of Gaelic publications and the like' (SED 1966). At the subsequent meeting, the government duly rejected An Comunn's principal requests, but agreed to make a direct grant of £5,000 to An Comunn to assist with the Mòd and a separate award of £5,000 to establish a Gaelic books council to support the publication and distribution of Gaelic books.[4] The books council stimulated considerable growth in Gaelic book publishing in the years following, some of them through Club Leabhar, a Gaelic book club which was in operation from 1968 to 1980 and had seven hundred members at its peak (Thompson 1986: 108–9).

In 1969 Parliament enacted the *National Mod (Scotland) Act 1969*, which authorised local authorities to give grants to support the Mòd, as was already permitted in relation to the Eisteddfod in Wales ([Thompson] 1968). The Act appears relatively insignificant in retrospect, but the fundamental principle of public funding for Gaelic remained controversial, so that Labour MP Peter Doig asked 'why should we be boosting up a language which is of its own free will dying out?' (*Irish Times* 1969).

In relation to An Comunn's demand that Gaelic should be granted 'equal validity in legal and administrative matters in the Gaelic-speaking area', Ross took the position 'that changes could only be justified if hardships and injustice could be shown to arise from the existing arrangements'. In this connection he contended that there was little demand for court interpreters from people with limited ability in English (SO 1966b). This was a somewhat skewed interpretation of the evidence the Scottish Office had gathered from court deputes with experience in the Gaelic areas. The Sheriff Clerk Depute for Portree noted that the local procurator fiscal conducted 'between 80 and 90% of his sudden death and fatal accident inquiries in Gaelic, not because the witnesses cannot understand English but because Gaelic is their normal speaking language and on matters of importance they prefer to speak in their native tongue, if given the opportunity' (Mackay 1966).

Although their public statements focused on operational issues, the authorities were well aware that these requests from Gaelic organisations and activists were primarily intended as efforts to elevate the public status of Gaelic rather than to meet the practical needs of non-English speakers (e.g. SO 1970, 1981). In 1966 a civil servant in the Scottish Office argued that questions concerning the knowledge of Gaelic should be retained in the 1971 census on the grounds that 'our defence against inordinate claims for the recognition of Gaelic for public purposes can conveniently be based on present fairly exact information about the extent to which it is spoken' (SO 1966).

In the 1960s and early 1970s officials stuck to a consistent line, rejecting comparison to Wales by pointing to the much larger number of monolingual speakers of Welsh (e.g. SO 1970a). Over time, as monolingual speakers disappeared from the scene in both countries, the argument shifted to a slightly different metric, that of the overall number of speakers. In 1981 the president of An Comunn, Donald MacCuish, wrote to the Scottish Secretary to express 'frustration' that the government's 'facile explanation that the differences in numbers of speakers of' Gaelic and Welsh had become 'stereotyped under successive administrations', with no recognition of the need to deal with minority languages on any more principled basis (ACG 1981b).

As noted above (p. 99), the use of Gaelic in Scottish courts was never prohibited by legislation. Instead, testimony in Gaelic by witnesses and parties was permitted at the discretion of the judge or sheriff. Following the adoption of the *Welsh Language Act 1967*, the government deflected demands for official status for Gaelic on the basis that there was no formal prohibition in Scots law on the use of Gaelic as there had been in relation to Welsh in Wales (e.g. SO 1969). This argument was disingenuous, as the 1967 Act established a fundamentally different policy regime which allowed the free use of Welsh even by parties and witnesses whose 'natural language' was English rather than Welsh. The government's position was conclusively refuted in 1982 when the High Court of Justiciary affirmed a sheriff's order precluding Gaelic activist Iain Taylor from using Gaelic in court (*Taylor* v. *Haughney* (1982); see p. 201 below). Surprisingly, there has been no subsequent push to remove this legal restriction, and the established monolingual principle still holds in all criminal cases and almost all civil cases, with the result that Gaelic continues to have almost no place in the Scottish legal system.

The government adhered to a similar line of argument in relation to demands to grant 'equal validity' with English. Given that there were no explicit statutory limitations on the use of Gaelic, the government asserted that Gaelic already enjoyed 'equal validity' with English, so that legislation establishing its official status would be redundant (SO 1970c). This position has been continually reasserted over the decades. In 2003 constitutional affairs spokesman Lord Evans of Temple Guiting drew the conclusion that Gaelic 'has [...] official status within the United Kingdom' on the basis of the UK's ratification in 2001 of the European Charter for Regional or Minority Languages (discussed on pp. 259–62 below), which 'signalled [the government's] clear commitment to maintain and promote the use of indigenous minority languages across the United Kingdom, including Gaelic' (Hansard 2003).

In response to demands for the production of Gaelic versions of official forms, the government again invoked the small number of Gaelic monoglots and took the position that such provision would not be justified given 'the substantial expenditure involved' (SO 1969). The government continued to adhere to this position in subsequent years, even as it began to issue forms in Welsh and in other languages (such as those for the 1971 census) as a response to the influx of Asian immigrants to Britain from the 1950s onwards (SO 1970a). When An Comunn noted the provision for Asian language speakers, the government distinguished the situation on the grounds that Asian immigrants had only limited English and relatively little contact with English speakers (SO 1973). The only official document published in Gaelic at this time was a summary of the 1961 census results in relation to Gaelic ([Thompson] 1968). Only in the 1980s did the publication of Gaelic versions of public documents become more common, but even then this was haphazard rather than systematic, as discussed below (pp. 202, 294–5).

Another line of argument from the Scottish Office involved the political acceptability of recognition for Gaelic to the English-monoglot majority in Scotland. As one civil servant expressed it in 1970, 'it is considered doubtful whether English speaking Scottish opinion would generally be in favour of a policy involving the introduction, even in the Gaelic speaking areas alone, of mandatory linguistic requirements for the conduct of public business' (Scottish Home and Health Department 1970).

Along with An Comunn, the GSL played an active role as a campaigning organisation from the late 1960s into the 1980s. In 1968 the Society convened a public meeting, addressed by Donald John MacKay and six MPs, which agreed a set of requests to the government concerning the status of Gaelic. These requests included a demand for a parliamentary bill to give Gaelic the same status afforded Welsh under the 1967 Act, for a 'more equitable provision of public funds' in support of Gaelic publishing, culture, education, signage and broadcasting, for the creation of 'a sociological research unit', and for an increase in the use of Gaelic by HIDB, including the appointment of more Gaelic-speaking staff (GSL 1969). These and other related demands would be pressed in a steady stream of correspondence in the years following, but there were no significant concessions from the government.

GAELIC AND ROAD SIGNS

The issue of bilingual road signage also emerged as a significant issue in the early 1970s. Here too Gaelic activists took the lead of Wales. Through the 1960s, the signage issue became intensely controversial, as Cymdeithas yr Iaith Gymraeg campaigned vigorously for Welsh road signs, often adopting the tactic of painting over monolingual English signs (Phillips 2004). In 1972, after almost a decade of agitation, the Bowen Report made the sweeping recommendation that all kinds of traffic signs on all roads in Wales should be bilingual (Committee of Inquiry into Bilingual Traffic Signs 1972). These moves in Wales inspired similar demands from Gaelic activists in relation to Scotland.

The first Gaelic–English bilingual signs had actually been erected in 1954 in Port Charlotte in Islay, as the result of an initiative by the Gaelic League of Scotland, which paid for the signs at no cost to Argyllshire County Council (*GH* 1954), but this did not lead to any wider adoption of the practice. This was not the first time a proposal of this kind had been made; as early as 1910 the Fort William town council considered a suggestion to erect bilingual street signs, but this did not come to fruition (*IC* 1909a, 1909b).

In 1970 the Scottish Office stated that the Scottish Secretary might authorise the erection of bilingual road signs on non-trunk roads 'if a good case can be made out by a local authority' (MacKinnon 1991: 109), but the government was unwilling to grant a blanket authorisation of the kind introduced in Wales (Scottish Home and Health Department 1969). The GSL then wrote to the sixty-four burgh and district councils in the Highlands and Islands urging them to adopt a policy of erecting bilingual road signs and public notices. This initiative met with a cool reception. Ten authorities, most of them in Ross-shire and Sutherland, replied favourably and agreed to adopt (or, in the case of Stornoway, retain) such a policy; eight refused and explained their reasons for doing so (most of them relating to cost); three refused without giving a reason; fourteen merely acknowledged the Society's letter; and twenty-nine did not reply at all (MacKinnon 1974: 93–4; *Scotsman* 1971).

Scottish Office civil servants reacted to developments in Wales by developing strategies to stifle similar moves in Scotland. Prior to the establishment of the Bowen Commission, the Scottish Office was consulted about the possible implications for Scotland of introducing bilingual signage in Wales. One civil servant worried that '[t]here is an obvious danger that the setting up of such a committee will stimulate a demand for a similar committee [. . .] in Scotland', but argued that any such pressure 'can readily be resisted', as there seemed 'little likelihood of a serious demand'. The fact that the GSL's 1970 initiative had 'received very little support and a certain amount of outright opposition' from councils was noted. Given this political calculation, it was felt that there would be 'no difficulty about defending the decision not to set up such a committee [in Scotland] and not to authorise the general use of bilingual English/Gaelic traffic signs' (Scottish Development Department 1971). There was evidence of flexibility from ministers, however; George Younger (who went on to play an important role in supporting Gaelic development in his role as Scottish Secretary in the 1980s (see pp. 195–6)) commented, 'I do not think this sort of matter is something upon which Governments should be dogmatic. If ever there were to be clear evidence that the majority of people in any area wanted signs in Gaelic, I see no reason why they should not be allowed' (SO 1971b).

The most important flashpoint in relation to signage arose in Skye in 1973–4, where Sir Iain Noble, owner of the Fearann Eilean Iarmain estate and founder of the Gaelic college Sabhal Mòr Ostaig (discussed below, pp. 217–19), succeeded in making Inverness-shire County Council erect bilingual signs on the outskirts of Broadford and Portree. Noble's landholdings included the areas on the edge of the two villages and he demanded the erection of bilingual signs as a condition for granting the council an easement to widen the road (*GH* 1973; Hutchinson 2005: 115–19). The convener of the Council, Lord Burton, did his best to resist Noble's demands and became something of a demon figure in Gaelic circles, even being compared by one writer to 'Butcher' Cumberland, leader of the government forces at Culloden (MacFhionghuin 1974: 153).

By 1977 Gaelic signs had appeared not only on roads but at a Department of Employment office in Portree, Forestry Commission land, a hydro-electric substation and several hotels and shops in the islands (MacAoidh 1975b; *Guardian* 1977). Over the following decades, Gaelic was slowly introduced to road signs in various parts of the Gàidhealtachd, especially in the Western Isles and Skye, as discussed below (pp. 182, 270–1, 324). It is notable, however, that in Scotland bilingual road signage has generally been limited to the names of settlements (and occasionally institutions such as hospitals), whereas in Wales, from the early 1970s onwards, all information, including instructions and advisories, has been provided in both languages.

GAELIC EDUCATION: POLICY SHIFTS

In the post-war decades the education authorities gradually began to allow more room for Gaelic within the school system. Formal statements of policy from the SED in the 1950s and 1960s suggested an increasingly favourable view of Gaelic, although the department was not proactive in steering the implementation of change on the ground. In contrast to the improvements in provision in the 1980s and beyond, discussed in subsequent chapters, most of these changes were not driven by external pressure from parents and campaigning organisations, but largely reflected the broader modernisation of Scottish education and changes in educational philosophy, with a growing emphasis on 'child-centred education', a principle embedded in the *Education (Scotland) Act 1945* (O'Hanlon and Paterson 2015: 309–11). The 1945 Education Act (and those of 1962, 1969 and 1980) also retained the obligation introduced in the 1918 Act to make 'adequate and efficient provision' for 'the teaching of Gaelic in Gaelic-speaking areas'.[5] There was no significant public controversy or parliamentary debate concerning the continuation of this obligation, and Gaelic campaigners did not undertake to clarify or strengthen this legal requirement, despite the difficulties that had become apparent in relation to the implementation of the 'Gaelic clause'.[6]

In 1943 An Comunn's Education Committee submitted two memoranda to the Advisory Council on Education for Scotland, setting out recommendations concerning Gaelic education (ACG 1943a, 1943b). An Comunn argued that with improving economic opportunities at home, educational provision in the Gàidhealtachd 'should no longer be based upon the assumption [. . .] that pupils must find their life-work outside the Highlands'. As such it contended that 'at all schools throughout the Highlands it is surely possible and desirable to have all the work conducted in an authentic Gaelic atmosphere'. It is not entirely clear what 'an authentic Gaelic atmosphere' would have entailed; full Gaelic-medium education throughout the Highlands would have involved an immense transformation. An Comunn also urged the extension of Gaelic teaching to 'large Lowland Centres', anticipating that there would be interest from Lowlanders as well as Highlanders and descendants of Highlanders, thereby implying that provision should not be limited to already fluent speakers (ACG 1943a).

An Comunn's second memorandum presented additional proposals and arguments. It suggested that even though 'in many districts Gaelic is not now the speech of the children this is no reason why they should not be taught the language of their parents', arguing that the presence of a minority of English speakers should not be a 'pretext for neglecting the teaching of Gaelic altogether'. In relation to secondary teaching, An Comunn recommended that Gaelic should 'be given equal status with any other language in the curriculum'.[7] This argument was set forth on national grounds: 'the relegation of Gaelic to the precarious position it now enjoys is unworthy of Scotsmen' (ACG 1943b).

In 1946–7 the Advisory Council issued two reports, one dealing with primary education and the other with secondary. The views expressed in the two reports concerning the role of Gaelic in the education system were strikingly different.[8] The report on primary education was couched in highly romantic terms and presented Gaelic as an important element of Scottish culture of relevance to all Scottish schoolchildren:

> The question of Gaelic studies has been too exclusively regarded as affecting only the 'Celtic fringe' of Scotland, and the language that of a scattered and diminishing remnant [...]
>
> We suggest a different attitude. This was the language of the whole land before a word of English was ever spoken in it. Even in the lowlands the great majority of the hills and streams have Celtic names. In varying amounts there must be Celtic blood in most native Scots, though they know not a word of Gaelic [...] People poor in this world's goods, and living somewhat apart from the main stream of civilisation, tend to maintain in their primitive life the dreams and thoughts and arts of an earlier age; and this is true of Gaelic Scotland.
>
> We think it is worth while cherishing this language and culture, not merely for those who are born into it, but for the sake of the rest of Scotland. We therefore recommend that all Scottish children should learn something of Gaelic life and legends and traditions. Some pupils as they grow older may wish to learn the Gaelic language and read its literature; and for those, opportunities at selected schools may one day be provided. As for the Gaelic-speaking areas themselves, we recommend that all possible steps be taken to get an adequate number of Gaelic-speaking teachers and an ample supply of suitable class books and texts in the Gaelic language. (Advisory Council on Education 1946: 80)

In contrast, the report on secondary education expressed a limiting and condescending view of the role of Gaelic and made a sharp distinction between provision for Gaelic-speaking children and the non-Gaelic-speaking majority. The Advisory Council recommended that Gaelic-speaking secondary pupils should give priority to Gaelic over foreign languages, as they could reach a higher level of competence and 'they have a key to a literature which, since it enshrines the experience of their own race, will come home to them with an intimacy of appeal no other could rival' (Advisory Council on Education 1947: 92). The Advisory Council also recommended that every secondary school in a Gaelic-speaking area should have a qualified Gaelic teacher and that 'in large centres, where there is a considerable population of Celtic origin, facilities for learning Gaelic should be available in one school at least' (Advisory Council on Education 1947: 92). But the Council's view of Gaelic provision more generally was much more negative:

> We cannot agree with An Comunn Gaidhealach that Gaelic should have complete parity with other European languages in all the secondary schools

of Scotland. Even were it possible to find all the specialist teachers required [. . .] we think the position untenable for the following reasons:–
(1) For the pupil with no previous knowledge, Gaelic is not easier but much harder than the romance languages [. . .]
(2) The utility value of Gaelic is not high.
(3) While Gaelic literature is rich in appeal for those to whom it is native, it could hardly be claimed that it has either the sustained greatness or the immense range and volume of the European Literatures. (Advisory Council on Education 1947: 92)

The Advisory Council's report compares unfavourably with the counterpart report of this period concerning the teaching of Welsh, which recommended that Welsh be taught to all secondary pupils in Wales, including non-Welsh speakers, a proposal that was duly implemented in all but two Welsh counties (Ministry of Education 1953).

The SED's main policy documents from the early 1950s onwards became steadily more favourable towards Gaelic. Its 1950 memorandum on the primary curriculum expressed a flexible view of Gaelic as a teaching medium:

> With the child whose mother tongue is Gaelic, the teacher should not hesitate to use it in the initial stages of his school life [. . .] In [primary 3 and primary 4], though English is the main medium of instruction, especially in arithmetic, Gaelic can have important auxiliary uses, especially in helping the students to understand what they might find difficult if it were presented in English alone. [. . .] In general, bilingual instruction in the hands of a competent teacher will not only sharpen the pupil's perceptions and develop his intelligence but will also provide him with new interests. (SED 1950: 68–70)

The counterpart memorandum on junior secondary education, published in 1955, was the first SED publication to suggest that the schools should play a role in Gaelic language maintenance (O'Hanlon and Paterson 2015: 309). The document asserted that Gaelic teachers should encourage children 'to regard their own language with respect, to find its study satisfying and rewarding, and to continue its use in the future' and emphasised the role of parents in 'co-operating with the schools in their efforts to preserve the language' (SED 1955: 275). The overall aim was 'to make the pupils completely bilingual' (SED 1950: 274).

From 1951 onwards, the SED's annual reports on education in Scotland also expressed a modernising view of Gaelic teaching, urging 'an emphasis on oral expression and on the use of Gaelic as a medium of instruction' (SED 1951a; 20–1). These recommendations were formalised in the *Schools (Scotland) Code 1956*, which remained in effect until 2005 and which provided that 'in Gaelic-speaking areas reasonable provision shall be made in schemes of work for the instruction of Gaelic-speaking pupils in Gaelic language and literature, and the Gaelic language shall be used where appropriate for instructing Gaelic-speaking pupils in other subjects' (s. 21(3)). This wording involved a significant change from the Code of 1950, which had used the more restrictive phrase 'so far as is necessary' (s. 21(3)) rather than 'where appropriate'.

The SED's 'Primary Memorandum' of 1965, which replaced the 1950 curricular memorandum, expressed the view that '[i]t is the duty of the primary school to maintain and develop Gaelic as a living means of communication and expression'. It advised that schools should 'not only teach the mother tongue as a subject in its own right but also use it functionally when appropriate as a means of instructing Gaelic-speaking pupils in other subjects', particularly in religious education, natural science, local history and local geography (SED 1965: 199, 201). It was further recommended that the teaching of 'reading and number should be in Gaelic until such time as the pupils have gained a working knowledge of English' (SED 1965: 199). The Department declared that '[i]t is important that [. . .] Gaelic should be treated as a living language' and 'that pupils should have the opportunity at all stages of improving their oral proficiency' (SED 1965: 200, 201). A decade later, however, school inspector Murdo Macleod observed that these recommendations 'received less attention than they should have commanded' (Macleod n.d.: 3).

These shifts in policy were not entirely specific to Gaelic; rather, as argued in 1968 by John A. Smith, the North Uist-born Vice-Principal of Jordanhill College, 'the change in official attitude has sprung mainly from a general change in educational outlook affecting not only Gaelic but also all other subjects. This change is based largely on acceptance of the principle that the education of a child should be child centred and not authoritarian' (Smith 1968: 62–3; see O'Hanlon and Paterson 2015: 309–11). Smith took pains to point out that even with these shifts in policy the SED was 'still far removed from the active policy of fully developed bilingualism with literacy in both languages' (Smith 1968: 63). Yet he also conceded that the majority of Gaelic-speaking parents, 'while kindly disposed, are apathetic and some are either secretly or actively hostile' to the teaching of the language' (Smith 1968: 65). Commonly articulated reasons for parental resistance to an increased role for Gaelic during this period included the view that Gaelic was of no practical use outside Gaelic areas, that more attention to Gaelic would divert time from learning English or other subjects, and that Gaelic had already declined too far to make such measures worthwhile (MacLeòid 1960: 252–3).

These small policy moves towards a more favourable treatment for Gaelic articulated with the findings of educational research projects. In 1948 Christina Smith published an important if brief study on mental testing of children in Lewis aged 8, 10 and 12, which concluded that the children performed better when tested in Gaelic than in English and that their general performance was lower than it should have been. She suggested that 'there is a case for making more use of the Gaelic language as a teaching medium in schools in Gaelic-speaking districts' and for 'postpon[ing] the learning of English from age five to a more mature stage'. In her view, the prevailing 'educational methods [...] have precluded the coherent development of the bilingual child's mental capacities' and '[t]he fact that testing in English gives rise to faulty assessments of ability is a serious reflection upon the present educational system' (Smith 1948: 31). As noted earlier, she attributed this inadequate system to the underlying 'tacit assumption' 'that Gaelic-speaking Scots form such a small minority that no special administration is needed' (Smith 1948: 9).

Between 1957 and 1961 the Scottish Council for Research in Education's Committee on Bilingualism conducted a comprehensive survey to assess the scale of Gaelic-speaking by pupils in primary school and the first year of secondary school. Its results were more negative than many had expected (MacDhòmhnaill 1962). The survey found that only 0.6 per cent of Scottish pupils had Gaelic as their first language,[9] but that 15 per cent of pupils in Argyll, Inverness-shire, Ross & Cromarty and Sutherland could speak Gaelic (Committee on Bilingualism 1961: 26). Within these four counties, there were great variations. The survey revealed that on the mainland, 'Gaelic has disappeared as the first language of infants entering school, except in isolated pockets of population in Wester Ross and Ardnamurchan' (Committee on Bilingualism 1961: 25); only 100 of 18,722 mainland pupils were first-language Gaelic speakers (Committee on Bilingualism 1961: 27). In the Argyllshire islands, 19 per cent were first-language speakers, in Skye 51 per cent, while in the Western Isles the proportions ranged between 66 per cent in Lewis[10] and 94 per cent in Harris (Committee on Bilingualism 1961: 29). In relation to the islands, the Committee gave an instructive summary of the dynamics of language shift:

> [T]he process of Anglicisation begins historically round the official centres of transport on the east side of the island opposite the mainland. Thereafter, an English 'pale' develops inland from the bridge or pier head. It may be some

time before the development makes any marked advance inland. This is still true of Stornoway in Lewis [it is also true of Tarbert (Harris), Lochmaddy (North Uist), Lochboisdale (South Uist) and Castlebay (Barra)]. In Skye, on the other hand, as can be seen around Portree and Kyleakin, the development once begun soon spreads. [. . .] Localities [. . .] that were traditionally Gaelic, tend to become anglicised for various local reasons, and then the whole front begins to break up. That process is now nearing completion in Mull and Islay. (Committee on Bilingualism 1961: 31)

The Committee also investigated the use of Gaelic as a teaching medium and the teaching of Gaelic as a subject:

Gaelic is quite often used as a teaching medium. It is often used incidentally by the teacher, especially in the purely Gaelic-speaking areas, in discussion and in the teaching of English reading and English vocabulary, when dealing with those children who come to school with little or no English. It is unlikely to be used as the sole teaching medium except in the teaching of Gaelic itself. Despite all this use of Gaelic, in the majority of schools there is no period definitely set aside for the teaching of Gaelic to these classes [. . .] The average amount of time that is usually given to Gaelic, when it is given, varies, with a few notable exceptions, from 1 to 2 periods a week. (Committee on Bilingualism 1961: 34–5)

This account broadly aligned with that found by An Comunn in 1936, except that a generation later language shift had advanced substantially in many areas.

An important three-day conference on Gaelic education was held at Jordanhill College in 1956. The report of the conference in *An Gaidheal* painted a bleak picture. The position of the language was described as 'desperate' and 'deplorable'; the teaching of Gaelic in the primary school was 'limited, spasmodic and unsystematic'; 'to an increasing extent' secondary teachers 'ha[d] to teach Gaelic from the beginning', with 'less and less [. . .] support of a living culture to maintain and enrich [their] instruction'. Improvements to Jordanhill's training programme were recommended, and the college indicated that it was 'ready to co-operate actively in the bolder, more systematic, and more extensive teaching of Gaelic on an experimental scale in primary schools in the Gaelic-speaking area' (*AG* 1957). This was to lead to the 'Inverness-shire Scheme', discussed below (pp. 168–9).

GAELIC IN LOWLAND SCHOOLS

Until the Second World War the teaching of Gaelic in the schools was confined to the Gàidhealtachd, but limited secondary provision in

Lowland areas began in the 1940s. This was an important development, but it did not lead to a rapid expansion of such provision; fewer than a dozen Lowland schools offered Gaelic before the 1980s.

Although Gaelic had been taught in Glasgow in classes organised by Gaelic organisations, and in continuation classes in the High School of Glasgow from 1888 onwards, teaching at secondary schools began only in 1947, following a formal request to the education authorities by An Comunn in 1943. Both An Comunn and the Gaelic League of Scotland had been pressing for Gaelic teaching in Glasgow and Edinburgh since the early 1930s (*GH* 1930; *Scotsman* 1936c, 1937d, 1939; [Paterson] 1939). Using a questionnaire prepared by the Federation of Highland Associations (Federation of Highland Associations 1945), the Glasgow Corporation Education Department identified 412 Gaelic-speaking pupils in the city's primary schools and a further 211 in the secondary schools (Glasgow Corporation Education Department 1947a). Although preparations had been made to commence Gaelic classes in 1945 (Glasgow Corporation Education Department 1947a), there was an insufficient show of interest from pupils, a shortfall An Comunn attributed to inadequate promotion (ACG 1946). Following 'more intensive publicity work' on the part of An Comunn (*GH* 1947), Gaelic classes began in Bellahouston and Woodside Senior Secondary schools in 1947 and were made available to first- or second-year secondary pupils who were graded A1 (the highest academic level) in the secondary Qualifying Examination (Glasgow Corporation Education Department 1947b). The decision to restrict Gaelic to A1 pupils while allowing all pupils to study French attracted criticism from the GLS (Oscar 1947: 8; *An Ceum* 1948a). Underpinning this policy was a view that Gaelic was an especially difficult language that only the most able pupils could manage to learn. The initiative was not without controversy, however, and a flurry of critical letters to the editor of the *Glasgow Herald* led the paper to express the view that Gaelic teaching should be limited to those of Highland background and not extended to the general Glasgow school population (*GH* 1948b).

Sixty-seven pupils at Bellahouston and Woodside were enrolled on Gaelic classes in 1947–8, and the total roll rose to 148 by 1952. More than two-thirds of the pupils studying Gaelic in 1952 were in the first or second year of secondary school, however, and very few continued to Higher level (Glasgow Corporation Education Department 1952). As early as 1954, the overwhelming majority of the Glasgow secondary pupils were learners rather than native speakers (*AG* 1954: 13). In a polemical lecture to the Gaelic Society of Inverness in 1966, the poet and secondary school headmaster Sorley MacLean lambasted 'the "prominent" Gaels of Glasgow' for failing to enrol their children in these classes, and instead 'act[ing] as we now expect platform Gaels to act' (MacLean 1969: 21).

In 1958 Gaelic was introduced at a school in Edinburgh and a school in Greenock. For 56 of the 89 first-year secondary pupils studying Gaelic that year (including 30 of the 31 Edinburgh pupils), neither parent spoke Gaelic ([MacThòmais] 1957a; Committee on Bilingualism 1961: 76).

Significant as these developments in Lowland Scotland were, they paled in comparison to contemporary developments in Wales, where the first public Welsh-medium primary school opened in 1947, in Llanelli, to be followed by twelve more Welsh-medium schools by 1951 (Davies 2014: 124). Education through the medium of Gaelic would not begin until 1985 and the first Gaelic-medium school would not open until 1999, as discussed in the next chapter.

Gaelic classes were also made available for primary pupils at two Glasgow secondary schools, and Saturday sessions were organised for nursery pupils at the Highlanders' Institute (MacKinnon 1991: 92). In 1964 Gaelic was introduced to three primary schools in Glasgow and then later extended to a further six (ACG 1964: 19; [R. MacThòmais] 1985). But this programme was never rolled out extensively in the city's schools and proved short-lived. Gaelic was also introduced in some primary schools in Inverness, Aberdeen and Stirling in 1966–7 (AG 1966; ACG 1967: 14), and provision for adults also increased during this period, with classes offered at seventy-nine centres in 1969, approximately half of them in the Lowlands (ACG 1970: 30).

Until the 1950s Gaelic teaching in the schools was conceived almost entirely in terms of instruction for native speakers and there was very little provision for learners of the language. Sorley MacLean characterised the issue of provision for learners as 'the most urgent question in Gaelic education today' and argued that 'it has always been the real touchstone of sincerity and genuine seriousness in Gaelic education' (MacLean 1969: 21). Although MacLean did not explicate his argument in detail, it is clear that provision for learners had the potential to produce significant numbers of new Gaelic speakers and thus contribute to the reversal of language shift, whereas provision for native speakers could at best lead only to language maintenance.

MacLean and the Oban-based teacher Donald Thomson then led a campaign to develop separate school qualification examinations for learners, as the existing examinations were designed for native speakers and were much more difficult than the counterpart papers in French and other modern languages (MacNeacail 1986). An Comunn had proposed this as early as 1947 but the SED rejected the suggestion (*AG* 1948). By 1957 inspectors were observing that native speakers had 'a distinct advantage over those whose first language is English' (SED 1957: 61), and the numbers of learners in secondary schools classes was increasing noticeably, not only in the Lowlands but also in the Highlands (*AG* 1951, 1954: 13).

New examinations designed for Gaelic learners were introduced at the Ordinary grade in 1962 (for fourth-year secondary school pupils) and then the Higher grade (for school leavers) in 1968. The numbers of pupils sitting the exams rose in the years following, but there was no dramatic expansion of provision. The overwhelming majority of secondary schools in Scotland continued to make no provision for Gaelic, a pattern that continues to the present. In 1966 only 18 secondary schools were teaching Gaelic, and only 12 teaching the language to Higher grade, five of them in greater Glasgow (Hansard 1966). The number of Higher candidates rose from 94 in 1967 to 182 in 1984, of whom 120 were learners; Ordinary candidates went from 132 in 1967 to 533 in 1985 (414 of whom were learners) (Scottish Certificate of Education Examinations Board 1967, 1984, 1985). In secondary schools where Gaelic was offered, it was typically timetabled against a different subject, usually another language, and the more intellectually able pupils were generally advised to choose the other subject (Smith 1968: 71), which might be presented to pupils as being 'more valuable to them in their later careers' (*AG* 1957: 24).

Critics in the 1960s complained that the way Gaelic was taught and presented in the schools (to native speakers in particular) tended to create a negative image of the language in pupils' minds. Gaelic could seem 'stuffy, old-fashioned', 'second-rate, parochial and obsolescent', associated with 'a bleak unadventurous life', 'old unhappy far-off things and battles long ago' (Nisbet 1963: 49; Smith 1968: 71). A series of surveys conducted among secondary school and college pupils in the Western Isles showed considerable ambivalence towards the maintenance of Gaelic language and culture, although by 1985 attitudes were more positive than they had been in 1968 and 1978 (Mac a' Ghobhainn 1989–90).

INITIATIVES IN BILINGUAL EDUCATION

From the mid-1950s onwards, several initiatives in bilingual education were implemented in different areas of the Gàidhealtachd, a process that would lead to the more ambitious Bilingual Education Project in the Western Isles in 1975–82 and the 'Gaelic-medium' immersion programmes launched in 1985. These initiatives emerged in an international context in which perceptions of bilingualism in general, and of bilingual education in particular, were becoming significantly more favourable. The most famous initiative was that begun at St Lambert, near Montreal, in 1965, where an experimental nursery was opened for English-speaking children to be immersed in a French 'language bath' (Lambert and Tucker 1972: 225).

From 1956 onwards, Inverness-shire County Council began to develop a programme of bilingual education, with the strong support of Director of Education John MacLean (*Gairm* 1956; MacLean 1964). In 1958 the council appointed Murdo Macleod as Supervisor of Gaelic, with the remit 'to supervise and guide the teaching of Gaelic in the schools' (Inverness-shire County Council 1958). In 1961 the Ross-shire Education Committee agreed to follow Inverness-shire's lead by bringing Gaelic into all schools in Lewis (*GH* 1961), and a counterpart post of Gaelic organiser was created in Ross-shire in 1963 (Ross & Cromarty Council 1963).

In 1960 a draft scheme of work for the teaching of Gaelic, based on the recommendations of panels of teachers in Skye, Harris, North Uist, South Uist and Barra, was issued to the schools in those areas, and the final version of this *Scheme of Instruction in Gaelic* was published in 1964. The Scheme of Instruction expressed 'two broad complementary aims': 'the general educational development of the Gaelic-speaking pupil' and 'the perpetuation of Gaelic as a spoken language' (Inverness-shire County Council 1964: 2). Given the weakening sociolinguistic position of Gaelic, the Scheme acknowledged the role of the school as an agent of language maintenance: 'the example which would have been expected from parents in the past must now be given by the schools, if the language is to have any chance of survival' (Inverness-shire County Council 1964: 2–3). In terms of educational attainment, it was stated that 'the minimum level [. . .] envisaged [. . .] is a reasonable fluency in oral expression, reading and writing, at the end of the primary school course'. A wider aim was 'to bring the pupils to understand that they belong to a race which has a distinguished history and a valuable individual culture' (Inverness-shire County Council 1964: 3).

The bilingual scheme received a positive though not uncritical response. John A. Smith described the Inverness-shire scheme as 'certainly the boldest, most imaginative, and best-organised attempt yet to deal positively and directly' with Gaelic in education. Even so, he noted that the amount of teaching time devoted to Gaelic was 'certainly not nearly enough to provide the desired literacy in the language by the end of the primary school and to produce literacy on a corresponding level with what is attained in English' (Smith 1968: 66). Sorley MacLean delivered a harsh criticism of the confinement of the scheme to the islands, 'which treats Gaelic as fit only for the lesser breeds beyond the Kyle of Lochalsh or the Minch' (MacLean 1968: 22). The scheme was later extended to some schools in mainland districts of the county, including Inverness, Lochaber and Badenoch (MacLeod 2009: 229), but even so its impact was not as wide or long-lasting as it might have been because participation was voluntary and much depended on the enthusiasm of school heads and individual teachers (MacLeòid 2011: 25, 53). In 1970 the SED highlighted substantial variation in the use of Gaelic in the primary schools in the islands, noting that 'some teachers make fairly wide use of the language and others tend to use it only in the teaching of infants whose knowledge of English is minimal' (SED 1970: 14).

From the late 1950s, a wider range of Gaelic children's books began to be produced, most of them for use in the schools. Murdo Macleod himself made an important contribution with his *Làithean Geala* (1961), and the popular miscellany *Rosg nan Eilean* followed in 1966. These books were intended for older primary pupils and secondary pupils. In a rather different vein, a collection of traditional rhymes and games, *Aithris is Oideas*, appeared in 1964 (Scottish Council for Research in Education 1964). In 1958 An Comunn published four children's books translated from Irish and in 1967 it followed with colourful editions of five classic tales by Hans Christian Andersen and others (Ferguson and Matheson 1984: 73). In 1969-71 Gairm Publications produced a range of simple books for very young children. Several titles in the 'Ladybird' series (often considered quintessentially English and middle-class) were published between 1970 and 1974 by the Joint Committee on Gaelic Text-books, which had been established in 1968. This output represented a significant improvement in provision, but this was from a very low base.

THE DEVELOPMENT OF GAELIC BROADCASTING

In the post-war decades there were incremental improvements in the level of Gaelic programming on the radio, and these were supplemented by limited provision on television from the 1960s onwards. Despite the efforts of Gaelic campaigners, the overall level of provision remained very low, and it was not until the early 1990s that significant expansion occurred. In the field of broadcasting, as elsewhere, developments in Wales played an important role, as provision for Welsh consistently outstripped what was offered for Gaelic and helped frame the demands of Gaelic campaigners. As they pressed for increased provision, though, Gaelic activists recognised the potentially negative impact that television might have on Gaelic communities. Derick Thomson worried in 1957 that television would add to radio and film as a modern medium that would convey the message to youth that all interesting things were in English ([MacThòmais] 1957b), and by the end of the century he concluded that the 'spread of television to the general populace, with its mesmeric and meretricious power [. . .] cut a terrible swathe through Gaelic life' (Thomson 1999: 639).

The BBC became progressively more forthright in the post-war period in acknowledging responsibilities towards Gaelic. In its memorandum submitted to the Beveridge Committee on Broadcasting in 1949–51, the BBC noted that it 'ha[d] accepted the obligation to help in preserving and fostering the Gaelic language to meet the needs of Gaelic-speaking listeners' (BBC 1951: 28). In its annual report for 1954–5 the BBC amplified its policy:

> It is incumbent on a public corporation to include in its programme items that are of minority interest and the remote isolation of many of the Gaelic-speaking listeners is an additional reason why they should be adequately catered for, though not at times of majority listening. The solution is found in placing most of the Gaelic items at late evening periods or in the afternoon . . . (BBC 1955: 31)

Notwithstanding this rhetoric, in 1957 the BBC cut the Gaelic radio news from ten minutes each week to fifteen minutes once a month, provoking a backlash from Gaelic organisations and campaigners and the reversal of the decision (Donald 1962: 84–5). In 1964 the BBC's Royal Charter was amended so as to include a reference to language, thus requiring the Broadcasting Councils for Wales and Scotland to have 'full regard to the distinctive culture, language, interests and tastes' of the national audiences (BBC 1964: [6]).

The level of radio provision on the Scottish Home Service (later Radio 4) increased, from approximately two hours per week in 1959 to approximately three in 1967 and four in 1970, before reducing this output in 1971 to between 2.25 and 2.75 hours per week (MacKinnon 1991: 103). As late as 1974, only three hours a week were broadcast. News broadcasts moved to a daily basis in 1965.

From the late 1940s, the range of Gaelic material on the radio became increasingly diverse, with considerable provision for drama, although much of the content still consisted of music or sermons (Donald 1962: 87). New technology allowed for use of field recordings in programmes and a move away from the previous 'stiffly scripted studio-based approach' (Pedersen 2019: 99). Finlay J. MacDonald, co-founder of *Gairm*, joined the BBC staff as a second Gaelic producer in 1945. A third Gaelic producer was appointed in 1965 and a daily news and music programme was launched thereafter (MacPherson 2003: 260).

Some of the BBC's Gaelic programming was aimed at learners of the language rather than fluent speakers. Following on from the initial learners' programmes of 1934, between 1949 and 1951 the BBC broadcast four series of Gaelic learning programmes on the Scottish Home Service. The programmes were fifteen minutes long and each series had ten lessons, as well as accompanying booklets entitled simply *Learning Gaelic* (Ferguson and Matheson 1984: 22). These programmes were repeated in 1956–7 and the booklets reprinted. More than ten thousand copies of the booklets were sold (Thomson 1981: 10). The BBC noted on several occasions that the audience for Gaelic song programmes was considerably larger than would be expected from the number of Gaelic speakers recorded in the census (e.g. BBC 1960: 36; BBC 1963: 108).

The BBC's audience research showed high levels of satisfaction with the Gaelic output, but campaigners criticised the failure to ask questions concerning listeners' appetite for additional Gaelic programming. Writing in 1962, Gordon Donald argued presciently that an upgraded radio news service would be useful for Gaelic language development, in terms of disseminating new terminology and familiarising the audience with different varieties and dialects of Gaelic (Donald 1962: 95–6; [Murchison] 1950). Benefits of this kind were indeed noted from the late 1980s onwards, when a substantial radio and television service finally began.

Gaelic television broadcasts from the annual Mòd began in 1952 but provision expanded only very slowly thereafter. The first regular programme began in 1964 (the light entertainment programme *'Se Ur Beatha*) and in 1970 the first current affairs programme, *Bonn Còmhraidh*, was launched (MacKinnon 1991: 103). *'Se Ur Beatha* routinely attracted audiences four or five times greater than the number of the Gaelic-speaking population (BBC 1968: 118). In 1972 the BBC appointed its first Gaelic television producer, Neil Fraser (MacPherson 2003: 263), who went on to play a key role in the development of the Gaelic service in later years. Commercial stations (ITV) also began to broadcast Gaelic programmes on an occasional basis from the late 1960s. The first Gaelic play was broadcast in 1967: *Ceann Cropic* by Dr Finlay MacLeod, who would play a key role in Gaelic development from the 1970s onwards (see pp. 184, 189–90 below). Scottish Television broadcast a Gaelic learners' programme, *Beagan Gàidhlig*, in 1971–4; 'supported by special booklets and gramophone records, it evoked a significant response' (Independent Television Authority 1972: 26). Through the 1970s, however, the average output of television programming was still only about ten hours per year.

It is notable that campaigners for improved Gaelic provision of broadcasting during this period focused their attention exclusively on established broadcasters, primarily the BBC. Derick Thomson proposed in 1957 that universities and Gaelic organisations could establish a Gaelic television channel of their own, but this suggestion, which was probably entirely unrealistic, was not acted upon ([MacThòmais] 1957b). There was no attempt to establish alternative 'pirate' media, in contrast to Ireland and Wales (Ó hÉallaithe 2012; Wales Online 2014). CNCA did float the idea of a Gaelic pirate radio station in 1972 (Thompson 1972), to the consternation of An Comunn (*P&J* 1972), but, like an earlier suggestion in Uist in the mid-1960s (Mac a' Phearsain 2011: 227–8), this did not actually materialise. When significant improvements in provision came in the 1980s, as discussed below, these all resulted from campaigns to lobby the public authorities.

CONCLUSION

The decades following the Second World War brought major improvements to the economy, infrastructure and social conditions of the Gàidhealtachd, more innovative and critical interpretations of Gaelic culture and the first stirrings of a more modern, dynamic approach to Gaelic language development. National and local education authorities began to take a more proactive approach to Gaelic in the education system, recognising language maintenance and revitalisation as a public responsibility. Government funding of Gaelic organisations from the 1960s reinforced the sense that government had an obligation to the Gaelic community. Despite these advances, substantive progress was relatively limited.

In his *The Lion's Tongue* of 1974, Kenneth MacKinnon argued that successful Gaelic initiatives could 'only be carried out from "inside" Gaelic society':

The experience of Gaelic movements like those of Ruaraidh Erskine, An Comunn Gaidhealach, the Gaelic League of Scotland, and [. . .] Comunn na Cànain Albannaich [. . .] all alike have demonstrated the utter futility of trying to influence Gaeldom from the outside. [. . .] If people want to 'do things for Gaelic', whether they are Gaels who have left the homeland, or others who wish to take up Gaelic culture, there is only one way of implementing the ideas or influencing public opinion and this is to relocate themselves within the Gaelic area and to commence to implement their ideas on the spot. (MacKinnon 1974: 90–1)

The next phase of Gaelic development, discussed in the following chapter, brought unprecedented success, precisely because it was driven from the Gaelic heartlands in the Western Isles and Skye.

6

Revitalisation, 1975–96

THE LAST QUARTER OF the twentieth century brought a dramatic change in the status of Gaelic in Scotland and the level of official support for the language. In the late 1970s and early 1980s there was a palpable increase in the Gaelic community's confidence, cultural pride and 'will to survive' (GRG 1982: 17). Some of this new sense of empowerment emerged from, and found expression in, a range of innovative community-based initiatives to promote the language in the Western Isles and Skye. The mid- and late 1980s then brought rapid and significant improvements to provision for Gaelic, in relation to education, broadcasting and language planning, measures which laid the foundation for Gaelic development down to the present day. Sometimes characterised as a 'Gaelic renaissance' (D. J. MacLeod 1989), this era was widely perceived as the turning point for the language.

It is not easy to provide a straightforward explanation as to why this dramatic change occurred when it did. The wider international phenomenon of the 'ethnic revival' was already well past its peak by the time Gaelic initiatives gathered real momentum, and the political climate of the period was not especially favourable. On the contrary, the 1980s are conventionally depicted as a period during which Scotland was under attack from an ideologically hostile Conservative government (in power from 1979 to 1997) that was destroying the country's traditional industrial base and was largely indifferent to Scottish concerns (e.g. MacWhirter 2013). Gaelic played a minimal role in the debates about Scottish self-government in the 1980s and in the accompanying cultural movement of the period (Hames 2020). Significantly, Gaelic activists have not themselves developed a clear explanatory narrative on the reasons for the major shifts in policy at this time (e.g. Hutchinson 2005: 86).

Without doubt, one factor that motivated action on behalf of Gaelic was the perception of crisis: a recognition that Gaelic–English language shift had reached a critical phase and penetrated even the strongest Gaelic areas in the Western Isles, the last redoubt of the language. Urgent action was therefore needed, and this new sense of crisis coincided with the establishment of a new local authority for the Western Isles, Comhairle nan Eilean, which gave new scope for focused Gaelic initiatives.

In contrast to the early period of revival, the great majority of the activists and policy-makers driving this key phase of Gaelic development were native Gaelic speakers from crofting villages in the Western Isles or Skye, born from c. 1940 to the mid-1950s. Most of this group were university educated, typically part of the first generation in their families to receive higher education and, in some cases, secondary education. Many had known each other since secondary school (most commonly Portree High School or the Nicolson Institute in Stornoway) or university (usually Aberdeen or Glasgow) (Caimbeul 2000: 63), and the tightness of these Gaelic networks prompted some observers to speak of a 'Gaelic mafia' (Cormack 1994: 116–17). This pattern of upward mobility driven by improved access to higher education was apparent throughout Scotland (Paterson 2017: 258–9), but it was particularly striking in strongly Gaelic areas such as the Western Isles, where the education system had typically functioned as a pathway to out-migration but where new employment opportunities emerged at home in the 1970s, most obviously through the establishment of Comhairle nan Eilean. As in earlier periods, men were heavily dominant in Gaelic organisations and initiatives during this period, although there were important exceptions. By the same token, native speakers have continued to occupy the great majority of leadership roles in Gaelic organisations in the twenty-first century, even as learners or 'new speakers' of Gaelic have become much more numerous.

Ethnologist Natalie Coffre-Baneux characterised the Gaelic movement in the Western Isles from the 1970s onwards as being driven by the middle classes (Coffre-Baneux 2001: 271–4), but did not make clear that these 'middle classes' were typically products of new social mobility whose origins were in the heart of the crofting community, rather than a long-established bourgeois element. In fact, sociolinguistic studies by Kenneth MacKinnon showed that Gaelic language maintenance and support for Gaelic development tended to be weakest among the managerial and professional classes in the islands (many of whom were incomers) (MacKinnon 1987: 2000).

In the Gaelic context, particularly in relation to the Western Isles, the 1970s appear in retrospect as a time of increasing community confidence, a new readiness to question established practices and think about new possibilities and opportunities. Within this, the 'native intelligentsia' identified by Colin Williams (1999: 267–8) as an important factor in modern Celtic language movements played an instrumental role. This new sense of empowerment also found expression in a wave of militance that became apparent among young Gaelic activists in the late 1970s and early 1980s.

Conversely, there is relatively little evidence of political calculation on the part of the government – the sense that improved provision for Gaelic constituted concessions in response to political pressure or reflected the pursuit of political advantage. The Conservative government could not have expected any direct political dividend in electoral terms, although Donald Meek has suggested that 'the government was anxious to portray itself as a benign and constructive force within the Gaelic areas which were dominated by Labour and Liberal constituencies' (Meek 2001b: 26). More generally, the government's support for Gaelic can be seen as a way of showing support for a distinctly Scottish agenda in a way that was reasonably cheap and did not go against its core economic and social policies (Pittock 2008: 125).

THE POLITICISATION OF GAELIC

From the late 1960s and through the 1970s, Gaelic became increasingly politicised, receiving extensive attention in the diverse political periodicals that flourished at this time, including *Crann-Tàra*, *Scotia Review* and *Scottish International*. This had also been the case with the interwar Scottish Renaissance but the Gaelic material of that era tended to be folkloric in nature, typically written in Gaelic but rarely addressing any of the contemporary political and social issues that were tackled in the English-language contributions. In the 1970s, by contrast, articles concerning Gaelic matters in Scottish cultural and current affairs journals were often highly political in nature, indeed militant, and almost always written in English.

Even with this increased politicisation, Gaelic played only a minimal role in the debates on devolution for Scotland that intensified after the striking success of the SNP in the General Elections of February and October 1974 and led to the unsuccessful referendum of 1979 on the establishment of a devolved Scottish assembly. Gaelic also received very little attention from activists in the broad-based campaign for legislative devolution that developed between 1979 and 1997. The landmark *Claim of Right for Scotland* of 1989, a manifesto setting out the consensus position of the Scottish Constitutional Convention, made almost no reference to Gaelic, while the leading political magazine of the devolution movement, *Radical Scotland*, ignored Gaelic issues almost entirely, suggesting that it was eminently possible to be intellectually engaged with the matter of 'radical Scotland' and yet not be meaningfully concerned with the Gaelic question.[1] The flourishing Scottish literary and cultural scene of the post-1979 period also had little engagement with Gaelic (Hames 2020).

At the same time, however, Gaelic culture gained new prominence in the 1970s and played an important role in building confidence in the Gaelic community and awareness in the wider Scottish population. From the early 1970s, Gaelic literature, especially Gaelic poetry, began to receive greater attention from the English-monoglot majority in Scotland, and this increasing cultural prestige brought new support for the language. In 1971 Iain Crichton Smith produced a new English translation of Sorley MacLean's landmark collection *Dàin do Eimhir*, which had been published in 1943 but attracted a new group of Anglophone readers in the 1970s. Another notable contribution was the 1976 collection *Nua-Bhàrdachd Ghàidhlig/Modern Scottish Gaelic Poems* (MacAulay 1976), which presented the work of the so-called 'Famous Five' (MacLean, George Campbell Hay, Donald MacAulay, Iain Crichton Smith and Derick Thomson). John McGrath's play *The Cheviot, the Stag and the Black, Black Oil* (McGrath 1974), an influential agitprop-style retelling of Highland and Scottish history that emphasised historical injustice and exploitation, toured across Scotland in 1973–4, including many small communities in the Highlands and Islands, and was broadcast across the UK in 1974 as part of the celebrated *Play for Today* series. The show included a Gaelic element in the dialogue and Gaelic songs performed by Dolina MacLennan. Most important of all, the pioneering folk-rock group Runrig, established in Skye in 1974, gave voice to a new sense of Gaelic cultural identity and confidence, expressed in a new modern idiom that showed young Gaels (and other Scots) that Gaelic was 'a living language with contemporary relevance' (Tranmer 2016: 137). Runrig's first album, *Play Gaelic* (1978), was entirely in Gaelic; later albums, several of which reached the UK Top 10, were bilingual. Runrig's songs addressed many political and social issues affecting the Gàidhealtachd and Scotland as a whole, from the Clearances to deindustrialisation, contributing significantly to the wider Scottish cultural revival of the period (Hutchinson 2005: 130–2; *Herald* 2018b).

From the late 1970s onwards, the issue of provision for minority languages began to gain increased attention from European political institutions – the European Union (originally the European Economic Community) and later the Council of Europe. While these developments had no immediate ramifications for Gaelic policy in Scotland, they slowly contributed to the emergence of a more favourable policy climate. Beginning in 1981, the European Parliament passed a series of resolutions calling on member states to take action in support of regional and minority languages (Wright 2015: 240–1). These resolutions led to the creation in 1982 of an international support organisation, the European Bureau for Lesser Used Languages (EBLUL). While EBLUL was only a non-governmental organisation and never had any official status within the European Union, it nevertheless developed significant expertise and a degree of political influence, and helped build international support networks for minority language activists, allowing them to 'exchang[e] ideas on what to do and how to do it, thereby establishing forms of mutual support and solidarity and building up their know-how and self-confidence in taking initiatives' (Johnstone 1994: 2). Gaelic was well represented in EBLUL, with officials from the development organisation Comunn na Gàidhlig (discussed below, pp. 195–8) playing an active role.

The issue of minority languages also began to receive greater academic attention from the mid-1970s onwards. Language activists were increasingly addressing all aspects of 'peripheral community development', with the 'language issue [. . .] seen as being inextricably interwoven with the social, cultural and economic weft of the communal whole' (GRG 1982: 19). Meic Stephens's magnum opus *Linguistic Minorities in Western Europe* (1976) was a landmark contribution, and from 1979 onwards a series of international conferences on minority languages was held, the first of them in Glasgow in 1980 (Haugen, McClure and Thomson 1981). Several important academic works on the history and sociology of Gaelic appeared (e.g. Chapman 1978; Dorian 1981; Durkacz 1983; MacKinnon 1977; Withers 1984), accompanying James Hunter's influential *The Making of the Crofting Community* (1976), a radical reinterpretation which 'attempt[ed] to write the modern history of the Gaelic Highlands from the crofting community's point of view' (Hunter 1976: 5). Coupled with new efforts to advance programmatic, strategic thinking on Gaelic development, as discussed below (pp. 192–7), this body of work demonstrated a new seriousness of purpose in relation to Gaelic. From the mid-1970s, dedicated conferences on Gaelic development began to be conducted with increasing regularity, and focused proposals for programmatic, concrete action were circulated and discussed (e.g. MacThòmais 1976).

COMHAIRLE NAN EILEAN AND GAELIC DEVELOPMENT

The reorganisation of local government in Scotland in 1974, pursuant to the *Local Government (Scotland) Act 1973*, led to the creation of a new authority for the Western Isles (Outer Hebrides), a development that gave considerable new latitude for innovative initiatives to promote Gaelic in public administration, education, community organisation, the arts and other fields. Prior to this reorganisation the islands had formed part of larger counties that were administered from the mainland and dominated by non-Gaelic speakers. Lewis was part of Ross & Cromarty, whose county town was Dingwall, and the islands from Harris southwards were part of Inverness-shire, whose county town was Inverness. The population of the Western Isles was overwhelmingly Gaelic- speaking at this time (77.6 per cent in 1971) (MacKinnon 1978: 29). In principle at least, this high density of Gaelic speakers should have made strong Gaelic language policies possible.

Although its formal legal name remained Western Isles Islands Council, the new authority adopted the working name Comhairle nan Eilean (CnE) or 'Council of the Isles' shortly after its establishment in January 1975, claiming the name once used for the ruling council of the medieval Lordship of the Isles.[2] As Boyd Robertson, former director of the Gaelic college Sabhal Mòr Ostaig, noted, this was the first time the Gaels were in control of the islands since the time of the Lordship (Robertson 2011). The council reinforced this evocative historical association by adopting the Lordship's symbol of the *birlinn* (galley) for its logo.

The council quickly undertook a raft of innovative measures to accommodate and promote Gaelic. The most important of these were its Bilingual Education Project, discussed in detail below (pp. 183–7), and its wider bilingual policy for public administration. In April 1975 the council's Policy and Resources Committee unanimously decided that the council should 'adopt a policy of bilingualism and that steps should be taken to afford the English and Gaelic language equal status' (CnE 1975: 110; SG 1975c). A policy of this kind was unprecedented in the history of Scottish local government, although in 1966 the district councils in the Western Isles (which were superseded by the new Comhairle) had agreed to allow the use of Gaelic in their meetings (*P&J* 1966). The council's chief executive, Roy Maciver, expressed the aim of this policy as follows: 'the Western Isles should be a fundamentally bilingual community in which Gaelic and English are used concurrently as media of communication, so that the people of the area can have the choice of either language in as many situations as possible' (CnE 1977: 1). Steven Rae, the council's first Director of Administration, reported that the decision attracted considerable attention from the media and 'congratulations and enthusiastic noises' '[f]rom every corner of the Gaelic diaspora' (Rae 1976: 6). According to the important *Cor na Gàidhlig* report of 1982, discussed below (pp. 192–4), the adoption of the bilingual policy 'created a mood of expectancy and renewed confidence which in turn led to new initiatives and demands for further use of the language in other areas' (GRG 1982: 22).

The first steps in the implementation of the policy were to use bilingual letterheads on correspondence and memoranda; publish official council communications in bilingual format; issue road directions and street signs in Gaelic only; and ensure that 'street furniture' (signage and so on) was bilingual. Booths for simultaneous interpretation of council meetings were planned and council officials were to be given time off to attend Gaelic courses; Gaelic-speaking school leavers and university graduates were to be encouraged to seek posts with the council; Gaelic-speaking staff were to be encouraged to use Gaelic when dealing with the public; and the public were notified that 'those preferring to discuss their problems in Gaelic with officials should do so' (CnE 1975: 110–11). Some activists urged the council to go further and adopt considerably more forceful policies to secure the position of Gaelic. In 1976, for example, Duncan MacLaren, a founding member of CNCA, called for 'a deliberately rigorous programme of linguistic discrimination' that would have included compelling 'non-Gaels living in the islands' to become competent in Gaelic 'within a generous amount of time before being able to reside permanently or buy a house in the islands' (MacLaren 1976). This more radical proposal was not adopted, and unlike in Ireland or Wales (*Irish Independent* 2005; Welsh Government 2017) there have almost[3] never been any kinds of Gaelic-language conditions attached to house purchases or planning permission in the Western Isles or elsewhere.

Above and beyond the language question, recruiting qualified staff proved to be a challenge from the outset, particularly as the council could not match the salaries paid by other Scottish local authorities. In the Administration and Legal Services department, none of those recruited for senior posts knew any Gaelic, and the only native speakers in the department were two administrative assistants. Some elements of the bilingual policy began to be implemented successfully, however. A bilingual chequebook was procured, bilingual stationery was commissioned, streets in new housing developments were given Gaelic names and staff enrolled on Gaelic classes (including literacy classes for fluent speakers) (Rae 1976: 7).

In the winter of 1977–8, the council conducted a public consultation to formalise the bilingual policy (CnE 1978a). The consultative document set out detailed proposals in relation to council members and officials, the delivery of services (including education) and dealings with other bodies (including the media). The council also proposed to appoint a Bilingual Development Officer to implement the bilingual policy and '[e]nable progress to be made in the use of Gaelic in other fields' beyond education (CnE 1978a: 19).

Thirty-nine responses to the consultation were received, eighteen of them from individuals and twenty-one from organisations (CnE 1978e). An Comunn praised the council for its 'uniquely conscientious view of its duties' in relation to Gaelic, but argued that 'it is vital to establish the "costs" of bilingualism as a normal element of administrative expenditure' and 'fores[aw] policy implementation being attended by recurring weaknesses' if this was not done (ACG 1978b). An Comunn's Western Isles Regional Council (North) was more critical, expressing concern at 'the "watering down" process already observable in a number of areas where operational considerations are outlined', particularly in relation to staff recruitment, advertising and education (ACG 1978a). An Comunn's head office argued that it would be necessary 'to make a strong case to central government' for additional funding 'to meet the extra costs of implementing a Bilingual Policy' (ACG 1978b). The Educational Institute of Scotland criticised 'a tendency to follow up some firm statement of some aspect of policy with a qualifying rider which has the effect of weakening the force of the first statement and giving an impression of inconclusiveness about the Council's real intentions' (Educational Institute of Scotland 1978: 2).

Several submissions had more fundamental criticisms, however. Of the political parties, the SNP was most supportive, the Liberals rather less so, while the Labour Party opposed the use of simultaneous interpretation of meetings, the production of bilingual minutes and reports, and the use of monolingual Gaelic signage. All three parties opposed the council's proposal to appoint a Bilingual Development Officer (Western Isles Constituency Association 1978; Western Isles Liberal Association 1978; Western Isles Constituency Labour Party 1978). The Free Presbyterian Church was concerned that 'a too *rigid* application of the bilingual policy' could deter inward investment and return migration to the islands (Free Presbyterian Church 1978), while the council's own Director of Social Work, a non-Gaelic-speaking incomer to the islands, expressed 'fear' at 'the possibility of a form of apartheid developing in the Western Isles [. . .] unless the policy is implemented with sensitivity' (CnE 1978b). The diversity of these concerns demonstrates the lack of ideological consensus in support of strong Gaelic language policies in the islands, a problem which has had significant repercussions over the decades.

Following the consultation, the council's Policy and Resources Committee approved the bilingual policy, making only a minor amendment in relation to signage (CnE 1978c: 205). In contrast to other areas where Gaelic was appearing on public signs, signage in the Western Isles was not bilingual but in Gaelic only, except in Stornoway and Benbecula, where there were significant numbers of non-Gaelic-speaking residents. This practice was justified on the grounds of linguistic economy: unlike the mainland Highlands, the great majority of village names in the Western Isles are of Norse rather than Gaelic origin, and the Gaelic names are actually corruptions of the original Norse, just as most of the English names in the Highlands are corruptions of the original Gaelic. The Bilingual Policy thus proposed 'to identify those names which could, without inconvenience, be rendered always in their Gaelic form and to introduce that name for all official purposes', including road signs (CnE 1978a: 12). The signage policy attracted a good deal of local controversy, much of it from Gaelic speakers (Martin 2011).

A strongly Gaelic policy for the council – requiring a knowledge of Gaelic on the part of all post holders – would have been impracticable given the need for experienced staff with specialist skills. This might have been tackled through a systematic language training programme, but there were no dedicated resources to introduce such full-scale bilingualisation, partly because CnE was operating in administrative isolation as the only local authority in Scotland, indeed the only public body in Scotland, that was endeavouring to institutionalise bilingualism. In Highland Region, the area with the second-highest proportion of Gaelic speakers, only 9.5 per cent of the population was Gaelic-speaking in 1981 (James 1991: 174), and even tentative steps to institutionalise Gaelic in council operations, such as circulating a questionnaire concerning employees' willingness to use Gaelic in their work, proved controversial (*WHFP* 1985a). The situation in Scotland was profoundly different from other countries in which bilingualisation was attempted, such as the Basque Autonomous Community (Martínez-Arbelaiz 1996) and Canada (Fraser 2006), where substantial resources were made available for retraining government staff and targeted language development work. In addition, there was no programme to develop the terminology and registers required in specific work environments or to assist Gaelic speakers to acquire the linguistic skills necessary to work through the medium of Gaelic (cf. Mac an Iomaire 1983).

Although it did not provide additional funding to facilitate the bilingualisation process, the Scottish Office raised no objections to the council's plans to institutionalise Gaelic and give preference in hiring to Gaelic speakers. Concepts of discrimination in employment, as set out in the *Race Relations Act 1976*, had not yet penetrated public discourse to any significant extent; in later decades, suggestions of giving preference to Gaelic speakers often gave rise to concerns of unlawfulness (McLeod 1998, 2009). In 1988 the council obtained a legal opinion from an Edinburgh advocate which concluded that there would be a clear defence of justification to any claims of racial discrimination in employment arising out of Gaelic requirements in job specifications (Gill 1988). No such litigation has actually ensued, in the Western Isles or elsewhere, but this may reflect the fact that Gaelic-related job requirements have not been widely adopted (McLeod 2009).

The council's implementation of its bilingual policy and support for other Gaelic initiatives became more difficult after 1979, following the election of the Conservative government and the imposition of a programme of budget cuts (Maciver 1991). By 1982 the *Cor na Gàidhlig* report found that there was a 'lack of impetus' to the policy (GRG 1982: 22). The bilingual policy was renewed on several occasions and then replaced by iterations of a statutory Gaelic Language Plan pursuant to the *Gaelic Language Act (Scotland) 2005*, but the council has never succeeded in becoming a genuinely bilingual organisation, in sharp contrast to the comparable local authority in the strongest Welsh-speaking area of Wales, Gwynedd (Carlin 2013). This challenge has become progressively more difficult over time, as the proportion of Gaelic speakers in the islands' population has dropped steadily since the 1970s, from 78 per cent in 1971 to 52 per cent in 2011.

THE BILINGUAL EDUCATION PROJECT

Comhairle nan Eilean also undertook pioneering steps in the field of education, laying the foundation for subsequent initiatives to use Gaelic as a medium of instruction in schools. In 1975 the council launched a Bilingual Education Project in the islands' primary schools, funded by the SED and under the direction of Jordanhill College of Education. The intellectual driver of the project was Dr Finlay MacLeod, a Lewis-born psychologist who was appointed Primary School Adviser at CnE. MacLeod had set out in detail his view of the educational needs of the Gaelic community and the potential of bilingual education in his 1970 doctoral thesis (F. MacLeod 1970). In MacLeod's view, there was a profound gulf between the schools and the Gaelic community, and bilingual education could equip children in the Western Isles to 'gain an elaborated form of Gaelic speech, and the confidence and originality to enable them, as they grew up, to be aware and critical of these forces in the environment which restrict their freedom and curtail their development' (F. MacLeod 1970: 228, 100). In advancing the Bilingual Education Project, MacLeod placed particular importance on the need to strengthen the link between the school and the community (MacLeòid 1976: 34, 36). The project appointed as its director John Murray, a teacher who had also established a reputation as a writer and who returned from the Central Belt to work in Lewis.

The stated educational aims of the Bilingual Education Project were 'to enable children from a Gaelic-speaking background to become literate and competent in the use of both Gaelic and English to a level comparable to that achieved by their peers elsewhere in the country, and to provide facilities throughout the school for children from a non Gaelic-speaking background to learn Gaelic as a second language' (Murray and Morrison 1984). These aims were therefore significantly more ambitious than those of the earlier Inverness-shire Scheme. It was decided that Environmental Studies would be the most appropriate subject to emphasise within the bilingual scheme, given the strong connection to children's community surroundings.

Phase I of the project lasted from 1975 to 1978 and involved twenty-four primary schools. Phase II lasted from 1978 to 1981 and encompassed thirty-four schools. The SED provided funding for both phases of the project, and on completion of the second phase the project was transformed into a bilingual curriculum support unit within Comhairle nan Eilean's education department, with its remit then extended to cover all fifty-six primary schools in the islands (Dunn and Robertson 1989: 45). The project received considerable international attention, including a report in *The New York Times* in 1976 (*The New York Times* 1976).

A major challenge for the bilingual project was the impact of language shift. The project was predicated on the assumption that the participating pupils would be native Gaelic speakers, and thus receiving education in their mother tongue, but it became increasingly apparent that language shift was starting to gather pace even in the rural districts of the Western Isles. Even at the outset of the project in 1974–5, only 7 per cent of pupils at the four primary schools in and around Stornoway (long a bastion of Anglicisation) spoke Gaelic fluently and 68 per cent had no Gaelic, while in the fifty-six rural schools, 88 per cent of pupils had some knowledge of Gaelic (with 68 per cent being fluent speakers) and 12 per cent had no Gaelic (*SG* 1975c). The impact of language shift in the late 1960s and early 1970s was clear: while only 4 per cent of the rural pupils in primary 7 (mostly born in 1963) had no Gaelic, 22 per cent of those in primary 1 (mostly born in 1969) were monolingual English speakers (M. Macleod n.d.: 2). By 1992 only 19.5 per cent of the islands' primary school pupils were fluent Gaelic speakers (*Herald* 1992).

Another important obstacle confronting the bilingual project was ideological resistance among parents and teachers. The devaluing of Gaelic and valorisation of English, especially in the educational context, were strongly entrenched. Based on his experiences at dozens of meetings over the years, Murray was keenly aware that many parents did not see the benefits of the initiative and that many teachers were also sceptical, although he reckoned that four-fifths of teachers had become supportive by the end of the project (Murray 1991). Teachers had themselves all been trained in an English-medium system and their professional competences and general outlook reflected that formation (M. Macleod 2004).

The shortage of suitable teaching resources, especially books, was another major challenge for the project. An initial tranche of six books was published in 1977 under the Cliath imprint; this was a multi-agency initiative, involving HIDB, CnE, the University of Strathclyde and An Comunn (Nicolson 1977). The Cliath books were praised for the attractiveness and the professionalism of their production, a contrast to the 'drab and predictable' material produced for children in earlier decades (Nicolson 1977). For the longer term, it was decided that a dedicated publishing house would be required to meet these needs on an ongoing basis. This led to the establishment of the publishing house Acair (Gaelic for 'anchor') in Stornoway in 1977. Most of the books published by Acair for the Bilingual Education Project focused on aspects of island life and culture, with illustrations showing croft and other community settings as opposed to the urban, often English scenes typical of existing schoolbooks. One of the enduring successes was the Spàgan series, involving a giant purple creature and his boy companion.[4] The Acair books also emphasised living, colloquial Gaelic rather than the more formal register typical of earlier children's books (MacLeòid 1976: 34), to the consternation of some commentators.[5]

Despite the contribution of Acair, the issue of school resources proved to be an ongoing difficulty in Gaelic education, particularly in the years after 1985, when Gaelic-medium education spread widely across Scotland, as discussed below (pp. 209–17). Teachers were often forced to resort to 'paste-overs': translating English books into Gaelic themselves, typing or printing out the Gaelic version and then pasting the Gaelic text over the English. Proposals and requests for funding to develop a national Gaelic resource centre were repeatedly advanced (e.g. SO Education Department 1994: 5) until in 1999 a dedicated unit, Stòrlann Nàiseanta na Gàidhlig, was finally established. The situation has much improved since then, although the diversity of school materials available in Gaelic remains hugely less than in English, a situation inherent in the minority language condition in contact with the hegemonic world language that is English.

After the Bilingual Education Project had been in place in primary schools for several years, the question of continuity to the secondary phase arose, but plans to extend Gaelic-medium teaching to secondary proved controversial. In June 1980 the Comhairle's Education Committee voted unanimously to develop Gaelic-medium teaching 'through a progressive programme of development initially located in selected secondary schools and involving a restricted range of subjects' (CnE 1980a: 332; SG 1980a). Three days later, however, this decision was reversed by a 10–9 vote of the full council, largely because councillors were made aware of 'a great deal of feeling about the matter in the town of Stornoway' (SG 1980b; CnE 1980b: 398–9). In August 1980 the matter returned to the council and it was agreed to accept the plan for bilingual secondary education, but that this would be 'implemented only after full consultation with Parent and Teacher Organisations' (CnE 1980c: 482). Derick Thomson summarised this episode as 'reveal[ing] the deep division that exists in the strongest Gaelic area, on the role of Gaelic in education' (Thomson 1981: 14).

When the council sought additional funding from the SED to extend the Bilingual Education Project to the junior secondary phase, the SED required that the project be subjected to an external evaluation, taking the view that key questions concerning project outcomes, especially in terms of pupil attainment, had not been adequately answered (SO 1981j). This decision to require external evaluation was perceived as an affront by Murray and MacLeod and others involved in the project (SO 1982c), and the SED's statement that its general position on the matter was one of 'benevolent neutrality, neither encouraging nor discouraging bilingual education' (e.g. SO 1982c) became notorious in Gaelic education circles for many years thereafter (e.g. GRG 1982: 21–2; Robasdan 2006: 97). The SED's decision to require an external review of the Bilingual Education Project also annoyed An Comunn, with education officer Colin Spencer expressing incredulity: 'If you question the validity of Gaelic in education you question its validity everywhere. It is as if the last 100 years of struggle for Gaelic had never happened' (*GH* 1981b). In September 1982, however, the council finally agreed to allow the independent evaluation (*TESS* 1982). A team from Stirling University, led by Dr Rosalind Mitchell, was appointed to carry out the research, which was eventually published in 1987 (Mitchell et al. 1987; see Mitchell 1992). While the research report identified varying degrees of success in relation to different aspects of the project, the main area of concern was the increasing number of non-fluent pupils in the islands' schools and the need to develop appropriate teaching models to meet their needs (Mitchell et al. 1987: 198).

While the external review held up the prospect of dedicated SED funding for bilingual secondary education, CnE did proceed to put in place a two-year pilot bilingual programme in two junior secondary schools in Lewis, using its own resources, which focused on social science subjects (Dunn and Robertson 1989: 48–9). Progress in subsequent years was constrained by budget cuts and a controversial programme of school closures.

Building on the bilingual project in the Western Isles, a separate bilingual education scheme was introduced in 1978 into five primary schools in Skye, where Highland Regional Council was the education authority (GRG 1982: 23). This began as a small-scale support programme involving two peripatetic teachers. It was recognised that more attention to the needs of non-Gaelic-speaking children was required in Skye, as language shift was further advanced there than in the Western Isles. By 1985 this programme had been extended to all nineteen of the island's primary schools, even though there were significant variations in the proportions of Gaelic-speaking pupils in the different schools and some schools had few if any Gaelic-speaking teachers (Dunn and Robertson 1989: 45, 49–50; Cunningham 1984). As Gaelic-medium units developed in Skye from the late 1980s onwards, however, pupils in the English-medium classes began to receive less and less Gaelic, highlighting the demarcation between the two streams.

Although the Bilingual Education Project in the Western Isles could be characterised as a 'top-down' initiative, given that it was originally proposed and promoted by the education authority, almost all subsequent Gaelic education initiatives have resulted from 'bottom-up' campaigning and pressure. From the late 1970s onwards, Gaelic activists in different parts of the country began informational and promotional campaigns to build support among parents for improved Gaelic provision. This tactic differed from the more 'top-down' approach of An Comunn and other activists in previous decades, which resistant authorities had been able to deflect on the grounds that there was no actual demand from parents. Surveys of parents in diverse parts of the Gàidhealtachd – Sutherland, Easter and Wester Ross and Mull – conducted between 1978 and 1981 all returned very large majorities in support of introducing or increasing Gaelic teaching in the local schools (*Gairm* 1978; Caimbeul 1979–80; Gray 1981; Withers 1984: 246).

By 1984, local campaigns for Gaelic education were under way in several areas: Glasgow, Inverness, Portree and Digg in Skye, as well as the Western Isles (Wilson 1984). To an increasing extent, campaigners began to press for 'Gaelic-medium education' (GME) rather than bilingual education. The difference between 'Gaelic-medium' provision and bilingual provision was only loosely defined but was essentially 'a matter of degree' in terms of a higher proportion of Gaelic used in teaching and a greater use of teaching materials in Gaelic (Wilson 1984). As in other areas of policy, educational campaigners looked to Wales as a model and an inspiration, and the secretary of the promotional body Parents for Welsh Education was invited to the 1984 Mòd to explain the nature of Welsh provision and how it had been achieved (Wilson 1984). These campaigns are discussed in detail below in relation to Glasgow, the most high-profile among them.

OTHER COMMUNITY INITIATIVES IN THE WESTERN ISLES

Another significant initiative in the islands during this period was Pròiseact Muinntir nan Eilean (the Western Isles Community Education Project), which was supported by the Netherlands-based Bernard van Leer Foundation. The Van Leer Project, as it came to be known, led to the establishment of a range of innovative community initiatives in the islands. These included pre-school playgroups (*cròileagain*) and local historical societies (*comuinn eachdraidh*), which helped build 'a more informed and analytical awareness [. . .] of the social and economic reality' of the islands 'past and present' (GRG 1982: 33; Hunter 1992). These pioneering projects, all of which incorporated Gaelic as a central element, helped empower local communities in different ways and build a new sense of confidence and cultural pride, 'potentially a powerful force for development' (GRG 1982: 79).

The Van Leer Project had three stages: a feasibility study based in Ness in Lewis in 1976–7, Phase 1 in 1977–82, which involved three sites (Ness, Harris and Iochdar in South Uist), and Phase 2 in 1982–7. The Van Leer Foundation changed its general mandate in the early 1980s and this meant that Phase 2 of the project focused specifically on the development of pre-school education as opposed to wider community initiatives (Mackay 1996: 11–12). As the original proposal explained, the project was intended as 'an enterprise in adult education' that aimed to '[p]rovide a programme for promoting social development by stimulating the people of the Western Isles to perceive their own community more clearly' (Mackay 1996: 16). The project director, Donald John MacLeod, identified the following factors as being crucial to sustainable community development:

(a) a stable and cohesive social environment;
(b) an awareness of and sense of pride on the part of the community in its culture, including its language;
(c) a realistic and analytical awareness of the past and its part in shaping the attitudes of the present – liberating the past as a force for, rather than against, progress;
(d) a conscious appreciation, on the part of developers, of the interdependence of the social, cultural and economic domains in community life. (GRG 1982: 34)

Building on these understandings, a wide range of community groups in the Western Isles came forward with different kinds of initiatives.

From the outset the language question was a political issue within the Van Leer Project. Finlay MacLeod commented that 'it has become a political act for Hebridean parents to bring up their children as Gaelic speakers, for almost every move they make has to be against the tide. They require all the skill and resources that an initiative such as the [Van Leer] project can offer' (quoted in Mackay 1996: 27). These dynamics were illustrated during the feasibility phase of the project when a mother who had moved into the islands proposed to organise a pre-school playgroup but wanted it to be held in English. This prompted a group of local mothers to establish their own group with 'a local flavour', which was held in Gaelic (F. MacLeod [1976b]: 3–4).

The Gaelic arts emerged as another significant area of activity from the late 1970s onwards, with the establishment of several innovative community arts initiatives in the Western Isles, encompassing theatre, film, traditional music and the visual arts. The idea of promoting the Gaelic arts was not a new one; in 1966 An Comunn had proposed to the

Scottish Committee of the Arts Council of Great Britain (forerunner of the Scottish Arts Council) that a special Gaelic committee within the Arts Council should be established, but this proposal was rejected in favour of retaining the existing policy of 'seeking out means of supporting [G]aelic cultural enterprises within its present organisation and practice' (Arts Council of Great Britain 1966: 4; see Galloway 2012). By the early 1980s, following successful initiatives in the Western Isles, the Scottish Arts Council had adopted a more supportive stance, 'recognis[ing] the outstanding contribution made by Gaelic culture to Scottish society as a whole' and declaring that it was 'anxious to do all it can to assist in rescuing the true tradition from neglect and abuse, and to ensure the continuance of a vital and living culture' (Scottish Arts Council 1982: 731).

In 1985 the Council commissioned Dr Finlay MacLeod to produce a report on the potential of the Gaelic arts (F. MacLeod 1986). MacLeod found that the existing provision was highly sporadic, lacking structure and coordination, and recommended that the Council should work with CnaG and An Comunn to establish a dedicated Gaelic arts project. In the first instance he proposed that a full-time Gaelic arts officer be appointed, based in Stornoway but with a national remit, working with existing groups and building links between them and the Arts Council (F. MacLeod 1986: 30–1, 34). MacLeod's recommendations were accepted and this led to the creation in 1987 of Pròiseact nan Ealan (the National Gaelic Arts Project [later Agency]). In the years following, Pròiseact nan Ealan 'carved out an outstanding development and promotional role', sponsoring a range of activities in different cultural fields and 'responding to grass-roots demand rather than imposing preconceived notions from above' (CnaG 1994: 7). The director of Pròiseact nan Ealan, Malcolm MacLean, had previously run the first arts centre and gallery in the Western Isles, An Lanntair (The Lantern), which was established in Stornoway in 1985. Among its important early initiatives was the politically incisive exhibition *As an Fhearann* to mark the centenary of the Crofters Act of 1886 (MacLean and Carrell 1986).

A particularly important element in this Gaelic arts activity was the development of local music festivals (known as *fèisean*), aimed particularly at children and youth. Up until then the traditional arts had very little place in the isles' schools, and there was a sense that the decline of traditional musical skills was intertwined with the decline of the language (Rennie 1994: 9–10). The first event of this kind, Fèis Bharraigh, was held in the Isle of Barra in 1980, at the urging of a local priest, Father Colin MacInnes, and with financial support from the Scottish Arts

Council. The two-week festival involved some two hundred local children in Gaelic music classes, including piping, fiddle, accordion, singing and dancing (GRG 1982: 35). The success of Fèis Bharraigh inspired many similar festivals throughout Scotland and led to the creation of the national umbrella organisation Fèisean nan Gàidheal in 1988, which is still in existence and organises a series of year-long youth musical training programmes and festivals across Scotland (Martin 2006). As the fèisean spread across different parts of Scotland, however, the role of Gaelic tended to diminish. Although all fèisean had some Gaelic content, and most included mandatory Gaelic classes, in 1995 only three of the twenty-five fèisean were run entirely through the medium of Gaelic (Cormack 1995). Even if the role of Gaelic was often relatively limited, the fèisean have played an important role in attracting young people to learn Gaelic, and the connection between Gaelic and the revitalisation of traditional music in recent decades has been an important source of energy and cultural dynamism.

Another early arts initiative was the community cinema and communications project Cinema Sgìre, which ran from 1977 to 1981. The project was funded by CnE, the Scottish Film Council, HIDB and the Calouste Gulbenkian Foundation (*Outline Report* 1981). The project director was Michael Russell, who went on to become a senior minister in the SNP governments after 2007. Cinema Sgìre used film education and the development of video not just as a means of entertainment but also 'as a community tool' of self-expression and 'a method for examining community problems', including the production of video documentaries about local history and issues (Galbraith 1981: 17; GRG 1982: 34). Among other things, the Cinema Sgìre project gave rise to the first Celtic Film Festival, held in Benbecula in 1980, which was attended by representatives from Wales, Ireland and Brittany. This event (now known as the Celtic Media Festival) has been held continuously ever since, in a different 'Celtic' country each year.

Gaelic drama emerged as another important area of arts activity. Although Gaelic drama had been developing since the early twentieth century (Ross 2016), it lacked a strong institutional foundation. The pioneering theatre company Fir Chlis was founded in Harris in 1978, with funding from the Scottish Arts Council, HIDB and CnE. The company devoted considerable attention to theatre in education, work that was coordinated with other current projects such as Van Leer and the Bilingual Education Project, while its work for adults sought 'to stimulate its audience to a fresh awareness of their own community and heritage' (Fir Chlis n.d.). However, Fir Chlis arguably overemphasised professionalism and 'pure theatre' rather than building 'a foundation more geared to the continuing needs of the Gaelic community', and the group proved short-lived (GRG 1982: 51; F. MacLeod 1986: 25). A national Gaelic drama group, Tosg, followed in 1996, continuing until 2007.

BUILDING A GAELIC DEVELOPMENT INFRASTRUCTURE

By the late 1970s, HIDB had become keenly interested in these various community development initiatives in the Western Isles and the organisation played a central role in the key steps that would lead in the 1980s to the creation of a real Gaelic development infrastructure for the first time. During the 1970s the organisation introduced a system of 'social grants' to support different kinds of community projects and this funding mechanism proved important in getting Gaelic-related initiatives off the ground (Hutchinson 2005: 109).

HIDB was particularly interested in developing and supporting community cooperatives (*co-chomuinn*) to deliver local services and enterprises of different kinds, drawing on a successful model from the Irish Gaeltacht. In 1977 HIDB appointed two field officers to work with the *co-chomuinn*, John Angus Mackay in Lewis and Harris and Coinneach MacLean in Uist and Barra. Mackay would go on to play a key role in Gaelic development in the following decades. *Co-chomuinn* in different island communities were involved in diverse activities such as knitting, equipment hire, machine peat cutting and bakeries, and Gaelic was 'discreetly and acceptably' established as the normal language of organisation and delivery (Pedersen 2019: 52–62: GRG 1982: 35).

As HIDB became increasingly proactive in funding these diverse grass-roots Gaelic-related development initiatives, their success and potential prompted HIDB to establish a Gaelic Report Group in 1981 with the remit to 'advise the Board on the need and scope for more effective forms of help for developments in the Gaelic community in the Highlands and Islands linked with the Gaelic language' (GRG 1982: 2). This initiative came at a time when the political environment surrounding Gaelic had become particularly tense, partly as a result of the failure of a parliamentary bill that would have given official status to Gaelic, discussed in the next section.

The Report Group's review built on earlier policy proposals, notably the small but important 1976 book *Gàidhlig ann an Albainn/Gaelic in Scotland*, edited by Derick Thomson, which was styled 'a blueprint for official and private initiatives' (MacThòmais 1976). The book contained chapters on different areas of activity by six expert commentators, setting out recommendations for development in relation to education, media, culture and public life.

The Report Group had seven members, with Donald John MacKay, former director of An Comunn, in the chair and Martin MacDonald as the rapporteur. The group's report, *Cor na Gàidhlig* ('The State of Gaelic'), published in 1982, explored the context for Gaelic development in great detail, pronouncing the current structure of provision profoundly inadequate and arguing that 'the current situation is characterised by fragmentation of effort, lack of liaison, and a quite alarming degree of ignorance and misconception', which 'lead to unnecessary dissipation of scarce resources and obstructive, ill-informed attitudes' (GRG 1982: 82).

Analysing the current position of the Gaelic community, the Report Group pointed to the demographic challenge posed by simultaneous out-migration and in-migration: while young people left the Gàidhealtachd 'seeking further training' or a 'wider range of job opportunities', incomers, many of them middle-aged, 'find in the Highlands opportunities that attract them, particularly in the tourist-related sector' (GRG 1982: 16). This in-migration from non-Gaelic areas was to intensify significantly in the following decades, as discussed below (pp. 236–7). The group pointed to a 'widespread fatalism' in the Gaelic community and 'an acceptance by substantial numbers of the population that Gaelic was irrelevant to the future welfare of their children' (GRG 1982: 14).

The *Cor na Gàidhlig* report, now recognised as a landmark in the history of Gaelic development, made a detailed series of policy recommendations. Chief among these was the proposal to establish a new dedicated Gaelic development agency, 'Comhairle na Gàidhlig', with 'the participation of the main bodies which have a major role to play in language-related development in the indigenous Gaelic areas', namely HIDB, CnE, Highland Regional Council, Strathclyde Regional Council and An Comunn (GRG 1982: 82). The report also specified eight recommendations for new ventures in relation to the Gaelic arts, publishing, pre-school education and tourism (GRG 1982: 88–98), and identified a list of priority actions for HIDB, including recommendations concerning its own operations and matters that should be communicated to the Scottish Office.

The main aims of the proposed Comhairle na Gàidhlig were 'to initiate and carry out projects and ventures beneficial to the Gaelic community from a linguistic viewpoint' and 'provide expert advice and guidance to organisations on formulating Gaelic policies and introducing

Gaelic initiatives' (GRG 1982: 83). An initial staff complement of four was proposed, under the direction of a nine-member council, with an annual budget of £90,000 (GRG 1982: 83–4).

Following submission of the report, HIDB requested authorisation from the Scottish Office to offer an annual grant of £100,000 for four years to establish Comhairle na Gàidhlig. The Scottish Office was deeply reluctant to grant this request, even though it was keenly aware of the expectations the proposal had generated in the Gaelic world and of HIDB's concern that 'unrest among youth in Gaeldom might increase' if the proposal were rejected (SO 1983e: 4). The government's main concerns involved duplication of effort with the work of An Comunn and the risk of failure on the part of the new organisation (SO 1983f). After protracted internal discussion, in 1984 the Scottish Office notified HIDB that support for the initiative should be limited to 50 per cent of the organisation's proposed budget (£50,000 a year for four years) and that the funds should either be given to an existing organisation such as An Comunn or that any new body should merge in due course with An Comunn or another existing organisation (SO 1984a).

As this reorganisation was being proposed, however, An Comunn was itself going through a period of unprecedented crisis. Although it remained the principal Gaelic organisation at the start of the 1980s, with a membership of around 2,600 (GRG 1982: 39), it was increasingly perceived as a 'spent force' by a new generation of 'young Turks' (Caimbeul 2000: 55; Hutchinson 2005: 159). For several years, younger Gaelic activists had been frustrated by the organisation's conservatism and perceived ineffectiveness, and the long-standing issue of the extent to which Gaelic would be used in the organisation's operations came to a head at the annual general meeting in 1983, where a resolution was adopted that only Gaelic should be used for committee meetings. In March 1984 this decision was reversed at an Extraordinary Meeting (MacThòmais 1984), prompting some forty activists to walk out of the meeting and form a splinter organisation, Gàidhlig air Thoiseach (Gaelic First) (*WHFP* 1984b).

In April 1984 HIDB convened a meeting to plan a way forward. This involved the steering committee appointed to implement the *Cor na Gàidhlig* report, An Comunn, the dissident faction of An Comunn and others. This meeting followed extensive preparatory discussions and negotiations among these interested parties, coordinated by Allan Campbell, a development officer at Highland Regional Council who was seconded to assist HIDB for this purpose (Hutchinson 2005: 159–60). The group eventually managed to agree a proposal by which An Comunn would retain its functions (and funding) relating to Gaelic 'cultural exposition', particularly the Mòd, but the new Comhairle na Gàidhlig (CnaG)[6] would take over educational and language development functions. The board of CnaG would consist of representatives of HIDB, An Comunn and the three local authorities in the Gàidhealtachd, and CnaG would also be structured as a public membership organisation (SO 1984b). A steering committee was appointed to develop this proposal and Campbell was commissioned to prepare a supporting report (HIDB 1984; Campbell 1984). Campbell's report projected a budget for CnaG of £130,000 in the first year of operation, with funding coming from the SED (diverting some of their existing funding of An Comunn) and local authorities in addition to HIDB (Campbell 1984: 9–10). This proposal was agreed by the Scottish Office, albeit without enthusiasm, and then by An Comunn's Executive and membership.

John Angus Mackay was appointed as director of CnaG and Donald John MacLeod, who had also been deeply involved in Gaelic community development activities in the Western Isles, became the Education Officer. The organisation, based in Inverness, quickly won praise for its 'impressive' 'slick approach, based on good strong professional standards' (MacThòmais 1986). In an independent review of CnaG's work in 1989, Martin MacDonald concluded that it had 'evolved a successful strategy for fulfilling the aims' of the *Cor na Gàidhlig* report (authored by MacDonald), in particular through an effective 'system of priorities' and 'project-based strategy', but that the organisation was 'critically understaffed' (CnaG 1989b: 2, 11).

In July 1985 CnaG and the Gaelic college Sabhal Mòr Ostaig (discussed below) organised an important policy conference at the college with the title 'Towards a National Policy for Gaelic'. Scottish Secretary George Younger attended the conference and promised government support for community initiatives to promote the language:

> Central government efforts cannot save the Gaelic language unless Gaelic-speaking communities act out their own convictions and commitment to their mother tongue. [. . .] This [. . .] is why it is so important that this conference should encourage voluntary initiatives involving the community at large and young people in particular. We are prepared to do our part [. . .] working in partnership with local authorities, voluntary organisations and individuals who wish to build on the foundations already laid in support of Gaelic. (CnaG 1986: 8)

Pressed by poet and activist Aonghas MacNeacail about the issue of official status for Gaelic, Younger proposed to take an incremental approach, 'to move forward in using Gaelic for documents and so on, where it is appropriate and useful to do so, edging forward the frontiers' (CnaG 1986: 9). Although Younger's statements at the conference lacked any real concreteness, his general expression of support and openness to legitimate demands from the Gaelic community came to be recognised as a watershed in terms of government policy towards the language (Hutchinson 2005: 188–9).

The conference agreed key recommendations in the fields of education, the arts, the media, training, government services and the law, which were then further developed in CnaG's post-conference report, also entitled *Towards a National Policy for Gaelic* (CnaG 1986). The report asserted:

> The basis of the national policy should be that every Gaelic speaker in Scotland has the right to use Gaelic in as many situations as possible. This minimum long-term objective [...] can only be realised when Government accepts positive responsibility for Gaelic and gives a lead to all public bodies in regard to the explicit recognition of this principle. (CnaG 1986: 3)

Rather than 'a comprehensive and detailed list of requirements', CnaG proposed to seek 'agreement on broad policy principles, coupled with an advisory structure, through which such a dialogue can proceed' (CnaG 1986: 3). CnaG recommended that it should serve as the Scottish Office's 'official advisory body on Gaelic', but with two preconditions: that it must 'continue to operate at the community level to assist needs and aspirations' and that it 'have access to the policy formation process in the Scottish Office – and other public bodies' (CnaG 1986: 3). The latter demand was not satisfied in any meaningful sense, and these points continue to pose key challenges for Gaelic policy, now in relation to Bòrd na Gàidhlig, which struggles to serve Gaelic communities effectively or to exert significant influence on decision-making by government or other public bodies.

The report then discussed a series of policy areas and set out specific recommendations for the Scottish Office, other UK government departments, local government, broadcasters and broadcasting authorities. These broadly involved what can be called 'mainstreaming', requiring Gaelic to be taken into account in relation to particular policies and services and embedded in policy-making structures (CnaG 1986: 4–6).

In a leader column, the *Glasgow Herald* characterised the report as 'sensible' and 'coolly worded' and suggested that the government should find its goals 'almost totally acceptable' and that a 'clear, thrustful' government policy on Gaelic was required (*GH* 1986a). Although much progress was made in Gaelic development in the years following 1985, the word 'towards' in the title proved to be optimistic, and it would not be until 2007 and 2010, with the publication of the first National Gaelic Language Plan by Bòrd na Gàidhlig and the Scottish Government's first Gaelic Language Plan (BnG 2007; SG 2010a), that an actual formal national policy would be issued.

In its early years, CnaG was active in a wide range of fields, including economic development, education, children and youth, broadcasting and the arts. Its work in the key areas of education and broadcasting is discussed in detail below. Working with local committees, CnaG also prepared a series of ten-year development plans covering particular areas of the Gàidhealtachd: the Western Isles, Skye, Islay, Mull and northwest Sutherland (CnaG 1987a, 1987b, 1987c, 1987d, 1992). According to Allan Campbell, chief executive of CnaG from 1993 to 2003, these were intended not as action programmes but more as a statement of what might be possible if sufficient resources were available (Campbell 2011).

Over time, the limits of the development infrastructure developed in the mid-1980s became apparent and activists' attention shifted to building a more secure structure. As Donald Meek summarised the situation:

> The Gaelic leadership became aware of a serious flaw in Gaelic language planning, namely the lack of an overall plan braced by legal statute and provision. Gaelic development had been fostered by a series of unco-ordinated initiatives. There was a need for a framework which was both politically secure and also realistic in terms of committing hard cash to tackling the needs of the future. (Meek 2001b: 27)

Again the example of Wales was invoked: new legislation, the *Welsh Language Act 1993*, had been enacted (superseding the *Welsh Language Act 1967*), which stated definitively that Welsh and English should be treated on a 'basis of equality' and required public bodies to give effect to this principle through formal Welsh language schemes. The ultimately successful efforts to secure counterpart legislation for Gaelic are discussed in the next chapter.

DONALD STEWART'S GAELIC BILL

Initiatives in Gaelic development in the 1980s were taking place in a rapidly changing environment. Gaelic became significantly more politicised during this period, and new kinds of militant rhetoric and tactics came to the fore. One of the most important triggers for this shift was essentially coincidental. In late 1980 Donald Stewart, SNP MP for the Western Isles, placed second in the annual lottery for private members' bills in the House of Commons, which allowed him to submit a bill of his choosing. Stewart used this opportunity to introduce a bill that would have granted official status to Gaelic. His *Gaelic (Miscellaneous Provisions) Bill* was short but wide-ranging, including provisions to designate formally the 'Gaelic-speaking areas' of Scotland (the phrase used in the 'Gaelic clause' in education acts from 1918 onwards) and impose on the education authorities in such areas a general obligation 'to provide education in Gaelic'; to authorise the use of Gaelic by parties and witnesses '[i]n any legal proceeding in Scotland'; to authorise the production of Gaelic versions of forms and official documents (a provision that aligned with the *Welsh Language Act 1967*); and to establish a Gaelic Broadcasting Committee 'to co-ordinate and develop Gaelic television and radio'. When the bill came for a second reading in February 1981, however, it was allowed to expire, having gathered only thirty-seven of the hundred votes required to close the debate and allow the bill to proceed to the next stage of the legislative process (Burton and Drewry 1983: 453). The lack of support for Gaelic, and the lack of understanding, indeed contempt, expressed by several MPs, surprised and dismayed many in the Gaelic movement and inspired a new wave of militance on the part of activists.

Although the government did not make its view of the bill public, from the beginning its private discussions were strongly negative. Undersecretary of State Alex Fletcher described the bill as 'preposterous' and claimed that the case against it was 'formidable' in terms of cost implications, 'the scope for trouble-making' and 'patent inadequacies of drafting'; even 'the publicity which a Committee Stage would give the Gaelic enthusiasts is reason enough for Ministers to seek to prevent it' (SO 1981c). Officials in the Scottish Office, Scottish Courts Administration and Procurator Fiscal's office concurred that the bill should be opposed, principally on the grounds that it would involve additional government expenditure (SO 1981b).

Although the Chief Whip's office originally considered dragging out the debate on the Stewart bill in order to block another pending private member's bill involving freedom of information, it was eventually decided simply to kill the Gaelic bill as quickly as possible (SO 1981a, 1981d). Scottish Secretary George Younger 'sought advice on the possibility of amending the bill to render it anodyne', so as to 'attract less unfavourable publicity than blocking' the bill outright' (SO 1981f), but this suggestion was dismissed on the grounds that '[it] would be difficult to draft amendments which would make the Bill anodyne but not be wrecking in themselves' (SO 1981g).

Three strands of argument dominated the brief but acrimonious parliamentary debate, which was marred by an extraordinary series of hostile attacks on Gaelic and patronising remarks. First, there were expressions of outright prejudice against Gaelic and Gaelic speakers, like that of Labour MP Martin O'Neill, who mused about potential difficulties that might arise from 'a drunken Highlander appearing in court on a Monday morning claiming the right to give evidence in Gaelic' (Hansard 1981: col. 1113). Second, there were sceptical queries about the need to expand Gaelic's role given its weak demographic position, and stereotypical comments characterising Gaelic as an outmoded language unsuited to the modern world. Conservative MP Ian Sproat suggested that once Gaelic achieved official status the government would be required to print 'income tax forms for Cornwall [. . .] in bilingual Cornish [sic]', while Labour's George Robertson argued that a knowledge of Esperanto would be more useful than a knowledge of Gaelic (Hansard 1981: cols 1135, 1098).

Third, and perhaps most important, there were challenges to Gaelic's past and future significance in the life of Scotland as a whole, rather than merely the Gàidhealtachd. Alex Fletcher questioned 'how far we should go in providing a formal position for Gaelic in those areas where there is no indigenous Gaelic linguistic or cultural tradition' (Hansard 1981: col. 1116). Fletcher argued that it would 'build up resentment' if a provision making Gaelic court interpreters available were to be applied throughout Scotland, while Sproat declared that the bill was 'a first step towards the foisting of Gaelic on people in Scotland who do not want it foisted upon them' (Hansard 1981: cols 1116, 1132).

Supporters of Gaelic were greatly offended by the parliamentary response to Stewart's bill. In May, a march in Edinburgh in support of Gaelic attracted some five hundred participants, small in scale in comparison to street demonstrations involving other political issues but unprecedented in relation to Gaelic; this remains the largest demonstration ever seen concerning the language. In July An Comunn presented a petition with six thousand signatures to the Scottish Office, demanding improvements in the status and funding of Gaelic (ACG 1981c; SO 1981h).

In the wake of the defeat, various Gaelic organisations and commentators criticised the bill as having been poorly drafted (Thompson 1981).[7] An Comunn's Directorate published a detailed post-mortem, disavowing responsibility for the wording of the bill, in particular the arguably over-broad section concerning education. An Comunn also challenged its more militant critics, arguing that 'following a setback like this An Comunn cannot afford an emotional outburst, condemning all and sundry, friend and foe alike'. It suggested that critics who were not prepared to follow An Comunn's rules should 'join or form another organisation' and warned that 'in the climate of today there is a tendency for those who get involved in causes that provoke strong feelings to turn towards actions that ignore the rules of law' (ACG 1981a).

In 1981–3 there were several direct action campaigns involving the painting out of monolingual English road signs, in the manner of Welsh language campaigners. Such action was not unprecedented; in 1977 a short-lived organisation called Comunn nan Còirichean Sìobhalta (The Civil Rights Society) painted over several English signs in Skye and Lochalsh (Thompson 1986: 123). The two main organisations that emerged in the early 1980s were Strì (Struggle) and Ceartas (Justice). Strì was established in the summer of 1980, with Finlay MacLeod[8] as its chair (*GH* 1980: 7). Strì's first campaign focused on broadcasting but it also emphasised the importance of Gaelic education (GRG 1982: 41). MacLeod argued that instead of 'quick solution[s]' such as Scottish independence or the adoption of formal policies, it was necessary to 'build a strong base and a steady structure' (MacLeòid 1981). Even so, Strì sometimes adopted militant rhetoric. For example, it charged Strathclyde Regional Council with 'cultural genocide' for its decision to downgrade the Gaelic post at Oban High School from that of principal teacher to assistant principal teacher (*GH* 1981b). Earlier that year, proposing a campaign to encourage Gaelic speakers to withhold payment of television licences, MacLeod declared 'we are being driven to desperate measures' (*GH* 1981a). In the event, the campaign did not gain significant momentum.

The most active direct action group was Ceartas, which was founded in the immediate aftermath of the vote on the Stewart Bill. Activists associated with Sabhal Mòr Ostaig had gathered in London in connection with the vote and on their return to Scotland they painted out English road signs and painted Gaelic slogans along main roads in Perthshire, Lochaber and Skye (Hutchinson 2005: 146–7). Three months later, following a conference at SMO, Ceartas defaced several more road signs in south Skye (*P&J* 1981). In the autumn, just before the Mòd in Fort William, all the signs on the A82 (the main road in the West Highlands) from Loch Lomond north bearing the name Fort William were plastered over with storm-proof marine plastic stickers bearing the Gaelic form, An Gearasdan. This operation did not involve Ceartas but a different team of activists, who were never identified or charged (MacKinnon 2011). Ceartas also threatened to destroy radio and television masts if provision for Gaelic was not improved (*Crann-Tàra* 1981a), but this did not materialise. The group was very small, with no more than fifteen activists in all (Taylor 2011).

Several of these sign-painting incidents led to prosecutions, including one that gave rise to an important precedent reaffirming the highly limited role of Gaelic in the Scottish legal system, involving Iain Taylor, then director of SMO and a Ceartas activist, for defacing road signs in Skye in May 1981. In September of that year Mark Wringe, an undergraduate at Edinburgh University (later to become a lecturer at Sabhal Mòr), was refused permission to enter a plea in Gaelic in relation to a prosecution for a minor traffic offence. The Crown Office, the principal prosecutorial agency, took the position that all pleas must be in English and that '[p]leading in Gaelic was similar to a person remaining mute' (*GH* 1981c). In 1983 Taylor, Wringe and Alan Esslemont (who went on to become a senior executive at the Gaelic television service MG ALBA) were also prosecuted in connection with a subsequent Ceartas campaign involving signs on the A9 (*WHFP* 1984d).

Taylor's trial was held in Portree Sheriff Court in April 1982. Taylor moved the court to have the trial conducted in Gaelic, but the request was denied in light of his ability to use English. (Taylor was in fact a learner of Gaelic, originally from Elgin; it has been argued that in the politically charged circumstances it might have been better had a native speaker taken the 'test case' (MacKinnon 1991: 115)). Taylor then took an appeal to the High Court, which rejected his claim, relying on that court's 1841 *Alexander McRae* decision, discussed in chapter 1, which had held it improper to allow a witness to testify in Gaelic, through an interpreter, when the witness could speak English 'with perfect distinctness'.

The *Taylor* decision simply ratified existing practice, whereby permission to testify in Gaelic was essentially a matter for the individual judge's discretion, and it did not prompt the authorities to revisit the issue and make any change to court practice. In 1983 a senior civil servant acknowledged the 'ordinary' practice as reasserted in *Taylor* but indicated that policy on the matter was settled: 'Successive administrations have considered that Scottish legislation similar to the [*Welsh Language Act 1967*] would not be justified' (SO 1983a). Other than a minor modification concerning civil cases in three sheriffdoms, discussed in the next chapter, there has been no change since then; the *McRae* precedent from 1841 remains in effect. As all Gaelic speakers are now bilingual in Gaelic and English, this nearly completely precludes the use of Gaelic in court. The divergence with Wales, where a broad right to use Welsh is set out in the *Welsh Language Act 1993* (s. 22), is stark.

Despite the failure of the Stewart Bill and the court decision in *Taylor*, over the course of the 1980s the government slowly began to make more use of Gaelic in various official contexts. To some extent, these changes resulted from campaigning pressure. In a letter to George Younger in 1983, Donald Stewart argued that the failure of the Scottish Office to print 'any official forms or information leaflets in Gaelic or bilingually' amounted to 'definitely institutionalised discrimination against the Gaelic language in Scotland', given the range of documents that was being produced in Welsh and various South Asian languages (Stewart 1983). Stewart's demand prompted a negative response from the Scottish Information Office, the section of the Scottish Office with responsibility for the production of public information: 'for strictly marketing and cost considerations SIO would be against the production of material in Gaelic' and that '[w]e can effectively penetrate the market in English, and to suggest otherwise is frankly bunkum' (SO 1983d). But this traditional line of reasoning was quietly set aside as more and more Gaelic came to be used in government publications of different kinds, albeit sporadically and without any formal announcement or explicit policy. These included a Gaelic version of a leaflet and claim form concerning benefits entitlements (Hansard 1984). By 1987 the SED had introduced bilingual stationery. There were other experiments to give symbolic validation to Gaelic: the Scottish Office began issuing some press releases bilingually (Hansard 1986) and (non-Gaelic-speaking) Scottish Office ministers began to use the language in parliamentary debates and at Gaelic events (SO 1988; Hansard 1988, 1995).

A more unlikely form of official recognition came in connection with the *British Nationality Act 1981*, which was enacted a few months after the debacle of the Stewart Bill. The Act enumerated among the requirements for naturalisation as a British citizen that the applicant 'has a sufficient knowledge of the English, Welsh or Scottish Gaelic language' (schedule 1, s.1-(1)(c)). This was a new concession on the government's part, as the predecessor *Immigration Act 1971* permitted applicants for naturalisation to show a knowledge of Welsh,[9] reflecting the grant of legal status in the *Welsh Language Act 1967*, but a proposal that this be extended to Gaelic was rejected (Hansard 1971). The clause concerning Gaelic in the 1981 Act originated with amendments placed in both Houses of Parliament, which the Home Office originally opposed. Scottish Secretary George Younger successfully urged the Home Secretary, William Whitelaw, to accept the amendments, arguing that this would be seen as a 'significant advance' by the Gaelic community and could bring 'real political advantage', while a government defeat on the amendment would be 'highly embarrassing' (SO 1981i). The proposal was recognised as 'entirely presentational' in that very few if any candidates were likely to apply for naturalisation based on their knowledge of Gaelic, but the government was concerned about other possible political ramifications: against the background of ongoing hunger strikes by Irish Republican Army prisoners, the use of the term 'Scottish Gaelic' was intended to make clear that Irish would not be covered by this provision (HO 1981; SED 1981c).

The 1981 provision relating to Gaelic was retained in the successor immigration statute, the *Borders, Citizenship and Immigration Act 2009*. These provisions are very largely symbolic, given demographic and sociolinguistic reality, as there were very few if any potential applicants for naturalisation who could speak Gaelic but not English. It was nevertheless interesting as an indicator of the fluid nature of British identity; it would be inconceivable, for example, for the French or Spanish government to allow an applicant to acquire citizenship on the basis of their knowledge of Basque.

Various public bodies and private organisations also began to make increased provision for Gaelic during this period. Sometimes campaigning pressure was applied, but for the most part this was a matter of gradual, sporadic cultural shift rather than any kind of programmatic development. For example, the three established banks in Scotland had begun to issue Gaelic chequebooks in the early 1970s and to install bilingual signage in Gaelic areas from the late 1970s, as did the ferry company Caledonian MacBrayne (GRG 1982: 28), while the Post Office followed suit from 1987 (*P&J* 1987). A number of public or charitable bodies began to produce Gaelic publications or develop Gaelic policies, including the National Museum of Scotland (Macintosh 1999: 461). Taken together, these various initiatives brought a new degree of prominence to Gaelic in Scottish public life.

THE ESTABLISHMENT OF GAELIC-MEDIUM EDUCATION

Following the groundbreaking initiatives in bilingual education in the Western Isles and Skye, the most important steps in Gaelic education began not in the traditional rural communities but in the cities. This involved a shift from bilingual programmes as they had developed in the Western Isles and Skye to 'Gaelic-medium' programmes in which the proportion of Gaelic used in teaching was considerably greater. The most important campaign emerged in Glasgow, culminating in the opening of a dedicated Gaelic-medium primary school unit in August

1985. Another Gaelic unit also opened in Inverness at the same time, following a similar campaign there.

A key feature of these initiatives, and subsequent initiatives in Gaelic education, is that they have been driven by parental demand. Initial expressions of demand have come through parental self-organisation so that the decision to enrol children in Gaelic-medium provision is a result of affirmative parental choice. This dynamic has rendered irrelevant the problem of parental 'apathy' that dogged Gaelic activists in earlier periods. Parents have always retained the option of English-medium education, however, in contrast to the Irish Gaeltacht and Gwynedd in northwest Wales, where no such provision is available.

By the late 1970s many of the institutions established by Glasgow's Gaelic community in the late nineteenth and early twentieth centuries had begun to decline. The most obvious manifestation of this transition was the closure of the Highlanders Institute (Aitreabh nan Gàidheal) in 1979, for financial reasons. The Institute had opened in 1925 and served for decades as the main site for events organised by the city's various Gaelic societies. The once-strong cultural organisation Ceilidh nan Gaidheal faded out as an older generation of members died off, as did the Gaelic League of Scotland, although it continued to offer Gaelic classes until the late 1980s (Campbell 2014). The Gaelic Society of Glasgow continued to offer its lecture series, however, and the stronger of the various island and district associations, such as the Glasgow Lewis and Harris Association, the Glasgow Skye Association and the Glasgow Uist and Barra Association, maintained their extensive programmes of social events.

Kenna Campbell, secretary of Comann Sgoiltean Dà-chànanach Ghlaschu (the Glasgow Gaelic Bilingual Schools Association), which led the campaign for Gaelic-medium education, said that it was 'extremely difficult to understand' why pressure for GME in Glasgow (as opposed to teaching the language as a subject) had not developed earlier (Wilson 1985a). Welsh-medium schools in Wales, in contrast, spread rapidly from the late 1940s onwards (Evans 2000). One reason for the new concern was that Gaelic-speaking parents, typically people who had migrated to the city from Gaelic-speaking areas, found that it was becoming more difficult to raise their children in Glasgow as Gaelic speakers, a pattern that had been reasonably common in earlier decades. The suburbanisation of the city in the post-war period, when many people left densely populated inner-city areas such as Partick and Govan, played a role, and the practice of returning to Gaelic-speaking island communities for long periods in the summer became less common. In Campbell's view, people may not have 'realised how quickly decline was setting in' (Wilson 1985a) – a common feature of language shift situations.

Organised campaigning for Gaelic provision in the city began in 1980 when Urras Brosnachaidh na Gàidhlig (the Gaelic Language Promotion Trust) commissioned Professor Nigel Grant of Glasgow University, an expert on bilingual education, to explore the prospects for increasing Gaelic provision in Strathclyde Region (including the Oban area as well as Glasgow) (Grant 1980). At the annual meeting of the Glasgow Skye Association in 1982, poet and activist Aonghas MacNeacail raised the issue of Gaelic provision in Glasgow as a matter of concern, and this led to a national conference on Gaelic education in Glasgow in October 1983, which addressed questions of current practice and parental demand. Following the 1983 conference, Grant prepared a report on the feasibility of establishing bilingual schools in mainland Scotland, which was then submitted to Strathclyde Regional Council (N. Grant 1983; see also J. H. Grant 1983). The campaigners' demands were shaped by input from those familiar with the situation in the Western Isles, notably CnaG director John Angus Mackay and Highland councillor the Rev. Jack MacArthur, who advised the Glasgow campaigners to press for GME rather than bilingual education (K. Campbell 2014). Campaigners formed Comann Sgoiltean Dà-chànanach Ghlaschu, which organised a series of public meetings to inform and encourage parents (Fraser 1989: 163). In their leaflet seeking support from parents, the association argued that

> Virtually all minority groups in Britain are striving to preserve their own culture and identity. Many of them have been delighted to discover support coming to them from official bodies. As usual the Gaels have been content to stay at the 'back of the queue'. No-one but ourselves will press our claim.
> Let's move now! (Comann Sgoiltean Dà-chànanach Ghlaschu [1984])

These arguments reflected the context of a large urban authority in the early 1980s, where (in line with practice in other British cities) policy-makers had begun to make educational and social service provision to address the needs of growing immigrant populations (McClure 1983).

The progress of the campaign encountered various difficulties along the way. Campaigners perceived the council's education officials as being resistant to their proposals (Robertson 2011; Campbell 2014; Smith 2014), and in turn CnaG reported that council officials viewed Comann Sgoiltean Dà-chànanach Ghlaschu as 'a somewhat extremist group whose activities could be prejudicial to a controlled and reasonable programme of development of Gaidhlig education in the area'

(CnaG 1985). In particular, a feasibility study commissioned by the council concluded that GME would only be suitable for children who already spoke Gaelic (Fraser 1989: 164). But the Gaelic campaigners were able to make important allies among key councillors, notably Malcolm Green, convener of the council's Education Committee, and Bernard Scott, another Education Committee member, and to a lesser extent Charles Gray, convener of the council. This support from elected politicians played a crucial role in overcoming the resistance of council education officials and securing approval for an 'experimental' programme on the immersion model (Strathclyde Regional Council 1985a; Fraser 1989: 164–5).

Although the parents had asked for provision in the northwest of the city, where parents who had expressed interest in Gaelic education were concentrated, the council was unable to find suitable space in that area. The council offered a building north of the city centre, but this was rejected as unsuitable, and the council then proposed classrooms in Sir John Maxwell Primary School, in Shawlands on the south side of the city. This would not be a full school, moreover, but only a Gaelic 'unit', part of a school in which other children would be taught through the medium of English (Fraser 1989: 165–6; Campbell 2014; Smith 2014). This 'unit' model was to become the norm in Gaelic-medium provision across Scotland, as discussed below (pp. 209–10, 264).

The Gaelic unit in Glasgow opened in August 1985, with two teachers and twenty pupils, some of them as old as nine. The children came from various parts of the city, most of them far away from the school, so that arranging transport to the school was a significant issue (Fraser 1989: 162). For the first few months a minibus service was organised and paid for by Comann Sgoiltean Dà-chànanach Ghlaschu, Urras Brosnachaidh na Gàidhlig and the parents themselves (Wilson 1985b). The council then assumed responsibility for funding transport (Strathclyde Regional Council 1985b) but the following summer a council sub-committee voted to discontinue this funding. Following a protest by the parents, this decision was reversed by the full Education Committee. According to Kenna Campbell, this decision averted 'the virtual closure of the unit, because without travel expenses most of the children could not continue to go'. Green, a Labour councillor, made the case for funding in political terms, arguing that a failure to provide this would amount to 'abhorrent' 'financial discrimination' and limit the unit to well-off parents (*GH* 1986b; Fraser 1989: 162). Provision of free transport was also analogised to the service provided for pupils attending the city's specialist music and dance schools (Fraser 1989: 162).

This agreement to provide free school transport set an important precedent and became the norm once GME began to be offered in other parts of Scotland. This pattern of provision has continued down to the present, although it has sometimes provoked controversy (*EEN* 2010b; *P&J* 2011). The availability of free transport, which makes accessing the provision much easier for families in logistical terms, has certainly facilitated the growth of GME in Scotland over the decades. The situation contrasts sharply with the position in Northern Ireland, where no free transport to Irish-medium schools is provided (*McKee* v. *Department of Education*).

By 1989 enrolment in the Gaelic unit in Glasgow had reached eighty-nine (Fraser 1989: 159) and it continued to grow in the years following. By the late 1990s parents had become increasingly dissatisfied with the Gaelic unit at Sir John Maxwell's, and began to press for a free-standing Gaelic school in which all pupils would receive GME, as discussed in the following chapter (pp. 264–5).

In Inverness, progress towards the establishment of the Gaelic unit was rather less convoluted. As discussed above, Highland Regional Council had been offering bilingual education in a number of schools in Skye from 1978 onwards, so the concept of GME was not as novel as it was for Strathclyde. Several important councillors were Gaelic speakers and were strongly supportive of the language, especially Duncan Grant and the Rev. Jack MacArthur (Prògram Choinnich 1995; Peacock 2012), and the council had established a working party on Gaelic in 1982 (O'Hanlon and Paterson 2015: 313). Former CNCA activist Iain MacIllechiar, by then a secondary Gaelic teacher, and primary teacher Lisa Storey were the principal organisers of parents in Inverness. As in Glasgow, several public meetings were organised (*P&J* 1984), and potential pupils for the school were also recruited by means of distributing leaflets at local nurseries and visiting interested families (Prògram Choinnich 1995; MacIllechiar 2012). As in Glasgow, provision was offered not as a full school but in a Gaelic unit, which opened at Central Primary School in August 1985, the same day as Glasgow's, and Storey became the first teacher. Of the ten pupils who enrolled in the first class, only three were fluent Gaelic speakers (Pàrantan airson Foghlam Gàidhlig 1986: 1). At the same time that it agreed to open the unit in Inverness, Highland Regional Council also accepted a proposal for Portree, but delayed commencement until August 1986 (*WHFP* 1985b).

It was significant that, from the outset and down to the present, campaigners for GME dedicated all their efforts to persuading the authorities to make provision in public schools rather than establishing independent Gaelic schools. In many other minority language communities, including Northern Ireland, Brittany, the Basque Country and Hawai'i, the approach has been very different; minority language education has begun in private schools, typically with a high degree of parental/community involvement and often in an adversarial relationship with the public education authorities. The different approach in Scotland can be seen as an indication of the ideologically moderate orientation of Gaelic language campaigners in contrast with more militant approaches taken elsewhere (e.g. Maguire 1991; Rogers 1997; López-Goñi 2003). At the same time, though, it is important to note that support for public education is deeply embedded in Scotland, so that proposing to establish private Gaelic schools would have been objectionable to many potential supporters. The approach of 'working within the system' has brought some clear positive results for Gaelic campaigners, but it has required Gaelic organisations and parents' groups to accept many compromises, and several campaigns have failed or stalled when education authorities have rebuffed parental demands, as discussed in the next chapter (pp. 265–6 and 301–4).

FUNDING GAELIC EDUCATION

As bilingual education developed in the early 1980s, the relevant education authorities endeavoured to secure additional funding to meet the additional costs involved. These efforts proved time-consuming and fraught with obstacles. In 1982 the three local authorities involved in the delivery of Gaelic education at that time – CnE, Highland and Strathclyde – submitted a detailed application to the Scottish Office asking the government to make regulations under section 73 of the *Education (Scotland) Act 1980* which would authorise the government to make payment of specific grants for Gaelic education (CnE 1982b). A statutory authorisation of this kind was already in place to promote education in Welsh (*Education Act 1980*, s. 21).

The initial reaction of Scottish Office civil servants was distinctly unreceptive. The issue was framed in political terms: referring to the unsuccessful efforts to secure legislative protection for Gaelic in 1981, it was noted that ministers' 'unsympathetic reaction to the two Private Members bills last year suggests that they have no strong desire to placate the Gaelic lobby, despite the embarrassing measures taken by the Welsh Office' (SED 1982b). The obvious course, for the civil servants, would have been to turn the application down flat, but it was suggested that '[i]f Ministers want to make any gesture at all, this might be confined to relatively minor increases in grants to the bodies already active in this field' (SO 1982a, 1982b). There was an additional complication in terms of the mechanism of local government finance, as the creation of new 'ring-fenced' central government grants had the knock-on effect of reducing the overall grant given by central government to local authorities. The Convention of Scottish Local Authorities (COSLA) was therefore opposed as a matter of principle to the introduction of new specific grants. Eventually, Scottish Office minister Alex Fletcher turned down the councils' request for the introduction of a Gaelic-specific grant (SO 1982d) and SED officials later clarified that no 'increase in resources' for Gaelic education would be provided through other mechanisms (SED 1983).

This setback proved only temporary, as COSLA changed its position and announced that it would be willing to accept a specific grant for Gaelic education (SED 1985a, 1985b). The necessary enabling regulations,[10] which came into effect in 1986, covered expenditure on 'the teaching of the Gaelic language or the teaching in that language of other subjects'. In the first year of availability, 1986–7, the SED allocated £250,000 to the Specific Grants scheme, which provided local authorities with up to 75 per cent of the costs of Gaelic provision. Of this, £90,000 went to CnE, £90,000 to Highland and £70,000 to Strathclyde (SED 1985d). The decision to agree this Specific Grant funding was perceived as 'an important concession to the Gaelic lobby' on the part of COSLA (*TESS* 1985).

By 1990 the grant budget had grown to £1.2 million per year, and the number of local authorities drawing funding from the scheme had risen to eight. More than thirty years after its introduction, the Specific Grants remain in effect and continue to play a vital role in the Gaelic education system. In 2018–19 the funding level was £4.5 million per year (SG 2019). The introduction of the grant was extremely important in political terms, as it helped dispel financial concerns as a reason for education authorities to resist the introduction of GME, particularly at a time of budget cuts (Martin 2011; Robertson 2011). If authorities had been required to meet all the costs of new Gaelic-medium provision from their existing budgets, it is likely that some authorities would have been much less willing to agree to offer such provision.

THE DEVELOPMENT OF GME AFTER 1985

Building on these successes in Glasgow and Inverness, other new Gaelic primary units in various parts of Scotland opened rapidly in the following years. Two units opened in 1986, 5 in 1987, 3 in 1988, 6 in 1989, 8 in 1990, 5 in 1991, 7 in 1992 and 7 in 1993 (D. J. MacLeod 2007: 14). The great majority of these units were in small towns and villages in the Highlands and Islands, although these included areas where the language had long gone out of community use, such as Tain and Newtonmore, as well as rural areas of the Western Isles where Gaelic was still widely spoken, beginning at Breasclete in Lewis in 1986. Several units were established in Lowland towns and cities, including Aberdeen, Bishopbriggs, Edinburgh, East Kilbride and Forfar. From 1994 the rate of growth slowed, with three units opening each year until 1997, then one in 1998 and three in 1999 (MacLeòid 2007: 14), a pattern which continued in the twenty-first century, as discussed below (p. 297). A few Gaelic units closed not long after they opened, including Invergordon and Peterhead, a particularly unlikely location in the northeast of Scotland. GME was (and is) confined to state schools and there has also been no provision in denominational schools (although the schools chosen for the units in Fort William and Oban were council-run Catholic schools).[11]

Although twenty-five Gaelic units were established in the Western Isles between 1986 and 1999, taking in a quarter of primary pupils in the islands (D. J. MacLeod 2003: 13–14; Hutchinson 2005: 161), the 'unit' model proved controversial in this context. John Murray distinguished the situation in the islands, where there was already 'a detailed bilingual policy in operation', from other areas where there was no Gaelic provision, questioning 'why it should be necessary to add on segments to primary schools in an apparently haphazard way' (Murray 1987: [5]) and thereby create a sense that Gaelic was 'separate' and 'special' (Thompson 1987: 5). Other Gaelic activists, notably Annie MacSween, whose long involvement in Gaelic development began with the Van Leer Project, argued that the system was divisive in island communities, as it meant that children in GME might be sent to a school other than their local one, damaging the sense of cohesion in what were often very small communities, and sometimes placing the viability of the local school in jeopardy. MacSween argued that a universal system of bilingual education would have been more appropriate and more effective (MacSween 2011; BBC Naidheachdan 2013b).

In most areas where Gaelic-medium provision was established, the pattern of development was broadly similar, with local groups of parents coming together to organise an expression of local demand. In these efforts they were assisted by CnaG and especially by Comhairle nan Sgoiltean Àraich (CNSA, the Gaelic Pre-schools Association), so that a successful pre-school playgroup became the basis for follow-on primary provision. The decentralised structure of the Scottish education system meant that the case for Gaelic provision needed to be mounted and won in a number of individual authorities, each with its own officials and elected members. In this respect the pro-Gaelic policy adopted in the early 1980s by the Labour Party (which controlled most councils) was helpful (*WHFP* 1989), as was 'the general principle' that children should 'be educated in accordance with the wishes of their parents', embedded in the *Education (Scotland) Act 1980* (s. 28). Even so, Gaelic advocates were confronted by a pervasive 'dìth eòlas is dìth thuigsinn [. . .] is dìth fhaireachdainn' (lack of knowledge, understanding or sympathy), according to Boyd Robertson, then of Jordanhill College, who played an important role in Comann Sgoiltean Dà-Chànanach Glaschu (Robertson 2011). Some local campaigns were more straightforward than others: CNSA perceived Central Regional Council as obstructive (Ross 1992a), while other authorities were willing to open Gaelic units with very small numbers of pupils, sometimes even as few as three (Jordanhill College 1994). The situation was more favourable than in Northern Ireland, where the authorities declined recurrent funding for Irish-medium schools unless they had at least twelve pupils (fifteen in the main urban areas) (Mercator-Education 2004: 17).

CNSA was established at a meeting at Sabhal Mòr Ostaig in May 1982 following a visit to Wales the previous year to see how Welsh-medium pre-school provision was working (Scammell 1985: 22–3). At this time there were only four Gaelic pre-school groups in Scotland, but by 1985 this number had grown to eighteen and by 1994 there were 148, attended by 2,600 children (Macintosh 1999: 459). In 1983 HIDB awarded CNSA a grant which made it possible to appoint a full-time national development officer for three years, and Finlay MacLeod (formerly of Strì) took up this post. Additional part-time staff were then appointed in different parts of the country. CNSA placed strong emphasis on encouraging local groups to organise new playgroups in their own communities. From the outset a key aim was to stimulate parent demand for Gaelic-medium primary education, which would build on the pre-school experience (MacLeòid 1989–90). This grass-roots organisation proved to be an effective strategy and MacLeod's pivotal role in the process is widely credited in Gaelic circles.

As Gaelic-medium provision expanded and developed, the issue of curricular structure received increasing attention. Immersion education had developed from the 1960s onwards, originally for Anglophone children in Canada who were acquiring French (Lambert and Tucker

1972). Different pedagogical structures and approaches were developed in different contexts, with important variations in relation to the extent to which the target language was used for instruction and teacher–pupil interactions and the stage of schooling at which the target language was introduced. Bilingual education programmes can thus be categorised as 'early full immersion', 'late partial immersion' and all the points in between (Baker and Wright 2017). GME in Scotland came to develop as a relatively strong early immersion model, with Gaelic being introduced at an early stage and English not brought in until relatively late (O'Hanlon and Paterson 2015: 314). The adoption of a relatively strong pedagogical model is perhaps somewhat surprising given the traditional unease in the Gaelic community about the role of Gaelic in the education system; elsewhere, minority language communities have sometimes preferred, or been required to accept, models of bilingual education in which the majority language is used earlier and more extensively.

The development of a dedicated Gaelic curriculum progressed through the 1980s. In 1980, following 'strenuous representations' from the Gaelic sector, the Scottish Consultative Council on the Curriculum established a dedicated Committee on Gaelic, which issued a detailed report in 1983 with recommendations for development of Gaelic education, although these met with some resistance from the Council (HM Inspectors of Schools 1989: 5–6; Dunn and Robertson 1989: 50). Work was then taken forward by a Joint Working Party on Gaelic established by the SED (Dunn and Robertson 1989: 50–2).

In the early years of GME there were some divergences in the models of delivery (Johnstone 1994: 49) – unsurprisingly given that fourteen different education authorities[12] were offering GME by the late 1990s. Practice was then regularised by the 5–14 curriculum guidelines published by the Scottish Office Education Department[13] in 1993 (SOED 1993), which brought an 'unprecedented degree of standardisation in the definition of Gaelic education' (O'Hanlon and Paterson 2015: 314). The most important principles of these guidelines were the designation of an immersion phase of at least two years' duration (for children aged 5–6) in which Gaelic would be used exclusively; over time this was usually extended to three years. English was introduced at the end of primary 3 or the beginning of primary 4 and then used to an increasing degree in the subsequent years of primary education, with 'the relative proportion of time allocated to Gaelic and English language [. . .] vary[ing] in accordance with the needs of the child at particular times' (SOED 1993: 6). These principles were retained in the new Curriculum for Excellence

(SG 2010b) and subsequent guidance and advice on Gaelic education (BnG 2017; Education Scotland 2015).

The 5–14 guidelines stated the aim that provision should bring pupils 'to the stage of broadly equal competence in Gaelic and English, in all the skills, by the end of P[rimary] 7' (SOED 1993: 7). This was a challenging aspiration, particularly in relation to the explicit statement that this 'broadly equal competence' should pertain to all language skills, i.e. speaking, listening, reading and writing, as international research on bilingual education indicates that children who acquire an additional language through immersion education tend to come close to the skills of native speakers in relation to the 'passive' skills of listening and reading but to lag behind in relation to the 'active' skills of speaking and writing (Baker and Wright 2017: 257, 260).

A key challenge for GME from the beginning was the mixed nature of the pupil cohort. Unlike 'pure' immersion programmes, where all the participating children come from homes and communities in which the target language is not known or used, GME catered both for learners of the language and for children who were exposed to Gaelic in the home and, in some cases, children who were Gaelic-dominant[14] when starting school (Johnstone 1994: 48, 53). Ongoing language shift has meant that this problem has become less significant over time; even by the early 1990s, research suggested that a clear majority of children enrolled in GME in the Western Isles were coming from homes in which Gaelic was not normally spoken (Johnstone 1994: 50), and the proportions of such children were much lower in other parts of Scotland.

Conversely, there was no effort to develop a Gaelic curriculum distinct in content from that delivered in English-medium education in Scotland. Indeed, the teaching materials used are often translated from English into Gaelic. Although performance aspects of Gaelic culture play a prominent role in GME – especially song and instrumental music – there is relatively little emphasis on other aspects of Gaelic culture and no dedicated effort to inculcate Gaelic norms and values or Gaelic ways of seeing the world (MacLeod 2006–9: 237). Gaelic academic Domhnall Uilleam Stiùbhart went so far as to argue that Gaelic was being taught 'as a mere heap of words, with little or no cultural or historical context to give it meaning or value' (*WHFP* 2005).

This approach is quite different from that adopted in relation to indigenous language education programmes in other countries, notably that of Māori education in New Zealand. In part this reflects the intake to GME; the system has always been open to children from non-Gaelic backgrounds and an increasing proportion of pupils have little or no

Gaelic family heritage. In addition, it reflects the assimilative impulse of the Gaelic community more generally; a separatist approach to the GME curriculum, with a strong emphasis on cultural differentiation, might have caused concern to parents. Important questions about the nature of Gaelic culture would also need to be confronted; there has been relatively little critical examination of what exactly this consists of and what aspects should be emphasised in the contemporary world. Despite the lack of curricular differentiation, advocates often promoted GME by invoking the idea that bilingual education allowed children to develop 'two windows on the world', an understanding rooted in the so-called Sapir-Whorf hypothesis, the controversial proposition that every language inherently gives its speakers a different form of perception and conceptualisation and thus a different perspective on the world (Glaser 2007: 134).

As the Gaelic-medium system grew, three policy issues became increasingly problematic: the development of follow-on secondary provision, the challenge of teacher recruitment, and the perennial issue of finance.

The issue of secondary provision had already proved controversial in relation to the Bilingual Education Project, and then came to a head in 1994, when the schools inspectorate published its report *Provision for Gaelic Education in Scotland*. This report was the culmination of several years' work and gave a detailed evaluation of Gaelic provision of all levels. While it reached favourable conclusions in relation to primary GME, the report expressed a much dimmer view of the prospects for the further development of Gaelic-medium secondary provision. In particular, the report 'conclude[d] that the provision of Gaelic-medium secondary education in a number of subjects, determined by the vagaries of resource availability, is neither desirable nor feasible in the foreseeable future' and that secondary provision should instead have 'a closer focus on transmission of Gaelic language and culture per se [. . .] including elements from history, geography, music, art and drama' (SO Education Department 1994: 3).

The report prompted a strongly negative response from Gaelic organisations. Comann nam Pàrant, the newly founded national organisation of parents with children in GME, characterised the report as 'negative, unhelpful and [. . .] untrue' (Zall 1994). Students at the University of Edinburgh organised a demonstration outside the Scottish Office (Lewin and Mac an Tuairneir 2017: 89), and students at the University of Glasgow circulated a petition criticising the report that attracted more than seven hundred signatures (Zall 1994). The Conservative government's approach to secondary GME was changed by the new Labour government in 1997, which issued instructions 'to support and extend

GME in specified subjects in the secondary curriculum' (Macintosh 1999: 460). Even so, the limited scope of secondary GME has remained an ongoing difficulty down to the present, as discussed below (pp. 298–300). Pupils typically experience a sharp drop in the proportion of their lessons taught through Gaelic as they progress from primary to secondary school, and then from lower secondary to upper secondary, when they study particular subjects linked to formal national certificate examinations (O'Hanlon, Paterson and McLeod 2012: 31–2).

Recruitment of sufficient numbers of teachers has been a major ongoing problem in the development of GME. By the mid-1990s the shortage of Gaelic teachers had become 'a sharp brake on momentum in the progress of Gaelic education' (*WHFP* 1994). While this had sometimes been a difficulty in previous decades, the expansion of the Gaelic sector came at a time when the number of Gaelic speakers entering the labour force was steadily declining as a result of language shift. Somewhat ironically, another complicating factor was the widening of career opportunities in Gaelic as a result of development initiatives in different fields, especially television; where once there were almost no jobs involving Gaelic other than teaching, a range of different opportunities now became available. Various measures have been put in place over the decades to tackle the teacher shortage, including targeted recruitment campaigns, dedicated bursaries and in-service training programmes of different kinds, but as of 2020 significant difficulties remain, as discussed below (pp. 307–9).

A more fundamental difficulty with the development of GME was the absence of an overall national policy or strategy. The decentralised structure of the Scottish education system complicated matters; each authority offering GME was responsible for decisions concerning policy in its area, although an Inter-Authority Standing Group on Gaelic Education was set up in 1986 to promote coordination between the different authorities that provided GME. In 1997 CnaG published a national policy on Gaelic education (CnaG 1997b), but this lacked the official force that a government policy would have had. No official national strategy on GME was published until 2007 and no formal statutory guidance until 2017 (BnG 2007, 2017). In the absence of formal national policies, the most important statements of policy were the general curricular guidance documents (which are not strictly binding in the Scottish system) and periodic guidance documents from the schools inspectorate (e.g. HM Inspectorate of Schools 2011).

Significantly, GME appeared to be successful in terms of educational outcomes. An important study commissioned by the Scottish Office and published in 1999 concluded:

pupils receiving Gaelic-medium primary education, whether or not Gaelic was the language of their home, were not being disadvantaged in comparison with children educated through English. In many though not all instances they out-performed English-medium pupils and in addition gained the advantage of having become proficient in two languages. (Johnstone et al. 1999: 4)

These results were in line with many other studies of bilingual education internationally (Baker and Wright 2017: ch. 12) and were helpful not only in allaying fears of Gaelic-speaking parents but also in attracting non-Gaelic speakers who were impressed by the educational quality of GME (see pp. 309–10). Another study of pupil attainment in GME in 2010 produced broadly similar positive findings (O'Hanlon, McLeod and Paterson 2010; see p. 309).

On the other hand, there were concerns about immersion pupils' level of attainment in Gaelic itself, which related in turn to questions about the extent to which children in GME were using the language outside the school in a way that would lead to growth in the actual use of the language. These concerns have continued over the decades and are discussed in more detail below (pp. 310–11). Sociolinguist Joshua Fishman long argued that education on its own was unlikely to bring about sustainable language revitalisation and that establishing the language in home and community settings was much more important in strategic terms. In particular, he expressed scepticism about the value of the schools as an instrument of language revitalisation (Fishman 1991: 368–80). In his influential 1991 volume *Reversing Language Shift*, Fishman warned that Gaelic activists in Scotland were concentrating almost exclusively on what he deemed the 'higher-order props' of education and broadcasting (Fishman 1991: 380). It is by no means the case that this advice has been ignored (e.g. MacLeod 2006–9: 242) but it is extremely difficult to implement in practical terms, as language activists around the world have discovered.

The parents who opted for GME, particularly in the cities, tended to be disproportionately middle-class (Fraser 1989: 163). Over time this fed the development of a negative discourse that GME catered to a privileged subgroup of parents whose children benefited from smaller class sizes and other forms of special treatment, such as free school transport (e.g. Sorooshian 2010). This was a striking inversion of earlier social dynamics, by which Gaelic was traditionally associated with an impoverished rural underclass and used almost exclusively in informal settings. This inversion was also apparent in the reversal of previous diglossic patterns in the use of Gaelic, as the language gained a new association with formal contexts, in the schools, the public sector and elsewhere. New vocabulary and idiom of professional and official Gaelic began to develop (McLeod 2000; McEwan-Fujita 200; see pp. 234–5), with the new breed of Gaelic professionals, working in development roles or the media, characterised as 'Gaels in suits' or 'cappuccino Gaels' (MacLeòid 2004). This pattern of 'reverse diglossia' is fairly typical of the dynamics of minority language revitalisation and institutionalisation (Smith-Christmas and Ó hIfearnáin 2015: 262–4).

THE DEVELOPMENT OF SABHAL MÒR OSTAIG

Perhaps the most surprising development in relation to Gaelic in the last quarter of the twentieth century – as well as one of the most significant – was the establishment of the Gaelic college Sabhal Mòr Ostaig in the Sleat peninsula in southeast Skye (Dunbar 2011; Gossen 2001; Hutchinson 2005). The college was the brainchild of Iain Noble,[15] a learner of Gaelic who had left a career in merchant banking, who in 1972 purchased a newly created estate sold by Lord MacDonald to which Noble gave the name Fearann Eilean Iarmain. The estate included a set of disused nineteenth-century farm buildings at Ostaig, including a large barn (*sabhal mòr* in Gaelic), and Noble decided that these buildings could be used as a Gaelic college (Hutchinson 2005: 102–6). This development was part of Noble's broader vision for the estate, which involved using Gaelic as the medium of all economic activities, a pioneering measure which signalled a new approach to Gaelic development, as discussed below (pp. 234–6).

Any proposal for a Gaelic college at this time would probably have been perceived as somewhat eccentric but the specific site Noble chose for his college was unlikely in a number of respects. Sleat was geographically isolated at the end of a long single-track road, and its population had been declining for many decades; James Hunter described it as 'the most run-down and depopulated part of a run-down and depopulated island' (Hunter 2014).[16] The use of Gaelic in the local community was also on the wane, as was the case throughout south Skye from at least the 1950s (Duwe 2006: 11–12, 28). Establishing a Gaelic college in a more densely populated area of the Western Isles, such as Lewis or Uist, where community use of Gaelic was stronger, would have been more logical as a language planning initiative, but the siting of the college was essentially accidental rather than planned.

In its early years, the college's programme was limited to summer courses in Gaelic and traditional music, which began in 1973. A grant from the Calouste Gulbenkian Foundation in 1974 supported the appointment of the first full-time director for a three-year period (*GH* 1974), and a library was slowly built up. In 1978 the college trustees established a committee to consider the feasibility of developing a full-time diploma programme. The committee's report, submitted in 1980, proposed to develop programmes 'which offer training in business and administrative skills, and which relate this training to the problems, way of life and potential of the area' (quoted in Hutchinson 2005: 133). The emphasis was therefore on the social, economic and cultural development of the Gàidhealtachd.

The SED validated the programme as a Higher National Diploma in 1982 and full-time diploma programmes were offered from 1983, beginning with Business and Gàidhealtachd Studies, with Business Studies and Information Technology following in 1987 (Hutchinson 2005: 137–8, 197). These programmes were taught almost entirely through the medium of Gaelic, which was itself nearly unprecedented, as the established university Gaelic courses were traditionally taught in English (CnaG 1999b: 11). Full degree courses in Gaelic Language and Culture and Gaelic with North Atlantic Studies began in 1999, in the context of the University of the Highlands and Islands initiative (see p. 220). Over time, however, the college began to place a stronger emphasis on provision for learners of the language, as it became apparent that its original model of business-oriented courses for fluent Gaelic speakers could not attract sufficient numbers of students (Hutchinson 2005: 205). Since 1994 the college has also offered a postgraduate diploma in Gaelic media, integrally connected with the training needs of the Gaelic television and media industries (Hutchinson 2005: 198), which have grown hugely since the early 1990s, as discussed below (pp. 232–4).

Student numbers have remained small, although they have increased considerably since the mid-2000s with the launch of internet-based distance learning courses. The 1980 feasibility study had envisioned an annual intake of twenty students. The original cohort on the diploma courses in 1983 consisted of only eight students and had only reached eleven by 1990. With the introduction of immersion language courses the intake reached thirty-five in 1998 (Hutchinson 2005: 203–4). Numbers then grew with the addition of three- and four-year degree programmes; there are now ninety students on degree programmes, 260 enrolled in distance learning and access programmes and up to eight hundred studying on short courses in the summer (Sabhal Mòr Ostaig n.d.).

Fundraising to support the development of the college proved to be an ongoing challenge, and there were several difficult episodes in terms of finance. Contributions were sought from charitable foundations, private businesses (including Scottish Television and Grampian Television), HIDB and the Scottish Office (Hutchinson 2005: 136–8, 183–6). Funding injections allowed for the periodic expansion of the Sabhal Mòr campus. The first expansion came in 1993 with a second set of buildings around a courtyard interlocking with the original farm buildings, to be followed in 1998 by a second campus (Àrainn Chaluim Chille) across the road from the original college, and then in 2008 by a new 'Centre for Culture and Creative Industries', known as Fàs ('growth'). The next phase of development involves a new village at Kilbeg, adjoining the college. This will include housing as well as offices and function spaces, and the first building, named after Iain Noble, opened in 2015 (Ross 2015).

Sabhal Mòr Ostaig has played a hugely significant role as the epicentre of Gaelic revival in Scotland. Its role over the decades in educating fluent, confident speakers of Gaelic, both native speakers and learners, has been very considerable, but arguably more important is its impact as an inspiring demonstration of how Gaelic can be used effectively in modern settings and function as a dynamic living language. This was a remarkable achievement in light of the sense of fatalism that many perceived in relation to Gaelic, not least in Skye itself, in the 1960s and 1970s (Wilson 2011). SMO is also notable in the wider context of provision for minority languages across the world; few if any other languages with as small a speaker base as Gaelic have benefited from a comparable educational institution.

Despite the remarkable success of SMO, there was no wider expansion in provision for Gaelic in further and higher education in the last third of the twentieth century. Four new universities were established in Scotland between 1964 and 1967, three of them existing institutions that were upgraded to university status but one, Stirling University, created as an entirely new institution. There was an unsuccessful campaign to locate the new university in Inverness rather than Stirling, where there might well have been some provision for Gaelic (Cameron 2017). As it happened, none of the four new universities made any provision for Gaelic; a campaign by Stirling's Gaelic Society in 1976 seeking the introduction of Gaelic at the university proved unsuccessful (*Scottish Worker* 1976). Even following the designation of six more universities in Scotland in 1992, the only institutions offering degree programmes in Gaelic were those that had introduced it before the end of the First World War (Aberdeen, Edinburgh and Glasgow), although Strathclyde University began to make some provision following its absorption in

1993 of Jordanhill College of Education, which had long been the principal centre for the training of Gaelic teachers. Indeed, in the late 1980s there was a risk that the Universities Funding Council might force the amalgamation of the three existing Celtic departments, but an intervention from CnaG succeeded in nullifying this proposal (W. Gillies 2011).

From the late 1980s, a new campaign to establish a University of the Highlands and Islands slowly began to gather strength, culminating in the granting of full university status in 2011. The proposed university was structurally very different from the traditional model of an integrated campus in a single location. Instead, fourteen existing institutions across the region, geographically distant from each other and varying considerably in their size and structure, were brought into a network with a federal governance structure, with its executive office in Inverness (Pedersen 2019: 147). SMO was one of the member institutions, as was Lews Castle College in Stornoway, which also participated in the university's Gaelic degree programmes, but the role of Gaelic in the other participating colleges was very limited.

PROVISION FOR ADULT GAELIC LEARNERS

Although there was no significant expansion in the late twentieth century in provision for Gaelic learners in secondary schools, in marked contrast to the rapidly growing Gaelic-medium sector, provision for adult learners of Gaelic strengthened from the 1980s onwards and became identified as a distinct field of activity within overall language development planning. The strategic potential of adult learners was repeatedly noted (e.g. MacCaluim 2007a, 2007b: McLeod, Pollock and MacCaluim 2010) but never attracted the attention or the resources committed to school education. On the other hand, the demand for Gaelic learning in the wider Scottish public has remained fairly modest – a telling indicator of the general status of the language in Scottish society. The Gaelic case is very different from that of Basque, where the production of adult learners in the 1980s and 1990s attracted large-scale investment from the public authorities and made an immense contribution to the expansion of the speech community (Azkue and Perales 2005).

Provision for adult learners of Gaelic had existed since before the Second World War, especially in the form of classes organised by the Gaelic League of Scotland, but Gaelic evening classes became more popular from the 1960s onwards. The increase in learners in the Lowlands was usually identified as the main reason for the rise in speaker numbers recorded in the 1971 census (e.g. Thomson 1981: 10). There was no real coordination of this adult provision until 1984, when a new organisation, Comunn an Luchd-Ionnsachaidh (CLI), was set up to promote the learning of Gaelic by adults. The initiative originally came from An Comunn (An Comunn 1983), and three-year initial funding was then approved by HIDB. Iain MacIllechiar took up the post of director in February 1984 (Comunn an Luchd-Ionnsachaidh 1984).

CLI aimed to improve resources for learning and encourage better coordination of provision. In 1992 CnaG and CLI commissioned a major report on needs of learners, which concluded that 'provision for adult Gaelic learners is fragmented, lacks co-ordination and needs a more structured approach' (CnaG/CLI 1992: 65). There was an over-reliance on evening classes, with few other means of learning being available. There were no immersion courses, few work-based courses and only limited distance-learning facilities. Classes tended to be 'one size fits all', with people at mixed levels of ability and attainment often being taught in composite classes, and the methods of teaching and areas of language taught failed to meet the needs or interests of all learners. Tutors tended to be native speakers with little or no formal training in language pedagogy, and the quality of teaching was patchy as a result. Other identified deficiencies included outdated or poor-quality teaching materials and a lack of Gaelic broadcast output that was suitable for learners.

During the 1990s, SMO gradually developed as the most important provider of adult learning courses, especially intensive courses lasting for a full academic year that had the potential to bring students to fluency. Traditional university or community classes had far fewer contact hours (MacCaluim 2007: 30). Over time, Sabhal Mòr's year-long language courses have produced considerable numbers of fluent speakers, many of whom have gone on to play important roles in Gaelic language development. Since 1999 these courses (offered at different levels, one aimed at fluent speakers) have served as the first-year element of bachelor's degree programmes, although many students do not continue beyond the first year.

In the 1990s similar kinds of *cùrsaichean bogaidh* (immersion courses) began to be offered at further education colleges in different parts of Scotland (Robertson 2001). These year-long courses offered learners the opportunity to make much more rapid progress than the traditional evening class model. At their peak in the 1990s, such courses were available at fourteen colleges in various parts of Scotland, including Clydebank, Falkirk and Perth (Robertson 2001). Over time, however, colleges slowly withdrew their provision for financial reasons.

The *Specific Grants for Gaelic Education* do not extend to further or higher education courses, although a short-lived support scheme from the Scottish Funding Council (the body responsible for funding colleges and universities) brought some benefits by allowing Gaelic courses to run with small enrolments (Scottish Funding Council 2009: 25–6). By 2012 only three immersion courses were left, at Sabhal Mòr Ostaig, Lews Castle College and Stow College in Glasgow.

In 1979 the BBC broadcast a twenty-part television series for Gaelic learners, *Can Seo* ('Say This'), which proved surprisingly popular. There were 11,000 requests for copies of the learning booklet that accompanied the series and a reprint was required to meet demand (Thompson 1986: 128). This was the first television programme of its kind and it had the effect of heightening awareness of the language among the general Scottish population. Another programme aimed at adult learners, *Speaking Our Language*, appeared on the private channel Scottish Television between 1993 and 1996, attracting audiences of up to 100,000 (Johnstone 1994: 60). Repeats of the seventy-two episodes are still aired today on the Gaelic channel BBC ALBA, but there are no plans to produce a new learner's programme.

The expansion of Gaelic learning opportunities, via immersion education or more traditional learners' classes in schools and through adult provision, slowly effected a widening of the social base of the Gaelic-speaking community. This had the consequence of creating differences in perspective between traditional and 'new' speakers, an important phenomenon discussed in the next chapters.

GAELIC RADIO AND TELEVISION

Along with education and the language development infrastructure, Gaelic broadcasting (on both radio and television) became an increasingly important area of development and campaigning during this period. Gaelic provision was planned in the broad context of UK broadcasting policy, so that Gaelic organisations and activists pressed their claims in the context of large-scale UK-wide government consultations and discussions. Provision for Gaelic in broadcasting increased rapidly from the mid-1980s, especially following the creation of the Gaelic Television Fund in 1990. The success of the campaign for improved television provision was certainly the most remarkable outcome of this period of Gaelic development.

The importance that Gaelic activists ascribed to broadcasting, and television in particular, reflected what Martin MacDonald characterised as the 'commonplace article of faith among all linguistic minorities nowadays' that 'survival depends on gaining adequate access to the media'. There was pervasive concern that the English-speaking 'childminder in the corner of the living room' might 'erode the very basis of [Gaelic-speaking children's] cultural identity' and that if Gaelic had 'no place in the television culture of the young' it would 'have little reality for them, and certainly no status' (MacDonald 1990: 22). Although such understandings dominated discussions and discourses concerning Gaelic broadcasting, scholars of minority language media have been rather more sceptical, as discussed below.

Another important element in the drive for improved media provision was the claim of a 'right to self-expression', as Martin MacDonald characterised it. For MacDonald, the Gaelic community

> has been portrayed and interpreted, to the outside world initially and then reflexively to itself, almost exclusively by outsiders. [. . .] The provision of an adequate broadcasting service, through which the Gaelic community could express and examine its own aspirations, and project them on as much of the outside world as cared to view them, might be a useful corrective to several centuries of performing under someone else's microscope. (MacDonald 1990: 23)

The Crawford Report of 1974, which considered the future of broadcasting in the UK, endorsed the BBC's plans for increasing Gaelic radio output in northern Scotland to 10–15 hours per week and additional transmission on the new VHF band (later known as FM), but recommended no change in relation to the Gaelic output on the national service (HO 1974: 55–6, 77). In relation to television, Crawford expressed the view that given the low proportion of Gaelic speakers in the Scottish population, 'the cost of programming and the strain on resources, we do not think that any substantial increase will be possible on television in the near future' (HO 1974: 36). But its vision for Welsh was strikingly different, asserting that when a fourth television channel became available 'it should in Wales be allotted as soon as possible to a separate service in which Welsh-language programmes should be given priority' (HO 1974: 42). This position was justified in political terms, as 'an investment in domestic, cultural and social harmony in the United Kingdom' in the context of other 'government expenditure which is being incurred to satisfy Welsh aspirations' (HO 1974: 41).

In 1974 the BBC began to shift much of its Gaelic radio programming to the VHF band, a move that was unpopular with the Gaelic audience as the VHF signal could not be received in many parts of the Highlands and Islands (Moireach 1975). Campaigners began to make badges and placards joking that VHF stood for 'Very Hard to Find' rather than Very High Frequency (Meek 2011). Writing in 1975, John Murray argued that the BBC had shown 'mì-rùn' and 'mì-mhodhalachd' (ill-will and rudeness) towards Gaelic, and that

> nach eil poilisi aca airson na Gàidhlig, nach eil fhios aca dé ni iad mu deidh-inn; gu bheil iad, anns an fharsaingeachd, ga faicinn mar 'problem' agus ga làimhseachadh mar 'phroblem' – ga cur air falbh a dh'Inbhirnis, no a Thaigh Iain Ghròt...
>
> (they do not have a policy for Gaelic, they don't know what to do about it; that in general they see it as a problem and deal with it as a problem – sending it off to Inverness, or the back of beyond [literally John O'Groats] ...) (Moireach 1975: 147)

In December 1974 students at the University of Glasgow organised a small demonstration, involving about twenty-five people, at BBC Scotland headquarters in Glasgow to demand improvements in Gaelic provision (*Gairm* 1974–5; MacKinnon 1991: 132). A larger demonstration against the BBC, with almost two hundred people, followed in January 1975, and there was then a third protest in May, organised by the new student organisation Comunn nan Oileanach Gàidhlig and attended by three MPs (*GH* 1975). The students' demands included a Gaelic station for the islands, improved educational programmes for schools, ten hours a week of Gaelic on national radio, and at least one hour per week on television (*Glasgow University Guardian* 1975). Although relatively small in scale, these were the first street demonstrations ever organised in relation to Gaelic, and have earned an enduring place in community memory as a result.

The BBC established a Gaelic Advisory Committee in 1976, with the purpose of ascertaining the 'views, expectations and reactions' of Gaelic speakers (Thompson 1986: 121). This committee provided an important forum for the Gaelic community to communicate its needs and desires to the Broadcasting Council for Scotland and thus to senior management in London.

The Crawford report was followed in 1977 by the report of the Annan Committee, which had a more wide-ranging remit to consider the future of broadcasting in the UK. Despite receiving what it described as 'a prodigious number of representations about broadcasting in Gaelic', the Annan Committee failed to recommend significant improvements to the level of Gaelic provision. The report took the view that 'clearly the amount of programming in Gaelic cannot be increased considerably, without the risk, of alienating the majority of people in Scotland, who do not speak Gaelic' (HO 1977: 412). Its vision for the future of Gaelic broadcasting was distinctly vague:

> There should be some increase in the Gaelic output. [...] Responsibility for providing programmes in Gaelic to the Gaelic speaking areas should be shared between Grampian Television and the proposed Local Broadcasting Authority. [...] The BBC should be responsible for providing some programmes in Gaelic throughout Scotland on both radio and television. In our view, a special effort should be made to provide some educational programmes and programmes for children in Gaelic. Perhaps occasional programmes in Gaelic will find a place on the fourth television channel in Scotland. (HO 1977: 412)

The government's subsequent White Paper on broadcasting struck a somewhat more positive note and emphasised the important strategic role of broadcasting in minority language policy:

> Broadcasting has an important role to play in the preservation of Gaelic and Welsh as living tongues and in sustaining the distinctive cultures based upon them. In Scotland, the extent to which broadcasting in Gaelic can be increased is limited by the fact that, although Gaelic speakers are widely scattered, they constitute a small minority of the population. Nevertheless, the broadcasting authorities have a clear responsibility to ensure that the needs of this section of the community are met, and the Government trusts that they will take note of the view expressed by the Annan Committee that there should be some increase in the output of Gaelic programmes, particularly educational programmes and programmes for children. (HO 1978: 22)

The government's proposals in relation to Welsh were much more robust than for Gaelic, reflecting its view that 'in Wales there are special needs of a different kind' (HO 1978: 22). As in other fields, the difference in treatment between the two cases was a source of both frustration and inspiration to Gaelic activists, who saw how focused campaigning succeeded in winning concessions from the authorities (Moireach 1975: 154).

From 1979 onwards, there were significant improvements in the Gaelic radio service. In 1979 BBC Radio nan Eilean was established in Stornoway as part of a network of local services that accompanied the creation of Radio Scotland in 1978, with CnE and HIDB providing additional financial support. In 1985 the BBC Gaelic service was reorganised as Radio nan Gàidheal (literally 'Radio of the Gaels'), which brought together broadcasts from studios in Glasgow, Inverness and Stornoway. By the late 1980s, about twenty-eight hours a week were being broadcast (up from 7.25 hours per week in 1980 (Thomson 1981: 14)), and the range of programming had increased considerably. In 1993 the reach of the service was extended more widely in the Highlands but significantly reduced in Central Scotland, down to six hours per week (Lexecon Ltd 1994). The downgrading of the service in Central Scotland was controversial (*Scotsman* 1993b) and CnaG continued to press for more systematic development, commissioning a report that set out an economic case for a national radio service (Lexecon Ltd 1994). In 1995 Radio nan Gàidheal was upgraded to a national service, broadcasting for approximately forty-five hours per week. The service was available in most parts of Scotland, but as late as 1999 there were considerable geographic gaps (CnaG 1999a: 13).

Gaelic radio has been very largely confined to the BBC, however. There are no community Gaelic radio stations, unlike Ireland's Raidió na Life and Raidió Fáilte, although some local commercial stations in the Gàidhealtachd, such as Isles FM and Cuillin FM, have a limited amount of Gaelic programmes.

Radio nan Gàidheal has played a very important role in the Gaelic world, in some respects more important than television. Its news service was much more extensive than anything available on television or in print. It helped make listeners familiar with different Gaelic dialects and introduced new terminology, particularly in connection with news and current affairs. Most importantly, it also helped 'draw[] the Gaelic community closer together and build a sense of connectedness' (MacLennan 2003).

The extent of output on television was much smaller and proved slower to grow. In the mid-1970s the BBC was broadcasting only two Gaelic programmes per week, and one of these was unavailable in much of the Gàidhealtachd because it was broadcast on VHF (Moireach 1975: 150–1). Gaelic arrived on commercial television only in 1976, when Grampian Television, which held the Channel 3 licence for the north of Scotland, broadcast its first programme in Gaelic. The other Channel 3 licensee in Scotland at the time, Scottish Television, which catered to the mainly non-Gaelic-speaking Central Belt, only broadcast its first programme in Gaelic in 1987. From the late 1970s, Grampian Television also began to improve its offer. The range of Gaelic content began to expand; for example, children's programmes began in 1977 with the series *Cuir Car* on Grampian, with BBC programmes following in 1982 (NicNèill 2018: 34; Dunn 1985: 54–5).

Campaigners continued to press the issue of broadcasting provision through the 1980s. Donald Stewart's abortive Gaelic bill of 1981 included a provision to establish a Gaelic Broadcasting Committee, which was to 'co-ordinate and develop Gaelic television and radio'. The government's view of Gaelic television at this stage was summarised in a 1981 minute by an SED official, who dismissed the 'considerable history of representations from the Gaelic lobby' as follows:

> We have always adopted the line that the amount and nature of Gaelic broadcasting are entirely up to the broadcasting authorities and companies to decide. Comparisons with Wales are inevitably made, but Scottish Gaels lack the numbers and (so far) the militant attitudes for such comparisons to be taken seriously. (SED 1981a)

The political sensibilities of the Gaelic broadcasting issue were regularly noted in government papers of the time. In 1980 Scottish Office minister Alex Fletcher wrote to the Home Secretary that Scots 'cannot help drawing the comparison between the relatively lavish provision being made for Wales, and the long-term and uncertain prospects for Scotland. I hope we can avoid discontent about broadcasting becoming a factor in the rekindling of Scottish nationalism' (SO 1980a).

Welsh television had been growing steadily since the 1960s but reached a crucial new stage in 1982 with the establishment of the all-Welsh channel Sianel Pedwar Cymru (S4C, 'Channel Four Wales'). In contrast, Scotland received essentially the same Channel Four service as England, carrying very little Gaelic programming.

In the mid- and late 1980s CnaG identified broadcasting as one of the key areas for language development and concentrated much of its efforts on securing improved provision on radio and television, by organising a series of conferences and workshops and making numerous submissions to the government, the BBC, the Independent Broadcasting Authority and individual private television companies. Over the course of the 1980s, there was significant expansion in the number of hours of television programming broadcast annually: in 1988 102 hours of Gaelic programming were transmitted (52 on the BBC, 37 on Grampian and 13 on Scottish) (Veljanovski 1989: 10). However, this still amounted to less than two hours per week. In the late 1980s new emphasis began to be placed on programmes for children, reflecting the perceived importance of this audience in language planning terms (Dunn 1987: 54–5).

In early 1988, in anticipation of new broadcasting legislation, CnaG submitted a policy paper that argued for a much-enhanced television service (CnaG 1988). This would involve about 520 hours of programming per year, with a 'wide spectrum of programming' including news, current affairs, light entertainment, drama, children's programmes and 'specialised programmes of relevance to the community'. Significantly, however, CnaG did not go so far as to recommend a separate Gaelic channel.

In 1988 the government published a White Paper setting out its plans for the new broadcasting legislation (HO 1988). The White Paper gave little basis for optimism in relation to Gaelic provision, suggesting only that new local private broadcasting franchises that were to be introduced

> may also provide the means of delivering additional services to Gaelic speakers in parts of Scotland. The Government recognises the importance of broadcasting to the Gaelic language and its future development and, while no change is implied in present policies towards Gaelic broadcasting at national or regional level, new local services could be an important means of meeting Gaelic needs. (HO 1988: 28)

In response, CnaG engaged a London-based lobbying firm to push the case for improved Gaelic provision, but it failed to make headway with the government (Pedersen 2019: 117). HIDB then commissioned a prominent free-market economist, Cento Veljanovski, to prepare an additional report setting out an economic case for a Gaelic broadcasting service (Veljanovski 1989). It had become apparent that cultural arguments or rights claims would be unlikely to prove persuasive to the Conservative government. With his keen awareness of the government's pro-market approach to broadcasting policy, Veljanovski aimed instead to develop a proposal by which 'competitive forces can be harnessed to privatise the provision of Gaelic broadcasting' using 'revenues taken directly from the broadcasting industry itself'. He characterised this as a mechanism which 'satisfies all the criteria which a market-oriented government could wish for – privatised minority broadcasting' (Veljanovski 1989: 4, 57). This would be accomplished by the creation of a new television fund to which broadcasters, including private licence holders on Channel 3, would submit competitive tenders for production and transmission of programmes (Veljanovski 1989: 2–3). Most of the funding for this would come from the private broadcasting industry (Channel 3 licence holders)[17] and some from BBC licence fee revenue. Underpinning this vision, however, was an acceptance that Gaelic television was not viable in conventional market terms (just as the government had suggested in its White Paper) and needed to be understood in terms of meeting legitimate cultural needs for which the market could not adequately provide (Veljanovski 1989: 5). The report did note, however, that the creation of the fund would bring economic benefits in terms of increasing employment in the independent production sector and help develop an 'enterprise culture' in Gaeldom by reinforcing cultural identity and creating 'a new awareness and self-sufficiency' (Veljanovski 1989: 6, 21).

CnaG's own submission (CnaG 1989a) argued that 'without a significant enhancement of Gaelic television provision, the planned improvements in the range and quality of English-language programming resulting from the new Act would 'effectively increase the comparative deprivation of the Gaelic community' (CnaG 1989a: 1(3)). The maintenance of Gaelic was a central part of CnaG's argument:

> The importance of adequate broadcasting provision for minority languages like Gaelic cannot be over-emphasised [...] There is widespread consensus on a global scale amongst all authorities dealing with small linguistic communities that broadcasting services – and in particular television – are vital to survival. (CnaG 1989a: 1(5))

CnaG specified a minimum figure of £21 million per year for the new Gaelic service (CnaG 1989a: 7).

Although the Scottish Office had been persuaded of the case for additional funding for Gaelic television by the summer of 1989 (SED 1989a), thanks to Veljanovski's report and CnaG's lobbying efforts, other government departments, including the Prime Minister's office and the Treasury, remained unconvinced (SED 1989a; HM Treasury 1989a; Department for Trade and Industry 1989). Above and beyond the key principle of whether funding for Gaelic television should be increased was a question concerning the appropriate mechanism. Television (including S4C) was generally funded through the Home Office budget but it was suggested that Gaelic television should be funded from the Scottish Office budget. Further, if responsibility was assigned to the Scottish Office, there was an issue as to whether its baseline budget would be increased accordingly. Without such a baseline increase, any additional allocation for Gaelic television would have had to be matched by cuts in other areas.

Ministers and civil servants clearly understood that the matter involved political sensitivities and that a decision not to make significant new provision for Gaelic 'would cause a major political storm in Scotland' and be 'greeted with shock and disappointment by the Gaelic community and with protests from the other political parties which have pledged support' (SED 1989a, 1989c). Liberal MP Ray Michie had secured a parliamentary debate on the issue in May, and in October students from the University of Glasgow presented a petition to the Scottish Office with more than ten thousand signatures demanding improvements to the Gaelic television service (P&J 1989). CnaG also engaged in an active lobbying campaign with key ministers, including Scottish Secretary Malcolm Rifkind and junior Scottish Office minister Michael Forsyth.

Disagreement within government concerning the way ahead was resolved through a decisive intervention by Prime Minister Margaret Thatcher, who communicated her view that 'some increase in Gaelic television services would be appropriate' but that 'any financing for this purpose must come from a cash limited Scottish vote' (Prime Minister's Office 1989). The Home Office found this 'concession very surprising' (SED 1989b). Although the key point of principle had been clarified, important questions remained concerning the specific budget mechanism, and there was a protracted dispute between Rifkind and the First Secretary to the Treasury, Norman Lamont. Lamont took the view that the new money for Gaelic broadcasting should come from the basic Scottish block grant, while Rifkind insisted it should be a distinct new allocation. Lamont also proposed to use this opportunity to rework the funding mechanism for Welsh television, so that the cost of S4C, hitherto a distinct Home Office budget line, would instead be charged to the Welsh block grant. This proposal triggered a furious response from the Welsh Secretary, Peter Walker, who protested that such a move would nullify years of work to de-politicise the Welsh language (Welsh Office 1989). In 1980 the leader of Plaid Cymru, Gwynfor Evans, had threatened to go on hunger strike in order to hold the Conservative government to its promise to establish the dedicated Welsh channel (Edwards, Tanner and Carlin 2011: 538–41). Rifkind reminded Lamont of this history as well, warning that the Gaelic community might draw 'unfortunate conclusions' if their 'relatively rational and moderate approach' was unsuccessful (SO 1989b).

Eventually the Treasury changed its position, preferring not to have the matter returned to the Prime Minister for resolution (SO 1989c). The Treasury agreed to 'shelter [the Scottish Office] block baseline from the costs of establishing this new service', provided that the Scottish Office 'accept that the expenditure at issue is borne on a cash limited vote within the Scottish block' (and thus not funded through the Home Office like the rest of the television budget) (SO 1989d). Lamont proposed to add 'about £8 million a year' to the Scottish Office block baseline, beginning in 1992–3 (HM Treasury 1989b). The Scottish Office accepted this compromise and the funding agreement was duly announced.

The figure of £8 million reflected the estimates provided by CnaG of the amount necessary to provide an additional two hundred hours of Gaelic programming per year. This was at the lower end of what had been sought; Rifkind had previously characterised this as 'the minimum meaningful concession' (SO 1989a). In accepting the Treasury proposal, Rifkind noted the risk that there would be pressure to increase the level of funding were programme production costs to rise and the Gaelic community to demand further improvements in provision (SO 1989e).

There has been much speculation in Gaelic circles as to why the government accepted the case for Gaelic television. Some suggested that Rifkind's support reflected his Jewish background and a sensitivity to the needs and concerns of minorities (MacIver 2011; Wilson 2011). Many years later, urging additional funding for the Gaelic channel BBC ALBA, Rifkind wrote that 'whereas the Conservatives were portrayed as not having Scotland's interests at heart', he and Forsyth 'were fighting behind-the-scenes to support a hugely important part of our history and culture' (Rifkind 2016). Forsyth himself was keen to see Gaelic given appropriate support, expressing a feeling of historical injustice towards the Highlands and a strong commitment to the regeneration of the region (Forsyth 2011; Ross 1992b).

Once the principle of a television fund and the initial budget had been agreed, extensive discussions followed concerning the structure by which the fund would be administered. This emerged through the revision of the Communications Bill that was introduced in December 1989 and passed in June 1990 as the *Broadcasting Act 1990*. Although CnaG had proposed the creation of a dedicated Gaelic Broadcasting Authority, this proposal was rejected in favour of the creation of a new body under the auspices of the Independent Television Commission, Comataidh Telebhisein Gàidhlig (CTG, the Gaelic Television Committee), which had the responsibility of awarding grants for 'financing the making of television programmes in Gaelic' and related purposes such as training and research (*Broadcasting Act 1990*, ss. 183–4).

The cost of the new television fund was thus borne entirely by the government and not through any kind of private financing, as was the case with S4C and as Veljanovski had recommended. However, under the *Broadcasting Act 1990* (s. 184(1)), Channel 3 licence holders in Scotland were also required to ensure that 'a suitable proportion' of their programmes were programmes in Gaelic 'other than [CTG-]funded productions' – meaning that the Channel 3 licence holders would have to produce Gaelic programming without CTG assistance. The Channel 3 licence holders were also required to broadcast 'a suitable proportion' of Gaelic programmes funded by the CTG at peak viewing times. The term 'suitable proportion' was not quantified, and over time the commercial broadcasters tried to interpret it increasingly narrowly.

Following a competitive tendering process, the Channel 3 licences in Scotland were awarded in 1991 to Grampian (covering the north of Scotland) and Scottish (covering most of the south).[18] Both companies made commitments to Gaelic – surprisingly strong commitments, in the views of some – in their successful bids, although Grampian broadcast rather more than Scottish (209 hours in 1995 as opposed to 157 (Case Associates 1996: 5)).[19] Yet as early as 1993 the commercial broadcasters were expressing complaints about poor ratings for Gaelic programmes (which affected the rates advertisers were willing to pay) and trying to keep Gaelic programmes at peak times to a minimum (*Stage and Television Today* 1993). Increasingly the commercial channels began pushing their Gaelic programmes to late-night slots and emphasising 'least common denominator Gaelic programming' with 'minimal Gaelic content', concentrating on subjects like music and wildlife (Case Associates 1996: 19, 27).

The arrival of the large new tranche of funding led to a dramatic increase in Gaelic television production. Working closely with the broadcasters (Pedersen 2019: 168), the CTG endeavoured to commission a wide range of programming, including programmes for children, news and current affairs programmes and a 'soap', *Machair*. Media scholar Mike Cormack characterised the CTG's strategy as involving 'an accent on youth, an attempt to present a modernised view of the Gaelic community avoiding traditional stereotypes, an attempt to move Gaelic to the centre of Scottish affairs, and the adoption of an optimistic and rather one-sided view of the language's future' (Cormack 1994: 117).

With the rapid expansion of provision came considerable opportunities for Gaelic speakers in television production and the new phenomenon of 'Gaels in suits', brutally satirised in Tormod MacGill-Eain's 1996 novel *Cùmhnantan* ('Contracts') (MacGill-Eain 1996; Maclean 2012). At the same time, many jobs in the Gaelic television industry, especially those of a more technical nature such as camera operation and editing, were carried out by non-Gaelic speakers, often in urban areas (mainly Glasgow) rather than in island Gaelic communities (Dunbar 2003a: 78).

Gaelic television brought significant economic benefits, as discussed below, but it also helped 'raise the profile' of the language (to use the prevailing idiom) by attracting large numbers of non-Gaelic speakers through the use of subtitles (Pedersen 2019: 156). *Machair* drew up to 516,000 viewers, almost eight times the number of Gaelic speakers (Cormack 1994: 125). Another successful programme was *Eòrpa*, now in its twenty-seventh year, 'a hard-hitting current affairs series looking at social, economic and political issues across Europe' from a Gaelic perspective (Pedersen 2019: 161). At the same time, there was also a degree of backlash from non-Gaelic speakers, with some viewers and commentators ridiculing Gaelic programmes or objecting to the removal of other English-language programmes to make room for them (*Scotland on Sunday* 1993a, 1993b). Resentment was also evident among non-Gaelic staff at the BBC and other broadcasters, who were sometimes 'faintly paranoid' about the rise of Gaelic speakers to senior positions and the dedicated resourcing for Gaelic television (Morton 2004).

Perhaps most important of all, it was unclear, and it remains unclear, to what extent television provision actually improves the prospects for Gaelic language maintenance. Media studies scholar Mike Cormack has called into question the key assumption that a greater quantity and range of media content in Gaelic (including different genres and platforms) 'necessarily lead[] to more use of the language'. In light of the current demography of Gaelic, in which most speakers live in households where not all members can speak the language, Cormack suggested that 'the mere presence of Gaelic in a programme may not have much of an effect' (Cormack 2006: 216, 215).

The structure put in place by the *Broadcasting Act 1990* meant that Gaelic programming was fragmented and sporadic, spread over different channels at times that varied from day to day, week to week and month to month. The funding mechanism also proved unsatisfactory: the original plan had been for the Gaelic Television Fund to cover two hundred hours of programming per year, but in 1993–4, when the Fund was set at £9.5 million, only 195 hours were produced, and this then fell to 162 hours in 1994–5, by which time funding had been reduced to £8.7m, despite steadily rising production costs (Case Associates 1996: 6–7). The substantial funding cut announced in late 1993 was greeted with 'utter bewilderment' by the CTG, which called it 'difficult to comprehend in the light of the success of the committee's activities in economic and cultural terms' (*Herald* 1993).

In 1996 a new Communications Bill was introduced into Parliament, ultimately enacted as the *Communications Act 1996*, and this provided another opportunity for improvement to Gaelic provision. The CTG commissioned another report from Cento Veljanovski (Case Associates 1996), which made a series of recommendations for a more sustainable and integrated service, including the adoption of an inflation-based funding escalator (Case Associates 1996: 30–3). The government proved unwilling to accept any of these proposals other than the widening of the remit of the CTG: the new Act changed the name of the CTG to Comataidh Craolaidh Gàidhlig/the Gaelic Broadcasting Committee

(CCG) and extended its remit to include radio and a consultative role in relation to digital broadcasting, a new technology which was then in its early phase but which would become increasingly important in proposals for enhanced provision in the twenty-first century.

By the late 1990s the deficiencies of the funding and delivery model developed under the 1990 Act were readily apparent, and this led to a campaign for a dedicated Gaelic channel, discussed in the next chapter.

GAELIC AND ECONOMIC DEVELOPMENT

From the 1970s onwards, proactive efforts were made to connect Gaelic to processes and discourses of economic development in the Gàidhealtachd. Gaelic became increasingly perceived and depicted as a potential vector for economic growth, rather than an obstacle, as had been the received understanding for well over a century.

Iain Noble's work at his Fearann Eilean Iarmain estate in Sleat played a critical role in this modernising shift in the economic role of Gaelic. Taking inspiration from the linguistic and economic revitalisation he had seen in the Faroe Islands (Hunter 1974), Noble established Gaelic as the working language of the estate operations and the various enterprises established along with it, which included a hotel, a whisky business and a knitting mill (GRG 1982: 32). From the late 1970s these initiatives attracted increasing support and attention from HIDB, which began to see Gaelic as a potential driver of regional economic growth which could help build community confidence and dynamism and with it the capacity for entrepreneurship and development. This new discourse of the 'Gaelic economy' (McLeod 2002) gained further importance in the 1980s and 1990s, as it aligned with the philosophy and policy priorities of Margaret Thatcher's Conservative government (Hutchinson 2005: 163). Research was commissioned in 1991 to demonstrate the positive economic impacts of government expenditure on Gaelic. This study indicated that almost one thousand full-time equivalent jobs had been created, directly or indirectly, in the new Gaelic 'sector', most of them relating to television. More than half of these were in the Western Isles or Skye and Lochalsh, the areas with the highest density of Gaelic speakers (Sproull and Ashcroft 1993; Sproull 1996). Subsequent research in the late 1990s demonstrated the successful economic impact of funding to promote the Gaelic arts (Sproull and Chalmers 1998, 2006). CnaG and other agencies used these findings to help promote a discourse that Gaelic could involve attractive job opportunities, challenging the long-established discourse that the language had no instrumental value and did not help improve one's life chances. This has become an important element in promotional strategies ever since. In particular, Highlands and Islands Enterprise, the successor to HIDB, has published several reports and research studies concerning Gaelic and the economy (Pedersen 2019: 159–60; Highlands and Islands Enterprise 2014).

As the discourse linking Gaelic and economic development became increasingly powerful, some critics began to question whether the economic rationale for Gaelic development had begun to overshadow the language planning rationale. Journalist Tormod Caimbeul expressed concern that 'what was a family culture may soon become only a career option or a marketing tool' (Caimbeul 2000: 65). To some extent, these economic arguments were tactical in nature, presented after claims framed in cultural terms or based on minority rights had failed to convince policy-makers or, indeed, to mobilise the Gaelic community. This new economic framing of language is of course a broad-based phenomenon of the neoliberal era (Duchêne and Heller 2012).

The new 'Gaelic economy' was distinctly limited in its scope, however. Crucially, almost all this new economic activity, and almost all the new jobs, resulted from public spending on Gaelic initiatives; there was no concomitant growth in the private, for-profit sector, from which Gaelic remained almost entirely excluded. In addition, it was by no means clear that all this Gaelic-related economic activity involved the uncommunicative use of the Gaelic language; in some cases, the language was used only symbolically (Cox 1998), or services were aimed at consumers without any knowledge of Gaelic (McLeod 2002).

A related modernising agenda involved the programmatic use of Gaelic in new contexts, including the world of commerce. From the mid-1970s onwards, those involved in the new wave of Gaelic activity, including Sabhal Mòr Ostaig, Fearann Eilean Iarmain and the various educational and community initiatives in the Western Isles, began to place increasing emphasis on the use of Gaelic as the ordinary language of their operations. Sabhal Mòr in particular encouraged the use of Gaelic in all contexts: teaching, college administration and every aspect of college life. In line with the diglossic pattern that is typical of minority language contexts (Jaffe 1999: 19–20), English had become established in formal domains in Gaelic communities and Gaelic confined to less formal and less prestigious environments (MacKinnon 1977). A new ideology of Gaelic language normalisation now began to emerge: Gaelic should be used in as many circumstances as possible, and proactively using the language in modern contexts such as business, local government and further education was seen an integral part of the revitalisation and modernisation of the language (Hutchinson 2005: 165). As new Gaelic organisations developed in the 1980s, especially CnaG, this new practice and culture became firmly rooted.

For some this transition has been awkward. As the language was adapted and developed for new purposes, new, unfamiliar terminology and phrasing was required, but for many Gaelic speakers, Gaelic was tightly associated with distinct contexts of home and community and its use in new domains could feel uncomfortable or unnatural (McEwan-Fujita 2008; see M. MacLeod 2008). With these shifts, some speakers unfamiliar with these new, formal registers can come to lose confidence and form the view that their command of the language is 'not good enough'. At worst, this can even lead to a sense of disconnection and alienation from the wider language revitalisation project.

IN-MIGRATION AND THE LAND QUESTION

From the 1960s onwards, and especially from the 1980s, traditionally Gaelic communities in the West Highlands and Islands began to experience significant levels of in-migration, which sometimes proved controversial. Incomers came overwhelmingly from Lowland Scotland or from England and very few acquired real communicative competence in Gaelic, although some took limited steps to learn the language and many expressed general support for it (Smith-Christmas 2014). In the nineteenth century and the first half of the twentieth, there had been many examples of linguistic assimilation of incomers in Gaelic communities (GRG 1982: 14), but by the closing decades of the twentieth century language shift was sufficiently advanced that it was eminently possible – and to a very considerable degree, socially acceptable – for people to move into a Gaelic community and not learn Gaelic. Because in-migration was taking place at the same time as underlying language shift among the established population, the sociolinguistic consequences of in-migration to Gaelic communities are not entirely clear, although it is unquestionable that the influx of non-Gaelic speakers into Gaelic areas tended to depress the use of Gaelic in community contexts. Already by 1982 the *Cor na Gàidhlig* report noted as a 'result of this influx Gaelic is being badly eroded as the communal language in village halls, shops, banks and other social and work situations where it formerly held sway' (GRG 1982: 17).

The linguistic consequences of in-migration to the Gàidhealtachd never became sharply politicised to the extent they did in Wales, however. One important point of difference involved the schools: GME has always been optional and parents could essentially opt out of Gaelic altogether, very much in contrast to the situation in the Welsh 'heartland' of Gwynedd, where Welsh-medium education was effectively made mandatory in the 1970s (Madgwick and Rawkins 1982: 835). Although there were suggestions in the 1970s that Gaelic activists should move into Gaelic areas and undertake grass-roots activity on behalf of the language (MacKinnon 1974: 90–1), such intentional linguistic migration did not become a significant phenomenon in the way it did in Brittany, where incomers seeking an alternative lifestyle were at the centre of a new wave of Breton language activism in the 1970s (McDonald 1989).

Housing became, and remains, an important matter of controversy in many parts of the Gàidhealtachd, such as Skye, with incomers (including those purchasing holiday homes) driving up house prices and pricing 'locals' out of the market. Yet there has been relatively little debate about the language issue per se in connection with in-migration. By the same token, Gaelic did not play any noticeable role in the campaigns for land reform and the wave of community buyouts of estates in places such as north Assynt, Eigg, Gigha, north Harris and South Uist that began in the early 1990s (Mackenzie 2012), although the Galson estate in north Lewis, acquired by the community in 2007, has taken significant steps to promote Gaelic (BnG 2018b). Over time, the linkage between Gaelic promotion and issues of peripheral community development has tended to weaken and Gaelic development has instead come to focus on language-specific initiatives in all parts of Scotland.

GAELIC AND THE CHURCHES

The role of Gaelic in the churches was a continuing concern in the late twentieth century. Most obviously, the number of Gaelic services declined rapidly, a decline which eventually reached the Western Isles. In 1966 there were 82 'Gaelic-essential' charges (45 on the Highland mainland, 33 in the islands and four in the cities) and another 82 'Gaelic-desirable' charges (almost all of them on the Highland mainland). In approximately half the Gaelic-desirable parishes, however, the minister could not in fact speak Gaelic (MacLeòid 1968: 30–1). In 1968 the Rev. Roderick Macleod warned that the matter was 'ann an làmhan a' Ghàidheil fhèin' (in the hands of the Gael himself), and that if Gaelic lost its position 'bidh sinne, na Gàidheil, ciontach' (we, the Gaels, will be guilty) (MacLeòid 1968: 34).

Cor na Gàidhlig included a detailed survey of Gaelic in the three Presbyterian denominations (Church of Scotland, Free Church and

Free Presbyterian Church) and the Roman Catholic Church. Its overall assessment was negative: despite the church's role as 'an influential and supportive bulwark of Gaelic in the past', it had become 'an anglicising influence' and could 'be accused of being party to cultural deprivation' (GRG 1982: 61). The report found that 'Gaelic is under threat as a language of worship in its last strongholds, hence the sense of crisis' (GRG 1982: 57). There were variations among the denominations, however. In the Church of Scotland, numerous parishes were downgraded from 'Gaelic essential' status to 'Gaelic desirable', which 'normally leads to the appointment of a non-Gaelic-speaking minister, so that Gaelic disappears from local worship' (GRG 1982: 58). The Free Presbyterian Church, although the most strongly Gaelic-speaking in its congregations, was least troubled about the decline of Gaelic provision, perceiving it 'as a continuing fact which is not a major concern of the Church' (GRG 1982: 58). The position of Gaelic in the Catholic Church in the heartland of Uist and Barra was much stronger: recruitment of priests had not become a difficulty, and Gaelic was well established as the language of worship. This was partly because the form of Gaelic used in Catholic services had been modernised in the 1960s (following Vatican II) and was 'far closer to colloquial Gaelic' than is the case in the Protestant churches (GRG 1982: 60). However, in Catholic areas of the mainland such as Kintail and Moidart the same pattern of withdrawal was seen.

The long-standing issue of clerical shortages intensified in the following decades. By 1997 barely a quarter of the ministers in the Free Presbyterian Church, the most conservative of the Presbyterian denominations, were Gaelic speakers, so that a leading minister declared that 'as far as the Free Presbyterian Church is concerned Gaelic is now at an end' and that it was 'God's providence that this be so' (MacAulay 1997). By the first decade of the twenty-first century, the Free Church was having difficulties recruiting Gaelic-speaking ministers in its heartland of Lewis and the Catholic Church was beginning to confront shortages of priests in Uist and Barra (*Scotsman* 2002c; O'Henley 2006). These problems have intensified in recent years, and the number of Gaelic services offered has continuously declined.

Several churchmen played an important role in Gaelic initiatives in the late twentieth century. The first administration of Comhairle nan Eilean was co-convened by the Rev. Donald MacAulay, a Free Church minister from Lewis, and Father Calum MacLellan, a Catholic priest from Barra/Eriskay, who were strongly supportive of the bilingual policy and the Bilingual Education Project (MacAulay 1991; MacLellan

1991). The Rev. Jack MacArthur, a member of Comhairle nan Eilean and then Highland Council, played a pivotal role in Gaelic development in the 1980s and 1990s (MacDonald 2002). In the twenty-first century, however, no ministers or priests have taken a prominent role in Gaelic development. For example, none of the dozens of individuals appointed to Bòrd na Gàidhlig since 2003 have been ministers or priests. This fading is undoubtedly connected to the broader weakening of the churches in Gaelic communities and the declining use of Gaelic within the churches, although it can also be seen as part of a more general withdrawal of clerics from public and cultural activity in Scotland (Ansdell 2016).

Probably the most important initiative in the religious domain was the preparation of a new translation of the New Testament in 2019. The existing translation was produced in 1801 and an increasing number of Gaelic speakers found its language inaccessible, 'an unfamiliar tongue', as it differed so greatly from modern vernacular Gaelic (Eglinton 2017). The project took ten years and involved an ecumenical team of translators from the Church of Scotland, Free Church and Roman Catholic Church (Church of Scotland 2019).

From 1973 onwards, the Church of Scotland regularly expressed concern 'about the erosion of Gaelic culture and the disintegration of the Gaelic community' (GRG 1982: 57) and urged the government to make improved provision for the language (e.g. Committee on Church and Nation 2005). In recent years the churches have begun to take a more strategic approach to Gaelic development. In 2015 the Church of Scotland organised a day conference on the role of Gaelic in the church, the first event of its kind, and in 2019 it appointed a Gaelic development officer (*The Herald* 2015; Church of Scotland 2019). The Gaelic Society of the Scottish Episcopal Church was founded in 1974 (Scottish Episcopal Church n.d.), and in 2019, a Catholic Gaelic Society was established to further the use of Gaelic in the church (*Scottish Catholic Observer* 2019).

HOSTILITY AND REJECTION: ANTI-GAELIC DISCOURSES

As provision for Gaelic grew from the 1980s, public rejection and denigration of the language became more prominent. Most notably, attacks on the language and its speakers in newspaper columns and letters to the editor proliferated. In one early example, a correspondent to the *Glasgow Herald* in 1973 opposed An Comunn's proposal for increased educational provision on the grounds that Gaelic was associated with 'centuries of indiscrim[in]ate killings, pillage and savage rape, hateful persecution and small-minded bigotry' (*GH* 1973b); in 1989 another *Herald* correspondent opposed proposals to expand Gaelic broadcasting on the grounds that '[l]ess than 2% of the population speaks this virtually unusable language, historically equated with feuds and bloodshed, squalor, dreary whisky drunks, and oppressive religious doctrine' (*GH* 1989). Attacks of this kind, rooted in the anti-Highlander discourses of earlier centuries, were not unknown in the earlier decades of the twentieth century but were much rarer, probably because there was less promotional activity to provoke any kind of opposition. In one early example, in 1950 a correspondent who adopted the pen name 'Saxon' challenged 'the current craze for the teaching and fostering of Gaelic' and queried whether the 'ability to speak the uncouth tongue of Scotland's one-time barbarian fringe [should] be considered a cultural achievement' (*Dundee Evening Telegraph* 1950).[20] Such media attacks on Gaelic remain a persistent feature of Scottish public life, even if the specific tropes have varied somewhat over time, and are not perceived by newspaper editors as violating the acceptable norms of public discourse in a way that attacks on other minorities might be (MacKinnon 2012).

New strands of rejectionist discourse began to develop as institutional support, and thus public expenditure, increased, particularly in connection with television after 1992. Gaelic speakers now became characterised as a pampered minority who received special treatment or as 'subsidy junkies' (Dunbar 2000: 70). This negativity and rejection tended to instil a degree of defensiveness on the part of the Gaelic community and Gaelic organisations. Constant fears of a 'backlash' acted as a constraint on development, in part because politicians were alert to this negativity when making decisions on Gaelic matters.

CONCLUSION

The 1980s proved to be a pivotal time of change in relation to Gaelic development, and indeed all advances have effectively built on the foundations laid during this period. Subsequent initiatives in terms of governance, development infrastructure, education and broadcasting can be understood as incremental, albeit sometimes substantial, improvements on measures that were introduced during this crucial period. It is a long-established trope in Gaelic circles, albeit sometimes asserted mainly for its shock value, that Margaret Thatcher's Conservative government was the best government Gaelic ever had (e.g. Hutchinson 2005: 189).

Policies and strategies adopted during this period also brought in other kinds of changes which continue to have ramifications down to the present, some of them controversial. One was the increasingly national approach to Gaelic, as GME became established in Lowland urban areas and television and radio services extended to all of Scotland. Over time this would tend to weaken the connection between Gaelic and regional development which had been so crucial to HIDB's support for Gaelic promotion, and stoke concerns that heartland communities were being neglected. Related to this was concern about the growing professionalisation and 'creeping bureaucracy' (D. J. MacLeod 1989: 226) of Gaelic language promotion once substantial government support was made available. Over time this perception tended to bring about a disconnect between Gaelic organisations and ordinary Gaelic speakers, a perceived lack of ownership and participation (Morrison 1997). The most obvious manifestation of this disconnect was the continuing fall in the numbers of Gaelic speakers recorded in the decennial censuses and in the intensity of community language use as measured by sociolinguistic surveys. To an increasing degree, the combination of strengthened formal provision and declining community language use served to create what Kenneth MacKinnon described as 'an overcoat wrapped around an invisible man' (MacKinnon 1998).

7

Restructuring, 1997–2005

THE CREATION OF THE Scottish Parliament in 1999, following a referendum in 1997, was a watershed in Scottish political history and brought with it a significant opportunity to develop a more coherent and focused approach to Gaelic policy. Legislative devolution was a commitment of the 'New Labour' government elected in 1997, and this change in government after a long period of Conservative rule gave Gaelic organisations and activists space to press for improved provision in relation to language planning structure, education and broadcasting. By 2006 a Gaelic Language Act had been enacted, the first stand-alone Gaelic primary and secondary schools had opened and tentative agreement had been reached to establish a dedicated Gaelic television channel. But progress towards these outcomes was far from steady or certain, and only came to fruition following sustained campaigning pressure from Gaelic organisations and the wider Gaelic community.

GAELIC AND THE SCOTTISH PARLIAMENT

The establishment of the Scottish Parliament provided an opportunity to institutionalise Gaelic within a centrally important national body. The *Scotland Act 1998*, the foundational legislation which created the Parliament and devolved key areas of policy such as health, education, transport and culture from Westminster to Edinburgh, made no mention of Gaelic. In contrast, the counterpart *Government of Wales Act 1998*, which established the National Assembly for Wales, included the principle (originating in the *Welsh Language Act 1993*) that 'the Assembly shall in the conduct of its business give effect [...] to the principle that the English and Welsh languages should be treated on a basis of equality' (s. 47(1)). The Scottish Parliament is distinct from the

Scottish Government (known as the Scottish Executive between 1999 and 2007), although the two are often conflated or confused among the general public in Scotland.

Preparations for the opening of the Parliament took Gaelic into account in relation to parliamentary procedures and the layout of the building itself, although this provision was relatively modest. Following the recommendations of the Consultative Steering Group on the shaping of the Parliament (SO 1998a; paras 57, 58, 60, 62), bilingual signage and simultaneous interpretation equipment were installed, members were permitted to make speeches in Gaelic with the permission of the Presiding Officer[1] and speeches made in Gaelic were to be published in the Official Report in the original Gaelic, with an English translation. Legislation enacted by the Parliament is published in English only, however. While this provision for Gaelic is much greater than anything seen at Westminster, the role of Gaelic is clearly marginal, and the Scottish Parliament bears little similarity to the Welsh Assembly, which expresses 'the ambition [...] to be recognised as a truly bilingual institution' (National Assembly for Wales 2013: 2).

Gaelic has been little used in actual parliamentary work, due principally to the low numbers of members who can speak the language fluently (only two of 129 in the first session (1999–2003)). When members have used Gaelic in debates and questions, it has almost always been for essentially symbolic purposes, when issues specifically concerning Gaelic are under consideration. By the same token, very few parliamentary staff are able to speak the language.

Even so, the Parliament has served as a vitally important body for the scrutiny of a broad range of issues concerning Gaelic. In its first session (1999–2003), for example, parliamentary committees produced detailed reports on Gaelic broadcasting and the role of educational and cultural policy in supporting Gaelic and other languages (SP 2001, 2003a). Matters of this kind had not been considered in such detail at Westminster, where Gaelic (like other distinctly Scottish issues) was a much lower priority and little parliamentary time was allocated to them. A Cross-Party Parliamentary Group on Gaelic has also provided an important forum for policy discussion, although, as is typical of these groups, its meetings have tended to attract few members (MSPs) as opposed to representatives of Gaelic organisations and civil society.

Over the years the Parliament has conducted numerous debates specifically focused on Gaelic policy, but these tend to involve representatives of the different parties expressing warm sentiments towards Gaelic but with little partisan disagreement on substantive policy questions (e.g. SP 2015, 2018). The first of these debates was held in 2000, which Donald Meek described as 'a remarkable mix of reality, romanticism, bonhomie, historical allusion, cultural celebrationism, and [. . .] "Gaelic Granny syndrome"' (Meek 2001b: 29).[2] The debate was also the subject of (largely) light-hearted mockery in the press (Brown 2000; McNeil 2000). In contrast to the dismissive and contemptuous rhetoric in the debate on the Stewart Bill in 1981 (see pp. 198–9), it has been unacceptable for members of the Scottish Parliament to make openly negative remarks about Gaelic. But this was by no means true of local councillors or newspaper columnists, as discussed below (pp. 280–1 and 298).

Gaelic activists have been keen to ensure that Gaelic attracted support from all the political parties in Scotland. The conventional view was summarised by Allan Campbell, former chief executive of CnaG and BnG: 'Gaelic must never be allowed to become a "party political football", such a division will create stagnation in all development, and Gaelic will die while politicians score cheap points of[f] each other' (Campbell 2002). This cross-party support has tended to mean that there are individual politicians in different parties who have a personal interest in Gaelic, rather than that the party as a whole has a commitment to the language as a basic principle of policy or ideology. Instead the various parties tend to express general but limited support for Gaelic, and although the SNP is perceived as most supportive, one senior member of the party described its approach as 'very cautious' (Bélanger et al. 2018: 80; Chhim and Bélanger 2017: 935–6). Gaelic activists' emphasis on ensuring cross-party support is therefore based in part on an awareness that no party can be relied upon to make the language a policy priority. In 1998, ahead of the first elections to the Scottish Parliament, Finlay (Strì) MacLeod proposed the creation of a separate Gaelic party (*Scotsman* 1998), but the idea did not gain traction.

By the end of the twentieth century, the Gaelic issue had become broadly associated with the liberal left, typically understood as a matter of minority rights, but it was far from a priority among most organisations and activists of the Scottish left. For some, as had been the case with Lewis Grassic Gibbon in the 1930s, Gaelic was a secondary, purely cultural issue of interest mainly to the middle classes and a distraction from bread-and-butter concerns such as housing and social welfare (Galloway 2003; MacLeòid 2014). Similarly, Gaelic has had almost 'no presence at all within the new radical' anti-capitalist movement in Scotland in the twenty-first century, and is essentially invisible to activists of this stripe (Johnstone 2003).

In 2000 the Parliament appointed a Gaelic officer, Alex O'Henley, a well-known broadcaster and writer, but he quit the post less than two years later on the grounds that the Parliament had not developed its use of Gaelic as he had been led to expect. O'Henley expressed frustration at the lack of support from a key manager at the Parliament, declaring that 'it is an inescapable conclusion that certain people are trying to hinder the development of Gaelic' (*Scotsman* 2002b). Following this setback, two new Gaelic officers were recruited and since then the Parliament has been fairly proactive in its support for the language, particularly through a succession of well-designed Gaelic language plans from 2008 onwards (Scottish Parliamentary Corporate Body 2008, 2013, 2018). In 1998 (before devolution) Gaelic was identified as a ministerial brief for the first time, and since then there has been a designated minister for Gaelic, although this responsibility sits amid a much wider portfolio. Since 2016, for example, the Gaelic brief has been assigned to John Swinney, Cabinet Secretary for Education.

THE ROAD TO THE GAELIC LANGUAGE ACT

From the 1990s onwards, a 'legislative turn' was apparent in relation to minority language protection regimes in a range of jurisdictions (Williams 2013a). Language activists and development professionals came to see language legislation as an essential component of strategies to sustain and revitalise minority languages. Although initiatives at the level of family and neighbourhood are considered fundamental (Fishman 1991), it became accepted that legislation can play a key role in shaping institutional provision, which in turn may significantly enhance the status of the language among both speakers and non-speakers alike. In short, legislation became perceived as a necessary, but not sufficient, instrument in a wider programme of language revitalisation (Williams 2006).

The campaign for a Gaelic Language Act began in the mid-1990s, as Gaelic organisations and the Gaelic community began to perceive that the policy provision and planning structure for Gaelic that had been built since the early 1980s (as discussed in the previous chapter) was precarious and overly dependent on the goodwill of the non-Gaelic majority (Caimbeul 1996; Campbell 2002). In particular, the unstable position of Gaelic-medium education – subject to constant threats of cutback and closure, and, unlike other aspects of educational provision, not regulated by law – was undermining parental confidence in the system and jeopardising its potential for growth. There were several instances in the late 1990s when local authorities, in South Lanarkshire,

Edinburgh, Highland and elsewhere, announced plans to restrict or close Gaelic units (Dunbar 1997; Caimbeul 2000: 62). In this climate of uncertainty, Wales again provided a model for Gaelic activists. In 1993 the *Welsh Language Act 1993* was enacted, which established the general principle that Welsh and English should be treated 'on a basis of equality', and required individual public bodies to 'giv[e] effect' to this principle through Welsh language schemes 'specifying the measures' they would 'take as to the use of the Welsh language in connection with the provision of [public] services' (s. 5). CnaG set up a Working Group on Status in 1996, chaired by the advocate (barrister) Roderick John MacLeod, to study the question of official status for Gaelic and to make appropriate recommendations. A number of consultation meetings were held in different parts of Scotland, and a petition backing the principle of legal status attracted more than four thousand signatures. The working group submitted an initial report to the Scottish Office in 1997, entitled *Inbhe Thèarainte dhan Ghàidhlig/Secure Status for Gaelic*.[3] The phrase 'secure status' was a neologism with no established meaning either in law or language planning theory, chosen in preference to 'official status', which was thought to suggest an overly rigid approach that might make the authorities uneasy

The *Inbhe Thèarainte* report made ten specific recommendations:

- the principle of equal validity for Gaelic and English should be set out in legislation;
- the new Scottish Parliament should make comprehensive provision for Gaelic in its operations;
- local authorities should appoint Gaelic officers;
- all public bodies in Scotland and departments of central government should be required by legislation to develop Gaelic language policies
- litigants in courts and tribunals should be entitled to use Gaelic
- local authorities should be required to make Gaelic-medium education available upon a showing of reasonable demand
- legislation should create a comprehensive Gaelic broadcasting service
- existing anti-discrimination legislation should be amended so as to give protection to Gaelic speakers
- a new legal remedy should be created to allow for the enforcement of Gaelic-related entitlements, and
- these diverse proposals should be enshrined in a comprehensive Gaelic Language Act. (CnaG 1997: 4–5)

CnaG followed up the *Inbhe Thèarainte* document with a more detailed 'draft brief' for a language act in 1999 (CnaG 1999a).

Statements from the new Labour government elected in 1997 suggested a more positive attitude towards Gaelic than that expressed by the outgoing Conservative administration, such that CnaG and the Gaelic community fully anticipated that the government would respond to the recommendations for 'secure status' with legislation along the lines proposed by CnaG. Instead, discussions between CnaG and the Scottish Office/Scottish Executive from 1997 onwards ran into the sand. Although civil servants in the Gaelic section responded favourably to the CnaG proposals and recommended creating a statutory duty for local authorities to provide GME, this proposal was overruled by senior officials (SO 1998b, 1998c). Following devolution in 1999, the new Scottish Executive took the position that language legislation was unnecessary. The first First Minister, Donald Dewar, declared that he did 'not want to go down the Welsh road and end up with a situation where public bodies in Scotland would have legal obligations to conduct their business in Gaelic' (Campbell 2000). Instead of legislating for Gaelic, the government announced that it was 'working towards secure status' through a variety of measures, most of them relatively minor adjustments to policies put in place under the former Conservative administration in fields such as education and broadcasting (Dunbar 2003b). According to Donald Meek, 'the political interpretation of "secure status" with the Scottish Executive [...] became one of *general process*, rather than a series of measures which flow directly from the passing of a Gaelic Act' (Meek 2001b: 30).

In 1999 the Executive attempted to deflect the secure status proposals by establishing a Taskforce on the Public Funding of Gaelic to make policy recommendations on Gaelic, with John Alick MacPherson, deputy director of the Gaelic Broadcasting Committee, serving as its chair. The taskforce's report, published in 2000 (Taskforce on the Public Funding of Gaelic 2000), was somewhat sketchy and was widely criticised for failing to make any reference to a language act among its recommendations. Among other things, the taskforce recommended a substantial increase in the level of Gaelic development funding, the establishment of a 'Department of the Gàidhealtachd', staffed by Gaelic speakers, within the Executive, and the creation of a Gaelic Development Agency.

MacPherson responded to criticisms concerning the failure to recommend a language act by stating that it had been the taskforce's assumption that legislation would be forthcoming and that its recommendations for the Gaelic policy infrastructure would be in addition to this legislative framework (Ross 2000). A second source of controversy was the report's emphasis on Gaelic provision in what it called the 'heartlands' and its limited concern with the status of Gaelic elsewhere. The report proposed that Gaelic policy should be based on a three-part division among (1) the 'heartland' in the far northwest of Scotland 'where the language is still vibrant but vulnerable', (2) the rest of the Gàidhealtachd, 'where Gaelic was once healthy but has declined more rapidly in recent years' and (3) 'the remainder of Scotland and the diaspora of Gaelic speakers all over the world' (Taskforce on the Public Funding of Gaelic 2000: 14). This approach was criticised by some commentators for giving too little attention to Lowland Scotland, given the distribution of the Gaelic-speaking population and the population of Scotland as a whole (MacCaluim with McLeod 2001).

Dissatisfaction with the MacPherson report and continuing pressure for a Gaelic language act led the Executive to establish a second advisory group in December 2001, the Ministerial Advisory Group on Gaelic (MAGOG), which was chaired by Professor Donald Meek of the University of Edinburgh. MAGOG recommended a raft of measures, including 'immediate action [. . .] to develop and implement a Gaelic Language Act', the creation of a dedicated Gaelic Development Agency and a Gaelic Liaison Unit within the Executive and significantly increased funding for Gaelic development (an additional £5 million in 2003–4) (Ministerial Advisory Group on Gaelic 2002: 24–5). While the Executive accepted many of MAGOG's recommendations, it continued to reject the call for a Gaelic Language Act, along with the recommendations for increased funding and the creation of a Gaelic policy unit (Caimbeul 2002a). It did accept the recommendation to establish a Gaelic development agency, Bòrd Gàidhlig na h-Alba,[4] with appropriate powers to undertake language planning for Gaelic at a national level. The refusal to accept the recommendations for legislation and increased funding for Gaelic development provoked a sharply negative response in the Gaelic community, with An Comunn chief executive Donald John MacSween expressing 'anger and disappointment' (*P&J* 2002) and veteran activist Iain MacIllechiar asserting that many people were 'air las le feirg, gu bheil a' phrais a' goil agus an impis a dhol thairis' (lit up with anger, and the pot is about to boil over) (Caimbeul 2002b). A petition to the Scottish Parliament demanding a Gaelic Language Act attracted more than four thousand signatures and was formally presented to the chair of the Petitions Committee at a demonstration in Edinburgh in 2002 involving some 125 activists (MacNeacail 2002).

In 1999 the Scottish Executive had introduced a bill in the Scottish

Parliament (ultimately enacted as the *Standards in Scotland's Schools etc Act 2000*) which addressed a range of issues relating to school education in Scotland. Gaelic organisations saw this bill as an opportunity to press for the statutory right to Gaelic-medium education recommended by CnaG in 1997, and they were successful in persuading SNP MSP Michael Russell (who later became a cabinet minister in the SNP administrations from 2007 on) and Liberal Democrat John Farquhar Munro to introduce an amendment that would have required local authorities to provide Gaelic-medium primary education upon a showing of reasonable demand from parents. The government refused to accept the amendment, however, and it was eventually voted down. A much weaker provision was added to the legislation, however, which required local authorities to provide an annual account of the ways or circumstances in which they would provide GME and, where they did provide GME, to give an account of the ways in which they would seek to develop their provision (s. 5(2)). The Act also included a reference to Gaelic within a new system of 'national priorities' in education (Dunbar 2000: 84–7). By 2004, however, the consensus among Gaelic organisations was that this reporting mechanism had had little impact on Gaelic education (SE 2004a), and over time it effectively became a dead letter.

The next parliamentary move occurred in 2002, after the publication of the MAGOG report, when Russell introduced a member's bill concerning Gaelic (the *Gaelic Language (Scotland) Bill*). The key provision of this bill tracked the wording of the central provision of the *Welsh Language Act 1993* (section 5(2)), so that public bodies in Scotland would be required to produce Gaelic language plans to 'give effect, so far as is both appropriate in the circumstances and reasonably practicable, to the principle that in the exercise of functions by public bodies the Gaelic and English languages should be treated on a basis of equality' (s. (1)(3)). The bill did not cover Scotland as a whole, however, only the local government areas of Highland, Western Isles, Argyll & Bute and the islands of Arran, Great Cumbrae and Little Cumbrae (which formed part of the North Ayrshire administrative area). This geographical limitation was strongly criticised by Gaelic organisations, who insisted that any legislation for Gaelic had to be Scotland-wide in scope (SP 2003b: II, 31, 134–5, 138–9, 142–3). Russell pointed out that under the terms of the bill it could be extended to other parts of Scotland by a simple order from the Scottish Ministers, and argued that the geographical restriction was made in the interests of practicability. Russell also argued that this limitation would reduce opposition to the bill (SP 2003c). In the end, the Executive declined to support a request to accelerate the legislative schedule for the bill, and it eventually died in early 2003 for lack of parliamentary time, shortly ahead of the parliamentary election held in May of that year.

In its manifesto for that election, however, Scottish Labour reversed its position on the issue of legislation for Gaelic and decided to make a commitment to introduce a Gaelic act. Following Labour's return to power, again in coalition with the Liberal Democrats, a draft *Gaelic Language (Scotland) Bill* was published for public consultation in September 2003. The bill set out a policy mechanism comparable in key respects to that established by the Welsh Language Act: Bòrd na Gàidhlig would become a statutory body with general duties for language promotion and the specific obligation to produce and oversee a National Gaelic Language Plan, and individual public bodies would be required to 'determine [...] whether it is appropriate' for them to develop Gaelic language plans (s. 5).

The response to the bill was substantial; more than three thousand submissions were received, then the largest number for any legislative consultation since the opening of the Parliament. It was also largely negative. Commentators in the Gaelic media and respondents to the consultation were disappointed by the weakness of the bill, especially the absence of any rights or obligations relating to Gaelic-medium education and the provision that public authorities should merely be asked to consider whether they should develop Gaelic language plans, not required to do so, as with the Welsh Language Act (e.g. Dòmhnallach 2003; MacLeòid 2003; Johnstone et al. 2004). In its response to the consultation, the Bòrd was candid in its criticism of the bill:

> [Chan] eil am Bile làidir gu leòr. Tha an t-eòlas a tha againn fhìn mar bhuidheann agus an fhianais agus rannsachadh a chuir sinn air dòigh a' cur an cèill ma thèid am Bile a reachdachadh gun atharrachadh nach coilean e a chuid amasan. [...] Gu mì-fhortanach cha tèid aig a' Bhile seo air crìonadh a' chànain a stad mar a tha e air a dhreachdachadh an-dràsta.

> The Bill is not sufficiently robust. Our own collective experience and the evidence and research we have marshalled and considered establish that if the Bill is enacted without amendment it will not achieve its objectives. [...] Sadly as presently drafted the Bill is too weak to stem the decline of the Gaelic language. (BnG 2003)

In relation to the proposed National Gaelic Language Plan, the Bòrd argued that the Plan should be legally binding and legally enforceable (BnG 2003). In its Policy Memorandum accompanying the bill (SP 2004b), the Scottish Executive rejected this view, arguing instead that

The Executive's view of the purpose of the national plan is that it is not to create enforceable burdens on all sections of Scottish public life, but instead to develop a holistic approach to Gaelic language development which will guide public authorities in their approach to the language. A consensual approach is the Executive's preferred means for the Bòrd to carry out its functions. The Executive considers that such an approach is in the long-term interests of the Gaelic language. (SP 2004b: 6)

The most controversial submission during the legislative process came from the Commission for Racial Equality, which argued that the Gaelic bill should be widened 'to include all of Scotland's languages'. The CRE argued that 'requiring authorities to prepare and publish a Gaelic language plan will impact on public authorities' ability to meet [their duties relating to racial equality. . . .] By focusing only on Gaelic, it could be argued that authorities are not giving due regard to promoting equality of opportunity and promote good relations between people of different racial groups.' The CRE went so far as to say that the proposed legislation 'could actually militate against new duties on public bodies in Scotland to promote race equality' and 'could send out an unhelpful message in terms of race relations' (Commission for Racial Equality 2003). The CRE's intervention was sharply criticised by a number of public officials and organisations, including the Education Committee itself (SP 2003b: I, 11, paras 61–2). The CRE's position on the Gaelic bill also contrasted sharply with the organisation's approach to language development in Wales, where the organisation entered into a concordat with the Welsh Language Board in 1996 (Welsh Language Commissioner 2016: 38), recognising their shared interest in equality, and developed and implemented a Welsh language scheme.[5]

Following the consultation, in September 2004 the Executive formally introduced the *Gaelic Language (Scotland) Bill* into the Scottish Parliament. This version incorporated significant changes from the consultation draft; most importantly, public authorities would now be required to develop Gaelic language plans and not merely asked to determine whether it would be appropriate for them to do so. Gaelic advocates perceived the bill as a substantial improvement to the earlier version, even if the continued failure to guarantee the right to Gaelic-medium education was seen as a major deficiency. Although it dealt with education only to a limited extent, the bill was scrutinised by the Parliament's Education Committee, which carried out its work on a cross-party basis, with no political differences coming to the fore.

Among the submissions to the committee was a warning from CnES that Bòrd na Gàidhlig should not simultaneously be given too much responsibility and too little power: 'It is important [...] that Bòrd na Gàidhlig is not cast in the role of a lone, national Gaelic policeman sent out by the Executive to browbeat recalcitrant organisations to sing from the Gaelic hymn sheet' (SP 2005: 20). The Education Committee 'fully endorsed th[is] view' (SP 2005: 20), but as discussed in the following chapter, the council's concern proved to be prescient.

The bill underwent some helpful revisions during the parliamentary process. An important amendment was introduced at the behest of the Education Committee (SE 2005a), to the effect that public authorities developing Gaelic language plans would be required to have regard not only to 'the extent to which the persons in relation to whom the authority's functions are exercisable use the Gaelic language' but also 'the potential for developing the use of the Gaelic language in connection with the exercise of those functions' (s. 3(5)(b)–(c)). In other words, authorities would have to consider not only the current position of Gaelic vis-à-vis the organisation but also how the organisation might contribute to the strengthening of Gaelic in the future. Taken at face value, section 3(5)(c) is potentially almost limitless in its scope – in theory, Gaelic could conceivably be 'developed' to the point of becoming the default language of the organisation's operations – but this provision clearly must be interpreted in line with the overall approach of the Act, which does not seek to impose unreasonable burdens.

At stage 2 of the legislative process, the Executive added new language concerning the work of the Bòrd, requiring that the Bòrd act 'with a view to securing the status of the Gaelic language as an official language of Scotland commanding equal respect to the English language'. This phrasing, analysed in more detail below, was much stronger than the wording in the consultation draft, which spoke only of 'securing the status of the Gaelic language as one of the languages of Scotland'. The SNP opposition introduced an amendment that would have strengthened this further by changing the formula of 'equal respect' to that of 'equal validity'. Gaelic Minister Peter Peacock argued against the amendment, contending that 'the phrase "equal validity" in the bill carries a significant risk that a court might rule that the bill conferred the right to demand the use of the language in a wider range of circumstances than is intended' (Scottish Parliament 2005). The Executive had already stated in its Policy Memorandum that it was unwilling to include any form of words 'which could result in any public authority anywhere in Scotland being placed under a legal duty to offer services in Gaelic on demand' (SP 2004b: para. 15). This was probably an unlikely interpretation; limiting phrases such as those used in the *Welsh Language Act 1993* – 'appropriate in the circumstances' and 'reasonably practicable' (s. 5(2)) – could readily have been found.

The Gaelic bill attracted relatively little public debate outside Gaelic circles and received little attention from the English-language media (but see Luckhurst 2005). Final approval in April 2005 was made on an unanimous vote. This consensus in support of the bill was a far cry from the response to the Stewart Bill in 1981 and demonstrated how much attitudes to Gaelic had improved in the intervening decades. At the same time, the lack of opposition demonstrates the relative weakness of the legislation; a more stringent and demanding bill would surely have provoked greater resistance.

THE GAELIC LANGUAGE ACT: KEY PROVISIONS AND OMISSIONS

The Gaelic Language Act is based to a considerable extent on the *Welsh Language Act 1993* (and bears some resemblance to the *Official Languages Act 2003* in the Republic of Ireland) but is rather less vigorous. Nevertheless, the Act is without doubt a landmark in the history of Gaelic policy in Scotland.

The preamble to the Act states the aim 'of securing the status of Gaelic as an official language of Scotland commanding equal respect with the English language'. Although the exact way this principle is expressed and positioned in the Act leaves considerable room for interpretation, it is nevertheless very important as a symbolic recognition of the status of Gaelic. The idea of Gaelic commanding 'equal respect' with English, after centuries of marginalisation and denigration, is extremely powerful, and the clear national association for the language ('an official language of Scotland') is also significant. The phrase 'official language' actually has no fixed meaning in law but is nevertheless resonant and symbolically powerful for the general population.

However, the Act does not actually contain any straightforward declaration of Gaelic's official status. This is in contrast to the *Welsh Language (Wales) Measure 2011*, which states unambiguously that 'the Welsh language has official status in Wales' and identifies seven kinds of enactments that give legal effect to this status (s. 1). The wording in the Gaelic Language Act is much more indirect: the phrase 'an official language of Scotland commanding equal respect with the English language' is actually preceded by 'with a view to securing the status of Gaelic as', a formula which suggests that this status is aspirational rather than actual. The Executive resisted including a more direct statement of Gaelic's status, noting the long-standing 'view of both the UK Government and the Executive that Gaelic already enjoys official status'[6] and making clear that the provision concerning official status was 'intended to be descriptive rather than confer particular rights of usage' (SE 2004e).

Nor is the principle of 'equal respect' directly linked to the Gaelic language plans that public authorities are required to prepare. This contrasts with the *Welsh Language Act 1993*, which specified that public bodies' Welsh language schemes have the 'purpose' of 'giving effect [. . .] to the principle that [. . .] the English and Welsh languages should be treated on a basis of equality' (s. 5). Instead, the phrase in the Gaelic Language Act concerning official status and equal respect relates only to the manner in which Bòrd na Gàidhlig is required to carry out its statutory functions (s. 1(3)). In any event, as discussed above in relation to the unsuccessful attempt to substitute 'equal validity' for 'equal respect', the phrase 'equal respect' has no recognised, operative legal meaning.

However, the principle of 'equal respect' does come into the plan process indirectly. Section 8(10) provides that 'in preparing guidance [concerning Gaelic language plans] and giving advice and assistance [concerning the development of Gaelic language plans], the Bòrd must seek to give effect, so far as is both appropriate in the circumstances and reasonably practicable, to the principle that the Gaelic and English languages should be accorded equal respect'.

The main operative sections of the Act concern the duties and powers of the Bòrd and the preparation of the National Gaelic Language Plan and individual public authorities' Gaelic language plans. A new agency, Bòrd na Gàidhlig, was established (replacing the earlier Bòrd Gàidhlig na h-Alba) and given a range of specified powers and responsibilities.[7] These include the obligation to prepare a National Gaelic Language Plan every five years and the power to issue guidance to local authorities in relation to GME. The Act is relatively unspecific about the content of the national plan, stating only that it 'must include proposals as to the exercise of [the Bòrd's] functions under this Act' and 'those proposals must include a strategy for promoting, and facilitating the promotion of [. . .] the use and understanding of the Gaelic language, and [. . .] Gaelic education and Gaelic culture' (s. 2(1) and (2)). As discussed in the next chapter (pp. 285–8), National Plans were published in 2007, 2013 and 2018. In many respects, the Bòrd was closely modelled on the existing Welsh Language Board, but the Welsh board did not have the obligation to produce a national language plan.

Under the Act, the Bòrd may require any public authority in Scotland to prepare a Gaelic language plan, although it is contemplated that such plans will vary according to 'the extent to which the persons in relation to whom the authority's functions are exercisable use the Gaelic language' and 'the potential for developing the use of the Gaelic language in connection with the exercise of those functions' (s. 3(5)(b)–(c)). This 'sliding scale' approach reflects the view of Gaelic organisations that different levels of provision for Gaelic are appropriate in different parts of Scotland, but that Scotland-wide coverage is essential given Gaelic's increasingly national rather than regional profile and the increasing dispersal of the Gaelic-speaking population (CnaG 1997; MacCaluim with McLeod 2001). In addition, a public authority cannot simply declare that there is no need to make provision for Gaelic on the grounds that there is no demand for it. As noted above, under section 3(5)(c) the organisation must consider 'the potential for developing the use of the Gaelic language', that is, how it might be able to grow and expand the use of Gaelic and the demand for Gaelic. A plan needs to be proactive rather than reactive.

The Act is not very specific in setting out the purposes and content of Gaelic language plans. In general, they must 'set out the measures to be taken by the relevant public authority in relation to the use of the Gaelic language in connection with the exercise of the authority's functions'. Importantly, however, these 'functions' are defined to mean both 'functions relating to [the authority's] internal processes' and 'the provision by the authority of any services to the public' (ss. 3(4)(a), 10(4)). The Act also provides that the government,[8] in consultation with Bòrd na Gàidhlig, may prepare regulations or guidance concerning the content of plans, and that public authorities 'must have regard to' such guidance when they prepare language plans (s. (3)(5)(e), (7) and (8); s. 8).

The government retains control over all stages of the language plan process; as one civil servant expressed it, 'there is a strong Ministerial veto running through the [Act] to ensure that the Bòrd carries out its functions appropriately' (SE 2004g). The government can quash the Bòrd's request for the preparation of a plan entirely (so that the public authority would not have to prepare a plan at all), it can modify the deadline for the plan, and it can modify the substantive terms of the plan (ss. 4(5)–(10), 5(5)–(8)). To date the government has not used any of these powers, but this arguably reflects the caution of the Bòrd in selecting the bodies to which it sends notifications, setting deadlines for the preparation of plans and agreeing the terms of plans.

The Bòrd's powers to enforce compliance with Gaelic language plans are weak and indirect. The Bòrd is entitled to request public authorities to provide reports concerning their compliance with their language plans, but the range of its investigatory power is not clear and it has no direct enforcement powers. Instead, under section 6 of the Act, 'where the Bòrd considers that a relevant public authority is failing to implement adequately measures in its Gaelic language plan, it may submit to the Scottish Ministers a report setting out its reasons for that conclusion', and the Ministers may then either 'lay a copy of the report before the Scottish Parliament' or 'direct the authority in question to implement any or all of the measures in its Gaelic language plan'. Gaelic language plans are therefore legally enforceable, but the power to require enforcement and the decision whether to use that power rest with the government and not with the Bòrd. In any event, to date the Bòrd has never reported a public authority to the government for non-compliance.

By the same token, the Act does not create any mechanism for the submission or investigation of complaints from the public concerning the implementation of public authorities' language plans. This stands in contrast to the counterpart language legislation in Ireland and Wales (*Official Languages Act 2003*, ss. 21, 23; *Welsh Language (Wales) Measure 2011*, s. 14).

In some respects, the omissions from the Act are more important than what is included. As an enactment of the Scottish rather than Westminster Parliament, the Act extends only to public authorities that operate solely within Scotland or that deal with 'devolved' matters (which do not include broadcasting, defence, financial regulation, foreign affairs, social security, trade and most forms of taxation).[9] This means that UK-wide public bodies, ranging from the Inland Revenue and the Department for Work and Pensions to the Post Office and Coast Guard, have no obligations under the Act. This disjuncture makes it difficult to develop an integrated strategy for Gaelic development in the public sector, and may lead to confusion and frustration for Gaelic speakers in terms of service provision. In contrast, the *Welsh Language Act 1993*, as a Westminster enactment, reaches all public bodies that operate in Wales. The Welsh Language Act does not extend to Crown bodies such as departments of the Westminster government (s. 21(1)), but the government gave a commitment when the Act went through Parliament that these bodies would prepare Welsh language schemes as if they were required to do so by the Act (Williams 2010: 51). No such commitment was made with regard to the Gaelic Act, although the Education Committee urged the Executive to 'seek a formal undertaking' to this effect and there were several, if ultimately inconclusive, discussions between the Scottish and UK governments concerning this issue (SP 2005: 18; SE 2004e).

Following the enactment of the Act, the Passport Office began including Gaelic (and Welsh) in UK passports (*Herald* 2005) and the Department for Work and Pensions installed Gaelic signage in its buildings in the Highlands and Islands (SG 2015). However, the Driver and Vehicle Licensing Agency indicated its unwillingness to provide services in Gaelic, despite doing so in Welsh (Penning 2012), and the Westminster government stated in 2015 that it had 'no plans' to introduce a policy of replying in Gaelic to correspondence in Gaelic (Hansard 2015). In 2012 Labour MP Tom Harris put down an Early Day Motion in the House of Commons 'urg[ing] the Government to establish Gaelic on equal terms with English and Welsh' (Early Day Motion 2822). The motion attracted twenty-nine members' signatures and although BnG stated that it 'would welcome such a move' (*P&J* 2012a), the proposal generated little public discussion and did not lead to any ongoing pressure for Westminster legislation. Gaelic advocates then pressed the issue to the Smith Commission, the body set up in the wake of the 2014 independence referendum to agree new powers that would be devolved to Scotland, but this proposal was not addressed in the Commission's report, which actually made no reference to Gaelic at all (Yes Alba 2014; Smith Commission 2014).

Another limitation is that there is nothing in the Act establishing rights to use Gaelic in the courts or other legal proceedings. This omission contrasts with the corresponding legislation in Ireland and Wales, both of which include such guarantees (*Official Languages Act 2003*, s. 8; *Welsh Language Act 1993*, s. 21). The issue is instead left to the Gaelic language plan process. Remarkably, to date the Bòrd has not requested the Scottish Courts and Tribunals Service, which regulates legal procedure in Scotland, to prepare a Gaelic language plan. The restrictive principle reiterated in the *Taylor* v. *Haughney* case therefore remains in effect, modified only by a minor amendment to procedure in civil cases in island courts (discussed below, p. 261). In 2019 the poet Mark Spencer-Turner was prevented from giving evidence in Gaelic in an assault case in the Edinburgh Justice of the Peace Court (BBC Naidheachdan 2019c).

Despite the attention given to the connection between Gaelic and the economy from the 1980s onwards, the Act does not address the private sector at all; indeed, the possibility of imposing obligations on private companies was never seriously contemplated. This limitation is typical of language legislation in minority contexts. The *Welsh Language (Wales) Measure 2011*, for example, only addresses narrowly defined categories of private companies. Linguistic regulation of private companies tends to appear only in enactments on behalf of more widely spoken languages, such as the legislation in France and Québec requiring the use of French in the workplace (Wright 2015: 140–1).

Most importantly, there is nothing in the Act concerning any right to receive, or obligation to deliver, Gaelic education, which Peacock recognised at the outset of the legislative process was '*the* key issue for the Gaelic community' (SE 2004d: [3]). According to one civil service minute, the Executive 'studiously avoided conferring rights to usage' (SE 2004g). None of the opposition parties introduced any amendments to establish a right to GME, as they had with the Standards in Scotland's Schools Bill in 1999. As concern about the instability of GME was the main driving force of the campaign for the Act, Gaelic advocates perceived this omission from the Act as a major setback. Provision for education would be addressed as one of the major elements in individual local authorities' Gaelic language plans, but in the absence of the 'stick' of a legally enforceable right, authorities have not been pushed to make significant changes in their offer in relation to Gaelic.

One common argument against the inclusion of such a right was that it would have been impossible to put into effect given the shortage of teachers (Campbell 2015). However, it is certainly possible that the 'stick' of legal obligation might prompt local authorities to seek significant changes in the structure of teacher education. For example, the Hawai'i Supreme Court has ruled that because the state is 'constitutionally required to make all reasonable efforts to provide access to Hawaiian immersion education', it should take practical steps such as giving greater financial or other incentives to attract immersion teachers, providing transportation, reworking workloads and timetables or partnering with community members with a knowledge of the language (*Clarabal* v. *Department of Education* (2019)). An enforceable legal right might bring the Gaelic teacher issue into sharper focus in the minds of education officials.

The Financial Memorandum submitted to the Parliament in connection with the Gaelic bill gave useful insight into the Executive's view of the Act and the likely trajectory of implementation. The memorandum stated that the Executive expected the Bòrd to produce only about ten language plans per year (SP 2004b: para. 82). Given that there are several hundred public authorities in Scotland, full implementation of the legislation at such a rate would take decades. As discussed below (pp. 288–90), the Bòrd only agreed about sixty plans in the first fourteen years of implementation, less than half this anticipated number. The Executive also advised that the Bòrd should not require bodies in areas with 'few' Gaelic speakers to produce plans 'in the years immediately after the enactment of the Bill' (SP 2004b: para. 92). It also indicated that it would establish a Gaelic Language Development Fund (now the Gaelic Language Act Implementation Fund) to assist public authorities in meeting some of the costs of implementing Gaelic language plans. This mechanism has helped take some of the political sting out of the implementation process, in the same way as the Specific Grants for Gaelic Education made it easier for local authorities to agree to introduce GME.

The Gaelic Language Act was an important milestone in the history of Gaelic development and introduced a much more complex language policy regime. National Gaelic Language Plans and individual public authorities' plans began to be published from 2007 onwards, giving rise to a range of operational and political issues. This policy trajectory is considered in detail in the next chapter.

THE EUROPEAN CHARTER FOR REGIONAL OR MINORITY LANGUAGES

The most important outcome of the growing attention to minority languages at the European level from the early 1980s was the Council of Europe's *European Charter for Regional or Minority Languages*, a treaty which seeks 'the protection of the historical regional or minority languages of Europe' as part of 'the maintenance and development of Europe's cultural wealth and traditions' (preamble). The Charter was opened to ratification by state parties in 1992 and entered into force in 1998, once it had been ratified by five states.[10] In 1996 the Conservative government announced that it would not ratify the Charter (Macintosh 1999: 467) but this decision was reversed by the Labour government in 2001. The UK government's decision to enter into a formal international treaty requiring the protection of Gaelic and other minority languages in the UK was symbolically important, but over time it has had little practical impact on the status of Gaelic in Scotland.

In order to accommodate the sociolinguistic situations of many different languages and the political interests of many different states, the Charter was carefully designed to allow substantial flexibility in terms of the commitments to which signatories would be bound. Under the Charter, all languages spoken in the state territory that meet the Charter's definition of a 'regional or minority language'[11] are automatically covered by Part II of the Charter, and thus included in the scope of Article 7, which sets out a number of general principles, including 'the need for resolute action to promote regional or minority languages in order to safeguard them'. Part III of the Charter is considerably more detailed and demanding, and here states may decide which languages to designate, and which particular paragraphs of Part III they will accept in relation to particular languages. Part III involves specific undertakings in relation to education, the judiciary, administrative authorities and public services, media, cultural activities and facilities, economic and social exchanges, and transfrontier exchanges (Grin 2003), and states then have considerable discretion to decide which of these undertakings they will accept. Crucially, the only enforcement mechanism under the Charter is a system of state reporting; it is not possible for a group or an individual to bring a court case alleging non-fulfilment of obligations. Under Article 15, paragraph 1 of the Charter, each state which has ratified the Charter must make an initial report within a year of its entry into force, specifying how it has complied with its commitments, and must then make subsequent reports every three years. A designated Committee of Experts then visits the country to investigate the actual situation, including meeting with representatives of language organisations, and submits an evaluative report which also includes recommendations. These recommendations are then transmitted to the Council of Ministers and, if accepted, sent on to the state party. But there is no further legal mechanism to require compliance.

The UK's ratification document was highly variegated. The government declared that it would apply the Charter to Gaelic, Welsh, Irish (in relation to Northern Ireland), Scots and Ulster Scots; in 2003 it added Cornish and Manx. Scots, Ulster Scots, Cornish and Manx were designated under Part II of the Charter only, while Gaelic, Welsh and Irish were designated under the more stringent Part III. However, the UK's strategy in relation to the Charter was to accept, as far as possible, only those undertakings that aligned with existing provision for the languages in question. Thus, out of a total of 68 paragraphs and subparagraphs set out in Part III, the government specified 52 for Welsh, 39 for Gaelic and only 36 for Irish, which was only one more than the minimum number that was required. These disparities reflected the significantly greater extent of provision for Welsh than for Gaelic or Irish, but the government did not use the opportunity of Charter ratification to bring provision for Gaelic and Irish up to the level of Welsh. By taking this minimalist approach, the UK effectively ensured that ratification of the Charter simply reiterated the status quo, rather than prompting any improvement of provision for the protected languages. Nor did ratification of the Charter involve any substantive review of policy to ensure that provision for the various languages was based on the equitable application of clear principles. Arguably then, the UK paid little attention to the *spirit* of the Charter.

In relation to Gaelic, the only change that the government made in order to meet the requirements of the Charter was a minor amendment to court rules to allow litigants or other parties to civil proceedings to give oral evidence in Gaelic in sheriff courts in three sheriff court districts, Portree, Lochmaddy and Stornoway, and in appeals to higher courts from those sheriff courts[12] (which collectively handle only about 0.5 per cent of the total volume of civil litigation (McLeod 2008c: 210)). Without this change the government would not have satisfied the requirement to accept at least one paragraph in relation to each Article of Part III, in particular Article 9, which deals with judicial authorities (McLeod 2008c: 206–7). The government declined to extend the Charter to cover criminal proceedings, based on its view that this would put 'additional pressure on court time' and 'raise significant cost implications to pay for the services of interpreters' (SE 2001). For all criminal cases throughout Scotland, the established *McRae* rule, ratified in the *Taylor* case, remained in place.

Another important commitment concerning Gaelic in the UK's instrument of ratification was its acceptance of Article 11 1 a 2, which provides that 'to the extent that radio and television carry out a public service mission' the government must 'encourage and/or facilitate the creation of at least one radio station and one television channel in' Gaelic. This had relevance for the ongoing discussions concerning the establishment of a dedicated Gaelic television channel, discussed in detail below.

With regard to Gaelic primary education, the UK bound itself to the 'most ambitious' of the available subparagraphs, article 8 1 b. i., which requires the authorities 'to make available primary education in the relevant regional or minority languages' (CoE 2004: 32). This demands more systematic, mainstreamed provision than that contemplated by subsection iv., under which such education need be provided only 'to those pupils whose families so request and whose number is considered sufficient'.

In its first monitoring report (CoE 2004), the Committee of Experts criticised several aspects of the UK's implementation of the Charter, notably in relation to Gaelic education and broadcasting. Among the recommendations to the UK government made by the Committee of Ministers in response to the Committee of Experts' report were that the UK authorities should make primary and secondary education in Gaelic generally available in the areas where the language is used, facilitate the establishment of a television channel or an equivalent television service in Gaelic and overcome the shortcomings in Gaelic radio broadcasting. The Committee of Experts found that provision for Gaelic in education was 'very patchy and is non-existent even in some places where there are significant numbers of Gaelic speakers', and was therefore 'insufficient to meet the requirements of the undertakings chosen by the UK' (CoE 2004: 32). This finding did not have any concrete ramifications in practice, however.

The Committee of Experts discreetly criticised the UK for its haphazard approach to the implementation of the Charter, observing that 'there appears to be comparatively little co-ordination or co-operation regarding language policy between the authorities in Wales, Northern Ireland and Scotland and the central government in London' and that 'each administration [in Wales, Scotland and Northern Ireland] has adopted a different approach, which seems to be largely dependent on the strength of political will to support regional or minority languages' (CoE 2004: 54, 8). The Committee was particularly critical of the Scottish Executive in this connection, noting that:

> There appears to be less emphasis on minority language policy on the part of the Scottish Executive, even though there is political will to protect the Gaelic language [...] The Scottish Executive [...] does not seem to have informed relevant administrations about the obligations deriving from the Charter, nor has it established concrete guidelines for the administrations on how to carry out their responsibilities under the Charter. (CoE, 2004: 57)

The Committee of Experts submitted three further evaluation reports, in 2007, 2010 and 2014, but these have not had any noticeable impact on Gaelic policy. Over time the Charter has lost significance for both Gaelic campaigners and policy-makers and is now rarely mentioned in policy discussions.

In 1998 the UK also ratified another Council of Europe legal instrument in the field of minority rights, the *Framework Convention for the Protection of National Minorities*. The UK government has taken an unusual approach to its implementation of the Framework Convention, by including groups whose presence in the UK is the 'result of recent migration flows' within the terms of the Explanatory Report on the Charter (CoE 1995). The Convention does not contain a definition of 'national minority', but is understood by most states to encompass only groups settled on the state territory for a lengthy period, at least a hundred years (Wicherkiewicz 2005). The UK has instead aligned its interpretation of the term with the definition developed under the *Race*

Relations Act 1976 (McLeod 1998), thereby including 'ethnic minority communities (or visible minorities) and the Scots, Irish and Welsh, who are defined as a racial group by virtue of their national origins', as well as 'Gypsies (and Travellers in Northern Ireland)' (CoE 1999: para. 2).

This approach to the Framework Convention may give rise to language-related commitments in relation to Gaelic and other language communities. Most obviously, article 10 provides as follows:

1 The Parties undertake to recognize that every person belonging to a national minority has the right to use freely and without interference his or her minority language, in private and in public, orally and in writing.

2 In areas inhabited by persons belonging to national minorities traditionally or in substantial numbers, if those persons so request and where such a request corresponds to a real need, the Parties shall endeavour to ensure, as far as possible, the conditions which would make it possible to use the minority language in relations between those persons and the administrative authorities.

The reference here to 'real need' raises an important issue. A key practical difference between speakers of the autochthonous languages designated under the Charter and speakers of the UK's allochthonous languages is that all the former can also speak English, while many of the latter have limited competence in English. A range of public services, including both translation of documents and oral interpretation, is provided to UK residents who cannot speak English, with the corollary being that such services will not be made available to individuals who can speak English. The City of Edinburgh Council, for example, has declined to provide translation and interpretation for Gaelic speakers on the grounds that Gaelic is a 'language of choice' rather than a language 'of need' (McLeod 2008c: 216–17).

This policy position is set out in the section of the UK's 1999 report relating to the Framework Convention that deals with article 10:

> In public administration, the Government's policy is to deal with non-English speakers on a basis of courtesy and respect for their linguistic preference. Persons from ethnic minorities may use their own language in their contacts with administrative authorities and public services.

This policy is not based on legislation or any kind of formal written statement, however, and the formulation given here is somewhat evasive. The reference to 'linguistic preference' might seem to encapsulate the principle of language choice, but the key limiting phrase here is 'non-

English speakers'. If a minority language speaker can speak English, he or she is no longer a 'non-English speaker' and is expected to speak English. Delivery of services is predicated on the inability to use English.

In 2009 Gaelic was authorised for use in European Union institutions, although its status was less than that of full working language, which was granted to Irish (as the first official language of a member state). Although the UK ambassador to the EU announced that this step would 'help to build a closer link between EU institutions and speakers of Scottish Gaelic by allowing them to raise their concerns and have them addressed directly in their native language' (*Times* 2009), it was understood that the measure was essentially symbolic. In 2010 Education Secretary Michael Russell took advantage of the new provision to use Gaelic for a speech to the EU's Education, Youth and Culture Council (*Times* 2010). Gaelic had actually been used in the European Parliament as far back as 1973, when Russell Johnston (an MEP and later an MP) used some Gaelic in a speech (Dòmhnallach 1973). With the withdrawal of the UK from the EU in 2020, however, this provision became moot. There was considerable concern about the impact of Brexit on Gaelic and other minority language communities in the UK, not only as a result of the cut-off of funding opportunities for projects directly relating to language but also for infrastructural support in outlying areas (*Irish Times* 2016). The Highlands and Islands have benefited very considerably from different EU support programmes over the decades.

GAELIC-MEDIUM EDUCATION: FROM UNITS TO SCHOOLS

From the late 1990s onwards, a major development in relation to Gaelic education has been the push to develop free-standing Gaelic schools in place of Gaelic units within English-medium primary schools. Gaelic advocates have viewed free-standing schools as providing a more immersive and supportive environment for language acquisition and the reinforcement of Gaelic identity. As discussed above, the unit model for GME originally arose out of a political compromise in Glasgow and Inverness in the mid-1980s and this structure was then replicated elsewhere as GME rolled out to different authorities. In other minority language jurisdictions such as Wales and Ireland, minority language education was much more likely to be delivered in dedicated schools.

The first push for a dedicated Gaelic school began in Glasgow, where by the late 1990s parents had become increasingly dissatisfied with the Gaelic unit at Sir John Maxwell School. Even though the number of Gaelic-medium pupils had reached a hundred by 1993 (University of Strathclyde 1994), growth then stalled. Some parents felt that the predominance of English at the school was increasing and some questioned the extent of the headteacher's support for GME. In one activist's view, 'bha e mar gu robh sinn a' loidseadh ann an taigh nach robh a' buntainn dhuinn' ('we felt as if we were lodging in a house that didn't belong to us') (Ó Gallchóir 2007: 103). These concerns led some parents to push for the creation of a dedicated Gaelic school, although others preferred to argue the case for a second Gaelic unit on the north side of the River Clyde (where most GME families lived). At a meeting of parents in 1998, it was agreed to push for a Gaelic school, and a discussion document setting out possible options was circulated among the parent group. At a subsequent meeting, the aim of a dedicated Gaelic school received the unanimous support of the parents in attendance. Parents examined various potential sites and focused on the school in Ashley Street in Woodside, near the West End of the city, when this became available. Through a well-organised lobbying campaign, the support of Glasgow councillors and the Scottish Executive was secured, and the Executive agreed to provide special funding of £300,000 (McCurdy 2000: 26; Ó Gallchóir 2007: 103–5). The new school, Bun-sgoil Ghàidhlig Ghlaschu (Glasgow Gaelic Primary School), eventually opened in 1999 with 109 pupils (*Herald* 1999). The original school in Ashley Street soon proved too small, however; enrolment had increased to 172 by 2004 (Glasgow City Council 2004). A second campaign was organised to secure an expanded primary school and a dedicated secondary. Following another round of intensive parental lobbying, the council acceded to the parents' demands and agreed to open a 3–18 school (from nursery through the end of secondary) at Woodside in the Finnieston area of the city. Again the Scottish Executive awarded dedicated funding for the project, this time a much larger grant of £3.8 million (Rogers and McLeod 2007: 369). These developments provoked a degree of opposition; one critic linked to the EIS, the teachers' union, characterised the dedicated Gaelic school as an undesirable affront to 'inclusion and diversity', a form of 'separate and exclusive provision' for a 'privileged minority group' (Donnelly 2004).

At the same time, a similar campaign by parents to establish a dedicated Gaelic school in Edinburgh proved unsuccessful. The City of Edinburgh Council was less supportive than Glasgow, and there were more divisions within the parent group. The campaign began in 1997, after council education officials raised the possibility of imposing a cap on the number of pupils entering the Gaelic unit at Tollcross Primary School, which had been established in 1988. Parents and supporters held a demonstration at the City Chambers and a working group was established by the local branch of Comann nam Pàrant. Discussions between the parent group, the council and the Scottish Office/Executive continued until early 2000, when the council rejected the proposals on the grounds that the predicted enrolment at a stand-alone school, based on the results of a survey of Tollcross parents, was only 67 pupils (86 per cent of those currently enrolled at Tollcross) instead of the 90–100 it deemed necessary for a viable separate school (*Herald* 2000). Some councillors were strongly opposed to the proposal in principle, with one Labour member going so far as to say that Gaelic parents were trying to establish educational 'apartheid' in the city (MacLeòid 2000; Armstrong 2018).

The council agreed to review the issue in 2002, but this resulted in another refusal to support the proposal for a stand-alone school, even though a survey showed that 463 parents (72 per cent of those who responded) agreed in principle with the establishment of a dedicated Gaelic school and 104 said they would send their child to such a school. Although this figure exceeded the 90–100 specified in 2000, the council asserted that past experience suggested that there would be a significant drop-off between statements of intent and actual enrolment (*EEN* 2002). It reiterated that position later that year, in response to Scottish Executive advice to examine Gaelic provision in connection with the UK's ratification of the European Charter for Regional or Minority Languages (City of Edinburgh Council 2002). In the event, it was not until 2013, following a lengthy second campaign (discussed in the following chapter, pp. 301–2), that a Gaelic school opened in Edinburgh.

In 2007 the second free-standing school opened in Inverness, with capacity for two hundred pupils. Two extensions to the school were subsequently built due to increasing demand for places (*P&J* 2018a). By 2001 there were obvious problems with capacity in the original Gaelic unit at Central Primary School, and thus there were no stumbling blocks in terms of securing political and financial support for the new Gaelic school from Highland Council and the Scottish Executive (*P&J* 2001; *TESS* 2002). Once open, however, the school had great difficulties recruiting a Gaelic-speaking head teacher. The post had to be re-advertised numerous times and the appointment of an interim head with little Gaelic brought a degree of reputational damage to Gaelic education generally. Only in May 2015 was the school able to appoint a permanent head (*Highland News* 2015). Proposals for a Gaelic high school in Inverness were advanced in 2006 (*P&J* 2006) and for a second primary in 2011 (*IC* 2011), but these have still not come to fruition.

It was notable that the push for free-standing schools first emerged in the cities rather than the rural 'heartlands', as had also been the case with the first Gaelic units back in 1985. In part this reflected sheer numbers: enrolling a hundred or more pupils in GME was considerably easier in Glasgow than in Skye or the Western Isles. But there were also significant political difficulties when campaigners sought to establish Gaelic schools in rural areas, as discussed in the next chapter (pp. 302–4).

THE PUSH FOR A GAELIC TELEVISION CHANNEL

As the shortcomings of the funding and regulatory regime for Gaelic television that had been established in 1989–90 became increasingly apparent, proposals for a dedicated Gaelic television channel began to gather pace after the election of the Labour government in 1997. Brian Wilson, the former publisher of the *West Highland Free Press* who had been elected to Parliament in 1987, was appointed as minister for Gaelic – the first time that Gaelic had ever been formally designated in a ministerial remit. Although Wilson ordered a £500,000 cut to the Gaelic television budget in 1997, the following year he made use of a departmental underspend to commission Neil Fraser to write a report on the viability of a dedicated channel (Fraser 1998). This was to be the first stage of what Fraser would later characterise as 'a long, tortuous and occasionally frustrating odyssey' that took almost a decade to complete (MG ALBA 2008: 4). These discussions took place at an important juncture for broadcasting provision more generally, as new digital technology was being introduced to replace the traditional analogue system, a process that involved immense technical challenges.

Fraser reviewed the fragmented provision for Gaelic and concluded that 'the concept of a Gaelic *service* remains elusive; the extended provision has become just a large collection of programmes randomly scheduled across several channels with no overall control of the range and quality of the programmes on offer' (Fraser 1998: 4). Unlike S4C, whose funding was increased annually in line with inflation, the funding of the CCG was not based on a non-discretionary formula. This meant that by 1998 the value of the fund available for Gaelic programming had fallen by 24 per cent in real terms since 1992. In 1999 the fund was sufficient to fund only about 160 hours instead of the intended 200, and by 2004 this had fallen to 149 hours (Fraser 1998: 6–7; CCG 2003: [2]).

Fraser concluded that 'the multi-channel, multi-service prospect on offer' from digital transmission provided 'a real opportunity to develop a coherent Gaelic television service', driven by a 'single Gaelic Broadcasting Authority'. This 'would overcome the present fractionation and lack of coherence' and 'enable a clear strategy for the quality, quantity and range of Gaelic output' (Fraser 1999: 19). In relation to funding, Fraser proposed 'a formula for a secure public contribution [...] based on the total terrestrial qualifying revenue' from the various commercial broadcasters alongside 'a more equitable disbursement from the BBC's annual licence take' (Fraser 1999: 17). No indicative budget figure was provided, although a table showed total income for 1998 of £96.9 million for S4C in Wales, £18.0 million for TG4 in Ireland and £11.13 million[13] for Gaelic television in Scotland (Fraser 1999: 16).

The government followed up the Fraser report by establishing a Gaelic Broadcasting Task Force chaired by Alasdair Milne, former Director-General of the BBC, in order 'to examine from the standpoint of technical feasibility, finance and programming the practicability of establishing a dedicated Gaelic television channel' (Gaelic Broadcasting Task Force 2000: 2). The Milne report recommended the creation of a stand-alone Gaelic Broadcasting Authority on the model of S4C, which would 'have overall responsibility for the scheduling and the broadcast' of Gaelic programmes. The Gaelic service would be made available 'free to air' on all digital platforms but with digital satellite prioritised in the first instance as it offered the most extensive coverage. The authority would be funded by a statutory formula designed to yield £44 million per year, adjusted annually for inflation (Gaelic Broadcasting Task Force 2000: 15–18, 22). This represented a quadrupling of the existing budget but was still considerably less than half that of S4C. Milne estimated that this budget would suffice to produce about three hours of original peak-time programming per day and increase employment in Gaelic broadcasting from about 316 full-time equivalent positions to about 802 (Gaelic Broadcasting Task Force 2000: 28).

The Milne recommendations received virtually universal support within the Gaelic community, but the response from government in both London and Edinburgh was much more negative. Both governments accepted that the current provision was unsustainable and that improvement was required, but both expressed dissatisfaction with Milne's proposals. In the formal DCMS reply to Milne, broadcasting minister Kim Howells stated that the 'core recommendations' for the creation of a Gaelic Broadcasting Authority with an annual budget of £44 million were 'not justified or acceptable' (DCMS 2002). Brian Wilson, who pushed the case for an enhanced service as a backbencher, later expressed the view that it had been tactically unwise to specify a figure, and that it would have been safer to concentrate on the nature and extent of the service that was being proposed (Wilson 2011).

From the outset, Milne's proposal for a substantially increased budget for Gaelic television was criticised by civil servants. The scale of the additional funding suggested was described as 'hard to justify' and it was argued that 'the Treasury is unlikely to accept an economic argument to support these proposals given the low numbers of Gaelic speakers' (Scotland Office 2001). An underlying difficulty was that civil servants in the Department for Culture, Media and Sport (DCMS) at Whitehall were unhappy that the department had to bear the expense of the budget for S4C (Wilson 2005; Laughton 2004: 9). Adding further expenditure for a second minority language was a very unwelcome proposition. Eventually, in 2010 the government was able to push most of the cost of S4C onto the BBC (which had previously had no responsibility for funding or operating the service) as part of its new licence fee agreement (Brown 2015).

A significant obstacle to the development of an acceptable new model for Gaelic television involved the structure of devolution and the funding arrangements for Gaelic broadcasting. Broadcasting was a reserved matter under the *Scotland Act 1998* and thus the principal authority responsible for policy decision-making was the DCMS. However, funding of the Gaelic Television Fund had passed from the Scottish Office, a Whitehall department, to the new Scottish Executive in Edinburgh, as part of the overall block grant provided by the UK Treasury.[14] DCMS took the position that any additional funding for Gaelic television should come from Holyrood rather than Westminster, even though the original funding in 1992 had been provided as a new tranche from the Treasury. Gaelic broadcasting thus became 'a devolution orphan', as John Angus Mackay expressed it (SE 2004f). Progress stalled for several years for a combination of reasons. These were technological as well as political and financial in nature: there were significant technical and regulatory complexities involved in the transition to the multi-platform, digital system that was developing rapidly during this period (Ofcom 2004).

The government's specific commitment under the European Charter to 'encourage and/or facilitate the creation' of a dedicated Gaelic channel played a small but useful role in these deliberations. Both Gaelic campaigners and government officials repeatedly drew attention to this obligation (e.g. Celtic Film and Television Festival 2004; Jowell 2004), which helped focus minds even if it was a relatively minor factor in the overall decision-making process.

As Westminster was preparing new broadcasting legislation in 2002 (enacted as the *Communications Act 2003*), the CCG and others endeavoured to bring the issue of a dedicated Gaelic channel onto the legislative agenda. Milne had recommended the creation of a new Gaelic Broadcasting Authority, but this proposal was not accepted; instead the Act reconstituted the CCG as Seirbheis nam Meadhanan Gàidhlig/ the Gaelic Media Service (GMS) and gave it 'additional powers to make programmes and co-ordinate the provision of a Gaelic media service' (CCG 2003).

After a protracted stalemate, the DCMS eventually accepted in 2004 that it had responsibility for developing the new Gaelic service but remained unwilling to commit significant new funding to pay for it (*Herald* 2004). Instead, the DCMS looked to the BBC to play a more significant role in funding and running the service. The BBC and the GMS set up a working group and, after lengthy planning and negotiations, in 2006 an agreement was reached between the GMS and the BBC to establish a new digital service, which was to be named BBC ALBA (Working Group 2006). The two organisations developed BBC ALBA as a joint partnership venture, an unprecedented arrangement for the BBC, which had previously maintained sole control over its various services, and signed a formal collaboration agreement in July 2007.

The funding arrangements for BBC ALBA were complex. The BBC increased its spend by £2.5 million annually (to £4.6 million) and the Scottish Executive by £3 million annually (from £8.5 million to £11.5 million), while DCMS provided only a token one-off allocation of £250,000. The Scottish Media Group (which now owned both Grampian and Scottish) also agreed to pay £1.2 million over three years in order to buy itself out of its obligation to broadcast Gaelic programmes. This meant a planned budget of £16.8 million a year, not much more than a third of what Milne had suggested was necessary (Working Group 2006: 7–8). It was intended that the channel would be on air for up to seven hours per day, concentrated in late afternoons and evenings, seven days a week, with 1.5 hours of new programming per day (increasing to three hours per day by 2013). The rest of the output was to consist of repeat programming, archival material, and daily news and weather supplied by the BBC (Dunbar 2010: 411). After clearing important regulatory hurdles, the service was launched in 2008, as discussed in the next chapter.

THE EXTENSION OF BILINGUAL ROAD SIGNS

Following early steps in Skye and the more important example of the Western Isles (see pp. 158 and 182 above), Gaelic campaigners continued to push for the wider roll-out of bilingual road signage, but changes were slow to materialise. From the late 1970s onwards, bilingual signage was erected on roads controlled by the local authority in various parts of the Highland Council[15] area, including Skye, Ardnamurchan, Moidart, Morvern and Assynt. Under the *Road Traffic Regulation Act 1967* (and then the successor statute of 1984) local authorities were required to obtain consent from the Scottish Office to install non-standard[16] signage of this kind, but this was granted without undue difficulty (Highland Regional Council 1984; *WHFP* 1984c). Matters became more complicated when authorisation was sought to erect signage on trunk (main) roads; civil servants were highly reluctant to grant such authorisation. In 1999 Transport Minister Sarah Boyack controversially refused Highland Council's request to erect signs on the A87 in Skye and a stretch of the A830 near Mallaig, citing safety concerns, but it emerged that her Westminster predecessor Calum Macdonald had actually overruled the civil servants earlier that year, before devolution, and ordered that permission be granted (*P&J* 1999). In 2001 Boyack reversed course and authorised the erection of bilingual signs on these two roads. In 2003 Boyack's successor Lewis Macdonald announced that bilingual signs would be erected on eight more trunk roads in the Highland and Argyll & Bute council areas, including the A82, the most important arterial road in the West Highlands (SE 2003). The underlying policy articulated by the Executive was that bilingual signs would be installed on trunk roads passing through a Gaelic-speaking community or that led directly to a ferry port serving a Gaelic community in the islands (SE 2004b). The A9, the main road from Central Scotland to Inverness, did not fulfil these criteria and was not included in this signage programme, to the disappointment of long-standing Highland councillor Dr Michael Foxley, who attributed the refusal to 'institutional racism' within the civil service (*WHFP* 2003; see also *Scotsman* 2002a).

Bilingual signage also began to appear on the rail network at this time. Beginning in 1996, bilingual signage giving the names of stations in both Gaelic and English was installed on the two Highland rail lines (from Glasgow to Oban and Mallaig and from Perth to Kyle of Lochalsh and Thurso).[17] The stations affected included Glasgow Queen Street station, the third busiest in Scotland. This programme sparked less controversy than the road signs, although this was to change when bilingual station signs were extended to all of Scotland, as discussed in the next chapter (pp. 324–5).

After bilingual signage was installed at the Scottish Parliament, bilingual signs were erected at the Edinburgh and London offices of the Scotland Office[18] (*Sunday Herald* 1999). Beginning in the mid-1990s bilingual signage also became increasingly common in private businesses, including supermarkets, snow sports centres centres, hotels and restaurants (CnaG 2010), often facilitated by grants from CnaG or HIE (Reference Economic Consultants 2011). This usage of Gaelic on such signage was usually confined to Highland areas but occasionally extended to parts of the urban Lowlands (*P&J* 2003). All of these initiatives contributed to 'raising the profile' of Gaelic, to use the conventional idiom of the time.

TERMINOLOGY AND CORPUS DEVELOPMENT

As Gaelic became more institutionalised, the need grew for specialist Gaelic terminology, so that the language could be used effectively in new situations and deal appropriately with new topics. Initiatives in this area have been relatively limited, however: status planning has significantly outpaced corpus development, so that Gaelic is sometimes insufficiently polished to be used effectively for the formal settings into which it has recently expanded (McLeod 2004b).

Limited work on terminology development was carried out at different points in the twentieth century, including work on terms for committees and meetings by An Comunn in the 1920s and 1930s, secretarial training courses and various initiatives on the part of the BBC, CnE, Fearann Eilean Iarmain and Sabhal Mòr Ostaig (Thomson 1985: 271). Sabhal Mòr initiated work on a Gaelic terminology database in the late 1980s and produced a basic collocation of terms in 1993 (Stòr-Dàta Briathrachais 1993), but no further outputs followed. Although the creation of new terminology requires painstaking linguistic work, an equally difficult challenge is that of circulation and acceptance by the user community (Ní Ghearáin 2007). The BBC, especially the news service of Radio nan Gàidheal, has played an important role in this field (Lamb 1999), but complaints are sometimes heard that the use of new terms relating to current affairs renders programmes inaccessible or even unintelligible to some listeners.

One important corpus planning initiative was *Faclair na Pàrlamaid*, a glossary of Gaelic terms for use in connection with the business of the Scottish Parliament (SE 2001). This was then followed by similar dictionaries for local government and public administration (European Language Initiative 2011, 2012). Due to the under-resourcing of these projects, however, the linguistic work underpinning these dictionaries is not always entirely satisfactory (McLeod 2001).

Initiatives in this area have been sporadic, however; there is no established terminology unit or specialist organisation that develops new terminology on an ongoing basis, even though the need for such terminology is constant and ongoing. The position contrasts unfavourably with Ireland and Wales, where dedicated terminology units have been established for decades (Nic Phaidín 2008; Hawke 2018), contributing significantly to the ongoing modernisation of Irish and Welsh and facilitating their use in a wide range of contemporary contexts.

CONCLUSION

Legislative devolution in 1998 ushered in a new era for Scotland and brought important new opportunities in relation to Gaelic. Although progress was slower than anticipated and various compromises had to be agreed, the enactment of the Gaelic Language Act, the opening of the first dedicated Gaelic school and the agreement to establish BBC ALBA between 1997 and 2005 were widely and rightly perceived as major steps forward for Gaelic development. Gaelic advocates were hopeful that these measures would mean significant advances for the language in the 'new Scotland' that followed devolution. The ambitious phrase 'secure status' was a resonant if highly ambitious one. The following years have brought significant new challenges in terms of implementation and advancement, as discussed in the next chapter.

8

Institutionalisation, 2006–20

THE IMPLEMENTATION OF THE Gaelic Language Act from 2006 onwards ushered in an important new stage in Gaelic policy in Scotland. Language planning for Gaelic has become increasingly institutionalised and diversified, with many more agencies and bodies now developing policies and undertaking initiatives in relation to the language, principally as a result of the statutory language plan process. This has brought a palpable increase in the prominence of Gaelic in Scottish public life. Education has remained the most important field of Gaelic activity, but recent developments in broadcasting and media have also been very significant. The digital television service BBC ALBA has transformed the Gaelic media landscape, and the fundamental technological changes involving electronic communication in recent years have been as important in the Gaelic context as elsewhere.

More generally, Scotland has undergone dramatic political change during this period. Since 2007 the Scottish National Party has become electorally dominant and the issue of Scottish independence has moved to centre stage. A second referendum on independence is now proposed, after the failed referendum of 2014. While Gaelic has played a minimal role in these wider shifts, the polarised political environment they have engendered may have important implications for the language and the fragile political consensus in support of its promotion.

Yet the evident decline of Gaelic as a community language in its traditional 'heartlands' remained a key concern that cast a shadow over progress achieved through growth and development elsewhere. A major study of language use in Shawbost in the Isle of Lewis (Mac an Tàilleir, Rothach and Armstrong 2010) produced sobering results, even if these essentially only confirmed the patterns observed in previous research (e.g. NicAoidh 2006) and reported in myriad anecdotal accounts.

Importantly, Shawbost was chosen for the research as it was 'one of the strongest "Gaelic-dominant" communities in Scotland'. Despite this, the report concluded that 'the language is falling apart and may be dead as a community language in Shawbost within one or perhaps two generations' (Mac an Tàilleir, Rothach and Armstrong 2010: 5, 4). These warnings were then reiterated in a wider study of language use in the Western Isles published in 2020 (Ó Giollagáin et al. 2020).

THE SNP ADMINISTRATION AND GAELIC POLICY

Although the SNP's coming to power in 2007 was a landmark in Scottish political history, in relation to Gaelic there has been ongoing broad continuity in policy from the late 1980s onwards. The SNP government has not introduced any major new policy initiatives concerning Gaelic. Instead, the previous pattern of path-dependent, incremental development of existing policies, originating in the 1980s, has continued, with successive improvements to existing programmes and structures building upon each other. Nevertheless, Gaelic appears to have become more politicised in recent years, particularly in the increasingly polarised political environment that has developed in the context of the independence debate. The nature of the policy cycle was such that several important Gaelic policy measures that were agreed by the previous Labour–Liberal Democrat coalition of 2003–7 only came into effect after the SNP's election victory in 2007, so that many casual observers came to perceive them as SNP initiatives or indeed 'nationalist vanity projects', as some media commentators had it (Grant 2010; Wilson 2017). Although the Gaelic Language Act had been enacted in 2005 and took effect in 2006, the first National Gaelic Language Plan was not published until May 2007, shortly after the SNP came to power, and public authorities' Gaelic language plans only began to appear from that autumn, including the Scottish Government's own language plan in 2010 (SG 2010a, 2017). Similarly, BBC ALBA was launched in 2008, but the plan for the service had been agreed by the previous administration following years of campaigning and negotiation, as discussed in the previous chapter.

An early indication of the SNP administration's lukewarm approach to Gaelic came in connection with the rebranding of the Scottish 'Executive' as the Scottish 'Government' in 2007. Although the Scottish Parliament decided in its first Gaelic Language Plan, published in 2007, to adopt a bilingual corporate identity for all purposes and to use a bilingual logo in all contexts (Scottish Parliamentary Corporate Body 2008: 17), the Scottish Government declined to make its bilingual logo the default. One senior civil servant was 'insistent that the English-only version of the mark be used', as 'Gaelic is not the secondary language of Scotland' (SG 2007). This bilingual logo was thus confined to a relatively limited range of contexts, and even then the Gaelic text was in a font only half the size of the English one (McLeod 2011). Only in 2013 was this practice changed, so that a bilingual logo is now used in all contexts, with Gaelic and English in the same size of lettering (SG 2017a: 23).

More controversially, the government refused to produce a Gaelic version of the ballot paper for the 2014 independence referendum. This decision was in line with existing practice in Scottish elections; in contrast to Wales, where bilingual ballot papers became standard following the *Welsh Language Act 1967*, no bilingual election ballot has ever been issued in Scotland, even in the Western Isles. The decision not to provide a Gaelic version of the referendum ballot was based on testing of the proposed question (in English) carried out by the Electoral Commission, which found that voters who speak Gaelic as a first language 'could understand the question easily and experienced no difficulty in completing the ballot paper' (SP 2013: [6]).[1] This rationale was highly problematic, as the principle that no provision would be made for Gaelic speakers except for those who cannot understand English is out of line not only with the Gaelic Language Act but with the basic principles of Gaelic policy as it had developed since the 1980s.

A petition demanding a bilingual ballot paper was submitted to the Scottish Parliament by Gaelic campaigner John Macleod, president of An Comunn (SP 2013). In the face of government opposition, the Parliament's Public Petitions Committee declined to support the proposal and no member sought to amend the pending Referendum Bill. It was unfortunate that the issue of bilingual ballots had not been raised earlier, in connection with a less decisive vote. Perhaps surprisingly, although Bòrd na Gàidhlig made a written submission in support of the proposal for a bilingual ballot paper (BnG 2013), it has not taken any steps to seek to alter the practice in subsequent elections.

If the decision not to provide a bilingual ballot disappointed Gaelic activists, the government's preparations for the referendum also gave a telling indication of the distinctly lower public status of Scots. The government produced a 670-page White Paper detailing its plans for an independent Scotland (SG 2013b), and summary versions of this very important document were produced in Gaelic and in fifteen other languages – but not in Scots. (The practice of issuing summaries rather than full versions of publications in Gaelic is a common, and obviously problematic, one.)

Language issues played only a minimal role in the vigorous and wide-ranging public debate ahead of the 2014 referendum, and very little discussion was carried out through the medium of Gaelic. The White Paper asserted that 'in an independent Scotland, Gaelic will have a central place in public life', but the document actually suggested policy continuity in relation to Gaelic rather than any kind of transformative change (SG 2013b: 314, 449, 532, 564). The SNP's caution might well have reflected an assessment of popular opinion: it is by no means the case that supporters of Scottish independence necessarily support the revitalisation of Gaelic. The Scottish Social Attitudes Survey of 2012 (discussed in more detail below) found that although those who supported Scottish independence were slightly more likely to express favourable views in relation to Gaelic, only 53 per cent of respondents who expressed support for independence stated that they wished to see an increase in the number of Gaelic speakers in Scotland over the next fifty years (Paterson et al. 2014: 443).

Although there have been few new Gaelic policy initiatives from the SNP administration, the government has been relatively generous in relation to financial matters, even if funding for BnG for 2011–12 and beyond was cut in line with the general reductions applied to all public bodies in the era of 'austerity' in the UK. Two particularly important decisions were the continuation of the Specific Grants for Gaelic Education scheme, notwithstanding the general abolition in 2007 of 'ring-fenced' central government grants to local authorities, and the creation of a Gaelic Schools Capital Fund in 2007 (BnG 2017: 33). This dedicated fund provided substantial grants (up to £1.8 million) for the development or expansion of Gaelic schools in Glasgow, Inverness and Edinburgh (City of Edinburgh Council 2011; SG 2018b). The scheme has since been renamed the Gaelic Capital Fund and given a wider scope, so as to allow for the funding of other kinds of Gaelic projects, such as the Cnoc Soilleir community hub in South Uist, which received £1 million in 2017 (SG 2017c). Also important was the development of the Gaelic Language Act Implementation Fund (GLAIF) scheme in relation to Gaelic language plans, discussed below (p. 293).

Even if there was little in the way of policy innovation, ministers in the SNP government sometimes produced strongly pro-Gaelic rhetoric. In 2007 then First Minister Alex Salmond declared that 'we must recognise that a vibrant Gaelic language and culture are central to what it means to be Scottish in the modern world' and that 'my Government's ambition is to see Gaelic emerge again as a truly national language' (Salmond 2007). Salmond is not a Gaelic speaker, and he had no reputation as a champion of the language. Two years later, Michael Russell (Education Secretary 2009–14) condemned criticism of spending on Gaelic as 'shockingly perverse' and 'as daft as it is offensive', arguing that such opposition 'is not a view, but a prejudice' (Russell 2009). On the other hand, Nicola Sturgeon, who succeeded Salmond as First Minister in 2014, was perceived in Gaelic circles as being less supportive of the language, and there has been little evidence of significant engagement with Gaelic matters on her part.

The SNP government has introduced some limited policy measures in relation to Scots, mostly in the field of education, but these have been much less comprehensive than some Scots activists had anticipated. Following the model used for Gaelic, a Ministerial Advisory Group on the Scots Language was established to make policy recommendations for language development. The Group's report, published in 2010, set out a range of proposals in relation to education, broadcasting, literature and the arts, international contacts, public awareness and dialects (Ministerial Advisory Group on the Scots Language 2010). Significantly, there was no suggestion of a Scots Language Act or a national language agency. The modesty of these proposals showed the influence of 'experienced civil servants' in the Group's membership and the view that 'initiatives must be shaped and pursued in the context of a given political and economic ambience in which even highly desirable moves may not be practically possible' (Ministerial Advisory Group on the Scots Language 2010: 4). This report was followed by the publication of a very brief Scots language policy in 2015 (SG/Education Scotland 2015).

There has also been a small amount of policy activity in relation to Scots from other bodies. This included the appointment of Scots Language Co-ordinators by the national education directorate Education Scotland, the development of a new qualification in Scots language by the Scottish Qualifications Authority and the publication of Scots language policies by Creative Scotland, the national arts agency, and Aberdeenshire Council (Eunson 2017; SQA n.d.; Creative Scotland 2015; Aberdeenshire Council 2017).[2] More significantly, the government agreed to the inclusion of a question concerning Scots in the 2011 census, a long-standing demand of Scots language activists. The census showed that 1.5 million people claimed to be able to speak Scots, 30 per cent of the population, but there was significant doubt about the reliability of the responses, given the widespread lack of clarity among the Scottish public concerning the distinction between Scots and English (Sebba 2019).

More substantial policy initiatives have been taken in relation to

British Sign Language (BSL). Following a long campaign by the signing community and key organisations, the Scottish Parliament adopted the *British Sign Language (Scotland) Act 2015*. This legislation was introduced by a backbench member but the government agreed to support the bill and, like the Gaelic Act of 2005, it was passed unanimously. The BSL Act is loosely based on the Gaelic Language Act and requires the Scottish Government to produce a National BSL Plan and certain named public bodies to produce BSL plans (De Muelder 2016). In contrast to the Gaelic Language Act, only the specific public authorities listed in the legislation are covered and no executive agency was created with the duty of implementing the Act, and the enforcement mechanism is minimal. The first National Plan was published in 2017 (SG 2017b) and numerous plans from other bodies have followed. Significantly, there has been no public controversy concerning the BSL plan process, much in contrast to the situation in relation to Gaelic language plans, as discussed below (p. 289).

PUBLIC OPINION ON GAELIC

Gaelic issues continue to have little political prominence in Scotland and only come to the attention of the wider population relatively rarely. Several surveys of public opinion conducted between 2003 and 2012 showed a broadly similar pattern of widespread but relatively shallow support for Gaelic, with negative views confined to a relatively small minority (Market Research UK 2003; West and Graham 2011; O'Hanlon et al. 2013; see also Chhim and Bélanger 2017).[3] These survey results were considerably more positive than those from the only previous national survey, conducted in 1981 (MacKinnon 1981; MacKinnon 2013). Gaelic organisations and supporters have been heartened by these results, although it is by no means clear that generally positive language attitudes necessarily signal commitment to strong and potentially expensive language support programmes. Comparable surveys in Ireland (e.g. Conradh na Gaeilge 2019) show considerably higher levels of support for Irish than the Scottish studies do for Gaelic, but this has not been transformed into backing for robust policies to promote the language.

The most detailed and authoritative of these studies, carried out as part of the Scottish Social Attitudes Survey in 2012, showed that 76 per cent of the Scottish population felt that Gaelic was 'very important' or 'fairly important' to Scottish cultural heritage, while only 21 per cent believed it was 'not very important' or 'not important at all' (Paterson et al. 2014: 438; see also MacKinnon 1981; West and Graham 2011). In contrast, only 14 per cent felt Gaelic was 'very important' or 'fairly important' to 'being truly Scottish', while 84 per cent said it was 'not very important' or 'not at all important' (Paterson et al. 2014: 438). Perceptions of territoriality were an important feature of these survey results; for example, 32 per cent of respondents felt that the use of Gaelic should be encouraged across Scotland, 55 per cent felt it should be encouraged 'where it is already spoken', and 11 per cent felt it 'should not be encouraged at all' (Paterson et al. 2014: 439). As Gaelic has become more visible in Lowland areas, especially as a result of signage at railway stations, as discussed below (pp. 324–5), this distinction in public opinion may become more significant. The survey also asked respondents about the level of government spending in support of Gaelic (then £24 million per year, or £4.80 per person in Scotland). 45 per cent thought this amount was about right, 33 per cent thought it was too much and 16 per cent thought it was too little; the remainder said they did not know (O'Hanlon et al. 2013: [8]). Bearing in mind that a certain proportion of the population would probably find spending on almost any kind of government programme excessive, these results were encouraging to Gaelic organisations and activists.

All these surveys were carried out before the 2014 independence referendum, and there is some evidence to suggest that negative attitudes towards Gaelic have spread and hardened among some voters who oppose independence and have come to associate Gaelic with the SNP, for the reasons discussed above. Much of this evidence comes from the traditional forum of letters to newspaper editors and the new platform provided by social media such as Twitter, and it may be risky to infer wider public attitudes from commentary of this kind. Nevertheless, some politicians have expressed concern about the increased polarisation of opinion on Gaelic along the axis of views on the independence question (*Herald* 2018a).

If this association between Gaelic and the SNP in some minds is relatively new, there are a number of more deeply rooted tropes in negative media commentary concerning Gaelic (see Chalmers, Calvert and Irwin 2011; MacKinnon 2012). Public signage or other noticeable provision for Gaelic is often objected to as 'shoving the language down our throats'. Sometimes the language itself is derided, sometimes Gaelic speakers. Gaelic is an 'obscure prehistoric dialect' that 'sounds more like someone chewing a cushion than actual human speech', while Gaelic speakers are 'bracken-munchers', 'sodden in whisky' (Brown 1998, 2000; Colgan 2003). Gaelic speakers are 'overindulged zealots' (Brown

2000), a pampered minority that receive special privileges at unreasonable cost to the taxpayer and that should be required to pay for Gaelic education, Gaelic media or other Gaelic services themselves (Donnelly 2004; Bowditch 2009). Although the frequency with which such hostile views are aired appears out of line with the results of opinion surveys, they may have an influence on policy-makers who come to see support for Gaelic as controversial or risky, and they often have a demoralising effect on Gaelic speakers, who can come to feel that their language and culture are under attack (Hebrides Writer 2018).

Much of this negative media coverage, especially in tabloid newspapers, has related to statutory Gaelic language plans. The most notorious example involved the claim that the Scottish Government planned to spend £26 million on bilingual road signs (*Daily Record* 2010), which became and remains a widely circulated trope on social media. The actual figure was a small fraction of the total road sign budget of £2 million (Wings over Scotland 2010), and in fact no large-scale bilingualisation programme was planned, as discussed below (pp. 323–4); £26 million actually was the total annual Gaelic budget, of which the largest share funded BBC ALBA.

BÒRD NA GÀIDHLIG: CHALLENGES AND CONTROVERSIES

Throughout its existence, Bòrd na Gàidhlig has struggled to establish strategic direction and marshal support from the Gaelic community, and several of its policy and funding decisions have been deeply controversial. Over time it has become a lightning rod for criticism concerning the full range of Gaelic issues, much like An Comunn in previous decades. In 2019 concerns about the performance of the Bòrd became more widely publicised with the publication of a critical consultants' report on the organisation's governance and management (Deloitte 2019). Overall the Bòrd has been a disappointment to many Gaelic advocates, and the future of the organisation is somewhat unclear.

One significant challenge has been unstable leadership: the Bòrd went through five chief executives and six chairs in the first thirteen years of its existence as a statutory body. Allan Campbell, formerly chief executive of CnaG, became the Bòrd's first chief executive in 2006 but resigned on health grounds in 2007,[4] to be replaced (after a gap of several months) by Kenneth Murray, who had no previous experience in the Gaelic sector and who himself resigned after less than a year (*Herald* 2008). An interim management team was in charge from August 2008 to September 2010, when John Angus Mackay, former chief executive of the Gaelic Broadcasting

Committee, was appointed as chief executive. Following Mackay's retirement in 2015, Iain Campbell took over the role but resigned after only two months; no public explanation was given but internal difficulties relating to the mishandling of staff compensation appears to have been the trigger. Following another period of interim management, in July 2016 Shona MacLennan was appointed as chief executive.

The Bòrd has arguably been underpowered in terms of staff, with a complement of approximately eighteen full-time equivalent, while the Welsh Language Board had eighty-four members of staff at its peak (Williams and Walsh 2017: 123 fn, 5). In particular, this understaffing has impeded the implementation of the language plan process, so that development of new plans has been relatively slow and their monitoring somewhat ineffective, as discussed below. The Bòrd has not recruited staff with specialist knowledge of language planning, and staff training has been limited.

In 2019 a report by the consulting firm Deloitte found significant failings in the Bòrd's management and governance. According to the report, Bòrd staff were 'united in feeling that the organisation is directionless, simply reacting and drifting from one crisis to the next' (Deloitte 2019: 8). The report found that the senior management team did 'not have the skillset or resources required to carry out their roles effectively' and that there was 'a clear lack of openness and transparency of decision-making' and 'a culture of secrecy in the organisation' (Deloitte 2019: 15, 30). The Auditor General ordered the Bòrd to 'deliver and demonstrate significant improvements' in response to the concerns raised (Auditor General for Scotland 2019).

It is significant that the Welsh Language Board, the principal model for BnG, was abolished in 2012 (pursuant to the *Welsh Language (Wales) Measure 2011*), with some of its functions transferred to the Welsh Assembly Government and others to the new Welsh Language Commissioner (Williams 2014). The creation of language commissioners – executive officers with powers to enforce compliance with language laws – has become an increasingly common model in minority language provision in recent years, with Ireland also having adopted this structure in 2003 (Amon and James 2019). Given the Bòrd's difficulties, a restructuring of this kind might prove suitable for Gaelic in Scotland, but to date there have been no detailed proposals to this effect (*Herald* 2017b). Similarly, although the Gaelic Act was based on the *Welsh Language Act 1993*, Wales has also dispensed with the ad hoc language plan model required by that act and moved to a system of sectoral standards in relation to Welsh language service provision. These standards set out benchmarks for all organisations of a similar nature (such as local authorities or health boards and trusts) and 'provide a much greater level of consistency and clarity in relation to the obligations of regulated bodies [...] than was the case with Welsh language schemes' (Dunbar 2019b: 13). In effect, then, Gaelic development continues to use a model that was deemed unworkable for Welsh a decade ago.

The Bòrd's effectiveness was also limited through the impact of budget reductions. A strategic planning report commissioned for the Bòrd in 2009 stated the aspiration of Gaelic organisations for a 5 per cent funding increase in 2011–12 and increases of 10 per cent in the two following years (Gillies and Thomson 2009: 22). Instead funding was cut, with obvious ramifications for organisational capacity.

Although this system is not commanded by the Gaelic Act, one of the Bòrd's most important functions in practical terms has been to serve as a conduit for government funding of Gaelic organisations. As might be expected of a body with responsibility for funding allocations, the Bòrd soon drew fire from various different sources. In particular, decisions to withdraw funding from established organisations and schemes, or to support unsuccessful new initiatives, attracted criticism. These included the removal of support for the monthly newspaper *An Gàidheal Ùr*, the pre-school education body Taic (formerly CNSA) and the learners' organisation Clì Gàidhlig on the one hand and difficulties relating to the funding of Gaelic classes for adults using the Ùlpan model and the unsuccessful social networking site mygaelic.com on the other.

An Gàidheal Ùr had been established in 1998 by An Comunn but never developed a sustainable financial model, surviving instead on interstitial tranches of funding, latterly from the Bòrd. Although the content of the paper left much to be desired, its loss in 2009 was a serious blow to print media in Gaelic, essentially reducing coverage (and fora for debate) to a handful of weekly columns in national and local newspapers or on websites such as Dàna (www.dana.org). There has been an increase in online written news content in recent years, principally on the BBC Naidheachdan website, but there have been no moves to develop a full online news service along the lines of tuairisc.ie in Ireland or Golwg360 in Wales, despite the fact that confining publication to the online format eliminates traditional production and distribution costs.

The decision to withdraw funding from Taic/CNSA sparked considerable controversy, principally because of the long-standing reputation of the organisation and its director, Finlay MacLeod, who was widely credited with playing a central role in the development of Gaelic education in the early 1980s (Pedersen 2019: 207–8). As discussed in earlier chapters,

CNSA had begun its work by establishing pre-school playgroups which in turn generated demand for Gaelic-medium primary education. Its role then began to change as new funding structures for nursery education came into effect, so that local authorities came to take responsibility for provision for children aged 3–5. MacLeod began to move the focus of the organisation away from early years provision and to express concerns about the effectiveness of the existing mechanisms for Gaelic language transmission. Matters came to a head when Taic failed to satisfy the Bòrd that its work programme was sufficiently aligned with the requirements of the Bòrd's 2009 development strategy *Ginealach Ùr na Gàidhlig* (discussed below) (BnG 2010). Following the withdrawal of funding for Taic, the Bòrd took over provision for children aged 0–3 itself.

The Bòrd's decision to grant funding of approximately £520,000 for a dedicated Gaelic social networking site, mygaelic.com (BnG 2011), also proved controversial. This site was not a grass-roots initiative from the Gaelic community but the brainchild of a Glasgow-based creative design and advertising company. Following its launch in 2009, mygaelic.com was quietly closed down in 2011, having failed to find a viable niche among Gaelic-speaking users. mygaelic required users to establish a separate profile and negotiate a separate platform but most people preferred to use the mainstream sites such as Facebook. Bilingual users tend to find mainstream sites and services more practical, as they are more effective for communication and interaction in their bilingual social networks (cf. Cunliffe, Morris and Prys 2013: 85). mygaelic was then subsumed into the new Gaelic learning site learngaelic.net (whose core function was very different).

The Bòrd's management of provision for adult learners was another controversial issue (Pedersen 2019: 208–9). The Bòrd was keen to develop a broad-based programme for adult learners and decided to concentrate on support for the Ùlpan model developed by the private company Deiseal Ltd. Ùlpan was based on the Israeli *ulpan*, Hebrew immersion courses designed for the linguistic integration of new immigrants, and its Welsh adaptation *wlpan* (Jones 1991). Ùlpan attracted criticism and a Bòrd-commissioned review of the programme found mixed success (M. MacLeod et al. 2015). The Bòrd subsequently withdrew its funding, which had exceeded £1 million in total (M. MacLeod et al. 2015: 42). In 2016 the Bòrd also withdrew funding from Clì Gàidhlig (formerly Comann an Luchd-Ionnsachaidh), forcing the directors of the organisation to wind up the organisation (Hebrides News 2016). The collapse of Clì followed rapidly from the demise of the Gaelic arts agency Pròiseact nan Ealan, which had its core funding from Creative

Scotland (the national arts body) withdrawn, rendering the organisation unviable (MacLean 2019). Although the decision to de-fund Pròiseact nan Ealan did not implicate the Bòrd directly, it contributed to a wider sense of crisis in the Gaelic sector (*WHFP* 2015).

More generally, the Bòrd attracted criticism for its distance from the Gaelic community. The decision to locate the Bòrd's main office in Inverness rather than the Western Isles was controversial. In addition, the annual congress (Còmhdhail) that CnaG had organised between 1995 and 2004 was discontinued. This event had served as an important forum for Gaelic professionals and activists to come together and consider major issues confronting the Gaelic world. Since 2006 the Bòrd has held only three public conferences, in 2008, 2010 and 2016.

The Bòrd has also been criticised for failing to publicise and promote Gaelic more effectively to the wider Scottish public, and to challenge attacks on the language by journalists and politicians more vigorously. At the same time, the Bòrd is also often criticised for its boosterism and over-optimistic 'spin' (e.g. http://iolairelochtreig.blogspot.com/), particularly against the backdrop of the obviously weakening situation of the language in the traditional communities in the islands.

NATIONAL LANGUAGE PLANS AND STRATEGIES

Under section 2 of the Gaelic Language Act, the Bòrd is required to prepare a National Gaelic Language Plan every five years, which 'must include a strategy for promoting, and facilitating the promotion of [...] the use and understanding of the Gaelic language, and [...] Gaelic education and Gaelic culture'. The first National Plan was published in 2007 and ran until 2012, followed by a second plan for 2012–17 and a third for 2018–22 (BnG 2007, 2012, 2018). In addition, in the middle of the life of the first National Plan, the government required the Bòrd to produce another language strategy, *Ginealach Ùr na Gàidhlig* (BnG 2010), which effectively eclipsed the first National Plan for the last two years of its life.

A key question concerning these plans is the extent to which they can truly be considered 'national' or have achieved significant stature and 'buy-in' from a wide range of organisations in different sectors. Under section 3(5)(a) of the Act, public authorities implementing Gaelic language plans are required to 'have regard' to the National Plan, but it is likely that many other organisations in Scotland, especially those outside the public sector, are minimally aware of its existence. Crucially, as explained earlier, the National Plan is not legally enforceable. It is also notable that, in contrast to other jurisdictions which have developed national language strategies, including Wales, Ireland, the Basque Country and Catalonia, the National Plan is not produced and delivered by the government itself,[5] but by a small executive agency with a relatively low public profile (Williams 2013b).

The 2007–12 National Plan was grounded in established language planning theory (Kaplan and Baldauf 1997) and was thus 'guided by four well-established and interrelated language planning principles': language acquisition, language usage, language status and language corpus (BnG 2007: 12). The plan set out an overarching 'vision [...] to create a sustainable future for Gaelic in Scotland in which the language will be the preferred language of an increasing number of people in Scotland, the mother tongue of an increasing number of speakers, supported by a dynamic culture in a diverse language community' (BnG 2007: 12). This was further explained as 'a vision which recognises Gaelic as a national asset and responsibility of Scotland[,] does not reduce the status of, or support for, other languages in Scotland [and] uses Gaelic to increase awareness and appreciation of Scotland's diverse linguistic heritage and society' (BnG 2007: 12). This phrasing was evidently intended to address political concerns about the status of Gaelic in Scotland as a whole, including potential concerns about the role of Scots and other more recently established community languages such as Punjabi and Cantonese. The idiom was very much in tune with the multicultural rhetoric that had become conventional in Scotland (McLeod 2019).

The plan then specified fifteen desired outcomes in relation to the four main areas of activity (acquisition, usage, status and corpus). For acquisition, the designated outcomes were 'an increase in the use and transmission of Gaelic in the home', 'an increase in the percentage of children acquiring Gaelic in the home', 'an increase in the uptake and availability of Gaelic-medium education' and 'an increase in adult Gaelic learners progressing to fluency' (BnG 2007: 12). The remaining eleven outcomes were all based on the same 'an increase . . .' formula, which was inherently problematic as even the most modest of increases (such as a handful more pupils enrolled in GME) would technically mean that the goal had been achieved.

However, the plan also set out a range of more specific targets. The structure here was unusual. The targets were grouped chronologically according to four milestones: 'the immediate future', 2021, 2031 and 2041. The specified years correspond to decennial censuses. No numerical targets were given for 'the immediate future' or for the 2011 census, as it was felt that this would come too soon for policy measures implemented from 2007 onwards to take effect. For 2021 onwards, ambitious numerical targets were set in relation to speaker numbers and enrolments in Gaelic education. The targets for 2021 included 4,000 entrants enrolled in first-year Gaelic-medium primary education (up from 313 in 2006–7); 65,000 Gaelic speakers recorded in Scotland (up from 58,652 in 2001); and 40,000 Gaelic speakers recorded in Scotland who could read and write the language (up from 31,218 in 2001). For 2031 the corresponding numbers were 10,000, 75,000 and 65,000, and for 2041 they were 15,000, 100,000 and 100,000 (BnG 2007: 15). These numerical targets proved to be the most controversial feature of the plan as they were widely perceived as being unrealistic. The targets in relation to GME were seen as particularly unattainable. Finally, the plan set out in detail fourteen 'priority areas' 'such as the home, education and adult learning' and a series of key projects (BnG 2007: 17).

In 2010 ministerial responsibility for Gaelic passed to Michael Russell, Cabinet Secretary for Education, who had extensive previous experience of Gaelic cinema and television. Russell was dissatisfied with the National Plan, which he felt was too wide-ranging and diffuse, and instructed the Bòrd to develop a new language strategy which focused more explicitly on increasing the acquisition of Gaelic. This new strategy, published in 2010 as *Ginealach Ùr na Gàidhlig*[6] (BnG 2010), effectively replaced the 2007 National Plan from then on. *Ginealach Ùr na Gàidhlig* identified five key action areas: Support for Parents, Promotion of Acquisition, Adult Learning, 0–5 Education and 5–18 Education (BnG 2010: 3). In effect, three of the 'four well-established and interrelated language planning principles' identified in the National Plan (BnG 2007: 12) – language usage, language status and language corpus – were sidelined in order to emphasise acquisition alone. For each of the five designated action areas, a number of specific actions (eighteen of them in all), outcomes and key performance indicators were specified, along with the date for delivery (BnG 2010: 9–14).

Work on the second National Plan began in 2011 and a draft was duly submitted for public consultation. The final version of the 2012–17 plan bore little relation to the consultation version, however, and appeared to overlook most of the points raised by consultees. It reflected instead the priorities and preferences of civil servants in the Scottish Government. The second plan was strikingly shorter than the first and only two numerical targets were specified: 'an increase in the number of children enrolling in Gaelic-medium education [. . .] doubling the current annual intake to 800 by 2017' and 'an increase in the number of adults acquiring Gaelic from the current total of around 2,000 to 3,000 by 2017' (BnG 2012a: 22, 26). This target of eight hundred entrants to primary 1 by 2017 was just one-fifth of the figure specified for 2021 in the 2007–12 plan, but even so this target was not reached, as discussed below. Unlike the first plan, the 2012 plan was not built on an obvious foundation in language planning theory. In terms of structure, the plan specified eight 'development areas', ten 'key outcomes' and thirty-two 'strategic priorities'. These development areas were Home & Early Years; Schools & Teachers; Post-school Education; Communities; Workplace; Arts & Media; Heritage & Tourism; and Corpus.

An evaluation of the second National Plan commissioned by the Bòrd identified several shortcomings. There was a widespread perception among the stakeholders and community members who were consulted that the plan did not set out its objectives and targets with sufficient clarity. It was also felt that the plan gave insufficient attention to language planning at a local level, especially planning to promote community language use. Finally, there was a perceived need for closer ongoing engagement between the Bòrd and key stakeholders (Jones et al. 2017).

The third National Plan, published in 2018, is shorter than the second plan and includes fewer targets. The general aim of the plan 'is that Gaelic is used more often, by more people and in a wider range of situations'. This entails action involving 'increasing the use of Gaelic', 'increasing the learning of Gaelic' and 'promoting a positive image of Gaelic' (BnG 2018: 15). For each of these heads, several 'priority areas' and 'key new commitments' were identified (BnG 2018: 39–53). The plan states that BnG 'will publish a detailed National Gaelic Language Plan 2018–23 Implementation Strategy within 6 months' of the launch of the plan (BnG 2018: 55), but in fact this strategy has never appeared. Instead, a key high-level mechanism is the 'Faster Rate of Progress' initiative, by which Education Secretary John Swinney, Minister for Gaelic, convenes periodic meetings of key organisations with Gaelic language plans to guide implementation.

Overall there has been a sense that the national plan mechanism has not maximised its potential for the strategic management of Gaelic development. It is striking how the plans have differed in their structure and become less concrete and specific in each iteration. If new language legislation is contemplated, or amendments are made to the 2005 Act, the National Plan mechanism probably warrants re-examination.

PUBLIC AUTHORITIES' LANGUAGE PLANS

Shortly after the Act's official commencement in 2006, the Bòrd began to issue notifications to public authorities to prepare Gaelic language plans. The first plans were agreed in 2007 and by 2020 more than sixty public authorities had published Gaelic language plans. The organisations involved included twenty-nine of Scotland's thirty-two local authorities,[7] a varied range of national bodies (especially in the heritage, cultural and education sectors), six universities and colleges, and two regional health trusts (http://gaeliclanguageplansscotland.org.uk). Plans are generally agreed for a term of five years (in accordance with section 7(2) of the Act), so that several organisations have moved on to prepare their second or third plans (or, in the Bòrd's parlance, 'iterations').

The first wave of Gaelic language plans, most of them directed to organisations in the Gàidhealtachd, attracted relatively little controversy (except in relation to the implementation of Highland Council's plan in Caithness, an area perceived as having relatively little Gaelic tradition (Rosie 2012)). Controversy grew considerably, however, when the Bòrd began issuing notices to high-profile national bodies, especially Police Scotland and the Scottish Ambulance Service (*EEN* 2016; *The Express* 2016), and to local authorities in areas of Scotland perceived as having little connection to Gaelic, such as Aberdeenshire, Dumfries & Galloway and Fife (*P&J* 2015; *Daily Record* 2016; *The Courier* 2015). The convener of Aberdeen's finance committee announced that he would do 'as little as legally possible' to implement the city council's plan, while a councillor in Moray denounced BnG as the 'Gaelic Gestapo' and urged the local authority to defy the legal requirement to produce a plan (*National* 2016; *P&J* 2017). In the end, however, all bodies notified by BnG have ended up agreeing a plan, although many of these involve very modest commitments, as discussed below.

Although resistance to the Gaelic plan process was often based on financial concerns, an important ground for objection was territorial in nature: the belief that Gaelic was 'never spoken' in a particular area and that Gaelic had no relevance there. In some cases it was asserted that provision for Scots would be more appropriate given the local linguistic tradition (e.g. *P&J* 2013; *Courier* 2019), but very few bodies undertook to develop provision for Scots on a voluntary basis, as numerous organisations had done for Gaelic prior to the passage of the 2005 Act. One exception to this pattern was Aberdeenshire Council's Scots Language Guidelines, adopted in 2017 (Aberdeenshire Council 2017).

As noted earlier (p. 258), the pace of plan development is significantly slower than the Executive had anticipated in 2005, and hundreds of public authorities in Scotland have yet to prepare a Gaelic plan. The rate of plan development is also slow compared to the progress of language schemes under the counterpart language acts in Wales and Ireland. By

2013, twenty years after the passage of the *Welsh Language Act 1993*, there were 558 Welsh language schemes in operation (Williams 2014: 246), while in Ireland 112 schemes were agreed in the ten years following the enactment of the *Official Languages Act 2003* (Ó Flatharta 2015: 386). One key factor distinguishing the Scottish case is the need for differentiation among plans to account for the significant variation in 'the extent to which the persons in relation to whom the authority's functions are exercisable use the Gaelic language' (*Gaelic Language (Scotland) Act 2005*, s. 3(5(b)). In contrast, section 5(2) of the *Welsh Language Act 1993* articulated a single overarching norm, that 'the English and Welsh languages should be treated on a basis of equality', and all Welsh language schemes were required to give effect to this principle, no matter what part of Wales the organisation was based in, or even if the body had a UK-wide remit. Welsh language schemes thus tended to vary relatively little and to follow closely the guidelines issued by the Welsh Language Board (Welsh Language Board 1996), and as such could be agreed more quickly than Gaelic plans.

Another important factor in the slow pace of Gaelic plan development was the lack of staff resource at the Bòrd. The Bòrd stated a 'preference [. . .] to issue notices [to prepare plans] commensurate to the support which officers can provide to authorities in the development of their plans (i.e. the Bòrd should not issue a large number of notices and leave public authorities to get on with it alone without any input from the Bòrd)' (BnG 2007c). Ongoing understaffing due to budget constraints necessarily meant that relatively few notices were issued. It also limited the Bòrd's capacity to monitor the implementation of plans in an effective manner (Jones et al. 2017).

Under section 3(5)(e) of the Act, public authorities preparing Gaelic language plans 'must have regard to' the Bòrd's guidance on the development of Gaelic language plans, which was published in 2007 (BnG 2007b). In accordance with the flexibility built into the Act, the guidance suggests that public authorities will have very broad latitude in shaping their institutional plans. The guidance identifies four principal 'corporate functions' which should be represented 'in some way' in every Gaelic language plan: 'identity', 'communications', 'publications' and 'staffing'. Within each of these functional areas, '[a]uthorities should consider developing a policy' for action with respect to a number of specific functions and offer several possibilities 'of what the different elements of that policy might be' (BnG 2007b: 19–27). With regard to the recruitment of Gaelic-speaking staff – a key element in building operational capacity in relation to the language – all that is given in the guidance is the suggestion, as one example of a possible measure in a possible policy, that 'the authority investigates and ascertains which posts, *if any*, could be designated Gaelic-essential and which could be designated Gaelic-desirable' (BnG 2007b: 26 (emphasis added)).

With regard to the 'sliding-scale principle' of varying levels of provision, the guidance 'identifie[s] four broad categories of expected Gaelic-language provision' according to the relative density or number of Gaelic speakers in the areas served by the body in question. The Bòrd's expectations are highest with respect to bodies serving areas where Gaelic speakers form a majority of the population, but even in this context the guidance contains several qualifications and limitations:

> the [Bòrd's] expectation is that the public authority will work towards, within a reasonable timescale and having regard to its particular circumstances, creating the conditions in which Gaelic can be used across all of its services to the public, and in which any employee who wants to use Gaelic in the execution of their duties can do so. (BnG 2007b: 17)

The 'sliding scale' approach of the Act was a mechanism to address a policy problem that had been apparent since the 1970s. Successive proposals to institutionalise Gaelic in public life, such as those prepared by An Comunn in 1975 and Donald John MacLeod in 1976 (ACG 1975; MacLeòid 1976), and then the MacPherson report, had offered various permutations on the idea of a core Gaelic territory, a semi-Gaelic territory and a residual, less Gaelic territory (Taskforce on the Public Funding of Gaelic 2000). Over time, however, the Gaelic-ness of the stronger territories had diminished steadily, while the perceived importance of the residual territory, especially the major cities, had tended to increase.

The key underlying difficulty is that the proportion of Gaelic speakers in the national population is so low, slightly over 1 per cent. In other jurisdictions where legislation has been enacted to promote minority languages in the public sector, the proportion of minority language speakers is significantly higher. More than 20 per cent of the population of Wales can speak Welsh, more than 30 per cent of the Basque Autonomous Community can speak Basque, and even in the Republic of Ireland, where only about 2 per cent of the population actually uses Irish on a daily basis, more than 40 per cent of the population claimed the ability to speak the language in recent censuses (Central Statistics Office n.d.).

Nor do countries where bilingualisation is confined to specific regions provide an obviously useful model. In Finland, municipalities with a density of 8 per cent minority language speakers are classified as bilingual (*Finland Language Act 2003*, ss 5–6); but in Scotland only one of the thirty-two local authorities had a density of 8 per cent Gaelic speakers in 2011 (CnES) and only three exceeded 5 per cent (Argyll & Bute, CnES and Highland). Over 75 per cent of the Scottish population lives in local authority areas where less than 1 per cent of the population speak Gaelic (NRS 2015). In some cases, the absolute number of speakers, not their density in the population, may be more meaningful. In Finland, a municipality may also be designated as bilingual if it has more than three thousand minority language speakers. If that criterion were applied in Scotland, only five local authorities would be covered (Argyll & Bute, CnES, Edinburgh, Glasgow and Highland). In the end, it may simply be that Gaelic development has relied too much on adapting models and approaches from other jurisdictions that may not actually be fully suitable to the Gaelic context, given the demographic thinness of the language.

The Bòrd's guidance explains the role of institutional language plans in terms very similar to those of the 'Catherine Wheel' model developed by Miquel Strubell, who envisioned a virtuous circle by which increasing the offer of minority language services would stimulate increased demand for such services, greater prestige for the language and a greater desire to acquire it (Strubell 1999: 239–42). This understanding was expressed by the Bòrd as follows:

> By providing for the use of Gaelic in the provision of services as well as in internal operations, Gaelic Language Plans will increase the profile and visibility of the language, helping to increase its status. This will help create a sense amongst users of Gaelic that their language is valued by public authorities, and by the wider society in which they live. In order to help deliver Gaelic provision, Gaelic language skills will become useful job skills in an increasingly wide range of employments. This will greatly enhance Gaelic users' perception of the usefulness of their language, and will create real incentives for increasing numbers of Gaelic speakers to pass on their language, for non-Gaelic speakers to learn it, and for all parents, Gaelic-speaking and non-Gaelic-speaking, to have their children educated in Gaelic. (BnG 2007b: 4)

Responding to concerns that the guidance was overly complex and difficult to interpret, in 2014 the Bòrd conducted a consultation on a revised version of the guidance and then prepared a new draft which it sent to the Scottish Government for approval (BnG 2014). This revised version was never published, however, and instead the Bòrd conducted a fresh consultation in 2019 (BnG 2019a). The original

2007 version has thus remained in effect in relation to the preparation of new plans.

An important aspect of the implementation of the Act was the role of dedicated funding made available by the Bòrd to help defray some of the costs of implementing Gaelic language plans. This funding scheme, the Gaelic Language Act Implementation Fund (GLAIF), was allocated £1.4 million in 2007, but the budget has since been cut as a result of the overall reduction of the Bòrd's budget. The implementation act mechanism is not unique to Gaelic but has been adopted in relation to other government programmes as well (Peacock 2012). GLAIF has been useful in political terms, as most of the objections that have been articulated in relation to Gaelic language plans have related to cost. At the same time, the Bòrd endeavoured 'to create a culture amongst all bodies that support Gaelic development that Gaelic services are normal, regular and must be planned for', so that in the long term 'Gaelic language expenditure should be mainstreamed and supported from existing budgets'. GLAIF was based on the recognition that 'in the short-term there is a need to pump-prime some particular areas of Gaelic development' (BnG 2007d).

To date there has been no comprehensive evaluation of the content and implementation of the various plans developed under the Act (Dunbar 2018: 162–3). However, it is clear that most of the plans, especially those of organisations operating in non-Gaelic areas, have not brought significant changes to the policies and practices of the organisations involved; many are essentially cosmetic, or very limited in their range. The offer of services through the medium of Gaelic is often very restricted. More surprisingly and more worrisomely, the plans of some organisations operating in the Gàidhealtachd are distinctly weak, notably that of NHS Eileanan Siar, the health trust serving the Western Isles, whose vague undertakings have been characterised as 'highly problematic' (Dunbar 2018: 166). On the other hand, the fact that important public organisations, including prestigious national bodies such as Historic Environment Scotland and the National Library of Scotland, are seen to be advancing the language represents a significant contribution to the public status of Gaelic.

In particular, Gaelic plans tended to make only weak commitments in relation to the appointment of Gaelic-speaking staff, even though bilingualisation of the workforce has been identified as the most effective means of providing bilingual services (as opposed to using translation and interpretation) (Walsh and McLeod 2008). With the small population of skilled personnel, recruitment of qualified Gaelic-speaking staff is often difficult, however. There are also persistent concerns about the acceptability of designating Gaelic skills as a criterion for employment, even if such concerns are often actually more political than legal in nature (McLeod 2009).

During the first phase of Gaelic institutionalisation from the late 1980s to the early 2000s, a number of public bodies in Scotland appointed dedicated Gaelic officers to manage Gaelic development. It might have been anticipated that this practice would become more widespread with the implementation of the Act as more organisations developed Gaelic plans, but this has only happened to a limited extent. The main phase of plan development and implementation coincided with a period of fiscal austerity in the UK which led to tightened budgets for all public bodies, so that making new staff appointments became difficult. Instead of appointing new Gaelic officers, many organisations assigned responsibility for the development and implementation of their language plans to existing members of staff without particular knowledge of the Gaelic situation and whose general duties and professional backgrounds lay in other areas.

In addition, most Gaelic officer posts have tended to be at a relatively low level within organisations, so that the officers lack clout with senior managers. Such officers often function as 'lone riders', receiving little support as they single-handedly try to promote Gaelic across the organisation. There is also a difficulty with career development for staff in the Gaelic sector, with limited opportunities for promotion and advancement.

At the same time, training for staff involved in plan implementation, including those working in Gaelic development organisations, has been perceived as inadequate. A recent review concluded that it was necessary to make 'an intentional effort to shift from a pattern of development characterised by ad hoc initiatives and anecdotal knowledge to development founded on professional expertise and on knowledge of international best practice in language planning for the survival of linguistic diversity' (M. Macleod et al. 2018: 153).

Many plans place considerable emphasis on the publication of Gaelic versions of different kinds of documents. This approach involves a combination of convenience for the organisation and, perhaps, a misconception on the part of those designing the plans. Only two-thirds of Gaelic speakers can read Gaelic, as noted above (p. 25), and there is almost certainly no one who can read Gaelic more easily than they read English. The overwhelming majority of these official Gaelic publications are drafted in English and translated into Gaelic, typically by an outside contractor. The total proportion of public documents produced in Gaelic remains very small, and thus these promotion efforts amount to much less than a move towards systematic official bilingualism, such as that practised by the federal government in Canada. The current practice of increasing but sporadic translation of public documents into Gaelic can be seen as characteristic of a particular stage in minority language development, in which the authorities take limited steps to accommodate the minority language in the public sphere but stop well short of operating on a genuinely bilingual basis.

Most bodies appear to produce Gaelic versions of documents on a fairly ad hoc basis. However, the Scottish Government's first Gaelic Language Plan articulated a number of criteria to determine whether particular official publications should be made available in Gaelic. Preparation of a Gaelic version would be more likely

> when a topic is of particular interest to those living within the geographical areas where Gaelic is more prevalent; deals with matter relating to the Gaelic language, culture or education; relates to a matter of national importance being distributed to all households via pamphlets or leaflets; [or] is being translated into other community languages. (SG 2010a: 45)

Overall, the Gaelic experience aligns closely with that of Māori, where 'despite an obvious increase in the volume and ease of access to [official documents in Māori since 2000], there is little obvious evidence that these documents themselves have directly or indirectly led to any further generation of Māori language civic discourse' (Stephens 2014: 79–80).

In Ireland, where the requirement to produce Irish versions of various official documents, including 'any document setting out public policy proposals', is embedded in the national language legislation (*Official Languages Act 2003*, s. 10), the cost of producing translations has attracted considerable public controversy (O'Connell and Walsh 2005), but this has been much less the case in Scotland. This is somewhat surprising given that aggressive attacks on spending on Gaelic initiatives are so common in Scotland, as noted above.

It is important to understand that Gaelic versions of public documents are prepared primarily for status rather than functional reasons, that is, because Gaelic speakers cannot read the English versions. Indeed, there is substantial evidence – albeit anecdotal in nature – to suggest that few Gaelic speakers actually make use of the Gaelic versions of public documents. Without question, one reason for this low rate of take-up is the historic marginalisation of Gaelic in public life, which meant that many Gaelic speakers became inured to public services being provided exclusively through English. Another is its marginalisation in the education system, which has meant that Gaelic speakers develop much better literacy skills in English than in Gaelic. The accessibility and quality of the Gaelic translations is also a factor, however. There are no training courses or certification structures for Gaelic translators,[8] some kinds of specialist terminology are underdeveloped, and the range of linguistic resources (dictionaries, thesauruses, databases) remains limited, despite substantial improvements in recent years.

The monitoring and enforcement of Gaelic plans has been somewhat weak. The Bòrd has commissioned several reviews of the implementation of particular bodies' plans but these have not been published, on the grounds that a public 'naming and shaming' of particular organisations would not be productive. The Bòrd's commissioned review of the National Plan in 2017 found that these reviews varied in their 'rigour and overall quality' (Jones et al. 2017: [21]). It also found 'considerable variation in the amount and quality of information provided by organisations with regard to the implementation of their' plans and shortcomings in the Bòrd's data-gathering and evaluation procedures (Jones et al. 2017: [21]). Significantly, although the Act establishes a procedure by which the Bòrd may present a report to the Scottish Government expressing its view that a public authority is 'failing to implement adequately measures in its Gaelic language plan' (s. 6(4)), to date this power has never been used. This reluctance on the part of the Bòrd may be seen as a sign of excessive caution, or as a reflection of its relative weakness and the risks of taking a more confrontational approach with public authorities.

Although some commentators have expressed scepticism about the value of the Act, it is clear that the language plan process has prompted public organisations that previously had little or no engagement with the language to make provision for Gaelic in various different ways and to pay attention to the 'Gaelic agenda', creating opportunities for Gaelic use in new and often prestigious contexts. However, in most cases Gaelic plans have had little impact on the functioning of organisations and have not brought about a significant increase in the actual use of Gaelic. Whether a reform of the language plan mechanism might yield meaningful improvements of this kind represents an important policy challenge.

DEVELOPMENTS IN GAELIC EDUCATION

The main developments in Gaelic education after 2006 involved efforts to increase the overall numbers of pupils enrolled in GME and to open more stand-alone Gaelic schools. Overall, progress has been relatively modest and there have been significant delays and political complications, particularly in relation to the creation of Gaelic schools. Teacher recruitment has remained challenging, and the provision of GME at secondary level continued to be limited. Gaelic learners' education grew considerably in some respects but declined in others; notably, the introduction of the '1+2' policy, by which all Scottish pupils are to study two languages in addition to their mother tongue (Scottish Government Languages Working Group 2012), did not lead to a major transformation in the role of Gaelic in the school system.

The number of primary pupils enrolled in GME rose from 2,068 in 2005–6 to 3,467 in 2018–19, an increase of more than two-thirds (University of Strathclyde 2006: [10]; BnG 2019b: 13). While this growth is considerable, the 2018–19 figure is still only 0.9 per cent of the national total (BnG 2019b: 13), so there remains great potential for a more dramatic expansion. However, the number of primary schools offering GME in 2018–19 was actually the same (fifty-nine) that it had been in 1999–2000 (MacLeod 2007: 14; BnG 2019b: 13). Despite the implementation of the Gaelic Language Act, no additional education authorities introduced GME after 2005; indeed, the most recent new addition was Inverclyde in 1999 (MacLeòid 2007: 14). In 2018–19 eighteen of the thirty-two local authorities did not offer GME in any of their primary or secondary schools, the same figure as in 1998.[9] Only four new Gaelic-medium units opened after 2006, three of them in the Highland Council area (Nairn in 2006, Drumnadrochit in 2011 and Thurso in 2013) and one in Perth & Kinross (Aberfeldy in 2013).[10] Importantly, however, by 2020 there were seven dedicated Gaelic primary schools, three in Glasgow (which opened in 1999, 2016 and 2020 respectively) and one each in Inverness (2006), Edinburgh (2013), Fort William (2015) and Portree (2018).

The mismatch between rising pupil numbers and declining numbers of providers indicates that the average size of Gaelic-medium schools and units was increasing. This growth was heavily concentrated in a few large urban schools, however. Between 2005–6 and 2018–19 the numbers of primary pupils rose from 195 to 699 in Glasgow, 90 to 375 in Edinburgh and 96 to 225 in Inverness (University of Strathclyde 2006: [7]–[9]; BnG 2019b: 13; Bun-sgoil Ghàidhlig Inbhir Nis 2019: 3). Enrolments in the Western Isles rose more slowly during this period, from 495 to 731,[11] an increase of 48 per cent, but this came against a rapidly falling school roll, so that the proportion of pupils enrolled in GME actually went up significantly, as discussed below. In contrast, some areas saw a decline, including Aberdeen (45 down to 40) and East Kilbride (84 down to 69). As noted earlier, BnG's second National

Gaelic Language Plan included the target of doubling the number of children entering primary 1 GME from 400 to 800 between 2012 and 2017. In the event, the increase was only 38 per cent (from 406 in 2011–12 to 559 in 2017–18).

The relatively slow rate of growth reflected different kinds of policy failure. The Gaelic Language Act authorised the Bòrd to promulgate regulations or guidance to establish good practice in relation to Gaelic education, but it took twelve years for the guidance to be published (BnG 2017). Eleven local authorities that were not previously offering GME have published statutory Gaelic plans, but BnG did not require them to begin offering GME as a condition for approving the plan.[12] These authorities made faint commitments to consider the possibility of beginning to offer such provision (e.g. Dundee City Council 2015: 14), but as of yet none have actually done so.

There was less progress at secondary level, continuing the pattern observed since the 1990s. By 2018–19 there were 1,423 secondary pupils in Gaelic medium, 0.5 per cent of the national total (BnG 2019b: 16). This figure cannot be compared directly to that for 2005–6, as a new, more expansive definition was adopted in 2012 by which pupils studying no subject other than Gaelic itself were classified as Gaelic medium. Since 2011–12, enrolments (using this new criterion) have risen by 29 per cent (from 1,104) (BnG 2012b: 1). There is still only one Gaelic-medium secondary school, in Glasgow.

The Glasgow school opened in 2006, seven years after the first stand-alone Gaelic primary school. This was in effect a natural development of the existing primary, as the Woodside campus was large and capable of housing a school catering for the full 3–18 spectrum. The secondary school grew steadily and by 2018–19 it had 343 pupils (BnG 2019b: 16). The status and profile of the school, and of GME in Glasgow more generally, were enhanced by its success in published 'league tables' of exam results. In recent years its pupils gained the best results of any council-run school in Glasgow on the Higher examinations, so that a leading newspaper characterised it as 'an ever-present amongst the top schools in Scotland over the past few years' (*Herald* 2019a). This pattern aligns with the academic success of Irish-medium secondary schools in the Republic of Ireland and Breton-medium schools in Brittany (*Irish Times* 2018; *Le Télégramme* 2013).

The Glasgow secondary school aimed to deliver all subjects through the medium of Gaelic, but this has not yet been achieved. As of 2019 approximately a third of the curriculum was still being delivered through English due to the lack of specialist teachers.

Compared to primary, recruitment of secondary teachers is more challenging as it requires Gaelic speakers with expertise in a wide range of subjects. Some schools have been more successful than others in offering an increasing number of secondary subjects through the medium of Gaelic. At the Nicolson Institute in Stornoway, this has now reached ten subjects. One possible solution, long mooted but slow to materialise, is the use of information and communications technology to allow teachers to deliver classes on a distance learning model. In 2016 the Scottish Government awarded funding of £700,000 to CnES to progress an 'e-sgoil' initiative (*Scotsman* 2016; www.e-sgoil.com).

In relation to secondary education, there is also an issue concerning the nature of parental demand. Success in qualifying examinations is recognised as being important for tertiary educational opportunities and occupational success, and some parents are concerned that studying through the medium of Gaelic might have adverse impacts on their children (O'Hanlon and Paterson 2015: 317–18). Along with issues concerning pupils' linguistic confidence in Gaelic, this factor may also help explain the disappointingly low uptake of the Gaelic-medium examination papers that have been developed for Geography, History, Mathematics and Modern Studies (SQA 2020).

The numbers of Gaelic learners in secondary schools increased by a fifth between 2005–6 and 2018–19, from 2,718 to 3,266, but the number of schools making such provision actually dropped from 36 to 29 (University of Strathclyde 2006; BnG 2019b: 18). Additionally, almost four-fifths of these learners were in the first two years of secondary school (BnG 2019: 18). Developing Gaelic learners' education at secondary level was much less of a policy priority for BnG and other agencies, based on the view that with limited resources (especially teachers) GME was more likely to produce competent, active speakers in the future (Milligan 2010). From 2015 onwards, concern developed about the impact of the restructuring of the secondary curriculum under the national Curriculum for Excellence, which meant that upper-level secondary pupils were permitted to take fewer subjects than had previously been the case (*The Courier* 2018). This had the effect of driving down registrations for Highers in Gaelic (and other languages). In 2019 only 61 pupils took the Learners Higher, a decline of 52 per cent since 2011. On the other hand, the number of pupils sitting the Higher for fluent speakers rose by 16 per cent over the same time period, from 116 in 2011 to 135 in 2019 (SQA 2011, 2019). Following a review, the Scottish Parliament's Education Committee concluded in 2019 'that a sharp drop in young people taking Gaelic qualifications in secondary school will have a direct impact on the number of young people who go on to become teachers of Gaelic and in Gaelic Medium Education' and recommended 'that the Scottish Government considers as a matter of urgency how Gaelic uptake can be supported to prevent this situation becoming worse' (SP 2019: 37).

An important anomaly of Gaelic provision is that there is so little Gaelic teaching to learners in comparison to those studying through the medium of Gaelic. This pattern is very much out of alignment with other minority language jurisdictions. In Wales in 2018–19, approximately 16.4 per cent of school pupils were studying through the medium of Welsh (with a further 9.7 per cent partly in Welsh), while some 6.5 per cent of pupils in the Republic of Ireland were studying through Irish, but all the remaining pupils learned Welsh or Irish as a subject (StatsWales 2019; Gaeloideachas 2019; Department of Education and Skills 2019). Even in New Zealand, where only 2.5 per cent of pupils were studying through Māori in 2018, a further 21.5 per cent were studying Māori as a language (Education Counts 2018).

A different kind of policy failure concerning Gaelic education involved the so-called 1+2 languages policy, a national scheme originating in the European Commission's languages strategy (European Commission 2004) that sought to ensure that all school pupils in Scotland studied two languages in addition to their mother tongue (SG Languages Working Group 2012).[13] This large-scale initiative could have been embraced as a significant opportunity to expand the role of Gaelic in the Scottish educational system, particularly as the class time dedicated to the second foreign language would be very limited. Such a transformation took place in Wales with the implementation of the *Education Reform Act 1988*, which made Welsh a mandatory subject in the national curriculum and brought about a rapid expansion in the provision of Welsh for learners (Williams 2014). Yet with Scotland's 1+2 policy there was never any real push to ensure that all school pupils studied Gaelic, either as an L2 or an L3, or even to ensure that a significant number of schools offered Gaelic (SG Languages Working Group 2012: 13). Instead, the overwhelming majority of local authorities and schools chose to offer other European or Asian languages, and in 2018–19 Gaelic was only being taught to learners in 128 of the 2,011 primary schools in Scotland (as an L2 in 68 of them and an L3 in 60). Of these, the overwhelming majority (103) were in the main Gaelic areas of Argyll & Bute, Highland and the Western Isles (BnG 2019: 20). This low level of provision was all the more remarkable given that an earlier programme, Gaelic Learners in the Primary School, had been in existence since 2000 (Johnstone et al. 2003) and provided a training and curricular foundation that could have been built upon.

THE GROWTH OF STAND-ALONE GAELIC SCHOOLS

The most important success in Gaelic education in the twenty-first century has been the growth of dedicated Gaelic schools. As had been the case from the early 1980s onwards, Glasgow was the trailblazer. The continuing growth of the existing Gaelic primary school in Glasgow, reaching 559 in 2015, meant that a second school became necessary. This new school, Bun-sgoil Ghàidhlig Ghleann Dail, located on the south side of the city, opened in 2016. Controversy broke out, however, when it became clear that even with the opening of the second school the number of places available was insufficient to meet demand. Initially the council proposed a cap on enrolments that would have excluded a significant number of children, including some who had been attending Gaelic nursery for two years, but following an outcry the number of places was increased (BBC Naidheachdan 2018). The council then moved forward with plans to open a third school at Gowanbank in the southwest of the city, but this plan was withdrawn in autumn 2017 when the public consultation showed strong opposition to the siting of the school (Glasgow City Council 2017). Eventually an acceptable plan was agreed and a third school, Cartvale, opened in Govan in 2020, initially as an annexe to the first school but then as a free-standing school. Plans for a fourth Gaelic primary in the Calton in the east end of the city, with a £2 million grant from the Scottish Government, were also announced in 2019 (*Scotsman* 2019). Impressive as this growth is, there were thirty-eight Irish-medium primary schools in Dublin in 2019, whose population is comparable to that of Glasgow (Gaeloideachas 2019).

In contrast to this steady progress in Glasgow, almost everywhere else proposals to develop dedicated Gaelic schools met with significant roadblocks and controversy. This was particularly the case in Edinburgh, where an initial campaign in the late 1990s had been rebuffed, as discussed above (pp. 265–6). A new campaign developed in the mid-2000s as numbers in the existing unit at Tollcross, founded in 1988, rose rapidly (Armstrong 2018). The campaign encountered significant resistance from the council, with education convener Marilyne MacLaren taking the view that it was 'difficult perhaps to see the value of Gaelic in a capital city when we're such a cosmopolitan city' (Murtagh 2011: 43). Opposition also came from the main local newspaper, which expressed the view that the school would be unduly expensive, that 'Mandarin would be more useful than Gaelic' and that the city had 'no historic Gaelic culture' (*EEN* 2010a). Through intensive lobbying of councillors, especially personal visits to councillors' surgeries, the parents' organisation was able to overcome this resistance. Bòrd na Gàidhlig chair Art Cormack played an active role in the campaign, and the Scottish Government was also supportive throughout, and agreed to provide a grant of £1.8 million from the Gaelic Schools Capital Fund. Eventually the council agreed to establish the school at the former Bonnington primary. It opened in 2013 with 213 pupils, under the name Bun-sgoil Taobh na Pàirce, and the roll now exceeds 400 (*Scotsman* 2012; Armstrong 2018: 24–5).

New controversies were to follow, however. A particularly difficult episode arose in spring 2017. Secondary Gaelic provision had been offered at James Gillespie's High School, a highly regarded school for which the nearby Tollcross primary had served as a 'feeder'. The relocation of primary GME to a different part of the city rendered this arrangement less obviously logical, and the council proposed to move provision away from Gillespie's, which was struggling with an expanding school roll. With minimal notice, the council proposed to send half the Gaelic pupils coming up from Bun-sgoil Taobh na Pàirce to a different school, Tynecastle High School. Parents mobilised rapidly, prompting an intervention from the Moderator of the Church of Scotland and, most importantly, an explicit threat from Bòrd na Gàidhlig to seek interdict against the council on the grounds that the statutory consultation required under the *Schools (Consultation) (Scotland) Act 2010* had not been carried out.[14] The council rescinded its proposal and agreed to establish a working group to develop a satisfactory solution to the issue of secondary GME provision (City of Edinburgh Council 2016). The new council elected in 2017 proved much more supportive of Gaelic than its predecessors, and is now considering plans to establish a dedicated Gaelic secondary school in the city (*EEN* 2018).

In the Highland Council area, proposals to develop dedicated Gaelic primary schools in addition to the one in Inverness (see p. 266 above) encountered significant difficulties. In the first iteration of its statutory Gaelic Language Plan, published in 2007, Highland Council undertook to 'react positively when opportunities arise to set up all-Gaelic schools', 'aiming at 2 schools in the Plan's lifetime' (i.e. by 2012) (HC 2007: 32). It was subsequently agreed that these would be built in Portree and Fort William, but as the UK government's austerity policy began to bite in the years following, capital projects were significantly delayed. The Fort

William school did not open until 2015 and the Portree school until 2018, eleven years after the council had agreed the project in principle, and there were several local controversies about siting and other issues along the way (*P&J* 2014a; *Times* 2018).

Other proposals for Gaelic schools in the Highland area proved unsuccessful. In 2006 there was a controversial proposal to turn Sleat Primary School, which adjoined Sabhal Mòr Ostaig, into a Gaelic school and require children who wished to receive English-medium education to go to the nearest other school. Unfortunately this was in Broadford, a full 15 miles away, so there would have been considerable inconvenience to families choosing English-medium education. In the end, Highland Council imposed a compromise solution by which Sleat Primary School would be designated as a Gaelic school with an English unit (*The Herald* 2006). Activists perceived this change as cosmetic, as it still meant that a significant proportion of the children in the school would not be able to speak or understand Gaelic, thus precluding the development of a Gaelic immersion environment. Similar 'Gaelic schools with English units' would be opened in the Western Isles in the years following.

The decision to retain English-medium education at the Sleat school gave rise to another controversy in 2019, when the council decided to house the English-medium nursery and Gaelic-medium nursery in the same building, against the wishes of the majority of parents. In the view of the council, which perceived 'unacceptable tension' in the local community, this approach 'would achieve the greatest level of inclusion' (*WHFP* 2019b). This then led to a much wider controversy, with the convener of the council announcing that the council would build no new dedicated Gaelic schools and suggesting that Gaelic-medium pupils had been treated unduly favourably compared to those in English medium (HC 2019). Several prominent activists and politicians sharply criticised the council for this new approach, which went against long-standing policies, and the campaigning group Misneachd submitted a formal complaint to the Bòrd, alleging that the council was failing to implement the commitments in its Gaelic language plan (BBC Naidheachdan 2019b).

Another dispute arose in 2005–6 in the mainland village of Morar. Lady Lovat Primary in Morar had an overwhelmingly Gaelic school roll, serving the villages of Morar, Mallaig (3 miles to the north) and Arisaig (5 miles to the south). Due to capacity issues, Highland Council proposed to move the Gaelic-medium pupils into a new Gaelic unit in Mallaig Primary School (HC 2005). The Gaelic-medium parents saw this as 'a golden opportunity' to develop a dedicated Gaelic school in Morar by moving the smaller group of English-medium pupils to Mallaig (Comann nam

Pàrant Rathad nan Eilean 2006), but their campaign proved unsuccessful and the council implemented the move of the Gaelic pupils to Mallaig. The Morar plan attracted much less publicity and controversy than the Sleat proposal, but it was actually more workable. More recently, in 2018 Argyll & Bute Council rejected a proposal for a dedicated Gaelic school in Oban on financial grounds, even though it recognised that there was sufficient demand among local parents (*P&J* 2018b).

In the Western Isles, all attempts to develop dedicated Gaelic schools have failed, for different reasons. As discussed earlier (p. 210), the GME model has been controversial in the islands because of its perceived negative effects on local communities. In 2006–8, Comhairle nan Eilean Siar surveyed Western Isles parents to assess their views on Gaelic-medium schools, but there was only limited support from parents, and the council decided not to proceed with its plans (CnES 2009). In Barra, parental support was stronger but the proposal was not taken forward (K. MacLeod 2017: 79–81). In 2010 the council surveyed parents of children in GME about the possibility of establishing a Gaelic school in Stornoway but concluded that there was 'not a strong mandate', with twenty-five submissions in favour and eighteen against (CnES 2010). In 2013 the council rejected suggestions from Bòrd na Gàidhlig that it should open a Gaelic school in Lewis, arguing that this would mean centralising Gaelic-medium provision in Stornoway and weaken the language in other parts of the island (BBC Naidheachdan 2013a).

In 2013 the Scottish Government granted CnES an additional £500,000 in funding to improve facilities and provide information technology infrastructure. Although the funding came from the government's Gaelic Schools Capital Fund, CnES agreed only to conduct a consultation about designating certain schools as Gaelic schools where Gaelic-speaking pupils are in the majority, not about establishing Gaelic schools without an English-medium stream (SG 2013). In 2015 six primary schools were duly redesignated as 'Gaelic schools', but they usually retained English-medium streams, in the manner of the Sleat school (*P&J* 2015a).

The council was more successful in its efforts to increase the proportion of primary school children entering GME, especially in South Uist and Barra. By 2019 the proportion of primary pupils in GME had reached 40 per cent and the council agreed a plan by which pupils entering primary school would automatically be enrolled in Gaelic medium unless parents affirmatively request that they be placed in English medium (CnES 2020). The approach of removing the English-medium option entirely, repeatedly urged by militant activists over the years (e.g. Misneachd 2018: 13), remains off the table, however.

The relatively weak demand for Gaelic education in the Western Isles appears to confirm Tadhg Ó hIfearnáin's observation that 'deeply rooted anxiety of parents' in relation to acquisition of English and the importance of the minority language 'can continue to be transmitted for generations even after changes in the majority opinion have led to a more encouraging environment for the minority language's speakers' (Ó hIfearnáin 2013: 118; see Gaelic Educationist 1948). However, in considering the overall pattern of demand it should be borne in mind that an increasing proportion of parents in the Western Isles are incomers without family links to the language who would be unaffected by such anxiety.

GAELIC EDUCATION: THE POLICY FRAMEWORK

As discussed in the previous chapter, a key driver of the campaign for a Gaelic Language Act was the wish to create a legally enforceable right to GME. When the Act as passed did not include any such right, Gaelic organisations and activists continued to press the issue, prompting the SNP to include a commitment in its manifesto to 'examine we how can introduce an entitlement to Gaelic-medium education where reasonable demand exists' (SNP 2011: 24). The meaning of the term 'entitlement', as opposed to 'right', was less than obvious. The ensuing legislation, the *Education (Scotland) Act 2016*, sets up a complex mechanism by which education authorities are required to respond to parental requests to assess the need to provide Gaelic-medium primary education.[15] The statutory process involves two stages, a preliminary and a full assessment, and authorities must take a wide range of factors into account, including evidence of demand and the views presented in a public consultation. Crucially, under section 12(7) of the Act, the authority is required to offer GME based on the outcome of the full assessment 'unless it would be unreasonable to do so'. This system is much less than a straightforward enforceable right to Gaelic education, but it does place more significant constraint on local authority discretion than had been the case previously. It is important in this context that parents also have no right to education through the medium of the minority language in either Ireland or Wales, although parents do enjoy a right to French- or English-medium education in Canada in certain circumstances (*Canadian Charter of Rights and Freedoms*, s. 23).

It remains to be seen how effective the Act will be in bringing about the introduction of GME in areas where it has not been offered up to now. One significant feature of the Act is section 9(6), which sets five children in a year cohort as the threshold to demonstrate the existence of potential demand and trigger the requirement to conduct a full assessment of need. In urban areas this is not a high bar but it may be a significant obstacle in thinly populated rural areas. The Act also imposes new obligations on education authorities to publicise the potential availability of GME and, in the case of authorities that are already providing it, to promote and support it (s. 15).

The first two attempts by parents to make use of the new legislation produced disappointing outcomes. In Argyll & Bute, parental demand prompted the council to agree to open a Gaelic unit at Bunessan on the Isle of Mull in 2017, but the procedure took so long that by the time the teaching post was advertised it was too late to attract candidates for the start of the next school year (BBC Naidheachdan 2017). Eventually a suitable applicant, a Canadian national, was recruited but was controversially denied a visa on the grounds that her salary would be insufficient to qualify (CBC 2018). More problematically, in East Renfrewshire a submission on behalf of forty-nine parents was rejected by the council following an 'initial assessment' which determined that there had not been a showing of demand of the requisite five children in the relevant year group (*Herald* 2017a; East Renfrewshire Council 2017b). The letter sent by the council to parents who had expressed an interest in GME was phrased in extraordinarily negative terms, suggesting strongly that if they chose GME for their children the parents would have to learn Gaelic and that indicating an interest at this preliminary stage, without being given any specific information concerning the Gaelic provision that would be offered, would preclude parents from securing a place for their children at their local primary school (East Renfrewshire Council 2017a). The former stricture had never been applied by any other authority, though non-Gaelic-speaking parents (who constitute the great majority in most areas) are encouraged and assisted to learn the language. The council insisted that it had followed the statutory guidance (BnG 2017) but the Bòrd disagreed. Under pressure from campaigners, Gaelic organisations and the Scottish Government, the council eventually agreed to consider a revised application once the guidance had been clarified (East Renfrewshire Council 2017b). In the event, however, no provision was made. In 2019 parents in North Ayrshire, another council which had never previously offered GME, were more successful; following an expression of demand on behalf of five children, the local authority agreed to make provision from 2020 onwards at a school in Kilwinning (North Ayrshire Council 2019).

Section 16 of the Education Act also effected an amendment to the

Gaelic Language Act in relation to the issuance of formal guidance on Gaelic education. Section 9 of the Gaelic Act had provided that Bòrd na Gàidhlig 'may prepare and submit to the Scottish Ministers guidance in relation to the provision of Gaelic education and the development of such provision' and this section was changed to the mandatory 'must'. Education authorities are required to 'have regard' to this guidance. Guidance had in fact been in development for some time, under the auspices of the national education support body Education Scotland, but the delay to this process prompted the government to include this section in the new Act and to assign the responsibility to BnG. In 2017 the Bòrd published its guidance document, which 'aims to explain the different elements that constitute Gaelic education in Scotland and to establish a consistent approach and a clear expectation of what Gaelic medium education (GME) is and how it should be delivered' (BnG 2017: 4). Together with a formal advice note from Education Scotland (2015), local authorities now have a clear blueprint to guide the design and delivery of Gaelic provision at all stages of education. However, as of 2020 schools inspectors were observing that 'overall, educators are not yet making sufficient use' of the statutory guidance (Education Scotland 2020: 11).

ISSUES INVOLVING GAELIC EDUCATION

A number of challenges continue to affect Gaelic education. The greatest and most enduring of these is that of teacher recruitment (Dunn 2013). Although a number of measures have been adopted to address the shortage, significant difficulties remain, and the demand for Gaelic-medium teachers continues to rise as the system undergoes continuous growth. BnG launched a teacher recruitment programme, Thig Gam Theagasg (Come Teach Me), but the pool of potential candidates with the necessary linguistic skills and commitment was very limited. New providers (the University of Edinburgh and the University of the Highlands and Islands) began to offer undergraduate Gaelic teacher education degree programmes in 2014 and 2016. These programmes added to those of the long-established lead provider in the sector, the University of Strathclyde, but at the same time the University of Aberdeen withdrew its programmes. Edinburgh offers a pathway for students with no prior knowledge of Gaelic, and this has helped widen the potential pool.[16] Notably, the growth of GME in the schools has not led to an expansion in the number of students earning degrees in Gaelic. Across the four universities with Gaelic programmes, the total number of graduates per year is usually under forty, and most of these are not attracted to a teaching career.

While BnG offers some small dedicated bursaries for teacher education students,[17] more substantial incentive programmes to attract Gaelic teachers have been ruled out. For example, the Scottish Government introduced £20,000 bursaries to attract new teachers of science, technology and mathematics (SG 2018), but has declined to provide comparable support for students intending to work in the Gaelic sector (*WHFP* 2020). Offering salary premiums to Gaelic-medium teachers has been considered politically unacceptable.

Continuing professional development for Gaelic-medium teachers has been very limited. This has become increasingly problematic as new entrants to the profession often lack confidence in some aspects of their Gaelic skills, especially grammar and formal usage. An increasing proportion of Gaelic-medium teachers are L2 speakers (Pollock 2010), and even those who consider themselves native speakers generally tend to lack the fluency and confidence of older generations (Bell et al. 2014).

Other programmes endeavoured to assist existing teachers to move from working in English medium to Gaelic medium. The online Streap course offered by SMO and the University of Aberdeen was aimed at fluent Gaelic speakers and aimed to build language skills and competence as well as confidence in teaching through Gaelic.[18] A more ambitious 'Gaelic Immersion for Teachers' (GIfT) course offered at the University of Strathclyde from 2014 onwards took teachers with an intermediate level of Gaelic out of the classroom for a year to receive intensive training in Gaelic language and bilingual pedagogy. This programme was expensive to run as the salaries of the participating teachers (approximately ten in a year cohort) needed to be paid. Most of this was covered by GLAIF, and the Scottish Government also contributed £100,000 per year. The course was loosely modelled on the retraining programme developed in the Basque Country in the 1980s to prepare teachers for Basque-medium teaching (Zalbide and Cenoz 2008), but on a far smaller scale. GIfT also encountered operational challenges: it was difficult to recruit sufficient numbers of teachers with an adequate linguistic foundation, and local authorities were sometimes unwilling to release teachers from their classroom for a full year.[19]

Teacher retention has also been an ongoing problem facing the Gaelic sector: many teachers who would be able to teach through Gaelic opt to teach through English instead. In 2014 more than a third of the primary teachers qualified to work in Gaelic medium were not doing so (Kidner 2015: 19). Some of these teachers will be working in English medium simply for geographical reasons, but there is also considerable 'leakage' as teachers choose to move out of Gaelic medium. Gaelic-medium teaching is recognised as being significantly more demanding than English medium. This is partly because of the inherent challenges of linguistic immersion pedagogy, partly because Gaelic-medium teaching materials and resources are so much more limited and teachers are still often required to create their own (Comann nam Pàrant 2017). In addition, the use of classroom assistants to support Gaelic-medium teachers has been reduced due to budget cuts, placing additional pressure on teachers. In recognition of the challenges of immersion teaching, Highland Council formerly set lower pupil–teacher ratios in Gaelic medium, but this policy was rescinded in 2010 in the name of equalisation (*WHFP* 2012). A government proposal in 2010 to establish lower ratios for GME on a national basis, in light of the 'extra responsibilities' involved and 'additional skills' required, was withdrawn in the face of opposition (*TESS* 2010). The belief that GME involves smaller class sizes remains vigorous among some critics, however (e.g. Sorooshian 2010).

Although no relevant data are systematically gathered, it is clear that over time a decreasing proportion of children in GME came from Gaelic-speaking homes, even in areas where Gaelic remains widely spoken in the community. In urban areas the overwhelming majority of parents cannot speak Gaelic, and most of these have no close family history or connection to Gaelic areas. Parents have been attracted to GME for a variety of reasons, often in combination. One important set of motivations involved parents' 'sense that Gaelic was part of their heritage', whether that be 'family heritage, general cultural heritage, heritage of the Highlands and Islands, and Scottish heritage' (O'Hanlon, McLeod and Paterson 2010: 46).

GME also developed a favourable reputation for educational quality. This included a perception that GME generally attracted parents who were interested in and committed to education, thereby creating a positive school culture and community (O'Hanlon, McLeod and Paterson 2010: 56–7). A 2010 study (O'Hanlon, McLeod and Paterson 2010) found that pupils in GME outperformed their English-medium counterparts in English reading, broadly confirming the findings of the Stirling research published in 1999 (Johnstone et al. 1999). Importantly, the study included controls for pupils' socio-economic status. Opponents of Gaelic often charge that positive educational outcomes are simply a consequence of the predominantly middle-class demographic that chooses GME (e.g. Hickey 2010).

Parents were also attracted by a more general belief in the 'benefits of bilingualism'. This did not refer to bilingualism as social practice, as promoted by Gaelic advocates in earlier decades, the idea that Gaelic speakers could know and use both Gaelic and English. Rather, these 'benefits' related to cognition and involved the understanding that bilinguals showed superior skills in terms of executive function, such as the ability to manage different kinds of tasks simultaneously. Such outcomes were indicated in a number of international studies, and investigations of Gaelic-medium pupils showed positive outcomes of this kind (Lauchlan, Parisi and Fadda 2012; Cape et al. 2018). Questions have been raised about the significance of these effects, however, as not all tests have yielded such results (Lehtonen et al. 2018).

Gaelic organisations have been keen to include claims about the 'benefits of bilingualism' in their promotional information (e.g. BnG n.d. a). In this context, there is a possibility that some parents may choose Gaelic education for its perceived intellectual and educational benefits but have relatively little engagement with the language and the language community. The constant policy pressure to expand Gaelic education and increase the numbers of children enrolled may mean tending to court the marginally committed. This may be a price that had to be paid; an approach that focused exclusively on families with a strong, demonstrated commitment to Gaelic would almost certainly not have generated sufficient demand to make provision politically viable, most obviously in places like Edinburgh.

Although overall educational attainment of GME pupils has been very encouraging, there have been ongoing concerns about their Gaelic language skills. O'Hanlon, McLeod and Paterson's 2010 study of attainment concluded that although a very high proportion of GME pupils in the final year of primary school had reached the level of attainment in Gaelic expected of pupils at that stage, levels of attainment after two years of secondary school were noticeably lower. Of primary 7 pupils, 81 per cent were judged to have reached the expected level in speaking Gaelic, but only 61 per cent of secondary 2 pupils, while for Gaelic writing the corresponding figures were 68 per cent and 54 per cent (O'Hanlon, McLeod and Paterson 2010: 22). Several other studies have shown weaknesses among GME pupils in terms of their grammatical accuracy in Gaelic (MacNeil and Galloway 2004; Müller 2006; MacLeod 2006–9: 233; NicLeòid 2016). These findings align with research on immersion programmes in Canada and elsewhere, which show that although immersion learners develop strong receptive skills in listening and reading, they tend to be weaker than native speakers in relation to the productive skills of speaking and writing, and 'do not always gain grammatical accuracy or competence in all dimensions' comparable to native speakers (Baker and Wright 2017: 257, 260). In addition, graduates of GME programmes tend to acquire a hybrid variety of Gaelic that shows elements of different dialects as well as influence from English; this issue is discussed below in connection with adult 'new speakers'.

International research also indicates that pupils enrolled in immersion education programmes tend not to use the language informally among themselves (M. Macleod et al. 2014: 9–11). Several studies have confirmed this pattern in relation to GME pupils (MacLeod 2006–9: 235; O'Hanlon, Paterson and McLeod 2012). According to Sìleas NicLeòid (2018: 54), because Gaelic does not 'function as a means for peer communication' it would be wrong to interpret GME learners' deviations from established linguistic norms 'as new language developments that can be understood as an expression of the speakers' distinct linguistic identity'. By the same token, suggestions that the Gaelic produced by immersion pupils in Glasgow, which shows marked influence from the phonology and intonation of Glasgow English, may give rise to a new 'Glasgow Gaelic' (Nance 2018), may be exaggerated: such usage may have little currency outside the classroom.

An important study by Stuart Dunmore addressed the overall sociolinguistic impact of GME in terms of Gaelic language use and transmission on the part of adults who had gone through GME in the early years of its existence (Dunmore 2015, 2019). Of the 46 former pupils who were interviewed, who were aged between 24 and 34 at the time of the investigation, 22 reported high current ability in Gaelic, 6 reported intermediate ability and 18 low ability (Dunmore 2015: 136). In terms of usage, however, only 10 interviewees reported high use of Gaelic in their daily lives, 12 reported intermediate to low use and 24 reported low use (Dunmore 2015: 117–26). In the 1980s and 1990s optimistic statements envisioned a scenario by which graduates of GME would become active, lifelong users of Gaelic who would transmit the language to their own children (Dunmore 2015: 74–5). Dunmore's findings align with Fishman's view that education on its own is unlikely to produce active speakers. However, it is also relevant that these pupils all attended Gaelic units rather than dedicated Gaelic schools, and had relatively little exposure to Gaelic in secondary school. A stronger model, including a richer secondary experience, might produce better outcomes. The fundamental challenges would remain in place, however: due to their home and local environments, the great majority of GME pupils have almost no contact with the language outside school.

ADULT LEARNERS AND 'NEW SPEAKERS'

Provision for adult Gaelic learners in the twenty-first century has tended to involve a step back for every step forward. The college immersion courses developed in the 1990s slowly withered away (see p. 222 above), removing the most viable learning pathways for many students. By 2010 a review for Bòrd na Gàidhlig concluded that provision for adult Gaelic learners 'tends to be patchy, uncoordinated, poorly promoted, inadequately funded and often lacking in professional rigour' (McLeod, Pollock and MacCaluim 2010: vi). The three National Gaelic Language Plans all made reference to adult Gaelic learning, but commitments were very general; the plan for 2018–23 states the intention to 'develop the existing resources for adult learners and ensure that gaps in support and provision are identified and addressed' (BnG 2018a: 49).

As noted earlier, Clì Gàidhlig lost its vigour and was eventually wound down, meaning that no organisation had specific responsibility for the strategic coordination of this sector. A new web-based learning service, learngaelic.net, was developed, providing information about learning opportunities and a wide range of learning materials. The materials on learngaelic.net make extensive use of digital technology, and this initiative was developed under the auspices of MG ALBA as part of its remit to expand the reach of the digital service BBC ALBA, discussed below. The promise of the Ùlpan learning system also dissipated, after the expenditure of significant funds, but an initiative to systemise Gaelic learning and map learning outcomes onto the Common European Framework of Reference for Languages,[20] Comasan Labhairt ann an Gàidhlig/Adult Gaelic Proficiency,[21] is in progress. A certification system for learners comparable to Teastas Eorpach na Gaeilge (European Certificate for Irish, www.teg.ie) is still some way away, however.

In late 2019 Gaelic was added to the language learning app Duolingo, and within a month of its launch more than 115,000 people – more than double the number of speakers recorded at the 2011 census – had signed up. The launch generated extensive media coverage (Massie 2019) and general goodwill, even if it is unlikely that many of these Duolingo users will progress to fluency and active use of the language.

As was the case in the 1990s (MacCaluim 2007), the scale of adult Gaelic learning remains modest, with little obvious potential for significant sociolinguistic impact. A survey conducted in November 2018 estimated that there were 5,460 adult learners in Scotland at that time, but of these only 22 per cent were under the age of thirty-five. Sixty per cent were at a beginner/elementary level (CEFR levels A1/2) and only

9 per cent were at the upper levels (B2/C1/C2). Fifty-seven per cent of learners were in Glasgow, Edinburgh, Highland or the Western Isles (Sellers and Carty 2019: 5, 11, 14, 35–6).

Several studies have investigated the motivations of adult Gaelic learners (e.g. MacCaluim 2007: 157–69; McLeod, Pollock and MacCaluim 2010: 26; Sellers and Carty 2019: 16). As is typical in relation to heritage language learning (Edwards 2010: 171–2), this research indicates that factors involving identity or culture tend to predominate over instrumental or communicative goals. In the most recent study, the most frequently identified reasons related to issues of cultural heritage: 13.4 per cent of responses[22] cited 'Gaelic is a part of Scotland's culture and heritage' as a motivation and 12.1 per cent 'to help preserve or revitalise the language'; 7.6 per cent involved an interest in Gaelic music, 6.1 per cent in place names, 5 per cent in Gaelic literature and 7.4 per cent a general interest in languages. Other reasons were cited less frequently: 'members of my family speak, or spoke, Gaelic' (4.9 per cent), 'I have Gaelic-speaking friends' (4.7 per cent) and 'my children/grandchildren are in Gaelic-medium education' (4.3 per cent). 'To get a job in the Gaelic sector' and 'I want to live in a traditionally Gaelic-speaking area' received particularly few citations (2.1 per cent and 1.8 per cent) (Sellers and Carty 2019: 16). The great majority of these responses came from learners who had not been learning Gaelic long, however, and evidence suggests that people often find that their motivations change over time (MacCaluim 2007: 158). As such, the factors identified by more advanced learners appear to be slightly different (McLeod, O'Rourke and Dunmore 2014: 11–14).

In the twenty-first century the concept of the 'new speaker' gained significant purchase in sociolinguistics (Smith-Christmas et al. 2018). The term 'new speaker' represents a refinement of earlier concepts such as 'L2 speaker' or 'learner'. Although there is as yet no universally agreed definition of the term, the most useful formulation entails 'people who did not acquire the language in the home when they were growing up, but have nevertheless acquired the language to a significant degree of competence and are now making active use of the language in their lives' (McLeod and O'Rourke 2015: 154). This is a much more specific term than 'learner', which encompasses individuals with limited language ability who are not able to use the language socially or professionally. In the Gaelic context, new speakers have become a much more obvious presence in the twenty-first century, although there are no reliable data to indicate how numerous they actually are (McLeod and O'Rourke 2015: 154).

To an ever-greater extent, there has been a decoupling of Gaelic language ability and active use on the one hand and family language background on the other, at least outside the core Gaelic communities in the islands. This has led to a more complex matrix of variegated Gaelic identities and less certainty about acceptance and belonging in the Gaelic community (Glaser 2007: 247–71). This issue may be most acute in the case of the very small number of new speakers from a Black or minority ethnic background (Ezeji 2015; Gessesse 2019).

One manifestation of this uncertainty is that the significance of the ethnonym *Gàidheal*/Gael[23] has become less clear. The principal issue is the centrality of the Gaelic language to Gaelic identity. Some people take the view that one can be a Gael without being able to speak Gaelic, usually on the basis of family and community origins, while conversely some people who can speak Gaelic are reluctant to label themselves as Gaels (MacAulay 1994: 42–3; Bechhofer and McCrone 2014). In practice, this can even mean that 'when Gaels are spoken of, no one is quite sure what one is and few claim to be one', as James Oliver has argued (2005: 21; see Dunmore 2015: 207–13). One means of overcoming this difficulty is to use language-based identifiers such as *luchd na Gàidhlig* (literally 'the people of the Gaelic language') in place of 'Gaels'. This usage has become increasingly common in recent decades (McLeod 2014). Overall, though, there is a considerable degree of intellectual and ideological confusion in this area, and no effective consensus has been reached. This contrasts with the situation of Basque, where a clear language-based understanding of group membership has been developed (Urla 2012: 60, 127–8).

Some of these 'new speakers' acquired their Gaelic through GME, others via long-term college or university courses, community classes or other means (McLeod and O'Rourke 2015: 158–9). However, the fact that such a high proportion of new speakers attributed their fluency in the language to having studied for a year or more at SMO or on full-time university Gaelic programmes demonstrates a weakness in the system, as such pathways are not viable for large numbers of potential learners.

New speakers, particularly those living in urban areas, often reported the shortage of opportunities to speak Gaelic as a significant obstacle to their language acquisition and development. Very few people reported learning Gaelic through immersion in a traditional Gaelic community, and some individuals found it more viable than others to enter or develop Gaelic social networks (McLeod and O'Rourke 2015). Proposals are now being advanced to develop Gaelic centres in urban areas that would serve as a social base or 'hub' for local Gaelic communities, including both native and new speakers. These would draw upon comparable initiatives in Wales and the north of Ireland, such as the Cultúrlann McAdam-Ó Fiaich in Belfast (Gruffudd and Morris 2012).

The changing nature of the Gaelic-speaking community, and the growth of new forms of Gaelic language usage in the media and other sectors, have also had important linguistic impacts in terms of increasing hybridisation and standardisation (McLeod 2017). The term 'middle of the Minch' Gaelic is often used to describe an imagined central form that draws on the dialects most widely spoken today, those of the Western Isles and Skye (which are separated by the strait known in English as the Minch). James Grant described the dynamic as follows:

> The centre of the Scottish Gaelic-speaking world now lies in the islands of the Northern Hebrides: Lewis, Harris, North Uist, Skye, Benbecula, South Uist and Barra. Amongst Scottish Gaelic speakers there seems to be a tacit agreement that Gaelic as spoken in and around the central districts of this island group should be accepted for most purposes as the standard form of the language. This is particularly apparent in broadcasting, where broadcasters, no matter their origin, seem unconsciously to adopt the pronunciations and usages which they think common to this area. (Grant 2004: 70)

The new Gaelic-medium workplaces that emerged in the 1980s often brought speakers of different dialects together, and with it a culture of linguistic accommodation (McLeod 2017: 189). For new speakers, including graduates of GME, hybridisation usually results from having numerous teachers speaking different dialects over the course of the language-acquisition journey (McLeod, O'Rourke and Dunmore 2014: 39).

The valorisation of 'authenticity' observed by Kathryn Woolard in the Catalan context and elsewhere is readily observable in the Gaelic context: the sense that 'a speech variety must be perceived as deeply rooted in social and geographic territory in order to have value' (Woolard 2016: 22). For some commentators, then, mid-Minch Gaelic is 'a disconcerting mixture that belongs to nowhere at all' (McLeod 2017: 194, 191). This unease is compounded by a sense that traditional Gaelic idiom and usage and the dialectal diversity of the language are thinning out, and that the language is losing its *blas* (richness of taste) (Bell et al. 2014).

BBC ALBA: SUCCESSES AND CONTROVERSIES

The launch of the Gaelic digital television service BBC ALBA on the Freeview digital terrestrial platform in 2011 represented the culmination of a drawn-out policy process stretching back to the 1990s. While the service continues to face significant challenges, all of them ultimately connected to funding, Scotland now has a universally available dedicated Gaelic television service, the long-sought objective of Gaelic language planners and campaigners. This milestone was reached almost thirty years later than in Wales, where the Welsh channel S4C was launched in 1982, and fifteen years later than in Ireland, where Teilifís na Gaeilge (renamed TG4 in 1999) was launched in 1996. Nevertheless, the creation of BBC ALBA was remarkable in the sense that no other European minority language community of comparable size benefits from such extensive television provision.

Funding has always been the principal challenge for Gaelic broadcasting. As discussed in earlier chapters, only a few years after the introduction of the Gaelic Television Fund in 1992, the inadequacy of the budget became apparent, and the protracted discussions that led to the development of BBC ALBA were predicated on the insistence that there could only be relatively small increases in the level of funding. The issue was ultimately political; budgets were decided according to what politicians in London and Edinburgh considered acceptable rather than what was needed to provide a viable service. Donald Campbell, chief executive of the Gaelic Media Service, perceived a 'glass ceiling' on the level of funding that would be politically acceptable to the non-Gaelic majority in Scotland, while his predecessor John Angus Mackay concluded that with persistently inadequate budgets 'Gaelic broadcasting is being asked to make bricks without straw' (MacLean 2018: 10, 14). As with the 1990 settlement, the financial position of BBC ALBA has deteriorated over time, and it has become increasingly difficult to provide a service with adequate quantity, quality and range of programming.

As discussed in the previous chapter, the lengthy policy discussions concerning the Gaelic channel from 1997 onwards concluded with the agreement to establish BBC ALBA as a partnership between MG ALBA and the BBC. Before the service could be launched, however, authorisation by the BBC Trust, the BBC's governing body, was required. This proved to be a lengthy and close-run process. In the course of its assessment the Trust conducted a so-called 'Public Value Test'. In 2007 the Trust announced the provisional conclusions of this review, ruling that it required additional evidence before it could 'conclude that the proposal would generate sufficient public value to justify the level of investment required'. In particular, the Trust was 'not convinced that the proposal for the service place[d] enough emphasis on the role of the service in attracting new speakers to the Gaelic language' and found 'very little evidence of a convincing plan for appealing to a wider audience in Scotland' (BBC Trust 2007: 11–12). In response, the BBC Executive submitted additional evidence. In 2008 the Trust announced the final conclusions of its review and approved the BBC Executive's application to launch the Gaelic digital service but only on satellite and cable, which only a minority of viewers were accessing. Rollout to the digital terrestrial service Freeview, the platform used by the great majority of viewers, was made conditional on the outcome of a further 'detailed review [...] to ensure that sufficient public value is being created in practice by the new service' (BBC Trust 2008: 6).[24] But the Trust imposed a number of conditions to its approval; in particular, BBC ALBA was required to demonstrate that it was attracting an audience of 250,000 viewers, i.e. 5 per cent of the Scottish total. This figure was very challenging, considering that in 2011 fewer than 50,000 people were recorded as being able to speak Gaelic and fewer than 90,000 to understand it. It was therefore essential for the service to attract large numbers of viewers who could not understand Gaelic, and this had significant consequences for programming strategy, as discussed below.

BBC ALBA was duly launched in 2008, but was initially available only via satellite. Plans to have the service made available via cable (a popular platform in urban areas) became bogged down with the private provider of this service (Virgin Media) and the channel did not actually become available on cable until 2011 (*Herald* 2011).

In order to make BBC ALBA available on Freeview, the BBC and MG ALBA proposed to free up additional bandwidth capacity for BBC ALBA by displacing several radio services, including the BBC World Service, during the periods when BBC ALBA was broadcasting (i.e. peak hours in the late afternoon and evening). This proposal predictably led to opposition from users of the services in question (*Express* 2010).

In 2010, following another review, the BBC Trust announced that it would authorise the launch of BBC ALBA on Freeview, again ruling that the evidence provided was sufficient to pass the public value test (BBC Trust 2010). The Trust concluded that the service was 'serving Gaelic speakers well', 'appealing more widely beyond Gaelic speakers' and 'operating effectively' (BBC Trust 2010: 6–10). It noted that there was 'strong public policy and political support for the proposal in Scotland', including support from the Scottish Government and Scottish Parliament, but observed that 'the views of audiences are more balanced' and that the issue of Freeview carriage for BBC ALBA was 'clearly an emotive one, as respondents to our consultation expressed strong – and opposing – views' (BBC Trust 2010: 16–17).

The Freeview launch in 2011 led to a significant increase in viewer numbers, as campaigners had predicted. Prior to the launch on Freeview, the total weekly reach for the channel (i.e. the proportion of Scottish viewers watching the service for at least 15 minutes per week) was 220,000 adults aged sixteen and over. In the three months following the launch, the weekly reach rose to 530,000 adults, or 12.9 per cent of the national total. Recalling that only 1.8 per cent of the population (92,000 people) can understand Gaelic, this was a remarkable achievement, but it meant that only a small fraction of the audience consisted of Gaelic speakers.

Since that time, however, there has been a gradual decline in viewing figures for BBC ALBA, for various reasons, including the rapidly changing technological environment for electronic media. Weekly reach peaked in 2013–14 at 17.6 per cent[25] but had declined to 10.3 per cent by 2018–19, while reach among the core Gaelic audience peaked in 2015–16 at 74 per cent but fell to 59 per cent by 2018–19. BBC ALBA programmes were introduced to the iPlayer catch-up service in 2011, with downloads peaking in 2014–15 at 7.4 million but declining to 3.9 million in 2018–19. The new category of social media viewership (e.g. clips on Facebook) increased from 1.24 million to 2.6 million between 2017–18 and 2018–19, however (MG ALBA 2014: 11; 2015: 24; 2016: 22; 2019: 21).

The position of S4C in Wales bears some similarity with that of BBC ALBA but the differences are perhaps more striking. The funding model for S4C is very different from that of BBC ALBA and has undergone profound change since 2010, although one constant is that its budget has always been four or five times higher. The viewership for S4C (measured according to weekly reach in Wales) has also declined considerably in recent years, down 34 per cent between 2011 and 2019 (S4C 2012: 29; S4C 2019: 47). The audience profile is very different from that of BBC ALBA: the S4C viewership of 314,000 in 2018–19 is equivalent to 56 per cent of the Welsh-speaking population at the 2011 census, whereas the BBC ALBA figure is a multiple of the Gaelic-speaking population in Scotland.

The most important reason for the declining viewership for BBC ALBA and S4C was the wider decline in viewership of broadcast television as audiences shifted to new kinds of non-broadcast services, including streaming services such as Netflix and video services such as YouTube. Between 2010 and 2018, average daily viewing of broadcast television in Scotland dropped by 27 per cent (Ofcom 2019: 10).

If changing consumption patterns created sector-wide challenges, BBC ALBA also faced distinct difficulties of its own. Continuing budget constraints meant that there was limited funding for new content, which meant a high level of repeats. As early as 2012, MG ALBA's chair warned that this was leading to 'audience fatigue' (*Herald* 2012). By 2019 only 25 per cent of BBC ALBA's schedule consisted of first-run programmes

(MG ALBA 2019: 7). Similarly, for financial reasons BBC ALBA has not been made available in High Definition, only Standard Definition, meaning that there was a noticeable difference in display quality, which MG ALBA characterised as a 'second-class service' (MG ALBA 2019: 9). In relation to the iPlayer platform, MG ALBA argued that 'promotional spend and ease-of-discovery favour big-budget, English-language content' and marginalised BBC ALBA material (MG ALBA 2019: 11).

Shifts in consumption patterns were most pronounced among young people, who were watching less and less conventional television and were increasingly drawn to services such as YouTube, typically using mobile phones (Graffmann 2014; NicNèill 2018). This shift presents a significant challenge to Gaelic broadcasting in terms of language planning, as children's programming has long been identified as a key element in the overall development strategy (e.g. Dunn 1987: 54). The power of the English-language mass media, backed by immense resources and presenting a vision in which everything glamorous, exciting and 'cool' happens in English, has long been identified as an important factor that pushes youth away from minority languages such as Gaelic, but this trend has intensified considerably with the new technologies introduced in recent years. Similarly, in the ever-more variegated media landscape it is now much more difficult for a single minority-language provider like BBC ALBA to find a viable niche.

The political and financial position of the service also became more difficult following the election of a Conservative UK government in 2015. The new government proposed sweeping changes to the BBC and called into question the financial viability of all the BBC's Celtic-language services. These included, from 2010 onwards, S4C, for which the government required the BBC to assume financial responsibility. At the same time, the BBC's Royal Charter, the basic agreement setting out its purpose and obligations, was up for renewal. The previous government, a coalition between the Conservatives and the Liberal Democrats, had been more favourably inclined towards Gaelic broadcasting and had created a new DCMS budget line of £1 million per year for BBC ALBA, but this was promptly rescinded following the 2015 election, in which the Conservatives secured an outright majority (SG 2015). The Scottish Government then decided to allocate an additional £1 million per year to make up for this cut (BBC News 2016) but this only meant that BBC ALBA was able to stand still, not improve its service. The value of the Scottish Government's contribution to the Gaelic television budget actually declined by 34.5 per cent in real terms between 2006 and 2018.[26]

In connection with the government's review and the BBC Charter renewal process, MG ALBA proposed that the BBC should increase the level of Gaelic programming it provided to BBC ALBA to the level of Welsh programming it provided to S4C (10 hours per week). This would have meant an increase from 230 to 520 hours per year (MG ALBA 2015: 2–3). In the event, the BBC agreed to increase its annual contribution by £1.2 million, but this was much less than MG ALBA had sought (BBC 2017a). By the end of 2018, ten years after the launch of BBC ALBA, MG ALBA declared that

> the overall framework for Gaelic media provision urgently needs to be reviewed and invigorated. The existing funding settlement, which has no long-term security, will not be sufficient to meet the public service rights of those we serve or to fully address the challenges ahead of us. [. . .] Consequently, MG ALBA will invite the BBC, Ofcom, the Scottish Government and the UK Government to engage in a dialogue aimed at reaching a new settlement for Gaelic broadcasting. (MG ALBA 2019: 7–8)

To date, there has been no movement of this kind.

These budgetary constraints, coupled with the political imperative to attract large numbers of non-Gaelic viewers, had a strong impact on the range of programming on BBC ALBA. The service developed a 'twin pole' strategy, with some programming aimed at the core Gaelic audience, which had little appeal to non-Gaelic speakers, and other content that was more attractive to the mass, non-Gaelic audience (McMahon 2017). There was a heavy emphasis on sport, music and 'reality' programmes, which could be produced at relatively little cost, but very little drama, which was much more expensive. Increasingly over time, the service ran more and more repeats, leading to audience fatigue. The notion of a single 'core' audience is itself problematic, as it is by no means the case that all Gaelic speakers share similar interests.

In 2018–19 three-quarters of the total new content (412 hours) consisted of sport (186 hours, 45 per cent of the total) and factual (mostly 'reality') programming (123 hours, 30 per cent). There were only 4.5 hours of new drama and comedy, 1.1 per cent of the total. Drama and comedy cost more than twenty times as much to produce as sport (£313,584 per hour compared to £13,262), so that more than 15 per cent of the content budget (£9.35 million) was spent on less than five hours' worth of drama and comedy (MG ALBA 2019: 71).

BBC ALBA also emphasised sports programming for strategic reasons, as large numbers of non-Gaelic-speaking viewers were attracted to football and rugby matches. Live commentary was provided in Gaelic but interviews and analysis were usually in English.[27] The channel's director of programming until 2016, Alan Esslemont, had previously adopted this approach at Ireland's TG4. The strategy was equally successful in Scotland, as lower-league football matches were not available in English, so that BBC ALBA was able to fill a niche in the market. For some critics of the channel, however, this strategy constituted 'cheating' (*The Express* 2009).

Another element in Esslemont's programming strategy was 'to tell Scottish stories that haven't been told' (Hepburn 2010), often through different kinds of 'reality' programmes. Many of these 'Scottish' stories focused on specific groups of English monoglots, such as 'Glasgow City FC' (2013), concerning a women's football team, and all the dialogue in these programmes was in English only, with no dubbing into Gaelic or Gaelic subtitles. For former government minister Kenny MacAskill, BBC ALBA was functioning as 'the repository for anything with a particularly Scottish perspective' rather than 'a dedicated Gaelic channel' (MacAskill 2016).

BBC ALBA's programming strategy also became increasingly controversial among some Gaelic activists, particularly in relation to its use of English voicing in some programmes and the use of 'burnt-in' English subtitles which viewers were unable to switch off. In 2015 a campaigning organisation, Gàidhlig-TV, was formed, led by teacher and publisher Lisa Storey. The campaign attracted support from a number of prominent figures and organisations in the Gaelic cultural world (Gàidhlig-TV 2015; Fèisean nan Gàidheal 2016). After a flurry of controversy, the issue has since died down somewhat, although a degree of alienation persists in a section of the Gaelic community, and as of 2020 technology to allow viewers to turn off subtitles (which would have cost implications) has not been introduced.

In 2019 the BBC launched a new English-language service called BBC Scotland, which potentially threatened the position of BBC ALBA (Ofcom 2018). The budget for the new service is more than 50 per cent higher (£32m per year), it will broadcast no more than 50 per cent repeats and its programming is available in high definition. The sense of BBC ALBA as 'poor relation' is palpable. BBC Scotland may also disrupt BBC ALBA's programming strategy given that a good deal of MG ALBA's programmes, especially 'reality' programmes, are of wider Scottish interest with no specifically Gaelic dimension.

The wider cultural impact of BBC ALBA, for the Gaelic community and for Scotland more generally, has not yet been fully assessed (but see MacKenzie 2018). Perhaps surprisingly, there has been little critical analysis of the content of Gaelic television programming, such as the long-running drama series *Bannan*, now in its sixth series (but see O'Donnell 2001; Chalmers 2011). It is not clear that the service has maximised its potential as a vehicle for Gaelic 'self-expression [...] through which the Gaelic community could express and examine its own aspirations' (MacDonald 1990: 23). Similar, despite its successes in terms of audience reach, it is not clear how much the service has managed to 'affirm the contemporary relevance and presence of Gaelic' to wider Scottish society (Chalmers et al. 2013: 218). The overall cultural impact of Gaelic television seems to have been less than for the counterpart Irish-language service TG4, which was widely credited with promoting a new, modern image for the language in the wider Irish population (Moriarty 2008; Ó Gairbhí 2017).

As in other minority-language jurisdictions, debates continue about the proper role of the Gaelic media in language revitalisation strategy. Proponents argue that investment in electronic media is necessary to promote a contemporary image for the language and to meet the needs of contemporary Gaelic speakers' lifestyles, but it is by no means clear that increased investment in Gaelic media will or can deliver concrete benefits in terms of Gaelic language acquisition and use (see Dunbar 2003a; Cormack 2006). These challenges have become ever-greater with the rapid pace of technological change, which demands constant innovation and makes the work of a single content provider like BBC ALBA all the more difficult.

Radio provision for Gaelic has attracted much less attention and controversy than television. BBC Radio nan Gàidheal continues to play an important role in reaching the Gaelic community, and its output has increased slightly in recent years. The content budget increased from £3.2 million in 2006–7 to £4 million in 2017–18 (BBC 2006: 142; BBC 2019: 43), but this nevertheless amounted to a 10 per cent cut in real terms. Weekly reach within the Gaelic audience declined from 69 per cent in 2015–16 to 56 per cent in 2018–19 (BBC 2017b: 41; BBC 2019: 43). The average time spent listening to the service declined from 8 hours 40 minutes in 2016–17 to 6 hours 39 minutes in 2018–19 (BBC 2017b: 41; BBC 2019: 43). As with television, the technological position of radio has changed immensely due to the greatly increased availability of services over the internet and the popularity of podcasts, trends which threaten the viability of a single service that attempts to attract the spectrum of Gaelic listeners. In contrast to BBC ALBA, Radio nan Gàidheal is much less concerned with attracting non-Gaelic speakers, although there are dedicated programmes for learners (*Beag air Bheag* and *Litir do Luchd-ionnsachaidh*), and many learners use the radio as a resource.

BILINGUAL SIGNAGE AND THE 'LINGUISTIC LANDSCAPE'

In the early twenty-first century Gaelic became significantly more visible in Scotland's 'linguistic landscape', largely as a result of a bilingual signage programme at railway stations and the implementation of Gaelic language plans by public authorities. The concept of linguistic landscape was first developed by Rodrigue Landry and Richard Bourhis, who used it to refer to the 'visibility and salience' of particular languages on 'public road signs, advertising billboards, street names, place names, commercial shop signs, and public signs on government buildings' (Landry and Bourhis 1997: 23, 25). In 1950 John Lorne Campbell wrote that 'it is possible to travel through the Outer Hebrides from one end to another and hear nothing but Gaelic spoken, and see nothing but English written' (Campbell 1950: 27–8). In the twenty-first century it is possible to undertake the same journey and hear almost nothing but English spoken but with written Gaelic prominent everywhere. Gaelic is also increasingly visible in urban centres such as Inverness, Glasgow and Edinburgh. Some private companies and organisations also introduced bilingual signage, notably major retailers such as supermarket chains and DIY stores. In the Gaelic context the increased prominence of Gaelic could be seen not only in the increased usage of bilingual signage in public spaces, but, with a broader understanding of the concept of linguistic landscape, in the adoption of bilingual logos by a range of public authorities[28] and the increased presence of Gaelic on the internet and in the broadcast media. Considered cumulatively, these initiatives have had a significant impact in increasing the profile of the language, especially in Lowland Scotland.

In its online guidance to organisations on creating a Gaelic language plan, the Bòrd explained the importance of including Gaelic in the linguistic landscape:

> Demonstrating equal respect for Gaelic and English in your corporate identity and in your organisation's signage has an immediate impact on the status of Gaelic, making it visible, accessible and valued. The inclusion of Gaelic has a strong awareness-raising effect both amongst the public and within the organisation, creating a positive image of the language and promoting its use. The presence of Gaelic in signage and corporate identities lets Gaelic users know that Gaelic is welcomed and valued by the organisation. (BnG n.d. b)

Many organisations developed bilingual logos when they adopted statutory Gaelic language plans, but several of these chose to display the Gaelic form below the English and in a significantly smaller font. This approach arguably goes against the Gaelic Language Act's principle of 'equal respect' (Puzey, McLeod and Dunbar 2013). As noted above, the Scottish Government initially took this approach, but has now redesigned the logo so that the same font size is used in both languages.

The issue of bilingual road signs became increasingly controversial after 2007, but the SNP administration has actually done relatively little to increase their presence. New Gaelic signs on a number of trunk roads in the West Highlands and Argyll were installed between 2003 and 2010 (thus continuing after the 2007 election), but as discussed earlier (p. 271) this development had been agreed under the previous Labour–Liberal Democrat administration (SE 2003; Transport Scotland 2016). Indeed, one of the more significant Gaelic policy decisions of the SNP government was to order a review of possible safety concerns before bilingual signs would be authorised on any additional trunk roads. This review, announced in 2009, was perceived by campaigners as a delaying tactic on the part of civil servants (*WHFP* 2009). When it was eventually published in late 2012, the Transport Research Laboratory's report concluded that while bilingual signs 'increase the demand of the driving task, drivers appear able to absorb this extra demand, or negate it by slowing down, which ultimately results in no detectable change in accident rates' (Kinnear et al. 2012: 1).

In the wake of the safety review, the government announced that bilingual signs would be installed on the A9, the principal trunk road in the north of Scotland (*Herald* 2012; Transport Scotland 2016), which had been refused by the previous administration (SE 2004). To date, however, no bilingual signs have yet been erected, as the bilingualisation programme is connected to a long-term project to make the road into a dual carriageway. No plans have been announced to install bilingual signs on any additional trunk roads.

Similarly, the increased use of Gaelic on 'Welcome' signs at points of entry to Scotland such as airports and the principal roads across the English border resulted from a report commissioned by the previous Labour–Liberal Democrat administration. This report on 'first impressions' of Scotland recommended that 'bilingual English and Gaelic signs should be used' at international points of entry 'to emphasise the sense of place' (SE 2005b). This was an important example of the symbolic use of Gaelic to index Scotland and Scottishness.

Since 2010, however, there has been a major expansion of bilingual signage in railway stations, especially in central Scotland, where most stations are situated. All station name signs on platforms (but not those outside stations) are now bilingual, except in cases where no Gaelic form exists or can be readily generated. This change of policy was never formally announced but resulted from behind-the-scenes discussions between the Scottish Government and First ScotRail, the private company which then held the franchise to operate rail services in Scotland. Publicly this was characterised as 'part of the overall ScotRail rebranding programme which was included at no extra cost as part of the arrangements to extend the ScotRail franchise contract in 2008' (Transport Scotland 2015). Technically, then, this Gaelic signage initiative is not a matter of government policy.

Although bilingual road signs have been limited to the Highlands and Islands, the new policy for railway stations extends to all parts of Scotland. The great majority of stations are located in areas where Gaelic has not been spoken for centuries (with the densest concentration in the greater Glasgow area) and include not only place names of Gaelic origin but new translations of non-Gaelic names, notably Margadh an Fheòir for Haymarket in Edinburgh. In addition, the new Gaelic presence on the railways was not confined to place names; the rebranding exercise also involved adding a Gaelic strapline on train carriages, with the Gaelic phrase 'Rèile na h-Alba' alternating with 'Scotland's Railway'. Around the same time, Gaelic was also added to police cars and ambulances operating across the country in connection with those services' Gaelic language plans.

The new wave of station signage gave rise to considerable controversy. This was the first time Gaelic was meaningfully represented in the linguistic landscape of Lowland Scotland, and thus for many observers the first time they had ever encountered the language in written form.[29] Some opponents argued that presenting Gaelic in Lowland stations gave a misleading impression of the importance of the language for Scotland (Jack 2010), 'overemphasising one slice of a many-banded core sample pulled from the earth', while others contended that it constituted a 'spurious' nationalist 'vanity project' that aimed to create an artificial symbolic difference between Scotland and England (Wilson 2017).

The bilingual signage policy was underpinned by language planning objectives. According to BnG's director of research, extension of bilingual signage into areas where Gaelic has not been spoken in recent centuries involves 'pushing the bounds for the language': 'it is about promotion, not the past, but using the past to lend credence to the promotion of the status of the language' (Morgan 2012: 54). In addition to status planning aspects, though, there are significant corpus planning issues involved in determining the correct (or most appropriate) Gaelic form of a particular name when this is not in widespread current use. A dedicated agency, Ainmean-Àite na h-Alba,[30] was established in 2006 to give authoritative advice to public bodies on these matters, underpinned by specialist research. In some cases, it is recommended not to produce a Gaelic form 'if a placename is of non-Celtic derivation, has an etymology not readily transparent to the average speaker of Scottish Standard English, and has no established Gaelic form or alternative' (Morgan 2012: 54).

The broader sociolinguistic impact of these various initiatives to increase the presence of Gaelic in the linguistic landscape is uncertain. Drawing on the Irish experience, Tadhg Ó hIfearnáin has warned:

> The institutionalisation of Gaelic in the public domain may lead to more confidence in the community of speakers, in turn leading to more usage and transmission to the youth and learners, but unless the development of this area of public policy is managed with this in mind, the linguistic landscape may simply come to reflect the position that Gaelic already has in the lives of the vast majority of the population. (Ó hIfearnáin 2010: 37–8)

Much then remains to be done to ensure that the strategic potential of these measures is secured.

GAELIC AS A WRITTEN LANGUAGE

One of the striking developments of the twenty-first century has been the significant growth in written Gaelic: without question, Gaelic is now more written than at any previous point in history. This growth has taken place in several distinct fields, from book publishing to official documents to social media, and has multiple different causes. Given the long-standing exclusion of Gaelic from education and formal domains, this has been a substantial shift, although there is a significant mismatch between production and consumption: some written Gaelic material may not actually be much read.

Formal planning initiatives are responsible for some of this transformation. As discussed above, status planning for Gaelic in the public sector has generated the production of Gaelic versions of many public documents and other kinds of web content, particularly in connection with the implementation of the Gaelic Language Act. Here in particular, it is not clear to what extent production generates actual consumption, or production is based upon actual demand; at worst, Gaelic material is produced as a 'box-ticking exercise'.

A very different kind of initiative has been the development of Gaelic prose fiction, particularly novels, since 2003, as the result of strategic development initiatives from the Gaelic Books Council, especially the Ùr-Sgeul project between 2003 and 2013 (Storey 2011). More than fifty novels for adults have been published in the twenty-first century, compared to fewer than a dozen before 2000. There are considerable challenges in relation to the distribution and consumption of Gaelic fiction, but the very fact of its production is important, in terms of developing the linguistic and indeed imaginative range of the language.

There has also been a significant growth in academic writing through the medium of Gaelic, including books, journal articles and university theses. Until the late 1990s almost no published academic work was written in Gaelic. Here the shift appears to have resulted from a culture change in the academic community rather than any kind of strategic initiative. SMO, which began offering Gaelic-medium undergraduate degrees in 2000, has played an important role, as has the biannual academic conference Rannsachadh na Gàidhlig (Researching Gaelic) that has been held from 2000 onwards (McLeod 2013b).

The rapid growth of various forms of electronic communication, especially text messaging and social media platforms such as Facebook and Twitter, has led to a major increase in the popular use of Gaelic, although it is clear that most Gaelic speakers tend to use English much more frequently than Gaelic for these purposes. Importantly, much in contrast to official documents or literary novels, this kind of written language use is typically informal, unregulated and 'bottom-up' in nature. The growing use of Gaelic for electronic communication, coupled with the ever-increasing amount of Gaelic content on the internet, has helped break down geographical barriers and build 'virtual Gaelic communities'. In the future, as the role of electronic communication increases and the role of the language in traditional communities continues to decline, the importance of such virtual communities is likely to increase. The nature of electronic communication is evolving so rapidly, however, that is difficult to predict how such communities will function in years to come.

DEVELOPMENTS IN CORPUS PLANNING AND LANGUAGE TECHNOLOGY

Corpus planning has been relatively neglected within Gaelic development, particularly in terms of work involving grammatical standardisation, terminological development, lexicography and style. A variety of language resources are vital if the language is to be used effectively in particular settings, especially those of a professional or specialist nature (McLeod 2004). There have been significant developments in corpus planning in the twenty-first century, however, with digital technology playing a central role in most of them. A range of computer-based language resources such as apps and games have been created (McEwan 2015). Commentators have argued that it is essential for minority languages to have a presence in the technological domain, given the importance of technology in the lives of young people. 'Through an association with technology a language may be perceived as relevant, modern, cool or even sexy and young people may be more inclined to use it', while 'if a language is seen as archaic, rural or old-fashioned, then people, especially young people, may be less inclined to use it' (Keegan and Cunliffe 2014: 388).

Proposals for a Gaelic Academy that would coordinate linguistic development work in Gaelic have received only limited support from the Bòrd and the Scottish Government. Instead of a 'bricks and mortar' academy, the Bòrd established a Corpus Support Group whose membership consists of expert native speakers. In this connection two important projects have been commissioned concerning linguistic development and standardisation. The first of these resulted in the *Dluth is Inneach* report on the linguistic and institutional foundations for Gaelic corpus planning (Bell et al. 2014). A second inter-university project, LEACAG, generated guidance on key issues in Gaelic grammar that give rise to uncertainty among users (Ross et al. [2018]).

A longer-term project is Faclair na Gàidhlig (www.faclair.ac.uk), an inter-university initiative to produce a historical dictionary of Gaelic. Over the course of the next several decades the project will generate multiple outputs and applications to serve different kinds of users. A related project is DASG (Digital Archive of Scottish Gaelic) (www.dasg.ac.uk), a large online repository of digitised texts and lexical resources for Gaelic, including the corpus which will serve as the basis for the dictionary (Pike 2019).

Am Faclair Beag ('The Little Dictionary') (www.faclair.com), perhaps the most widely used new language resource, is unusual because it was developed without any official support. This initiative involved digitising Dwelly's classic dictionary from the early twentieth century and supplementing it with new words reflecting current usage. It was developed by two individual technicians, Michael Bauer and Will Robertson.

CONCLUSION

With the Gaelic Language Act and the launch of BBC ALBA, provision for Gaelic in Scotland reached a new level of institutionalisation. The implementation of the Act and other initiatives has clearly brought greatly enhanced status and prominence to the language. The language has greater visibility than ever before and the range of actors making provision for the language has expanded very considerably.

Even so, by 2020 there was a widespread sense of disappointment at the direction of Gaelic development and unease about the overall situation of the language. In the eyes of many, the Gaelic Language Act has brought relatively limited results and Bòrd na Gàidhlig has not been able to provide astute or inspiring leadership. Alongside this, there was pervasive concern about the decline of the language in the traditional communities and the perceived 'disconnect between the carriers of the language and the professionalised language and media sector' (Maclean 2019: 255). For every indicator of regeneration or growth, then, there are other, less positive, indicators.

Despite this widespread unease, there has been little focused discussion on alternative strategic approaches. One possibility that has been advanced is that of new language legislation. This might entail replacing the current Gaelic Language Act with an act that gives more concrete rights to Gaelic speakers, with a language commissioner overseeing compliance. On the other hand, the recent history of both the *Welsh Language (Wales) Measure* and the *Official Languages Act* in Ireland suggests that designing effective and politically acceptable language legislation is no simple matter.

However, it is not necessarily the case that Bòrd na Gàidhlig's difficulties really result from the Gaelic Language Act itself. More could clearly be done within the existing framework, particularly if the Bòrd had greater capacity in terms of the number of staff and the range of their skills. Audit Scotland's critical 2019 report on the Bòrd may provide a valuable opportunity for a careful re-examination of the purpose, capacity and potential of the Bòrd. More importantly, such an evaluation might allow for fresh strategic thinking concerning the future course of Gaelic development more generally. If there is to be meaningful progress, however, new ideas would need to be backed by significantly increased funding, and this would require a level of political will that has been lacking up to now.

Conclusion

IN THE TWENTY-FIRST CENTURY the position of Gaelic in Scotland has become increasingly paradoxical. In terms of day-to-day community use, Gaelic is the weakest it has ever been, while the public status of the language and the level of institutional provision increase every year. This situation may well be unsustainable.

With the revitalisation initiatives that began in the 1970s, accelerated in the 1980s and solidified in the twenty-first century, Gaelic has come to play a much more prominent role in Scottish life than it has in many centuries. In symbolic terms, Gaelic has become an 'icon of nationhood' in Scotland (Paterson et al. 2014: 447). In functional terms, the language is now embedded in national and local government and other important public institutions, visible in the linguistic landscape and strongly present in the broadcast and digital media. Gaelic has widened its social base with the growth of GME and attracted a wide range of new speakers, all of whom find different kinds of appeal and meaning in the language. Most obviously in Glasgow, there can often be a sense of dynamism, cultural energy and optimism surrounding the language. This feeling could not be more different from the fatalism concerning the future of Gaelic that was so pervasive in the middle of the twentieth century.

Yet despite all the improvements in formal status and institutional recognition in recent decades, the demographic decline of the language continues. The number of people speaking Gaelic has dropped by at least three-quarters since 1891. Indeed, the decline can be considered even more severe than this, as the figures from recent censuses include some people with only a modest command of the language and many who use it relatively infrequently, as against the Gaelic speakers of the nineteenth century, most of whom used it as their principal if not exclusive means of communication. In year after year, decade after decade, once solidly

Gaelic communities have come to use more and more English and less and less Gaelic, sometimes through active choice, sometimes through acquiescence to changing community norms, sometimes perhaps almost unconsciously.

Taking a broad view of the various efforts at language revitalisation since the late nineteenth century, a key factor is the failure to achieve critical mass. Not enough people were directly engaged in Gaelic language organisations and movements, and not enough people were quietly supportive of their efforts. As a result, politicians and policy-makers rarely felt significant pressure to introduce or improve provision for Gaelic. Where one thing might have led to another and then another, as happened in Wales, there was relatively little cumulative progress in Scotland. Even with the recent advances, provision for Gaelic in the education system today is less extensive than it was for Welsh in the 1950s, before the modern period of Welsh language revitalisation even began.

There were two main reasons for this failure to achieve critical mass. Within the traditional ethnolinguistic Gaelic community, Gaelic revitalisation was undermined by assimilationism, through which large numbers of Gaels did not see value in the transmission of the language and resisted (actively or quietly) attempts to institutionalise the language, most obviously in the education system. Some became 'Xians v. Yish', to use Joshua Fishman's terminology (Fishman 2001: 481 fn. 1), no longer using the Gaelic language but finding cultural practices or markers other than language that allowed them to assert some kind of continuing Gaelic identity. Indeed, this approach was long evident within An Comunn itself, with its tartan-clad choir members who often could speak almost no Gaelic. In a more direct way, exogamous marriages and consequent non-transmission of the language brought about a steady diminution of the language community.

At the same time, calls to attract the wider Scottish population to Gaelic never succeeded on a large scale, as has happened in the Basque Country since the return of democracy in the 1970s (Urla 2012). Determining the reasons that something does not occur is an inherently difficult undertaking but the best explanation for this failure to awaken is the extent of the social dislocation of Gaelic in Scotland. By the end of the nineteenth century, Gaelic was spoken by less than 7 per cent of the Scottish population and retained social vitality only in some of the poorest and remotest parts of the country. The great bulk of the Scottish population were living in areas where Gaelic had not been spoken for more than half a millennium and most of them would have had no awareness that the language had ever been used in their own families and communities. Generations of campaigners pressed the case for recognising Gaelic as a key element in Scottish identity, yet recent surveys suggest that these claims have penetrated only to a modest extent. Some activists have expressed the belief that the wider transformative impact of Scottish independence, should that arrive, might bring a dramatic change in the fortunes of Gaelic in Scotland, but there is little concrete evidence that might support this optimistic view.

The case was thus very different from that of Irish in Ireland, even though the social base of Irish speaking in isolated, impoverished rural communities was very similar to that of Gaelic. Irish had been spoken by a majority of the Irish people until at least the end of the eighteenth century (FitzGerald 1984) and most people retained some sense of familial connection to the language (even if the process of language shift had often been traumatic and given rise to complex, often negative feelings). This sense of connection made it possible for Conradh na Gaeilge to attract support from a substantial section of Irish society for its programme of language revival, and more importantly for that revivalist vision to become embedded in the foundational ideology of the Irish Free State from 1922 onwards. Even so, the limited success of the Irish revival project after 1922 testifies to the challenges of revitalising a minority language that has undergone severe sociolinguistic dislocation.

In the case of Gaelic in Scotland, it is possible to imagine various ways in which different kinds of political and cultural movements might have emerged in the Gàidhealtachd and could have integrated language revitalisation into a wider programme of social and economic transformation. This could have happened in the late nineteenth century with the crofters' movements, for example, or with the post-1945 programme of modernisation. Counterfactual speculation is usually of limited value but in this instance it is easy to identify the difficulties. Gaelic was already too sociolinguistically and ideologically marginalised and could not be effectively incorporated into the dominant visions of the future, whether that be the promise of Britishness and Empire, industrialisation and 'progress' in the nineteenth century or the post-war prospect of modernisation, consumerism and the new welfare state.

By the same token, it might have been possible for the SNP to have incorporated a stronger Gaelic element into its ideology and political programme following its successes from the 1960s onwards, but this would have gone against the grain of nationalist politics for most of the twentieth century, and its electoral appeal would probably have been limited. Even today, the SNP's approach to Gaelic remains cautious. At the same time, though, it is unquestionable that the main force that has brought about increased institutional and popular support for Gaelic in recent decades is the sense of Gaelic as a national concern that is important for Scotland as a whole. Without this perceived national dimension for Gaelic, it is certain that much of the current provision, most notably the television service, would not exist.

It is also possible to imagine how other approaches to Gaelic development strategy might have brought different outcomes. Was the gradual, albeit rarely explicit, shift to a national, Scotland-wide rather than regional approach after the 1980s appropriate? Might greater emphasis on strong language support programmes in the core Gaelic areas have brought better outcomes? Certainly it is not difficult to imagine that 25,000 speakers in a solidly Gaelic Western Isles, with Gaelic secure as the normal language of community interaction and institutions, would be a stronger foundation for the survival of Gaelic than the actual situation of 57,000 speakers, most of them scattered in low-density sociolinguistic environments and with language use and transmission breaking down even in core areas such as Shawbost. Arguments to this effect are commonplace, indeed stereotyped, in Gaelic circles (e.g. J. MacLeod 2005).

Yet such speculation again fails to engage with the social and ideological reality. In social, economic and institutional terms, the Western Isles are tightly integrated with the rest of Scotland, and in-migration and tourism have had a significant impact on community dynamics. Language policy in the Western Isles, including its educational aspects, reflected the choices and preferences of the people of the islands, including their choices at the ballot box. Much stronger policies were adopted in northwest Wales but these were the outcomes of democratic decision-making – local parents demanded a strong role for Welsh in education in a way that their counterparts in the Western Isles did not. In the Western Isles, deeply rooted language ideologies that devalued Gaelic remained in play, often reinforced by people's direct personal experience that Gaelic had brought them no benefit in life (Campbell 2011).

Crucially, no basis for a viable programme to stem Gaelic–English language shift in rural communities – a process that took effect in district after district, decade after decade – has yet been developed. Indeed, the challenges have become ever-greater given the recent decline of Gaelic in the Western Isles. Today, even in the rural districts more than a third of the local population does not know Gaelic, so that broad-based community-level interventions or support programmes involving employment or housing, such as those proposed by the campaigning group Misneachd (2018), become ever-more impracticable as mechanisms to secure language maintenance and transmission. The deep-rooted structural problems affecting the islands go far beyond issues of language, and are mirrored in many other rural areas of Europe.

If sights are lowered and specific aspects of language policy are considered in more detail, it is more plausible to imagine that outcomes in particular fields could have been more favourable, and that incremental, cumulative progress could have brought provision for Gaelic a good deal further along. To consider the field of education, all of the following scenarios were far from impossible, even taking into account the actual constraints that were presented. School boards' expressed interest in Gaelic teaching in the 1870s might have been harnessed more effectively; the 'Gaelic clause' in the *Education (Scotland) Act 1918* might have been applied more vigorously; Gaelic teaching might have spread to many more Lowland schools in the 1950s and beyond; the Bilingual Education Project of the 1970s might have developed into a viable programme to ensure that all pupils in the Western Isles left school with a solid command of Gaelic; the rapid geographical expansion of GME might have continued after the end of the 1990s; effective secondary GME might have developed in the Western Isles and elsewhere from the 1990s onwards; the college immersion courses of the late 1990s might have been strengthened and expanded, rather than allowed to wither; Bòrd na Gàidhlig might have pushed local authorities to increase significantly their provision for Gaelic education in their statutory Gaelic language plans; and Gaelic might have obtained a secure position in the '1+2' languages programme. Taken together, all of these developments would have produced a much more robust Gaelic education system.

If this failure to achieve critical mass for Gaelic meant that there was too little progress, much of the progress that has been made also probably came too late. For example, by the time CnE was established and it introduced its bilingualisation programme, a 'tipping point' in terms of language shift (Mertz 1989) had already been reached in island communities, so that a large proportion of the schoolchildren served by the Bilingual Education Project were not first-language Gaelic speakers. If such measures had been introduced a generation earlier, when community language use was stronger, their impact might have been more significant. More generally, the institutional provision that began to thicken in the 1980s and gathered pace in the twenty-first century came at a time when the position of Gaelic in traditional communities had already become very precarious. This 'too little too late' dynamic appears to be typical of minority language revitalisation initiatives, however, as language shift only tends to attract significant concern once it has become undeniable (Edwards 2010: 48–9).

The unduly pessimistic predictions of the 1950s that Gaelic would be dead by 2020 suggest that it may be unwise to make confident forecasts concerning the future of Gaelic. As use of the language in traditional island communities declines even as 'energy centres' develop elsewhere, it seems that the most likely scenario is that Gaelic will become a language of second-language speakers in specific social networks of different degrees of thickness, some of them in the Gàidhealtachd, some elsewhere, often sustained through institutional structures such as school education and facilitated by information and communication technology. For most of these speakers Gaelic might then be used only in particular contexts and situations rather than as their main language of daily life. A growing number might be so-called 'neo-native' speakers, however, acquiring Gaelic in the home in early childhood from a parent or parents who themselves learned Gaelic.

For many observers, linguistic survival of such a kind would be artificial or even meaningless. For some, Gaelic would become something like Latin, which continued as an ecclesiastical and intellectual language long after it went out of popular use. Others question whether such a kind of survival is viable at all. At the moment, in Scotland as in Wales and Ireland, rural communities with dense networks of speakers have served as 'a core reserve sending out pulses of speakers which keep the language alive over a broader territory' (Aitchison and Carter 2004: 134; see Ó Tuathaigh 2008: 41). Urban Gaelic communities rely heavily on such speakers, and on the idea of a 'heartland', as a source not only of linguistic authority and authenticity but also of social and cultural meaning. It may be that much of the energy driving Gaelic revitalisation at the national level would dissipate without the continuing production of speakers in traditional communities.

Not all observers despair of this new dynamic. The novelist Andrew Dunn, a native speaker from Lewis, expressed a different perspective:

> Every single one of us who speaks the language is a Gael, and to hell with when we learned the language or whether we had a Gaelic family or what dialect we speak or where we're from or what colour our skin is [. . .] We can see people from all over the world who have learned Gaelic taking part in our culture, and some of them even writing songs or books in Gaelic.
>
> Perhaps now the time has come to grow used to the concept of the new community: that we are all a part of the Gaelic diaspora, and that we don't need to pine for the communities of old. Those communities are gone, and will never come back; that way of life is lost, and it had a lot of aspects we

wouldn't want to get back anyway. Shouldn't we instead look to the future, and work together to build community ties in a form that's suitable for the age we live in? I don't see any other way to go, myself. (Dunn 2015)

To return to Kenneth Jackson's prediction, given in the Introduction, that Gaelic would 'be quite extinct by the middle of the next century' and that nothing would be left other than 'a few people' in Lewis 'who can remember it' (Jackson 1958: 230, 232), it is entirely possible that such a wholesale language decline might have taken place in the absence of the support programmes brought in from the 1970s onwards. Simply put, many thousands of people know and use Gaelic today who would not do so if there had not been such great improvements in the status of the language and provision to support its maintenance over the last forty years. From the perspective of 2020, it is difficult to foresee a more fundamental transformation in the sociolinguistic position of the language, but it is important to recognise the impact of the successful policies that have been introduced, even if the degree of that success is much less than many observers would desire.

Notes

INTRODUCTION

1. Legal citations for all statutes, treaties and court decisions referred to in the text are given at the end of the Bibliography.
2. This organisation is typically known as 'An Comunn', which literally means simply 'The Association'. The English title 'The Highland Association' was formerly used alongside the Gaelic version but the organisation is now always known by its Gaelic name. The abbreviation ACG is used in this book for referencing purposes but is not common.
3. MacKinnon's 1991 *Gaelic: A Past and Future Prospect* is essentially an expanded and updated version of his 1974 *The Lion's Tongue*. The Gaelic version of Hutchinson's 2005 *A Waxing Moon* is significantly shorter but contains information not given in the English version.
4. There have been extensive debates concerning the terminology and concepts applicable to these fields (e.g. Sallabank 2014: 8–11, 24–8). This book uses the most widely accepted terms and does not attempt to make a further contribution to these debates.

CHAPTER 1

1. The distinction between so-called P- and Q-Celtic languages relates to a sound change by which the proto-Celtic sound $*k^w$ became a p (voiceless labial stop) in the P-Celtic languages (Fife 2009: 5–6).
2. Gaelic remained in use in the far southwest, in Galloway and Carrick, until at least the sixteenth century (Livingston 2012). In this part of Scotland the language was introduced not through the expansion of the kingdom of Alba but by the hybrid Norse-Gaelic settlers known as the Gall-Ghàidheil (Clancy 2011: 374).
3. This passage is quoted in almost all accounts of Highland and Gaelic history, but the translation here is taken from Grant 1994: 76–7 and

4. The Latin word *Scotus* is the ethnonym corresponding to 'Gael' so that using the same root form to refer to the language spoken by this people is effectively unavoidable. The claim that the Gaels 'gave Scotland its name' is a common discursive trope (e.g. Campbell 1950: 15).
5. This usage is connected to the English set phrase 'the Highlands and Islands', directly mapped on to Gaelic as 'a' Ghàidhealtachd 's na h-Eileanan'.
6. James became James VI of Scotland in 1567 and then James I of England in 1603 following the death of his distant cousin Queen Elizabeth.
7. The principal enactment was *An act for the abolition and proscription of the Highland dress*.
8. An earlier version of the Bible in Classical Gaelic, the literary form used by the learned classes of Ireland and Scotland in the late Middle Ages, had been introduced in 1690, but this had limited circulation and impact (Durkacz 1983: 20–3).
9. This idea has become something of a trope, even used by Prince Charles in a speech at Sabhal Mòr Ostaig in 2004 (Prince of Wales 2004).
10. Data for this table is taken from Withers and MacKinnon 1983; General Register Office for Scotland 2005; and NRS 2015.
11. No census was conducted in 1941 due to the Second World War. The figure for intercensal change given here therefore represents twenty years rather than ten. The rate of change per decade between 1931 and 1951 was −14.9, close to the figures for 1921–31 and 1951–61.
12. The term 'Western Isles' traditionally referred to all the Hebridean islands off the west coast of Scotland, in contradistinction to the 'Northern Isles' of Orkney and Shetland. The use of 'Western Isles' for the so-called Long Island from Lewis to Barra is of relatively recent origin but is now firmly established.
13. There are no reliable data for the numbers of Gaelic speakers outside Scotland. In the 2011 census, fifty-eight residents of England and Wales declared Gaelic to be their 'main language', but the number with speaking ability would certainly be much higher (www.nomisweb.co.uk/census/2011, Table QS204EW). In the Canadian census of 2016, 3,980 people reported that they could conduct a conversation in Gaelic (Statistics Canada 2017).
14. Conversely, in 2011 47.1 per cent of children aged 3–15 who could speak Gaelic did not have a Gaelic-speaking parent (NRS 2014, CT_0217_2011), reflecting the decision of non-Gaelic-speaking parents to send their children to Gaelic-medium education.

Note: the list begins mid-item with "Barrow 1980: 146, rather than the more commonly used version by Felix Skene (Skene 1871: 38), whose accuracy has been questioned. On the dating of the text, see Broun 2009."

CHAPTER 2

1. This enactment is now conventionally known as the Act of Union of 1536 but the formal title is *An Acte for Laws & Justice to be ministred in Wales in like fourme as it is in this Realme* (Owen 1908: 87).
2. In 1961 there were 656,002 Welsh speakers in Wales, 26 per cent of the population, as against 80,978 Gaelic speakers in Scotland, 1.6 per cent of the population. In 2011 the respective figures were 562,016 (19 per cent) and 57,602 (1.1 per cent) (Davies 2014: 104; Statistics for Wales 2012).
3. In Macpherson's 'Ossian', the legendary warrior Fionn mac Cumhaill became 'Fingal' and his warrior-band the 'Fingalians' rather than the Fianna.
4. This designation is now commonplace in Scotland even though there was no Queen Elizabeth I in Scotland, the first English queen of that name having reigned prior to the Union of Crowns in 1603.
5. Prince Charles has become something of an enthusiast for Gaelic, adding a substantial Gaelic section to his personal website (http://www.princeofwales.gov.uk/gaidhlig/) alongside the Welsh. At the 2010 Mòd, held in Caithness, the prince even waded into a current controversy concerning the implementation of Highland Council's Gaelic Language Plan in Caithness (BBC News 2010a).
6. NRS CH8/212/1, ff. 81–3 (quoted in Withers 1988: 15).
7. These included three of Scotland's ducal families, the highest aristocratic rank (the dukes of Argyll, Atholl and Montrose).
8. Weekly newspapers were produced in 1892–1904 (*Mac-Talla*), 1908–9 (*Alba*) and 1920–1 (a second iteration of *Alba*). *Sruth* was published fortnightly between 1967 and 1970 (and with less frequency until 1979) and *An Gàidheal Ùr* monthly between 1998 and 2009.

CHAPTER 3

1. The word *Gàidhealach* should be spelled with a grave accent according to the current Gaelic Orthographic Conventions (SQA 2009), and An Comunn now uses the accent on its name, but usage in the past was variable.
2. This phrase was used by Sir Donald Walter Cameron of Locheil in a speech in 1930 (*EEN* 1930).
3. There is no connection between this publication and the previous journal with this title published between 1871 and 1877. The abbreviation *AG* is used for both in bibliographic entries, however.
4. Suspicions were raised concerning the identity of 'Fiona MacLeod' almost immediately. Among other things, Fiona is not a traditional Gaelic name and would have been very uncommon among native Gaels in the late nineteenth century. It actually appears to have been invented by James Macpherson.

5. Erskine wrote 'Marr' with two rs instead of the established 'Mar' used by the earls of that name since the Middle Ages. His name is often misspelled as a result. The Gaelic form of his name that he adopted was Ruaraidh Arascainn is Mhàirr and the doubling of the r may have been intended to align with the Gaelic spelling, also used for the region in Deeside (Ó Baoill 2000). The Christian name Ruaraidh is more commonly spelled Ruairidh; another prominent user of the spelling Ruaraidh was the Gaelic scholar and poet Ruaraidh MacThòmais (Derick Thomson).
6. The phrase 'aiseirigh na seann chànain Albannaich' ('resurrection of the old Scottish language') was an allusion to the title of the first Gaelic poetry collection, published by Alasdair mac Mhaighstir Alasdair (Alexander MacDonald) in 1751.
7. The Earl of Mar in 1907 was actually named Walter rather than John. The reference in the document appears to be to the Earl of Mar who led the Jacobite forces in the rising of 1715.
8. In fact, the 1901 census showed that there were 55,003 Gaelic speakers in Inverness-shire and 37,741 in Argyllshire, as against 22,530 in Glasgow.
9. For one exception, see 'Thule' (1924), who challenged the claim that Gaelic was once spoken in the Lowlands, characterising Gaelic as 'a sickly plant which droops and dies away from its own soil' and the Gaels as 'ever famed for [. . .] lawlessness and barbarity'.
10. The International Celtic Congress holds an annual conference, including one in Perth in 2017. It is not to be confused with the International Congress of Celtic Studies, an academic conference that has been held quadrennially since 1959.
11. This labelling of Ireland as 'Scotia Major' and Scotland as 'Scotia Minor' was typical of what might be called the 'superiority complex' that has characterised Irish views of Gaelic Scotland since the Middle Ages (see McLeod 2004a, 2008a).
12. The department was known as the 'Scotch' Education Department until 1918, when it became the Scottish Education Department. In 1991 it became the Scottish Office Education Department and (following several intermediate changes) its functions are now carried out by the Learning Directorate of the Scottish Government and the executive agency Education Scotland. The use of the adjective 'Scotch' was common in Scotland in the nineteenth century but its acceptable use is now limited to a few particular contexts, notably whisky.
13. At this time the Lord President was the cabinet member responsible for the education system, among other duties. The office of Secretary for Scotland (Secretary of State for Scotland after 1926) was created in 1885.
14. The first footnote related to Article 17(i) of the Code and the second to Article 19 c 3. The kind of 'person' in question was a pupil teacher.
15. For a useful summary of the system of school finance in this period, see M. K. MacLeod 1981: 51–3.

16. Such meetings were held in, for example, 1874, 1876, 1878, 1886, 1897, 1904, 1905, 1906, 1908 and 1917 (e.g. *Courier & Argus* 1874; GSI 1878b: 11; *Aberdeen Weekly Journal* 1878; *GH* 1886; *Aberdeen Weekly Journal* 1897; *Celtic Monthly* 1904; Mackay 1906; GSI 1910; *DG* 1908a, 1917b).
17. The same school logbook also contains a remarkable entry from 26 February 1864 (possibly several decades before the other incident): 'Master reproved scholars for speaking Gaelic to one another & exhorted them to form the habit of expressing themselves in Victoria's language' (Perth & Kinross Archives MS CC1/5/7/33). It is entirely possible that pupils who failed to form this habit might have been punished physically, and the phrase 'Victoria's language' is significant in itself.
18. The Aberdeen chair has been vacant since 2002, however, when the first Professor, Donald Meek, moved to the University of Edinburgh.
19. *Martin* v. *MacLean*, [1844] 6 Dunlop 981.
20. The legislation concerning Wales, the *Proceedings in Courts of Justice Act 1730* and the *Courts in Wales and Chester Act 1732*, was repealed by the *Civil Procedure Acts Repeal Act 1879* and superseded by the *Welsh Language Act 1967* (s. 1) and then by the *Welsh Language Act 1993* (s. 22). The *Proceedings in Courts of Justice Act* did apply to the Scottish Court of Exchequer, which dealt with issues concerning customs and excise, revenue, stamp duty and probate, until its abolition in 1856. The Irish legislation, the *Administration of Justice (Language) Act (Ireland) 1737*, remains in effect in Northern Ireland and a recent application for judicial review challenging its continuing validity was dismissed (*In Re MacGiolla Cathain's Application for Judicial Review*, [2009] NIQB 66).
21. A sheriff in Scotland is not a law enforcement officer but a lower-court judge.
22. 'Procurator fiscal' is the term used in Scotland for a prosecutor in the lower courts.
23. The comparative data are taken from the 1891 census (Parry and Williams 1999: 455; Census Office 1893).
24. The notice is reproduced in Maclean and Carrell 1986: cover and 31.
25. The notice is reproduced on the NRS website, www.nrsscotland.gov.uk/about-us/our-history.
26. A copy of the notice is held in the Special Collections at the University of Edinburgh Library, shelfmark RB.P.129.4.
27. For examples of such private sector posts, see *Greenock Telegraph*, 2 November 1866, 2; *Scotsman*, 31 July 1889, 11; *IC*, 18 February 1908, 1; 23 March 1909, 8; 4 May 1909, 3; 25 May 1909, 8.
28. For example, the Army published bilingual recruitment advertisements in the Gaelic periodical *Gairm* in the 1960s.
29. Five leaflets by Liberal and Conservative candidates for the Argyllshire constituency in the General Elections of 1885, 1892, 1906 and 1910 are held in the Special Collections of Edinburgh University Library, shelfmark

RB.P.129. Among those who issued Gaelic or Gaelic–English materials in other parts of the Gàidhealtachd were Sir William Stirling-Maxwell, Conservative candidate for Perthshire in 1874, and George James Bruce, Highland Land League candidate for Inverness in 1918 (Stirling-Maxwell 1874; Bruce 1918).
30. By denomination, these consisted of Church of Scotland 235, Free Church 166, Roman Catholic Church 36, Baptist Church 12, Episcopal Church 9 and Congregational Church 3 (Murchison 1955: 4).

CHAPTER 4

1. In contrast, in 1929 An Comunn president Sheriff J. MacMaster Campbell expressed the hope that the workforce at the new industrial installations would be composed very largely of Highlanders and 'predicted the opening of big branches of An Comunn at the new Highland industrial centres' (*AG* 1929). This was not to be.
2. The form 'Clann Albain' is grammatically or orthographically incorrect, but the standard form Albann and the dialectal variant Albainn were also sometimes used (Lorimer 1997: 290 fn. 92). The name means 'Children of Scotland'.
3. The use of Gaelic to facilitate exclusion from Australia was not unprecedented. In an earlier incident without such political overtones, Gaelic was used in a dictation test to secure the deportation of three Africans in 1927 (Laing 1959).
4. A small number of the Gaelic speakers living in the Western Isles in 1971 would have been educated elsewhere, in areas not subject to the 'Gaelic clause', but this factor would not have made a significant difference to the overall position. Literacy levels were significantly lower in Catholic communities than Protestant ones, suggesting that some of the reported literacy skills were imparted through the Protestant churches rather than the state education system (MacKinnon 1985: 11–12).
5. In 1930, pursuant to the *Local Government (Scotland) Act 1929*, the separate education authorities established under the 1918 Act in place of the previous school boards were abolished and education became a responsibility of county councils.
6. By 1921 the proportion of Gaelic speakers in the two most Gaelic parishes of Perthshire, Kenmore and Fortingall, had declined to 49.7 per cent and 41.6 per cent respectively, down from 71.9 per cent and 77.5 per cent in 1891 (Duwe 2005: 23). A restrictive understanding of the term 'Gaelic-speaking area' could reasonably have excluded these districts; given that language shift typically involved the breakdown of intergenerational transmission, there would have been few Gaelic-speaking children in the area by the 1920s. In 1925 a request was made to allow for the teaching of Gaelic at one school in the area (Lawers, on Loch Tay-side) but the SED denied

the request on the grounds that it would impose an excessive burden on the single teacher in the school (Young 2016: 191–3).
7. Examples included schools in Ferintosh in the Black Isle in 1923 and Dulnain Bridge near Grantown-on-Spey in 1936 (Ross 1923: 11; *Scotsman* 1936d).
8. Father of Professor Derick Thomson, who played a critical role in the Gaelic movement from the 1950s to the 1990s.
9. The data given to An Comunn may have been incomplete, however, as six students graduated with a degree in Celtic from Aberdeen in 1931. There were three graduates from Edinburgh and twenty-eight from Glasgow that year (*AG* 1932).

CHAPTER 5

1. However, the book received a sharply critical review from the Rev. T. M. Murchison, editor of *An Gaidheal* and a key figure in Gaelic and Highland development in the post-war period (Murchison 1945).
2. The use of the definite article with 'Gaelic' is common and appears to reflect the usage of Gaelic speakers who transferred to English the Gaelic use of the definite article with the names of languages. Nowadays this usage is considered mildly pejorative.
3. This provision was retained in successor legislation, including the currently operative *Crofting Reform (Scotland) Act 2010* (Schedule 1, s. 4).
4. Gaelic publishing was in a poor state at this time, with only about fifteen books published between 1961 and 1965 (MacGill-Fhinnein 1965–6: 135–44). The situation has now improved very significantly; approximately five hundred Gaelic books were published in the period 2005–19.
5. *Education (Scotland) Act 1945*, s. 1(1); *Education (Scotland) Act 1962*, ss. 1(1), 2(2(c), 3(2)(b) and 4(d); *Education (Scotland) Act 1969*, s. 1(1); *Education (Scotland) Act 1980*, s. 1(5)(a)(iii) and 1(5)(b)(iv).
6. In the House of Lords debate on the Education (Scotland) Bill in 1969, an amendment was introduced that would have extended the obligation to include provision for teaching Gaelic to Gaelic-speaking children in non-Gaelic-speaking areas. The amendment was withdrawn in response to the government's argument that this would prove too complex to administer (Hansard 1969).
7. This proposal that Gaelic 'should be given equal status with any other language in the curriculum' was initially advanced in An Comunn's 1936 report on the teaching of Gaelic (ACG 1936: 10).
8. The reports had different authors: the report on primary education was written primarily by W. D. Ritchie, Director of Education for Ayr, and the report on secondary education by J. J. Robertson, Headmaster of Aberdeen Grammar School (Young 1986: 252–7).
9. Different definitions of the term 'first language' were used in the 1957 survey

of primary pupils and the 1959 survey of secondary pupils (Committee on Bilingualism 1961: 23–4).
10. The figure for Lewis was depressed by Stornoway, where only 4 per cent of children were first-language Gaelic speakers. The figures for the parishes in west Lewis were higher than anywhere else in Scotland, with a maximum of 96 per cent in Uig (Committee on Bilingualism 1961: 32).

CHAPTER 6

1. *Radical Scotland* grew out of the earlier journal *Crann-Tàra*, but the name was changed in 1981 as it was felt that the Gaelic title 'drives away potential readership' (*Crann-Tàra* 1981b).
2. Only eleven of the twenty councillors voted for this particular version of the name, with the remainder preferring 'Comhairle nan Eilean Siar', i.e. 'Council of the Western Isles' or 'Western Isles Council' (*SG* 1975a). This alternative version was eventually adopted as the formal legal name in 1997, pursuant to the *Local Government (Gaelic Names) (Scotland) Act 1997*.
3. Sir Iain Noble did propose to attach a Gaelic language condition in relation to a housing development in Sleat in 2001, but this was rejected by the local community council (*WHFP* 2001).
4. The Spàgan books were actually translated from English, with the series having been originally known as *The Monster*.
5. The use of more demotic Gaelic in schoolbooks was not uncontroversial; Derick Thomson decried the use of 'the grossest localisms' and saw the 'high degree of English interference in the Gaelic [...] taught in schools' in the Western Isles as 'the theory of the lowest common denominator', characterised by 'an unpleasant narrowness and parochialism', in contrast to what he described as his own sense of 'historical pride' and 'frankly elitist attitude' (Thomson 1981: 18). Linguistic controversies involving purism or modernising compromises are common in minority language revitalisation contexts (Dorian 1994).
6. During the process of discussion and deliberation, the name of the proposed body was changed from 'Comhairle na Gàidhlig' to 'Comunn na Gàidhlig', which was perceived as being more appropriate for a membership organisation (Campbell 1984: 4).
7. Later in 1981, two further bills concerning Gaelic were introduced in Parliament (*Gaelic Language*, 1980/81 Bill 76; *Gaelic Language* (No. 2), 1980/81 Bill 100) but neither was enacted. These were very limited in scope but would have established a Gaelic Broadcasting Authority, defined the 'Gaelic-speaking areas' and imposed a duty on local authorities in Gaelic-speaking areas to promote the Gaelic arts.
8. MacLeod is not related to Dr Finlay MacLeod. In Gaelic circles the former is known as 'Fionnlagh Strì' or 'Finlay Playgroups', the latter as 'Dr Finlay'.

9. *Immigration Act 1971*, Schedule 1, Appendix A, s. 5A(2)(d).
10. *The Grants for Gaelic Language Education (Scotland) Regulations 1986*, SI 1986 No. 410.
11. Private schools play a very minor role in the Scottish education system, enrolling only 4.1 per cent of pupils (Scottish Council of Independent Schools 2018). Catholic schools are publicly funded and run by the local authorities.
12. Following the restructuring in 1973, the structure of Scottish local government was changed again in 1996, with thirty-two local authorities replacing the nine regional authorities and three island councils.
13. The name of the education department was changed in 1991.
14. Although there are no reliable data, it appears that by the mid-1980s the number of children entering primary school without a good knowledge of English was very small.
15. Noble became a baronet in 1987 and was thereafter referred to as Sir Iain.
16. The population of the parish of Sleat peaked at 2,957 in 1831 but had dropped to a mere 452 in 1971, a decline of almost 85 per cent. By 2011 this had recovered to 913, more than double the 1971 figure. The population of Skye as a whole increased by only 39 per cent between 1971 and 2011.
17. Since its creation, S4C had been funded principally through a levy on independent television licence holders, including, somewhat anomalously, the Scottish companies Grampian and Scottish, who were paying approximately £2.7 million a year. Veljanovski proposed reallocating this funding stream. Further funds would come from the proceeds from the auction of future franchise rights for Channel 3 services (Veljanovski 1989: 56).
18. Borders Television covered the Scottish Borders and Dumfries & Galloway areas and did not make any provision for Gaelic, but these areas had very few Gaelic speakers. Viewers in the Borders area did receive the Gaelic programmes on BBC Scotland and Channel 4, however.
19. In 1995 the BBC broadcast slightly less than either Grampian or Scottish (138 hours) but the share of CTG-funded programmes was significantly higher (60 per cent as against 34 per cent for Grampian and 31 per cent for Scottish). Channel 4 broadcast only four hours in the entire year (Case Associates 1996: 5).
20. Similarly, in 1939, 'Lowlander' complained about Gaelic programming on the radio in terms which would become familiar in later decades, decrying the 'continued pampering' of 'a small minority' who should 'pay for a station to be used for their own particular needs' ('Lowlander' 1939).

CHAPTER 7

1. Specifically, the Standing Orders of the Parliament provide that 'the Parliament shall normally conduct its business in English but members may speak in Scots Gaelic or in any other language with the agreement

of the Presiding Officer' (*Scotland Act 1998 (Transitory and Transitional Provisions)(Standing Orders and Parliamentary Publications) Order 1999*, Schedule, s. 7(1)). The form 'Scots Gaelic' is somewhat unusual. The *British Nationality Act 1981* refers to 'Scottish Gaelic' while other relevant legislation refers simply to 'Gaelic'. The adjectival form 'Scots' is now rare but is always used in the important context of 'Scots law'.

2. With his term 'Gaelic Granny syndrome', Meek was referring to the tendency of politicians who do not speak Gaelic to discover 'Gaelic grannies', Gaelic speakers somewhere in the family tree through whom a connection to Gaelic can be asserted, in warm and fuzzy terms.
3. This report and the follow-up Draft Brief for a Gaelic Language Act were principally drafted by Rob Dunbar and the author.
4. Bòrd Gàidhlig na h-Alba was then replaced with a statutory body with the slightly simpler name Bòrd na Gàidhlig. This body does not have an English title but translates as 'the Gaelic [Language] Board'.
5. In its subsequent submission concerning the actual Gaelic bill in 2004, the CRE stated that it was fully supportive of the general principles of the bill, but expressed 'concerns about the lack of progress on the Scottish Executive's commitment to introduce a National Language Strategy' (CRE 2004).
6. In the course of the legislative process, Peacock gave an updated explication of the basis for the government's view that Gaelic already enjoyed official status, citing 'the fact that we incur spending on the language, that there is a minister with responsibility for it; that various acts of Parliament refer to it; that the Gaelic Language (Scotland) Bill has been introduced; that we answer parliamentary questions in it; [and] that we have debates in Gaelic in the chamber' (SP 2004c, col. 1974).
7. Somewhat surprisingly, the Act does not require that members of the Bòrd have a knowledge of Gaelic. In practice, almost all appointees have been Gaelic speakers, but meetings of the Bòrd are often attended by non-Gaelic-speaking civil servants and thus simultaneous interpretation is provided at meetings.
8. As is conventional in Scottish legislation, the Act actually refers to 'the Scottish Ministers' rather than the Scottish Executive (the term in use in 2005) or the Scottish Government.
9. The Lord Advocate (the chief law officer in Scotland) actually advised that 'while the arguments are finely balanced, it would be within the competence of the Scottish Parliament to include reserved bodies within the scope' of the Act (SE 2004c).
10. The Charter has now ratified been by twenty-five states. The Council of Europe is an international organisation of forty-seven member states that was established in 1949 and is based in Strasbourg. It is entirely separate from the European Union and thus the UK's withdrawal from the European Union has no impact on its commitments under the Charter.

11. The Charter defines 'regional or minority languages' as languages that are 'traditionally used within a given territory of a State by nationals of that State who form a group numerically smaller than the rest of the State's population' and are 'different from the official language(s) of that State' (CoE 1992: Article 1(a)). Importantly, this definition 'does not include either dialects of the official language(s) of the State or the languages of migrants'. In the Scottish context, then, languages that are widely spoken as the result of migration flows, such as Polish, Cantonese or Punjabi, are not covered. The government's designation of Scots under the Charter was seized upon by some activists as an official determination that Scots does not constitute a 'dialect' of English, as otherwise it could not be covered by the Charter.
12. *Act of Sederunt (Rules of the Court of Session Amendment No. 4) (Miscellaneous) 2001*, 2001 No. 305; 'Practice – Use of Gaelic in Civil Proceedings', Act of Court of the Sheriff Principal of Grampian, Highlands and Islands, 11 June 2001.
13. This figure included £1.5 million from the BBC, £650,000 from Grampian and £480,000 from STV in addition to the £8.5 million from the Scottish Office.
14. This was an unforeseen consequence of the compromise of 1989 by which the new funding for Gaelic television was allocated to the budget for the Scottish Office rather than the Home Office (see p. 230).
15. The authority was known as Highland Regional Council until 1996 and Highland Council thereafter. Until 1996 there was an additional layer of district councils, including Lochaber District Council, which authorised the erection of bilingual village name signs in Moidart in 1979 (ACG 1979: [2]).
16. The issue here was not strictly a matter of language; civil servants stated that monolingual Gaelic signs would be compliant with the standard design specifications set out in the relevant legislation. Bilingual signs involved a deviation from these specifications.
17. www.scot-rail.co.uk/page/Gaelic+Station+Names+before+2008 (last accessed 5 January 2020).
18. Following devolution, the former 'Scottish Office' was renamed the 'Scotland Office'.

CHAPTER 8

1. In 2010 the Labour peer Lord Foulkes unsuccessfully introduced an amendment in the House of Lords that would have required the question in the 2011 referendum on the alternative vote system to be given in Gaelic as well as English in Scotland (Hansard 2010). Pursuant to section 8 of the subsequently enacted *Parliamentary Voting System and Constituencies Act 2011* the question was put in Welsh in Wales. The SNP does not make

nominations for the House of Lords and so did not take a position on this issue. In 1984 the SNP had proposed that Gaelic versions of ballot papers be prepared in General Elections (Hansard 1984), but this suggestion has not been taken forward since then.
2. Creative Scotland's Scots policy contained only three pages of substantive content, compared to twenty-four in its current Gaelic Language Plan (Creative Scotland 2019).
3. Chhim and Bélanger's study considered public perceptions of the relative significance of Gaelic and Scots for Scottish identity. West and Graham's study was carried out on behalf of the Scottish Government, which also commissioned a parallel study on attitudes to Scots (TNS-BMRB (2010), but without a comparative Gaelic–Scots element.
4. Campbell had served as the chief executive of the non-statutory Bòrd Gàidhlig na h-Alba since 2003.
5. Note, however, that under section 2(6) of the Act, the National Plan must be approved by the Scottish Ministers.
6. Although this document was published in English only, unlike the two National Plans, it did not have an English title. It translates as 'the new Gaelic generation'.
7. The authorities which have not been notified to prepare a plan are Orkney, Shetland and Scottish Borders.
8. Heriot-Watt University ran short courses in interpretation in 2013, but these did not lead to any formal certification.
9. Several of these authorities pay for transport for pupils wishing to access GME in adjoining authorities (using Specific Grant funding). Such arrangements typically mean long journey times for these pupils, which may deter parents from choosing this option.
10. There was no increase in the overall number of Gaelic units because of school closures in the Western Isles due to falling school rolls. GME was offered in twenty-five primary schools in the Western Isles in 2000–1 but only twenty in 2018–19 (University of Strathclyde 2001; BnG 2019: 13).
11. However, there were 643 Western Isles pupils in GME in 1998–9, when the national total was 1,816. Over the twenty years between 1998–9 and 2018–19, then, the rate of increase in the Western Isles was only 13.7 per cent as against 133 per cent in the rest of Scotland.
12. The authorities in question were Aberdeenshire, Clackmannanshire, Dumfries & Galloway, Dundee, East Renfrewshire, Fife, Moray, North Ayrshire, South Ayrshire, Renfrewshire and West Dunbartonshire. As explained on p. 306, North Ayrshire will offer GME from 2020 onwards.
13. For pupils in GME, English was designated as the first additional language for purposes of the 1+2 scheme, even though it was in fact the mother tongue of the overwhelming majority of them.
14. Schedule 1, section 1 of this Act requires education authorities to consult with parents and other stakeholders if it wishes to 'discontinue the provi-

sion of Gaelic medium education' at any school where it is offered. In Scots law 'interdict' corresponds to an injunction under English and American law, i.e. a prohibitory court order.
15. Section 14 of the Act also authorises the Scottish Ministers to extend the Act by regulations to cover early years and childcare.
16. Information concerning these various programmes is given at www.teagasg.com (last accessed 4 January 2020).
17. https://www.gaidhlig.scot/bord/fundraising/ (Gaelic Education Grants) (last accessed 4 January 2020).
18. www.abdn.ac.uk/study/postgraduate-taught/degree-programmes/959/gaelic-medium-education/ (last accessed 30 November 2019).
19. www.teagasg.com/en/transfer-to-gaelic-education/gaelic-immersion-course-for-teachers/. The author has been involved in the development and delivery of this programme and observations made here are based upon personal knowledge.
20. www.coe.int/en/web/common-european-framework-reference-languages (last accessed 30 November 2019).
21. www.gla.ac.uk/schools/humanities/research/celticgaelicresearch/researchprojects/comasanlabhairtannangaidhlig/ (last accessed 30 November 2019).
22. The survey was completed by 867 learners but they were permitted to cite as many reasons as they liked. The total number of reasons identified was 3,792.
23. The widespread use of the term 'Gael' in English is relatively new; the traditional English form corresponding to *Gàidheal* was 'Highlander' (Watson 1923: 66–7), which now has a rather dated ring to it.
24. There had actually been a limited presence of Gaelic on digital television since 1998, under the terms of the *Multiplex Licence (Broadcasting of Programmes in Gaelic) Order 1996*, which required 'that Gaelic programming be carried for at least 30 minutes per day between the hours of 6pm and 1030pm'. This was provided via a service called TeleG, which re-broadcast programming from STV and later BBC ALBA for an hour each day (Pedersen 2019: 175–7). Once BBC ALBA became available on Freeview, the 1996 order was repealed (*Multiplex Licence (Broadcasting of Programmes in Gaelic) (Revocation) Order 2011*) and TeleG was taken off air.
25. One particular reason for the surge in viewership at this point was that BBC ALBA was broadcasting matches involving Rangers FC, one of the two most popular football teams in Scotland, which had gone into administration in 2012 and subsequently re-entered the lowest division of the Scottish football league (MacKenzie 2018: 17). Rangers quickly achieved promotion, however, and this viewership duly disappeared.
26. This figure is calculated using www.bankofengland.co.uk/monetary-policy/inflation/inflation-calculator, with budget data from Scottish Government 2018 (£11.9 million in 2006–7 and £12.8 million in 2018–19).

27. For rugby matches, a 'red button' was provided that allowed viewers to access commentary in English, but this controversial service was not extended to football matches, which attracted much larger audiences (MacKenzie 2018: 78; *WHFP* 2014).
28. A minor form of institutionalisation that developed in recent years is the official designation by legislation of Gaelic names of public bodies. These include Creative Scotland/Alba Chruthachail, Historic Environment Scotland/Àrainneachd Eachdraidheil na h-Alba and the Scottish Fire and Rescue Service/Seirbheis Smàlaidh agus Teasairginn na h-Alba (*Public Services Reform (Scotland) Act 2010*, s. 36(1); *Historic Environment Scotland Act 2014*, s. 1(1); *Police and Fire Reform (Scotland) Act 2012*, s. 101(1)).
29. The 2012 Scottish Social Attitudes Survey (see pp. 279–80) found that 58 per cent of respondents reported having seen Gaelic on a public sign in the preceding month (O'Hanlon et al. 2013: [2]). It is highly unlikely that the figure would have been anywhere near as high before the introduction of bilingual signs at Lowland railway stations.
30. This organisation does not have an English version of its name but translates as 'Placenames of Scotland'.

Appendix: Timeline of Gaelic Policy from 1871

1871   Gaelic Society of Inverness established
1872   *Education (Scotland) Act 1872* enacted
1882   Chair of Celtic created at the University of Edinburgh
1885   'Highland Minute' grants new concessions for Gaelic in education
1886   *Crofters (Scotland) Act 1886* enacted
1891   An Comunn Gaidhealach established
1892   First Mòd held
1918   'Gaelic clause' added to *Education (Scotland) Act 1918*
1923   First Gaelic radio broadcast
1930   Gaelic League of Scotland established
1947   Gaelic introduced in first Lowland schools
1952   Journal *Gairm* established
       First Gaelic television broadcast
1954   First Gaelic street signs erected, in Port Charlotte, Islay
1956   Bilingual scheme begins in Inverness-shire primary schools
1965   Highlands and Islands Development Board established
1968   Gaelic Books Council established
1974   Sabhal Mòr Ostaig established
1975   Comhairle nan Eilean established; Bilingual Policy agreed; Bilingual Education Project begins in primary schools
1979   Unsuccessful referendum on establishing a Scottish Assembly
1981   Donald Stewart introduces unsuccessful Gaelic bill in Parliament
1982   *Cor na Gàidhlig* report published
1984   Comunn na Gàidhlig established
1985   Gaelic-medium education begins, in Glasgow and Inverness
       Radio nan Gàidheal established
1986   Specific Grants for Gaelic Education scheme established

1990 Gaelic Television Fund established pursuant to the *Broadcasting Act 1990*
1997 Comunn na Gàidhlig publishes recommendations on Secure Status for Gaelic
1999 Opening of the Scottish Parliament
First dedicated Gaelic primary school opens, in Glasgow
2001 UK government ratifies the European Charter for Regional or Minority Languages
2005 *Gaelic Language (Scotland) Act 2005* enacted; Bòrd na Gàidhlig established
2006 First dedicated Gaelic secondary school opens, in Glasgow
2007 First National Gaelic Language Plan and first statutory Gaelic language plans published
2008 BBC ALBA television service launched
2014 Unsuccessful referendum on Scottish independence
2016 *Education (Scotland) Act 2016* places new obligations on local authorities to respond to demands for Gaelic-medium education

Bibliography

Aberdeen Daily Journal (1903), 'Gaelic for the Army', 4 June, 4.
Aberdeen Daily Journal (1921), 'The Decline of the Gaelic', 30 December, 4.
Aberdeenshire Council (2017), *Aberdeenshire Council – Scots Language Guidelines*, http://dywaberdeenshire.org/wp-content/uploads/2017/08/Aberdeenshire-Doric-Guidelines-Feb-17.pdf (last accessed 12 October 2019).
Aberdeen University Review (1916), 'Lectureship in Celtic', 3, 172–3.
ACG (1891), *Manifesto*, Oban: ACG.
ACG (1893), *Scottish Gaelic as a Specific Subject*, Oban: ACG.
ACG (1904), Appeal for the Magazine Fund, Oban: ACG.
ACG (1907a), *Feill a' Chomuinn Ghaidhealaich/Highland Association Bazaar*, Glasgow: ACG.
ACG (1907b), *The Teaching of Gaelic in Highland Schools*, Glasgow: ACG.
ACG (1918a), *Facal do na Gàidheil/A Word to the Gaidheal*, Glasgow: ACG.
ACG (1918b), Letter from Margaret Macdonald, Interim Secretary, to Robert Munro, Scottish Secretary, 2 July (NRS ED14/87).
ACG (1928), 'Taghadh Buill Ùghdarrais an Fhoghluim', *AG*, 23, 67–9.
ACG (1930), Memorial by An Comunn Gàidhealach to the Right Honourable The Secretary of State for Scotland and H.M. Lord Advocate for Scotland (NRS HH83/233).
ACG (1935), *Forty-fourth Annual Report*, Glasgow: ACG.
ACG (1935), *Gearr–iomradh air Obair agus Riaghailtean–earalaichaidh Comunn na h–Òigridh/A brief preliminary note on the new Youth Movement in the Gaidhealtachd*, Glasgow: ACG.
ACG (1936), *Report of the Special Committee on the Teaching of Gaelic in Schools and Colleges*, Glasgow: ACG.
ACG (1938a), *Bonn–steidh agus Riaghailtean/Frith-Laghannan / Constitution and Rules/Bye–Laws*, Glasgow: ACG.
ACG (1938b), *Am Measg nam Bodach*, Glasgow: ACG.

ACG (1943a), 'Memorandum for the Advisory Council on Education for Scotland by the Education Committee of An Comunn Gaidhealach', *AG*, 38, 66.

ACG (1943b), 'Additional Memorandum for the Advisory Council on Education for Scotland', *AG*, 38, 88.

ACG (1946), Letter from Neil Shaw, Secretary, to H. Stewart MacIntosh, Director of Education, City of Glasgow Corporation, 27 December (Glasgow City Archives (Mitchell Library) D–ED 11.1.191).

ACG (1948), *Fifty-Seventh Annual Report 1947–48*, Glasgow: ACG.

ACG (1958), *Sixty-Seventh Annual Report 1957–58*, Glasgow: ACG.

ACG (1964), *Seventy-Third Annual Report 1963–64*, Glasgow: ACG.

ACG (1966), Memorandum to William Ross MP, Scottish Secretary, 14 February (NRS HH41/1657/A/3).

ACG (1968), *Annual Report 1967–68*, Inverness: ACG.

ACG (1970), *Annual Report 1969*, Inverness: ACG.

ACG (1972), 'Highland Information Pamphlets' [advertisement], *Gairm*, 79, 196.

ACG (1975), *Polasaidh do'n Ghàidhlig/A Policy for Gaelic*, Inverness: ACG.

ACG (1976), *Bilingual Traffic Signs: Director's Report to the Management Committee*.

ACG (1978a), Letter from Domhnall I. MacIomhair, An Comunn, to Steven Rae, CnE, 26 January (CnE/SG).

ACG (1978b), Letter from Colin Spencer, Education Director, to Roy MacIver, Chief Executive, CnE, 15 February (CnE/SG).

ACG (1979), *Cuairtlitir* (An Giblean), Inverness: ACG.

ACG (1981a), 'The Gaelic (Miscellaneous Provisions) Bill: An Assessment by An Comunn Directorate', *Carn*, 35, 3–5.

ACG (1981b), Letter from Donald MacCuish, President, to George Younger, Scottish Secretary, 5 February (NRS ED61/185).

ACG (1981c), Letter from Dolina MacLennan to George Younger MP, Scottish Secretary, 7 July (NRS HH41/2712).

ACG (1983), 'Proposals on a Scheme to Foster the Learning of Gaelic by Adults' (NRS ED61/196).

Advisory Council on Education in Scotland (1946), *Primary Education: A Report of the Advisory Council on Education in Scotland*, Edinburgh: HMSO.

Advisory Council on Education in Scotland (1947), *Secondary Education: A Report of the Advisory Council on Education in Scotland*, Edinburgh: HMSO.

AG (1872), 'New College – Dr M'Lauchlan's Gaelic Class', 1, 100.

AG (1874a), 'Highland and Welsh Gatherings', 3, 228.

AG (1874b), 'Comunn Ur Gaidhealach', 3, 312–13.

AG (1874c), 'Gaelic Schools of the Church of Scotland', 3, 324.

AG (1877), 'The Reply of the School Boards to the Circular of the Scotch Education Department on the Subject of Teaching Gaelic', 6, 155–60.
AG (1925), 'Executive Meeting', 20, 73–4.
AG (1927), 'The Welsh Report', 23, 40–1.
AG (1929), 'Forward the Gaels', 24, 105.
AG (1930), 'Conference at Inverness', 25, 181–2.
AG (1932), 'The M.A. in Gaelic', 27, 14.
AG (1939), 'Summer School of Gaelic', 34, 119.
AG (1946), 'Litreachas Gàidhlig air son Feachdan an Rìgh', 42, 2.
AG (1948), 'General Council', 43, 72–3.
AG (1949), 'Annual Meeting', 44, 159, 161.
AG (1951), 'Learners' School at Swordale', 46, 94.
AG (1952), 'Notes and Comments – Higher Gaelic', 47, 10.
AG (1954), 'Honouring a Great Gael', 49, 11–14.
AG (1955), 'Executive Council', 50, 114–16.
AG (1957), 'Following Up the Conference: Suggestions for Action', 52, 23–4.
AG (1962), 'Conference Report', 57, 79–82.
AG (1964), 'Gaidhlig is Comunn', 59, 73–4.
AG (1966), 'A Year's Endeavour', 61, 110.
Ahlander, Per G. L. (2009), 'Marjory Kennedy-Fraser (1857–1930) and Her Time: A Contextual Study', PhD thesis, University of Edinburgh.
Aitchison, John and Carter, Harold (2004), *Spreading the Word: The Welsh Language 2001*, Talybont: Y Lolfa.
Aitken, Keith (2004), 'Living language looks dead on its feet to me', *The Express*, 9 September.
Alba (1920a), 'Maighstirean-Sgoile agus a' Ghàidhlig', 1(11), 2.
Alba (1920b), 'Clàr-Iomairt a' Mhòid', 1(16), 4.
Amon, Hermann and James, Eleri (eds) (2019), *Constitutional Pioneers: Language Commissioners and the Protection of Official, Minority and Indigenous Languages*, Toronto: Thomson Reuters.
Anderson, Michael (2012), 'The Demographic Factor', in T. M. Devine and Jenny Wormald (eds), *The Oxford Handbook of Modern Scottish History*, Oxford: OUP, 39–61.
Anderson, R. D. (1995), *Education and the Scottish People 1750–1918*, Oxford: Clarendon Press.
Andrews, Liam (1997), '*The very dogs in Belfast will bark in Irish*: The Unionist Government and the Irish language 1921–43', in Aodán Mac Póilin (ed.), *The Irish Language in Northern Ireland*, Belfast: Iontaobhas Ultach, 49–94.
Ansdell, Douglas (1998), *The People of the Great Faith – The Highland Church 1690–1900*, Stornoway: Acair.
Ansdell, Douglas (2016), personal communication with the author, 9 September.
Argathalian (1876), 'Malairt ann an Gailig', *AG*, 5, 150–1.
Argyll & Bute Council (2017), 'Gaelic Education and Gaelic Specific Grant Funding' (paper for Community Services Committee, 9 March), https://www.

argyll–bute.gov.uk/moderngov/documents/s116878/GaelicSpecificGrantv4. pdf (last accessed 12 October 2019).

Armstrong, Timothy Currie (2018), 'The Language of the Playground: Activists Building Consensus on the Language Policy and Ethos of a New Gaelic Immersion School', in M. MacLeod and Smith-Christmas (2018), 17–31.

Arnold, Matthew (1867), *On the Study of Celtic Literature*, London: Smith, Elder & Co.

Arnold, Matthew (1889), 'General Report for the Year 1852', in Francis Sandford (ed.), *Reports on Elementary Schools 1852–1882 by Matthew Arnold (One of Her Majesty's Inspectors of Schools)*, London: Macmillan, 1–20.

Arts Council of Great Britain, Scottish Committee (1966). Minute of meeting, 17 November (NRS ED61/76).

Aucamp, Anna Jacoba (1926), *Bilingual Education and Nationalism with Special Reference to South Africa*, Pretoria: J. L. Van Schaik.

Auditor General for Scotland (2019), *The 2018/19 audit of Bòrd na Gàidhlig: Governance and transparency*, www.audit-scotland.gov.uk/uploads/docs/report/2019/s22_191213_bord_gaidhlig.pdf (last accessed 3 January 2020).

Azkue, Jokin and Perales, Josu (2005), 'The teaching of Basque to adults', *International Journal of the Sociology of Language*, 174, 73–83.

Baker, Colin and Wright, Wayne J. (eds) (2017), *Foundations of Bilingual Education and Bilingualism*, 6th edn, Bristol: Multilingual Matters.

Ball, Martin and Müller, Nicole (eds) (2008), *The Celtic Languages*, London: Routledge.

Bannerman, John M. (1954), 'President's English Address', *AG*, 49, 82–3.

Barère de Vieuzac, Bertrand (1794), 'Rapport du Comité de salut publique sur les idiomes', http://www.axl.cefan.ulaval.ca/francophonie/barere-rapport.htm (last accessed 1 November 2019).

Barrow, G. W. S. (1980), *The Anglo-Norman Era in Scottish History*, Oxford: Clarendon Press.

Barrow, Geoffrey (2nd edn, 2003). *The Kingdom of the Scots: Government, Church and Society from the Eleventh to the Fourteenth Century*, Edinburgh: EUP.

Basque Autonomous Community Department of Education, Language Policy and Culture (2013), *Fifth Sociolinguistic Survey*, Vitoria-Gasteiz: Basque Autonomous Community.

Bateman, Meg (2015), 'Niall MacLeòid, Bard of Skye and Edinburgh', in Christopher MacLachlan and Ronald W. Renton (eds), *Gael and Lowlander in Scottish Literature: Cross-currents in Scottish Writing in the Nineteenth Century*, Glasgow: Association for Scottish Literary Studies, 172–89.

BBC (1939), *Twelfth Annual Report 1938*, London: BBC.

BBC (1951), 'BBC Memorandum – General Survey of the Broadcasting Service', in *Report of the Broadcasting Committee, 1949 – Appendix H: Memoranda Submitted to the Committee*, London: HMSO, 1–74.

BBC (1955), *Annual Report and Accounts for the Year 1954–55*, London: HMSO.
BBC (1960), *Annual Report and Accounts for the Year 1959–60*, London: HMSO.
BBC (1963), *Annual Report and Accounts for the Year 1962–63*, London: HMSO.
BBC (1964), *BBC Royal Charter*, London: BBC.
BBC (1968), *Annual Report and Accounts for the Year 1967–68*, London: HMSO.
BBC (2007), *BBC Group Annual Report and Accounts 2006/2007*, London: BBC.
BBC (2017a), 'Biggest BBC investment in Scotland in twenty years', www.bbc.co.uk/mediacentre/latestnews/2017/scotland-investment (last accessed 15 October 2019).
BBC (2017b), *BBC Group Annual Report and Accounts 2016/17*, London: BBC.
BBC (2019), *BBC Group Annual Report and Accounts 2018/19*, London: BBC.
BBC Naidheachdan (2013a), 'Comhairle a' diùltadh sgoil Ghàidhlig', www.bbc.co.uk/naidheachdan/23341115 (last accessed 5 January 2020).
BBC Naidheachdan (2013b), 'Crìonadh mòr sa Ghàidhlig anns na h-Eileanan', www.bbc.co.uk/naidheachdan/24954480 (last accessed 12 October 2019).
BBC Naidheachdan (2016), 'Crìochan gan cur air sgoiltean Gàidhlig', www.bbc.co.uk/naidheachdan/35417887 (last accessed 12 October 2019).
BBC Naidheachdan (2017), 'Aonad Gàidhlig ùr san Ros Mhuileach', www.bbc.co.uk/naidheachdan/40458066 (last accessed 12 October 2019).
BBC Naidheachdan (2019a), 'Foghlam Gàidhlig an Glaschu a' fàs', www.bbc.co.uk/naidheachdan/49446895 (last accessed 12 October 2019).
BBC Naidheachdan (2019b), 'Gearain oifigeil fo Achd na Gàidhlig', www.bbc.co.uk/naidheachdan/50019548 (last accessed 12 October 2019).
BBC Naidheachdan (2019c), 'Casg air a' Ghàidhlig sa chùirt', www.bbc.co.uk/naidheachdan/50247522 (last accessed 14 November 2019).
BBC Naidheachdan (2019d), '5% de chòmhraidhean am Barraigh sa Ghàidhlig', www.bbc.co.uk/naidheachdan/48199065 (last accessed 14 November 2019).
BBC News (2010a), 'Prince Charles comments on row over Gaelic in Caithness', www.bbc.co.uk/news/uk-scotland-highlands-islands-11541611 (last accessed 26 October 2019).
BBC News (2016), 'Gaelic broadcaster gets £1m Scottish government funding', www.bbc.co.uk/news/uk-scotland-35855438 (last accessed 26 October 2019).
BBC Trust (2007), *Gaelic Digital Service: Public Value Test provisional conclusions*, London: BBC Trust.
BBC Trust (2008), *Gaelic Digital Service: Public Value Test final conclusions*, London: BBC Trust.
BBC Trust (2010), *BBC ALBA review: Final conclusions*, London: BBC Trust.

Bechhofer, Frank and McCrone, David (2014), 'What makes a Gael? Identity, language and ancestry in the Scottish Gàidhealtachd', *Identities: Global Studies in Culture and Power*, 21, 113–33.
Bélanger, Éric, et al. (2018), *The National Question and Electoral Politics in Quebec and Scotland*, Montreal: McGill-Queen's University Press.
Bell, Susan, et al. (2014), *Dlùth is Inneach – Final Project Report: Linguistic and Institutional Foundations for Gaelic Corpus Planning*, Inverness: BnG.
Benson, Arthur Christopher and Viscount Esher (eds) (1908), *The Letters of Queen Victoria: A Selection From Her Majesty's Correspondence Between the Years 1837 and 1861, Volume 2, 1844–1853*, London: John Murray.
Billings, Cathal (2017), 'Speaking Irish with hurley sticks: Gaelic sports, the Irish language and national identity in revival Ireland', *Sport in History*, 37, 25–50.
Black, Ronald (1986), 'The Gaelic Academy: The Cultural Commitment of the Highland Society of Scotland', *SGS*, 14, 1–38.
Black, Ronald (1999), 'Introduction' to *An Tuil: Duanaire Gàidhlig an 20mh Linn/Anthology of 20th Century Scottish Gaelic Verse*, Edinburgh: Polygon, i–lxx.
Black, Ronald (2008), 'I Thought He Made It All Up: Context and Controversy', in Domhnall Uilleam Stiùbhart (ed.), *The Life & Legacy of Alexander Carmichael*, Port of Ness: Islands Book Trust, 57–81.
Black, Ronald (2010), 'Gaelic Orthography: The Drunk Man's Broad Road', in M. Watson and Macleod (2010), 229–61.
Blackie, John Stuart (1876), 'Ought Gaelic to be Taught in Highland Schools?' *AG*, 5, 343–52.
Blackie, John Stuart (1876), *The Language and Literature of the Scottish Highlands*, Edinburgh: Edmonston and Douglas.
BnG (2003), Consultation submission on the Gaelic Language Bill.
BnG (2007a), *Plana Nàiseanta na Gàidhlig 2007–2012/The National Gaelic Language Plan 2007–2012*, Inverness: BnG.
BnG (2007b), *Stiùireadh air Deasachadh Phlanaichean Gàidhlig/Guidance on the Development of Gaelic Language Plans*, Inverness: BnG.
BnG (2007c), 'Implementation of the Gaelic Language (Scotland) Act 2005 and the National Plan for Gaelic: Public Authority Language Plans' (paper for Bòrd meeting, 1 May) (WCM/FOI).
BnG (2007d), 'Gaelic Language Act Implementation Fund: Draft Policy for Distribution 2007/08' (paper for Bòrd meeting, 1 May) (WCM/FOI).
BnG (2010), *Ginealach Ùr na Gàidhlig: Plana Gnìomha gus àireamh luchd-labhairt na Gàidhlig a mheudachadh/An Action Plan to increase the numbers of Gaelic speakers*, Inverness: BnG.
BnG (2010), Letter from Daibhidh Boag, Director of Language Planning, to Finlay MacLeod, Taic, 7 July (WCM).
BnG (2011), Letter from Alasdair MacKinnon, Head of Finance & Corporate Affairs, to Ronald MacDonald, 13 July, www.whatdotheyknow.com/

request/mygaeliccom_web_site_costdetails#incoming–193473 (last accessed 1 November 2019).
BnG (2012a), *National Gaelic Language Plan 2012–2017: Growth & Improvement*, Inverness: BnG.
BnG (2012b), *Dàta Foghlaim Ghàidhlig/Gaelic Education Data 2011–12*, Inverness: BnG.
BnG (2013), Submission to the Referendum (Scotland) Bill Committee, www.parliament.scot/S4_ReferendumScotlandBillCommittee/Ref_03_Bord_na_Gaidhlig.pdf (last accessed 1 November 2019).
BnG (2014), *Dreachd dhen Stiùireadh Airson a Bhith Dealbh Phlanaichean Cànain Gàidhlig/Draft Guidance on the Development of Gaelic Language Plans*, Inverness: BnG.
BnG (2017), *Statutory Guidance on Gaelic Education*, Inverness: BnG.
BnG (2018a), *National Gaelic Language Plan 2018–2023*, Inverness: BnG.
BnG (2018b), 'Gaelic focus for Urras Oighreachd Ghabhsainn (Galson Estate Trust)', www.gaidhlig.scot/gaelic-focus-for-urras-oighreachd-ghabhsainn-galson-estate-trust/ (last accessed 6 January 2020).
BnG (2019a), *Public Consultation: Draft Plans Guidance*, www.gaidhlig.scot/bord/gaelic-you/public-consultation-draft-plans-guidance/ (last accessed 1 November 2019).
BnG (2019b), *Dàta Foghlaim Ghàidhlig/Gaelic Education Data 2018–19*, Inverness: BnG.
BnG (n.d. a), 'HOW to develop a Gaelic Language Plan', www.gaeliclanguageplansscotland.org.uk/en/how-to-develop/guidance (last accessed 1 November 2019).
BnG (n.d. b), 'Fiosrachadh do Phàrantan', https://fdp.gaidhlig.scot/ (last accessed 3 January 2020).
Board of Agriculture and Fisheries (1913), *Annual Report of the Intelligence Division, Part II*, London: HMSO.
Board of Agriculture for Scotland (1919), *Seventh Report of the Board of Agriculture for Scotland*, Edinburgh: HMSO.
Board of Agriculture for Scotland (1921), *Ninth Report of the Board of Agriculture for Scotland*, Edinburgh: HMSO.
Board of Education for Scotland (1878), *Third Annual Report*, London: HMSO.
Board of Education, Welsh Division (1927), *Welsh in Education and Life*, London: HMSO.
Board of Supervision for the Relief of the Poor in Scotland (1849), *Third Annual Report*, Edinburgh: HMSO.
Board of Supervision for the Relief of the Poor and of Public Health in Scotland (1867), *Twenty-Second Annual Report*, Edinburgh: HMSO.
Board of Supervision for the Relief of the Poor and of Public Health in Scotland (1895), *Forty-Ninth Annual Report*, Edinburgh: HMSO.
Boardman, Steve (2005), 'Pillars of the Community: Campbell lordship and architectural patronage in the fifteenth century', in Richard Oram and Geoff

Stell (eds), *Lordship and Architecture in Medieval and Renaissance Scotland*, East Linton: Tuckwell Press, 122–59.

Bone, T. R. (1968), *School Inspection in Scotland 1840–1966*, London: University of London Press.

Boudreau, Annette and Dubois, Lise (2008), 'Français, acadien, acadjonne: Competing discourses on language preservation along the shores of the Baie Sainte-Marie', in Alexandre Duchêne and Monica Heller (eds), *Discourses of Endangerment: Ideology and Interest in the Defence of Languages*, London: Continuum, 98–120.

Bowditch, Gillian (2009), 'Allow Gaelic to thrive without taxpayers' cash', *The Sunday Times*, 11 October, 27.

Boyd, Gavin (2013), *Fascist Scotland: Caledonia and the Far Right*, Edinburgh: Birlinn.

Brand, Jack (1978), *The National Movement in Scotland*, London: Routledge & Kegan Paul.

Broun, Dauvit (2009), 'Attitudes of *Gall* to *Gaedhel* in Scotland before John of Fordun', in Broun and MacGregor (2009), 49–82.

Broun, Dauvit and MacGregor, Martin (eds) (2009), *Mìorun Mòr nan Gall, 'The great ill-will of the Lowlander'? Lowland Perceptions of the Highlands, Medieval and Modern*, Glasgow: Centre for Scottish and Celtic Studies, University of Glasgow.

Brown, Allan (1998), 'Gael warning', *Sunday Times*, 18 October.

Brown, Allan (2000), 'A tongue lashing from the Gaels', *Sunday Times*, 20 February.

Brown, Maggie (2015), 'Will S4C return to bleak times?', *The Guardian*, 19 July, 32.

Brown, W. Oliver (1934), 'Gaelic and Politics', *The Scots Independent*, 8, 201.

Brown, Tom (2000), 'It might be Gaelic but they're still talking nonsense', *Daily Record*, 3 March, 8.

Browne, Donald R. and Uribe-Jongbloed, Enrique (2013), 'Introduction: Ethnic/Linguistic Minority Media – What their History Reveals, How Scholars Have Studied Them and What We Might Ask Next', in Haf Gruffydd Jones and Uribe-Jongbloed (2013), 1–28.

Bruce, George J. (1918), 'Do Luchd–taghaidh Siorramachd Inbhir–Nis', Inverness: Highland News Printing and Publishing Works.

Buchanan, Joni (2002), 'The Gaelic Communities', in Gerry Hassan and Chris Warhurst (eds), *Anatomy of the New Scotland*, Edinburgh: Mainstream, 270–6.

Bun-sgoil Ghàidhlig Inbhir Nis (2019), 'Ar Sgoil/Our School', https://bunsgoil-ghaidhliginbhirnis.wordpress.com/about/ (last accessed 9 October 2019).

Bureau of Education, India (1920), *Selections From Educational Records, Part I: 1781–1839*, Calcutta: Superintendent, Government Printing.

Burnett, John A. (2011), *The Making of the Modern Scottish Highlands 1939–1965*, Dublin: Four Courts Press.

Burnett, Ray (1998), 'The long nineteenth century: Scotland's Catholic Gaidhealtachd', in Raymond Boyle and Peter Lynch (eds), *Out of the Ghetto? The Catholic Community in Modern Scotland*, Edinburgh: John Donald, 163–92.

Burnett, Ray (2016), '"They will never understand why I am here": The irony of Connolly's Scottish connections', in Kirsty Lusk and Willy Maley (eds), *Scotland and the Easter Rising: Fresh Perspectives on the Easter Rising*, Edinburgh: Luath Press, 56–62.

Burnley Campbell, Margaret (1912), 'An Comunn – Its Membership', *DG*, 7, 192–3.

Burton, Ivor and Drewry, Gavin (1983), 'Public Legislation: A Survey of the Session 1980/81', *Parliamentary Affairs*, 36, 436–59.

Caber-Feidh (1897), 'Litir a Lunnainn', *Mac-Talla*, 6:6, 1.

Caimbeul, Aonghas (1973), *Suathadh ri Iomadh Rubha*, Glasgow: Gairm.

Caimbeul, Aonghas Pàdraig (1996), 'Gàidhlig agus heroin', *An Cànan*, 64, 1.

Caimbeul, Aonghas Pàdraig (2002a), 'Dòigh eile air am bonnach a roinn', *The Scotsman*, 27 February, 17.

Caimbeul, Aonghas Pàdraig (2002b), 'Daoine "air las le feirg" mu làimhseachadh na Gàidhlig', *The Scotsman*, 29 May, 16.

Caimbeul, Maoilios (1979–80), 'Gàidhlig ann an Sgoiltean Earraghàidheal', *Gairm*, 109, 66–8.

Caimbeul, Seonaidh (2011), 'Mod and Gaelic are not quite in tune', *The Scotsman*, 18 October.

Caimbeul, Tormod (2000), 'The Politics of Gaelic Development in Scotland', in McCoy with Scott (2000), 53–66.

Cameron, A. C. (1877), 'On Gaelic and its Teaching in Highland Schools', *The Celtic Magazine*, 2, 181–7, 236–40.

Cameron, A. D. (1986), *Go Listen to the Crofters: The Napier Commission and Crofting a Century Ago*, Stornoway: Acair.

Cameron, Donald (2018), 'Time to take politics out of the debate over Gaelic', *The Herald*, 28 April 17.

Cameron, Ewen A. (1996), 'The Scottish Highlands: From Congested District to Objective One', in T. M. Devine and R. J. Finlay (eds), *Scotland in the Twentieth Century*, Edinburgh: EUP, 153–69.

Cameron, Ewen A. (1997), 'The Scottish Highlands as a special policy area, 1886 to 1965', *Rural History*, 8, 195–215.

Cameron, Ewen A. (1998), 'Embracing the past: the Highlands in nineteenth-century Scotland', in Dauvit Broun, R. J. Finlay and Michael Lynch (eds), *Image and Identity: The Making and Re-making of Scotland Through the Ages*, Edinburgh: John Donald, 177–94.

Cameron, Ewen A. (2000), *The Life and Times of Fraser Mackintosh Crofter MP*, Aberdeen: Centre for Scottish Studies, University of Aberdeen.

Cameron, Ewen A. (2010), *Impaled Upon a Thistle: Scotland Since 1880*, Edinburgh: EUP.

Cameron, Ewen A. (2017), 'University Realities: The Inverness Campaign to Establish Scotland's Fifth University', *TGSI*, 67, 9–50.

Campbell, Allan (1984), 'C.N.A.G. – Report on Practical Implementation' (report for HIDB) (NRS ED61/196).

Campbell, Allan (2002), email to Russel Henderson (office of Murdo Fraser MSP), 2 April (WCM).

Campbell, Allan (2011), interview with the author, Inverness, 4 July.

Campbell, Allan (2015), 'Beachd Ailein', *Oban Times*, 30 April, 4.

Campbell, Angus Peter (2000), 'Gaelic: Dewar "won't go down the Welsh road"', *WHFP*, 8 September.
 [see also Caimbeul, Aonghas Pàdraig]

Campbell, John Lorne (1950), *Gaelic in Scottish Education and Life*, 2nd edn, Edinburgh: Saltire Society.

Campbell, John Lorne (1978), 'Notes on Hamish Robertson's "Studies in Carmichael's *Carmina Gadelica*", *SGS*, 13:1, 1–17.

Campbell, John Lorne (ed.) (1984), *Highland Songs of the Forty-five*, 2nd edn, Edinburgh: Scottish Gaelic Texts Society.

Campbell, Kenna (1983), 'Gaelic', in J. Derrick McClure (ed.), *Minority Languages in Central Scotland*, Aberdeen: Association for Scottish Literary Studies, 11–14.

Campbell, Kenna (2014), interview with the author, Glasgow, 29 April.

Cape, Ruth, et al. (2018), 'Cognitive effects of Gaelic medium education on primary school children in Scotland', *International Journal of Bilingual Education and Bilingualism*, DOI: 10.1080/13670050.2018.1543648.

Carlin, Patrick (2013), 'On Both Sides of the Menai? Planning for the Welsh Language in North-West Wales', *Revista de Llengua i Dret*, 59, 92–110.

Carmichael, Alexander (ed.) (1900), *Carmina Gadelica/Ortha nan Gaidheal*, vol. 1, Edinburgh: T. & A. Constable.

Carney, Sébastien (2015), *Breiz Atao! Mordrel, Delaporte, Lainé, Fouéré: une mystique nationale (1901–1948)*, Rennes: Presses Universitaires de Rennes.

Case Associates (1996), *Gaelic Television & the Broadcasting Bill: Assessment and Proposals*, London: Case Associates.

Catholic Church (1834), *Iùl a' Chrìostaidh*, ed. by Raonull MacRaing, Aberdeen: Catholic Church.

CBC (2018), 'Scottish politician takes up cause of N.S. woman who wants to teach Gaelic in Scotland', https://www.cbc.ca/news/canada/nova-scotia/gaelic-teacher-nova-scotia-scotland-education-1.4648227 (last accessed 20 December 2019).

CCES (1875), *Report of the Committee of Council on Education in Scotland; with Appendix, 1874–75*, London: HMSO.

CCES (1878), *Report of the Committee of Council on Education in Scotland; with Appendix, 1877–78*, London: HMSO.

CCES (1879), *Report of the Committee of Council on Education in Scotland; with Appendix, 1878–79*, London: HMSO.

CCES (1880), *Report of the Committee of Council on Education in Scotland; with Appendix, 1879–80*, London: HMSO.
CCES (1884), *Report of the Committee of Council on Education in Scotland; with Appendix, 1883–84*, London: HMSO.
CCES (1885), 'Education (Scotland) Grants to Highland Schools' (minute dated 30 April 1885), London: Eyre & Spottiswoode.
CCES (1898), *Report of the Committee of Council on Education in Scotland. 1897–98*, London: HMSO.
CCES (1899), *Report of the Committee of Council on Education in Scotland. 1898–99*, London: HMSO.
CCG (2003). *Towards a Gaelic Media Service: From CCG to GMS*, Stornoway: CCG.
Ceilidh nan Gaidheal (1947), *Ceilidh nan Gaidheal, Glaschu 1896–1946: Leabhar na h-Ard-Fheise*, Glasgow: Ceilidh nan Gaidheal.
Celtic Film and Television Festival (2004). Letter from Celtic Film and Television Festival to Tessa Jowell MP, SoS for Culture, Media and Sport, 8 April (WCM/FOI).
The Celtic Monthly (1904), 'Highland Societies and Gaelic Teaching', 12, 190.
The Celtic Review (1912), 'An Comunn Gaidhealach', 8, 95–6.
Census Office (1874), *Eighth Decennial Census of the Population of Scotland Taken 3d April 1871, with Report*, Edinburgh: HMSO.
Census Office (1893), *Tenth Decennial Census of the Population of Scotland Taken 5th April 1891, Supplement to Vol. 1, with Report*, Edinburgh: HMSO.
Central Statistics Office (n.d.), Census of Population 2016 – Profile 10 Education, Skills and the Irish Language, www.cso.ie/en/releasesandpublications/ep/p-cp10esil/p10esil/ilg (last accessed 3 January 2020).
An Ceum (1948a), 'Activities of the League', 2:5, 8.
An Ceum (1948b), 'An Oidhche Chaledonach', 2:6, 8.
Challan, Maighread A. (2012), *Air Bilean an t-Sluaigh: Sealladh air Leantalachd Beul-Aithris Ghàidhlig Uibhist a Tuath*, Belfast: Cló Ollscoil na Banríona.
Chalmers, Douglas (2011), 'Eòrpa: taking Europe from the periphery to the core', in David Hutchison and Hugh O'Donnell (eds), *Centres and Peripheries: Metropolitan and Non-metropolitan Journalism in the Twenty First Century*, Newcastle: Cambridge Scholars Publishing, 128–48.
Chalmers, Douglas, Calvert, Julian and Irwin, Andrea (2011), *Appraisal of Written Media Attitudes to Gaelic: Final Report*, Glasgow: Glasgow Caledonian University.
Chalmers, Douglas, et al. (2013), 'The Contribution of BBC Alba to Gaelic: A Social and Economic Review', in Haf Gruffydd Jones and Uribe-Jongbloed (2013), 212–23.
Chambers, William (1877), 'The Gaelic Nuisance', *Chambers's Journal*, 723, 689–91, and 740, 129–32.

Chapman, Malcolm (1978), *The Gaelic Vision in Scottish Culture*, London: Croom Helm.
Chapman, Malcolm (1992), *The Celts: The Construction of a Myth*, Basingstoke: Macmillan.
Charles-Edwards, Thomas (2007), 'The Lure of Celtic Languages, 1850–1914', in Marios Costambeys, Andrew J. Hamer and Martin Heale (eds), *The Making of the Middle Ages: Liverpool Essays*, Liverpool: Liverpool University Press, 15–35.
Cheape, Hugh (2010), 'Gheibhte breacain charnaid ("Scarlet Tartans Would be Got ..."): The Re-invention of Tradition', in Ian Brown (ed.), *From Tartan to Tartanry: Scottish Culture, History and Myth*, Edinburgh: EUP, 13–31.
Cheape, Hugh (2014), '"Tha feum air cabhaig": The Initiative of the Folklore Institute of Scotland', *Scottish Studies*, 37, 53–62.
Chhim, Chris and Bélanger, Éric (2017), 'Language as a public good and national identity: Scotland's competing heritage languages', *Nations and Nationalism*, 23, 929–51.
Church of Scotland (2019), 'New Bible resources for Gaelic speakers released', www.churchofscotland.org.uk/news-and-events/news/2019/new-bible-resources-for-gaelic-speakers-released (last accessed 5 January 2020).
City of Edinburgh Council (2002), 'Provision for Gaelic Language' (paper for Executive of the Council, 10 September).
City of Edinburgh Council (2011), 'Outcomes Arising from Consultation on Proposals for the Future Development of Nursery and Primary Gaelic Medium Education' (Report No. CEC/50/11–12/CF).
City of Edinburgh Council (2016), 'Recent Developments in Gaelic Education Provision in Edinburgh' (paper for Education, Children and Families Committee, 24 May), Edinburgh: City of Edinburgh Council.
Civil Service Commissioners (1921), 'Regulations Respecting Open Competitive Examinations for the Admission of Girls to the Clerical Class of the Civil Service' and 'Regulations Respecting Open Competitive Examinations for the Admission of Boys to the Clerical Class of the Civil Service', *The Edinburgh Gazette*, 9 December, 2130, 2132.
Clancy, Thomas Owen (2011), 'Gaelic in Medieval Scotland: advent and expansion', *Proceedings of the British Academy*, 167, 349–92.
Clancy, Thomas Owen (2015), 'Early Celtic Poetry (to 1500)', in Carla Sassi (ed.), *The International Companion to Scottish Poetry*, Glasgow: Scottish Literature International, 6–14.
Clancy, Thomas Owen and Crawford, Barbara E. (2001), 'The Formation of the Scottish Kingdom', in R. A. Houston and W. W. J. Knox (eds), *The New Penguin History of Scotland: From the Earliest Times to the Present Day*, London: Allen Lane/Penguin Press, 28–95.
Clann na h-Alba (1912), *Brosnachadh*, London: Clann na h-Alba.
CnaG (1985), Letter from John Angus Mackay, Director, to Robin Banks, Secretary, Gaelic Language Promotion Trust, Oban, 16 April (WCM).

CnaG (1986), *Poilisidh Nàiseanta airson na Gàidhlig/Towards a National Policy for Gaelic*, Inverness: CnaG.
CnaG (1987a), *A' Ghàidhlig anns na h-Eileanan an Iar: Plana Leasachaidh Deich Bliadhna/Gaelic in the Western Isles: A Ten-Year Development Plan*, Inverness: CnaG.
CnaG (1987b), *A' Ghàidhlig anns an Eilean Sgitheanach: Plana Leasachaidh Deich Bliadhna/Gaelic in Skye: A Ten-Year Development Plan*, Inverness: CnaG.
CnaG (1987c), *A' Ghàidhlig ann an Ìle: Plana Leasachaidh Deich Bliadhna/ Gaelic in Islay: A Ten-Year Development Plan*, Inverness: CnaG.
CnaG (1987d), *A' Ghàidhlig ann am Muile: Plana Leasachaidh Deich Bliadhna/ Gaelic in Mull: A Ten-Year Development Plan*, Inverness: CnaG.
CnaG (1988), *Towards a Gaelic Television Service*, Inverness: CnaG.
CnaG (1989a), *The Case for a Gaelic Broadcasting Service: Response to the White Paper 'Broadcasting in the 90s'*, Inverness: CnaG.
CnaG (1989b), *Adhartas na Gàidhlig 1982–1989/Gaelic Progress Report 1982–1989*, Inverness: CnaG.
CnaG (1992), *Plana Leasachaidh Deich Bliadhna ann an Iar Thuath Chataibh/A Ten-Year Gaelic Development Plan for North and West Sutherland*, Inverness: CnaG.
CnaG (1994), *Gàidhlig 2000: A Strategy for Gaelic Development into the 21st Century*, Inverness: CnaG.
CnaG (1997a), *Inbhe Thèarainte dhan Ghàidhlig/Secure Status for Gaelic*, Inverness: CnaG.
CnaG (1997b), *Innleachd Airson Adhartais: Poileasaidh Nàiseanta airson Foghlam Gàidhlig/Framework for Growth: A National Policy for Gaelic Education*, Inverness: CnaG.
CnaG (1999a), *Dreach iùl airson Achd Gàidhlig/Draft brief for a Gaelic Language Act*, Inverness: CnaG.
CnaG (1999b), *Gàidhlig plc – Plana Leasachaidh Cànain – A Development Plan for Gaelic*, Inverness: CnaG.
CnaG (2010), 'Support for bilingual signs at Scottish Ski Centres', http://cnag.org/index.php/en/news/older-news/56-news-2010/361-support-for-bilingual-signs-at-scottish-ski-centres (last accessed 4 November 2019).
CnaG and Comann an Luchd-Ionnsachaidh (1992), *Feumalachdan Luchd-Ionnsachaidh – Rannsachadh Nàiseanta/Provision for Gaelic Learners: A National Survey*, Inverness: CnaG.
CNCA [1971a]), Constitution (NLS MS Acc. 12130/2).
CNCA (1971b), 'Campaign of Irritation by Language Society' (press release) (NLS MS Acc. 12130/3).
CNCA (1974), 'Gaelic Language Group Rebuff An Comunn Criticisms' (press release) (NLS MS Acc. 12130/3).
CnE (1975), Minute of Meeting of the Policy and Resources Committee, 15 April (CnES–SG).

CnE (1977), 'The Bilingual Policy', report by Chief Executive for Policy & Resources Committee meeting, 19 May (item 32) (CnES–SG).
CnE (1978a), *The Bilingual Policy: A Consultative Document*, Stornoway: CnE.
CnE (1978b), Memorandum from H. M. Garland, Director of Social Work, to Donald Martin, Deputy Director of Administration, 3 February (CnES/SG).
CnE (1978c), Minute of Meeting of the Policy and Resources Committee, 30 March (CnES–SG).
CnE (1980a), Minute of Meeting of the Education Committee, 17 June (CnES–SG).
CnE (1980b), Minute of Meeting of the Council, 20 June (CnES–SG).
CnE (1980c), Minute of Meeting of the Council, 21 August (CnES–SG).
CnE (1982a), *Bilingual Education Policy Implementation Review*, Stornoway: CnE (CnES–SG).
CnE (1982b), Letter from Donald Macaulay, Convener, CnE, to George Younger, Scottish Secretary, 25 February (NRS ED61/20).
CnES (2006), 'Gaelic Policy Implementation – Pilot Phase', www.cne-siar.gov.uk:8000/media/7571/gaelicpolicyimplementationpilotphase.pdf (last accessed 7 December 2019).
CnES (2007), *Plana Gàidhlig 2007–2012/Gaelic Language Plan 2007–2012*, Stornoway: CnES.
CnES (2009), 'Gaelic Policy Implementation: Delivery of Gaelic Medium Education', https://www.cne-siar.gov.uk/media/CommitteeArchive/OldCommitteeDocs/education/agendas/february2009/cdr03125%20%20delivery%20of%20gm%20education.pdf (last accessed 7 December 2019).
CnES (2010), 'Review of Educational Provision – Survey Regarding a Standalone Gaelic School' (Education and Children's Services Committee, 24 August), www.cne-siar.gov.uk:8000/Media/CommitteeArchive/OldCommitteeDocs/education/agendas/august2010/JKR30109%20Gaelic%20School%20Survey%20240810.pdf (last accessed 29 October 2019).
CnES (2020), 'Circular No. 2020/01 – P1 Enrolment: Gaelic', 15 January, Stornoway: CnES.
CoE (1995), *Explanatory Report to the Framework Convention for the Protection of National Minorities*, Strasbourg: CoE.
CoE (2004), *Application of the Charter in the United Kingdom*, Strasbourg: CoE.
Coffre-Baneux, Natalie (2001), *Le Partage de Pouvoir dans les Hébrides Écossaises: Pasteurs, Élus et Managers*, Paris: L'Harmattan.
Colgan, Jenny (2003), 'Tha Telebhisean Gàidhlig cac', *The Guardian*, 23 September.
Comann nam Pàrant (2017), Submission to the Education and Skills Committee, Scottish Parliament on teacher workforce planning for Scotland's schools, www.parliament.scot/S5_Education/Inquiries/20170427ComannnamParantNaionalgroupTeacherWorkforce.pdf (last accessed 29 October 2019).

Comann nam Pàrant Rathad nan Eilean (2006), 'Highland Council's Formal Consultation: "Concerns and Inaccuracies"' (WCM).
Comann Sgoiltean Dà-chànanach Ghlaschu ([1984]), *Register of Membership* (recruitment leaflet), Glasgow: Comann Sgoiltean Dà-chànanach Ghlaschu (WCM).
Commission for Racial Equality (2003), 'Submission from the Commission on Racial Equality', in SP, Education, Culture and Sport Committee 2003, vol 2.
Commission for Racial Equality (2004), 'CRE Response to call for evidence on Stage 1 of the Gaelic Language (Scotland) Bill', in SP Education Committee 2005a, vol. 3.
Commissioners of HM Inland Revenue (1909), *Fifty-Second Report of Commissioners of His Majesty's Inland Revenue*, London: HMSO.
Committee for Informal Education (1950a), *Constitution*, Glasgow: ACG (NRS ED27/272).
Committee for Informal Education (1950b), *Statement of Functions of Regional Organisers*, Glasgow: ACG (NRS ED27/272).
Committee on Bilingualism of the Scottish Council for Research in Education (1961), *Gaelic-speaking Children in Highland Schools*, London: University of London Press.
Committee on Church and Nation, General Assembly of the Church of Scotland (2004), 'Gaelic Language Bill: Consultation Response', Edinburgh: Church of Scotland.
Committee of Inquiry into Bilingual Traffic Signs (1972), *Bilingual Traffic Signs/ Arwyddion Ffyrdd Dwyieithog: Report of the Committee of Inquiry under the Chairmanship of Roderic Bowen, Esq., Q.C., M.A., LL.D, 1971–72*, Cardiff: HMSO.
Committee of Inquiry into the Functions and Powers of the Islands Councils in Scotland (1984), *Report*, Edinburgh: Scottish Office.
An Comunn Albannach ([1977]), Manifesto: 'For a Gàidhlig Scotland', Glasgow: An Comunn Albannach.
Comunn an Luchd-Ionnsachaidh (1984), *Cuairt Litir Ionnsachaidh*, 1, Inverness: Comunn an Luchd-Ionnsachaidh.
Comunn Gailig Ghlascho (1891), *Proceedings of the Gaelic Society of Glasgow, Vol. 1 – 1887–91*, Glasgow: Archibald Sinclair.
Comunn na h-Òigridh (1937). *Clàr-innse Campa Comunn na h-Òigridh 1937*, Glasgow: ACG.
Comunn na h-Òigridh (1955), *Riaghailtean agus Clàr-Obrach*, Stirling: A. Learmonth & Son.
Comunn nan Albannach ([1908?]), *Brosnachadh do na Gàidheil/A Manifesto to the Scots People*, London: Kenneth MacKenzie.
Comunn nan Gaidheal (1918a), membership recruitment letter, Edinburgh and London: Comunn nan Gaidheal.
Comunn nan Gaidheal (1918b), 'Achd an Fhog[h]luim Neo-Albannach', *The Scottish Review*, 41, 79–88.

Conradh na Gaeilge (2019), *Céard é an Scéal? Tuairimí an Phobail i Leith na Gaeilge/Public Opinion on the Irish Language*, Dublin: Conradh na Gaeilge.

Cooper, Robert L. (1990), *Language Planning and Social Change*, Cambridge: CUP.

Cormack, Arthur (2011), 'Additional submission from Arthur Cormack – Cathraiche (Chair) of Bòrd na Gàidhlig' to the Scottish Parliament, Education and Culture Committee, www.parliament.scot/parliamentarybusiness/CurrentCommittees/53360.aspx#annb (last accessed 12 October 2019).

Cormack, Mike (1993), 'Problems of Minority Language Broadcasting: Gaelic in Scotland', *European Journal of Communication*, 8, 101–17.

Cormack, Mike (1994), 'Programming for Cultural Defence: The Expansion of Gaelic Television', *Scottish Affairs*, 6, 114–31.

Cormack, Mike (2006), 'The media, language maintenance and Gaelic', in McLeod (2006a), 211–19.

Costa, James (2009), 'Language history as charter myth? Scots and the (re)invention of Scotland', *Scottish Language*, 28, 1–25.

Costa, James (2017), 'On the pros and cons of standardizing Scots: Notes from the North of a small island', in Pia Lane, James Costa and Haley De Korne (eds), *Standardizing Minority Languages: Competing Ideologies of Authority and Authenticity in the Global Periphery*, London: Routledge, 47–65.

The Courier (2015), 'Claims of "bigotry" as councillors clash over promotion of Gaelic in Fife', 4 February.

The Courier (2018), '"Catastrophic" drop in exam passes blamed on declining subject choice by Curriculum for Excellence architect', 9 August.

The Courier (2019), 'Gaelic language plan will see bilingual Angus street signs', 1 June.

The Courier and Advertiser (1934), 'Scathing Attack on Mod Policy', 19 October, 7.

The Courier and Advertiser (1935), 'Lord Scone's Question', 6 February, 12.

Cowan, Edward J. (2000), 'The Discovery of the Gàidhealtachd in Sixteenth Century Scotland', *TGSI*, 60, 259–84.

Cox, Richard A. V. (1998), 'Tokenism in Gaelic: the language of appeasement', *Scottish Language*, 17, 70–81.

Cox, Richard A. V. and Armstrong, Timothy Currie (eds) (2011), *A' Cleachdadh na Gàidhlig: slatan-tomhais ann an dìon cànain sa choimhearsnachd*, Sleat: Clò Ostaig.

Craig, Cairns (2018), *The Wealth of the Nation: Scotland, Culture and Independence*, Edinburgh: EUP.

Craigie, W. A. (1924), 'The Present State of the Scottish Tongue', in W. A. Craigie et al., *The Scottish Tongue: A Series of Lectures on the Vernacular Language of Lowland Scotland*, London: Cassell & Co., 1–46.

Craik, Henry (1884a), *Report on Highland Schools*, London: HMSO.

Craik, Henry (1884b), *The State in its Relation to Education*, London: Macmillan.
Craik, Henry (1901), *A Century of Scottish History: From the Days Before the '45 to Those Within Living Memory*, Edinburgh: W. Blackwood & Sons.
Crann-Tàra (1981a), 'Ceartas', 13, 7–8.
Crann-Tàra (1981b), 'Editorial', 15, 3.
'Creag Shnidheasdail' (1933), 'An Comunn Gaidhealach' (letter to the editor). *Scots Independent*, 7, no. 75 (January).
Creative Scotland (2015), *Scots Leid Policie/Scots Language Policy*, Edinburgh: Creative Scotland.
Creative Scotland (2019), *Plana Cànain Gàidhlig 2019–22/Gaelic Language Plan 2019–22*, Edinburgh: Creative Scotland.
The Crofters Commission (1888), *Report by the Crofters Commission as to their Proceedings . . . for the Period from 25th June 1886 to 10th December 1887*, Edinburgh: HMSO.
Cruickshank, Catherine (2002), 'The Role of the Gaelic Society of Inverness in the Representation and Promotion of Gaelic Life and Culture, 1871–1914', MLitt thesis, University of Aberdeen.
Cruickshank, Janet and Millar, Robert McColl (eds), *After the Storm: Papers from the Forum for Research on the Languages of Scotland and Ulster triennial meeting, Aberdeen 2012*, Aberdeen: Forum for Research on the Languages of Scotland and Ireland.
Cunliffe, Daniel, Morris, Delyth and Prys, Cynog (2013), 'Investigating the Differential Use of Welsh in Young Speakers' Social Networks: A Comparison of Communication in Face-to-Face Settings, in Electronic Texts and on Social Networking Sites', in Haf Gruffudd-Jones and Uribe-Jongbloed (2013), 75–86.
Cunningham, Maggie (1984), 'Skye bilingual scheme to cover all schools', *WHFP*, 8 February, 7.
Daily Mail (2015), 'Police Scotland are blasted after spending taxpayers' money rebranding their force helicopter in Scots Gaelic', 31 August.
Daily Record (1940), 'No M. I. Posters in Gaelic', 7 February, 3.
Daily Record (1944), 'Scotland's Own Broadcasting? "Home Rule" on Radio', 21 September, 5.
Daily Record (1975), 'Judge tells former PC "You are free"', 21 March, 5.
Daily Record (2010), '£26m drive for Gaelic', 9 July, 2.
Daily Record (2016), 'Dumfries and Galloway councillor slams Gaelic action plan as "fantastic waste of money"', 31 March.
Dauenhauer, Nora Marks and Dauenhauer, Richard (1998), 'Technical, emotional, and ideological issues in reversing language shift: examples from Southeast Alaska', in Lenore A. Grenoble and Lindsay J. Whaley (eds), *Endangered Languages: Language Loss and Community Response*, Cambridge: CUP, 57–98.

Davidson, Neil (2001), 'Marx and Engels on the Scottish Highlands', *Science & Society*, 65, 286–326.
Davies, Gwilym Prys (2000), 'The Legal Status of the Welsh Language in the Twentieth Century', in Geraint H. Jenkins and Mari A. Williams (eds), *'Let's Do Our Best for the Ancient Tongue': The Welsh Language in the Twentieth Century*, Cardiff: UWP, 217–48.
Davies, Janet (2nd edn, 2014), *The Welsh Language: A History*, Cardiff: UWP.
Day, John Percival (1918), *Public Administration in the Highlands and Islands of Scotland*, London: University of London Press.
DCMS (2002), Letter from Dr Kim Howells MP, Minister for Culture, Media & Sport, to Alasdair Milne, May (date unspecified) (WCM/FOI).
DCMS (2004), Letter from Tessa Jowell MP, SoS for Culture, Media and Sport, to the Celtic Film and Television Festival, 21 May (WCM/FOI).
De Barra, Caoimhín (2018), *The Coming of the Celts AD 1860: Celtic Nationalism in Ireland and Wales*, Notre Dame, IN: University of Notre Dame Press.
De Meulder, Maartje (2016), 'The influence of deaf people's dual category status on sign language planning: the British Sign Language (Scotland) Act (2015)', *Current Issues in Language Planning*, 18, 215–32.
Deloitte (2019), *Bòrd na Gàidhlig: Report to the Audit and Risk Management Committee – Leadership and Governance*, www.audit-scotland.gov.uk/uploads/docs/report/2019/aar_1819_bord_gaidhlig_wider_scope.pdf (last accessed 10 January 2020).
Department of Agriculture for Scotland (1954), *Report of the Commission of Enquiry into Crofting Conditions*, Edinburgh: HMSO.
Department of Education and Skills (2019), 'Key Statistics 2017/2018 and 2018/2019', www.education.ie/en/Publications/Statistics/Key-Statistics/key-statistics-2018-2019.pdf (last accessed 27 August 2019).
Department of Trade and Industry (1989), Letter from Nicholas Ridley, SoS for Trade and Industry, to David Waddington, Home Secretary, 31 October (NRS ED 29/114).
de Varennes, Fernand and Kuzborska, Elżbieta (2019), 'Minority Language Rights and Standards: Definitions and Applications at the Supranational Level', in Hogan-Brun and O'Rourke (2019), 21–72.
Devine, T. M. (1988), *The Great Highland Famine*, Edinburgh: John Donald.
DG (1906), 'The Training of Gaelic-Speaking Teachers', 1, 128.
DG (1908a), 'Report of Deputation on the Teaching of Gaelic', 3, 145–7.
DG (1908b), 'An Comunn Gaidhealach and the Education (Scotland) Bill', 3, 183–4.
DG (1908c), 'Gaelic in the Schools', 3, 229.
DG (1908d), 'Education (Scotland) Bill', 4, 20.
DG (1909a), 'Education (Scotland) Bill – The Gaelic Amendment', 4, 57–8.
DG (1909b), 'Gaelic and the Impending School Board Elections', 4, 80.
DG (1910), 'Timchioll an Teallaich', 5, 155.

DG (1912a), 'Gaelic-Speaking Ministers', 7, 135–6.
DG (1912b), 'The Churches on Gaelic', 7, 195.
DG (1914a), 'The Churches and the Scarcity of Gaelic Preachers', 9, 148–9.
DG (1914b), 'Mrs. Kennedy-Fraser and Songs of the Hebrides', 9, 171–2.
DG (1916a), 'The Department and Gaelic', 11, 87–8.
DG (1916b), 'Comunn News', 11, 142.
DG (1916c), 'Special Meeting of An Comunn Gaidhealach Executive', 12, 20–1.
DG (1917a), 'Gaelic-Speaking Priests', 12, 85.
DG (1917b), 'The Teaching of Gaelic in Schools – Interview with Secretary for Scotland', 12, 110–11.
DG (1917c), 'Scheme of the Church of Scotland for Promoting the Education of Gaelic-Speaking Students for the Ministry', 12, 188–9.
Diack, William (1918), 'The Future of the Scottish Labour Party', *The Scottish Review*, 41, 165–96.
Dickson, Tony (1985), 'Marxism, Nationalism and Scottish History', *Journal of Contemporary History*, 20, 323–36.
Dinwoodie, Robbie (1993), 'Last flight to bleak exile', *The Herald*, 9 June, 10.
Dombrowski, Lindsay Milligan, et al. (2013), 'Initial teacher education for minority medium-of-instruction teaching: the case study of Scottish Gaelic in Scotland', *Current Issues in Language Planning*, 15, 119–32.
Dòmhnallach, Aonghas (2003), 'Bille leth pruidh bho dhaoine meagh-bhlàth', *P&J*, 13 October, 12.
Dòmhnallach, Màrtainn (1973), column, *WHFP*, 23 February, 2.
Dòmhnallach, Màrtainn (1981), 'Dà chànan bheò bho bheul na h–òigridh', *North 7*, 44, 8–10.
 [see also MacDonald, Martin]
Donald, Gordon (1962), 'Roinn a Mhic 's an Athar? (Gàidhlig air a' Bh.B.C.)', *Gairm*, 41, 84–100.
Donnelly, Hugh (2004), 'Gaelic puts up the barriers in Glasgow', *TESS*, 26 November.
Dorian, Nancy C. (1981), *Language Death: The Life Cycle of a Scottish Gaelic Dialect*, Philadelphia: University of Pennsylvania Press.
Dorian, Nancy C. (1994), 'Purism vs. compromise in language revitalization and language revival', *Language in Society*, 23, 479–94.
Dorian, Nancy C. (2011), 'The ambiguous arithmetic of language maintenance and revitalization', in Joshua A. Fishman and Ofelia Garcia (eds), *The Handbook of Language and Ethnicity*, Vol. 2, New York: OUP, 459–69.
[Drever, James] (1948), 'Scottish Survey', *Scots Review*, 9, 130–1.
Duchêne, Alexandre and Heller, Monica (eds), *Language in Late Capitalism: Pride and Profit*, New York: Routledge.
Dumville, David (1996), 'Ireland and Britain in *Táin Bó Fraích*', *Études Celtiques*, 32, 175–87.

Dunbar, Rob (1997), 'East Kilbride wake-up call for Gaelic activists', *WHFP*, 28 February, 7.

Dunbar, Robert (2000), 'Legal and Institutional Aspects of Gaelic Development', in McCoy with Scott (2000), 67–87.

Dunbar, Robert (2003a),'Gaelic-medium Broadcasting: Reflections on the Legal Framework from a Sociolinguistic Perspective', in Kirk and Ó Baoill (2003), 73–82.

Dunbar, Robert (2003b), *The ratification by the United Kingdom of the European Charter for regional or minority languages*, Mercator–Legislation Working Paper 10, Barcelona: Mercator–Legislation.

Dunbar, Robert (2010), 'BBC ALBA and the Evolution of Gaelic Television Broadcasting: A Case Study', *European Yearbook of Minority Issues*, 9, 389–418.

Dunbar, Robert (2011), 'A unilingual minority language college in a multilingual university: Sabhal Mòr Ostaig', *European Journal of Language Policy*, 3, 197–214.

Dunbar, Robert (2018), 'Organisational Language Planning: Gaelic Language Plans in the Public Sector', in M. MacLeod and Smith-Christmas (2018), 156–72.

Dunbar, Robert (2019a), 'Gaelic periodicals and the maintenance and creation of networks: Evidence from the Eastern Canadian Gàidhealtachd', in Michel Byrne and Sheila M. Kidd (eds), *Lìontan Lìonmhor: Local, National and Global Gaelic Networks from the 18th to the 20th Century*, Glasgow: Celtic & Gaelic, University of Glasgow, 108–52.

Dunbar, Robert (2019b), '*An Coimisinéir Teanga* and *Comisiynydd y Gymraeg*: The Challenges of a Changing Legislative Environment', in Amon and James (2019), 101–24.

Dundee City Council (2015), *Dundee City Council's Gaelic Language Plan 2015–2020*, Dundee: Dundee City Council.

Dundee Courier and Advertiser (1938), 'Gaelic Atmosphere For This School – An Comunn Plan to Develop Highlands', 3 October, 4.

Dundee Courier (1981), Leader concerning the Gaelic (Miscellaneous Provisions) Bill, 27 January, 8.

Dundee Evening Telegraph (1892), 'Gaelic Translations of Gladstone's Speeches', 17 August, 2.

Dundee Evening Telegraph (1916), 'Should Gaelic be Taught in Schools? Arbroath School Board Discussion', 27 June, 2.

Dundee Evening Telegraph (1950), 'Teaching of Gaelic' (letter to the editor from 'Saxon', Dundee), 31 October, 3.

Dunmore, Stuart (2015), 'Bilingual life after school? Language use, ideologies and attitudes among Gaelic-medium educated adults', PhD thesis, University of Edinburgh.

Dunmore, Stuart (2019), *Language Revitalisation in Gaelic Scotland: Linguistic Practice and Ideology*, Edinburgh: EUP.

Dunn, Anndra (2015), 'Conaltradh'/'Communication', in Kevin MacNeil (ed.), *Struileag: Shore to Shore/Cladach gu Cladach*, 64–9, 70–4, Edinburgh: Polygon.

Dunn, Catherine (1987), 'Mediating Gaelic', *Media Education Journal*, 5, 53–6.

Dunn, Catherine (2013), *Long-Term Plan to Increase Numbers in Gaelic-Medium Education*, Inverness: BnG.

Dunn, Catherine and Robertson, A. G. Boyd (1989), 'Gaelic in education', in Gillies (1989), 44–55.

Durkacz, Victor E. (1983), *The Decline of the Celtic Languages: A Study of Linguistic and Cultural Conflict in Scotland, Wales and Ireland from the Reformation to the Twentieth Century*, Edinburgh: John Donald.

Duwe, Kurt (2005), *Gàidhlig (Scottish Gaelic) Local Studies, Vol. 27: Siorrachd Pheairt & Sruighlea (Perthshire & Stirling)*, Wedel, Germany: Hydromod, www.linguae-celticae.org/dateien/Gaidhlig_Local_Studies _Vol_27_Peairt_Sruighlea_Ed_II.pdf (last accessed 13 October 2019).

Duwe, Kurt (2006), *Gàidhlig (Scottish Gaelic) Local Studies, Vol. 12: An t-Eilean Sgitheanach: Port Righ, An Srath & Slèite (Isle of Skye: Portree, Strath & Sleat)*, Wedel, Germany: Hydromod, www.linguae-celticae.org/dateien/Gaidhlig_Local_Studies_Vol_12_Port_Righ_Sleite_Ed_II.pdf (last accessed 13 October 2019).

Dwelly, Edward (2001 [1901–11]), *Illustrated Gaelic–English Dictionary*, Edinburgh: Birlinn.

Dziennik, Matthew (2015), *The Fatal Land War, Empire, and the Highland Soldier in British America*, New Haven: Yale University Press.

Earra-Ghaidheal (1933), 'The Truth About An Comunn Gaidhealach', *The Free Man*, 2, 35, 6.

East Renfrewshire Council (2017a), Letter from Mhairi Shaw, Director of Education, concerning Gaelic Medium Primary Education: Initial Assessment, 18 April (WCM).

East Renfrewshire Council (2017b), 'Gaelic Medium Education: Outcome of a Request for an Assessment', Education Committee, 21 June, 63–6, https://www.eastrenfrewshire.gov.uk/CHttpHandler.ashx?id=20402&p=0 (last accessed 30 November 2019).

Easton, Norman (1982), 'The People's Tongue: Socialist Thochts on Scotlan's Languages', *Radical Scotland*, 1, 16–19.

Eckert, Penny (1983), 'The Paradox of National Language Movements', *Journal of Multilingual and Multicultural Development*, 4, 289–300.

Education Commission (Scotland) (1865), *First Report by Her Majesty's Commissioners Appointed to Inquire into the Schools in Scotland*, Edinburgh: HMSO.

Education Commission (Scotland) (1867), *Second Report by Her Majesty's Commissioners. Elementary Schools*, Edinburgh: HMSO.

Education Commission (Scotland) (1867), *Third Report by Her Majesty's Commissioners. Burgh and Middle-Class Schools*, Edinburgh: HMSO.

Education Counts (2018), 'Māori Language in Education', www.education-counts.govt.nz/statistics/maori-education/maori-in-schooling/6040 (last accessed 12 October 2019).
Education Scotland (2015), *Advice on Gaelic Education*, Edinburgh: Education Scotland.
Edwards, Andrew, Tanner, Duncan and Carlin, Patrick (2011), 'The Conservative governments and the development of Welsh language policy in the 1980s and 1990s', *The Historical Journal*, 54, 529–51.
Edwards, Hywel Teifi (1990), *The Eisteddfod*, Cardiff: UWP.
Edwards, John (2009), *Language and Identity: An Introduction*, Cambridge: CUP.
Edwards, John (2010), *Minority Languages and Group Identity: Cases and Categories*, Amsterdam: John Benjamins.
Edwards, Owen Dudley (ed.) (1989), *A Claim of Right for Scotland*, Edinburgh: Polygon.
EEN (1883), 'The Supply of Gaelic Speaking Ministers', 22 November, 3.
EEN (1891), 'Unionists Pose As Land Law Reformers', 17 August, 2.
EEN (1893), 'Stubborn Gaelic Witnesses in Edinburgh', 27 July, 2.
EEN (1901), 'A Man Who Struck King Edward', 19 February, 2.
EEN (1904), 'Marquis of Tullibardine and Gaelic', 3 February, 2.
EEN (1906), 'A Gaelic Manifesto', 11 January, 3.
EEN (1930), 'Cannot Speak Gaelic. – Confession by Cameron of Locheil. – Nationalists Criticised', 10 October.
EEN (2002), 'Anger as city opts to block all-Gaelic primary', 14 March, 8.
EEN (2010a), 'Gaelic education', 9 June, 14.
EEN (2010b), 'War of words over free bus travel for Gaelic school pupils', 19 June, 7.
EEN (2016), 'Critics say police's Gaelic plans are "waste of time"', 30 December.
EEN (2018), 'Edinburgh Council to open new Gaelic schools by 2024', 10 October.
Educational Institute of Scotland (1978), Letter from John MacAskill, Hon. Secretary, Lewis Branch, to Steven Rae, CnE, 8 February (CnES/SG).
Eglinton, James (2017), 'Why Gaelic speakers talk about God in English', *The Scotsman*, 7 December.
Ellis, Peter Berresford (1985), *The Celtic Revolution: A Study in Anti-Imperialism*, Talybont: Y Lolfa.
Ellis, Peter Berresford (2001), 'The Wordsmith – Edward Dwelly', in Dwelly (2001), vii–xxiv.
Ellis, Peter Berresford and Mac a' Ghobhainn, Seumas (1971), *The Problem of Language Revival*, Inverness: Club Leabhar.
Engels, Friedrich (2010 (electronic edn) [1849]), 'The Magyar Struggle', in *Karl Marx, Frederick Engels: Collected Works*, London: Lawrence & Wishart, vol. 8, 227–38.

Erskine, Ruaraidh, of Marr (1904), 'The Church and the Highlands', *GB*, 1, 1–11.
Erskine, Ruaraidh, of Marr (1905), 'Malairteachd', *An Claidheamh Soluis*, 25 November, 8.
Erskine of Marr, Ruaraidh (1906), 'Gaelic Confederation', *GB*, 3, 11–25.
Erskine of Marr, Ruaraidh (1912), 'Progress', *GB*, 9, 494–501.
Erskine, Ruaraidh, of Marr (1923a), 'Fo Chromadh an Taighe', *The Scottish Chapbook*, 1, 221–8.
Erskine, Ruaraidh, of Marr (1923b), 'Là de na Làithibh', *The Scottish Chapbook*, 2, 52–3.
   [see also Erskine, S. R.]
Erskine, S. R. (1900), 'Gaelic and the Gaels', *Outlook*, 6, 599.
   [see also Erskine, Ruaraidh, of Marr]
Eunson, Bruce (2017), ''23 Months 4 Coordinators 1 Aim: a discussion on attempts to develop the place of Scots language in education across Scotland', in Cruickshank and Millar (2017), 98–106.
European Commission, Directorate-General for Education, Youth, Sport and Culture (2004), *Promoting Language Learning and Linguistic Diversity: An Action Plan 2004–06*, Brussels: European Communities.
European Language Initiative (2011), *Faclair airson Riaghaltas Ionadail: Gàidhlig agus Beurla/Dictionary for Local Government: Scottish Gaelic and English*, Milton Keynes: European Language Initiative.
European Language Initiative (2012), *Faclair Rianachd Phoblaich: Gàidhlig agus Beurla/Dictionary for Public Administration: Scottish Gaelic and English*, Milton Keynes: European Language Initiative.
Evans, A. C. (1982), 'Use of Gaelic in Court Proceedings', *Scots Law Times*, 1982, 286–7.
Evans, W. Gareth (2000), 'The British State and Welsh-Language Education 1914–1991', in Jenkins and Williams (2000), 343–69.
The Express (2009), 'BBC's Gaelic boss "fiddles" TV ratings with football', 15 September, 12.
The Express (2010), 'BBC Alba kicks radio stations off Freeview', 22 December, 18.
The Express (2016), 'Gaelic logo plan for ambulance service', 17 January.
Ezeji, Cassie (2015), 'Whose Gaelic is it Anyway? Identity and Perception', https://mapmagazine.co.uk/whose-gaelic-it-anyway-identity-and-perception (last accessed 14 October 2019).
Fairney, Janice (2006), 'Highlanders from home: the contribution of the Highland Society and the GSL to Gaelic culture, 1778–1914', PhD thesis, University of Edinburgh.
Farquharson, Rev. Archibald (1875), 'Highlanders at Home and Abroad', *TGSI*, 3, 9–25.
Federation of Highland Associations (Glasgow) (1945), Letter from Kenneth Macdonald, Honorary Secretary, to H. Stewart MacIntosh, Director of

Education, City of Glasgow Corporation, 9 February (Glasgow City Archives (Mitchell Library) D–ED 11.1.191).

Fèisean nan Gàidheal (2016), 'BBC consultation on nations' radio, BBC Alba and news and current affairs on TV and online in the devolved nations: Response from Fèisean nan Gàidheal', Portree: Fèisean nan Gàidheal.

Fenyö, Krisztina (2000), *Contempt, Sympathy and Romance: Lowland Perceptions of the Highlands and the Clearances During the Famine Years, 1845–1855*, East Linton: Tuckwell Press.

Ferguson, Duncan (2011), interview with the author, Plockton, 21 June.

Ferguson, Mary and Matheson, Ann (1984), *Scottish Gaelic Union Catalogue: A List of Books Printed in Scottish Gaelic Since 1567*, Edinburgh: NLS.

Fife, James (2009), 'Typological Aspects of the Celtic Languages', in *The Celtic Languages*, in Ball and Müller (2008), 3–21.

'Fingal' (1967–8), 'Chan ann saor a mhàin ach Gàidhlig – not only free but Gaelic', *Scottish Vanguard*, 1(2), 15 and 2(2), 9–11.

Finlay, Richard J. (1994), *Independent and Free: Scottish Politics and the Origins of the Scottish National Party, 1918–1945*, Edinburgh: John Donald.

Finlay, Richard J. (2004a), *Modern Scotland: 1914–2000*, London: Profile.

Finlay, Richard (2004b), 'Gaelic, Scots and English: the politics of language in inter-war Scotland', in William Kelly and John R. Young (eds), *Ulster and Scotland, 1600–2000: History, Language and Identity*, Dublin: Four Courts Press, 133–41.

Fir Chlis (n.d.), Promotional leaflet (CnE–SG).

Fishman, Joshua A. (1978), *Language Loyalty in the United States*, New York: Arno.

Fishman, Joshua A., et al. (1985), *The Rise and Fall of the Ethnic Revival: Perspectives on Language and Ethnicity*, Berlin: Walter de Gruyter.

Fishman, Joshua A. (1991), *Reversing Language Shift: Theoretical and Empirical Foundations of Assistance to Threatened Languages*, Clevedon: Multilingual Matters.

Fishman, Joshua A. (1993), *The Earliest Stage of Language Planning: The 'First Congress' Phenomenon*, Berlin: Walter de Gruyter.

Fishman, Joshua A. (ed.) (2001), *Can Threatened Languages Be Saved? Reversing Language Shift, Revisited: A 21st Century Perspective*, Clevedon: Multilingual Matters.

Fishman, Joshua A. (2006), *Do Not Leave Your Language Alone: The Hidden Status Agendas Within Corpus Planning in Language Policy*, Mahwah, NJ: Lawrence Erlbaum.

FitzGerald, Garrett (1984), 'Estimates for baronies of minimum level of Irish-speaking amongst successive decennial cohorts, 1771–1781 to 1861–1871', *Proceedings of the Royal Irish Academy*, 84C, 117–55.

Forsyth, Michael (Baron Forsyth of Drumlean) (2011), telephone interview with the author, 17 August.

Fraser, Anne (1989), 'Gaelic in primary education: a study of the development of Gaelic bilingual education in urban contexts', PhD thesis, University of Glasgow.
[see also Gillies, Anne Lorne]
Fraser, Graham (2006), *Sorry, I Don't Speak French: Confronting the Canadian Crisis That Won't Go Away*, Toronto: McClelland & Stewart.
Fraser, James E. (2009), *From Caledonia to Pictland: Scotland to 795*, Edinburgh: EUP.
Fraser, Neil (1998), 'A Review of Aspects of Gaelic Broadcasting' (Report by Fraser Production and Consultancy for the Scottish Office Education and Industry Department, Arts and Cultural Heritage Division).
Fraser, Neil (2014), interview with the author, Glasgow, 4 September.
Free Presbyterian Church, Outer Isles Presbytery (1978), 'Observations on "The Bilingual Policy: A Consultative Document"' (CnES/SG).
Fry, Michael (2000), 'They didn't say yes, they didn't say no, so there could not be a conclusion', *Scottish Daily Mail*, 3 March, 11.
Fry, Michael (2007), 'Let's switch off the subsidies – Gaelic is a language of the past', *Sunday Times*, 25 November, 18.
Gaelic Broadcasting Task Force (2000), *Gaelic Broadcasting Task Force Report*, Edinburgh: SE.
A Gaelic Educationist (1948), 'The Present Position of Gaelic', *Alba*, 1, 10–13.
Gaelic Review Group (1982). Cor na Gàidhlig: Language, Community and Development – The Gaelic Situation. Inverness: Highlands and Islands Development Board.
The Gaelic Story at the University of Glasgow (2019), '20th Century: The Department of Celtic', https://sgeulnagaidhlig.ac.uk/20th-c-department-ofceltic/ (last accessed 17 December 2019).
Gaeloideachas (2019a), 'Statistics', https://gaeloideachas.ie/i-am-a-researcher/statistics/ (last accessed 27 August 2019).
Gaeloideachas (2019b), 'Primary Schools in Dublin', https://gaeloideachas.ie/county-region/primary-schools-in-dublin/ (last accessed 27 August 2019).
Gàidhlig-TV (2015), Open letter to Maggie Cunningham, Chair, MG ALBA, and Kenneth MacQuarrie, Controller, BBC Scotland, 23 April (WCM).
Gailig (1923), 'The Inverness Conference', 19, 10–15.
Gairm (1956), 'Cothrom na Féinne do'n Sgoil Ghàidhlig', 16, 360–1.
Gairm (1974–5), 'Cath Rathad na Bàn–rìgh Mairearad', 89, 22–3.
Galbraith, Neil (1981), 'The Western Isles: A New Context', in *Off the Beaten Track: Studies of Education in Rural Areas of Scotland*, 15–19, Edinburgh: SED.
Galloway, George (2003), 'Prepare For a Storm If We're Forced to Be Gaels', *Sunday Mail*, 24 October.
Galloway, George (2008), 'Gaelic Station Is A Turn-Off For Viewers', *Sunday Mail*, 4 February, 15.

Galloway, Susan (2012), 'The Arts Council and the Gaelic Arts', *Northern Scotland*, 3, 98–131.
GB (1905), 'Càs no Bàs', 2, 300–8.
GB (1906), 'A' Ghaidhlig anns na Sgoilean', 3, 97–101.
GB (1907a), 'Sinn Féin', 4, 1–13.
GB (1907b), 'Gàidheil is Comunnairean', 4, 384–91.
GB (1908a), 'Na Comuinn Ghaidhealach an Glaschu', 5, 38–45.
GB (1908b), 'The Recent Crisis in the Gaelic Movement', 5, 233–50.
General Register Office (1975), *Census 1971 Scotland: Gaelic Report*, Edinburgh: HMSO.
General Register Office for Scotland (2005), *Cunntas-Sluaigh na h-Alba 2001: Aithisg Ghàidhlig/Scotland's Census 2001: Gaelic Report*, Edinburgh: General Register Office for Scotland, https://www.nrscotland.gov.uk/statistics-and-data/census/2001-census/results-and-products/reports-and-data/gaelic-report (last accessed 1 November 2019).
Gessesse, Naomi (2019), 'What it's like being black in the Scottish Gaelic community', http://gal-dem.com/what-its-like-being-a-person-of-colour-in-the-scottish-gaelic-community/ (last accessed 1 November 2019).
GH (1870), 'Nairn – Imprisonment for Contempt of Court', 17 November, 3.
GH (1888), 'Gaelic in Highland Churches', 1 June, 9.
GH (1897), 'The Gaelic Question (By a Gaelic-speaking Highlander)', 17 April, 3.
GH (1930a), 'Instruction in Gaelic – Facilities in Glasgow Schools Desired', 19 April, 5.
GH (1933), 'Gaelic Culture in Scotland' (leader), 29 September, 10.
GH (1939), 'Letters in Gaelic From Soldiers', 14 October, 5.
GH (1943a), 'Gaelic Culture – Essentials for Survival', 16 April, 6.
GH (1943b), 'Gaelic in Schools' (leader), 1 December, 4.
GH (1946), 'Appeal for Glasgow Chair of Celtic', 14 October, 4.
GH (1947), 'Gaelic in Schools' (letter to the editor from Farquhar MacRae, ACG), 16 May, 4.
GH (1948), 'Future of Gaelic' (leader), 29 May, 2.
GH (1954), 'Street Names in Gaelic – Islay Innovation', 7 January, 2.
GH (1961), 'Extension of Gaelic in Lewis Schools – Removal of Handicap', 30 December, 13.
GH (1962), 'Gaelic and the Civil Service – Proposal Rejected', 30 May, 6.
GH (1973a), 'Gaelic signs to point the way', 8 February, 7.
GH (1973b), 'Savage tongue?' (letter to the editor from I. T. Bryden, Fincastle, Perthshire), 17 August, 8.
GH (1974), '£8700 grant for Gaelic college', 29 October, 7.
GH (1975), 'Gaels protest to BBC', 5 May, 2.
GH (1980), 'The Mod under attack from Gaeldom's young dissidents', 10 October, 7.
GH (1981a), 'Gaelic group calls for a TV licence rebellion', 7 April, 7.

GH (1981b), '"Contempt" claim over Gaelic post', 28 August, 3.
GH (1981c), 'Protest as court rejects a plea made in Gaelic', 11 September, 7.
GH (1986a), 'Gaelic upsurge', 5 February, 12.
GH (1986b), 'Travel costs to be met for pupils attending Gaelic unit', 7 August, 6.
GH (1989), 'Gaelic air-time' (letter to the editor from Kenneth Dunn, Pitlochry), 26 July, 8.
Gibb, Andrew Dewar (1930), *Scotland in Eclipse*, London: Humphrey Toulmin.
Gill, Brian (1988), Note for Western Isles Islands Council (Education and Bilingual Policies) (CnES–SG).
Gillies, Anne Lorne (2000), 'Creating Culture', in McCoy with Scott (2000), 96–104.
[see also Fraser, Anne]
Gillies, H. Cameron (1885), 'Highland Education', *The Highland Magazine*, 1(1), 38–52, 1(2), 113–20.
Gillies, H. Cameron (1885), 'Gaelic in Schools – The Special Minute', *The Highland Magazine*, 2(7), 54–61.
Gillies, Norman (2011), interview with the author, Armadale, Skye, 20 June.
Gillies, Norman and Thomson, Nicola (2009), 'Bòrd na Gàidhlig – Gaelic Organisations: The Way Forward' (report for BnG) (WCM/FOI).
Gillies, William (1988–90), 'Liam MacGill'Iosa: A Friend of the Gael', *TGSI*, 56, 503–33.
Gillies, William (ed.) (1989a), *Gaelic and Scotland/Alba agus a' Ghàidhlig*, Edinburgh: EUP.
Gillies, William (1989b), 'A Century of Gaelic Scholarship', in Gillies (1989a), 3–21.
Gillies, William (1991), 'Gaelic Songs of the 'Forty-Five', *Scottish Studies*, 30, 19–57.
Gillies, William (1996), 'Foreword', in Cathair Ó Dochartaigh (ed.), *Survey of the Gaelic Dialects of Scotland*, vol. 1, Dublin: Dublin Institute for Advanced Studies, vii–ix.
Gillies, William (2008), 'Scottish Gaelic', in Ball and Müller (2008), 230–304.
Gillies, William (2011), personal communication with the author, 14 June.
Glasgow City Council (2004), 'Future Gaelic Medium Provision', 8 September (WCM).
Glasgow City Council (2009), 'Draft Gaelic Language Plan 2009 to 2012: Public Consultation Exercise September to December 2008', Glasgow: Glasgow City Council.
Glasgow City Council (2017), *Response to the Consultation – Proposal: To Open a New Gaelic Medium Education (GME) Primary School in the South West of the City and to Define New Catchment Areas for Primary-aged Children Attending Glasgow Gaelic School/Sgoil Ghàidhlig Ghlaschu and*

Glendale Gaelic School/Bunsgoil Ghàidhlig Ghleann Dail and the New School, Glasgow: Glasgow City Council.

Glasgow Corporation Education Department (1947a), Note for Director, 'Gaelic' (JD/ABB), 16 January (Glasgow City Archives (Mitchell Library) D-ED 11.1.191).

Glasgow Corporation Education Department (1947b), Circular letter to primary school head teachers from H. Stewart MacIntosh, Director of Education, 13 May (Glasgow City Archives (Mitchell Library) D-ED 11.1.191).

Glasgow Corporation Education Department (1952), 'Gaelic in Secondary Schools' (GSF/MWS), 17 December (Glasgow City Archives (Mitchell Library) D-ED 11.1.191).

Glasgow University (1934), *Glasgow University Students' Handbook 1934–1935*, Glasgow: University of Glasgow.

Glasgow University Guardian (1975), 'Suas Leis a' Ghàidhlig', 30 January, 12.

Glaser, Konstanze (2007), *Minority Languages and Cultural Diversity in Europe: Gaelic and Sorbian Perspectives*, Clevedon: Multilingual Matters.

Glen, Duncan (1964), *Hugh MacDiarmid (Christopher Murray Grieve) and the Scottish Renaissance*, Edinburgh: W. & R. Chambers.

GLS (1931), 'Constitution', Glasgow: GLS.

GLS (1935), circular letter soliciting donations, from Jean Douglas, Honorary Treasurer, 5 January (NLS MS Acc. 4721, file 474).

Gondek, Meggan (2007), 'Pictish symbol stones: caught between prehistory and history', in Aron D. Mazel, George Nash and Clive Waddington (eds), *Art as Metaphor: The Prehistoric Rock-art of Britain*, Oxford: Archaeopress, 69–89.

Gossen, Andrew (2001), 'Agents of modern Gaelic Scotland: curriculum, change and challenge at Sabhal Mòr Ostaig, the Gaelic College of Scotland', PhD thesis, Harvard University.

Gove, Michael (2009), 'Don't let Hebridean Gaelic culture go the way of the auk', *The Scotsman*, 19 September.

Graffman, Katarina (2014), *Media behaviour among young Gaelic-speakers: A comparative study in Scotland, Sweden and Finland: Report for MG ALBA*, Stockholm: Inculture.

Grannd, Nigel (1984), 'A' Ghàidhlig agus Foghlam air a' Ghaidhealtachd 's a' Ghalldachd an Alba', *Gairm*, 127, 205–11.

[see also Grant, Nigel]

Grant, Alastair (1934), 'Highlands and Lowlands', *Scots Independent*, 8, no. 91, 100–1.

Grant, Alexander (1991), *Independence and Nationhood: Scotland 1306–1469*, Edinburgh: EUP.

Grant, Alexander (1994), 'Aspects of National Consciousness in Medieval Scotland', in Claus Bjørn et al. (eds), *Nations, Nationalism and Patriotism in the European Past*, Copenhagen: Academic Press, 68–95.

Grant, Donald (1965), 'The President's Address', AG, 60, 129–32.

Grant, J. H. (1983), 'An investigation into the feasibility of establishing Gaelic/English bilingual schools on the mainland of Scotland', MPhil dissertation, University of Glasgow.
Grant, James (2004), 'The Gaelic of Islay, a North Channel Dialect?', in Ó Háinle and Meek (2004), 69–95.
Grant, James Shaw (1972), 'James Shaw Grant on Gaelic's Role', *WHFP*, 20 October, 5.
Grant, Nigel (1980), *Gaelic School Study: Report to the Gaelic Language Promotion Trust of the Feasibility Study Conducted by the Research Team of the Department of Education, University of Glasgow*, Glasgow: Gaelic Language Promotion Trust.
Grant, Nigel (1983), *Report to the Gaelic Language Promotion Trust on the Feasibility of Gaelic–English Bilingual Schools on the Mainland of Scotland*, Glasgow: Gaelic Language Promotion Trust.
Grant, Nigel (1984), 'A Case for Gaelic–English Bilingual Primary Schools in Strathclyde Region', n.p.
Grassic Gibbon, Lewis (2001), *Smeddum: A Lewis Grassic Gibbon Anthology*, ed. by Valentina Bould, Edinburgh: Canongate.
Gray, Hamish (1981), Letter from Hamish Gray MP to Alexander Fletcher MP, Under-Secretary of State for Scotland, 17 November (NRS ED48/2601).
Grégoire, Henri (1794), *Rapport sur la nécessité et les moyens d'anéantir les patois et d'universaliser l'usage de la langue française*, https://archive.org/details/rapportsurlanece00greg (last accessed 1 November 2019).
Grieve, C. M. (1926), *Contemporary Scottish Studies, First Series*, London: Leonard Parsons.
Grieve, C. M. (1969 [1931]), 'The Caledonian Antisyzygy and the Gaelic Idea', in Duncan Glen (ed.), *Selected Essays of Hugh MacDiarmid*, London: Jonathan Cape, 56–74.
Grieve, C. M. (2004 [1923]), 'A Theory of Scots Letters', in McCulloch (2004), 27–8 (excerpted from *The Scottish Chapbook*, 1 (1923), 210–12).
    [see also MacDiarmid, Hugh]
Gruffudd, Heini and Morris, Steve Morris (2012), *Canolfannau Cymraeg and Social Networks of Adult Learners of Welsh: Efforts to Reverse Language Shift in comparatively non-Welsh-speaking Communities*, Swansea: South West Wales Welsh for Adults Centre.
GSL (1969), Letter from Alasdair MacKenzie MP, Chief, and J. A. Lynn, Secretary, GSL, to William Ross, Scottish Secretary, 10 February (NRS HH41/1994).
The Guardian (1977), 'Hydro board bows to Gaelic power', 27 October, 2.
Gunn, Hugh (1931), *The Distribution of University Centres in Britain: A Plea for the Highlands of Scotland*, Glasgow: Airlie Press.
Haf Gruffydd Jones, Elin and Uribe-Jongbloed, Enrique (eds) (2013), *Social Media and Minority Languages: Convergence and the Creative Industries*, Bristol: Multilingual Matters.

Hagemann, Susanne, '"Bidin natural": Identity Questions in Scottish Twentieth-Century Renaissance Literature', *Scottish Literary Journal*, 21(1), 44–55.
Hames, Scott (2020), *The Literary Politics of Scottish Devolution: Voice, Class, Nation*, Edinburgh: EUP.
Hanham, H. J. (1969), *Scottish Nationalism*, London: Faber & Faber.
Hanoa, Rolf Otto (1969), 'A meeting with European language movements', in Holmestad and Lade (1969), 9–15.
Hansard (1898), Reply from Andrew Graham Murray MP to question from James Galloway Weir MP, HoC Debates, 17 May. Vol. 57, col. 1554.
Hansard (1908), Reply from David Lloyd-George MP to question from James Galloway Weir MP, HoC Debates, 30 November, vol. 197, col. 1059.
Hansard (1927), Question to Sir John Gilmour, Scottish Secretary, from Neil MacLean MP, and reply thereto, 12 April, vol. 205, cols 202–3.
Hansard (1932), Question to Archibald Skelton MP from Lord Scone MP, and reply thereto. HoC Debates, 30 June, vol. 267, col. 2016.
Hansard (1943), Gaelic (Instruction in Primary Schools), HoC Debates, 30 November, vol. 395, col. 186.
Hansard (1965a), Debate on Highland Development (Scotland) Bill, HoC Debates, 19 March, vol. 708, col. 1095.
Hansard (1965b), Reply from William Ross MP, Scottish Secretary, to question from Malcolm Macmillan MP, HoC Debates, 3 November, vol. 718, cols 1011–12.
Hansard (1966), Reply from William Ross MP, Scottish Secretary, to written question from Russell Johnston MP, HoC Debates, 2 February, vol. 723, col. 245W.
Hansard (1969), Debate on Education (Scotland) Bill, House of Lords Debates, 1 July, vol. 303, col. 482.
Hansard (1971), Debate on Registration as Citizen, Crown Service etc., HoC Debates, 19 October, vol. 823, cols 651–5.
Hansard (1981), Debate on the Gaelic (Miscellaneous Provisions) Bill, HoC Debates, 13 February, vol. 998, cols 1088–1152.
Hansard (1984), Debate on Representation of the People Bill, HoC Debates, 10 December, vol. 69, col. 808.
Hansard (1986), Reply from Malcolm Rifkind MP to question from Donald Stewart MP, HoC Debates, 15 July, vol. 101, cols 100–1W.
Hansard (1988), Debate on Gaelic Language (TV Programmes), HoC Debates, 27 July, vol. 138, col. 396.
Hansard (1995), Reply from Lord James Douglas-Hamilton to question from Paul Flynn MP, HoC Debates, 25 January, vol. 253, col. 357.
Hansard (2003), Reply from Lord Evans of Temple Guiting to written question from Lord Mackenzie of Culkein, House of Lords Debates, 12 June, vol. 649, col. 70WA.
Hansard (2010), Debate on amendment 31 to the Parliamentary Voting System

and Constituencies Bill, House of Lords Debates, 8 December, vol. 723, cols 185–236.

Hansard (2015), Government departments: Scots Gaelic Language: Written question – 10755, 20 October.

Harvie, Christopher (1998), *No Gods and Precious Few Heroes: Twentieth-Century Scotland*, Edinburgh: EUP.

Harvie, Christopher and Jones, Peter (2000), *The Road to Home Rule: Images of Scotland's Cause*, Edinburgh: EUP.

Haugen, Einar (1966), *Language Conflict and Language Planning: The Case of Modern Norwegian*, Cambridge, MA: Harvard University Press.

Haugen, Einar, McClure, J. Derrick and Thomson, Derick S. (eds) (1981), *Minority Languages Today*, Edinburgh: EUP.

Hawke, Andrew (2018), 'Coping With an Expanding Vocabulary: The Lexicographical Contribution to Welsh', *International Journal of Lexicography*, 31, 229–48.

Hay, George Campbell (1947), 'Gael Warning', *The Scots Review*, 8:7, 104–5.

Hay, J. C. MacDonald (1937), 'The Present Position of Gaelic', *AG*, 33, 3–5.

HC (2005), 'Consultation on Proposals to Change Provision of Education in Lady Lovat Primary School – Report by the Area Education Manager', Inverness: HC.

HC (2006), 'Consultation on Proposals to Designate Sleat Primary School as a Dedicated Gaelic School – Report by Director of Education, Culture and Sport', Inverness: HC.

HC (2007), *The Highland Council Gaelic Language Plan 2007–2011*, Inverness: HC.

Highland Council (2012), *The Highland Council Gaelic Language Plan 2012–2016*, Inverness: HC.

HC (2019), Letter from Margaret Davidson, Convener, to Alasdair Allan MSP, Convener, Cross-Party Parliamentary Group on Gaelic (WCM).

Hebrides News (2016), 'Gaelic learners' association to fold', www.hebrides-news.com/cli-to-fold-141116.html (accessed 3 January 2020).

Hebrides Writer (2018), 'Time to tackle anti-Gaelic xenophobia masquerading as journalism', https://www.hebrideswriter.com/2018/05/25/2751/ (last accessed 10 January 2020).

Henderson, Angus (1918), 'The Hon. R. Erskine of Marr', *The Celtic Annual 1918–1919: Year Book of Dundee Highland Society*, 6, 5–7.

Henderson, Angus (1937), 'Our Highland Pioneer', *Perthshire Advertiser*, 17 March, 12.

Hepburn, Iain (2010), 'Looking at the bigger picture over Gaelic TV and BBC Alba', *Daily Record*, 1 August.

The Herald (1992), 'Only 20% of isles children fluent in Gaelic', 13 May, 2.

The Herald (1993), 'Gaelic TV lobby condemns "demoralising" grant cut', 16 December, 5.

The Herald (2003), 'Ministers to take tough line in backing Gaelic', 11 October, 8.
The Herald (2004), 'Jowell takes TV control', 10 June, 2.
The Herald (2005), 'Passports to feature Gaelic language', 7 February, 6.
The Herald (2006), 'Green light for English unit at Gaelic school', 22 September, 12.
The Herald (2008), 'Gaelic development chief resigns after months in job', 7 August, 5.
The Herald (2011), 'Freeview launch for BBC Gaelic channel', 8 June, 8.
The Herald (2012), 'BBC Alba audience warning', 7 September, 8.
The Herald (2012), 'Bilingual road signs for A9 after safety fears allayed', 12 September, 9.
The Herald (2015), 'Church of Scotland holds conference to promote Gaelic language', 21 March.
The Herald (2017a), 'Gaelic school rejected after council shuns parents' bid', 7 October.
The Herald (2017b), 'Call for Gaelic language czar for Scotland', 16 October.
The Herald (2018a), 'Tory MSP tells "unionist ultras" to dial down rhetoric on Gaelic', 28 April.
The Herald (2018b), 'Alba no more. Skye no more. Loch Lomond no more. Runrig say farewell', 11 August.
The Herald (2019a), 'Gaelic education tells you all about the culture of Scotland with music, traditions and history', 20 March, 6.
The Herald (2019b), 'Drive to spread Gaelic is no more than political subterfuge' (letter from Bill Brown, Milngavie), 12 June, 15.
Hickey (2010), column, *The Express*, 18 November, 15.
HIDB (1966a), Letter from J. A. Macaskill to A. M. Hamilton, SAFS, 22 April (NRS SEP12/277).
HIDB (1966b), Minute of Meeting between Sir Robert Grieve, Chairman, and Donald John MacKay and Rory MacKay, ACG, 27 June (N.V. 118/66) (NRS SEP12/277).
HIDB (1982), *Cor na Gàidhlig: Language, Community and Development: The Gaelic Situation*. Inverness: HIDB.
HIDB (1984), Staff Paper 5155 – Progress on Gaelic Council (CNAG) (NRS ED61/196).
The Highlander (1879), 'The Highlander', 6 June, 1–2.
Highland News (2015), 'Head finally found for Gaelic school in Inverness', 1 May.
Highland Regional Council, Strathclyde Regional Council and Western Isles Islands Council (1982), Submission on Behalf of Highland Regional Council, Strathclyde Regional Council and Western Isles Islands Council for the Making of Regulations for Specific Grants for the Teaching and Use of Gaelic under Section 73 of the Education (Scotland) Act 1980 (NRS ED61/20).
Highland Regional Council (1984), Minutes of Meeting of Committee on Gaelic Language and Culture, 5 July (HC Archives, HRC 1/1/18).

Highland Regional Council (1985), Letter from R. H. Stevenson, chief executive, to Secretary, SED, 4 June (NRS ED61/190).

Highlands and Islands Enterprise (2014), *Ar Stòras Gàidhlig: The economic and social value of Gaelic as an asset*, Inverness: Highlands and Islands Enterprise.

HM Inspector of Constabulary (1865), *Seventh Report of Her Majesty's Inspector of Constabulary of Scotland*, London: HoC.

HM Inspectors of Schools (2011), *Gaelic Education: Building on the Successes, addressing the barriers*, Livingston: HMIE.

HM Inspectors of Schools, Northern Division (1989), 'Some Recent Developments in Gaelic Education' (NRS ED61/160).

HM Treasury (1989a), Minute from Nigel Lawson, Chief Secretary to the Treasury, to the Prime Minister, 25 October (NRS ED 29/114).

HM Treasury (1989b), Letter from Norman Lamont, Chief Secretary to the Treasury, to Malcolm Rifkind, Scottish Secretary, 29 November (NRS ED 29/114).

HO (1873), 'Dynamite, Horsley's Blasting Powder, &c – Nitro-Glycerin Act, 1869 (32 & 33 Vict., cap. 118)', *The London Gazette*, 31 January, 427–9.

HO (1974), *Report of the Committee on Broadcasting Coverage*, London: HMSO.

HO (1977), *Report of the Committee on the Future of Broadcasting*, London: HMSO.

HO (1978), *Broadcasting*, London: HMSO.

HO (1981), Minute from M. J. Addison, B4 Division, to Miss Kippax, 9 September (NRS HH41/2712).

HO (1988), *Broadcasting in the '90s: Competition, Choice and Quality – The Government's Plans for Broadcasting Legislation*, London: HMSO.

HO (1989), Minute from Douglas Hurd, Home Secretary, to the Prime Minister, 17 October (NRS ED 29/114).

Hogan-Brun, Gabrielle and O'Rourke, Bernadette (eds) (2019), *The Palgrave Handbook of Minority Languages and Communities*, London: Palgrave Macmillan.

Holmestad, Einar and Lade, Arild Jostein (eds) (1969), *Lingual Minorities in Europe*, Oslo: Det Norske Samlaget.

Howell, David (1986), *A Lost Left: Three Studies in Socialism and Nationalism*, Chicago: University of Chicago Press.

Hughes, Robert (2017), 'The Role of Welsh-language Journalism in Shaping the Construction of Welsh Identity and the National Character of Wales', PhD thesis, Liverpool John Moores University.

Hulbert, John (ed.) (1985), *Gaelic: Looking to the Future*, Longforgan: Andrew Fletcher Society.

Hunter, James (ed.) (1986), *For the People's Cause: From the Writings of John Murdoch, Highland and Irish Land Reformer*, Edinburgh: HMSO.

Hunter, James (2000 [1976]), *The Making of the Crofting Community*, 2nd edn, Edinburgh: John Donald.
Hunter, James (2014), 'Scottish independence: Highlanders stand proud', *The Scotsman*, 2 September.
Hunter, Janet (1992), '*Comuinn Eachdraidh*: The Development of Local History Societies in the Western Isles, 1977–1991', MLitt thesis, University of Aberdeen.
Hunter, William (1974), 'Gaelic – the vital spark of the isles', GH, 6 May, 12.
Hussain, Asifa M. and Miller, William (2006), *Nationalism: Islamophobia, Anglophobia, and Devolution*, Oxford: OUP.
Hutchinson, Roger (2005), *A Waxing Moon: The Modern Gaelic Revival*, Edinburgh: Mainstream.
Hutchinson, Roger, with Dick, Criosaidh (2005), *Gealach an Fhàis: Ùr Bheothachadh na Gàidhlig*, Edinburgh: Mainstream.
Hyde, Douglas (1894), 'The Necessity for De-Anglicising Ireland', in *The Revival of Irish Literature*, London: T. Fisher Unwin, 115–61.
'Ian' (1904), 'Degenerate Highlanders', *The Celtic Monthly*, 12, 210.
IC (1908a), 'Gaelic in Schools', 22 May, 3.
IC (1908b), 'Inverness Teachers and the Gaelic Amendment', 5 June, 4.
IC (1908c), 'Islay School Board and Gaelic Teaching' and 'Lewis Boards and Gaelic', 9 June, 4.
IC (1908d), 'The Teaching of Gaelic', 19 June, 6.
IC (1909a), 'Town Council', 7 May, 2.
IC (1909b), 'Town Council', 11 June, 7.
IC (2011), 'Changes needed before second Gaelic school', 8 July.
Independent Television Authority (1972), *Annual Report and Accounts 1971–72*, London: HMSO.
Inspector-General of Recruiting (1870), *Memorandum by the Inspector-General of Recruiting*, London: HMSO.
Inverness County Council Education Committee (1958), Minutes of meeting, 8 October (HC Archives CI/5/19/9/2/1).
Inverness County Council Education Committee (1964), *Scheme of Instruction in Gaelic*, Inverness: Inverness County Council.
Irish Independent (2005), 'New homes in Gaeltacht must now be sold to Irish speakers', 23 April.
Irish Times (1969), 'M.P. opposes aid for Scottish Gaelic', 22 May, 7.
Irish Times (2016), 'Brexit a "potential disaster" for minority languages', 22 June.
Irish Times (2018), 'Irish medium schools continue to outperform on Feeder lists', 4 December.
Jack, Ian (2010), 'Saving a language is one thing, but I'm saddened by Scotland going Gaelic', *The Guardian*, 11 December, 43.
Jackson, Kenneth (1958), 'The Situation of the Scottish Gaelic Language, and the work of the Linguistic Survey of Scotland', *Lochlann*, 1, 229–34.

Jaffe, Alexandra (1999), *Ideologies in Action: Language Politics on Corsica*, Berlin: Mouton de Gruyter.
James, Alan (2013), 'P-Celtic in Southern Scotland and Cumbria: a review of the place-name evidence for possible Pictish phonology', *Journal of Scottish Name Studies*, 7, 29–78.
James, Clive (1991), 'What Future for Scotland's Gaelic-speaking Communities?', in Colin H. Williams (ed.), *Linguistic Minorities, Society and Territory*, Clevedon: Multilingual Matters, 173–218.
Jarvie, Grant (1991), *Highland Games: The Making of the Myth*, Edinburgh: EUP.
Jenkins, Geraint H. and Williams, Mari A. (eds) (1998), *The Welsh Language in the Nineteenth Century*, Cardiff: UWP.
Johnstone, Euan (2003), 'Mura Dèan an-Dràsta, Cuin?/If Not Now, When?', *Cothrom*, 35, 18–20.
Johnstone, Richard (1994), *The Impact of Current Developments to Support the Gaelic Language: Review of Research*, Stirling: Scottish CILT.
Johnstone, Richard, et al. (1999), *The attainments of pupils receiving Gaelic-medium primary education in Scotland*, Stirling: Scottish CILT.
Johnstone, Richard, et al. (2003), *Gaelic Learners in the Primary School (GLPS) in Argyll & Bute, East Ayrshire, North Lanarkshire, Perth & Kinross and Stirling: Evaluation Report*, Stirling: Scottish CILT.
Johnstone, Richard et al. (2004), *Draft Gaelic Language Bill Consultation Analysis: Report to the Scottish Executive and Bòrd na Gàidhlig*, Sleat: Lèirsinn.
Jones, Christine M. (1991), 'The Ulpan in Wales: a study in motivation', *Journal of Multilingual and Multicultural Development*, 12, 183–93.
Jones, Kathryn, et al. (2017), *Assessment of the Impact of the National Gaelic Language Plan 2012–17: Final Report for Bòrd na Gàidhlig*, Edinburgh: IAITH/Celtic & Scottish Studies, University of Edinburgh.
Jones, Peter (1981), 'New mood of militancy', *P&J*, 9 October, 10.
Jones, Rhys, Merriman, Peter and Mills, Sarah (2016), 'Youth organizations and the reproduction of nationalism in Britain: the role of Urdd Gobaith Cymru', *Social and Cultural Geography*, 17, 714–34.
Jordanhill College of Education, Gaelic Department (1994), 'Gaelic-medium units in Primary Schools: Pupil numbers 1993–94', Glasgow: Jordanhill College of Education.
Judge, Anne (2007), *Linguistic Policies and the Survival of Regional Languages in France and Britain*, Basingstoke: Palgrave.
Kaplan, Robert B. and Baldauf, Richard B. (1997), *Language Planning: From Practice to Theory*, Clevedon: Multilingual Matters.
Kavanagh, Paul (2011), 'Scotland's Language Myths: 4. Gaelic has nothing to do with the Lowlands', https://newsnet.scot/archive/scotlands-language-myths-4-gaelic-is-only-a-highland-language/ (last accessed 1 November 2019).
Keating, Michael (2010a), 'The End of Union? Scottish Nationalism and the UK State', in Keith Breen and Shane O'Neill (eds), *After the Nation?*

Critical Reflections on Nationalism and Postnationalism, London: Palgrave Macmillan, 103–19.

Keating, Michael (2010b), *The Government of Scotland: Public Policy Making After Devolution*, 2nd edn, Edinburgh: EUP.

Keene, Catherine (2013), *Saint Margaret, Queen of the Scots: A Life in Perspective*, New York: Palgrave Macmillan.

Kelly, Jamie (2016), 'The Mission at Home: The Origins and Development of the Society in Scotland for Propagating Christian Knowledge, 1709–1767', *e-sharp*, 24.

Kelta (1836), 'Professorship of the Gaelic Language and Literature', *Thistle; or, Anglo-Caledonian Journal*, 1, 470–3.

Kennedy, Michael (2002), *Gaelic Nova Scotia: An Economic, Cultural, and Social Impact Study*, Halifax: Nova Scotia Museum.

Kidd, Colin (2008), *Union and Unionisms: Political Thought in Scotland, 1500–2000*, Cambridge: CUP.

Kidd, Sheila (ed.) (2007), *Glasgow: Baile Mor Nan Gaidheal: City of the Gaels*, Glasgow: Department of Celtic and Gaelic, University of Glasgow.

Kidd, Sheila (2008), 'Burning issues: reactions to the Highland Press during the 1885 election campaign', *SGS*, 24, 286–307.

Kidd, Sheila (2010), 'A Thaghdairean Gaedhealach: Early Gaelic Electioneering', in Kenneth E. Nilsen (ed.), *Rannsachadh na Gàidhlig 5*, Sydney, NS: Cape Breton University Press, 116–33.

Kidd, Sheila (2015), 'The Language Barrier and Welfare Provision in the Nineteenth Century', paper presented at the International Congress of Celtic Studies, Glasgow, 13–17 July.

Kidner, Camilla (2015), *SPICe Briefing: Education (Scotland) Bill*, Edinburgh: SPICe.

Kinnear, Neale, et al. (2012), *Analyses of the Effects of Bilingual Signs on Road Safety in Scotland*, Wokingham: Transport Research Laboratory.

Kirk, John M. (2011), 'Scotland and Northern Ireland as Scots-speaking Communities', in John M. Kirk and Dónall P. Ó Baoill (eds), *Sustaining Minority Language Communities: Northern Ireland, the Republic of Ireland and Scotland*, Belfast: Cló Ollscoil na Banríona, 193–205.

Kirk, John M. and Ó Baoill, Dónall P. (eds) (2003), *Towards Our Goals in Broadcasting, the Press, the Performing Arts and the Economy: Minority Languages in Northern Ireland, the Republic of Ireland, and Scotland*, Belfast: Cló Ollscoil na Banríona.

Kirk, Neville (2007), *Custom and Conflict in the 'Land of the Gael': Ballachulish, 1900–1910*, Monmouth: The Merlin Press.

Knooihuizen, Remco (2005), 'The Norn-to-Scots Language Shift: Another Look at Socio-historical Evidence', *Northern Studies*, 39, 105–17.

Laing, Uisdean (1959), 'Mar a Chum a' Ghàidhlig Astralia Geal', *Gairm*, 29, 19–22.

Lamb, William (1999), 'A Diachronic Account of Gaelic News-speak: The Development and Expansion of a Register', *SGS*, 19, 141–71.
Lambert, Wallace E. and Tucker, G. Richard (1972), *The Bilingual Education of Children: The St. Lambert Experiment*, Rowley, MA: Newbury House.
'L[àmh] L[àidir]' (1898), 'Comunnan Gàidhlig', *Mac-Talla*, 6, 273.
Landry, Rodrigue and Bourhis, Richard Y. (1997), 'Linguistic Landscape and Ethnolinguistic Vitality: An Empirical Study', *Journal of Language and Social Psychology,* 16:1, 23–49.
Lauchlan, Fraser, Parisi, Marinella and Fadda, Roberta (2012), 'Bilingualism in Sardinia and Scotland: Exploring the cognitive benefits of speaking a "minority" language', *International Journal of Bilingualism*, 17, 43–56.
Laughton, Roger (2003), *S4C: An Independent Review*, London: DCMS.
The Laws of Scotland: Stair Memorial Encyclopedia (2017) (available via ww.lexisnexis.com).
Lehtonen, Minna, et al. (2018), 'Is bilingualism associated with enhanced executive functioning in adults? A meta-analytic review', *Psychological Bulletin*, 144(4), 394–425.
Leneman, Leah (1991), *Fit for Heroes? Land Settlement in Scotland After World War I*, Aberdeen: Aberdeen University Press.
Lewin, Custal y and Mac an Tuairneir, Marcas (eds) (2017), *Comann Ceilteach Oilthigh Dhùn Èideann: 180 Bliadhna/Edinburgh University Highland Society: 180 Years*, Edinburgh: Comann Ceilteach Oilthigh Dhùn Èideann.
Lewis, Saunders (1986), 'Tynged yr Iaith', in *Ati, Wy'r Ifainc*, ed. by Marged Dafydd, Cardiff: UWP, 88–98.
Lewis, Saunders (1971), 'The Fate of the Language', trans. by Elizabeth Edwards, *Planet*, 4, 13–27.
Lexecon Ltd (1994), *The Case for a National Gaelic Radio Service*, London: Lexecon Ltd.
Linklater, Eric (1938), 'Scotland To-Day', *Journal of the Royal Society of Arts*, 86, 810–12.
Linklater, Magnus (2002), 'Gaelic must take its chances as arts funding crisis bites', *The Scotsman*, 17 November, 20.
Livingston, Alistair (2012), 'The Decline of Gaelic in Galloway 1370–1500', www.academia.edu/1534013/The_Decline_of_Gaelic_in_Galloway_1370-1500 (last accessed 20 December 2019).
Lo Bianco, Joe (2001), *Language and Literacy Policy in Scotland*, Stirling: Scottish CILT.
Local Government Board for Scotland (1910), *Fifteenth Annual Report of the Local Government Board for Scotland*, Edinburgh: HMSO.
López-Goñi, Irene (2003), 'Ikastola in the twentieth century: an alternative for schooling in the Basque Country', *History of Education*, 32, 661–76.
Lorimer, Hayden (1997), '"Your Wee Bit Hill and Glen": The Cultural Politics of the Scottish Highlands, *c.* 1918–1945', PhD thesis, Loughborough University.

Lotz, Jim (1969), 'Regional Planning and Development in the Highlands and Islands of Scotland', *Canadian Public Administration*, 12, 372–86.
[Lovat-Fraser], J. A. (1917), 'The Duke of Argyll', *The Celtic Monthly*, 1–2.
'Lowlander' (1939), 'Gaelic Broadcasts' (letter to the editor), *Daily Record*, 22 February, 10.
Luckhurst, Tim (2005), 'So what is the Gaelic for utterly pointless quango?' *Daily Mail*, 4 February, 14.
Lynch, Peter (2013), *SNP: The History of the Scottish National Party*, 2nd edn, Cardiff: Welsh Academic Press.
Mac a' Ghobhainn, Dùbhghlas (1989–90), 'Beachdan Òigridh Innse Gall', *Gairm*, 149, 76–82.
Mac a' Ghobhainn, Seumas (1969), 'Over to You' (letter to the editor), *Sruth*, 50, 11.
Mac a' Ghobhainn, Seumas (1972), 'Ruaraidh Arascainn is Mhàirr', *SG*, 19 February, 4.
Mac a' Ghobhainn, Seumas (1973), 'A Most Unusual Scottish Patriot', *A' Bhratach Ùr*, 2(1), 4–5.
Mac a' Ghobhainn, Seumas (1973), 'Iain MacPheadruis and the Gaelic League of Scotland', *A' Bhratach Ùr*, 3(1), 4–5.
Mac a' Ghobhainn, Seumas (2000 [1977]), 'A' Ghàidhlig – The Scottish Language', in Peter Berresford Ellis, *Scotland Not Only Free But Gaelic – A Tribute To Seumas Mac a' Ghobhainn*, ed. by Risnidh MagAoidh, Glasgow: Celtic Editions, [14]–[17].
Mac a' Ghreidir, Gillechriosd (1929), 'Gaelic Literature Surveyed', *The Scots Independent*, 3(10), 131.
[see also Grieve, C. M.]
Mac a' Phearsain, Seonaidh Ailig (2011), *Steall à Iomadh Lòn*, Inverness: CLÀR.
[see also MacPherson, John A.]
MacAilpein, Tòmas (2017), 'Cultar agus an comann-sòisealta ann an Ìle, mu 1890 gu 1960', PhD thesis, University of Glasgow.
Mac an Iomaire, Peadar (1983), 'Tionchar na tionsclaíochta ar Ghaeilge Chonamara Theas', *Teangeolas*, 16, 9–18.
Mac an Tàilleir, Iain, Rothach, Gillian and Armstrong, Timothy Currie (2010), *Barail agus Comas Cànain: Aithisg rannsachaidh airson Bòrd na Gàidhlig*, Sleat: SMO.
[MacAoidh, Garbhan] (1975a), '"Fine Ghàidheil" – An Gàidheil iad?', *Crann-Tara: Newsletter of Comunn na Cànain Albannaich*, 10, 2.
MacAoidh, Garbhan (1975b), 'Cogadh nan Comharraidhean', *Gairm*, 92, 317–19.
MacArthur, John (1885), 'The Future of the Gaelic Language', *The Celtic Magazine*, 10, 251–6, 299–305.
MacAskill, Kenny (2016), 'Let us see ourselves and the world through our own TV lens', *Sunday Herald*, 7 September.

MacAulay, Donald (1966), 'On Some Aspects of Modern Gaelic Verse', *SGS*, 11, 136–45.
MacAulay, Donald (1972), Letter to the Editor, *SG*, 15 July.
MacAulay, Donald (ed.) (1976), *Nua-Bhàrdachd Ghàidhlig/Modern Scottish Gaelic Poems*, Edinburgh: Southside.
MacAulay, Donald (1994), 'Canons, myths and cannon fodder', *Scotlands*, 1, 35–54.
MacAulay, Rev. Donald (1991), Video interview with Calum Ferguson (Bliadhna na Gàidhlig), Box 70, Museum nan Eilean, Stornoway.
MacAulay, Peter (1997), 'Loosening link between Gaelic and the churches', *WHFP*, 21 November, 7.
Macbean, Lachlan (1876), *Elementary Lessons in Gaelic*, Inverness: The Highlander.
MacCaluim, Alasdair (2007a), *Reversing Language Shift: The Social Identity and Role of Adult Learners of Scottish Gaelic*, Belfast: Cló Ollscoil na Banríona.
MacCaluim, Alasdair (2007b), '"More than interesting": a' Ghàidhlig sa Bhaile Mhòr', in McLeod (2007), 19–30.
MacCaluim, Alasdair, with McLeod, Wilson (2001), *Revitalising Gaelic? A Critical Analysis of the Report of the Taskforce on Public Funding of Gaelic*, Edinburgh: Celtic and Scottish Studies, University of Edinburgh.
MacColla, Eòbhann [MacColl, Evan] (1886), *Clàrsach nam Beann*, Glasgow: Archibald Sinclair.
'MacColla, Fionn' [Thomas Douglas MacDonald] (1975), 'The Cultural Situation in Alba', *Am Baner Kernewek*, 1:3, 8–10.
MacCurdy, Edward (1943), 'The Case for Gaelic', *The Spectator*, 5996, 497.
MacCurdy, Edward (1944), 'The Present Disabilities of Gaelic', *AG*, 39, 41–3.
MacDhòmhnaill, Fionnlagh I. (1962), Review of Committee on Bilingualism 1961, *Gairm*, 39, 281–3.
 [see also MacDonald, Finlay J.]
MacDhunlèibhe, Donnachadh (1961), 'Teagasg Na Gàidhlige Sna Sgoiltean', *Gairm*, 37, 35–7.
MacDiarmid, Hugh (1997 [1929]), 'Towards a Scottish Renaissance: desirable lines of advance', in Angus Calder, Glen Murray and Alan Riach (eds), *The Raucle Tongue: Hitherto Uncollected Prose, Volume II: 1927–1936*, Manchester: Carcanet, 79–81.
 [see also Grieve, C. M.]
Macdonald, Catriona (2009), *Whaur Extremes Meet: Scotland's Twentieth Century*, Edinburgh: John Donald.
Macdonald, Finlay J. (1958), 'Last Days of Gaelic', *Saltire Review*, 5, 14–20.
 [see also MacDhòmhnaill, Fionnlagh I.]
MacDonald, Fraser (2011), 'Doomsday Fieldwork, or, How to Rescue Gaelic Culture? The salvage paradigm in geography, archaeology and folklore, 1955–1962', *Environment and Planning D: Society and Space*, 29, 309–35.

MacDonald, John (ed.) (1927), *Voices from the Hills (Guthan o na Beanntaibh): A Memento of the Gaelic Rally, 1927*, Glasgow: ACG.
MacDonald, John A. (1957), 'Green Light for Gaelic', *Ossian 1957*, 10–11.
MacDonald, Martin (1976), 'The Media', in MacThòmais (1976), 67.
MacDonald, Martin (1990), 'The Gaelic language and Scottish broadcasting', *Media Education Journal*, 9, 21–3.
MacDonald, Martin (2002), 'Champion of Gaelic whose personal skills helped build an effective ministry', *The Herald*, 13 December, 20.
   [see also Dòmhnallach, Màrtainn]
MacDonald, Murdoch (1937), 'The Present Position of Gaelic', *AG*, 33, 37–8.
MacDonald, Peter (2017), 'Myth buster: Was tartan really banned after Culloden?', *The Scotsman*, 31 October.
Macdonald, Sharon (1997), *Reimagining Culture: Histories, Identities and the Gaelic Renaissance*, Oxford: Berg.
MacEwen, Sir Alexander (1931), 'The Highlands: The Spirit of the Gael', *AG*, 26, 50–3.
MacEwen, Sir Alexander (1932), *The Thistle and the Rose: Scotland's Problems Today*, Edinburgh: Oliver & Boyd.
MacFarlane, Sir D. H. (1895), Bilingual election leaflet to the electors of Argyllshire, July 1895 (NLS MS Acc 9736/82).
MacFarlane, Malcolm (1889), *The Phonetics of the Gaelic Language*, Paisley: J. & R. Parlane.
[MacFarlane, Malcolm] (1906), 'Only a Medley', *DG*, 1, 148–50.
MacFarlane, Malcolm (1912), *Am Briathrachan Beag/The School Gaelic Dictionary*, Stirling: Eneas Mackay.
MacFarlane, Malcolm (1929), 'Half a Century of Vocal Gaelic Music', *TGSI*, 32 (1924), 251–71.
MacFhionghuin, Coinneach, NicRath, Criosaidh and Galloway, Iain (2007), *Bòrd na Gàidhlig: Dreachd de Phlana Nàiseanta na Gàidhlig agus Dreachd den Stiùireadh air Planaichean Gàidhlig – Aithisg mun Cho-chomhairleachadh Phoblach*, Inverness: BnG.
   [see also MacKinnon, Kenneth]
MacFhionghuin, Ruairidh (1974), 'Nàimhdeas do'n Ghàidhlig', *Gairm*, 86, 153–6.
MacGaraidh, Seumas (1935), 'Suas Alba! Save the Language', *New Scotland*, 10(1), 3.
MacGill-Eain, Tormod (1997), *Cùmhnantan*, Inverness: CLÀR.
MacGille Iosa, Liam (1920), 'Eire', *Alba*, 24.
MacGille Sheathanaich, Niall (1936), 'An Comunn Gaidhealach', *Outlook*, 1(9), 104–6.
MacGill-Fhinnein, Gordon (1965–6), 'Ath-bheòthachadh na Gàidhlig an Èirinn agus an Albainn', *Gairm*, 51, 201–5; 53, 55–9; 53, 135–44.
MacGregor, John (1897), *Luinneagan Luaineach (Random Lyrics)*, London: David Nutt.

MacGregor, Martin (2009), 'Gaelic Barbarity and Scottish Identity in the Later Middle Ages', in Broun and MacGregor (2009), 7–48.
MacIllechiar, Iain (2012), telephone interview with the author, 8 February.
Mac 'Ill Fhialain, Aonghas (1972), *Saoghal an Treabhaiche*, Inverness: Club Leabhar.
Macinnes, Allan (1996), *Clanship, Commerce, and the House of Stuart, 1603–1788*, East Linton: Tuckwell Press.
MacInnes, John (2006), 'The Gaelic Perception of the Lowlands' and 'The Panegyric Code in Gaelic Poetry and its Historical Background', in Michael Newton (ed.), *Dùthchas nan Gàidheal: Selected Essays of John MacInnes*, Edinburgh: Birlinn, 34–47, 265–319.
MacIntosh, Farquhar (1999), 'The Prospects for Gaelic', in Ronald Black, William Gillies and Roibeard Ó Maolalaigh (eds), *Celtic Connections: Proceedings of the Tenth International Congress of Celtic Studies*, East Linton: Tuckwell Press, 457–69.
Maciver, Rev. Angus (1918), Letter to Sir John Struthers, Secretary, SED, 24 July (NRS ED14/87).
MacIver, Matthew (2011), interview with the author, Edinburgh, 21 January.
Maciver, Roy (1991), Video interview with Calum MacFhearghuis, 'Mar chaidh poileasaidh dà-chànanach a stèidheachadh','Bliadhna na Gàidhlig' project (Museum nan Eilean, Stornoway).
Maciver, Ruairidh (2018), 'The Gaelic Poet and the British military experience, 1756–1856', PhD thesis, University of Glasgow.
Mackay, David (1996), *We did it ourselves* – Sinn fhein a rinn e: *an account of the Western Isles Community Education Project* Pròiseact Muinntir nan Eilean *1977–1992*, The Hague: Bernard van Leer Foundation.
Mackay, D. (1966), Letter to K. J. MacKenzie, Scottish Office Home and Health Department (NRS HH41/1657).
Mackay, Donald J. (1969a), 'The lingual minority in Scotland', in Holmestad and Lade (1969), 137–41.
Mackay, Donald J. (1969b), 'Educational problems in Scotland', in Holmestad and Lade (1969), 142–5.
Mackay, Rev. G. W. (1917), 'The Gaelic Question in Scotland', *An Deo-Gréine*, 13, 19–24.
MacKay, I. R. (1976 [1966]), *Who Are the Highlanders?*, Inverness: An Comunn Gàidhealach.
MacKay, John (2002), *Highlanders! Stand Shoulder to Shoulder: A History of the Gaelic Society of Perth*, Perth: Gaelic Society of Perth.
Mackay, John Angus (2011), interview with the author, Edinburgh, 13 June.
Mackay, J. G. (1899), *Easy Gaelic Syntax*, London: David Nutt.
Mackay, Margaret A. (2013), 'The First Sixty Years of the School of Scottish Studies: An Overview', in Bob Chambers (ed.), *The Carrying Stream Flows On: Celebrating the Diamond Jubilee of the School of Scottish Studies*, Kershader: Islands Books Trust, 1–33.

Mackay, William (1893), *Urquhart and Glenmoriston: Olden Times in a Highland Parish*, Inverness: Northern Counties Newspaper and Printing and Publishing Co.

Mackay, William (1906), 'The Teaching of Gaelic in Schools', *The Celtic Monthly*, 14, 237–8.

Mackenzie, A. Fiona D. (2012), *Places of Possibility: Property, Nature and Community Land Ownership*, Oxford: Blackwell.

[Mackenzie, Alexander] (1881), 'A Gaelic Court', *The Celtic Magazine*, 6, 463.

[Mackenzie, Alexander] (1885), 'Highland Judges and the Gaelic Language', *The Celtic Magazine*, 10, 441–4.

Mackenzie, Compton (1933), 'Quo Vadis', *Ossian*, 1933, 10.

Mackenzie, Compton (1998 [1936]), 'Catholic Barra', in John Lorne Campbell (ed.), *The Book of Barra*, Stornoway: Acair, 1–25.

MacKenzie, D. F. (1948), 'Highland Pseudo-Culture', *Alba*, 1, 63–5.

MacKenzie, Gordon H. (2018), 'Minority language media, status planning & linguistic attitudes in Scotland: the sociolinguistic impact of the Gaelic television channel BBC Alba', MLitt thesis, University of Glasgow.

MacKillop, Andrew (2001), *More Fruitful Than the Soil: Army, Empire and the Scottish Highlands, 1715–1815*, East Linton: Tuckwell Press.

MacKinnon, Donald (1875), 'Gaelic Language in Highland Schools', *AG*, 4, 23–7.

MacKinnon, Kenneth (1970–2), 'The School in Gaelic Scotland', *TGSI*, 47, 374–91.

MacKinnon, Kenneth (1974), *The Lion's Tongue: The Story of the Original and Continuing Language of the Scottish People*, Inverness: Club Leabhar.

MacKinnon, Kenneth (1977), *Language, Education and Social Processes in a Gaelic Community*, London: Routledge & Kegan Paul.

MacKinnon, Kenneth (1978), *Gaelic in Scotland 1971: Some Sociological and Demographic Considerations of the Census Report for Gaelic*, Hatfield: Hatfield Polytechnic.

MacKinnon, Kenneth (1981), *Scottish Opinion on Gaelic: A report on a national attitude survey for An Comunn Gàidhealach undertaken in 1981*, Hatfield: Hatfield Polytechnic.

MacKinnon, Kenneth (1985), *The Scottish Gaelic Speech-Community – Some Social Perspectives*, Hatfield: Hatfield Polytechnic.

MacKinnon, Kenneth (1987), 'Gender, Occupation and Educational Factors in Gaelic Language-Shift and Regeneration', in Gearóid Mac Eoin, Anders Ahlqvist and Donncha Ó hAodha (eds), *Third International Conference on Minority Languages: Celtic Papers*, Clevedon: Multilingual Matters, 47–71.

MacKinnon, Kenneth (1991), *Gaelic: A Past and Future Prospect*, Edinburgh: Saltire Society.

MacKinnon, Kenneth (1998), 'Neighbours in Persistence: Prospects for Gaelic Maintenance in a Globalising English World' (oral version of paper published in another form in McCoy with Scott (2000), 144–55).

MacKinnon, Kenneth (2001), 'Identity, Attitudes and Support for Gaelic Policies: Gaelic Speakers in the Euromosaic Survey 1994/95', in John M. Kirk and Dónall P. Ó Baoill (eds), *Language Links: The Languages of Scotland and Ireland*, Belfast: Cló Ollscoil na Banríona, 171–80.

MacKinnon, Kenneth (2009), 'Celtic Languages in a Migration Society: Economy, Population Structure and Language Maintenance', in John M. Kirk and Dónall Ó Baoill (eds), *Language and Economic Development: Northern Ireland, the Republic of Ireland, and Scotland*, Belfast: Cló Ollscoil na Banríona, 166–74.

MacKinnon, Kenneth (2011), interview with the author, Edinburgh, 28 June.

MacKinnon, Kenneth (2012), '"Never spoken here", "Rammed down our throats" – the rhetoric of detractors and disparagers of Gaelic in the press: Gaelic in Press Discourse and Public Attitudes. Evidence to The Leveson Inquiry, September 2012', https://discoverleveson.com/evidence/Witness_Statement_of_Professor_Kenneth_MacKinnon/11480/media (last accessed 12 October 2019).

MacKinnon, Kenneth (2013), 'Public Attitudes to Gaelic: a comparison of surveys undertaken in 1981, 2003 and 2011', in Cruickshank and Millar (2017), 1–19.

[see also MacFhionghuin, Coinneach]

MacKinnon, William (1885), *Do Luchd-taghaidh Ball-Pàrlamaid air son Siorramachd Earra-ghàidheal*, Glasgow: Robert Maclehose.

Mackintosh, John P. (1974), 'The new appeal of nationalism', *New Statesman*, 27 September, 408–12.

MacLabhruinn, Donnchadh (1970), 'Comunn na Cànain Albannaich ("Tìr Gun Chànain, Tìr Gun Anam")', *Sruth*, 77, 10–11.

MacLaren, Duncan (1976), 'Good signs for Gaelic', *Question*, 14, 5.

[see also MacLabhruinn, Donnchadh]

MacLaren, James (1923), *MacLaren's Gaelic Self-Taught*, Glasgow: Archibald MacLaren.

MacLauchlan, Rev. Thomas (1875), 'Mu 'n Ghailig a Bhi air a Teagasg 's na Sgoilibh', *AG*, 4, 16–18.

MacLean, Diane (2018), 'Gaelic Television: Building Bricks Without Straw', *International Journal of Scottish Theatre and Screen*, 11, 6–28.

MacLean, J. A. (1964), 'Gaelic–English Scheme a Success', *AG*, 59, 44–6.

MacLean, John (1978), *In the Rapids of Revolution: Essays, articles and letters 1902–23*, ed. by Nan Milton, London: Allison & Busby.

MacLean, Magnus, 'The Gaelic Outlook', in MacDonald (1927), 295–6.

Maclean, Malcolm (2000), 'Parallel Universes: Gaelic Arts Development in Scotland, 1985–2000', in McCoy with Scott (2000), 105–25.

Maclean, Malcolm (2011), interview with the author, Stornoway, 8 June.

Maclean, Malcolm (2019), 'The Place of Gaelic in Today's Scotland', in Gerry Hassan and Simon Barrow (eds), *Scotland the Brave? Twenty Years of Change and the Future of the Nation*, Edinburgh: Luath Press, 252–9.

Maclean, Malcolm and Carrell, Christopher (eds) (1986), *As an Fhearann/From the Land*, Edinburgh: Mainstream.
MacLean, Norman (2012), *Contracts*, Edinburgh: Birlinn.
MacLean, Sam [Sorley] (1969), 'Problems of Gaelic Education' [I], *Catalyst*, 2:4, 21–2.
MacLean, Sam [Sorley] (1970), 'Problems of Gaelic Education' [II], *Catalyst*, 3:1, 9–10.
MacLellan, Father Calum (1991), Video interview with Calum Ferguson (Bliadhna na Gàidhlig), Box 68, Museum nan Eilean, Stornoway.
MacLennan, Gordon (1966), 'New Hope for Gaelic', in Frank Thompson (ed.), *Recent Developments in the Celtic Countries: Annual Book of the Celtic League 1966*, Dublin: Celtic League, 68–73.
MacLennan, Hugh Dan (1998), 'Shinty dies hard "Scotland's national game": A re-assessment and re-definition, with particular reference to its survival and development in the nineteenth century in Australia, Canada, England and Ireland', PhD thesis, University of Aberdeen.
MacLennan, Ishbel (2003), 'BBC Craoladh nan Gàidheal: Cò sinn?', in Kirk and Ó Baoill (2003), 67–72.
MacLennan, R. (1932), 'The National Question and Scotland', *Communist Review*, 4, 505–10.
MacLeod, Donald John (1969), 'The sellers of culture: a look at interpretations and some false interpreters of Gaelic culture', *Scottish International*, 8, 49–52.
MacLeod, Donald John (1970), 'Twentieth Century Gaelic Literature: A description Comprising Critical Study and a Comprehensive Bibliography', PhD thesis, University of Glasgow.
MacLeod, Donald John (1974–6), 'Gaelic Prose', *TGSI*, 49, 198–230.
MacLeod, Donald John (1989), 'Gaelic: the dynamics of a Renaissance', in Gillies (1989a), 222–9.
MacLeod, Donald John (2006–9), 'Reversing the Decline of Gaelic: The Contribution of Gaelic Medium Education', *TGSI*, 65, 228–43.
   [see also MacLeòid, Dòmhnall Iain]
MacLeod, (Dr) Finlay (1970), 'An Experimental Investigation into Some Problems of Bilingualism', PhD thesis, University of Aberdeen.
MacLeod, (Dr) Finlay (1976a), 'Gaelic in Primary Schools', in *Full Report of the One Day Conference on Scottish Studies and Gaelic in Scottish Schools*, Aberdeen: Aberdeen College of Education, 1–3.
MacLeod, (Dr) Finlay ([1976b]), 'Western Isles Community Education Project' (CnES–SG).
MacLeod, (Dr) Finlay (1986), *Gaelic Arts: A Way Ahead – A Report for the Scottish Arts Council*, Edinburgh: Scottish Arts Council.
MacLeod, (Dr) Finlay (1986), 'The ORACLE has spoken', *WHFP*, 8 May.
   [see also MacLeòid, (An Dr) Fionnlagh]
MacLeod, Finlay (Strì) (1981), Letter to the Editor, *Càrn*, 33, 5.

[see also MacLeòid, Fionnlagh]

Macleod, John (2005), 'With so much rubbish on TV does it matter if some of it's in Gaelic?' *Daily Mail*, 3 November, 14.

Macleod, John (2015), *When I Heard the Bell: The Loss of the* Iolaire, Edinburgh: Birlinn.

MacLeod, Kirstie (2017), 'Gaelic in Families with Young Children: Education and Language Choice', PhD thesis, University of Edinburgh.

Macleod, Mairi (2004), 'Teachers and change in the Western Isles', PhD thesis, University of Cambridge.

[MacLeod, Malcolm C.] (1912), 'A Course of Gaelic Instruction', *The Celtic Annual 1912: Year Book of Dundee Highland Society*, 2, 7.

MacLeod, Malcolm (1914), 'An Comunn Gaidhealach', *Scottish Review*, 37, 365–75.

[MacLeod, Malcolm C.] (1915), 'Malcolm MacFarlane', *The Celtic Annual 1916: Year Book of Dundee Highland Society*, 5, 27–8.

[MacLeod, Malcolm C.] (1919), 'Foreword – The Gaelic Movement', *The Celtic Annual 1918–1919: Year Book of Dundee Highland Society*, 6, 2–3.

Macleod, Rev. Malcolm (1930), 'The Highland Pulpit and the Preservation of the Gaelic Language', *AG*, 26, 12–14.

[Macleod, Rev. Malcolm] (1942), 'An Cogadh', *AG*, 38, 1.

[Macleod, Rev. Malcolm] (1944), 'A' Ghàidhlig agus Aoradh Follaiseach', *AG*, 39, 73–4.

MacLeod, Marsaili (2008), 'The Meaning of Work in the Gaelic Labour Market in the Highlands and Islands of Scotland', PhD thesis, University of Aberdeen.

MacLeod, Marsaili, et al. (2015), *Libhrigeadh Gàidhlig do dh'Inbhich tro Ùlpan/Delivery of Gaelic to Adults through Ùlpan*, Inverness: BnG.

MacLeod, Marsaili and Smith-Christmas, Cassie (eds) (2018), *Gaelic in Contemporary Scotland: The Revitalisation of an Endangered Language*, Edinburgh: EUP.

MacLeod, Mary K. (1981), 'The interaction of Scottish educational developments and socio-economic factors on Gaelic education in Gaelic-speaking areas, with particular reference to the period 1872–1918', PhD thesis, University of Edinburgh.

Macleod, Michelle, et al. (2014), *Young Speakers' Use of Gaelic in the Primary Classroom: A multi-perspectival pilot study*, Aberdeen: University of Aberdeen.

Macleod, Michelle, et al. (2018), 'Planning for Growth: The Professionalisation of the Taskforce for Gaelic Revitalisation', in M. MacLeod and Smith-Christmas (2018), 141–55.

MacLeod, Morag (1996), 'Folk Revival in Gaelic Song', in Munro (1996), 124–37.

MacLeod, Murdo (1963), 'Gaelic in Highland Education', *TGSI*, 43, 305–34.

MacLeod, Murdo (n.d.), 'Scottish Gaelic: Its Roles and Functions Within and Outside the Curriculum' (unpublished paper held at the SMO Library).

[see also MacLeòid, Murchadh]

MacLeod, Murray (2009), 'Minister's wrong turn on bilingual signs', *WHFP*, 3 April, 11.

MacLeod, Roderick John (2012), 'Gaelic at the Court', in *No Ordinary Court: 100 Years of the Scottish Land Court*, Edinburgh: Avizandum, 101–10.

MacLeòid, Aonghas (2014), 'Know Your Place – Gaelic and Elements of the Left', *Bella Caledonia*, 6 February, https://bellacaledonia.wordpress.com/2014/02/06/know-your-place-gaelic-and-elements-of-the-left/ (last accessed 29 November 2019).

MacLeòid, Calum (1944), 'A' Ghàidhealtachd agus a' Ghàidhlig', in *Am Feachd Gàidhealach*, Glasgow: ACG, 26–9.

MacLeòid, Coinneach (1912), 'O Leanabas gu Fearalas', *DG*, 7, 186–8.

MacLeòid, Dòmhnall Iain (1970), 'Innleachdan airson cor na Gaidhlig 'san deachad tha romhainn', *Sruth*, 85, 4, 12; 86, 4, 9; 87, 12; 88, 3, 12; 89, 3, 12.

MacLeòid, Dòmhnall Iain (1976), 'A' Ghàidhlig am Beatha Fhollaiseach an t-Sluaigh', in MacThòmais (1976), 12–27.

MacLeòid, Dòmhnall Iain (2007), 'Sùil air ais', in Mairead NicNeacail and Mata M. MacÌomhair (eds), *Foghlam tro Mheadhan na Gàidhlig*, Edinburgh: Dunedin Academic Press, 1–15.

MacLeòid, Dòmhnall Iain (2011), *Dualchas an Aghaidh nan Creag: The Gaelic Revival 1890–2020*, Inverness: Clò-beag.

[see also MacLeod, Donald John]

MacLeòid, (An Dr) Fionnlagh (1976), 'Na Bun-sgoiltean', in MacThòmais (1976), 28–35.

[see also MacLeod, (Dr) Finlay]

MacLeòid, Fionnlagh (Strì) (1981), 'Strì – Airson na Gàidhlig', *Càrn*, 34, 2–3.

MacLeòid, Fionnlagh (Strì) (1989–90), 'Facal bho ar Stiùiriche', *Comh-Ràdh*, 7, 4.

[see also MacLeod, Finlay]

MacLeòid, Murchadh (1960), 'A' Ghàidhlig agus an Sgoil', *Gairm*, 31, 249–55.

[see also MacLeod, Murdo]

MacLeòid, Murchadh (2000), 'Cainnt mhaslach mu sgoil Ghàidhlig', *The Scotsman*, 23 February.

MacLeòid, Murchadh (2003), 'Bile ùr na Gàidhlig: tillibh gu'n bhòrd-deasachaidh gus na tuill a lìonadh', *Scotland on Sunday*, 12 October.

MacLeòid, Murchadh (2004), 'Bu leinne an oidhche ann am pàrlamaid na h-Alba', *Scotland on Sunday*, 28 November.

MacLeòid, Ruairidh (1968), 'A' Ghàidhlig ann an Eaglais na h-Alba', *Gairm*, 65, 29–34.

MacMaster Campbell, John (1930), 'The Highlands and the Revival of Gaelic', *AG*, 25, 50–3.

Mac na Ceàrdaich, Domhnall (1928), 'C' Ainm a Th' Ort?', *The Scots Independent*, 2, 170.

MacNeacail, Aonghas (1977), 'Cliath: An Auspicious Beginning'. *WHFP*, 19 August.
MacNeacail, Aonghas (1986), 'Questions of Prestige: Sorley MacLean and the Campaign for Equal Status for Gaelic in Scottish Education', in Raymond J. Ross and Joy Hendry (eds), *Sorley MacLean: Critical Essays*, Edinburgh: Scottish Academic Press, 201–10.
MacNeacail, Aonghas (2002), 'Smuaintean air deamo na Gàidhlig', *The Scotsman*, 25 September.
MacNeacail, Aonghas (2011), interview with the author, Edinburgh, 18 August.
MacNeacail, H. C. (1920), 'The Scottish Language', *The Scottish Review*, 43, part 97, 59–68.
MacNeil, Morag and Galloway, John M. K. (2004), *Patterns of Gaelic speech at key stages in secondary education: An exploratory study*, Sleat: Lèirsinn Research Centre, SMO.
MacNéill, Rev. Iain Deòrsa (1892(?)), *Mallachd na Misg*, Glasgow: Free Church Temperance Society.
MacPhaidein, Iain (1917), 'Ciod Iad na Cunnartan a tha Cuartachadh na Gàidhlig?', *DG*, 12, 76–8, 92–4.
MacPherson, D. C. (1879), *Practical Lessons in Gaelic for the Use of English-Speaking Students*, Edinburgh: Maclachlan & Stewart.
Macpherson, J. Iain (1929–30), 'Speech by the Rt Hon. J. Iain Macpherson, K. C.', *TGSI*, 35, 171–7.
MacPherson, John A. (1998–2000), 'The Development of Gaelic Broadcasting', *TGSI*, 61, 251–79.
[MacPhie, Donald] (1914), 'Uilleam-Gun-Chèill – Plàigh na Roinn Eòrpa', *DG*, 10, 1–3.
Mac Póilin, Aodán (2007), 'Nua-Ghaeltacht Bhéal Feirste: ceachtanna le foghlaim?', in McLeod 2007, 31–59.
Mac Póilin, Aodán (2018), 'What about Ullans? Ulster Scots and the Irish language', in Róise Ní Bhaoill (ed.), *Our Tangled Speech: Essays on Language and Culture*, Belfast: Ulster Historical Foundation, 44–79.
Macrae, Farquhar (1957), 'President's English Address', *AG*, 52, 102–3.
MacSween, Annie (2011), interview with the author, Cross, Isle of Lewis, 7 June.
Mac-Talla (1904), 'Facal 'San Dealachadh', 12, 197.
MacThòmais, Frang (1975), 'Gaelic on the move', *Crann-Tara: Newsletter of Comunn na Cànain Albannaich*, 10, 4–5.
MacThòmais, Frang (1978), 'On the Gaelic Front', *Càrn*, 23, 4.
MacThòmais, Frang (1981), 'On the Gaelic Front', *Càrn*, 34, 3.
MacThòmais, Frang (1984), 'On the Gaelic Front', *Càrn*, 46, 5.
MacThòmais, Frang (1986), 'On the Gaelic Front', *Càrn*, 54, 5.
MacThòmais, Frang (1987), 'On the Gaelic Front', *Càrn*, 59, 4–5.
[see also Thompson, Frank]

[MacThòmais, Ruaraidh] (1957a), 'Air an Spiris', *Gairm*, 19, 203.
[MacThòmais, Ruaraidh] (1957b), 'Air an Spiris', *Gairm*, 21, 11.
MacThòmais, Ruaraidh (1958), 'Na Sgoilean Gàidhlig (2)', *Gairm*, 23, 268–70.
MacThòmais, Ruaraidh (ed.) (1976), *Gàidhlig ann an Albainn/Gaelic in Scotland: A blueprint for official and private initiatives*, Glasgow: Gairm.
MacThòmais, Ruaraidh (1981), 'Bile na Gàidhlig', *Gairm*, 114, 111–14.
[MacThòmais, Ruaraidh] (1985), 'Air an Spiris', *Gairm*, 132, 299.
[MacThòmais, Ruaraidh, and MacDhòmhnaill, Fionnlagh I.] (1955a), 'As a' Chathair', *Gairm*, 13, 11.
[MacThòmais, Ruaraidh, and MacDhòmhnaill, Fionnlagh I.] (1955b), 'Na Rocaidean', *Gairm*, 14, 123–31.
   [see also Thomson, Derick]
MacThòmais, Seumas (1928), 'Cor na Gàidhlig', *AG*, 24, 30–1.
MacUisdein, Seorus A. Cléireach [George Aitken Clark Hutchison] (1910), 'Do Luchd-taghaidh Fir-ionaid 'sa Phàrlamaid air son Siorramachd Earraghaidheal', n.p.: Seorus MacUisdein (EUL RB.P.129/9).
MacWhirter, Iain (2013), *Road to Referendum*, Glasgow: Cargo Publishing.
Madgwick, Peter and Rawkins, Phillip (1982), 'The Welsh Language in the Policy Process', in Peter Madgwick and Richard Rose (eds), *The Territorial Dimension in United Kingdom Politics*, London: Macmillan, 67–99.
Maguire, Gabrielle (1991), *Our Own Language: An Irish Initiative*, Clevedon: Multilingual Matters.
Marfany, Joan-Lluis (2004), '"Minority" Languages and Literary Revivals', *Past and Present*, 184, 137–67.
Market Research UK (2003), *Attitudes to the Gaelic Language*, Glasgow: Market Research UK.
Márkus, Gilbert (2017), *Conceiving a Nation: Scotland to AD 900*, Edinburgh: EUP.
Martel, Angéline (1999), 'Heroes, Rebels, Communities and States in Language Rights Activism and Litigation', in Miklos Kontrá et al. (eds), *Language: A Right and a Resource – Approaching Linguistic Human Rights*, Budapest: Central European University Press, 47–80.
Martin, Donald (2011), interview with the author, Stornoway, 9 June.
Martin, Kate (2006), *Fèis: The First Twenty-five Years of the Fèis Movement*, Portree: Fèisean nan Gàidheal.
Martínez-Arbelaiz, Asun (1996), 'The language requirement outside the academic setting: The case of the Basque administration', *Journal of Multilingual and Multicultural Development*, 17, 360–72.
Mason, John (1954), 'Scottish Charity Schools of the Eighteenth Century', *Scottish Historical Review*, 33, 1–13.
Mason, Keith (2014), 'The saga of Egon Kisch and the White Australia Policy',

[2014 Summer] *Bar News: The Journal of the New South Wales Bar Association*, 64–7.

Massie, Alex (2019), 'I'm talking the talk with Gaelic, so to speak', *The Times*, 1 December, 34.

Masson, David (ed.) (1891), *The Register of the Privy Council of Scotland, Vol. X, A.D. 1613–1616*, Edinburgh: HM Register House.

May, Stephen (2012), *Language and Minority Rights: Ethnicity, Nationalism and the Politics of Language*, 2nd edn, London: Routledge.

McAllister, Laura (2001), *Plaid Cymru: The Emergence of a Political Party*, Bridgend: Seren.

McCoy, Gordon, with Scott, Maolcholaim (eds) (2000), *Aithne na nGael/ Gaelic Identities*, Belfast: Institute of Irish Studies, Queen's University Belfast/ULTACH Trust.

McCrone, David (2017), *The New Sociology of Scotland*, London: SAGE Publications.

McCulloch, David (1934), 'An Comunn is Doing Great Work for the Highlands', *P&J*, 20 April, 6.

McCulloch, Margery Palmer (ed.) (2004), *Modernism and Nationalism: Literature and Society in Scotland 1918–1939*, Glasgow: Association for Scottish Literary Studies.

McCulloch, Margery Palmer (2007), 'Reshaping Scotland: Ireland, Europe and the Interwar Scottish Literary Renaissance Movement', *Journal of Irish and Scottish Studies*, 1, 179–90.

McCurdy, Mike (2000), 'Achieving a Gaelic-medium School in Glasgow', in *Sgoil Ghàidhlig airson Baile Dhùn Éideann: Latha Fiosrachaidh/A Gaelic-medium School for Edinburgh: Information Day*, Edinburgh: Comann nam Pàrant (Dùn Èideann agus Lodainn), 26–7.

McDonald, Maryon (1989), *We Are Not French! Language, Culture and Identity in Brittany*, New York: Routledge.

McEwan, Emily (2015), 'Scottish Gaelic Information Technology', https://gaelic.co/gaelic-tech/ (last accessed 3 January 2020).

McEwan, Emily (2018), 'Anti-Gaelic Bingo Revisited', https://gaelic.co/anti-gaelic-bingo-revisited/ (last accessed 14 December 2019).

McEwan-Fujita, Emily (2008), 'Working at "9 to 5" Gaelic: speakers, contexts, and ideologies of an emerging minority language register', in Kendall A. King et al. (eds), *Sustaining Linguistic Diversity: Endangered and Minority Languages and Language Varieties*, Washington, DC: Georgetown University Press, 81–93.

McEwan-Fujita, Emily (2010a), 'Sociolinguistic ethnography of Gaelic communities', in Watson and Macleod (2010), 172–217.

McEwan-Fujita, Emily (2010b), 'Ideologies and experiences of literacy in interactions between adult Gaelic learners and first-language Gaelic speakers in Scotland', *SGS*, 26, 87–114.

McGrath, John (1974), *The Cheviot, the Stag and the Black, Black Oil*, Kyleakin: West Highland Publishing.
McIlvanney, William (2000), 'Money alone can't pump life into dying language', *Scotland on Sunday*, 17 September, 19.
McKechnie, Alexander (1934), *Introduction to Gaelic Scotland*, London and Glasgow: Blackie & Son.
McKenna, Kevin (2011), 'It would be unspeakable to lose Gaelic', *The Guardian*, 9 October, 39.
McLeod, Wilson (1998), 'Autochthonous language communities and the Race Relations Act', *Web Journal of Current Legal Issues*, no. 1.
McLeod, Wilson (2000), 'Official Gaelic: Problems in the Translation of Public Documents', *Scottish Language*, 19, 100–16.
McLeod, Wilson (2001), *Faclair na Pàrlamaid: A Critical Analysis*, Edinburgh: Celtic and Scottish Studies, University of Edinburgh.
McLeod, Wilson (2002), 'Language Planning as Regional Development: The Growth of the Gaelic Economy', *Scottish Affairs*, 38, 51–72.
McLeod, Wilson (2003), 'Language politics and ethnolinguistic consciousness in Scottish Gaelic poetry', *SGS*, 21, 91–146.
McLeod, Wilson (2004a), *Divided Gaels: Gaelic Cultural Identities in Scotland and Ireland, c.1200–c.1650*, Oxford: OUP.
McLeod, Wilson (2004b), 'The challenge of corpus planning in Gaelic development', *Scottish Language*, 23 (2004), 68–92.
McLeod, Wilson (ed.) (2006), *Revitalising Gaelic in Scotland: Policy, Planning and Public Discourse*, Edinburgh: Dunedin Academic Press.
McLeod, Wilson (ed.) (2007), *Gàidhealtachdan Ùra: Leasachadh na Gàidhlig agus na Gaeilge sa Bhaile Mhòr/Nua-Ghaeltachtaí: Cur chun cinn na Gàidhlig agus na Gaeilge sa Chathair*, Edinburgh: Celtic and Scottish Studies, University of Edinburgh.
McLeod, Wilson (2008a), 'Linguistic pan-Gaelicism: a dog that wouldn't hunt', *Journal of Celtic Linguistics*, 12, 87–120.
McLeod, Wilson (2008b), '"Fanndaigeadh na Gàidhlig" aig Iain MacGriogair: Aisling molaidh don Ghàidhlig?', in Colm Ó Baoill and Nancy R. McGuire (eds), *Caindel Alban: Fèill-Sgrìobhainn do Dhòmhnall E Meek (SGS, 24)*, 419–40.
McLeod, Wilson (2008c), 'An opportunity avoided? The European Charter and UK language policy', in Gwynedd Parry and Robert Dunbar (eds), *The European Charter for Regional or Minority Languages: Legal Challenges and Opportunities*, Strasbourg: CoE, 201–18.
McLeod, Wilson (2009), 'Expanding the Gaelic Employment Sector: Strategies and Challenges', in John M. Kirk and Dónall Ó Baoill (eds), *Language and Economic Development: Northern Ireland, the Republic of Ireland, and Scotland*, Belfast: Cló Ollscoil na Banríona, 153–65.
McLeod, Wilson (2011), 'Gaelic language plans and the issue of bilingual logos', in John M. Kirk and Dónall P. Ó Baoill (eds), *Strategies for Minority*

McLeod, Wilson (2013a), '"Chan eil e *even* ann an Dwelly's!": The Continuing Legacy of Edward Dwelly's Gaelic Dictionary', in Katherine Campbell et al. (eds), *'A Guid Hairst': Collecting and Archiving Scottish Tradition – Essays in Honour of Dr Margaret A. Mackay*, Aachen: Shaker Verlag, 163–70.

Languages: Northern Ireland, the Republic of Ireland, and Scotland, Belfast: Cló Ollscoil na Banríona, 203–11.

McLeod, Wilson (2013b), 'A' Ghàidhlig sgoilearail: cothroman is cnapan-starra', in Colm Ó Baoill and Nancy McGuire (eds), *Rannsachadh na Gàidhlig 6*, Aberdeen: An Clò Gàidhealach, 289–304.

McLeod, Wilson (2013c), 'Gaelic poetry and the British military, 1756–1945', in Carla Sassi and Theo van Heijnsbergen (eds), *Within and Without Empire: Scotland Across the (Post)colonial Borderline*, Newcastle: Cambridge Scholars Publishing, 61–76.

McLeod, Wilson (2014), '*Luchd na Gàidhlig* and the "detritus of a nation"', in Virginia Blankenhorn (ed.), *Craobh nan Ubhall: A Festschrift for John MacInnes (Scottish Studies*, 36), 149–54.

McLeod, Wilson (2017), 'Dialectal diversity in contemporary Gaelic: perceptions, discourses and responses', in Cruickshank and Millar (2017), 183–211.

McLeod, Wilson (2018), 'New speakers of Gaelic: a historical and policy perspective', in MacLeod, M. and Smith-Christmas (2018), 79–93.

McLeod, Wilson (2019), 'Conceptions and discourses of linguistic justice: some illustrations from the Scottish context', *Sociolinguistica*, 33, 45–62.

McLeod, Wilson and O'Rourke, Bernadette (2015), '"New speakers" of Gaelic: perceptions of linguistic authenticity and appropriateness', *Applied Linguistics Review*, 6, 151–72.

McLeod, Wilson, O'Rourke, Bernadette and Dunmore, Stuart (2014), *'New Speakers' of Gaelic in Edinburgh and Glasgow*, Edinburgh: Soillse.

McLeod, Wilson, Pollock, Irene and MacCaluim, Alasdair (2010), *Adult Gaelic Learning in Scotland: Opportunities, Motivations and Challenges – A Research Report for Bòrd na Gàidhlig*, Edinburgh: Celtic and Scottish Studies, University of Edinburgh.

McMahon, Conor (2017), 'Why TG4's boss has his eye on an Irish-language Oscar win', https://fora.ie/tg4-alan-esslemont-3640530-Oct2017/ (last accessed 10 January 2020).

McMahon, Timothy G. (2008), *Grand Opportunity: The Gaelic League and Irish Society, 1893–1910*, Syracuse, NY: Syracuse University Press.

McNeil, Robert (2000), 'Gaelic flavours a peculiarly Scottish debate', *The Scotsman*, 3 March, 1.

McNeir, Clive Leo (ed.) (2001), *Faclair na Pàrlamaid: Dictionary of Terms*, Edinburgh: SE.

Meek, Donald E. (1990), 'Language and Style in the Scottish Gaelic Bible (1767–1807)', *Scottish Language*, 9, 1–16.

Meek, Donald E. (ed.) (1995), *Tuath is Tighearna: Tenants and Landlords*, Edinburgh: Scottish Gaelic Texts Society.

Meek, Donald E. (1996), *The Scottish Highlands: The Churches and Gaelic Culture*, Geneva: World Council of Churches.

Meek, Donald E. (2001a), 'The Language of Heaven?: The Highland Churches, Culture Shift and the Erosion of Gaelic Identity in the Twentieth Century', in Robert Pope (ed.), *Religion and National identity: Wales and Scotland c. 1700–2000*, Cardiff: UWP, 307–37.

Meek, Donald E. (2001b), 'From disparagement to devolution: reviving Gaelic in Scotland, 1980–2000', in David Dickson et al. (eds), *Ireland and Scotland: nation, region, identity; náisiún, régiún, céannacht; nàisean, ceàrn tìre, fèineachd*, Dublin: Centre for Irish–Scottish Studies, TCD, 25–31.

Meek, Dòmhnall E. (2002), 'An Aghaidh na Sìorraidheachd? Bàird na ficheadamh linn agus an Creideamh Crìosdail', in Colm Ó Baoill and Nancy McGuire (eds), *Rannsachadh na Gàidhlig 2000*, Aberdeen: An Clò Gàidhealach, 103–16.

Meek, Donald E. (2004), 'Religion, riot and romance: Scottish Gaelic perceptions of Ireland in the 19th century', in Ó Háinle and Meek (2004), 173–93.

Meek, Donald (2011), interview with the author, Polmont, 11 August.

Meek, Donald E. (2012), 'Derick Thomson: A colossus of twentieth-century Scotland', *WHFP*, 20 April, 18.

Meek, Dòmhnall E. (2013a), 'From Magnus MacLean to Angus Matheson: Glasgow and the Making of Celtic Studies in Scotland', http://meekwrite.blogspot.co.uk/2013/03/celtic-studies-glasgow-and-making-of.html (last accessed 29 November 2019).

Meek, Dòmhnall E. (2013b), '*Gairm* agus Saoghal nan Gàidheal', http://meekwrite.blogspot.co.uk/2013/03/twentieth-century-gaelic-literature.html (last accessed 29 November 2019).

Mercator-Education (2004), *The Irish language in education in Northern Ireland*, 2nd edn, Leeuwarden: Mercator-Education.

Mertz, Elizabeth (1989), 'Sociolinguistic creativity: Cape Breton Gaelic's linguistic "tip"', in Nancy Dorian (ed.), *Investigating Obsolescence: Studies in Language Contraction and Death*, Cambridge: CUP, 103–16.

MG ALBA (2008), *Annual Report and Accounts 2007/08*, Stornoway: MG ALBA.

MG ALBA (2014), *Annual Report and Accounts 2013/2014*, Stornoway: MG ALBA.

MG ALBA (2015), 'BBC Charter review consultation– MG ALBA Response', www.mgalba.com/downloads/consultations/tomorrows-bbc201511.pdf?lang=en (last accessed 7 December 2019).

MG ALBA (2016), *Annual Report and Accounts 2015/2016*, Stornoway: MG ALBA.

MG ALBA (2019), *Annual Report and Accounts 2018/2019*, Stornoway: MG ALBA.

Mill, John Stuart (1991 [1861]), 'Considerations on Representative Government', in John Gray (ed.), *On Liberty and Other Essays*, Oxford: OUP, 203–467.

Millar, Robert McColl (2018), *Modern Scots: An Analytical Survey*, Edinburgh: EUP.
Milligan, Lindsay (2010), 'The role of Gaelic (Learners) Education in reversing language shift for Gaelic in Scotland', PhD thesis, University of Aberdeen.
Ministerial Advisory Group on Gaelic (2002), *Cothrom Ùr don Ghàidhlig/A Fresh Start for Gaelic*, Edinburgh: SE.
Ministerial Advisory Group on the Scots Language (2010), *Report of the Ministerial Advisory Group on the Scots Language*, Edinburgh: SG.
Ministry of Education, Central Advisory Council for Education (Wales) (1953), *The Place of Welsh and English in the Schools of Wales*, London: HMSO.
Misneachd (2018), *Plana Radaigeach airson na Gàidhlig: Freagairt don Phlana Cànain Nàiseanta Gàidhlig 2018–23/A Radical Plan for Gaelic: A Response to the National Gaelic Language Plan 2018–23*, https://issuu.com/misneachd/docs/misneachd-plana_radaigeach_airson_n (last accessed 2 November 2019).
Mitchell, James (1996), *Strategies for Self-Government: The Campaigns for a Scottish Parliament*, Edinburgh: Polygon.
Mitchell, James (2003), *Governing Scotland: The Invention of Administrative Devolution*, Basingstoke: Palgrave Macmillan.
Mitchell, Rosamond (1992), 'The "Independent" Evaluation of Bilingual Primary Education: A Narrative Account', in J. Charles Alderson and Alan Beretta (eds), *Evaluating Second Language Education*, Cambridge: CUP, 100–40.
Mitchell, Rosamond, et al. (1987), *Report of an Independent Evaluation of the Western Isles' Bilingual Education Project*, Department of Education, University of Stirling.
Mitchison, Naomi (1942), 'Gaelic with an Oxford Accent', *Scots Independent*, 178, 2.
Moireach, Iain (1975), 'Craobh-sgaoileadh agus a' Ghàidhlig', *Gairm*, 90, 140–54.
Moireach, Iain (1987), 'Alba', in *Congress '87 – Language: Mother Tongue and Bilingualism*, [2]–[6], Inverness: International Celtic Congress.
  [see also Murray, John]
Moore, Dafydd (ed.) (2017), *The International Companion to James Macpherson and The Poems of Ossian*, Glasgow: Scottish Literature International.
Morgan, Peadar (2012), 'Lifting the Blanket: dual-naming for Gaelic language planning', in *Placenames Workshop 2012 – Theme: Management and dissemination of toponymic data online*, 24–25 August, Fiontar, Dublin City University, 49–55, www.logainm.ie/placenames2012/pdf/proceedings_imeachtai.pdf (last accessed 2 November 2019).
Morrison, John (1997), 'Time to return power to the Gaelic community', *WHFP*, 27 June, 7.
Morton, Brian (2004), 'Paranoia, guilt . . . and vision: the Gaels at the BBC', *Sunday Herald*, 11 April.

Mudie, Robert (1822), *A Historical Account of His Majesty's Visit to Scotland*, Edinburgh: Oliver & Boyd.

Mufwene, Salikoko (2017), 'Language vitality: The weak theoretical underpinnings of what can be an exciting research area', *Language*, 93, 202–23, 306–16.

Muir, Edwin (1982 [1936]), *Scott and Scotland: The Predicament of the Scottish Writer*, Edinburgh: Polygon.

Mulholland, Robert (1972), 'Scotland's Future – Ends Before Means', *Scotia Review*, 1, 16–19.

Muller, Janet (2010), *Language and Conflict in Northern Ireland and Canada: A Silent War*, Basingstoke: Palgrave Macmillan.

Müller, Martina (2006), 'Language use, language attitudes and Gaelic writing ability among secondary pupils in the Isle of Skye', in McLeod (2006a), 119–38.

Munro, Ailie (1991), 'The Role of the School of Scottish Studies in the Folk Music Revival', *Folk Music Journal*, 6:2, 132–68.

Munro, Ailie (1996), *The Democratic Muse: Folk Music Revival in Scotland*, Aberdeen: Scottish Cultural Press.

Munro, D. Fraser (1918), Letter to Sir John Struthers, Secretary, SED, 20 July (NRS ED14/87).

Munro, Gillian and Mac an Tàilleir, Iain (eds) (2010), *Coimhearsnachdan Gàidhlig An-diugh/Gaelic Communities Today*, Edinburgh: Dunedin Academic Press.

[see also Rothach, Gillian]

Munro, Neil (1984), 'As Irish slips back, and the Welsh remain cautious, where stands Gaelic?', *WHFP*, 30 March, 13.

Murchison, T. M. (1945), Review of John Lorne Campbell, *Gaelic in Scottish Education and Life*, *AG*, 40, 61–2.

[Murchison, T. M.] (1946), 'Gàidhlig a' BhBC', *AG*, 41, 47–8.

Murchison, T. M. (1955), 'Story of An Comunn', *AG*, 50, 3–4, 14–18, 22–5, 32–4, 45–8, 52–3, 62–4, 71–2, 87–8, 112.

[Murchison, T. M.] (1950), 'Gàidhlig a' Bh.B.C.', *AG*, 50, 33.

Murray, John (1991), Video interview with Calum Ferguson (Bliadhna na Gàidhlig), Box 74, Museum nan Eilean, Stornoway.

Murray, John and MacLeod, Finlay (1981), 'Sea change in the Western Isles of Scotland: the rise of locally relevant bilingual education', in Jonathan P. Sher (ed.), *Rural Education in Urbanized Nations: Issues and Innovations*, Boulder, CO: Westview Press, 235–54.

Murray, John and Morrison, Catherine (1984), *Bilingual Primary Education in the Western Isles, Scotland: Report of the Bilingual Education Project, 1975–81*, Stornoway: Acair.

Murray, John, and Dunn, Catriona (1989), 'Gaelic education and the Gaelic community', in Gillies (1989a), 56–63.

[see also Moireach, Iain]

Murtagh, Cera (2011), 'Balancing act', *Holyrood Magazine*, 31 January, 42–3.
Nance, Claire (2018), 'Linguistic Innovation Among Glasgow Gaelic New Speakers', in Cassie Smith-Christmas et al. (eds), *New Speakers of Minority Languages: Linguistic Ideologies and Practices*, London: Palgrave Macmillan, 213–30.
Napier, Theodore (1907), 'Gaelic Manifesto – Brosnachadh', *Fiery Cross*, 22, 5–6.
The National (2016), '"I'll do as little as legally possible to promote Gaelic" vows Aberdeen council finance chief', 12 August.
National Assembly for Wales (2013), *Official Languages Scheme*, Cardiff: National Assembly for Wales.
Neill, William (1967), 'The Despised Tongue', *Catalyst*, 1:1, 2–4.
Neville, Cynthia (2010), *Land and Law in Medieval Scotland*, Edinburgh: EUP.
The New York Times (1927), 'To Seek Funds Here for Gaelic College', 27 February, E20.
The New York Times (1976), 'In Scotland's Outer Hebrides, the Defenders of Gaelic Still Hope to Have the Last Word', 30 March, 8.
Ní Annracháin, Máire (2003), 'Literature in Irish', in J. R. Hill (ed.), *A New History of Ireland Volume VII: Ireland 1921–84*, Oxford: OUP, 573–86.
NicLeòid, Sìleas (2018), 'Gaelic Amongst Schoolchildren: Ideas on Language Change and Linguistic Changes in Gaelic', in M. MacLeod and Smith-Christmas (2018), 45–61.
NicNèill, Catrìona (2018), 'Telebhisean mar ghoireas poileasaidh cànain: a chleachdadh aig cloinn dà-chànanaich', PhD thesis, University of Aberdeen/ University of the Highlands and Islands.
Nic Phaidín, Caoilfhionn (2008), 'Corpus Planning for Irish: Dictionaries and Terminology', in Nic Phaidín and Ó Cearnaigh (2008), 93–107.
Nic Phaidín, Caoilfhionn and Ó Cearnaigh, Seán (eds), *A New View of the Irish Language*, Dublin: Cois Life.
Ní Ghearáin, Helena (2007), 'Lexical Modernisation in Irish: possibilities for the development of Scottish Gaelic?', in Jean-Michel Eloy and Tadhg Ó hIfearnáin (eds), *Langues proches – Langues collatérales/Near Languages – Collateral Languages*, Paris: L'Harmattan, 207–17.
Nicolaisen, W. F. H. (2001), *Scottish Place-names: Their Study and Significance*, Edinburgh: John Donald.
Nicolson, Alexander (1866), *Report on the State of Education in the Hebrides*, Edinburgh: HMSO.
[Nicolson, Alexander N.] (1927), 'Introduction', *TGSI*, 31, v–xii.
Nig Uidhir, Gabrielle (2006), 'The Shaw's Road urban Gaeltacht: role and impact', in Fionntán de Brún (ed.), *Belfast and the Irish Language*, Dublin: Four Courts Press, 136–46.
Nilsen, Kenneth (2010), ''A' Ghàidhlig an Canada: Scottish Gaelic in Canada', in Watson and Macleod (2010), 90–107.
Nisbet, John (1963), 'Bilingualism and the School', *SGS*, 10, 44–52.

NRS (2014), *Scotland's Census 2011: Shaping Scotland's Future*, www.scotlandscensus.gov.uk (last accessed 6 January 2020).

NRS (2015), *Scotland's Census 2011: Gaelic report (part 1)*, Edinburgh: NRS.

North Ayrshire Council (2019), Initial Assessment (letter from Caroline Amos, Head of Service, Education & Youth Employment) (9 March) (WCM).

North Star and Farmers' Chronicle (1907), 'Here and There: Earl of Mar's Manifesto', 24 January, 4.

Ó Baoill, Colm (1974), 'Gaeilge na hAlban – Gaeilge gan ghluaiseacht', in Anraí Mac Giolla Chomhaill (ed.), *Meascra Uladh*, Monaghan: An tUltach, 89–92.

Ó Baoill, Colm (2000), 'Of Mar', *SGS*, 20, 165–9.

Ó Baoill, Colm (2010), 'A History of Gaelic to 1800', in Watson and Macleod (2010), 1–21.

Ó Ceallaigh, Seosamh (2006), *Coláiste Uladh, 1906–2006*, Donegal: Seosamh Ó Ceallaigh.

Ó Conchubhair, Brian (2009), *Fin de Siècle na Gaeilge*, Indreabhán: Cló Iar-Chonnacht.

Ó Giollagáin, Conchúr, et al. (2020), *The Gaelic Crisis in the Vernacular Community: A Comprehensive Sociolinguistic Survey of Scottish Gaelic*, Aberdeen: Aberdeen University Press.

O'Connell, Eithne and Walsh, John (2005), 'The translation boom: Irish and language planning in the twenty-first century', *Administration*, 54:3, 22–34.

Ó Cuív, Brian (1989), 'Irish language and literature, 1845–1921', in W. E. Vaughan (ed.), *A New History of Ireland VI: Ireland Under the Union 1870–1921*, Oxford: OUP, 385–435.

O'Donnell, Hugh (2002), 'Peripheral Fissions? Soap Operas and Identity in Scotland, Ireland and the Basque Country', *EnterText*, 2.1.

O Dughaill, Colman (1918), 'Some New Gaelic Terms for Educational Use', *The Celtic Annual 1918–1919: Year Book of Dundee Highland Society*, 6, 33–47.

Ó Fiannaí, Seán (1995), *Conradh na Gaeilge (Gaelic League) in Scotland*, Glasgow: Conradh na Gaeilge.

Ó Flatharta, Peadar (2015), 'Language schemes – a useful policy tool for language planning?', *Current Issues in Language Planning*, 16, 378–91.

Ó Gairbhí, Seán Tadhg (2017), *Súil Eile*, Dublin: Cois Life.

Ó Gallchóir, Seán (2007), 'Foghlam tro mheadhan na Gàidhlig ann an Glaschu', in McLeod (2007), 103–8.

Ó Háinle, Cathal (1994), 'Ó Chaint na nDaoine go dtí an Caighdeán Oifigiúil', in Kim McCone et al. (eds), *Stair na Gaeilge*, Maynooth: Department of Old Irish, St Patrick's College, 745–93.

Ó Háinle, Cathal and Meek, Donald E. (eds) (2004), *Unity in Diversity: Studies in Irish and Scottish Gaelic Language, Literature and History*, Dublin: School of Irish, Trinity College.

O'Hanlon, Fiona, McLeod, Wilson and Paterson, Lindsay (2010), *Gaelic-

Medium Education in Scotland: choice and attainment at the primary and early secondary school stages, Inverness: BnG.

O'Hanlon, Fiona, Paterson, Lindsay and McLeod, Wilson (2012), *Language Models in Gaelic-medium Pre-school, Primary and Secondary Education*, Edinburgh: Soillse/Scottish Government.

O'Hanlon, Fiona, et al. (2013), *Soillse Research Digest 3/Geàrr-iris Rannsachaidh Shoillse 3: Public Attitudes to Gaelic in Scotland/Beachdan a' Phobaill air a' Ghàidhlig ann an Alba*, Inverness: Soillse.

O'Hanlon, Fiona and Paterson, Lindsay (2015), 'Gaelic Education Since 1872', in Freeman, Mark, Anderson, R. D. and Paterson, Lindsay (eds), *The Edinburgh History of Education in Scotland*, Edinburgh: EUP, 304–25.

Ó hÉallaithe, Donncha (2012), '"TnaG" – an teilifís bradach a lag an lóchrann 25 bliana ó shin', *Gaelscéal*, 10 October, 8, https://cs.slu.edu/~scannell/gaelsceal/2012-10-10.pdf (last accessed 1 November 2019).

O'Henley, Ailig (2006), 'An Eaglais Chaitligeach a' call dìleab nan sagairtean Ghàidhlig', *WHFP*, 8 December, 12.

Ó hIfearnáin, Tadhg (2008), 'Irish-speaking society and the state', in Ball and Müller (2008), 539–86.

Ó hIfearnáin, Tadhg (2010), 'Institutionalising Language Policy: Mismatches in Community and National Goals', in Munro and Mac an Tàilleir (2010), 35–47.

Ó hIfearnáin, Tadhg (2013), 'Institutional Breton language policy after language shift', *International Journal of the Sociology of Language*, 233, 117–35.

O'Leary, Philip (1986), '"Children of the same mother": Gaelic relations with the other Celtic revival movements, 1882–1916', *Proceedings of the Harvard Celtic Colloquium*, 6, 101–30.

Ó Torna, Caitríona (2005), *Cruthú na Gaeltachta, 1893–1922: Samhlú agus Buanú Chonstráid na Gaeltachta i Rith na hAthbheochana*, Dublin: Cois Life.

Ó Tuathaigh, Gearóid (2008), 'The State and the Irish Language: An Historical Perspective', in Nic Phaidín and Ó Cearnaigh (2008), 26–42.

Oban Times (1891), 'Lord Archibald Campbell and the Gaelic', 19 September, 3.

Oban Times (1911), 'An Comunn Gaidhealach – The Comunn Secretaryship – List of Candidates – The Speaking of Gaelic', 24 June, 2.

Oban Times (1937), 'Teaching of Gaelic – Inverness-shire MP's Views', 20 November, 4.

Ofcom (2004), *Looking to the Future of Gaelic Broadcasting*, London: Ofcom.

Ofcom (2014), *PSB Report 2014: Annex 3.iii Audience opinions – BBC ALBA*, London: Ofcom.

Ofcom (2018), *BBC Scotland Competition Assessment Final determination*, London: Ofcom.

Ofcom (2019), *Media nations: Scotland 2019*, London: Ofcom.

Oliver, James (2005), 'Scottish Gaelic Identities: Contexts and Contingencies', *Scottish Affairs*, 51, 1–24.
Oram, Richard D. (ed.) (2014), *The Lordship of the Isles*, Leiden: Brill.
Ó Riagáin, Pádraig (2018), *Measures of Language Proficiency in Censuses and Surveys: A Comparative Analysis and Assessment*, Berlin: Springer.
Oscar (1947), 'Gàidhlig anns na Sgoilean', *An Ceum*, 1:7, 7–8.
Outline Report on Cinema Sgire Community Cinema and Communications Project in the Western Isles, September 1977 to March 1981, Stornoway: CnE.
Owen, Ivor (ed.) (1908), *The Statutes of Wales*, London: T. Fisher Unwin.
P&J (1922), 'The Teaching of Gaelic – Sinn Fein Highlander's Protest', 20 January, 5.
P&J (1932), 'Work of Mod Attacked', 20 October, 8.
P&J (1935), 'Australian "Slur" on Gaelic Resented', 19 January, 7.
P&J (1937), 'An Comunn Singing Called Death-Knell of Gaeldom', 6 October, 7.
P&J (1939), 'Gaels Want Some of Czech Gift', 27 February, 7.
P&J (1950), 'The Election – in Gaelic and in Welsh', 30 January, 6.
P&J (1966), 'Gaelic gets boost in isles', 9 November, 4.
P&J (1972), 'Gaelic Pirate Radio Bid', 17 May, 1.
P&J (1981), 'More signs defaced by Gaelic group', 16 May, 3.
P&J (1984), 'New group to fight for Inverness Gaelic primary', 21 April, 25.
P&J (1985), 'Grants for Gaelic are on the way', 6 October.
P&J (1987), 'Gaelic signs get stamp of approval from P.O.', 25 May, 3.
P&J (1989), 'Protest over lack of Gaelic broadcasting', 28 October.
P&J (1999), 'Gaelic signs KO'd by civil servants with a little help from devolution', 2 October, 1.
P&J (2002), 'City councillors give their backing for new Gaelic project', 7 November, 6.
P&J (2002), 'Isles fury as Gaelic survey findings are placed on hold', 22 February.
P&J (2003), 'Gaelic signs spark anger in Doric stronghold', 26 March, 16.
P&J (2006), 'Pressure grows for Gaelic High School to be built in Inverness', 23 August, 6.
P&J (2011), 'Storm over taxis for Gaelic pupils', 26 April, 3.
P&J (2012a), 'End "mistreatment" of Gaelic', 6 March, 11.
P&J (2012b), 'Anger at Gaelic school "road to nowhere" plan', 22 August, 10.
P&J (2013), 'Gaelic school action pledge', 9 February, 8.
P&J (2014a), 'Parents back objectors to view-blocking Gaelic school', 14 August, 10.
P&J (2014b), 'Gaelic promoted in Doric heartland', 12 September, 4.
P&J (2015a), 'Teachers to ditch English and use Gaelic only in six Western Isles schools', 6 February.
P&J (2015b), 'Aberdeenshire Council could spend £300,000 promoting Gaelic in north-east's Doric heartland', 14 September.

P&J (2017), 'Councillor blasts "Gaelic Gestapo" as region is forced to promote the language', 22 March.
P&J (2018a), 'Plans for new nursery building next to Inverness Gaelic primary', 22 November.
P&J (2018b), 'Parents "cha toir e seachad" on Gaelic school for Oban', 12 December.
Pan-Celtic Congress (1903), 'The Annexation of the Highlands', *Celtia*, 3, 89–91.
Pàrantan airson Foghlam Gàidhlig (1986), *Sgoil Ghàidhlig: General Information*, Inverness: Pàrantan airson Foghlam Gàidhlig.
Parry, Gwenfair and Williams, Mari A. (1999), *The Welsh Language and the 1891 Census*, Cardiff: UWP.
[Paterson, John M.] (1939), 'Am Fear Eagair' (editorial), *Crois Tara*, 8, 2.
Paterson, Lachy (2010), 'Print Culture and the Collective Māori Consciousness', *Journal of New Zealand Literature*, 28, 105–29.
Paterson, Lindsay (1994), *The Autonomy of Modern Scotland*, Edinburgh: EUP.
Paterson, Lindsay (2003), *Scottish Education in the Twentieth Century*, Edinburgh: EUP.
Paterson, Lindsay (2011a), interview with the author, Edinburgh, 7 July.
Paterson, Lindsay (2011b), email to the author, Edinburgh, 7 July.
Paterson, Lindsay (2017), 'Scottish Education and Scottish Society', in McCrone 2017, 246–65.
Paterson, Lindsay, et al. (2014), 'Public Attitudes to Gaelic and the Debate about Scottish Autonomy', *Regional and Federal Studies*, 24, 429–50.
Paterson, Lindsay and O'Hanlon, Fiona (2015), 'Public views of minority languages as communication or symbol: the case of Gaelic in Scotland', *Journal of Multilingual and Multicultural Development*, 36, 555–70.
Peacock, Peter (2012), interview with the author, Gollanfield, Nairn, 5 December.
Pearse, Patrick (1905), 'Gleó na gCath', *An Claidheamh Soluis*, 25 November, 7.
Pedersen, Roy (2011), interview with the author, Inverness, 5 July.
Pedersen, Roy (2019), *Gaelic Guerrilla: John Angus Mackay, Gael Extraordinaire*, Edinburgh: Luath Press.
Penning, Mike (2012), Letter from Mike Penning MP, Parliamentary Under SoS, Department of Transport, to Tom Harris MP (WCM).
Perthshire Advertiser (1914a), 'Celtic Literature – Royal Patronage for Comunn Litreachais na h'Albann', 21 January, 6.
Perthshire Advertiser (1914b), 'County and District News – Callander', 8 April, 6.
Phillips, Dylan (2000), 'The History of the Welsh Language Society 1962–1998', in Jenkins and Williams (2000), 463–90.
Pike, Lorna (2019), 'Faclair na Gàidhlig', in Meg Bateman and Richard A. V.

Cox (eds), *Cànan is Cultar/Language and Culture: Rannsachadh na Gàidhlig 9*, Sleat: Clò Ostaig, 269–80.

Pittock, Murray (2008), *The Road to Independence? Scotland Since the Sixties*, London: Reaktion Books.

Pollock, Irene (2010), 'Learning from Learners: Teachers in Immersion Classrooms', in Munro and Mac an Tàilleir (2010), 117–25.

Powell, Ashley (2010), 'Broadening Horizons? A look at the role of religion and nationalism in *Guth na Bliadhna*', in Moray Watson and Lindsay Milligan (eds), *From Vestiges to the Very Day: New Voices in Celtic Studies*, Aberdeen: AHRC Centre for Irish and Scottish Studies, 53–66.

Prattis, J. I. (1981), 'Industrialisation and Minority-Language Loyalty: the Example of Lewis', in Haugen, McClure and Thomson (1981), 21–31.

Premier Business Development Ltd (2009), *Gaelic Education Needs: Feasibility Study for the City of Edinburgh Council*, Edinburgh: Premier Business Development Ltd, www.edinburgh.gov.uk/download/meetings/id/19567/gaelic_feasibility_study (last accessed 3 November 2019).

Prime Minister's Office (1989), Letter from Paul Gray, Private Secretary to the Prime Minister, to Sara Dent, HO, 2 November (NRS ED 29/114).

Prince of Wales (2004), 'A speech by HRH The Prince Charles, Duke of Rothesay, at Sabhal Mor Ostaig, Isle of Skye', www.princeofwales.gov.uk/speech/speech-hrh-prince-charles-duke-rothesay-sabhal-mor-ostaig-isle-skye (last accessed 3 November 2019).

Prògram Choinnich (1995) (BBC Radio nan Gàidheal, 14 June), http://tobaran-dualchais.co.uk/en/fullrecord/2537 (last accessed 20 December 2019).

Province of Nova Scotia (2019), *Gaelic Nova Scotia: A Resource Guide*, Halifax: Province of Nova Scotia.

Puzey, Guy, McLeod, Wilson and Dunbar, Robert (2013), *Approaches to Bilingual Corporate Identity*, Edinburgh: Soillse.

Queen Victoria's Journals (1849), Journal entry, Balmoral Castle, 23 August 1849, www.queenvictoriasjournals.org/ (last accessed 3 November 2019).

Rae, Steven (1976), 'Gaelic and Comhairle nan Eilean', *New Edinburgh Review*, 33, 4–10.

Ravenstein, E. G. (1879), 'On the Celtic Languages in the British Isles; a Statistical Survey', *Journal of the Statistical Society of London*, 42, 579–643.

Rea, F. G. (1997 [1964]), *A School in South Uist: Reminiscences of a Hebridean Schoolmaster, 1890–1913*, Edinburgh: Birlinn.

Reference Economic Consultants (2011), *Evaluation of Bilingual Signs & Marketing Scheme*, Inverness: Reference Economic Consultants.

Registrar-General for Scotland (1874), *Eighth Decennial Census of the Population of Scotland Taken 3d April 1871, With Report*, vol. 2, Edinburgh: HMSO.

Reid, Duncan (1895), *A Course of Gaelic Grammar*, Glasgow: J. Thomlinson.

[Reid, Duncan] (1909), 'Teagasg na Gàidhlig anns na Sgoiltean' and 'School Boards and Gaelic', *DG*, 4, 141–2.

[Reid, Duncan] (1910), 'Facal Earail do na Gaidheil' and 'An Appeal to Highlanders', *DG*, 5, 29–30.
Reid, Irene A. (2013), 'Shinty, Nationalism and National Autonomy in Scotland, 1887–1928', *International Journal of the History of Sport*, 30, 2098–2114.
Rennie, Frank (1994), *Case Studies in Rural and Community Development No. 1, Fèis Bharraigh*, Perth: Rural Forum Scotland.
Report of the Imperial Education Conference (1911), London: HMSO.
Rifkind, Sir Malcolm (2016), 'BBC must invest in continuing progress of Gaelic television', *The Times*, 30 December, 26.
'Rob Roy' (1907), 'Celticism – The Mod', *The Scotsman*, 19 September, 7.
Robasdan, Boyd (2006), 'Foghlam Gàidhlig bho linn gu linn', in McLeod (2006), 87–118.
[see also Robertson, Boyd]
Roberts, Alasdair (2006), 'Maighstir Eobhan Mac Eachainn and the Orthography of Scots Gaelic', *TGSI*, 63, 358–405.
Roberts, Peter R. (1997), 'Tudor Legislation and the Political Status of "the British Tongue"', in Geraint H. Jenkins (ed.), *The Welsh Language Before the Industrial Revolution*, Cardiff: UWP, 123–52.
Robertson, Angus (1923), 'The Gaelic Outlook', *AG*, 19, 18–22.
Robertson, Boyd (2001), *Aithisg air Solarachadh Chùrsaichean Bogaidh Gàidhlig an Alba/Report on Gaelic Immersion Course Provision in Scotland*, Glasgow: SQA.
Robertson, Boyd (2011), interview with the author, Ostaig, Skye, 21 June.
[see also Robasdan, Boyd]
Robertson, Bruce (2016), 'We must be proud of the rise of Gaelic education', *TESS*, 16 September, 20–1.
Robertson, James (1979), 'Memories of Rannoch', *TGSI*, 51, 199–301.
Rogers, Vaughan (1997), 'Cultural pluralism under the one and incorrigible French republic: Diwan and the Breton language', *Nationalism and Ethnic Politics*, 2, 550–81.
Rosie, Michael (2012), '"Areas cannot be selective": Caithness and the Gaelic Road-Sign Saga', *Scottish Affairs*, 80, 33–61.
Ross & Cromarty Council (1963), Minute of Meeting of [Education Committee] Staffing Sub-Committee, 12 March, 1024–5 (HC Archives CRC 3/2/13).
Ross, David (1991), 'Gaelic on the run to stop the rot', *The Herald*, 11 October.
Ross, David (1992a), 'Chance to grow up with Gaelic', *The Herald*, 15 May, 15.
Ross, David (1992b), 'Unexpected friend of Gaeldom', *The Herald*, 3 December, 19.
Ross, David (2015), 'Centre that speaks to our past as well as our future', *The Herald*, 21 October, 13.
Ross, David (2018), *Highland Herald: Reporting the News from the North*, Edinburgh: Birlinn.
Ross, John (2000), 'Dewar pledges his support for Gaelic . . . or does he?', *The Scotsman*, 9 September, 7.

[Ross, Rev. Neil] (1926), 'A' Ghàidhlig anns an Eilean Sgiathanach', *AG*, 21, 177–8.
[Ross, Rev. Neil] (1930), 'Na Tionail Cheilteach', *AG*, 25, 129–30.
Ross, Susan (2016), 'Identity in Gaelic Drama 1900–1949', *International Journal of Scottish Theatre and Screen*, 9, 39–60.
Ross, Susan, et al. (2018), *Stiùireadh Gràmair*, https://dasg.ac.uk/grammar/grammar.pdf (last accessed 3 November 2019).
Ross-shire Journal (1912), 'Scarcity of Gaelic-speaking Divinity Students', 17 May, 4.
Rothach, Gillian, Mac an Tàilleir, Iain and Dòmhnallach, Brian (2016), *Comas is Cleachdadh Cànain sa Choimhearsnachd, agus an Cunntas-sluaigh 2011*, Sleat: SMO.
   [see also Munro, Gillian]
Royal Commission on the Crofters and Cottars in the Highlands and Islands of Scotland (1884), *Report of Her Majesty's Commissioners of Inquiry into the Condition of the Crofters and Cottars in the Highlands and Islands of Scotland*, Edinburgh: Neill & Co.
Royal Commission on Scottish Affairs, 1952–1954 (1954), *Report*, Edinburgh: HMSO.
Rubin, Joan and Jernudd, Björn H. (1971), *Can Language Be Planned? Sociolinguistic Theory and Practice for Developing Nations*, Honolulu: University Press of Hawaii.
Russell, Michael (2009), 'Sabhal Mòr Ostaig Lecture: Turning the Tide', www.scotland.gov.uk/News/Speeches/Speeches/smarter/SabhalMorOstaig (last accessed 3 November 2019).
Sabhal Mòr Ostaig (n.d.), 'The College', www.smo.uhi.ac.uk/en/colaiste/ (last accessed 3 January 2020).
Sallabank, Julia (2014), *Attitudes to Endangered Languages: Identities and Policies*, Cambridge: CUP.
Salmond, Alex (2007), 'Sabhal Mòr Ostaig Lecture: Government plans for Gaelic'. Speech delivered at St Cecilia's Hall, Edinburgh, 19 December, www.scotland.gov.uk/News/Speeches/Speeches/First-Minister/sabmorsot07 (last accessed 3 November 2019).
'Sandy' (1908), 'Compulsory Gaelic' (letter to the editor), *GH*, 10 June, 12.
Scammell, Keith (1985), 'Pre-school Playgroups', in Hulbert (1985), 21–7.
Scothorne, Rory and Gibbs, Ewan (2018), 'Origins of the present crisis? The emergence of "left-wing" Scottish nationalism, 1956–81', in Evan Smith and Matthew Worley (eds), *Waiting for the Revolution: The British Far Left from 1956*, Manchester: Manchester University Press, 163–80.
Scotland Office (2001), Memorandum from Stuart MacDonald to PS/Minister of State, 14 February (WCM/FOI).
Scotland on Sunday (1993a), 'Backlash builds as Gaels enjoy broadcasting boom', 27 June.
Scotland on Sunday (1993b), 'Scottish minds its language', 14 November.

The Scotsman (1824), 'The Gaelic', 27 October, 1.
The Scotsman (1838a), 'Scots Parliamentary Business', 26 May, 4.
The Scotsman (1838b), 'Scots Parliamentary Business', 20 June, 4.
The Scotsman (1839), 'Scots Parliamentary Business', 6 July, 4.
The Scotsman (1876), 'Lochalsh', 9 October, 5.
The Scotsman (1908), 'A lively skirmish', 18 June, 6.
The Scotsman (1909), 'A Speech in Gaelic – Unionist Candidate for Ross and Cromarty', 18 December, 11.
The Scotsman (1911), 'The Gaelic Mod: Business Meeting', 2 October, 8.
The Scotsman (1912), 'Comunn Gaidhealach – Annual Meeting', 30 September, 6.
The Scotsman (1915), 'Gaelic Speaking Chaplains for the Troops', 21 July, 6.
The Scotsman (1922), 'Position of Gaelic Language – Official Survey Since New Education Act', 16 May, 4.
The Scotsman (1930a), 'Value of Gaelic – Discussion at Inverness Conference – Educationists' Views', 16 August, 12.
The Scotsman (1930b), 'The Claim for Gaelic: Language of Dreams and Visions', 15 December, 12.
The Scotsman (1933), 'An Comunn Gaidhealach – Executive's All-Gaelic Meeting – The Provincial Mods', 11 March, 16.
The Scotsman (1935), 'Sheriff Court Witnesses Who Prefer Gaelic', 12 January, 10.
The Scotsman (1936a), 'Teaching of Gaelic – Suggestions by Council of "An Comunn" – Higher Status Wanted', 25 January, 16.
The Scotsman (1936b), 'Gaelic in the Schools', 11 June, 10.
The Scotsman (1936c), 'Edinburgh Classes for Teaching of Gaelic' (letter to the editor from T. Douglas Macdonald), 5 November, 13.
The Scotsman (1936d), '1938 Mod for Glasgow – In Conjunction With Exhibition – Highland Village Plan', 23 November, 12.
The Scotsman (1937a), 'Knowledge of Gaelic – Desirable but not Essential – Inverness-shire Post', 6 May, 8.
The Scotsman (1937b), 'Gaelic in Schools', 30 September, 8.
The Scotsman (1937c), 'The Position of Gaelic', 30 September, 10.
The Scotsman (1937d), 'Gaelic in Edinburgh Schools', 14 October, 16.
The Scotsman (1937e), 'Director of Education – Fife Man Appointed at Inverness – Non-Gaelic Speaker', 22 October, 8.
The Scotsman (1938), 'An Comunn – Executive Uses Gaelic Exclusively – Youth Movement Grows', 2 April, 12.
The Scotsman (1939a), 'Gaelic Folk School – An Comunn Rejects Canna Scheme', 18 March, 18.
The Scotsman (1939b), 'An Comunn Executive – Teaching of Gaelic in Schools – Duncraig Scheme Progress', 8 April, 13.
The Scotsman (1948), 'Gaelic Teaching in Primary Schools – Minimum Period Urged', 17 January, 6.
The Scotsman (1971), 'Few back signs in Gaelic', 5 January.

The Scotsman (1993b), 'Gaels voice anger over interference with radio', 21 October, 4.
The Scotsman (1998), 'Activists may start Gaelic political party', 7 October, 2.
The Scotsman (2002a), 'Civil servants accused of 'anti-Gaelic racism''', 24 May, 11.
The Scotsman (2002b), 'Parliament's Gaelic chief quits over language barrier', 25 May, 9.
The Scotsman (2002c), 'Wee Frees face shortage of ministers', 12 December, 10.
The Scotsman (2007), 'Call for international Celtic festival to replace "boring, outdated Mod"', 23 August, 7.
The Scotsman (2012), 'Timetable set for city's first Gaelic school', 17 July.
The Scotsman (2016), 'Ambitious virtual Gaelic school wins £700,000 boost', 24 August.
The Scotsman (2018), 'SNP should spend money on policing not more Gaelic signs' (letter from William Loneskie, Oxton), 17 July.
The Scotsman (2019), 'Scottish Government pledges £2m for further Gaelic education', 11 October.
Scott, Priscilla (2014), '"With heart and voice ever devoted to the cause": Women in the Gaelic Movement, 1886–1914', PhD thesis, University of Edinburgh.
Scott, W. R. and Cunnison, J. (1924), *The Industries of the Clyde Valley During the War*, Oxford: Clarendon Press.
Scottish Arts Council (1982), 'Memorandum Submitted by the Scottish Arts Council', in House of Commons Education, Science and Arts Committee, Session 1981–82, *Public and Private Funding of the Arts, Minutes of Evidence* (1981/82 HC 49-v, 29 March), London: HoC.
Scottish Catholic Observer (2019), 'Catholic Gaelic society hold inaugural Mass', 19 July.
Scottish Certificate of Education Examinations Board (1967), *Report for 1967*, Dalkeith: Scottish Certificate of Education Examinations Board.
Scottish Certificate of Education Examinations Board (1984), *Report for 1984*, Dalkeith: Scottish Certificate of Education Examinations Board.
Scottish Certificate of Education Examinations Board (1985), *Report for 1985*, Dalkeith: Scottish Certificate of Education Examinations Board.
Scottish Council for Civil Liberties (1981), 'Statement by the Scottish Council for Civil Liberties in Support of the Gaelic Language (Miscellaneous Provisions) Bill' (NRS HH41/3389).
Scottish Council for Research in Education (1964), *Aithris is Oideas: Traditional Gaelic Rhymes and Games*, London: Scottish Council for Research in Education.
Scottish Council of Independent Schools (2018), 'Annual Census', www.scis.org.uk/facts-and-figures/ (last accessed 20 December 2019).

Scottish Economic Committee, Committee on the Highlands and Islands (1938), *The Highlands and Islands of Scotland: A Review of the Economic Conditions with Recommendations for Improvement*, Glasgow: Scottish Economic Committee.

Scottish Episcopal Church (n.d.). 'The Gaelic Society of the Scottish Episcopal Church', https://www.scotland.anglican.org/gaelic-society-scottish-episcopal-church/ (last accessed 5 June 2020).

Scottish Funding Council (2009), *Gaelic Language Plan*, Edinburgh: Scottish Funding Council.

The Scottish Highlander (1893), 'Gaelic in the Highland Law Courts', 30 November, 6.

Scottish Home Department (1950), *A Programme of Highland Development*, Edinburgh: HMSO.

Scottish Home and Health Department (1970), Letter from T. D. Ewing to Kenneth MacKinnon, Leigh-on-Sea, Essex, 22 April (WCM).

Scottish Home and Health Department (1980), 'Background Note – PQ Question 12 – Mr Donald Stewart' (NRS HH41/1994).

Scottish Parliamentary Corporate Body (2008), *Gaelic Language Plan 2008–2013*, Edinburgh: SP.

Scottish Parliamentary Corporate Body (2013), *Gaelic Language Plan 2013–18*, Edinburgh: SP.

Scottish Parliamentary Corporate Body (2018), *Gaelic Language Plan 2018–23*, Edinburgh: SP.

Scottish Universities Commission (1863), *General Report of the Commissioners Under the Universities (Scotland) Act, 1858*, Edinburgh: HMSO.

Scottish Worker (1976), 'The Fight for the Gaelic Language', 3:3, 8.

SE (2001), Letter from Jim Wallace, Deputy First Minister, to Sarah Boyack MSP, 31 August (WCM).

SE (2002), 'Advice to NDPBs and Local Authorities' (concerning the European Charter for Regional or Minority Languages), 14 February (WCM).

SE (2003), 'Bilingual signs rolled out', www.gov.scot/News/Releases/2003/01/2947 (last accessed 30 November 2019).

SE (2004a), 'Gaelic Bill – Meeting with Education Interests' (minute from Douglas Ansdell, Gaelic Unit, to Minister for Education and Young People), March (date unspecified) (WCM/FOI).

SE (2004b), Letter from Nicol Stephen MSP, Minister for Transport, to Councillor Hamish Fraser, HC, 26 July (WCM/FOI).

SE (2004c), Minute from Peter Peacock, Minister for Education & Young People, to First Minister and Deputy First Minister, 'Gaelic Language (Scotland) Bill: Pre Introduction 6 September 2004' (WCM/FOI).

SE (2004d), Letter from David Brew, Head of Cultural Policy Division, to David Crawley, Head of Scotland Office, 14 September (WCM/FOI).

SE (2004e), Letter from Peter Peacock, Minister for Education & Young People, to Duncan Ferguson, Chair, BnG, 16 September (WCM/FOI).

SE (2004f), 'Gaelic Language Bill – Public Meeting at Royal National Mod, A K Bell Library – 14 October 2004' (WCM/FOI).
SE (2004g), email from Steven MacGregor, Gaelic Unit, to Minister for Education and Young People, 10 November (WCM/FOI).
SE (2005a), 'Gaelic Language (Scotland) Bill – Stage 2: Education Committee recommendations for amendments' (WCM/FOI).
SE (2005b), *Review of First Impressions of Scotland: Report to Ministers*, Edinburgh: SE.
Sebba, Mark (2019), 'Named into being? Language questions and the politics of Scots in the 2011 census in Scotland', *Language Policy*, 18, 339–62.
SED (1873), *Minute of the Board of Education for Scotland Submitting Draft Articles of a Code for That Country*, London: HMSO.
SED (1875), *Code of Regulations*, London: HMSO.
SED (1877), *Return to an Address of the Honourable House of Commons, dated 26 February 1877*, London: HoC.
SED (1885), *Minute on Special Conditions of Parliamentary Grant Applicable to Certain Specified Counties in Scotland*, Parliamentary Papers 1885, vol. 41 (Cmnd 4399).
SED (1893), *Scotch Code of Regulations for Evening Continuation Schools, with Schedule and Appendix*, London: HMSO.
SED (1905), *Secondary Education (Scotland): Report for the Year 1905 by J. Struthers, Esq.*, London: HMSO.
SED (1907a), *Memorandum on the Teaching of English in Scottish Primary Schools*, London: HMSO.
SED (1907b), *Memorandum on the Study of Languages*, London: HMSO.
SED (1950), *The Primary School in Scotland: A Memorandum on the Curriculum*, Edinburgh: HMSO.
SED (1951a), *Education in Scotland in 1950*, Edinburgh: HMSO.
SED (1951b), Minute from Marion M. Lawson, SED to Mr Stephenson, 16 November (NRS ED27/272).
SED (1953a), Minute from K. Dawson, SED, 4 May (NRS ED27/272).
SED (1953b), Minute from Marion M. Lawson, SED to Mrs Montgomerie, 11 June (NRS ED27/272).
SED (1953c), Minute from L. M. Collinson, SED to R. S. Stewart, SED, 14 October (NRS ED27/272).
SED (1955), *Junior Secondary Education*, Edinburgh: HMSO.
SED (1957), *Education in Scotland in 1956*, Edinburgh: HMSO.
SED (1961), *Education in Scotland in 1960*, Edinburgh: HMSO.
SED (1965), *Primary Education in Scotland*, Edinburgh: HMSO.
SED (1966), Minute to Mr Law, 22 April (NRS HH41/1669).
SED (1970), *Education in Scotland in 1970*, Edinburgh: HMSO.
SED (1981a), Minute from M. J. P. Cunliffe, Division V, SED to Mr Connelly, 30 January (NRS ED61/185).

SED (1981b), Minute from PS/SED to PS/Mr Fletcher, 5 August (NRS HH41/2712).

SED (1981c), Letter from N. Pittman, SED to J. A. Ingman, HO, 4 September (NRS HH41/2712).

SED (1982a), Minute from P. A. Cox, SED to Secretary, SED, 25 March (NRS ED61/20).

SED (1982b), Minute from J. A. M. Mitchell, SED to P. A. Cox, SED, 2 April (NRS ED61/20).

SED (1983), 'Note of a Meeting with Local Authorities to Discuss Possible Developments in Gaelic Education', 5 April (NRS ED61/190).

SED (1985a), Letter from D. A. Campbell, SED to G. H. Spiers, COSLA, 31 July (NRS ED61/190).

SED (1985b), 'Minutes of Meeting Between the Secretary of State for Scotland and the Convention of Scottish Local Authorities', 4 October (NRS ED61/190).

SED (1985c), Minute from G. I. McCran, PS/CS, to PS/Under SoS, 'Specific Grant for Gaelic', 8 October (NRS ED61/190).

SED (1985d), Minute from M. R. Lamond to Mr Stewart, 'Specific Grants', 21 October (NRS ED61/190).

SED (1989a), Minute from Alan McPherson, SED to Margaret MacLean, 1 August (NRS ED29/114).

SED (1989b), Minute from Margaret MacLean, SED, to PS/SoS, 10 November (NRS ED29/114).

SED (1989c), Minute from W. A. P. Weatherston, SED to PS/SoS, 29 November (NRS ED29/114).

Sellers, Daniel, Borge Consulting and Carty, Nicola (2019), *Inbhich a tha ag ionnsachadh Gàidhlig – 2018/Adults learning Gaelic – 2018*, Inverness: BnG.

S4C (2012), *Annual Report and Statement of Accounts 2012*, Cardiff: S4C.

S4C (2019), *Annual Report and Statement of Accounts for the 12 month period to 31 March 2019*, Cardiff: S4C.

SG (2007), Notes from Name Change Group Meeting 15/08/07 (WCM/FOI).

SG (2010a), *Plana Gàidhlig/Gaelic Language Plan*, Edinburgh: SG.

SG (2010b), *Curriculum for Excellence: Literacy and Gàidhlig – Principles and Practice*, Edinburgh: SG.

SG (2013a), 'Maoin son foghlam Gàidhlig', https://news.gov.scot/news/maoin-son-foghlam-gaidhlig (last accessed 29 November 2019).

SG (2013b), *Scotland's Future: Your Guide to an Independent Scotland*, Edinburgh: SG.

SG (2015), Letter from Nicola Sturgeon, First Minister, to Alasdair MacCaluim, Glasgow, 18 July (WCM).

SG (2016), *Summary statistics for schools in Scotland No. 7: 2016 Edition*, Edinburgh: SG.

SG (2017a), *The Scottish Government Gaelic Language Plan 2016–2021*, Edinburgh: SG.

SG (2017b), *British Sign Language (BSL) National Plan 2017–2023*, Edinburgh: SG.
SG (2017c), 'Funding for Gaelic Centre', https://news.gov.scot/news/funding-for-gaelic-centre (last accessed 2 November 2019).
SG (2018a), *Independent Review of Hate Crime Legislation in Scotland: Final Report*, Edinburgh: SG.
SG (2018b), 'Treas sgoil Ghàidhlig ann an Glaschu', www.gov.scot/news/third-glasgow-gaelic-school/ (last accessed 2 November 2019).
SG (2018c), 'Annual spend on support for Gaelic since 1999: FOI release', https://www.gov.scot/publications/foi-18-01112/ (last accessed 15 October 2019).
SG (2018d), '107 new STEM teachers funded by bursary', www.gov.scot/news/107-new-stem-teachers-funded-by-bursary (last accessed 29 October 2019).
SG (2019), 'Scheme of Specific Grants for Gaelic, budget and allocation: FOI release', https://www.gov.scot/publications/foi-18-03763/ (last accessed 20 December 2019).
SG/Education Scotland (2015), *Scots Language Policy*, Edinburgh: SG.
SG Languages Working Group (2012), *Language Learning in Scotland: A 1+2 Approach*, Edinburgh: SG.
SG (1975a), 'Gaelic Title – "Comhairle nan Eilean"', 1 February, 5.
SG (1975b), 'Teaching Gaelic in Schools – The Future Looks Bright', 29 March, 1.
SG (1975c), 'New Council Approve Vigorous Bi-Lingualism', 19 April, 1.
SG (1980a), 'Am I Living in "Cuckoo" Land?', 21 June, 1.
SG (1980b), 'Council Throw Out Gaelic Plan for Secondaries', 28 June, 1.
SG (2015), 'Funding cut to Gaelic TV "cultural vandalism"', 6 December.
Sharp, William ('Fiona MacLeod') (1910 [1900]), 'The Gael and his Heritage', in *The Winged Destiny: Studies in the Spiritual History of the Gael*, London: William Heinemann, 223–60.
Shaw, Michael (2020), *The Fin-de-Siècle Scottish Revival: Romance, Decadence and Celtic Identity*, Edinburgh: EUP.
[Shaw, Neil] (1955), 'President's English Address', *AG*, 50, 102–3.
Shohamy, Elena (2006), *Language Policy: Hidden Agendas and New Approaches*, London: Routledge.
Sinclair, Andrew (1981), Letter from Andrew Sinclair, Wick, to Sandy Lindsay (former Councillor, Highland Regional Council), 3 June (HC Archives D127/1).
Sìol nan Gaidheal (n.d.) (a), 'History of Our Movement' (URL: www.siol-nan-gaidheal.org/hstoom.htm).
Sìol nan Gaidheal (n.d.) (b), 'The Gaelic Language' (URL: www.siol-nan-gaidheal.org/gaelic.htm#freedom).
Sìol nan Gaidheal (n.d.) (c), 'Seamus Mac Garaidh – Portrait of A Patriot' (www.siol-nan-gaidheal.org/garaidh.htm).

Skene, William F. (ed.) (1871), *John of Fordun's Chronicle of the Scottish Nation*, trans. by Felix J. H. Skene, Edinburgh: Edmonston & Douglas.
Small, Mike (2018), 'On Myths of Genocide', *Bella Caledonia*, 21 February, http://bellacaledonia.org.uk/2018/02/21/on-myths-of-genocide/ (last accessed 15 November 2019).
Smith, Anthony D. (1981), *The Ethnic Revival*, Cambridge: CUP.
Smith, Christina A. (1948), *Mental Testing of Hebridean Children in Gaelic and English*, London: University of London Press.
The Smith Commission (2014), *Report of the Smith Commission for further devolution of powers to the Scottish Parliament*, www.smith-commission.scot (last accessed 15 November 2019).
Smith, Iain Crichton (1986), 'Real People in a Real Place', in *Towards the Human: Selected Essays*, Edinburgh: Macdonald Publishers, 13–70.
Smith, John A. (1968), 'The Position of Gaelic and Gaelic Culture in Scottish Education', in Derick S. Thomson and Ian Grimble (eds), *The Future of the Highlands*, London: Routledge & Kegan Paul,, 59–91.
Smith, John A. (1978–80), 'The 1872 Education (Scotland) Act and Gaelic Education', *TGSI*, 51, 1–67.
Smith, Mina (2014), interview with the author, Glasgow, 29 April.
Smith-Christmas, Cassie (2014), *Language and Integration: Migration to Gaelic-Speaking Areas in the Twenty-First Century*, Stornoway: Soillse.
Smith-Christmas, Cassie and Ó hIfearnáin, Tadhg (2015), 'Gaelic Scotland and Ireland: Issues of class and diglossia in an evolving social landscape', in Dick Smakman and Patrick Heinrich (eds), *Globalising Sociolinguistics: Challenging and Expanding Theory*, London: Routledge, 256–69.
Smith-Christmas, Cassie, et al. (eds.) (2018), *New Speakers of Minority Languages: Linguistic Ideologies and Practices*, Basingstoke: Palgrave Macmillan.
SNP (1978), 'A' Ghàidhlig: na tha romhainn a dhèanamh', *Gairm*, 104, 301–11.
SNP (2011), *Scottish National Party Manifesto 2011*, Edinburgh: SNP.
SO (1930a), Minute to Mr Laird concerning ACG 1930, 30 May (Ref. 31054/14) (NRS HH83/233).
SO (1930b), Letter from John Lamb, SO, to Neil Shaw, Secretary, ACG, 23 June (NRS HH83/233).
SO (1959), *Review of Highland Policy*, London: HMSO.
SO (1966a), Note for the Secretary of State's meeting with ACG, 29 April (NRS HH41/1657).
SO (1966b), 'Mr Ross Meets An Comunn Gaidhealach – Aid Asked for Gaelic Language' (NRS HH41/1669).
SO (1966c), Minute from G. P. Belfourd, SHHD, to the Registrar General, 2 December (NRS HH41/1669).
SO (1968b), Letter from William Ross MP, Scottish Secretary, to Malcolm Macmillan MP, 29 May (NRS HH41/1669).
SO (1969), Letter from J. Cormack, Private Secretary to the Scottish Secretary,

to Mrs J. A. Lynn, Honorary Secretary, GSL, 2 April (GSL Archive, University College London Library).

SO (1970a), Letter from William Ross MP, Scottish Secretary, to Russell Johnston MP, 19 February (NRS HH41/1994).

SO (1970b), Minute from Duncan Dee, SHHD, to Mr Findlay and Mr J. A. Scott, 8 July (NRS HH41/1994).

SO (1970c), Letter from Gordon Campbell MP, Scottish Secretary, to Kenneth MacKinnon, Leigh-on-Sea, Essex, 10 July (WCM).

SO (1973), Letter from E. G. Christie, SHHD, to Gordon Burns, ACG, 22 January (NRS HH41/1994).

SO (1975), Letter from Robert Hughes to Norman Burns, ACG, 24 June (NRS DD4/5634).

SO (1980a), Letter from Alex Fletcher MP to Leon Brittan, Home Secretary, 20 March (NRS ED61/185).

SO (1980b), Minute from V. C. Stewart, General Record Office Scotland, to Mr Ogilvie, SHHD, 25 April (NRS HH41/1994).

SO (1981a), Minute from Jack Reynolds, Dover House, to Parliamentary Secretaries to SED and SHHD, 14 January (NRS HH83/674).

SO (1981b), Gaelic (Miscellaneous Provisions) Bill – Note of meeting, 15 January (NRS HH41/3389).

SO (1981c), Minute from A. J. Rushworth, Parliamentary Clerk to Under-SoS, to Parliamentary Clerk, 19 January (NRS HH41/3389).

SO (1981d), Extract of minute of meeting of Scottish Ministers, 21 January (NRS HH83/674).

SO (1981e), Minute from E. C. Reavley, SHHD, to David Connelly, SED, 27 January (NRS ED61/185).

SO (1981f), Teleprint message from PS, Scottish Secretary to PS/SED, 29 January (NRS HH83/674).

SO (1981g), Minute from Boyd McAdam, PS/Minister of State, to PS/Scottish Secretary, 2 February (NRS HH83/674).

SO (1981h), Minute from Godfrey Robinson, PS/SoS to PS/SED, 7 July (NRS HH41/2712).

SO (1981i), Letter from George Younger, Scottish Secretary, to William Whitelaw, Home Secretary, 24 September (NRS HH41/2712).

SO (1981j), Minute from R. S. Johnstone, SED to W. J. Fearnley, SED, 22 December (NRS ED48/2601).

SO (1982a), Minute from P. A. Cox, SED to Secretary, SED, 25 March (NRS ED61/20).

SO (1982b), Minute from J. A. M. Mitchell, SED to P. A. Cox, SED, 2 April (NRS ED61/20).

SO (1982c). Minute from W. Nicol, SED, to W. J. Fearnley, SED, 28 April (NRS ED48/2601).

SO (1982d), Letter from Alex Fletcher, Minister for Industry and Education, to

Alexander Matheson, Convener, Western Isles Islands Council, 5 October (NRS ED61/205).

SO (1983a), Letter from D. F. Middleton, PS/Minister of State, to Lord Campbell of Croy, 2 June (NRS HH41/2712).

SO (1983d), Minute from David Beveridge, Scottish Information Office, to J. L. Ross, SED, 'Green Folder – Mr Donald Stewart MP – Discrimination Against the Gaelic Language in Scottish Office Leaflets and Forms', n.d. [11] August (NRS ED29/80).

SO (1983e), Minute from J. S. B. Martin, Scottish Economic Planning Department, to PS/SEPD, PS/Mr Stewart and PS/Minister of State, 29 August (NRS ED61/196).

SO (1983f), Minute from R. G. L. McCrone, Industry Department, to Mr Stewart, Minister of State and Secretary of State, 7 November (NRS ED61/196).

SO (1983g), Minute from Andrew Chisholm, PS to Mr Stewart, to PS/Minister of State, 14 November (NRS ED61/196).

SO (1984a), Letter from J. S. B. Martin, Industry Department, to Iain MacAskill, Secretary, HIDB, 16 January (NRS ED61/196).

SO (1984b), Minute from M. MacLeod to D. A. Campbell, SED, 24 April (NRS ED61/196).

SO (1988), Minute from D. A. Campbell, SED to PS/Mr Forsyth, 26 July (NRS ED29/69).

SO (1989a), Minute from Malcolm Rifkind, Scottish Secretary, to the Prime Minister, 26 October (NRS ED 29/114).

SO (1989b), Letter from Malcolm Rifkind, Scottish Secretary, to Norman Lamont, First Secretary of the Treasury, 1 December (NRS ED29/114).

SO (1989c), Minute from Margaret MacLean, SED to PS/SofS, 12 December (NRS ED29/114).

SO (1989d), Minute from Margaret MacLean, SED to PS/SofS, 15 December (NRS ED29/114).

SO (1989e), Letter from Malcolm Rifkind, Scottish Secretary, to Norman Lamont, First Secretary of the Treasury, 18 December (NRS ED29/114).

SO (1998a), *Report of the Consultative Steering Group on the Scottish Parliament: 'Shaping Scotland's Parliament'*, Edinburgh: SO.

SO (1998b), Minute from Francis Brewis, EID-ACH, to PS/Mr Wilson and PS/SoS, 30 April (NRS 61/233/138–42).

SO (1998c), Minute from John Elvidge to Mr Lonie (NRS 61/233/158).

SO Education Department (1993), *National Guidelines for Curriculum and Assessment in Scotland: Gaelic 5–14*, Edinburgh: SO Education Department.

SO Education Department (1994), *Solarachadh na Gàidhlig ann am Foghlam ann an Albainn/Provision for Gaelic Education in Scotland*, Edinburgh: SO Education Department.

Sorooshian, Roxanne (2010), 'Leave endangered languages to die in peace', *Sunday Herald*, 19 September, 5.

SP (2000), 'Gaelic', Official Report, 2 March, cols 382–426.

SP, Education, Culture and Sport Committee (2001), *Report on the Gaelic Broadcasting Committee*, Edinburgh: SP.

SP, Education, Culture and Sport Committee (2003a), *Report on Inquiry into the role of educational and cultural policy in supporting and developing Gaelic, Scots and minority languages in Scotland*, Edinburgh: SP.

SP, Education, Culture and Sport Committee (2003b), *Stage 1 Report on the Gaelic Language (Scotland) Bill*, Edinburgh: SP.

SP (2003c), debate on the Gaelic Language (Scotland) Bill: Stage 1, 6 March, http://www.parliament.scot/parliamentarybusiness/report.aspx?r=4434&i=31840&c=796673&s=gaelic (accessed 3 December 2019).

SP (2004a), *Gaelic Language (Scotland) Bill: Explanatory Notes (and Other Accompanying Documents)*, Edinburgh: SP.

SP (2004b), *Gaelic Language (Scotland) Bill: Policy Memorandum*, Edinburgh: SP.

SP, Education Committee (2004c), 'Gaelic Language (Scotland) Bill: Stage 1', www.parliament.scot/parliamentarybusiness/report.aspx?r=465&mode=pdf (last accessed 3 December 2019).

SP, Education Committee (2005a), *Stage 1 Report on the Gaelic Language (Scotland) Bill*, vol. 3, Edinburgh: SP.

SP (2013), Reply by Nicola Sturgeon MSP to question S4W-12829 from Angus MacDonald MSP, www.parliament.scot/S4_ChamberDesk/WA20130225.pdf (last accessed 13 November 2019).

SP (2015), Debate on the 10th Anniversary of the Gaelic Language (Scotland) Act 2005, Edinburgh: SP, www.parliament.scot/parliamentarybusiness/report.aspx?r=10002&i=91801#ScotParlOR (last accessed 3 December 2019).

SP (2018), Debate on National Gaelic Language Plan 2018–23, Edinburgh: SP, www.parliament.scot/Gaelic/DebateonGaelicNationalLanguagePlan2018.pdf (last accessed 3 December 2019).

SP, Education Committee (2019), *Subject choices in schools*, SP Paper 575, 6th Report, 2019 (Session 5), Edinburgh: SP.

Spolsky, Bernard (2010), 'Ferguson and Fishman: Sociolinguistics and the Sociology of Language', in Ruth Wodak, Barbara Johnstone and Paul E. Kerswill (eds), *The SAGE Handbook of Sociolinguistics*, London: SAGE Publications, 11–23.

Spolsky, Bernard (2012), *The Cambridge Handbook of Language Policy*, Cambridge: CUP.

Sproull, Alan (1996), 'Regional economic development and minority language use: the case of Gaelic Scotland', *International Journal of the Sociology of Language*, 121, 93–117.

Sproull, Alan and Ashcroft, Brian (1993), *The Economics of Gaelic Language Development*, Glasgow: Glasgow Caledonian University.

Sproull, Alan and Douglas Chalmers (1998), *The Demand for Gaelic Artistic*

Bibliography

and *Cultural Products and Services: Patterns and Impacts*, Glasgow: Glasgow Caledonian University.

Sproull, Alan and Douglas Chalmers (2006), *The Demand for Gaelic Arts: Patterns and Impacts – A 10 year longitudinal study*, Stornoway: Gaelic Arts Strategic Development.

SQA (2009), *Gnàthachas Litreachaidh na Gàidhlig/Gaelic Orthographic Conventions*, Glasgow: SQA.

SQA (2011), *Statistics 2011 – Higher*, www.sqa.org.uk/sqa/57517.html (last accessed 10 January 2020).

SQA (2018), *SQA Provision for Gaelic*, Glasgow: SQA.

SQA (2019), *Attainment Statistics (December) 2019*, www.sqa.org.uk/sqa/64717.html (last accessed 10 January 2020).

SQA (2020), Enrolment data for Gaelic-medium examinations, Glasgow: SQA.

SQA (n.d.), 'Scots Language Award', https://www.sqa.org.uk/sqa/70056.html (last accessed 20 December 2019).

Sruth (1967), 'Na Cananan Beaga', 12, 1.

Sruth (1968), 'Am Mod' (leader), 41, 4.

Stage and Television Today (1993), 'Poor primetime ratings put Gaelic committee on defensive', 25 November, 24.

Statistics Canada/Statistique Canada (2017), *Census Profile, 2016 Census Nova Scotia [Province] and Canada [Country]*, www12.statcan.gc.ca/census-recensement/2016/dp-pd/prof/details/Page.cfm?Lang=E&Geo1=PR&Code1=12&Geo2=&Code2=&Data=Count&SearchText=Nova%20Scotia&SearchType=Begins&SearchPR=01&B1=All&GeoLevel=PR&GeoCode=12 (last accessed 31 January 2018).

Statistics for Wales (2012), 'Welsh speakers by local authority, gender and detailed age groups, 2011 census', Cardiff: Welsh Government, https://statswales.gov.wales/Catalogue/Welsh-Language/Census-Welsh-Language/welshspeakers-by-localauthority-gender-detailedagegroups-2011census (last accessed 20 December 2019).

StatsWales (2019), 'Pupils by local authority, region and Welsh medium type', https://statswales.gov.wales/Catalogue/Education-and-Skills/Schools-and-Teachers/Schools-Census/Pupil-Level-Annual-School-Census/Welsh-Language/pupils-by-localauthorityregion-welshmediumtype (last accessed 27 August 2019).

Stephens, Mamari (2014), 'A House With Many Rooms: Rediscovering Māori as a Civic Language', in Rawinia Higgins, Poia Rewi and Vincent Olsen-Reeder (eds), *The Value of the Māori Language*, Wellington: Huia Publishers, 53–84.

Stephens, Meic (1976), *Linguistic Minorities in Western Europe*, Llandysul: Gomer Press.

Stewart, Rev. Alexander (1801), *Elements of Galic Grammar*, Edinburgh: Peter Hill.

Stewart, Charles (1906), 'The Teaching of Gaelic in Highland Schools', *The Times*, 21 July, 8.
Stewart, Donald (1983), Letter from Donald Stewart MP to George Younger MP, Scottish Secretary, 7 July (NRS ED29/80).
Stewart, Donald (1994), *A Scot at Westminster*, Sydney, NS: Catalone Press.
Stewart, Ian B. (2015), 'Of crofters, Celts and claymores: the *Celtic Magazine* and the Highland cultural nationalist movement, 1875–88', *Historical Research*, 89, 88–113.
Stirling-Maxwell, Sir William (1874), 'Sir Uilleam S-Maxwell agus a' Ghàidhlig', *AG*, 3, 10–11.
Storey, John (2011), 'Contemporary Gaelic fiction: development, challenge and opportunity', in Emma Dymock and Wilson McLeod (eds), *Lainnir a' Bhùirn/The Gleaming Water: Essays on Modern Gaelic Literature*, Edinburgh: Dunedin Academic Press, 23–39.
An Stòr-Dàta Briathrachais Gàidhlig/The Gaelic Terminology Database (1993), *Leabhar 1/Vol. 1*. Sleat: Clò Ostaig.
Strathclyde Regional Council (1985a), Minutes of Education Committee, 10 July (p. 728) (Mitchell Library, Glasgow).
Strathclyde Regional Council (1985b), Letter from Keir Bloomer, Education Officer, to Donald MacLennan, Chairman, Comann Sgoiltean Dà-chànanach Ghlaschu, 8 November (WCM).
Stringer, Keith (2005), 'The emergence of a nation-state, 1100–1300', in Jenny Wormald (ed.), *Scotland: A History*, Oxford: OUP, 38–68.
Stroh, Silke (2017), *Gaelic Scotland in the Colonial Imagination: Anglophone Writing from 1600 to 1900*, Evanston, IL: Northwestern University Press.
Strubell, Miquel (1999), 'From Language Planning to Language Policies and Language Politics', in Peter J. Weber (ed.), *Contact+ Confli(c)t: Language Planning and Minorities*, Bonn: Dümmler, 237–48.
Sunday Herald (1999), 'Scots Secretary's residence to showcase art and design', 31 October, 3.
Tange, Hanne (2000), 'Writing the Nation: Four Inter-War Visions of Scotland', PhD thesis, University of Glasgow.
Taskforce on the Public Funding of Gaelic (2000), *Revitalising Gaelic – A National Asset: Report by the Taskforce on Public Funding of Gaelic*, Edinburgh: Scottish Executive.
Taylor, Iain (2011), telephone interview with the author, 2 August.
Taylor, Simon and Gilbert Márkus, *The Place-names of Fife, Vol. 5*. Donington: Shaun Tyas.
Taylor, S. W. (1968), 'The Language Question', *Scottish Vanguard*, 2(4–5), 10–11.
Le Télégramme (2013), 'Carhaix. Diwan meilleur lycée de France?', 1 October.
TESS (1982), 'Western Isles agree to evaluation', 17 September, 1.

TESS (1985), 'Gaelic grants concession uses old money for new', 11 October.
TESS (2002), 'Gaelic school comes a step closer', 23 August, 6.
TESS (2010), 'Bid to cut Gaelic class size', 6 August, 1.
TGSI (1872), 'Coimh-Dhealbhadh/Constitution', 1, iv–vi.
TGSI (1878a), 'Introduction', 6, xiii–xv.
TGSI (1884), 'The Gaelic Census', 10, 51–8.
TGSI (1915a), 'Annual Dinner', 27, 1–19.
TGSI (1915b), 'Annual Assembly', 27, 41–7.
TGSI (1924), 'Annual Dinner', 30, 84–100.
TGSI 1929), 'Annual Dinner', 30, 49–67.
TGSI (1932), 'Annual Dinner', 33, 252–77.
Thomas, Frank (1998), 'Gaelic in the Census of Population in Scotland, 1881 to 1991', in Kenneth MacKinnon (ed.), *Compass: Proceedings of the Colloquium on Minority-language Population-censuses*, Hatfield: University of Hertfordshire, n.p.
Thomas, James (ed.) (2015), *Grains of Gold: An Anthology of Occitan Literature*, London: Francis Boutle Press.
Thomas, Ned (1971), *The Welsh Extremist: A Culture in Crisis*, London: Gollancz.
Thompson, Frank (1963), 'The Voice of Scotland', in Ceinwen Thomas (ed.), *The Celtic Nations: Book of the Celtic League 1963*, Cardiff: Celtic League, 40–4.
Thompson, Frank (1968), 'The New Face of Gaelic', *Sruth*, 40, 10–12.
Thompson, Frank (1971–2), 'Gaelic in Politics', *TGSI*, 48, 67–100.
Thompson, Frank (1972), 'Scottish Language Society', *Crann-Tara*, 4, 5.
Thompson, Frank (1978), 'Gaelic in Scotland', *Resurgence*, 69, 16–18.
Thompson, Frank (1985), 'How Strong the Horsehair?', in Hulbert (1985), 1–10.
Thompson, Frank (1992), *History of An Comunn Gaidhealach: The First Hundred (1891–1991) – Centenary of An Comunn Gaidhealach*, Inverness: ACG.
  [see also MacThòmais, Frang]
Thomson, Derick S. (1964–6), 'The Role of the Writer in a Minority Culture', *TGSI*, 44, 256–71.
Thomson, Derick S. (1981), 'Gaelic in Scotland: Assessment and Prognosis', in Haugen, McClure and Thomson (1981), 10–20.
Thomson, Derick S. (ed.) (1983a), *The Companion to Gaelic Scotland*, Oxford: Basil Blackwell.
Thomson, Derick S. (1983b), 'Publishing, Gaelic', in Thomson (1983a), 244–7.
Thomson, Derick S. (1985), 'The Renaissance of Scottish Gaelic as a Component of National Identity', in P. Sture Ureland (ed.), *Entshehung von Sprachern und Völkern*, Berlin: De Gruyter, 261–72.
Thomson, Derick S. (ed.) (1996), *Alasdair mac Mhaighstir Alasdair: Selected Poems*, Edinburgh: Scottish Gaelic Texts Society.

Thomson, Derick S. (1997–8), 'Gaelic Renaissance *c*. 1900–1930', *TGSI*, 60, 285–301.
Thomson, Derick S. (1999), 'Scottish Minorities', in Herve ar Bihan (ed.), *Breizh ha Pobloù Europa/Bretagne et Peuples d'Europe*, Rennes: Hor Yezh, 635–44.
Thomson, Derick S. (2004), 'Erskine, Stuart Richard (1869–1960)', *Oxford Dictionary of National Biography*, www.oxforddnb.com/view/article/40311 (last accessed 15 November 2019).
[see also MacThòmais, Ruaraidh]
'Thule' (1924), 'The Absurd Pride of Race' (letter to the editor), *The Weekly Scotsman*, 9 February, 7.
The Times (1892), 'House of Commons', 17 February, 7.
The Times (1955), 'Mod Rejects Child Vocalists – Gaelic Below Standard', 28 September, 5.
The Times (2009), 'Scottish Gaelic – as spoken in Brussels and Luxembourg', 8 October, 22.
The Times (2010), 'Minister masters Gaelic jargon for Brussels speech', 12 May, 20.
The Times (2018), 'Gaelic-only school "cause of inequality"', 20 April, 3.
Tiree & Coll Gaelic Partnership (2011), *Ministers and Deep Sea Captains: The Schools of Tiree*, Tiree: Tiree & Coll Gaelic Partnership.
Titley, Alan (2011), 'The Ravelling of Narratives: Irish and Scottish Gaelic Life Stories Compared', in *Nailing Theses: Selected Essays*, Belfast: Lagan Press, 402–13.
TNS–BMRB (2010), *Public Attitudes Towards the Scots Language*, Edinburgh: SG Social Research.
Transport Scotland (2015), Letter from William Clark, Franchise Management Unit, to Adam Smith, 7 April, www.whatdotheyknow.com/request/total_cost_so_far_of_gaelic_sign (last accessed 25 October 2017).
Transport Scotland (2016), Letter from Graeme McQuaker, Head of Standards Branch, Trunk Roads and Bus Operations, to Craig McComb, 12 December, https://www.whatdotheyknow.com/request/gaelic_road_signs (last accessed 25 October 2017).
UK Government (1999), *Report Submitted by the United Kingdom Pursuant to Article 25, Paragraph 1 of the Framework Convention for the Protection of National Minorities*, London: UK Government.
Ulster Loyalist Anti-Repeal Union (1886), *Teagasg nan 'Home Rulers'*, Belfast: Ulster Loyalist Anti-Repeal Union.
University of Edinburgh (1898), *Report on Statistics by the University Court of the University of Edinburgh . . . for the Academical Year from 1st October 1896 to 30th September 1897*, London: HMSO.
University of Edinburgh (1902), *Report on Statistics by the University Court of the University of Edinburgh . . . for the Academical Year from 1st October 1900 to 30th September 1901*, London: HMSO.
University of Glasgow (2016), '20th Century Department of Celtic', http://sgeul

nagaidhlig.ac.uk/20th-c-department-of-celtic (last accessed 15 November 2019).

University of Strathclyde, Gaelic Department (2001), *Pupil Numbers in Gaelic Education 2000–01*, Glasgow: University of Strathclyde.

University of Strathclyde, Gaelic Department (2006), *Pupil Numbers in Gaelic Education 2005–06*, Glasgow: University of Strathclyde.

Urchardainn, Daibhidh (1927), 'A' Ghaidhlig anns na Sgoilean', in MacDonald (1927), 245–7.

Urla, Jacqueline (2012), *Reclaiming Basque: Language, Nation, and Cultural Activism*, Reno, NV: University of Nevada Press.

Veljanovski, Cento (1989), 'The Case for a Gaelic Broadcasting Service', London: Putnam, Hayes & Bartlett.

'Verb Sap.' (1933), 'An Comunn Gaidhealach' (letter to the editor), *Scots Independent*, 7, no. 76, 61.

Victoria, Queen (1878), *Duilleagain a Leabhar Cunntas ar Beatha anns a Ghadhalltachd [sic] bho 1848 gu 1861*, trans. by Rev. I. P. St Clair, Edinburgh: Edmonston & Co.

Victoria, Queen (1886), *Tuilleadh Dhuilleag bho M' Leabhar-latha mu Chunntas Mo Bheatha Anns a' Ghaidhealtachd bho 1862 gu 1882*, trans. by Mary MacKellar, Edinburgh: William Blackwood & Sons.

W (1884), 'Gaelic in schools', *The Celtic Magazine*, 9, 435–9.

Wales Online (2014), 'How a group of Welsh nationalists became pirate radio pioneers', https://www.walesonline.co.uk/news/wales-news/how-group-welsh-nationalists-became-6527184 (last accessed 15 November 2019).

Wallace, Stuart (2006), *John Stuart Blackie: Scottish Scholar and Patriot*, Edinburgh: EUP.

Walsh, John (2011), *Contests and Contexts: The Irish Language and Ireland's Socio-Economic Development*, Bern: Peter Lang.

Walsh, John and McLeod, Wilson (2008), 'An overcoat wrapped around an invisible man? Language legislation and language revitalisation in Ireland and Scotland', *Language Policy*, 7, 21–46.

Warner, Gerard (2000), 'In defence of Gaelic', *Sunday Times*, 12 October, 3.

Watson, Moray and Macleod, Michelle (eds) (2010), *The Edinburgh Companion to the Gaelic Language*, Edinburgh: EUP.

Watson, W. J. (1906), 'The Oban Conference', *DG*, 1, 146–7.

Watson, W. J. (ed.) (1915), *Rosg Gàidhlig: Specimens of Gaelic Prose*, Inverness: ACG.

Watson, W. J. (ed.) (1918), *Bàrdachd Ghàidhlig: Specimens of Gaelic Poetry 1550–1900*, Inverness: ACG.

Watson, W. J. (1923), 'The Position of Gaelic', *Gailig*, 18, 51–2, 66–8, 82–3, 98–100.

Watson, W. J. and Nicholson, Alexander N. (1929), 'Introduction and Review', *TGSI*, 32 (1929), v–xvi.

Watt, Rev. Lauchlan MacLean (1937), 'Celtic Glimpses', *TGSI*, 38, 10–45.

Webb, Keith (1977), *The Growth of Nationalism in Scotland*, Glasgow: Molendinar Press.
Welsh Government (2017), *Technical Advice Note 20: Planning and the Welsh Language*, Cardiff: Welsh Government.
Welsh Government & Welsh Language Commissioner (2015), *Welsh language use in Wales, 2013–15*, Cardiff: Welsh Government & Welsh Language Commissioner.
Welsh Language Board (1996), *Welsh Language Schemes: Their preparation and approval in accordance with the Welsh Language Act 1993*, Cardiff: Welsh Language Board.
Welsh Language Commissioner (2016), *Recruitment: Welsh Language Considerations*, Cardiff: Welsh Language Commissioner.
Welsh Nation (1973), 'Language society produces 5-year plan for Gaelic', 23 November, 2.
Welsh Office (1965), *Legal Status of the Welsh Language: Report of the Committee under the Chairmanship of Sir David Hughes Parry, Q.C., LL.D., D.C.L. 1963–1965*, London: HMSO.
Welsh Office (1972), *Bilingual Traffic Signs/Arwyddion Ffyrdd Dwyieithog: Report of the Committee of Inquiry under the Chairmanship of Roderic Bowen, Esq., Q.C., M.A., LL.D. 1971–72*, Cardiff: HMSO.
Welsh Office (1989), Letter from Peter Walker MP, Welsh Secretary, to Nigel Lawson MP, Chief Secretary to the Treasury, 3 November (NRS ED 29/114).
West, Catriona and Graham, Alastair (2011), *Attitudes Towards the Gaelic Language*, Edinburgh: SG Social Research.
Western Isles Constituency Association of the SNP (1978), 'Submission by the Western Isles Constituency Association of the Scottish National Party' (CnES/SG).
Western Isles Constituency Labour Party (1978), 'Submission by the Western Isles Constituency Labour Party on "The Bilingual Policy: A Consultative Document"' (CnES/SG).
Western Isles Liberal Association (1978), 'Comments by the Western Isles Liberal Association on the Pamphlet "The Bilingual Policy: A Consultative Document" Issued by Comhairle nan Eilean' (CnES/SG).
WHFP (1984a), 'Comann Luchd-ionnsachaidh: giving new vigour to the Gaelic learner', 10 February, 9.
WHFP (1984b), 'The language of dissent: Move to set up alternative to An Comunn' and 'Sgaradh 's a Chomunn', 23 March, 1.
WHFP (1984c), 'Green light for bilingual signs after four years', 7 July, 1.
WHFP (1984d), 'No Gaelic in court, as two are found guilty of damaging signs', 3 August, 14.
WHFP (1985a), 'Deadlock as staff, council fail to agree on "Gaelic-essential" staff post', 11 October, 16.

WHFP (1985b), 'August 1986 start date for Gaelic-medium primary class at Portree', 15 November, 14.
WHFP (1989), 'Labour pledge on Gaelic', 20 October.
WHFP (1994), 'Lobbying campaign underway to tackle Gaelic teacher shortage', 22 July.
WHFP (2000), 'Gaelic: Dewar "won't go down the Welsh road"', 8 September.
WHFP (2001), 'Breakthrough on Sleat housing shortage: Noble "Gaelic speakers preferred" stipulation is rejected', 7 December.
WHFP (2003), 'Bilingual road signs approved, despite battle against "racist" civil servants', 24 January.
WHFP (2005), Letter to the editor from Domhnall Uilleam Stiùbhart, Edinburgh, 4 November.
WHFP (2009), 'Minister's wrong turning on bilingual signs', 3 April, 11.
WHFP (2012a), 'Parents campaign against Gaelic medium staff cuts', 1 June.
WHFP (2014), 'Freagairt do dhraghan mu MG ALBA', 11 September.
WHFP (2015), 'A bad fortnight for Gaelic must not be allowed to get worse', 4 December.
WHFP (2019a), 'Gaelic's "worrying decline" at secondary school level threatens future of the language', 14 March.
WHFP (2019b), 'Swinney stresses full Gaelic immersion is "essential"', 6 September, 3.
WHFP (2020), 'Fresh bid to recruit more Gaelic teachers', 3 January, 1.
Wicherkiewicz, Tomasz (2005), 'Collateral/regional languages in the new EU member states', paper presented at the Near Languages (Collateral Languages 2) conference, Limerick, June 16–18.
Williams, Colin H. (1999), 'The Celtic World', in Joshua A. Fishman (ed.), *Handbook of Language and Ethnic Identity*, Oxford: OUP, 267–85.
Williams, Colin H. (2010), 'From Act to Action in Wales', in Delyth Morris (ed.), *Welsh in the Twenty-First Century*, Cardiff: UWP, 36–60.
Williams, Colin H. (2013a), 'Perfidious Hope: The Legislative Turn in Official Minority Language Regimes', *Regional and Federal Studies*, 23, 101–22.
Williams, Colin H. (2013b), *Official Language Strategies in Comparative Perspective*, Cardiff: NPLD.
Williams, Colin H. (2014), 'The Lightening Veil: Language Revitalisation in Wales', *Review of Research in Education*, 38, 242–72.
Williams, Colin H. and Walsh, John (2017), 'Minority Language Governance and Regulation', in Hogan-Brun and O'Rourke (2019), 101–30.
Wilson, Brian (1984), 'Important distinction between Gaelic-medium education and bilingualism', *WHFP*, 26 October, 5.
Wilson, Brian (1985a), 'Gaelic primary education inaugurated in Glasgow', *GH*, 15 August, 14.
Wilson, Brian (1985b), 'Now it's "joy, joy, joy all the way" for Glasgow Gaels', *WHFP*, 16 August, 5.

Wilson, Brian (2005), 'Let's talk Gaelic before it's too late', *The Observer*, 20 April.

Wilson, Brian (2011), interview with the author, Uig, Lewis, 6 June.

Wilson, Eliot (2017), 'Gaelic signs a spurious vanity project for SNP', *The Scotsman*, 12 May.

Wings over Scotland (2010), 'The lesser of two stupids', https://wingsoverscotland.com/the-lesser-of-two-stupids/ (last accessed 29 October 2019).

Withers, Charles W. J. (1984), *Gaelic in Scotland 1698–1984: The Geographical History of a Language*, Edinburgh: John Donald.

Withers, Charles W. J. (1998), *Urban Highlanders: Highland–Lowland Migration and Urban Gaelic Culture, 1700–1900*, East Linton: Tuckwell Press.

Withers, Charles W. J. and MacKinnon, Kenneth (1983), 'Gaelic speaking in Scotland, demographic history', in Thomson (1983a), 109–14.

Witt, Patrick (2013), 'Connections across the North Channel: Ruaraidh Erskine and Irish Influence in Scottish Discontent, 1906–1920', www.theirishstory.com/2013/04/17/connections-across-the-north-channel-ruaraidh-erskine-and-irish-influence-in-scottish-discontent-1906-1920/#.Xbhq0PZ2t9A (last accessed 29 October 2019).

Wmffre, Iwan (2007), *Breton Orthographies and Dialects: The Twentieth-Century Orthography War in Brittany*, Oxford: Peter Lang.

Woolard, Kathryn (2016), *Singular and Plural: Ideologies of Linguistic Authority in 21st Century Catalonia*, Oxford: OUP.

Woolf, Alex (2007), *From Pictland to Alba 789–1070*, Edinburgh: EUP.

Working Group of the BBC and Seirbheis nam Meadhanan Gàidhlig (2006), 'Gaelic Digital Service: Position Statement' (WCM/FOI).

Wright, Sue (2016), *Language Policy and Language Planning: From Nationalism to Globalisation*, 2nd edn, Basingstoke: Palgrave.

Yes Alba (2014), *Submission to the Smith Commission*, Glasgow: Yes Alba, https://yesalba.files.wordpress.com/2014/11/yes-alba-smith-commission.pdf (last accessed 29 October 2019).

Young, Helen (2016), 'The small rural school and community relations in Scotland, 1872–2000: an interdisciplinary history', PhD thesis, University of Stirling.

Young, James D. (1983), 'Marxism and the Scottish National Question', *Journal of Contemporary History*, 18, 141–63.

Young, John (1986), 'The Advisory Council on Education in Scotland: 1920–1961', PhD thesis, University of Edinburgh.

'Z' (1876), 'The Lochalsh School Board and Gaelic in Schools', *The Scotsman*, 16 October, 3.

Zalbide, Mikel and Cenoz, Jasone (2008), 'Bilingual education in the Basque Autonomous Community: Achievements and challenges', *Language, Culture and Curriculum*, 21(1), 5–20.

Zall, Carol (1994), 'A chance to end the suppression of Gaelic', *TESS*, 12 August.

LEGISLATION AND OTHER ACTS

Specific sections relating to Gaelic or linguistic matters are noted when applicable.

(a) Primary Legislation

Act and remitt in favour of the synod of Argyll (1695), Records of the Scottish Parliaments 1695/5/180
An Acte for Laws & Justice to be ministred in Wales in like fourme as it is in this Realme ['Act of Union'], 1536 (27 Hen. 8) c. 26 (s. 20)
An act for the more effectual disarming the highlands in Scotland ['Act of Proscription'], 1746 (19 Geo. 2), c. 39
Act for the Settlement of Parochial Schools, 1616 (Scottish Privy Council) (Masson 1891: 671–2)
Act for settling of schools, 1696 c. 26 (SP)
Administration of Justice (Language) Act (Ireland) 1737, 1737 (11 Geo. 2) c. 6 (s. 1)
Borders, Citizenship and Immigration Act 2009, 2009 c. 11 (s. 40(3))
British Nationality Act 1981, 1981 c. 61 (s. 1(1)(c))
British Sign Language (Scotland) Act 2015, 2015 asp 11
Broadcasting Act 1990, 1990 c. 42 (s. 183)
Broadcasting Act 1996, 1990 c. 55 (ss. 32, 95)
Communications Act 2003, 2003 c. 21 (ss. 208–10)
Courts in Wales and Chester Act 1732, 1732 (6 Geo. II) c. 14
Crofters (Scotland) Act 1955, 1955 (3 & 4 Eliz. 2) c. 21 (s. 1(4))
Crofters (Scotland) Act 1993, 1993 c. 44 (s. 1(5))
Crofting Reform (Scotland) Act 2010, 2010 asp 14 (s. 4(1)–(2))
Crofters Holdings (Scotland) Act 1886, 1886 (49 & 50 Vict.) c. 29 (s. 17)
Crown Charters (Scotland) Act 1847, 1847 (10 & 11 Vict.) c. 51
Education Act 1980, 1980 c. 20 (s. 21)
Education Reform Act 1988, 1988 c. 40 (s. 3)
Education (Scotland) Act 1872, 1872 (35 & 36 Vict.) c. 62
Education (Scotland) Act 1908, 1908 (8 Edw. 7) c. 63 (s. 10(1))
Education (Scotland) Act 1918, 1918 (8 & 9 Geo. V) c. 48 (s. 6(1))
Education (Scotland) Act 1945, 1945 (8 & 9 Geo. 6) c. 37 (s. 1(1))
Education (Scotland) Act 1962, 1962 (10 & 11 Eliz. 2) c. 47 (ss. 1(1), 2(2)(c), 3(2)(b) and 4(d))
Education (Scotland) Act 1969, 1969 (17 & 18 Eliz. 2) c. 49 (s. 1(1))
Education (Scotland) Act 1980, 1980 c. 44 (s. 1(5)(a)(iii) and (b)(iv))
Education (Scotland) Act 2016, 2016 asp 8 (ss. 7–18)

Elementary Education Act 1870, 33 & 34 Vict. c. 75
Gaelic Language (Scotland) Act 2005, 2005 asp 7
Government of Wales Act 1998, 1998 c. 38
Highlands and Islands Development (Scotland) Act 1965, 1965 c. 46
Historic Environment Scotland Act 2014, 2014 asp 19 (s. 1(1))
Immigration Act 1971, 1971 c. 77
Land Reform (Scotland) Act 2016, 2016 asp 18 (ss. 4(1) and 11(2))
Land Settlement (Scotland) Act 1919, 1919 (9 & 10 Geo. 5) c. 7
Local Government (Scotland) Act 1929, 1929 (19 & 20 Geo. 5) c. 25
Local Government (Scotland) Act 1973, 1973 c. 65
Local Government (Gaelic Names) (Scotland) Act 1997, 1997 c. 6
National Mod (Scotland) Act 1969, 1969 c. 41
Parliamentary Voting System and Constituencies Act 2011, 2011 c. 1
Police and Fire Reform (Scotland) Act 2012, 2012 asp 8 (ss. 1(1) and 101(1))
Proceedings in Courts of Justice Act 1730, 1730 (4 Geo. II) c. 26
Public Services Reform (Scotland) Act 2010, 2010 asp 8 (s. 36(1))
Race Relations Act 1976, 1976 c. 74
Registration of Births, Deaths and Marriages (Scotland) Act 1854, 1854 (17 & 18 Vict.) c. 80
Road Traffic Regulation Act 1967, 1967 c. 76
Road Traffic Regulation Act 1984, 1984 c. 27
Schools (Consultation) (Scotland) Act 2010, 2010 asp 2 (sched. 1, s. 1)
Scotland Act 1998, 1998 c. 46
Scottish Crown Estate Act 2019, 2019 asp 1 (s. 1(1))
Scottish Land Court Act 1993, 1993 c. 45 (s. 1(5))
Small Landholders (Scotland) Act 1911, 1 & 2 Geo. 5 c. 49 (s. 3(3))
Standards in Scotland's Schools etc. Act 2000, 2000 asp 6
Titles to Land Consolidation (Scotland) Act 1868, 1868 (31 & 32 Vict.) c. 101 (s. 90)
Welsh Courts Act 1942, 1942 (5 & 6 Geo. 6) c. 40
Welsh Language Act 1967, 1967 c. 66
Welsh Language Act 1993, 1993 c. 38
Welsh Language (Wales) Measure 2011, 2011 nawm 1
Immigration Restriction Act 1901 (Australia), No. 17 of 1901
Canadian Charter of Rights and Freedoms, s. 15, Part I of the *Constitution Act, 1982*, being Schedule B to the *Canada Act 1982* (UK), 1982, c. 11
Language Act (Finland), (No. 423/2003)
Gaeltacht Industries Act, 1957 (Republic of Ireland), No. 29 of 1957
Official Languages Act 2003 (Republic of Ireland), No. 32 of 2003

(b) Statutory Instruments

Act of Sederunt (Rules of the Court of Session Amendment No. 4) (Miscellaneous) 2001, SSI 2001 No. 305

The Education (National Priorities) (Scotland) Order 2000, SSI 2000 No. 443

The Gaelic Medium Education (Assessment Requests) (Scotland) Regulations 2016, SSI 2016 No. 425

The Grants for Gaelic Language Education (Scotland) Regulations 1986, SI 1986 No. 410

The Multiplex Licence (Broadcasting of Programmes in Gaelic) Order 1996, SI 1996 No. 2758

The Multiplex Licence (Broadcasting of Programmes in Gaelic) (Revocation) Order 2011, SI 2011 No. 1169

The Schools (Scotland) Code 1950, SI 1950 No. 915

The Schools (Scotland) Code 1956, SI 1956 No. 894

The Scotland Act 1998 (Transitory and Transitional Provisions)(Standing Orders and Parliamentary Publications) Order 1999, SI 1999 No. 1095, Schedule, s. 7(1)

The Traffic Signs Regulations and General Directions 2016, SI 2016 No. 362, Schedule 12

(c) Acts of Court

'Practice – Use of Gaelic in Civil Proceedings', Act of Court of the Sheriff Principal of Grampian, Highlands and Islands, 11 June 2001

PARLIAMENTARY BILLS AND MOTIONS

Gaelic (Miscellaneous Provisions), 1980/81 Bill 24 (HoC)
Gaelic Language, 1980/81 Bill 76 (HoC)
Gaelic Language (No. 2), 1980/81 Bill 100 (HoC)
Gaelic Language (Scotland) Bill, SP Bill 69, Session 1 (2002)
Gaelic Language (Scotland) Bill, SP Bill 25, Session 2 (2004)
Official Status of the Gaelic Language, Early Day Motion 2822, Session 2010–12 (HoC) (tabled 5 March 2012)

LEGAL CASES

Clarabal v. Department of Education of the State of Hawai'i, SCAP-16-0000475 (Hawai'i Supreme Court) (2019)

In re Mac Giolla Catháin's Application for Judicial Review, [2009] NIQB 66 (High Court of Justice in Northern Ireland)

McKee v. Department of Education, [2011] NIQB 98 (High Court of Justice in Northern Ireland)
M'Lean and Others (Tiree Crofters) [1886], 1 White 232 (High Court of Justiciary)
Myles Martin and Others (Borniskitaig Crofters) [1886], 1 White 297 (High Court of Justiciary)
Martin v. MacLean, [1844] 6 Dunlop 981 (Court of Session)
R v. Alex McRae (1841), Bell's Notes 270 (High Court of Justiciary)
R v. Wilson ex parte Kisch, [1934] HCA 63 (High Court of Australia)
Taylor v. Haughney, 1982 *Scottish Criminal Cases Reports* 360 (High Court of Justiciary)

EUROPEAN ARRANGEMENTS AND RESOLUTIONS

Council of the European Union, *Administrative Arrangement between the Government of the United Kingdom of Great Britain and Northern Ireland and the Council of the European Union* (2008/C 194/04), *Official Journal of the European Union*, 31 July 2008, C 194/7
Resolution on a Community Charter of Regional Languages and Cultures and on a Charter of Rights of Ethnic Minorities [Arfé Resolution], *Official Journal of the European Communities* 1981 C287/106 (European Parliament, 16 October 1981)

TREATIES

European Charter for Regional or Minority Languages, ETS No. 148 (CoE) (1992)
Framework Convention for the Protection of National Minorities, ETS No. 157 (CoE) (1994)
International Covenant on Civil and Political Rights, UNTS No. 14668, ss. 27, 30 (United Nations) (1976)

Index

Aberdeen, 135, 166, 210, 298; *see also* University of Aberdeen
Aberdeenshire Council, 278, 289
Aberfeldy, 297
Acair, 185
Acts of Proscription (1747), 12
Advisory Council on Education for Scotland, 159–61
Ainmean-Àite na h-Alba, 325
Alba (newspaper), 54n
Alba, kingdom of, 7–8
Albert, Prince, 60
American Iona Society, 131
Annan Committee, 224–5
Àrd Chomhairle na Gàidhlig, 108
Ardnamurchan, 22, 89, 163, 271
Argyll, 7, 12, 59, 62, 69, 125, 133, 142, 324
  Gaelic education in, 77–8, 125, 126, 128–9, 164, 272, 300, 304, 306
Argyll & Bute Council, 292, 304
Argyll Commission, 76, 82
Argyll, eighth duke of, 76, 96
Argyll, tenth duke of, 123
Argyllshire County Council, 122, 133, 157
Arnold, Matthew, 29
Arran, Isle of, 126
Assynt, 271
Aucamp, Anna Jacoba, 81
Auditor General for Scotland, 282
Australia, 15, 97, 116–17

Badenoch, 169
Bain, Rev. John, 134
Ballachulish, 73, 123
Bannan, 321
Bannerman, John, 128
Barère, Bertrand, 28
Barke, James, 116

Barra, Isle of, 164, 168, 190–1, 192, 238, 304, 315
Basque language, 26, 29, 55, 30, 182, 203, 208, 220, 286, 291, 308, 331
BBC
  and Gaelic, 36, 134–5, 170–2, 222, 223, 223–7, 233, 272, 283
BBC ALBA, 2, 222, 274
  audience figures, 312, 317–18
  creation of, 2, 35, 270, 273, 275, 315
  funding, 231, 268, 270, 281, 316, 318, 319–20
  impact of, 321–2
  programming, 222, 318, 319, 320–1
  regulatory requirements, 316–17, 320
  subtitling, 321
  see also Gaelic media, television
Beasley, Eileen and Trevor, 152
Belfast, 314
Bell, William, 146
Bellahouston Senior Secondary School, 166
Benbecula, Isle of, 182, 315
Berresford Ellis, Peter, 148
Bilingual Education Project, 32, 34, 168, 183–7, 214, 238, 334
bilingualism, 91, 115, 126–7, 162, 168, 179, 181, 183, 295, 309–10
Bishopbriggs, 210
Blackie, John Stuart, 96
Board of Education for Scotland, 77
Board of Supervision for Relief of Poor, 101
Bòrd na Gàidhlig, 35, 38, 111, 196, 239, 285–96
  and corpus planning, 108, 328
  criticism of, 52, 282, 283–5
  establishment of, 248, 250, 252, 254
  and Gaelic education, 298, 299, 302, 304, 306, 307–8, 310, 312, 334
  leadership of, 281–2, 329

Bòrd na Gàidhlig (cont.)
    see also Gaelic Language (Scotland) Act 2005
Borders, Citizenship and Immigration Act 2009, 203
Boudreau, Annette, 27
Bourhis, Richard, 323
Boyack, Sarah, 271
Brand, Jack, 145
Breasclete, 210
Breton language, 28, 54, 237, 298
British Empire, 12, 15, 72, 81, 332
British Nationality Act 1981, 202–3, 243n
British Sign Language (Scotland) Act 2015, 279
Brittany, 71, 116, 208, 237, 299
Brittonic language, 7
Broadcasting Act 1990, 231, 233
Broadford, 158, 303
Brown, George Mackay, 74–5
Bunessan, 306
Bun-sgoil Ghàidhlig Ghlaschu, 265, 301
Bun-sgoil Ghàidhlig Ghleann Dail, 301
Bun-sgoil Ghàidhlig Inbhir Nis, 266, 302
Bun-sgoil Ghàidhlig Phort Rìgh, 302–3
Bun-sgoil Taobh na Pàirce, 302
Burnley Campbell, Margaret, 60, 62
Burns, Norman, 158
Burton, Lord, 158
Busby, Adam, 146

Caimbeul, Tormod, 235
Caithness, 43n, 77–8, 289, 297
Caledonian MacBrayne, 203
Calouste Gulbenkian Foundation, 191, 217
Calvinism, 13
Campbell, Allan, 194–5, 197, 244, 281
Campbell, Angus, 89
Campbell, Lord Archibald, 59, 64
Campbell, Donald, 316
Campbell, Iain, 282
Campbell, John Lorne, 132, 139
Campbell, Kenna, 204–5, 206
Canada
    emigration to, 15, 112
    Gaelic in, 15, 20, 22n, 97, 109
    language policy in, 51, 183, 211, 295, 305, 310
Canna, Isle of, 132
Cantonese language, 259n, 286
Carmichael, Alexander, 66, 87
Carmichael, Ella, 62, 81
Carmina Gadelica, 66, 67
Carrick, 8, 9n
Castlebay, 164
Catalan language, 58, 286, 315
Catholic Church, 13, 39, 71, 72

and Gaelic, 105, 106, 124n, 210, 238, 239
Ceartas, 200–1
Ceilidh nan Gaidheal, 57, 65, 204
Celtic Congress, 71
Celtic Film Festival, 191
Celtic languages, 6–7
Celtic Revival, 65–7
Celtic League, 148
Celtic Twilight, 66, 118
Celtic Union, 57
Central Primary School (Inverness), 208, 266
Central Regional Council, 211
Chambers, William, 91
Channel 4, 227, 232n
Charles, Prince, 17n, 43
Cinema Sgìre, 191
The Cheviot, the Stag and the Black, Black Oil, 177
Church of Scotland, 13, 42, 45, 75
    Gaelic and, 104–5, 106, 237–8, 239, 302
Church of Scotland Ladies' Gaelic School Association, 76
Cinema Sgìre, 191
Clann Albain, 116
Clann an Fhraoich, 122
Clann na h-Alba, 37
Clark, Angus, 120
Clì Gàidhlig, 284
Cliath, 185
Club Leabhar, 154
Cnoc Soilleir, 277
co-chomuinn, 192
Coffre-Baneux, Natalie, 175
Comann nam Pàrant, 214, 266, 303
Comann Sgoiltean Dà-chànanach Ghlaschu, 204–6
Comhairle nan Eilean (Siar), 238, 239
    creation of, 175, 179
    and Gaelic, 34, 179–87, 225, 304, 334
Comhairle nan Sgoiltean Àraich, 210–11, 283–4
Commission for Racial Equality, 251
Committee for Informal Education, 122
Committee of Council on Education in Scotland, 92
An Comunn Albannach, 146
Comunn an Luchd-Ionnsachaidh, 221, 284
comuinn eachdraidh, 188
An Comunn Gàidhealach, 2, 4, 37, 53, 67, 114, 117, 143, 147, 153, 173, 189–90, 272
    aims of, 46, 49–50, 60, 63, 103, 149, 194–5
    and broadcasting, 135, 172
    criticism of, 50, 61, 70, 118, 120–1, 123, 135, 149, 150, 281

and Gaelic education, 49–50, 56, 62–3, 79, 82, 83–6, 124, 127–31, 159–61, 165, 167, 169, 185, 187, 188, 221, 239
  establishment of, 57, 59–60
  membership of, 52, 59–60, 61–2, 123, 148, 149, 194, 332
  Mòd, 43, 56, 59, 60–1, 120
  publications, 54, 64–5, 149–50, 283
  and status of Gaelic, 102, 105–6, 132–3, 141, 149, 151, 153–6, 181, 199–200, 248, 276, 291
  summer schools, 63
  use of English in, 54, 61, 63–4, 194, 332
  youth work, 121–2
Comunn Litreachas na h-Albann, 108
Comunn na Camanachd, 67
Comunn na Cànain Albannaich, 146, 149, 150–1, 173
Comunn na Gàidhlig, 111, 178, 190, 272, 285
  and community development, 197
  and economic development, 234, 236
  establishment of, 193–5
  and Gaelic education, 205, 210, 215, 220, 211
  and Gaelic broadcasting, 226, 227–31
  and secure status campaign, 246–9
Comunn na h-Òigridh, 122
Comunn nan Còirichean Sìobhalta, 200
Comunn nan Gàidheal, 84–5
Comunn nan Oileanach Gàidhlig, 224
Communications Act 1996, 233–4
Communications Act 2003, 269–70
communism, 74, 115, 116, 145
Congested Districts Board, 16
Convention of Scottish Local Authorities, 209
Conradh na Gaeilge (Gaelic League), 4, 62–3, 123, 332
Conservative Party, 43, 231, 234, 240, 319
Cor na Gàidhlig, 17, 345, 180, 193–4, 195, 236, 237–8
Cormack, Arthur, 38, 302
Cormack, Mike, 232, 233
Cornish language, 54, 199, 260
corpus planning *see* Gaelic, corpus planning
Council of Europe, 178, 259, 262
Craik, Sir Henry, 79, 80
Crawford Report, 223
Crann-Tàra, 176, 177n
Creative Scotland, 278, 285
Crofters Commission, 99
Crofters Holdings (Scotland) Act 1886, 16, 99
Crofters (Scotland) Act 1955, 152
Crofters' War, 16

crofting, 16, 41, 52, 62, 79, 83, 99–100, 140, 175, 178
Crois-Tara, 123–4
Crùisgean, 139
Culloden, battle of, 12, 40, 51, 139, 153, 158
Curriculum for Excellence, 212–13, 299
cùrsaichean bogaidh, 221
Cymdeithas yr Iaith Gymraeg, 150, 152, 156–7
Czechoslovakia, 117

Dál Riata, 7
Dàna, 283
David I, king, 9
Day, John Percival, 100
Deiseal Ltd, 284
An Deò-Ghréine, 54, 64–5
diglossia, 216–17, 235
Department for Culture, Media and Sport, 269–70, 319
devolution, 36, 145, 146, 176–7, 243, 269, 271, 273
  and Gaelic, 145, 177
Dewar, Donald, 247
Dickson, Tony, 73
diglossia, 216–17, 235
Disruption (1843), 13
Doig, Peter, 154
Donald, Gordon, 171
Driver and Vehicle Licensing Agency, 257
Drumnadrochit, 85, 125, 297
Dublin, 301
Dubois, Lise, 27
Dumfries and Galloway, 289
Dunbar, Rob, 52, 246n
Dunmore, earl of, 103–4
Dunmore, Stuart, 311
Dundee, 73, 298
Dwelly, Edward, 109, 328

East Kilbride, 210
East Renfrewshire Council, 306
Easter Rising, 71, 72
Easton, Norman, 38
Edinburgh, 51, 57, 58, 59, 65, 82, 129, 145, 199, 242, 248, 258, 268, 269, 271, 316, 323, 325
  Gaelic education in, 165, 166, 210, 265–6, 277, 297, 301–2, 313
  see also City of Edinburgh Council; University of Edinburgh
Education Scotland, 278, 307
Education (Scotland) Act 1872
  concessions, 78–82
  impact of, 74–5
  origin of, 76

Education (Scotland) Act 1872 (cont.)
  provisions of, 31, 76–7
  school boards and, 77–8
Education (Scotland) Act 1908, 83–4
Education (Scotland) Act 1918
  enactment of, 84–6
  implementation of, 124–30, 135, 159, 334
  interpretation of, 86, 124–5, 159, 198
Education (Scotland) Act 1945, 86, 159
Education (Scotland) Act 1962, 86, 159
Education (Scotland) Act 1980, 159, 208, 211
Education (Scotland) Act 2016, 305–7
Educational Institute of Scotland, 84, 181, 265
Edward VII, King, 60, 109
Edwards, John, 47
Eisteddfod, 59, 154
Electoral Commission, 276
English language, 18, 29–30, 48, 93–4, 160, 185, 186, 203
Eòrpa, 232–3
Erskine, Ruaraidh, 38, 39, 60, 68–72, 73–4, 108, 109, 110, 114, 115, 119, 123, 144, 173
e-sgoil, 299
Esslemont, Alan, 201, 320
ethnic revival, 3, 147, 174
European Bureau for Lesser Used Languages, 178
European Charter for Regional or Minority Languages, 259–62, 266, 269
European Parliament, 264
European Union, 178, 259n, 264
Evans, Gwynfor, 230
Evans of Temple Guiting, Lord, 155
Ewing, Winnie, 145

Farquharson, Rev. Archibald, 90
Faroe Islands, 234
fascism, 115–16
Fearann Eilean Iarmain, 158, 217, 234, 236
Federation of Celtic Societies, 57
Federation of Highland Associations, 165
Fèis Bharraigh, 190–1
Fèisean nan Gàidheal, 191
Fichte, Johann Gottlieb, 37, 41
Fife, 119, 289
Fine Gaidheil, 146
Finland, 291–2
First Scotrail, 324–5
Fishman, Joshua, 216, 311, 331
Fletcher, Alex, 198, 199, 209, 227
folk revival, 138
folklore, 60, 66, 135, 138
Folklore Institute of Scotland, 138

Forestry Commission, 158
Forfar, 210
Forsyth, Michael, 230, 231
Fort William, 117, 157, 200, 210, 297, 302–3
Foulkes, Lord, 276n
Foxley, Dr Michael, 271
Framework Convention for the Protection of National Minorities, 262–4
Fraser, D. Munro, 85
Fraser, Neil, 171, 267–8
Fraser Mackintosh, Charles, 87, 103
Free Church College, 106
Free Church Ladies' Gaelic School Association, 75
Free Church of Scotland, 13, 75
  Gaelic in, 106, 237–8, 239
Free Presbyterian Church, Gaelic and, 106, 181–2, 238
French language, 28–9, 77, 258

Gaelic
  and aristocracy, 8, 52, 57, 59, 60, 61, 121, 123, 149
  arts, 190–2, 196, 197, 234, 284–5, 288
  attitudes towards, 4, 10–11, 13, 19, 27, 29–31, 40, 41–2, 44–7, 54, 90, 93–4, 105, 120, 138, 141–2, 162–3, 167, 233, 239–40, 253, 279–81
  ban on use of, 12, 30–31, 33, 86–7, 91, 155
  and Britishness, 12, 43–4, 73, 203, 332
  in census, 19–26, 82, 102–3, 124, 142, 143, 154, 156, 171, 220–1, 312
  and churches, 12–13, 14, 75–6, 104–6, 237–9
  in cities, 12, 15, 53, 57, 69, 72–3, 74, 134, 143, 203, 204, 267, 291
  corpus planning, 53–4, 107–9, 272–3, 326, 327–8
  demographic history, 6–10, 17–26
  demonstrations for, 51, 199, 214, 224, 248, 265
  dialects of, 54, 107, 120, 135, 171, 226, 311, 315, 335
  dictionaries, 108, 109, 272, 296, 328
  digital resources, 312, 327–8, 330
  direct action on behalf of, 51, 150–1, 200–1
  drama, 61, 134, 171, 191–2, 320
  and economy, 29, 34, 45–6, 58–9, 93, 114, 136, 140–1, 142, 197, 217, 226, 228–9, 232–3, 234–5, 257, 269
  in education *see* Gaelic education
  in elections, 68, 103, 244, 250, 276, 305
  government funding for, 32, 33, 51, 77, 78, 79, 84, 137–8, 149, 154, 172, 181, 184, 186–7, 195, 199, 206, 208–9,

219, 222, 229–31, 233–4, 247–8, 259, 265, 267–70, 277, 283, 293, 299, 304, 316, 318, 320, 329
identity, 37, 41–2, 54, 57, 92, 115, 144, 150, 177, 213–14, 223, 229, 264, 311, 313, 314, 331
and labour movement, 72–4, 116
language use surveys, 25, 26, 241, 274–5, 311
learners of, 25, 32, 52, 60, 62–3, 68, 94, 105, 108–9, 122, 125–6, 129, 142, 144, 150, 165–7, 171–2, 175, 213, 218, 219, 220–2, 283, 284–5, 299–301, 310–14
in legal system, 98–100, 132–3, 154, 155, 199, 201–2, 257, 261
literacy, 14, 25, 75, 87, 91, 94, 124, 126, 162, 169, 181, 184, 213, 296, 310
literature, 53, 60–1, 70, 84, 93, 94, 96, 108, 110, 118, 119–20, 123, 131, 132, 142, 143, 160–1, 162, 177, 313, 326
in Lowlands, 8–9, 12, 15, 17, 20, 22–3, 37, 39, 40, 53, 68, 69, 142, 144, 159–60, 164–6, 167, 220, 241, 248, 272, 280, 323, 325, 334; see also Edinburgh; Glasgow
and military, 12, 102, 153
and monarchy, 43–4, 60
monolingual speakers, 24, 28, 33, 154–5
music, 57, 60, 61, 64, 67, 120, 123, 132, 134, 138, 143, 171, 177, 189, 190–1, 213, 214, 217, 232, 313, 320
as national language, 3, 4, 7, 35, 36–40, 49, 63, 68–9, 115, 123, 150, 240–1, 249, 252, 253, 255, 277, 333
new speakers, 25, 175, 222, 310, 313–15, 330
official status, 35, 38, 146, 151, 155, 195–6, 198–9, 246–7, 252–4
official use of, 31, 32–4, 98–103, 132–4, 153, 155–6, 179–83, 202–3, 242–3, 288–96, 326
organisations, 49–55, 56–9, 217, 241, 283, 329; see also Bòrd na Gàidhlig; An Comunn Gàidhealach; Comunn na Cànain Albannaich; Comunn na Gàidhlig; Gaelic League of Scotland
periodicals, 14, 54–5, 64–5, 70–1, 106, 109–10, 139, 142–3, 149–50, 176, 283
placenames, 40, 160, 182, 325
and political left, 53, 72–4, 115–17, 145–6, 244
and political parties, 43, 53, 103, 115, 181, 229, 243–4; see also Conservative Party; Labour Party; Liberal Party; Scottish National Party

prominence of, 4, 53, 81, 177, 203, 232–3, 255, 272, 274, 279, 292, 323, 325, 328, 330
publishing, 14, 54, 70, 108, 109, 110, 127, 154, 157, 169, 185, 193, 326–7
signage, 44, 156–8, 180, 181, 182, 203, 243, 257, 270–2, 280, 323–6
and social class, 52, 57, 58, 59, 61, 72–3, 119, 123, 175, 216, 244, 310
and social media, 39, 280, 281, 284, 318, 327
stereotypes, 10–11, 13, 117, 167, 232, 240, 280–1
terminology see corpus planning, Gaelic
and unionism, 43–4, 275, 280
women, role of, 52–3, 60
Gaelic Advisory Committee (BBC), 224
Gaelic Athletic Association, 67
Gaelic Books Council, 154, 326
Gaelic Broadcasting Committee, 234, 267, 269–70
Gaelic education
and corporal punishment, 86–90
curriculum, 32, 79, 85, 128, 129, 159, 161, 167, 212–14, 299
demand for, 90, 126, 162–3, 185, 188, 204, 205, 210–11, 216, 220, 264–6, 284, 299, 301–6, 308–10
enrolment levels, 77–8, 79–80, 125, 127–8, 165, 207, 210, 265–7, 287, 297–302, 305–6
examinations, 32, 79–80, 166–7, 298, 299–300
funding of, 32, 78–9, 83–4, 186–7, 208–9, 222, 259, 265, 266, 277, 297n, 299, 301, 302, 304, 308
free-standing schools v. units, 206, 207, 210, 264–7, 298, 301, 304, 311
Gaelic-medium education, origins of, 203–7
Gaelic-medium education, growth of, 207, 209–11, 264–6, 287–8, 297–9, 301–3
learners, provision for, 32, 62, 122, 129, 166–7, 299–300, 309
opposition to, 28, 46, 51, 69, 81, 85–6, 88, 90–1, 93–4, 111, 126, 129–30, 160–1, 217, 237, 240, 265–6, 301–2, 304–5, 306, 309, 333
policy, 25, 31–2, 39, 74–82, 83–6, 124–6, 158–63, 165–9, 183–8, 203–17, 261, 264–7, 287–8, 296–311
pre-school, 150, 166, 188–9, 210–11, 284, 301, 303
pupil attainment, 86, 124, 168, 186, 215–16, 309–10
research on, 127–9, 163–4, 186–7, 213, 215–16, 309–11

Gaelic education (*cont.*)
  secondary, 32, 79–80, 86, 127, 129, 160–2, 164, 165–7, 186–7, 214–15, 265, 266, 298–300, 302, 310, 311, 334
  teachers, 77–80, 82, 84, 93, 95, 96, 126–9, 160–1, 164, 168–9, 185–6, 187, 200, 206, 207, 215, 220, 258, 266, 297, 298–300, 307–9, 315
  teaching materials, 108–9, 127, 169, 171, 172, 185–6, 222, 309, 312
  and universities, 95–7, 130–2, 219–20, 307, 327
Gaelic Immersion for Teachers, 308
Gaelic Language Act Implementation Fund, 259, 277, 293, 308
Gaelic Language (Scotland) Act 2005, 35, 55, 183, 242, 276
  campaign for, 245–51
  implementation of, 258–9, 275, 277, 285–96, 326, 328–9
  omissions from, 256–8, 305
  provisions of, 35, 38, 253–6, 279, 298, 306–7, 323
Gaelic (Miscellaneous Provisions) Bill, 198–200
Gaelic Language (Scotland) Bill, 249–3
Gaelic League *see* Conradh na Gaeilge
Gaelic League of Scotland, 114, 117, 121, 122–4, 130, 157, 165, 173, 204, 220
Gaelic Learners in the Primary School, 300–1
Gaelic media
  criticism of, 225, 233, 240, 272, 317, 321
  funding, 33, 200, 223–31, 267–70, 281, 316–20, 322
  impact of, 135, 171, 226, 232–3, 321–2
  programming content, 134–5, 171–2, 225, 227–8, 232–3, 266, 272, 232–3, 319, 320–2
  radio, 32, 134–5, 150, 169–72, 198, 222, 223–7, 234, 241, 261–2, 272, 322
  social *see* Gaelic, and social media
  television, 19, 33, 35, 54, 170, 171–2, 198, 200, 201, 215, 218, 219, 222–34, 240, 241, 243, 261–2, 267–70, 274, 315–22, 333
Gaelic Schools Capital Fund, 277, 302, 304
Gaelic Schools Society, 75, 76
Gaelic Society of Glasgow, 58, 204
Gaelic Society of Inverness, 56, 57–8, 83, 88, 94, 102, 112, 114, 124, 165
Gaelic Society of London, 57, 58, 82, 83, 114, 120, 125, 148, 152, 156, 157
Gaelic Television Committee, 231–2, 233, 234

Gaelic Television Fund, 35, 222, 233, 269, 316
Gaeltacht Industries Act, 1957, 140
Gaeltarra Éireann, 140
An Gàidheal (1871–7), 56
An Gàidheal (1905–67), 54, 65, 106, 121, 164
An Gàidheal Ùr, 54n, 283
Gàidhealtachd
  Clearances, 14–16, 40, 51, 117, 139, 177
  definition, 11
  economy, 14–16, 18, 34, 74, 111, 113–14, 121, 131–2, 135, 136, 137, 139–41, 142, 149, 151, 153, 159, 172, 188, 189, 197, 217, 218, 229, 234–5, 257, 332, 333
  education in, 14, 75–9, 82–3, 91, 159, 184; *see also* Gaelic education
  in-migration, 19, 182, 193, 236–7
  out-migration from, 15, 17, 20, 112, 193
Gàidhlig-TV, 321
Gairm, 54, 142–3, 153, 169
Galloway, 8, 9n, 232n, 289
George IV, King, 13, 43
Gibb, Andrew Dewar, 115
Gillies, Anne Lorne, 58
Gillies, H. Cameron, 108
Gillies, William, 12
Gilmour, Sir John, 133
Glasgow, 51, 59, 61, 102, 119, 134, 135, 151, 178, 224, 225, 232, 271, 323, 325, 330
  Gaelic community in, 15, 22, 69, 72–3, 166, 204–5
  Gaelic education in, 32, 80, 165–6, 167, 188, 203–7, 222, 264–5, 267, 277, 297, 298, 301, 311, 313
  Gaelic organisations in, 43, 57, 58, 62, 65, 120–4, 149, 204
  see also University of Glasgow
Glasgow City Council, 265, 292, 301
Glasgow Corporation, 165
Glasgow Skye Association, 204, 205
Government of Wales Act 1998, 243
Grampian Television, 219, 225, 226, 227, 228n, 232, 270
Grant, Duncan, 207
Grant, James, 315
Grant, James Shaw, 46
Grant, Dr Lachlan, 113
Grant, Nigel, 205
Gray, Charles, 206
Grassic Gibbon, Lewis, 119, 244
Green, Malcolm, 206
Grieve, Sir Robert, 141
Gunn, Hugh, 131
Gunn, Neil, 119

Guth na Bliadhna, 54, 70–1, 84, 119
Gwynedd Council, 34, 183, 237

Harris, Isle of, 133
Hawai'ian language, 208, 258
Hay, George Campbell, 115, 117, 120, 177
Henderson, Angus, 89, 109
Herder, Johann Gottfried, 37, 41
Heriot-Watt University, 296n
Highland Clearances, 15–16, 18, 40, 51, 117, 139, 177
Highland Council, 17n, 266, 271, 289, 297, 302–4, 309
Highland Development League, 113
Highland games, 67
Highland–Lowland divide, 9–11, 13, 17, 36–7, 39–40, 69, 144, 159–61, 165, 240–1, 248, 280, 289, 325
Highland regiments, 12, 102
Highland Regional Council, 182, 187, 193, 194, 207
Highland societies *see* Gaelic, organisations
Highland Society of Edinburgh, 57
Highland Society of London, 57
The Highlander, 56, 96, 110
Highlands *see* Gàidhealtachd
Highlanders Institute, 166, 204
Highlands and Islands Development Board, 16, 34, 140–1, 192–5
and Gaelic, 34–5, 140–1, 152, 156, 185, 191, 192–5, 211, 219, 211, 228, 234–5, 241
Highlands and Islands Development (Scotland) Act 1965, 140, 152
Highlands and Islands Enterprise, 16, 235
Hilleary Report, 113
Historic Environment Scotland, 294
Home Office, 202, 229, 230, 269n
House of Commons, 83, 135, 152, 198, 257
Howells, Kim, 268
Hughes Parry Report, 152, 153
Hunter, James, 16, 178, 217
Hyde, Douglas, 55

immersion *see* language immersion
Immigration Act 1971, 202
Immigration Restriction Act 1901 (Australia), 117
Inbhe Thèarainte dhan Ghàidhlig, 246
India, 93–4
Inter-Authority Standing Group on Gaelic Education, 215
Inverclyde Council, 297
Invergordon, 140, 210
Inverness (city), 57, 98, 131, 141, 151, 220, 225, 285
Gaelic education in, 32, 127, 166, 204, 207, 264, 266, 297, 302
Inverness-shire, 69, 77, 78, 101, 122, 124, 125, 126, 127, 142, 163, 179
Inverness-shire County Council, 125, 126, 133, 158, 168
'Inverness-shire Scheme', 168–9, 184
Iochdar, 189
Iolaire, 112
Iona, Isle of, 139, 144
Ireland, 55, 66, 67, 72, 332
nationalism in, 71–2, 82, 103
Scottish Gaels' attitudes towards, 72, 103
Irish language, 6, 8, 24, 67, 101, 102, 103, 110, 169, 180, 264, 280, 283, 286, 291, 312, 316, 322, 326, 332
corpus planning, 107, 273
Gaeltacht, 11, 13, 63, 122, 140, 141, 192, 204, 335
language movement, 4, 49, 51, 52, 54–5, 62–3, 71, 123
and legislation, 98, 203, 253, 256, 257, 282, 289, 290, 295, 329
media, 65, 172, 268, 283, 315, 320, 322
in Northern Ireland, 31, 49, 52, 98n, 207, 208, 211, 260, 262, 314
in schools, 79, 80, 81, 82, 111, 204, 265, 298, 300, 301, 305
in universities, 96, 97
Islay, Isle of, 157, 164, 197

Jackson, Kenneth, 1, 336
Jacobitism, 12, 31
James VI and I, King, 11
James Gillespie's High School, 302
John of Fordun, 10–11
Johnson, Dr Samuel, 13, 66
Johnston, Russell, 264
Jolly, William, 94–5
Jordanhill College, 162, 164, 184, 211, 220
Jura, Isle of, 89

Kennedy-Fraser, Marjory, 67, 134
Kerr, Daniel, 88
Kilwinning, 306
Kingussie, 127
Kinlochleven, 113–14
Kintail, 238
Kisch, Egon, 116–17
Kyleakin, 164

Labour Party, 139, 145, 181, 199, 206, 211, 214, 247, 250, 259, 266, 267, 275, 324
Lallans, 118; *see also* Scots language
Lamont, Norman, 230
land raids, 16, 113

land reform, 16, 99–100, 237
Land Reform (Scotland) Act 2016, 152n
Land Settlement (Scotland) Act 1919, 113
Landry, Rodrigue, 323
language academies, 108, 328
language commissioners, 282, 329
language ideology, 14, 27, 29–30, 36, 44, 54, 55, 68, 90–5, 182, 185, 235–6, 333
language immersion, 168, 212–13, 216, 221–2, 258, 284, 303, 309, 310–11
language legislation, 152, 155, 197–8, 201, 245, 247, 256–8, 279, 288, 291–2, 295, 329; *see also* Finland; *Gaelic Language (Scotland) Act 2005*; Irish language; Welsh language
language planning, 35, 142, 148, 197, 227, 235, 246, 248, 274, 282, 286, 287, 288, 294, 319, 325
language revitalisation, 4, 50, 114, 122, 216–17, 245, 322, 331–2, 334–5
language rights, 85, 98, 147, 152, 196, 199, 201, 249, 252, 258, 263, 305
language shift, 216
  in Ireland, 63, 107, 332
  in Scotland, 6–9, 15, 17–26, 45, 69, 74, 89, 93, 105, 112, 125, 163–4, 166, 175, 184–5, 187, 204–5, 213, 215–16, 236, 333
  theoretical explanations, 17–18, 113, 205
An Lanntair, 190
Latin language, 8, 93, 335
Lewis, Isle of, 1, 16, 19, 62, 89, 100, 112, 113, 126, 163, 164, 175, 179, 189, 192, 217, 237, 238, 274–5, 315, 336
  Gaelic education in, 89, 126, 163, 168, 186, 187, 210, 299, 304
Lewis, Saunders, 55, 152
Lews Castle College, 220, 222
Liberal Party, 176, 181, 229, 249, 250
linguistic landscape, 322–6, 330; *see also* Gaelic, signage
Linguistic Survey of Scotland, 17
Livingstone, Duncan, 89
Llanelli, 166
Lochaber, 113–14, 140, 169, 200
Lochaber District Council, 271n
Lochalsh, 88, 200, 234
Lochboisdale, 164
Lochmaddy, 132, 164
Lordship of the Isles, 10, 179
Lowlands *see* Gaelic, in Lowlands

Mac a' Ghobhainn, Seumas, 144, 148, 150
MacArthur, Rev. Jack, 205, 207, 239
MacArthur, John, 88
MacAskill, Kenny, 321
MacAulay, Donald, 75, 143, 177
MacAulay, Rev. Donald, 238
MacAulay, Thomas Babington, 93–4
MacColl, Evan, 88
MacColla, Fionn, 39, 119, 144
MacCormick, John, 114
MacCuish, Donald, 155
MacDiarmid, Hugh, 38, 115–16, 118–19
MacDonald, Alexander (Alasdair mac Mhaighstir Alasdair), 36, 68n
MacDonald, Alexander, 124
Macdonald, Calum, 271
MacDonald, Finlay J., 141, 153, 171
Macdonald, John, 141
Macdonald, Lewis, 271
MacDonald, Martin, 193, 195, 222–3
MacDonald, Sir Murdoch, 130
MacDonald, Sharon, 19
MacEwen, Sir Alexander, 114, 132
MacFarlane, Malcolm, 108
MacGaraidh, Seumas, 115
MacGill-Eain, Tormod, 232
MacGille Ìosa, Liam, 71–2, 108
MacGregor, Dr John, 58
Machair, 232
MacIllechiar, Iain, 207, 221, 248
MacInnes, John, 37, 41
Maciver, Rev. Angus, 85
Maciver, Roy, 179
MacKay, Donald John, 148, 149, 156, 193
Mackay, Rev. G. W., 47
MacKay, J. G., 108
Mackay, John Angus, 192, 195, 205, 269, 281–2, 316
Mackay, William, 64, 83, 88
Mackenzie, Alexander, 98, 99
Mackenzie, Compton, 120–1, 134
Mackenzie, D. F., 141
MacKinnon, Donald, 92, 96
MacKinnon, Jonathan G., 109
MacKinnon, Kenneth, 17–18, 139, 172, 175
Mackintosh, John P., 145
MacLaren, Duncan, 180
MacLaren, Marilyne, 302
MacLauchlan, Rev. Thomas, 91–2
MacLean, Coinneach, 192
MacLean, John (1879–1923), 74–5
MacLean, John (1903–92), 168
MacLean, Magnus, 121, 126
MacLean, Malcolm, 190
MacLean, Neil, 133
MacLean, Sorley, 119, 143, 166, 169, 177
MacLellan, Angus, 89
MacLennan, Father Calum, 238
MacLennan, Dolina, 177
MacLennan, R., 116
MacLennan, Shona, 282

MacLeod, Donald John, 53, 71, 143, 189, 195, 291
MacLeod, Dr Finlay, 172, 184, 186, 189, 190
MacLeod, Finlay (Strì), 200, 211, 283–4
MacLeod, Fiona, 66
Macleod, John, 276
MacLeod, Sir John Lorne, 129
MacLeod, Rev. Kenneth, 61, 67
MacLeod, Malcolm C., 111
Macleod, Rev. Malcolm, 105
MacLeod, Murdo, 168, 169
MacLeod, Rev. Roderick, 237
MacLeod, Roderick John, 246
MacMaster Campbell, Sheriff J., 114n
Macmillan, Malcolm, 115, 153
MacNeacail, Aonghas, 195, 205
MacNeacail, H. C., 69
MacPhee, Hugh, 135
Macpherson, J. Iain, 86, 127
Macpherson, James, 13, 38n, 67
Macpherson, John Alick, 247–8
MacPherson of Cluny, Cluny, 58
MacPherson Report, 247–8
Alexander McRae (Court of Justiciary, 1841), 98, 201
MacSween, Annie, 210
MacSween, Donald John, 248
Máel Coluim III, 8–9
Mallaig, 271, 303–4
Man, Isle of, 71
Manx language, 260
Māori language, 51, 109, 213, 295, 300
Margaret, Queen, 8
Marloch, 112
Masson, David, 59
Matheson, Angus, 131
Matheson, John Carstairs, 73
McIver, Dr Isa H., 117
McKechnie, Alexander, 64
Meek, Donald, 131, 176, 197, 244, 247, 248
Metagama, 112
MG ALBA, 201, 312, 316–21
Michie, Rae, 229
Mill, John Stuart, 29–30
Milne, Alasdair, 268
Milne Report, 268–70
Ministerial Advisory Group on Gaelic, 248
Ministerial Advisory Group on the Scots Language, 278
minority languages
 attitudes towards, 27, 28, 44, 141, 305, 327–8
 characteristics of, 13, 19, 54, 58, 186, 217, 235
 movements, 33–4, 51, 53–5, 58, 107, 108, 147–8, 149, 178, 185n, 208, 212, 334–5
 provision for, 28, 155, 178, 212, 219, 225, 229, 245, 259–64, 282, 291–2, 295, 300, 305, 316, 319, 327, 332
 revitalisation *see* language revitalisation
minority rights, 137, 142, 147–8, 235, 244, 262
Misneachd, 151, 303, 304, 333
Mitchell, Rosalind, 187
Mitchison, Naomi, 114
Mòd *see* An Comunn Gàidhealach
modernism, 118
Moidart, 238, 271
Montgomery Committee, 33
Montrose, duke of, 52n, 130
Morar, 303–4
Moray Council, 289
Morrison, Murdo, 124
Morvern, 19, 271
Muir, Edwin, 119
Mull, Isle of, 164, 188, 197, 306
Munich Agreement (1938), 137
Munro, John Farquhar, 249
Munro, Robert, 86
Murchison, Rev. T. M., 135, 136, 139n
Murdoch, John, 18, 73, 92, 96
Murray, John, 184–6, 210, 224
Murray, Kenneth, 281
music *see* Gaelic, music
mygaelic.com, 284

Nairn, 98, 297
Napier Commission, 16, 79, 98–9
Napier, Theodore, 69
National Assembly for Wales, 242, 243
National Gaelic Language Plans, 35, 50, 197, 250–1, 254, 275, 285–8, 312
National Library of Scotland, 293
National Mod (Scotland) Act 1969, 154
National Museum of Scotland, 203
nationalism, 37, 41, 68, 81
 Gaelic, 36–7, 41, 62, 67, 70, 73, 113
 Irish, 63, 72, 82, 203
 Scottish, 36–8, 42–3, 68–70, 71, 115, 119, 120, 145, 146, 227, 275, 325, 332
 Welsh, 42, 147, 230
Neill, William, 144
Ness, 189
Newton, Michael, 90
Newtonmore, 210
NHS Eileanan Siar, 293
Nicolson, Alexander, 76, 79
Nicolson Institute, 175, 299
Norse language, 7, 10, 61, 182
North Ayrshire Council, 298n, 306
North of Scotland Hydro-Electric Board, 139

North Uist, Isle of, 162, 164, 168, 315
Nova Scotia, 15, 20, 97, 109

Ó Baoill, Colm, 49
O'Henley, Alex, 244–5
Ó hIfearnáin, Tadhg, 305, 326
O'Neill, Martin, 199
Oban, 59, 60, 61, 65, 85, 200, 205, 210, 304
Occitan language, 110
Ofcom, 320
Official Languages Act 2003 (Ireland), 253, 290
1+2 languages policy, 297, 300–1, 334
Orkney, 48, 100, 289
Ossian, 13, 40, 59, 66, 67

Pan-Celticism, 71–2
Passport Office, 256–7
Paterson, John M., 123
Peacock, Peter, 252, 254n, 258
Pearse, Patrick, 72
Perth & Kinross, 297
Perthshire, 77, 78, 82, 105, 125, 128, 131, 200
Peterhead, 210
Pictish language, 7
Pinkerton, John, 40
Plaid Cymru, 42, 147, 230
Police Scotland, 289
Polish language, 259n
Port Charlotte, 157
Portree, 154, 158, 164, 188, 201, 207, 261, 297, 302–3
Portree High School, 175
Prebble, John, 139
Pròiseact nan Ealan, 190, 284–5
Protestantism, 11, 12, 14, 71, 72, 124n, 143, 238
Punjabi language, 259n, 286

Quebec, 168, 258

Race Relations Act 1976, 183, 262
Radical Scotland, 177
Radio nan Eilean, 225
Radio nan Gaidheal, 225–6, 272, 322
Rae, Steven, 180
Rannsachadh na Gàidhlig, 327
Ravenstein, E. G., 103
referendums
    1979 (establishing Scottish Assembly), 176
    1997 (establishing Scottish Parliament), 2, 242
    2014 (Scottish independence), 42, 44, 257, 274, 276, 277, 280
Reformation, 11, 39, 48, 71

Registrar-General for Scotland, 29
Registration of Births, Deaths and Marriages (Scotland) Act 1854, 100
Reid, Duncan, 108
Rifkind, Malcolm, 230–1
Robertson, Angus, 131
Robertson, Boyd, 179, 211
Robertson, George, 199
Romansch language, 54
romanticism, 13, 37, 40, 47, 67, 160, 244
An Ròsarnach, 70, 119
Ross & Cromarty, 77, 78, 101, 125, 126, 127, 157, 163
    Easter Ross, 140
    Wester Ross, 163, 188
Ross & Cromarty Council, 122, 168
Ross, Donald, 90, 93–4
Ross, Rev. Neil, 106, 130, 133
Ross, William, 152, 153–4
Runrig, 138, 177
Russell, Michael, 191, 249–50, 264, 278, 287

Sabhal Mòr Ostaig, 54, 107, 158, 195, 200, 201, 211, 217–19, 220, 221, 222, 235, 272, 303, 308, 314, 327
St Francis Xavier University, 97
Salmond, Alex, 277–8
Sapir-Whorf hypothesis, 214
School of Scottish Studies, 138
Schools (Consultation) (Scotland) Act 2010, 302
Schools (Scotland) Code 1950, 162
Schools (Scotland) Code 1956, 161–2
Scotland Act 1998, 242, 269
Scotland Office, 271
Scots language, 7, 8, 38, 47–9, 118, 144, 146, 286
    in census, 48, 278
    diversity within, 48, 118
    linguistic status of, 7, 118, 278
    policy towards, 48, 118, 260, 278, 289
    see also Ulster Scots
Scots National League, 84
Scott, Bernard, 206
Scottish Ambulance Service, 289
Scottish Arts Council, 190, 191
Scottish Borders, 289n
Scottish Celtic Review, 97
Scottish Chapbook, 117–18, 119
Scottish Courts and Tribunals Service, 257
Scottish Education Department, 153, 195, 202, 227
    and Gaelic, 77–8, 79–81, 84, 85, 96, 105, 122, 124, 125, 127, 137, 158, 161, 162, 167, 169, 184, 186–7, 209, 212, 218

Scottish Executive, 243, 247, 248, 250, 262, 265, 266, 269, 270
Scottish Funding Council, 222
Scottish Gaelic Studies, 120
Scottish Gaelic Texts Society, 108, 120
Scottish Government, 197, 243, 275–6, 279, 281, 287, 292, 296, 317, 319, 320, 323, 324, 328
  and Gaelic education, 299, 300, 301, 302, 304, 306, 308
Scottish Land Commission, 100
Scottish Land Court, 99–100
Scottish Land Court Act 1993, 99
Scottish Media Group, 270
Scottish National Liberation Army, 146
Scottish National Party, 42–3, 114–15, 145, 176, 274, 278–9
  and Gaelic, 42–3, 114–15, 145, 147, 181, 197, 244, 249, 252, 275–8, 280, 305, 323–4, 332
Scottish Office, 35, 143, 154, 183, 193, 194–6
  and bilingual signage, 157, 271
  and Gaelic education, 208–9, 212, 214, 215, 219, 266
  and official status of Gaelic, 132, 154, 156, 198, 199, 202, 246–7
  and Gaelic television, 227, 229–30, 269
Scottish Parliament, 2, 38, 42, 242–5, 246, 248, 251, 256, 271, 272, 275, 276, 279, 299, 317
Scottish Qualifications Authority, 278
Scottish Renaissance, 38, 117–19, 176
Scottish Republican Socialist Party, 146
Scottish Review, 70
Scottish Television, 172, 219, 222, 226, 270
Sharp, William, 66–7
Shaw, Neil, 89
Shawbost, 274–5, 333
Shetland, 7, 100, 289n
shinty, 67, 135
Sianel Pedwar Cymru (S4C), 227, 228n, 229, 230, 231, 267–9, 315, 318–19
Sime, Donald, 92–3
Sìol nan Gaidheal, 146
Sir John Maxwell Primary School, 266–7, 264
Skene, W. F., 97
Skye, Isle of, 16, 20, 22, 54, 139, 163, 164, 174, 175, 177, 197, 217, 219, 234, 237, 315
  Gaelic education in, 168, 187, 188, 203, 207, 267, 303, 304
Sleat, 180n, 217, 234, 303, 304
Sleat Primary School, 303, 304
Small Landholders (Scotland) Act 1911, 100

Smillie, Robert, 73
Smith, Christina, 163
Smith, Iain Crichton, 177
Smith, John A., 51, 162, 168
Smith Commission, 257
Society for the Support of the Gaelic Schools in the Highlands and Islands, 44
Society in Scotland for Propagating Christian Knowledge, 14, 75, 87
social media, 280, 281, 318, 326, 327
Sorbian language, 54, 108
South Lanarkshire Council, 245
South Uist, Isle of, 89, 152–3, 168, 189, 237, 277, 304, 315
Specific Grants for Gaelic Education, 33, 208–9, 221–2, 259, 277
Spencer, Colin, 187
Spencer-Turner, Mark, 257
Sproat, Ian, 199
Standards in Scotland's Schools etc Act 2000, 249
Statutes of Iona, 11, 51
Stephens, Meic, 178
Stewart, Rev. Alexander, 92
Stewart, Charles, 91
Stewart, Donald, 145, 197–9, 202, 226–7
Stirling, 166; see also University of Stirling
Stiùbhart, Domhnall Uilleam, 213
Stòrlann Nàiseanta na Gàidhlig, 186
Stornoway, 100, 112, 132, 133, 157, 163n, 164, 175, 182, 185, 186, 190, 220, 225, 261, 299, 304
Storey, Lisa, 207, 321
Streap, 308
Struthers, Sir John, 80
Stow College, 222
Strathclyde Regional Council, 193, 200, 205–6, 208–9
Strì, 200
Strubell, Miquel, 292
Sturgeon, Nicola, 278
Sutherland, 78, 125, 126, 127, 157, 163, 188, 197
Sutherland, dukes of, 59, 130
Swinney, John, 245, 288

Taic, 283–4
Tain, 210
Tarbert, 164
Taskforce on the Public Funding of Gaelic, 247–8
Taylor, Iain, 155, 201
Taylor v. Haughney, 155, 201–2, 257, 261
television
  declining use of, 318, 319
  digital technology, 35, 234, 267, 268, 269, 270, 312, 315, 316

television (cont.)
　importance for minority languages, 19, 170, 222–3, 232–3, 321–2
　see also Gaelic media, television; Welsh language, media
TG4 (Ireland), 268, 315, 321, 322
Thatcher, Margaret, 230, 234, 240
Thompson, Frank, 82, 148, 149, 150
Thomson, Derick, 62, 131, 143, 153, 170, 172, 177, 185n, 186, 192
Thomson, Donald, 166
Thomson, James, 126
Thurso, 297
Tiree, Isle of, 16, 19, 20, 22, 90, 129
Tollcross Primary School, 255–6, 301

Uist, 112, 172, 192, 217; see also Benbecula; North Uist; South Uist
Ùlpan, 283, 284, 312
Ulster Scots language, 49
unionism, 42–4, 49, 50
University of Aberdeen, 80, 95, 96–7, 130, 175, 307, 308
University of Edinburgh, 1, 59, 80, 91, 95–6, 106, 138, 201, 214, 248, 307
University of Glasgow, 80, 95, 96–7, 130–1, 175, 214, 224, 229
University of Oxford, 96
University of St Andrews, 95, 130
University of Stirling, 187, 219, 309
University of the Highlands and Islands, 220, 307
Ùr-Sgeul, 326
Urras Brosnachaidh na Gàidhlig, 205, 206
Urdd, 122

Van Leer Project, 188–9, 191, 210
Veljanovski, Cento, 228–9, 233
Victoria, Queen, 43–4, 60, 88 n17, 96

Wales, 8, 26, 29, 34, 40, 42, 47, 55, 59, 70, 73, 122, 147, 154, 170, 180, 183, 225, 227, 236–7, 242–3, 247, 251, 262, 273, 331, 333, 335; see also Welsh language
Walker, Alexander, 82
Walker, Peter, 230
War Office, 102
Warre Cornish, W. H., 81
Watson, James Carmichael, 130
Watson, W. J., 88, 91, 125
Watt, Rev. Lauchlan MacLean, 114
Welsh language, 7, 8, 29, 30, 40, 42, 47, 138, 147, 230, 247, 249, 251, 273
　demographics, 24, 34, 73, 81, 99, 154–5, 291, 335
　in education, 32, 76, 88, 124, 161, 166, 188, 204, 211, 237, 264, 268, 300, 305, 331, 333
　in legislation, 30, 32, 35, 98, 152, 155, 156, 197, 198, 201, 202, 208, 242–3, 246, 250, 253–4, 256, 257, 282–3, 290, 329
　media, 15, 135, 139, 170, 172, 223, 225, 227, 229, 230, 267–9, 283, 315, 318–19
　movement, 34, 51, 55, 81–2, 111, 147, 151–2, 156–7, 230, 331, 333
　other provision for, 34, 55, 98, 99, 102, 157–8, 152, 155, 156–7, 183, 202, 257, 276, 286
Welsh Assembly see National Assembly for Wales
Welsh Assembly Government, 282
Welsh Courts Act 1942, 152
Welsh Language Act 1967, 98n, 152, 155, 197, 198, 201, 202, 276
Welsh Language Act 1993, 35, 98n, 197, 201, 242, 246, 249, 253, 254, 256, 257, 282, 290
Welsh Language Board, 251, 254, 282, 290
Welsh Language Commissioner, 282, 329
Welsh Language (Wales) Measure 2011, 253, 257, 282–3
West Highland Free Press, 139, 267
Western Isles, 20n, 34, 66, 112, 115, 139, 145, 149, 158, 167, 174, 175, 179, 180, 182, 183, 217, 235, 237, 270, 276, 293, 312
　community development, 188–92
　economy, 34, 175, 234, 333
　Gaelic education in, 32, 78, 125, 168, 183–7, 188, 203, 205, 210, 213, 267, 297, 300, 303, 304–5, 333
　Gaelic speaking in, 20, 22, 24, 26, 62, 125, 163, 179, 315, 333
　language shift in, 22, 24, 26, 163–4, 175, 185, 213, 275, 333
　see also Barra; Comhairle nan Eilean (Siar); Harris; Lewis; Uist
Western Isles Community Education Project, 188–9
Williams, Colin, 142, 176
Wilson, Brian, 267, 269
Withers, Charles, 55
Woodside Senior Secondary School, 165
Workers' Party of Scotland (Marxist-Leninist), 145–6
Wringe, Mark, 201

Yeats, William Butler, 66
Young, James D., 73
Younger, George, 158, 195–6, 198, 202

Zeuss, Johann Kaspar, 97

EU representative:
Easy Access System Europe
Mustamäe tee 50, 10621 Tallinn, Estonia
Gpsr.requests@easproject.com

www.ingramcontent.com/pod-product-compliance
Lightning Source LLC
Chambersburg PA
CBHW052053300426
44117CB00013B/2110